INFORMATION MODELLING AND KNOWLEDGE BASES XV

Frontiers in Artificial Intelligence and Applications

Series Editors: J. Breuker, R. López de Mántaras, M. Mohammadian, S. Ohsuga and W. Swartout

Volume 105

Recently published in this series

Vol. 104. A. Abraham et al. (Eds.), Design and Application of Hybrid Intelligent Systems
Vol. 103. B. Tessem et al. (Eds.), Eighth Scandinavian Conference on Artificial Intelligence – SCAI'03
Vol. 102. C. Turchetti, Stochastic Models of Neural Networks
Vol. 101. G.L. Torres et al. (Eds.), Advances in Intelligent Systems and Robotics – LAPTEC'03
Vol. 100. I. Aguiló et al. (Eds.), Artificial Intelligence Research and Development
Vol. 99. D. Šuc, Machine Reconstruction of Human Control Strategies
Vol. 98. H. Fujita and P. Johannesson (Eds.), New Trends in Software Methodologies, Tools and Techniques – Proceedings of Lyee_W03: The Second International Workshop on Lyee Methodology
Vol. 97. H.U. Hoppe et al. (Eds.), Artificial Intelligence in Education – Shaping the Future of Learning through Intelligent Technologies
Vol. 96. S. Handschuh and S. Staab (Eds.), Annotation for the Semantic Web
Vol. 95. B. Omelayenko and M. Klein (Eds.), Knowledge Transformation for the Semantic Web
Vol. 94. H. Jaakkola et al. (Eds.), Information Modelling and Knowledge Bases XIV
Vol. 93. K. Wang, Intelligent Condition Monitoring and Diagnosis Systems – A Computational Intelligence Approach
Vol. 92. V. Kashyap and L. Shklar (Eds.), Real World Semantic Web Applications
Vol. 91. F. Azevedo, Constraint Solving over Multi-valued Logics – Application to Digital Circuits
Vol. 89. T. Bench-Capon et al. (Eds.), Legal Knowledge and Information Systems – JURIX 2002: The Fifteenth Annual Conference
Vol. 87. A. Abraham et al. (Eds.), Soft Computing Systems – Design, Management and Applications
Vol. 86. R.S.T. Lee and J.H.K. Liu, Invariant Object Recognition based on Elastic Graph Matching – Theory and Applications
Vol. 85. J.M. Abe and J.I. da Silva Filho (Eds.), Advances in Logic, Artificial Intelligence and Robotics – LAPTEC 2002
Vol. 84. H. Fujita and P. Johannesson (Eds.), New Trends in Software Methodologies, Tools and Techniques – Proceedings of Lyee_W02
Vol. 83. V. Loia (Ed.), Soft Computing Agents – A New Perspective for Dynamic Information Systems
Vol. 82. E. Damiani et al. (Eds.), Knowledge-Based Intelligent Information Engineering Systems and Allied Technologies – KES 2002
Vol. 81. J.A. Leite, Evolving Knowledge Bases – Specification and Semantics
Vol. 80. T. Welzer et al. (Eds.), Knowledge-based Software Engineering – Proceedings of the Fifth Joint Conference on Knowledge-based Software Engineering
Vol. 79. H. Motoda (Ed.), Active Mining – New Directions of Data Mining
Vol. 78. T. Vidal and P. Liberatore (Eds.), STAIRS 2002 – STarting Artificial Intelligence Researchers Symposium
Vol. 77. F. van Harmelen (Ed.), ECAI 2002 – 15th European Conference on Artificial Intelligence
Vol. 76. P. Sinčák et al. (Eds.), Intelligent Technologies – Theory and Applications

ISSN 0922-6389

Information Modelling and Knowledge Bases XV

Edited by

Yasushi Kiyoki

Keio University, Japan

Eiji Kawaguchi

Kyushu Institute of Technology, Japan

Hannu Jaakkola

Tampere University of Technology, Finland

Hannu Kangassalo

University of Tampere, Finland

IOS Press

Amsterdam • Berlin • Oxford • Tokyo • Washington, DC

ISBN 1 58603 396 4
Library of Congress Control Number: 2003115510

Publisher
IOS Press
Nieuwe Hemweg 6B
1013 BG Amsterdam
The Netherlands
fax: +31 20 620 3419
e-mail: order@iospress.nl

Distributor in the UK and Ireland
IOS Press/Lavis Marketing
73 Lime Walk
Headington
Oxford OX3 7AD
England
fax: +44 1865 75 0079

Distributor in the USA and Canada
IOS Press, Inc.
5795-G Burke Centre Parkway
Burke, VA 22015
USA
fax: +1 703 323 3668
e-mail: iosbooks@iospress.com

PRINTED IN THE NETHERLANDS

Preface

This book includes the papers presented at the 13th European-Japanese Conference on Information Modelling and Knowledge Bases. The conference held in June 2003 in Kitakyushu, Japan, continues the series of events that originally started as a co-operation initiative between Japan and Finland, as early as the second half of the 1980's. By 1991, the geographical scope of these conferences had expanded to cover the whole of Europe and other countries, too.

The aim of this series of conferences is to provide research communities in Europe and Japan with a forum for the exchange of scientific results and experiences achieved using innovative methods and approaches in computer science and other disciplines. These communities have a common interest in understanding and solving problems on information modelling and knowledge bases, as well as applying the results of research to practice.

The research topics at this conference belong to the domain of the theory and practice of information modelling, conceptual modelling, design and specification of information systems, software engineering, databases and knowledge bases. We also aim to recognize and study new areas of modelling and knowledge bases, such as philosophy and logic, cognitive science, knowledge management, linguistics and management science. They are relevant too, and should be paid more attention. This time the selected papers cover many areas of information modelling, e.g.:

- concept theories
- database semantics
- knowledge bases and systems
- WWW information managements
- context-based information access spaces
- ontological technology
- 3D visualization
- temporal and spatial databases
- document data managements.

The published papers are formally reviewed by an international program committee and selected for the annual conference, a forum for presentations, criticism and discussions. All this is taken into account in the final published versions. Each paper has been reviewed by three or four reviewers. The selected papers are printed in this volume.

This effort had not been possible without support from many people and organizations. In the Program Committee there were 28 well-known researchers from the areas of information modelling, logic, philosophy, concept theories, conceptual modelling, databases, knowledge bases, information systems, linguistics, and related fields important for information modelling. In addition, 24 external referees gave invaluable help and support in the reviewing process. We are very grateful for their careful work in reviewing the papers. Professor Yasushi Kiyoki and Professor Hannu Kangassalo acted as co-chairmen of the program committee.

Kyushu Institute of Technology at Kitakyushu, Japan hosted the conference. Professor Eiji Kawaguchi acted as conference leader. His team took care of the practical aspects which were necessary to run the conference, as well as all those things which were important to create an innovative and creative atmosphere for the hard work during the conference days.

The Editors

Yasushi Kiyoki
Eiji Kawaguchi
Hannu Jaakkola
Hannu Kangassalo

Program Committee

Yasushi Kiyoki (co-chairman), Keio University, Japan
Hannu Kangassalo (co-chairman), University of Tampere, Finland

Pierre-Jean Charrel, Universite Toulouse 1, France
Xing Chen, Kanagawa Institute of Technology, Japan
Olga De Troyer, Vrije Universiteit Brussel, Belgium
Marie Duží, Technical University of Ostrava, Czech Republic
Tsutomu Endo, Kyushu Institute of Technology, Japan
Yutaka Funyu, Iwate Prefectural University, Japan
Yoshihide Hosokawa, Nagoya Institute of Technology, Japan
Seiji Ishikawa, Kyushu Institute of Technology, Japan
Yukihiro Itoh, Shizuoka University, Japan
Manfred A. Jeusfeld, Tilburg University, The Netherlands
Eiji Kawaguchi, Kyushiu Institute of Technology, Japan
Isabelle Mirbel-Sanchez, Universite de Nice Sophia Antipolis, France
Yoshihiro Okada, Kyushu University, Japan
Antoni Olivé, Universitat Politecnica Catalunya, Spain
Jari Palomäki, Massey University, New Zealand
Alain Pirotte, University of Louvain, Belgium
Michael Schrefl, University of Linz, Austria
Cristina Sernadas, Instituto Superior Tecnico, Portugal
Yasushi Shinjo, University of Tsukuba, Japan
Arne Sølvberg, Norwegian University of Science and Technology, Norway
Yuzuru Tanaka, University of Hokkaido, Japan
Bernhard Thalheim, Brandenburg University of Technology at Cottbus, Germany
Takehiro Tokuda, Tokyo Institute of Technology, Japan
Benkt Wangler, University of Skövde, Sweden
Esteban Zimanyi, Universite Libre de Bruxelles (ULB), Belgium
Jeffery Yu, The Chinese University of Hong Kong, Hong Kong

Organizing Committee

Eiji Kawaguchi, Kyushu Institute of Technology, Japan
Hannu Jaakkola, Tampere University of Technology, Pori, Finland
Hannu Kangassalo, University of Tampere, Finland
Yasushi Kiyoki, Keio University, Japan
Ulla Nevanranta (Publication), Tampere University of Technology, Finland
Yurika Suzuki (Publication), Keio University, Japan

Permanent Steering Committee

Hannu Jaakkola, Tampere University of Technology, Pori, Finland
Hannu Kangassalo, University of Tampere, Finland
Eiji Kawaguchi, Kyushu Institute of Technology, Japan
Setsuo Ohsuga, Japan (Honorary member)

Additional Reviewers

Kazuhiro Asami, Tokyo Institute of Technology, Japan
Per Backlund, University of Skövde, Sweden
Sven Casteleyn, Vrije Universiteit Brussel, Belgium
Thomas Feyer, Brandenburg University of Technology at Cottbus, Germany
Paula Gouveia, Lisbon Institute of Technology (IST), Portugal
Ingi Jonasson, University of Skövde, Sweden
Steffen Jurk, Brandenburg University of Technology at Cottbus, Germany
Makoto Kondo, Shizuoka University, Japan
Stephan Lechner, Johannes Kepler University, Austria
Michele Melchiori, University of Brescia, Italy
Erkki Mäkinen, University of Tampere, Finland
Jyrki Nummenmaa, University of Tampere, Finland
Günter Preuner, Johannes Kepler University, Austria
Roope Raisamo, University of Tampere, Finland
Jaime Ramos, Lisbon Institute of Technology (IST), Portugal
Joao Rasga, Lisbon Institute of Technology (IST), Portugal
Yutaka Sakane, Shizuoka University, Japan
Jun Sakaki, Iwate Prefectural University, Japan
Mattias Strand, University of Skövde, Sweden
Tetsuya Suzuki, Tokyo Institute of Technology, Japan
Eva Söderström, University of Skövde, Sweden
Mitsuhisa Taguchi, Tokyo Institute of Technology, Japan
Shiro Takata, ATR, Japan
Yoshimichi Watanabe, Yamanashi University, Japan

Contents

Information Modelling and Knowledge Bases XV
Y. Kiyoki et al. (Eds.)
IOS Press, 2004

VOLYNE: Viewpoint Oriented Requirement Engineering for Lyee Methodology

Pierre-Jean CHARREL, Laurent PERRUSSEL, Christophe SIBERTIN-BLANC
Université Toulouse 1 & Institut de Recherche en Informatique de Toulouse,
21 Allée de Brienne, F-31042 Toulouse Cedex, France.
Tel: (33) 561 12 87 99. Fax: (33) 561 12 88 80
Email: charrel@univ-tlse1.fr

Abstract. Lyee methodology regards the requirements elicitation process of new software from the principle that each actor of the project expresses intentions on an object to be designed. In order to improve the process, these actors are here considered from the so-called Viewpoint Paradigm, which considers the conditions for an object to be designed to acquire sense from multiple sources. The base of this paradigm is stated as follows: the sense of an object to be designed is the integration of the viewpoints which are exerted on it. The two concepts of Viewpoint and of Viewpoint Correlation are considered. Two Correlations are presented. The first aims at recognizing Viewpoints and their Correlations starting from the written documents produced during the requirements elicitation process. The second aims at managing the inconsistencies which occur during the process. The implementation specifications of these principles in LyeeAll™ CASE are finally addressed.

1. Introduction

The Lyee[1] methodology is a method for software generation, based on the principle that software reflects the intentions of all people interested by the future product, i.e. the clients and users. Practically, LyeeAll™ CASE is able to automatically generate programs from a set of specifications [16], [21]. These specifications are issued from an interactive requirements elicitation stage.

The aim of a requirement engineering activity is to define what future software must do. So the goal is to obtain a complete and consistent set of its features [20]. Viewpoint Oriented Requirements Engineering has been aiming since the early 90s' at handling in a better way a software specification and thus improving the quality of the output produced by the requirements elicitation and modeling stage. At the end of the requirements process, the resulting specification – of the services that has to be provided by future software – has to be consistent and complete. In a distributed specification activity, each Actor produces a specification fragment of future software [20]. Each fragment must have the ability to fit in with the others so as to produce at the end of the process a complete and consistent set of specifications. This managing principle spares the obligation to seek global consistency permanently but implies to tolerate inconsistencies during the process. Global consistency is only needed at the end of the process. Nothing dictates that the two tasks should be conducted simultaneously [5], [8].

---

[1] This paper hereof is contributed to the Lyee International Collaborative Research Project sponsored by Catena Corp. and The Institute of Computer Based Software Methodology and Technology. Lyee stands for GovernmentaL MethodologY for SoftwarE ProvidencE.

Within Viewpoint Oriented Requirements Engineering, each Actor – individual or group – produces a specification fragment. I. Sommerville and P. Sawyer [23] propose to distinguish two kinds of Viewpoints:

1. Viewpoints associated with the stakeholders, i.e. the Actors;
2. Viewpoints associated with organizational approach; they usually bring constraints on future software (cost, safety...).

The first kind of Viewpoints is close to the principle of Lyee since it directly addresses the entries of each individual Actor of a designing project. Thus we focus on this first case where each Viewpoint is exerted by one Actor. A Lyee requirements engineer elicits the data and their associated processes and takes into account the particular requirements related to LyeeAll™ environment. Usually a Viewpoint maintains high level goals describing its needs. Goals help to scope the Viewpoint [24] (cf. Fig. 1).

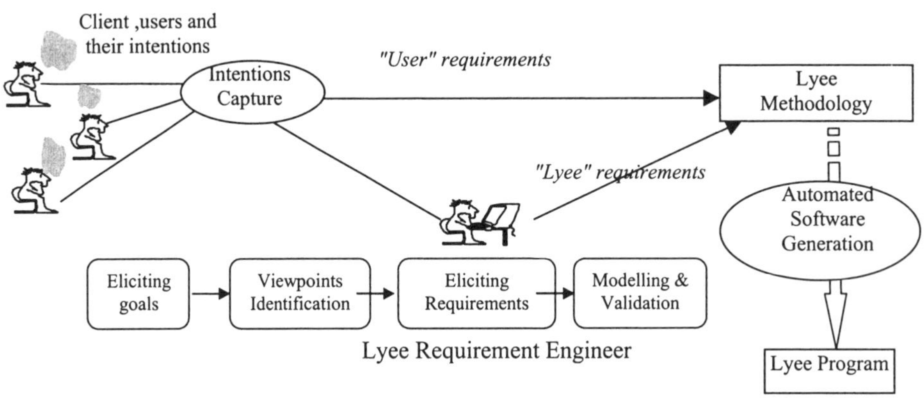

Fig. 1. Principle of a Multi-Viewpoint requirement process in Lyee

During the early designing phases, i.e. the phases during which requirements are elicited and analyzed, software exists only from the intentions of all the *Actors* of the project: the client, the future users, the contractor, and the members of the project team. In order to design software, these Actors will be called upon to come up with a series of intermediate, transitory and accessory artefacts, as well as specifications, prototypes, test sets, beta versions, etc., which can be seen as traces of the different *Viewpoints* exerting an influence on future software. These artefacts appear during the validation phases of the project when the Actors confront their own Viewpoints each other, correlate them, and at last let them converge towards a final consensual valid set of specifications. These artefacts are a series of *Representations* of future software. In other words, they are the traces of software signification process, i.e. the constitution process of its *sense*.

Section 2 describes the priniple of Lyee methodology. Section 3 presents the elements of the *Viewpoint Paradigm* and reconciles the precepts of semiotics on the conditions necessary for an Actor to give an Object sense. Section 4 defines the two key elements issued from the Viewpoint Paradigm when used in a requirements elicitation process: the two concepts of *Viewpoint* and *Viewpoints Correlation*. Section 5 presents two models of Viewpoint and Viewpoints Correlation closely related to Lyee methodology: sub-section 5.1 describes an experimental framework aiming at eliciting Viewpoints and their relationships on the basis of written documents produced during the requirement collecting stage. It gives rise to operational concerns related to the intelligibility and control of the requirement process; sub-section 5.2 presents a model of Correlation which aims at managing inconsistencies during the process by means of a logical framework. Section 6 sketches the implementation of these principles in LyeeAll™ CASE. Finally, we present issues to pursue this work.

2. Basic Principles of Lyee Software Generation Methodology

Lyee methodology [21] aims at transforming into executable code user requirements which are mainly described in terms of variables (words), control structures between variables (functions), sources (screen, database). When the requirements are defined, Lyee leaves all subsequent processing to predefined algorithms. The LyeeAll™ tool offers an interactive interface for a requirements engineer to enter the appropriate Lyee terms and generates corresponding software. The present LyeeAll™ tool generates VB code. Other target languages are planned to be implemented.

The Lyee designer needs to enter the *Defined* and its components, which are called the *Items*. A Defined corresponds to a window or a database access description. An Item is a database field or a button on a screen. An Item in LyeeAll tool has a type (numeric, text, buttons, mage). Then the designer creates the *Process Route Diagram (PRD)*. A PRD specifies the navigation between the various components of the application. A PRD is an ordered graph with a unique start node, intermediate nodes and one or several ending nodes. The nodes, which are called *Scenario functions*, have three control modules, called *Pallets*: *W04* Pallet controls the display of information to screens or insert in databases, including data manipulation and output generation; *W02* pallet controls the recovery of input from the screens or databases, including data-validity checking; *W03* controls the conditions for displaying information, including pre conditions checking and routing to another control Pallet. Another control strucutre, called the *Routing word*, is used to distribute the control over the various Scenario Functions of a *PRD*. In particular, these Words are handling over the control from one Pallet to another.

1. DEFINED DATA
    2. ITEMS DATA
3. PROCESS ROUTE DIAGRAM DATA
    4. SCENARIO FUNCTION DATA
        5. LOGICAL UNITS (PALLETS) DATA
            6. DOMAIN WORDS (SIGNIFICATION VECTORS) DATA
            7. ACTION VECTORS DATA
                7(a). Input Vectors
                7(b). Output Vectors
                7(c). Structural Vectors
                7(d). Routing Vectors

Fig. 2. Data Elements in LyeAll Requirements [1]

Pallets components are called *Domain Words*, and Words are grouped into *Logical Units*. Logical Units implement the behaviours of Defineds, and Words implement the behaviour of Items. *Vectors* can also be regarded as Words. There are two main classes of Vectors: *Signification Vectors* are composed of Domain Words; *Action Vectors* implement input and output actions, the initialization of screen elements such as fields or buttons, and the navigation between the application components. Figure 2 [1] shows the data elements for the LyeeAll™ input requirements and the steps to be followed in entering data into the

LyeeAll™ tool: the numbering of the data elements specifies the order to be followed in entering data. For instance: a Defined needs to be entered before entering its Items; a PRD must be defined before its Scenario functions are entered, followed by Logical Units and Domain Words.

3. Viewpoints as a Paradigm to Design Requirements: a Semiotic Foundation

The sense of a paradigm given by Thomas Kuhn and whose characteristics are defined by Edgar Morin in [15] is the following: a paradigm is a vision of the world that is neither verifiable nor disprovable, which is accepted as an axiom, excludes the issues it does not recognize, generates a feeling of reality and is recursively connected to the reasoning and systems it generates. Viewpoints, as a social issue, could be the key of such a paradigm. The statement on which this so-called *Viewpoint Paradigm* is founded is the following:

The sense of an object to be is the integration of the viewpoints exerted on it.

Two key points give rise to a definition of the elements in this paradigm: the Viewpoint concept is central to two processes, the process whereby Actors in the requirement elicitation process communicate amongst each other and the process whereby software, as a particular Object to be, achieves sense.

The first key point arises out of the following observation: the act of eliciting requirements brings into play a great many technical, organizational and financial skills to find solutions to problems such as technical constraints, controlling cost prices, managing and coordinating teams, over a period that may last for a very long time. It can be said that all Actors contributing one of these skills to the project has his/her "own" software that must be *integrated* with that of his/her partners. The quality of communications between project participants is therefore a key factor to the success of the requirement elicitation process. Indeed, in this concurrent engineering activity, the Actors are exchanging partial, incomplete and even contradictory information.

The second key point is to take into consideration the sense of an Object and the Actors that give this Object sense. In this way, the Object to be designed and an Actor participating in the project are not isolated entities: the Object gets sense when it is connected to how it is interpreted by an Actor in a Context through a Representation that takes on the form of a statement using a symbology. Any Representation of an Object is thus subjective and contextual.

This position is conducive to a global – systemic – view of Objects, Actors, Representations and the requirement elicitation process: it identifies the Object's sense and the result of the process used to design this Object.

3.1. Viewpoints and Communication Process

The first steps in software requirement elicitation process generally involve producing documents in natural language. "Formal" specification documents are only produced at the end of the process. We encounter the first semiotic foundation of the Viewpoint concept, in connection with the French approach of semiotics.

According to this approach [3], [11], semiotics provides a tool for visiting a document like a monument. It thus presents text as being inseparable from the author and the reader: the sense of a text is that given to it by its author, which is also the sense retrieved by the reader. Thus we may observe that a text is a communication medium if a reader is able to retrieve a sense from it, albeit a different one. A text thus only contains conditions placed by the author for retrieving the sense, these conditions being relative to the form – structure, presentation –, the literary genre, the language – English, terminology –, the style, etc. A co-authored text is the product of a pooling of several sense retrieval conditions, i.e. those recognized by its authors.

The French semiotic method is conducive to highlighting the differences in a text. These differences are considered as the very sources of sense. They are elicited using three types of analysis. The first analysis consists of identifying *narrative programs* or *contracts*: these feature an *actant* – person or thing – that performs or has an action performed which is then evaluated. Its opposite is an anti-narrative program which creates an opposition and is a source of sense. The second analysis looks at how the roles and interaction of the actants combine. Roles are expressed on the basis of canonical types. The third analysis identifies the *isotopies* of the text, i.e. its themes and the related elements of the text.

All these constructions are Representations of the text. They throw direct light on invisible aspects of it. These are, in fact, relationships that can be presented in the form of graphs showing terms and concepts that although present in the text, cannot be isolated from it because of the latter's linear form.

Elements linked to the Viewpoint concept are thus found in these French semiotic analysis schemas: Actor, Object, Representation, and relations between Actors and Objects.

3.2. Viewpoints and Signification Process

Peirce's semiotics defines a sign as "something that takes the place of something for someone with some respect for some reason" [18]. According to Umberto Eco [6] "*With some respect*" means "that the sign does not represent the entirety of the object but rather – through various abstractions – represents it from a certain viewpoint or with a view to a certain practical use". Thus, according to Peirce, "nothing is a sign if it is not interpreted as such", and a sign only acquires the status of a Representation of an Object in a relationship of three terms encompassing the Object, the sign as a signifier or Expression, and the signified as the Content of the Expression. The triad < Object, Expression, Content > is often represented in the *semiotic triad*. Fig. 2 shows this triad and gives some of the equivalent terms used by Saussure, Morris, and Hjelmslev [6].

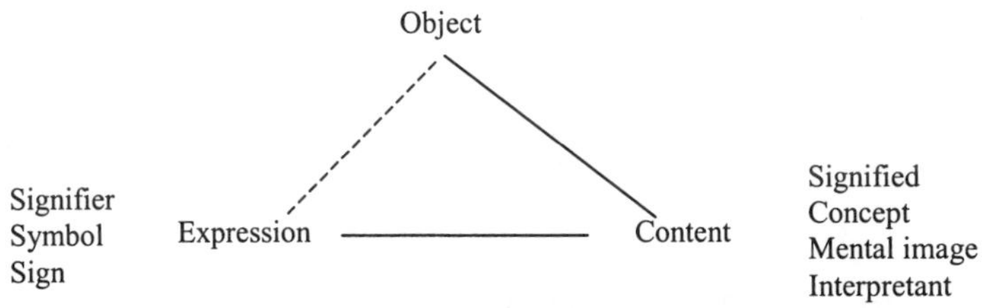

Fig. 2. Peirce's semiotic triad

Peirce adds two notions to his semiotic triad: the first is that a Content can itself be an Expression (a sign), and the second is that the Context decides which Content has to be associated with the Expression to give it sense.

In the archetype of the signification process represented by the semiotic triad we find several elements connected with our Viewpoint concept: the Object and the conditions for an Expression to be qualified to be a Representation of this Object.

4. Viewpoint and Viewpoints Correlation in a Requirement Elicitation Process: Semi-formal Definitions

Reconciling the Viewpoint notion with semiotics first leads to a set based representation of the basic concept of Viewpoint and then to this of Viewpoint Correlation. Let us assume a given universe of discourse.

Viewpoint. A *Viewpoint* implements the conditions for an *Actor* A to interpret the sense of an *Object* O to be: it is defined by the Object on which the interpretation is performed, the Actor performing it, the *Expression* E and *Content* CO of the interpretation of the Object by the Actor, and the *Context* C in which this interpretation is performed.

A Viewpoint thus comprises five poles: the Actor holds at least one Viewpoint, in the Context of which he/she produces an interpretation of the Object to be; the Object is interpreted by an Actor exerting a Viewpoint on it; the Context is the condition governing the way the Actor exerts his/her Viewpoint – e.g. the place from which the Viewpoint is exerted, the moment in time it is exerted, the tool used by the Actor to exert his/her Viewpoint, etc –; the Expression is a statement, formalised in a symbolic system, that is attached to the Object by the Actor within the Context of the Viewpoint to express his/her interpretation of the Object; the Content is the sense given within the Context by the Actor to the Object by means of Expression.

The semiotic triad does neither mention the Context in which the Expression – the signifier – is produced nor the Actor that produces it. A Viewpoint can be considered to be a semiotic triad *situated* for its Actor in his/her interpretation Context (cf. Fig. 3). The Content, certainly the most "abstract" of the five poles, contributes knowledge given by the Viewpoint on the Object. When the symbolic system used in Expression is a formal one, i.e. when semantics is associated with each statement, the two poles Expression and Content merge and correspond to what we already termed *Representation* at an earlier stage. In the following, R designates the Representation of a Viewpoint.

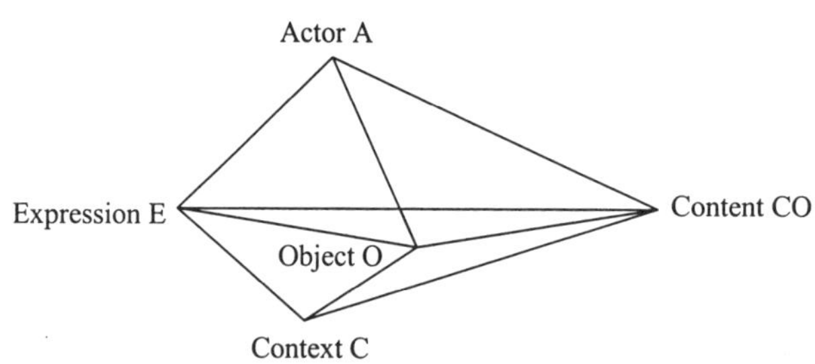

Fig. 3. Viewpoint and semiotic triad

Universe of Viewpoints. The *Universe* P of Viewpoints is the Cartesian product:

$$P = A \times O \times C \times E \times CO$$

in which A, O, C, E, CO designate respectively the aggregate of Actors, Objects, Contexts, Expressions, and Contents, each one being referred as a pole of the Universe.

We use dotted notation to designate one component of a Viewpoint. For example, p.a designates Actor a of Viewpoint p in universe P.

For the following definitions, the Universe is implicit. Actually, it is the reference from which all the Viewpoints can be defined.

<X>-Correlation. We use *<X>-Correlation* to designate any transitive relationship on X x X, where X designates one of the five poles.

This notion is extended to Viewpoints in the following way: two Viewpoints p1 and p2 are said to be <X>-correlated if an <X>-Correlation exists between two of their corresponding poles.

<X>-Correlator. An *<X>-Correlator* is a function:

$$cr: X \rightarrow X$$

where X is one of the poles.

Remark

The transitive closure of each <X>-Correlator cr defines an <X>-Correlation:

$$\{(x, cr(x)), x \in X\}$$

This notion is extended to Viewpoints in the same way as <X>-Correlation.

Examples

In the universe of an information system to be computerized, the relationship "works in the same department" is an <A>-Correlation; "is the hierarchical superior of" is an <A>-Correlator over all Viewpoints; if the Expressions of Viewpoints p1 and p2 are two knowledge bases made of logical formulae, an <E>-Correlator can define the formulae of p2 deducible from the formulae of p1.

System of Viewpoints. A *System of Viewpoints* is defined as the couple:

$$S = < P, CR >$$

where P is a universe of Viewpoints and CR is a set of <X>-Correlators defined on P.

Graph of Viewpoints. A System S of Viewpoints is called a Graph of Viewpoints iff each Viewpoint in S is <X>-Correlated to another through an <X>-Correlator of CR :

$$\forall p1, p2 \in P, \exists cr \in CR, (p1, p2) \in cr \text{ or } (p2, p1) \in cr$$

A Requirement Elicitation Process as a Graph of Viewpoints. According to the Viewpoint Paradigm, the process whereby requirements are collectively designed gives rise to a particular subset of <X>-Correlated Viewpoints which can be represented by a graph.

Reasoning on Viewpoints and the process facilitates the discovery and management of all significant differences. Here, the Contexts of all Viewpoints are the various milestones of the requirement elicitation process. The first and last nodes of the Graph respectively relate to two Viewpoints whose Actor is the project's customer, and the intermediate nodes are the various Viewpoints exerted throughout the process (cf. Fig. 4)..

For the initial Viewpoint of the graph, the Object is the assignment on the Actor-client's purchase order, the Context is the instant the project is launched, and the Representation is the entire set of documents produced by the Actor-client to the Requirements team.

For the final Viewpoint of the graph, the Object is the produced set of requirements – and all knowledge acquired on its maintenance and operation –, the Expression is the integration of all the Expressions of the Viewpoints in the final Context, and the Content then represents the formal acceptance by the Actor-client of the Object. The process is complete when the final Viewpoint of the Actor-client is able to prevail. At last, the Object acquires its sense for all the Actors involved in the requirements elicitation process, who exerted a Viewpoint on it.

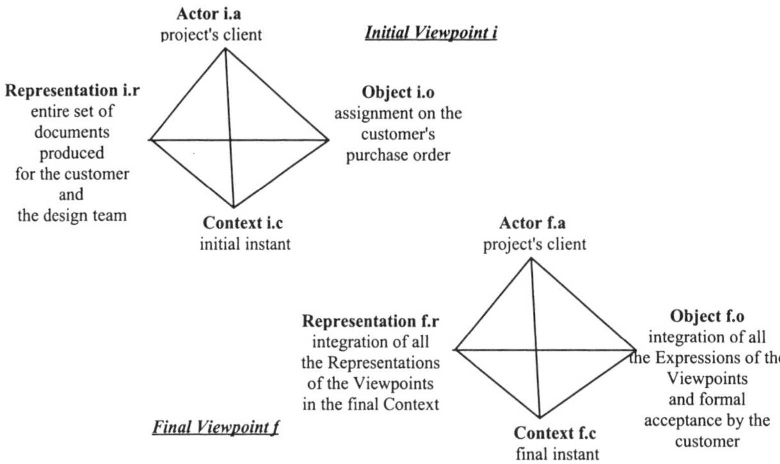

Fig. 4. Initial and final nodes of the Graph of Viewpoints of a requirement process

Dynamic and Static <X>-Correlators in a Requirement Elicitation Process.
We classify the <X>-Correlators into Dynamic and Static ones. *Dynamic <X>-Correlators* are relative to the requirements elicitation process and support the intelligibility of the process: they ensure its visibility and consistency. The Context pole represents the time scale of the process. So, Dynamic <X>-Correlators are <C>-Correlators, where Context is Time. *Static <X>-Correlators* are all <X>-Correlators defined at the other poles. They can take on the form of reasoning on Viewpoints to organize, when necessary, their consistency.

Examples

- "Validate a Representation" is a Static <R>-Correlator which links the Viewpoint p1 of the Actor who produces the Representation to be validated and the Viewpoint p2 of the Actor who validates it. The <E> component is the identity relationship, and the <CO> component is the Boolean function: p1.co → {true, false} (cf. Fig. 5).
- Objects are created throughout the process. They are assembled and modified in order to constitute the final body of requirements. Let us consider the history of the different versions of an Object produced by the same Actor during the process. Each version is related to one Viewpoint, and all these Viewpoints are linked to each other by <A,O,C>-Correlators where the <A> and <O> components are the identity relationship, and the <C> component is the relationship "*next step*" (cf. Fig.6).

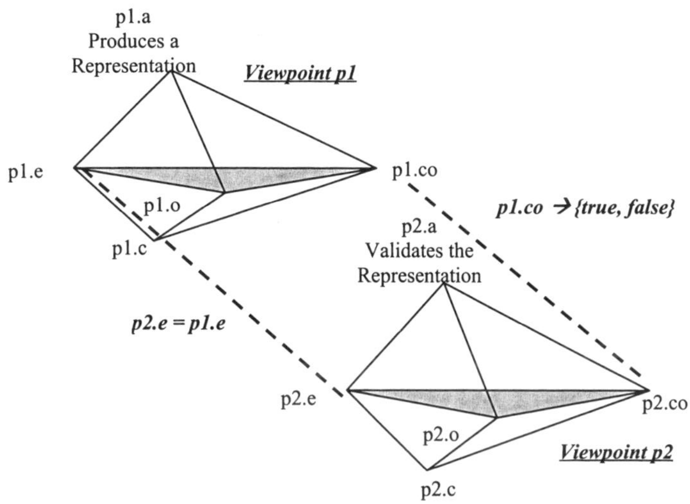

Fig. 5. An <R>-correlator "Validate a Representation"

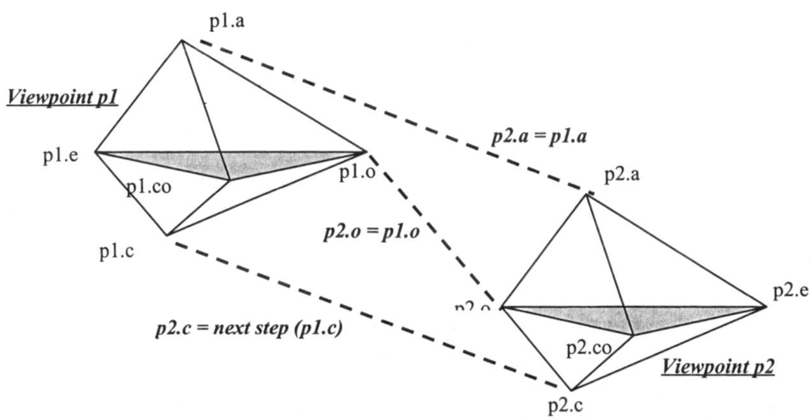

Fig. 6. An <A, O, C>-Correlator "History of the versions of an Object produced an Actor"

5. The Viewpoint Paradigm for the Intelligibility of a Lyee Requirements Elicitation Process

The Viewpoint Paradigm generates specific representation models: Viewpoint models and Correlation models. Two Correlation models are presented in this section, associated to issues relative to managing knowledge generated by Viewpoints exerted in a requirements elicitation process in the context of Lyee methodology. The first model is particularly adapted to Lyee because it aims at improving the elicitation of the *Words* by the production of significant lexical networks from which *Words* can be extracted. The second model uses a logical framework to address the management of consistency between requirements.

5.1 Infometrical Correlation

The first <X>-Correlation aims at gathering the so-called *Words* of Lyee from the written documents produced during the requirements elicitation process.

Let us summarize a research experience the overall objective of which was to demonstrate that the notions of Viewpoint and Viewpoint Correlation could be used and useful to structure, understand and process the results of the content analysis of a discourse [9]. The discourse was the transcript of a conversation between three space technology engineers, in the framework of a project for designing the architecture of a new small sized spacecraft. The objective was to provide tools to elicit the Viewpoints brought into play during the requirements elicitation process and to highlight those which have effectively contributed to the success of the process.

A proposition for a specification was drawn up during a meeting between the project manager, named D1, and two engineers, named D2 and D3. The meeting lasted three hours. An audio-video recording and the written transcription of the discussions held during the meeting constitute the raw data collected during the process.

Several analyses were carried out on the discussion transcript. We stress one of them, carried out by C. Vogel [9]. This analysis used a statistical representation of the text – by means of SEMIOLEX™ tool – as the source and not the text itself. The text was divided into six periods of thirty minutes. A glossary of keywords, called the *terms*, was selected from the general index of keywords constructed automatically from the transcript. The keywords in the glossary occur at least twice in the index. On the basis of this glossary, the statistical analysis combines the two data representation planes built from the various samples: frequency distribution tables and co-occurrence tables of the keywords.

Part of the results of statistical analysis is represented graphically by networks of terms, which are named *lexical networks* (cf. Fig. 7). Each of them is composed of at most ten terms attached to the co-occurrences. The analysis categorized several *shapes* of networks, according to the links between terms and the links with the neighbouring networks. Fig. 7 illustrates an example of a network and the excerpts from the relevant text: this example shows the term "shielding" as central for neighbouring terms such as "pumped propellant" or "pressure" and so defines a kind of proximity between them. Other terms like "impact" or "technology" join this network to neighbouring networks where they also take a part of. These lexical networks allowed terms of the discourse appear brightly to the analyst – the requirement engineer – and the three designers across the experiment.

Let us formulate this situation in the Viewpoint Paradigm. The conversation transcript is the trace of the interventions of the Actors D1, D2 and D3, but also of other Actors mentioned by D1, D2 and D3 – individuals, companies –, of Objects produced by the latter – “shielding”, “pumped propellant” –, and of their interactions during the process with respect to the components of the Object being designed – layout of the satellite’s propellant tanks, size of the antennae, mass of the components, etc. This transcription can be interpreted as the trace of the requirements elicitation process of this Object and its operating environment.

The analyst of the situation – the requirement engineer – is himself/herself an Actor of the requirements elicitation process who exerts a peculiar Viewpoint: its Object is this process and its related graph of Viewpoints; the Context is the period of time the meeting lasted between the initial instant at which the Object was non-existent and the final instant at which the conversation was stopped by the project manager D1; and the Representation is the transcription of the discussion. This Representation is also that of the Viewpoints exerted by the three Actors in the meeting on the Object to be designed. The Representations of these

Viewpoints are the transcripted interventions of the Actors during the meeting, and their Contexts are the instants at which these interventions took place. The Object is constructed as dialogue progresses by adding and updating Representations in the Viewpoints brought into play.

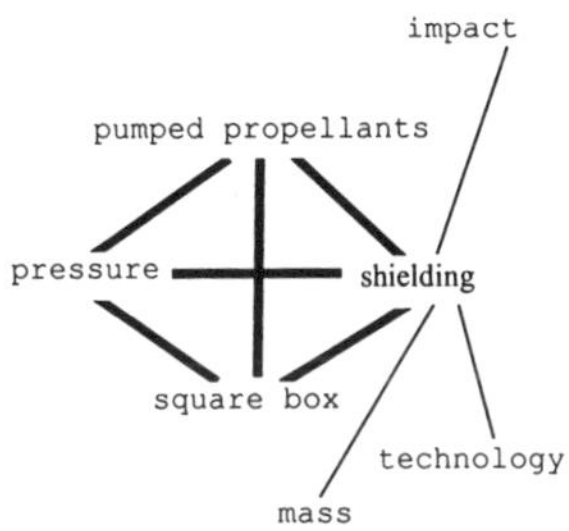

-- excerpt 472 -- D1: I would like to know if we shouldn't look deeper into the shielding thickness that would be required to significantly reduce the impact

-- excerpt 487 -- D2: Let me tell you. I don't understand why we don't use the--- since we're using pumped propellants, there's no pressure so we can make a square box! And place the electronics in it!. Let's put square boxes right there!

-- excerpt 870 -- D3: for the missions we're talking about, we need a minimum strength at these rates because that puts a constraint on technology at some point! Or maybe on the mass, since, if we have to increase the shielding, well, maybe not the shielding, you can see how quickly we reach the max!

Fig. 7. Text excerpts with the lexical network which represent them

This experiment led to define a general Dynamic <R>-Correlation, the *Infometrical Correlation* based on these lexical networks. The infometrical aspect of the Viewpoints enriches the analysis, by offering selected views of the corpus owing to the networks of co-occurrences. Among these views are: the network local to a Viewpoint, by selecting terms which co-occur with the Actor of the Viewpoint; the network limited to a given instant of the designing project; the networks whose shape stand out.

Let us consider how this experimental framework can contribute to Lyee methodology. First let us sum up another view of the major features of Lyee and LyeeAll™ tool. This complements former section 2

According to Lyee methodology, software automatic generation requires (1) the reduction of software requirements to the description of so-called *Words* and (2) to generate the control structure that processes these words to produce the expected result. Classical approaches design data structures and associated control structures, but LyeeAll™ generates the control structures from an "appropriate description of the former" [21]. This approach is close to declarative approaches: Lyee distinguishes input and output Words; the former are information provided by the environment, the latter are produced information. Lyee uses formulae to produce output Words; the production order is not required. LyeeAll™ is similar to a forward inference engine which saturates formulae until all the output Words are determined. But these formulae are not inference rules: they are procedural rules activated by the so-called Process Route Diagram (PRD) Lyee specific program structure. A PRD is composed of Scenario Functions, which are composed of Pallets, which are composed of Vectors. The PRD generates its own Words to distribute the control over the various components of a PRD.

The notion of *term* has to be replaced by the Lyee Words, such that Lyee engineer is able to recognize easily the Lyee concepts in the final lexical networks. They are to be recognized in the transcriptions of interviews of the Actors-clients and Actors-users and so improve the capture of the corresponding entries of LyeeAll™ CASE tool. For example, the term *client ID* is expected to meet the other terms *screen*, *database*, *input*, *and output* in lexical networks such as this of Fig. 7.

Fig. 8 presents an excerpt of the class schema in the UML notation [22] which suits as the Infometrical Correlation of the Viewpoints. The corpuses of written documents, from which words are issued, are accessible via the *source documents* method of class Representation. The *classification* method of Viewpoint class represents the access to classification tools like that used in the experiment described above.

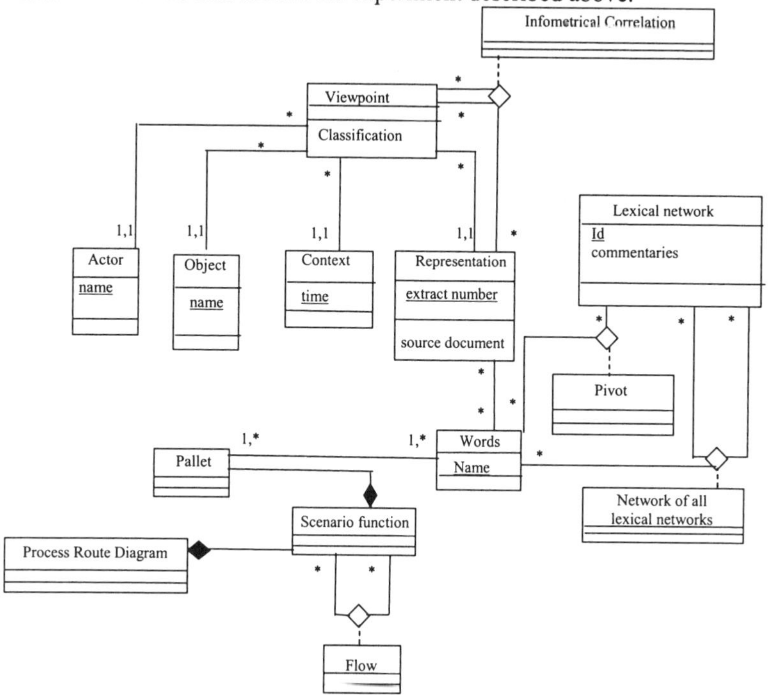

Fig. 8. Object-oriented conceptual model of an Infometrical Correlator in Lyee

This Infometrical <R>-Correlator, according to its implementation model, gives access to several analyses. A query language or a navigation tool may give access to the number of links between a Word and other Words or other networks; the integration or isolation of a network – number of adjacent networks –, the density of a network – number of linked Words, number of links in the network; the dimension of the network constituted by all the networks – number of nodes, number of links; the network density – maximal distance between two nodes, ratio number of networks / number of terms, ratio number of networks / number of links.

In the requirements elicitation process of a software designing project, chronology is a significant parameter of the corpus of related written documents. A computer-aided management tool of the history of the Representations of the Viewpoints would provide qualitative measures like: the trajectory of a Word in the different Viewpoints, i.e. its appearance and disappearance, increase of co-occurrences with other Words or progressive isolation; scenarios issued from an infometrical analysis, i.e. recognition of regularities in the networks with reference to types of scenarios, acquisition of new scenarios.

5.2 Management of Consistency between Requirements

The Viewpoint Paradigm gets rid us of the constraint of a permanent and total consistency between the different Representations. This tolerance for inconsistencies allows to not restraining prematurely the requirements elicitation process, and, for example, allows a better investigation of alternatives. In contrast with a centralized process whose goal is to prevent any inconsistency in the requirements, the goal in a Viewpoint oriented approach is to manage the inconsistencies. These characteristics are also found in the ideas put forward by S. Easterbrook et al. [5], [4] or by B. Nuseibeh et al. [8], [17]. Notably they claim that removing the perfect consistency constraint allows a better concentration on the requirement activity. Thus, the requirement expression appears less important than the expression of relationships between different Representations, i.e. the <R>-Correlations of the Viewpoint Paradigm. Here, we focus on the Expression of particular <R>-Correlations.

At some instants of the requirements elicitation process, Actors must confront part of their produced requirements with those of the other Actors. In concrete terms, in each Representation, there are some elements which allow establishing an <R>-Correlator cr with some elements of the other Representations:

$$\forall p1, \exists p2, p1.r \neq p2.r \text{ and } (p1,p2) \in cr$$

A similar formulation of these <R>-Correlations is also found in [17]. Now, we have to deal with the different kinds of <R>-Correlations. For instance, let us consider semantic links where Actors agree – or seem to agree – according to a common ontology.

Let p1.r and p2.r the respective Representations of two Viewpoints p1 and p2 of P. Each Representation is a set of items (e.g. the statement of an atomic requirement expressed as a logical formula). The consistency of Viewpoints p1 and p2 can be evaluated by means of <R>-Correlations like the following six ones [19], where e is an element of p1.r and e' is an element of p2.r deduced from e by means of some transformation:

- $(p1,p2) \in R1$ iff $p1.r \neq \phi \Rightarrow p2.r \neq \phi$; if the Representation p1.r exists then the Representation p2.r must also exist;
- $(p1,p2) \in R2$ iff $e \in p1.r \Rightarrow p2.r \neq \phi$; if an element e is present in p1.r then p2.r is not empty;
- $(p1,p2) \in R3$ iff $e \in p1.r \Rightarrow e' \in p2.r$; if an element e is present in p1.r then another element e' must be present in p2.r;
- $(p1,p2) \in R4$ iff $e \in p1.r \Rightarrow e \in p2.r$; if an element e is present in p1.r then e must also be present in p2.r.
- $(p1,p2) \in R5$ iff $e \in p1.r \Rightarrow e' \notin p2.r$; if an element e is present in p1.r then another element e' must not be present in p2.r;
- $(p1,p2) \in R6$ iff $e \in p1.r \Rightarrow e \notin p2.r$; if an element e is present in p1.r then e must not be present in p2.r.

These general rules allow detecting inconsistencies. These rules represent templates which can be instantiated according to the formalism of Lyee like in the following examples.

Examples

- R2: if there is a Process Route Diagram prd which is not atomic, then there must exist a second Process Route Diagram prd' which must describe it;
- R4: if a Word w is linked to a W02 Pallet, there exists a Scenario Function which produces w;
- R6: if a Word is produced by a Pallet, then this Word cannot be produced by another.

6. Implementation of the Viewpoint Paradigm to Lyee

We share with researchers in the Requirement Engineering field [4], [7], [8], [12], [13], [14], [17], [24], [25] the opinion that diversity is an unavoidable feature of new software system to be designed. But two statements distinguish the quoted works from our proposition. At first, Requirement Engineering is generally considered as the earliest stage of a design process. In the Viewpoint Paradigm applied to Lyee methodology, we try to act still earlier, i.e. on requirements expressed by natural language. The Viewpoint Paradigm allows dissociating Expression and Content, and thus allows us to consider Expressions which are not provided with formal semantics, like those of natural language.

The second statement is concerned with the relationships between Viewpoints. In many works, the objective is to ensure above all the formal consistency between Viewpoints. We consider that consistency is one possible <E>-Correlation, but is far from being the only pertinent one. In fact, the Infometrical Correlation is a tool to manage consistency, as one of the parameters of the completeness state of a requirements elicitation process.

Lyee methodology mainly consists of capturing the intentions of the different Actors and considers the requirements elicitation process of the *Object to be* as the expression of these intentions; in a complementary way the Viewpoint Paradigm considers the requirements elicitation process of the Object as the process producing the sense of this Object. For us it is important to render this process intelligible.

The next step of the work is to validate the presented models in the Lyee and LyeeAll™ framework. There appears a necessary new skill in the Lyee methodology: the Lyee Knowledge Engineer, whose task is to organize the elicitation of the users' intentions. According to the Viewpoint Paradigm, this skill corresponds to a pivotal Actor who will help to provide the Representations corresponding to what must feed LyeeAll™ CASE tool. It is indeed consistent with Lyee methodology and the Viewpoint Paradigm to render all the Actors responsible of their *intentions* towards software to be.

The requirements elicitation process is iterative until the completeness is observed by the Lyee Knowledge Engineer. At the end of the process, the entries of LyeeAll™ will be complete and consistent in the sense of the Viewpoint Paradigm, and the generation step can be executed properly. The question of the computerized support of the models will be studied, in order to integrate it to LyeeAll™ as an easy to use tool. We intend to support a Viewpoint-Oriented CASE tool for a Lyee Knowledge Engineer to the gathering of a complete and consistent set of entries for LyeeAll™.

To achieve his objective, five stages must be followed. These stages constitute the five iterative actions the Lyee Knowledge Engineer must achieve to obtain the expected set of requirements, as shown in Fig. 9.

Stage 1: Viewpoint elicitation: Words capture and translation with text classification tools

The first stage is a text mining stage: it constitutes a written transcription obtained from all the interviews and other forms of expression of needs collected during the initial stage of the *words* capture process. The result of this stage is the ontology of the domain and the elicitation of the Viewpoints involved in the requirements elicitation process.

Stage 2: Infometrical analysis: Implementation of the Infometrical Correlation

The statistical text processing tools will issue lexical networks in place of classical raw material. The Lyee Knowledge Engineer must complete the typology of all the Words issued to characterize the inputs of Lyee and LyeeAll.

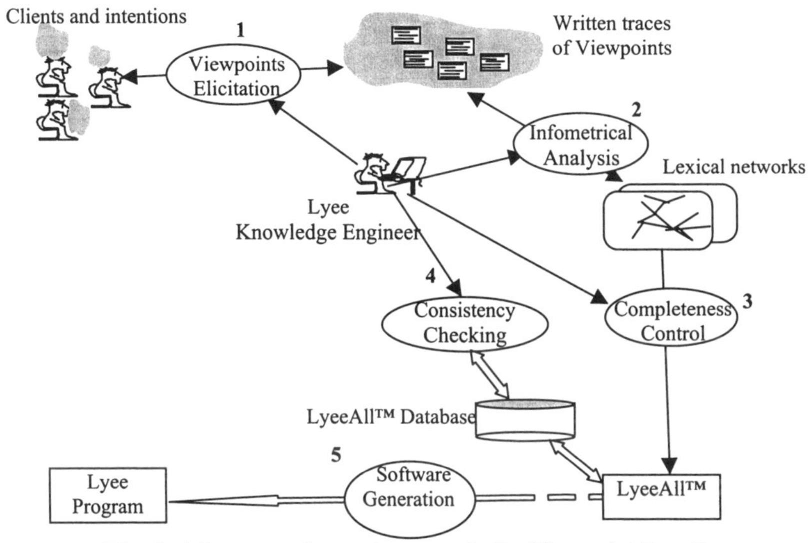

Fig. 9. A Lyee requirement process in the Viewpoint Paradigm

Stage 3: Completeness control of the requirements elicitation process

The requirement process has to converge towards a state where all the Actors implied in the process agree that the set of collected data is complete and consistent. The third stage of the iterative process helps to answer questions like: What are qualitative and quantitative data related to the completeness of the process? How to collect these data? How to render them visible?

We do not constrain the Representations of the Viewpoints to be homogeneous. Actually, either Viewpoints have an autonomous existence before their cooperation, or domain constraints can impose to an Actor of the project to express the Representations of its Viewpoints in a specific formalism. So the Context pole of Viewpoints is defined on two dimensions: Domain, and Time.

The completeness of the process can be viewed by means of a particular <A>-Correlator which defines the state of the cooperation between the different Actors who exert their Viewpoints. We define seven states:

1. isolation: initial state at the beginning of the process;
2. interoperability: the Viewpoints are exerted on the same Object in spite of heterogeneous formalisms;
3. compatibility: the Viewpoints share the Domain dimension of their Contexts;
4. correlation: the Viewpoints are interoperable and compatible;
5. connection: an Actor requests the Representation of several Viewpoints in order to look for inconsistencies, or fusion them; a connection generates a new Viewpoint and <R>-Correlator edges in the Graph of Viewpoints between this new Viewpoint and each of the first ones;
6. connectability: two Viewpoints are connectable if there exists at least one path between them in the Viewpoints Graph;
7. completeness: it is a measure of a *distance* between two Viewpoints, exerted by two Actors, this who orders the project and that who manages the project; this distance can rely

upon quantitative criteria, such as history of connections between Viewpoints, their number and frequency, etc.

We intend to define a model for this <A>-Correlator based on a Multi-Agent System: Roughly, each Viewpoint will be supported by an Agent and different <X>-Correlations can be simulated by the communication rules defined as the strategies of the system. This system has to be coupled with the statistical parser of the previous stage. In this framework, the requirements elicitation process will be assisted by a system which, in a living way, will show the different Actors what we could define as the *general quality of the process*.

Before LyeeAll™ code generation, the content of the LyeeAll™ metamodel database has to be merged with the production of this system. The different states of completeness will be notified by logical rules during the requirement process.

Stage 4: Implementation of the Consistency Management <R>-Correlation: organization of the requirements towards LyeeAll™

The entries of LyeeAll™ are still wrapped in their Viewpoint container. The aim of the consistency management tool dedicated to the Lyee Knowledge Engineer is to check the consistency among the Viewpoints. The inputs of this tool are all the outputs of the previous stage: the tool applies instances of the six Ri rules presented in section 5.2 to deduce the affectation of the Words to the Scenario Functions and their respective Pallets. The rules and the tool which supports them will be helpful for producing all the entries of the automatic program generation of Lyee.

Stage 5: Code Generation

This stage is the present generation stage of LyeeAll™ tool.

7. Conclusion

Lyee methodology regards new software from the principle that each Actor who is involved in the project expresses his/her own intentions on software to be designed. In order to improve the requirement elicitation process, these Actors have been considered from the so-called Viewpoint Paradigm, which deals with the conditions for an object to be designed to acquire sense from multiple sources. This paradigm, whose funding statement is that the sense of an Object to be is the integration of the Viewpoints which are exerted on it, leads to define the two concepts of Viewpoint and Viewpoint Correlation. Two kinds of Correlations were presented. The first aimed at recognising Viewpoints starting from the corpus of intentions statements produced by the users during the requirements elicitation process. The second aimed at managing the inconsistencies which occur during the process. We claim that the early step of the Lyee methodology can be greatly supported by the Viewpoint Paradigm by providing a so-called Lyee Knowledge Engineer with appropriate tools that produce the entries required by the code generator of LyeeAll™ tool.

A longer term issue is the following: What about designing complete Information Systems using Lyee? According to J. Goguen and C. Linde: "There are very good reasons why clients often do not, or cannot, know exactly what they need; they may want to see models, explore alternatives, and envision new possibilities" [10]. The Viewpoint Paradigm allows considering an Information System as a persistent requirements elicitation process. Each Actor of the Information System has "to find or give sense" to it, despite the evolution of intentions. This takes part of the dynamic – living? – feature of an Information System. Fig. 10 sketches an answer to this issue, considering a persistent loop towards the intentions of Actors, and a sixth stage assisted with computerised tools. These tools are extensions of those proposed here.

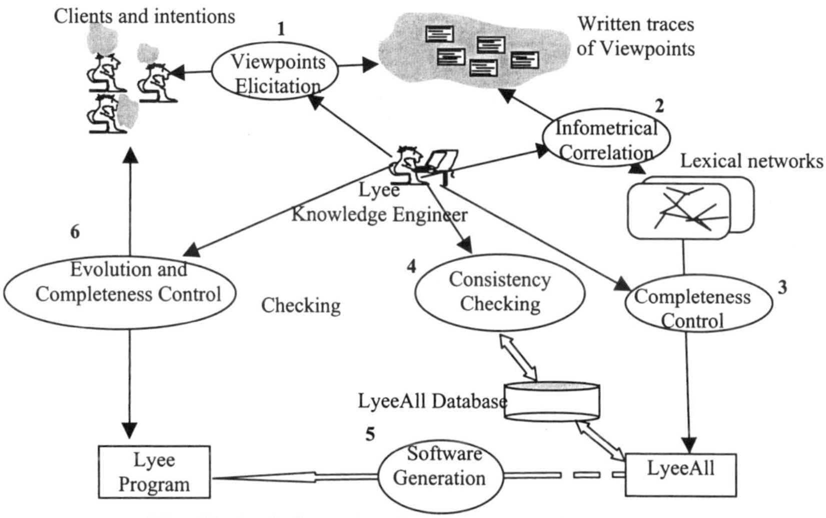

Fig. 10. An Information System as a persistent designing process

References

[1] B. Amon *et al.*, Automated Word Generation for the Lyee Methodology, *New Trends in Software Methodologies, Tools and Techniques,* H. Fujita and P. Johannesson (Eds.), IOS Press, 2002, pp. 357-374.

[2] G. v. Bochmann, Describing Requirements in Lyee and in Conventional Mehods: Towards a Comparison, *New Trends in Software Methodologies, Tools and Techniques*, ed. H. Fujita and P. Johannesson, IOS Press, 2002, pp. 343-356.

[3] G. Deledalle, Lire Peirce aujourd'hui, D. Giovannangeli, (Ed), Le point philosophique, De Boeck Bruxelles, 1990.

[4] S.M. Easterbrook *et al.*, Co–ordinating Distributed Viewpoints: the anatomy of consistency check, *Proceedings of Concurrent Engineering Research and Applications*, West Bloofield, USA, 1994.

[5] S.M. Easterbrook and B.Nuseibeh, Managing Inconsistencies in an Evolving Specification, *Requirement Engineering '95*, York, IEEE C.S. Press, 1995.

[6] U. Eco, Segno, Arnoldo Mondadori Editore, 1980.

[7] A. Finkelstein and H.Fuks, Multi–party Specification, *Proceedings of the 5th Workshop on Software Specification and Design*, Pittsburgh, IEEE C.S. Press, 1989.

[8] A. Finkelstein *et al.*, Inconsistency Handling in Multi-Perspective Specifications, *IEEE Transactions on Software Engineering* 20, 1994.

[9] D. Galarreta *et al.*, Study of Dynamic Viewpoints in Satellite Design, *Proceedings of the 9th Symposium IFAC Information COntrol in Manufacturing systems INCOM'98*, Nancy, June 24-26, 1998.

[10] J. Goguen and C. Linde, Techniques for Requirements Elicitation, *Proceedings Requirements Engineering '93*, S. Fickas and A. Finkelstein (Editors), IEEE Computer Society, 1993, pp. 152-164.

[11] A.J. Greimas, Sémantique structurale, Larousse, Paris, 1966.

[12] G. Kotonya and I. Sommerville, Viewpoints for Requirements Definition, *IEEE Software Engineering Journal* 7, 1992, pp. 375-387.

[13] J.C.S.P. Leite, and P.A. Freeman, Requirements Validation Through Viewpoint Resolution, *IEEE Transactions on Software Engineering* 17 (12), 1991.

[14] J.C.S.P. Leite, Viewpoint resolution in requirements elicitation, PhD Thesis, University of California Irvine, 1988.
[15] E. Morin, La complexité humaine, Champs l'Essentiel, Flammarion, 1991.
[16] F. Negoro, A Proposal for Requirement Engineering, *Proceedings of ADBIS2001, Advances in Database and Information Systems 2,* Vilnius, Lithuania, 2001.
[17] B. Nuseibeh *et al.*, Expressing the Relationships between Multiple Views in Requirements Specification, *IEEE Transactions on Software Engineering* 20 (10), 1994, pp. 760-773.
[18] C.S. Peirce, Collected papers, Harvard U.P., 1932.
[19] L. Perrussel, Expressing Inter-Perspective relationships: A logical Approach, *Proceedings of APSEC '95,* Brisbane, Australia, IEEE CS Press, December 1995.
[20] K. Pohl, The Three Dimensions of Requirement Engineering, *Proceedings of Software Engineering - ESEC '93, 4th European Engineering Conference*, Garmish-Partenkirchen, Germany, September, 1993.
[21] C. Rolland, A User Centric View of Lyee Requirements, *New Trends in Software Methodologies, Tools and Techniques,* H. Fujita and P. Johannesson (Eds.), IOS Press, 2002, pp. 155-169.
[22] J. Rumbaugh *et al.*, The Unified Modelling Language Reference Manual, Addison-Wesley, 1998.
[23] I. Sommerville and P. Sawyer, Viewpoints: Principles, Problems and a Practical Approach to Requirements Engineering, Lancaster University, Computing Department, Technical Report CSEG/15/1997, 1997.
[24] I. Sommerville *et al.*, Managing Process Inconsistency using Viewpoints, Lancaster University, Computing Department, Technical Report CSEG/9/1997, 1997.
[25] P. Zave, Classification of Research efforts in Requirement Engineering, *Computing Surveys* 29(4), 1997, pp. 315-321.

Information Modelling and Knowledge Bases XV
Y. Kiyoki et al. (Eds.)
IOS Press, 2004

Component-based Interaction Design

Thomas Feyer and Bernhard Thalheim

Computer Science Institute
Brandenburg University of Technology at Cottbus, FRG
{feyer, thalheim}@informatik.tu-cottbus.de

Abstract

It has been recognized that there exist dialog structures which re-occur in several applications and even in different application domains [11, 15, 3]. Examples are navigation and search support structures, help facilities, human error handling, and guided tours. Even though applications generally provide an implicit composition of such structures, it is often possible to identify and separate them from one another. So-called interaction patterns (see, for example, [11, 3]) provide an approach to reuse these structures. They define a framework to informally describe common, system-independent interactive structures, their relations, and usage. Besides their usefulness according to reuse, they lack support for verification and composition.

In this paper, we use interaction nets (a slight extension of coloured petri nets) to model, verify, and compose interactive system behavior. It is suited for the domain of information services, since it permits to specify structures of human-computer dialogs as well as interaction in general which comprises interaction with databases in particular. Besides the known dynamic semantics of nets, we introduce a component semantics which considers nets as black-boxes with an interface. The component semantics is well-founded since the behavior of a net composition coincides with the composition of the black-box behavior. It opens the opportunity to combine the advantages of a net-based specification with those of component approaches. More precisely, it permits (i) to specify and verify interaction by a net model, (ii) to consider interaction patterns as implementation-independent black-box specifications called components, and (iii) to infer properties of compositions from properties of elementary specifications.

1 Introduction

The design of appropriate dialog structures comprises an essential part of the design process of information services [8, 16]. To decrease time and costs of the design process and its verification, methods of reuse are applied to this area. For this purpose, dialog structures that re-occur in several applications are first identified and afterwards described and categorized as so-called *interaction pattern*. Examples are navigation and search support structures, help facilities, human error handling, and guided tours. Some models are rather informal but system independent descriptions as, for example, [11, 3] which basically comprise a pattern name, problem description, solution, pattern relations, and examples. Others are rather formal but system dependent as, for example, [15, 10] which focus on web applications.

There also exists several formal and system independent models for interaction design and verification. For example, [1, 6, 13] apply net-based approaches to design user interfaces. However, compositionality is commonly neglected by these approaches.

In [9], we proposed a formal net-based model which is system independent on the one hand, and permits composition on the other. We chose a net-based approach because of several advantages: (i) The granularity of input and output elements can be varied by the designer. It allows to model interaction at different levels of abstraction. (ii) According to composition, nets offer a natural framework to model parallelism and synchronization. (iii) Functional abstraction/specialization is achieved by refining transitions. (iv) Nets possess a formal semantics. (v) Net specifications may be system independent. (vi) There exist graphical representations.

In this paper, we extend the model of [9] to coloured petri nets which provide a more practical design model in comparison to elementary place transition nets. We call according interaction specifications *interaction nets.* To state properties about composite nets, it is generally required to know the net structure of its sub-nets. However, on the one hand this knowledge does not always exist (for example, interactive components which are not specified by a net model), and on the other it is not always desired, since it increases the costs by additional analysis. In a more efficient approach, properties are verified for elementary (net) specifications locally. Afterward, properties of composite specifications can be derived from the properties of its sub-specifications without analyzing the composite net itself. We realize this feature by defining a component semantics for interaction nets adopted from [4]. It considers components as black-boxes with (i) an external interface and (ii) a behavior specification defined by a relation between input streams and output streams. Thereby, a stream represents a finite or infinite sequence of messages. A composition operator then derives the black-box behavior of composed interaction nets from its sub-nets without knowing the particular net structures.

In the paper, we mainly target at user interaction instead of interaction in its general sense. Nonetheless, the proposed interaction model and its component semantics is not restricted to user interaction only.

The reminder of the paper is organized as follows. In Section 2, we describe the application of coloured petri nets [12] for interaction specification and introduce interaction nets and their composition. Section 3 states a brief overview about the component model of Broy et. al. [4]. In Section 4, we define a component semantics for interaction nets and an according composition operator. Afterwards, we state a theorem which proves that the behavior of net compositions can be derived from the component semantics of its sub-nets. Sections 5 and 6 discuss future work and conclude the paper.

2 Interaction Nets

We base interaction nets on the model of coloured petri nets which is briefly introduced in the following. For a more comprehensive introduction, we refer to an introductory book as, for example, [12].

Definition 2.1 *A* (non-hierarchical) coloured petri net (CP net) *is a tuple* $\mathcal{N} = (\Sigma, P, T, A, N, C, G, E, I)$ *which satisfies the following requirements:*

(i) Σ *is a finite set of non-empty data types, called* colour sets.

(ii) $P \subset \mathbf{P}$ *is a finite set of places.*

(iii) $T \subset \mathbf{T}$ *is a finite set of transitions.*

(iv) $A \subset \mathbf{A}$ *is a finite set of arcs.*

(v) $N : A \rightarrow P \times T \cup T \times P$ *is a* node *function that associates arcs with pairs of nodes.*

(vi) $C : P \rightarrow \Sigma$ *is a* colour *function that associates places with data types.*

(vii) $G : T \rightarrow EXP$ *is a* guard *function that associates transitions with expressions such that:*

$$\forall t \in T.\ type(G(t)) = bool \wedge type(var(G(t))) \subseteq \Sigma,$$

where type(e) denotes the data type of an expression e, type($\{e_1, e_2, \ldots\}$) denotes the set of data types of expressions $e_1, e_2, \ldots$, var(e) denotes the set of free variables of an expression e, and EXP denotes the set of all expression.

(viii) $E : a \to EXP$ *is an* arc expression *function that associates arcs with expressions such that:*

$$\forall a \in A.\ type(E(a)) = C(p(a))_{MS} \wedge type(var(E(a))) \subseteq \Sigma,$$

where p(a) is the place of N(a), and 't_{MS}' denotes type 'multi-set of type t'.

(ix) $I : P \to EXP$ *is an* initialization *function that associates places with closed expressions such that:*

$$\forall p \in P.\ type(I(p)) = C(p)_{MS}.$$

Thereby, **P**, **T**, and **A** denote countable infinite sets of places, transitions, and arcs respectively, such that $\mathbf{P} \cap \mathbf{T} = \mathbf{P} \cap \mathbf{A} = \mathbf{T} \cap \mathbf{A} = \{\}$. *Node* function N maps each arc into a pair of nodes where the first element represents the source node and the second the destination node. *Colour* function C defines the data types of places. Thereby, a place p may contain a multi-set of data elements of type $C(p)$ only. The type system builds up on base types like *int* (integers), *real*, *string*, *bool*, and *unit* (denoting a single colour only), and enables to define new types by type constructors *subset*, *product* (tuple constructor), *record* (named tuple constructor), *union*, and *list*. *Expressions* basically correspond to a variant of typed lambda calculus. The language used for CP nets is CPN ML which is an adapted version of Standard ML (SML) [12]. Thus, the evaluation of an expression is defined by means of reducing the respective lambda expression. *Guards* $G(t)$ provide an additional opportunity to control the firing of transitions t. If the guard expression evaluates to 'false', the corresponding transition must not fire. Commonly, missing guard expressions are considered as the closed expression 'true'. *Arc expression* function E associates each arc with an expression. It controls which multi-sets of data elements are consumed or produced by transitions. *Initialization* function I corresponds to the initial marking of elementary petri nets. It associates places with expressions that represent accordingly typed data elements.

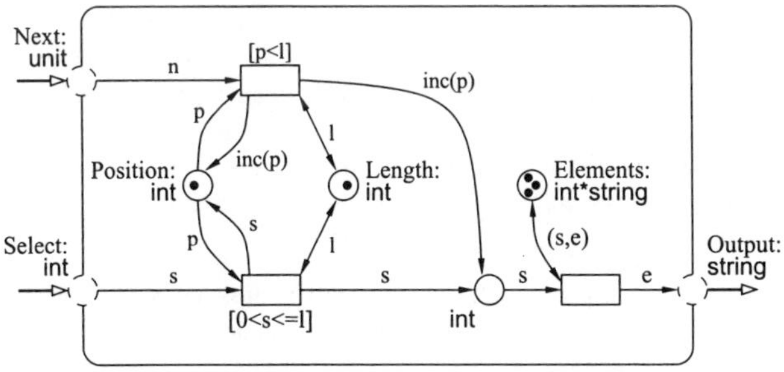

Figure 1: A CP net which provides an event-driven navigation through lists

Figure 1 represents an exemplary CP net. It realizes a simplified event-driven navigation through lists assumed that places 'Position', 'Length', and 'Elements' are initialized by an initial position, the number of elements in the list, and the list elements respectively. If a 'Next' event is initiated by the user, the current position is incremented (if possible), and the corresponding list element is provided at the output place. In the case of an 'Select' event, the list element at the selected position (if existing) is provided. In the figure, we abstractly represented initial data elements by simple dots within places. According to the definition of dynamic semantics of CP nets, we refer to [12]. A brief introduction is attached to the end of the paper.

Since we intend to compose nets, we extend net specifications by an interface. The interface consists of places which are used to receive data from or provide data to externally connected components.

Definition 2.2 *An* interaction net $\mathcal{N}^i = (\mathcal{N}, P^i, P^o)$ *is defined by a CP net* $\mathcal{N} = (\Sigma, P, T, A, N, C, G, E, I)$ *and two disjunctive place sets* $P^i, P^o \subseteq P$, *assumed that* $\mathcal{N}$ *satisfies the following conditions:*

$$\forall a \in A, p \in P, t \in T. \quad (t,p) \in N(a) \Rightarrow p \notin P^i, \tag{1}$$

$$\forall a \in A, p \in P, t \in T. \quad (p,t) \in N(a) \Rightarrow p \notin P^o. \tag{2}$$

The union $P^i \cup P^o$ *is denoted by* P^{io}. *Elements of* P^i, P^o, *and* P^{io} *are called* input places *(or* i-places*),* output places *(or* o-places*), and* input/output places *(or* i/o-places*) respectively.*

Conditions (1) and (2) ensure that input places are exclusively used for receiving data and output places are exclusively used for providing data. Figure 1 represents an interaction net, if dashed circles are interpreted as i/o-places. More precisely, places 'Next' and 'Select' are input places, place 'Output' is an output place.

At a pragmatic point of view, we distinguish input places, output places, context places, and transitions:

Input places are i/o places where external components may write into. Examples are input places which correspond to (i) events initiated by a user – for example, logging in, (ii) parameters published by another net – for example, the task history of the current session, or (iii) controlling information used for synchronization – for example, an activation signal.

Output places are i/o places where external components may read from. The interaction net conveys information via output places. If an external component connected to an output place represents a subsystem (or driver), output places represent an abstraction of external actions. For example, if an output place is externally consumed by a user interface driver or database manipulation driver, producing elements into an output place corresponds to outputting information to the user or initiating a manipulation request to a database.

Context places are non-i/o-places. They represent the internal context of the net during the execution of interactive scenarios. They can be interpreted as situation predicates since the elements in each context place characterize a single facet of the current situation. For example, elements in context places may represent which subtasks a user already accomplished within an interactive task as well as preferences of the current user.

Transitions define context changes. In particular in user interaction, the context of interacting parties changes after each utterance (input) [17, 14, 5]. To act/react properly, these changes must be reflected in the system. They are realized by transitions that compute the new context by altering the situation predicates depending on the utterance.

To enable associativity and commutativity of the composition, we introduce a rename operator. It renames places to prepare nets for their composition.

Definition 2.3 *A* renaming $\rhd_f$ *of an interaction net* $(\mathcal{N}, P^i, P^o)$ *with* $\mathcal{N} = (\Sigma, P, T, A, N, C, G, E, I)$ *is defined by a total, injective function* $f : P \to \mathbf{P}$. *The renamed interaction net* $(\mathcal{N}', P'^i, P'^o) := \rhd_f(\mathcal{N}, P^i, P^o)$ *with* $\mathcal{N}' = (\Sigma', P', T', A', N', C', G', E', I')$ *is defined as*

$$\Sigma' := \Sigma,\ P' := f(P),\ P'^i := f(P^i),\ P'^o := f(P^o),\ T' := T,\ A' := A,\ G' := G,\ E' := E,$$

$$N'(a) := \begin{cases} (f(p), t) : & N(a) = (p, t) \wedge p \in P, \\ (t, f(p)) : & N(a) = (t, p) \wedge p \in P. \end{cases} \quad \text{for all } a \in A,$$

$$C'(p') := C(f^{-1}(p')) \quad \text{for all } p' \in P',$$

$$I'(p') := I(f^{-1}(p')) \quad \text{for all } p' \in P',$$

where $f(P) := \bigcup_{p \in P}\{f(p)\}$, *and* f^{-1} *denotes the inverse function of* f.

If function f is not total on P, we can generally apply the comprehension of f as $f \cup \{p \to p \mid p \in P \wedge f(p) \text{ is undefined}\}$.

Figure 2 demonstrates renaming. Nets $\mathcal{N}_2'$ and $\mathcal{N}_3'$ result from rename operations $\rhd_{f_2}(\mathcal{N}_2)$ and $\rhd_{f_3}(\mathcal{N}_3)$ with functions $f_2 := \{p_2 \to p_5\}$ and $f_3 := \{p_4 \to p_1\}$. For readability, we omit minor details from the example nets in the paper as long as they are not significant.

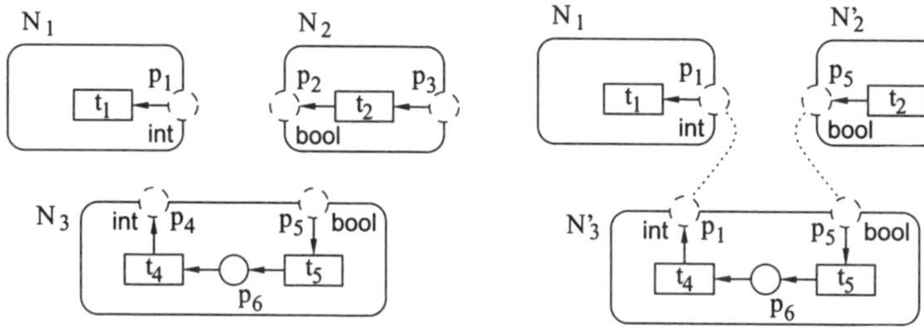

Figure 2: *Left:* Nets $\mathcal{N}_1, \mathcal{N}_2, \mathcal{N}_3$; *Right:* Renamed nets $\mathcal{N}_2' := \rhd_{f_2}(\mathcal{N}_2)$, $\mathcal{N}_3' := \rhd_{f_3}(\mathcal{N}_3)$

The composition of interaction nets is defined by merging shared input/output places:

Definition 2.4 *The* composition $\mathcal{N}_1^i \circ \mathcal{N}_2^i$ *of interaction nets* $\mathcal{N}_1^i = (\mathcal{N}_1, P_1^i, P_1^o)$, $\mathcal{N}_2^i = (\mathcal{N}_2, P_2^i, P_2^o)$ *defines a CP net* $\mathcal{N}^i = (\mathcal{N}, P^i, P^o)$ *as*

$$\Sigma := \Sigma_1 \cup \Sigma_2,\ P := P_1 \cup P_2,\ P^i := (P_1^i \cup P_2^i) \setminus (P_1^o \cup P_2^o),\ P^o := (P_1^o \cup P_2^o) \setminus (P_1^i \cup P_2^i),$$
$$T := T_1 \cup T_2,\ A := A_1 \cup A_2,\ N := N_1 \cup N_2,\ G := G_1 \cup G_2,\ E := E_1 \cup E_2, \text{ and}$$

$$C(p) := \begin{cases} C_1(p) : & p \in P_1 - P_2 \ \vee \ p \in P_1^i \cap P_2^o, \\ C_2(p) : & p \in P_2 - P_1 \ \vee \ p \in P_2^i \cap P_1^o. \end{cases}$$

$$I(p) := \begin{cases} I_1(p) : & p \in P_1 - P_2, \\ I_2(p) : & p \in P_2 - P_1, \\ I_1(p) + I_2(p) : & p \in P_1 \cap P_2. \end{cases}$$

assumed that $T_1 \cap T_2 = \{\}$, $A_1 \cap A_2 = \{\}$, *and*

$$\forall p.\ p \in P_1 \cap P_2 \ \Rightarrow \ \begin{array}{l} (p \in P_1^i \cap P_2^o \ \wedge \ C_2(p) \preceq C_1(p)) \ \vee \\ (p \in P_1^o \cap P_2^i \ \wedge \ C_1(p) \preceq C_2(p)). \end{array} \tag{3}$$

Thereby, the union of functions $f_1 \cup f_2$ is defined as $(f_1 \cup f_2)(x) = f_1(x)$ if $x \in dom(f_1)$, and $(f_1 \cup f_2)(x) = f_2(x)$ if $x \in dom(f_2)$ assumed that $dom(f_1) \cap dom(f_2) = \{\}$. The union of place sets $P_1 \cup P_2$ yields that equally named places merge. Condition (3) verifies that (i) interaction nets may be connected at i/o-places only, i.e., non-i/o-places must be pairwise different, and (ii) established connections must be compatible, i.e., output places may be connected to input places only, and the data type of output places must be a sub-type of the data type of input places.

The composition $(\mathcal{N}_1 \circ \mathcal{N}_2') \circ \mathcal{N}_3'$ of the nets in Figure 2 is shown in Figure 3.

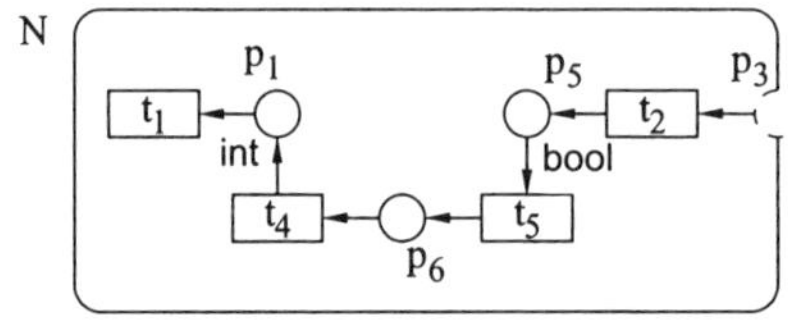

Figure 3: Composed net: $\mathcal{N} := \mathcal{N}_1 \circ \mathcal{N}_2' \circ \mathcal{N}_3'$

Because of the following proposition, we can generally omit parenthesis in multiple compositions, and may neglect the order of the composition sequence.

Proposition 2.1 *The composition operator $\circ$ is associative and commutative.*

Proof By the definition, associativity and commutativity can be reduced to the associativity and commutativity of the set operators union ($\cup$) and intersection ($\cap$) and the multi-set union operator (+). □

3 Stream-based Component Model

3.1 An Introduction

In [4], Broy et. al. define a system independent component model based on streams. *Streams* are finite or infinite sequences of data elements, called *messages*. They denote the communication histories of *directed channels*.

Definition 3.1 *Given a set* **M** *of* messages. *A* stream $s = \langle m_1, m_2, m_3, \ldots \rangle$ *is a finite or infinite sequence of messages.* $\mathbf{M}^*$, $\mathbf{M}^\infty$, *and* $\mathbf{M}^\omega := \mathbf{M}^* \cup \mathbf{M}^\infty$ *denote the set of all finite streams, the set of all infinite streams, and the set of all streams respectively.*

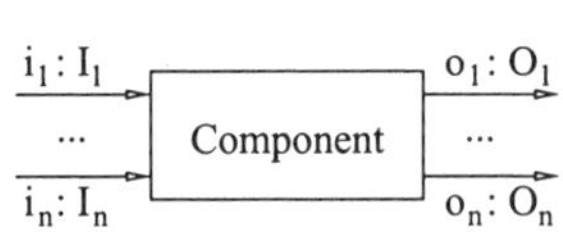

Figure 4: Abstract representation of a component

For example, the stream $\langle m_1, m_2, m_3, m_1 \rangle$ observed at a communication channel indicates that first m_1 was transmitted, followed by m_2 and m_3, and finally m_1 was transmitted again. Components are connected to input and output channels. Streams received on input channels are called *input streams*, streams transmitted through output channels are called *output streams* (see Figure 4). An essential aspect of the component definition is that beside its syntactic structure, the behavior of a component must be defined formally. Basically, the behavior of a component is characterized by the relationship between input streams and output streams.

Definition 3.2 *An* elementary component $\mathcal{C}$ *consists of*

(i) *a name,*

(ii) *a list of* frame labels, *for example, 'timed', 'untimed',*

(iii) input declarations, *i.e., a list* $\langle i_1 : I_1, \dots, i_n : I_n \rangle$ *of declarations of input channels where a* declaration $c : T$ *is a pair of a channel and a data type,*

(iv) output declarations, *i.e., a list* $\langle o_1 : O_1, \dots, o_m : O_m \rangle$ *of declarations of output channels, and*

(v) *a* body, *i.e., a formula in predicate logic.*

The frame labels impose syntactic and semantic constraints onto a component. For example, timed components are labeled by 'timed'. Input and output declarations associate the component with an interface which accepts messages of according data types. The body specifies the behavior of the component. It defines the relationship between input streams and output streams. Besides the use of predicate logic, Broy et. al. propose different specification styles, for example, a style which is based on state transition diagrams.

Dynamic semantics of components:

We use the following abbreviations:

$$\begin{aligned} i_S &:= i_1, \dots, i_n & o_S &:= o_1, \dots, o_m \\ I_S &:= I_1, \dots, I_n & O_S &:= O_1, \dots, O_m \\ B_S &:= Body & & \\ I_S{}^{\underline{\infty}} &:= I_1{}^{\underline{\infty}}, \dots, I_n{}^{\underline{\infty}} & i_S \in I_S{}^{\underline{\infty}} &:= i_1 \in I_1{}^{\underline{\infty}}, \dots, i_n \in I_n{}^{\underline{\infty}} \end{aligned}$$

where $M^{\underline{\infty}}$ denotes *timed* streams of messages of type M. Timed streams may contain so-called *time ticks* '$\surd$' which represent time periods where no messages were transfered. For example, the stream $\langle \surd, m_1, m_2, \surd, \surd, m_3, m_1, \surd, \dots \rangle$ represents a timed version of the untimed stream $\langle m_1, m_2, m_3, m_1 \rangle$. By help of these notations, we represent the syntactic interface of a component by $i_S : I_S \rhd o_S : O_S$.

Definition 3.3 *The denotation* $[\![\mathcal{C}]\!]$ *of a timed elementary component* $\mathcal{C}$ *is defined by the formula:*

$$[\![\mathcal{C}]\!] \;:=\; i_S \in I_S{}^{\underline{\infty}} \;\wedge\; o_S \in O_S{}^{\underline{\infty}} \;\wedge\; B_S\,. \tag{4}$$

The free variables in formula (4) correspond to the input and output streams of the component. This logical formula determines a predicate $\mathcal{R}_S$ through

$$(i_S, o_S) \in \mathcal{R}_S \;\Leftrightarrow\; B_S\,. \tag{5}$$

The i/o-behavior of component $\mathcal{C}$ is then specified by relation $\mathcal{R}_S$. The transition function from component specification $\mathcal{C}$ to its associated i/o behavior relation $\mathcal{R}_S$, we denote by $\mathbf{io}(\mathcal{C})$.

The behavior definition of untimed elementary components can generally be reduced to the timed case. Therefore, we focus on the more general timed case in the paper.

To specify component behavior by logical formulas, operators on streams are employed. In Section 4, we will use the following operators: (i) *length* $\#s$: provides the length of stream s, (ii) *concatenation* $s_1 \frown s_2$: provides the concatenation of streams s_1, s_2, (iii) *rest* $rt.s$: provides stream s with its first message removed, and (iv) *truncation* $s|_n$: provides a stream which consists of the first n messages of stream s.

The component model permits the composition of components. An essential property of component composition is that the behavior of the composition is completely determined by the behavior of the elementary components.

Definition 3.4 *A* composite component $\mathcal{C} = \otimes\{\mathcal{C}_1, \ldots, \mathcal{C}_k\}$ *is defined by a name and a set of components* $\mathcal{C}_1, \ldots, \mathcal{C}_k$*, that satisfy the following condition: if* $c : T_1$ *and* $c : T_2$ *occur in channel declarations of two (not necessarily distinct) components* $\mathcal{C}', \mathcal{C}'' \in \{\mathcal{C}_1, \ldots, \mathcal{C}_k\}$*, then*

(i) data types T_1 *and* T_2 *are equal, and*

(ii) pair $(c : T_1, c : T_2)$ *denotes a pair of an input and an output declaration.*

While condition (i) verifies type compatibility of the interface, condition (ii) ensures that connections are established exclusively by associating output channels with input channels. We call these internally connected channels *local channels.* The list of local channels is denoted by l_S, their corresponding data types by L_S. Figure 5 demonstrates an exemplary composition of two components. The resulting composite component provides as interface a single input channel and a single output channel.

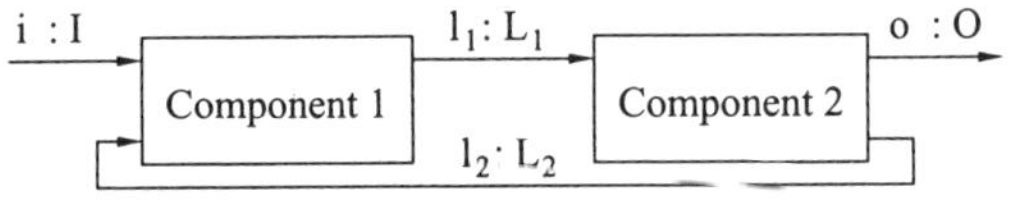

Figure 5: An exemplary composition of two components

Definition 3.5 *The denotation* $[\![\mathcal{C}]\!]$ *of a component* $\mathcal{C}$ *composed by sub-components* $\mathcal{C}_1, \ldots, \mathcal{C}_k$ *is defined by the formula:*

$$[\![\mathcal{C}]\!] \;:=\; \exists l_S \in L_S.\ \wedge_{j=1}^{k} [\![\mathcal{C}_j]\!]\,.$$

The existentially quantified channel indicators realize the desired semantics that output streams of a component $\mathcal{C}_1$ correspond to the input streams of a connected component $\mathcal{C}_2$.

3.2 Behavioral Characterization of Composition

It is straightforward to consider behavior relations specified by a component as (albeit infinite) database relations. The syntactic interface $i_S : I_S \rhd o_S : O_S$ defines an according relation schema by (i) identifying attribute names with channels and (ii) identifying attribute domains with streams of according message types. We denote a corresponding relation schema by $S_{\mathcal{C}} = (\bar{i}_S, \bar{o}_S)$.

We consider the composition of two components $\mathcal{C}_1$ and $\mathcal{C}_2$. Their according relation schemes can be represented as $S_{\mathcal{C}_1} = (\bar{i}_{S_1}, \bar{l}_{S_1}, \bar{o}_{S_1})$ and $S_{\mathcal{C}_2} = (\bar{i}_{S_2}, \bar{l}_{S_2}, \bar{o}_{S_2})$. Thereby, $\bar{l_S}$ denote local streams, $\bar{i_S}$ denote (unconnected) input streams, and $\bar{o_S}$ denote (unconnected) output streams (cf. Figure 5). By this agreement, the behavior of the composition is characterized as follows:

Proposition 3.1 *Given a composite component $\mathcal{C} = \mathcal{C}_1 \otimes \mathcal{C}_2$, respective i/o behavior relations $io(\mathcal{C}_1)$, $io(\mathcal{C}_2)$, and associated relation schemes $S_{\mathcal{C}_1} = (\bar{i}_{S_1}, \bar{l}_{S_1}, \bar{o}_{S_1})$ and $S_{\mathcal{C}_2} = (\bar{i}_{S_2}, \bar{l}_{S_2}, \bar{o}_{S_2})$. Then the composite i/o behavior relation $io(\mathcal{C})$ is determined by*

$$\begin{aligned} io(\mathcal{C}) = \{ & (i_{S_1}, i_{S_2}, o_{S_1}, o_{S_2}) \mid \\ & \exists l_S.\ (i_{S_1}, l_S, o_{S_1}) \in io(\mathcal{C}_1) \ \wedge \ (i_{S_2}, l_S, o_{S_2}) \in io(\mathcal{C}_2) \} . \end{aligned} \tag{6}$$

Proof The proposition is directly derived from Definition 3.5 and Statement (5). □

By applying operators of the relational algebra [7], this characterization can be expressed more compactly. Although database relations are generally finite, according operators can be applied to infinite relations as well. In particular, we may apply projection operation π and natural join operation $\bowtie$.

Proposition 3.2 *Given a composite component $\mathcal{C} = \mathcal{C}_1 \otimes \mathcal{C}_2$, respective i/o behavior relations $io(\mathcal{C}_1)$, $io(\mathcal{C}_2)$, and associated relation schemes $S_{\mathcal{C}_1} = (\bar{i}_{S_1}, \bar{l}_{S_1}, \bar{o}_{S_1})$ and $S_{\mathcal{C}_2} = (\bar{i}_{S_2}, \bar{l}_{S_2}, \bar{o}_{S_2})$. Then the composite i/o behavior relation $io(\mathcal{C})$ is determined by the natural join:*

$$\begin{aligned} \mathcal{R} &= \pi_{\bar{i}_{S_1}, \bar{i}_{S_2}, \bar{o}_{S_1}, \bar{o}_{S_2}} (io(\mathcal{C}_1) \bowtie io(\mathcal{C}_2)) \\ &= io(\mathcal{C}_1) \,\overline{\bowtie}\, io(\mathcal{C}_2) , \end{aligned}$$

where $\overline{\bowtie}$ denotes the natural join with a subsequent projection onto the non-joined attributes.

Proof Statement (6) of Proposition 3.1 corresponds to the definition of the natural join operator. In addition, local streams l_S are projected out from the result. □

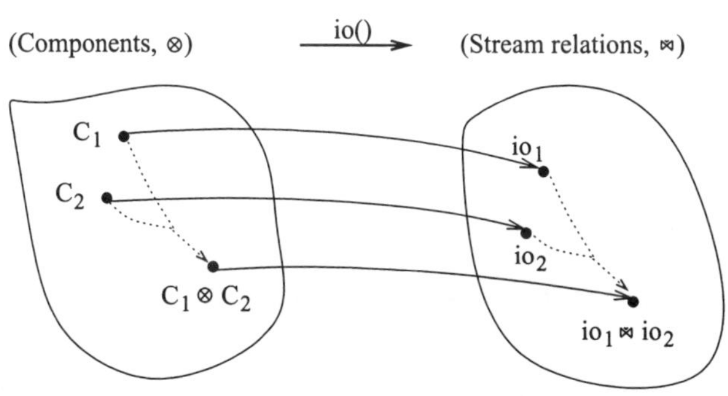

Figure 6: $io(\mathcal{C}_1 \otimes \mathcal{C}_2) = io(\mathcal{C}_1) \,\overline{\bowtie}\, io(\mathcal{C}_2)$

Proposition 3.2 implies that there exists a (partial) homomorphism from component specifications to according component behavior. More precisely, transition function $io()$ represents a partial homomorphism from component specifications (together with component composition $\otimes$) to behavior relations (together with behavior composition $\overline{\bowtie}$). The homomorphism mapping is graphically illustrated in Figure 6. We speak of a *partial* homomorphism, since composition operator '$\otimes$' is partially defined on components only. Therefore, the i/o behavior of component composition is completely determined by the i/o behavior of its elementary components.

4 Component Semantics of Interaction Nets

In Section 2, we defined formal syntax and semantics of interaction nets and their composition. Thereby, the dynamic behavior of a net is precisely defined by the net structure itself. In this Section, we will introduce a characterization of the external net behavior which is based on stream relations. In contrast to the first, it abstracts from the particular realization of a net. It opens the opportunity (i) to view dynamics of interaction nets as black-box components and (ii) to infer properties of composite nets from properties of their sub-nets.

In the following treatment, we assume that i/o-places of interaction nets are initially empty which does not restrict their expressive power.

4.1 I/O-Behavior of Interaction Nets

In the following, we will consider interaction nets as black-box components. While the internal net structure is assumed to be unknown, we may only obtain information about a black-box net through its interface. To investigate the external behavior, we employ the notion of an observer (see, for example, [2]). Technically, an observer is an interaction net itself which is connected to the investigated black-box net. As illustrated in Figure 7, an observer explores the behavior of a black-box by recording the relation between sent messages and received responses.

Definition 4.1 *An interaction net $\mathcal{O}$ is called* observer of $\mathcal{N}$, *if $\mathcal{N}$ is an interaction net, and the composition $\mathcal{N} \circ \mathcal{O}$ exists. We denote the set of observers of $\mathcal{N}$ by $ob(\mathcal{N})$.*

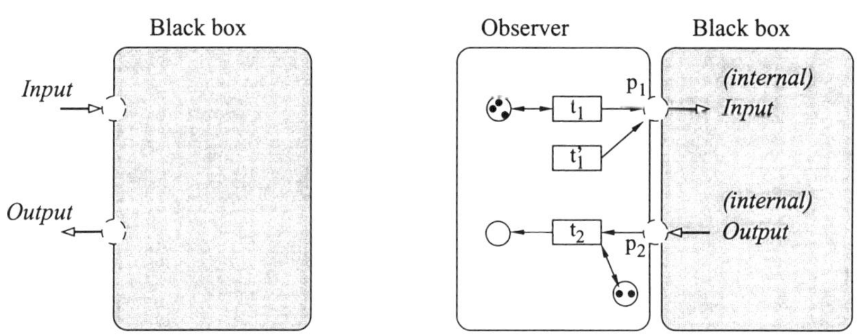

Figure 7: *Left:* A black-box; *Right:* An observer investigates the i/o-behavior of a black-box

To approach a stream based characterization of net dynamics, we record the flow of data elements within runs. Accordingly recorded histories, we call *traces*. We use the intuition that tokens consumed from a place p by a transition t at an occurrence of a step Y "flow" from place p through an arc a to transition t. If a transition does not fire at a step, then according traces correspond to the empty multi-set (shortly denoted as '$\surd$'). For readability, we will generally use $\mathcal{N}$ in the following to denote an interaction net $\mathcal{N}^i$ and its underlying CP net as well. We use $step(\mathcal{N})$ to denote the set of possible steps of net $\mathcal{N}$ and $run(\mathcal{N})$ to denote the set of possible runs of net $\mathcal{N}$.

Definition 4.2 *Given a CP net $\mathcal{N} = (\Sigma, P, T, A, N, C, G, E, I)$.*

Trace $tr(Y)[a]$ of step Y wrt. arc a *is defined as the multi-set of tokens the transition t connected to arc a produced/consumed through this arc during an occurrence of step Y, i.e.,*

$$tr(Y)[a] \;:=\; \sum_{(t,b)\in Y} E(a) < b > .$$

Input trace $tr(Y)[p^+]$ of step Y wrt. place p *is defined as the multi-set union of the traces of step Y wrt. all arcs $a \in A$ with p as its destination node, i.e.,*

$$tr(Y)[p^+] \;:=\; \sum_{a\in A,(t,p)\in N(a)} tr(Y)[a] .$$

Output trace $tr(Y)[p^-]$ of step Y wrt. place p *is defined as the multi-set union of the traces of step Y wrt. all arcs $a \in A$ with p as its source node, i.e.,*

$$tr(Y)[p^-] \;:=\; \sum_{a\in A,(p,t)\in N(a)} tr(Y)[a] .$$

Input trace $tr(r)[p^+]$ of a sequence of steps $r = \langle Y_1, Y_2, \ldots\rangle$ wrt. place p *is defined as the sequence of input traces of steps Y_k wrt. place p, i.e.,*

$$tr(r)[p^+] := \langle tr(Y_1)[p^+],\, tr(Y_2)[p^+],\, \ldots\rangle .$$

Output trace $tr(r)[p^-]$ of a sequence of steps $r = \langle Y_1, Y_2, \ldots\rangle$ wrt. place p *is defined as the sequence of output traces of steps Y_k wrt. place p, i.e.,*

$$tr(r)[p^-] := \langle tr(Y_1)[p^-],\, tr(Y_2)[p^-],\, \ldots\rangle .$$

Trace $tr(r)[\mathcal{N}]$ of a sequence of steps $r = \langle Y_1, Y_2, \ldots\rangle$ wrt. net $\mathcal{N}$ *is defined as the tuple of input and output traces of sequence r wrt. all places of $\mathcal{N}$, i.e.,*

$$tr(r)[\mathcal{N}] := (tr(r)[p_1^+], \ldots, tr(r)[p_k^+], tr(r)[p_1^-], \ldots, tr(r)[p_k^-]), \quad \textit{if } P = \{p_1, p_2, \ldots, p_k\}.$$

Trace $tr(\mathcal{N})$ of net $\mathcal{N}$ *is defined as the set of traces of all runs of net $\mathcal{N}$, i.e.,*

$$tr(\mathcal{N}) := \bigcup_{r\in run(\mathcal{N})} tr(r)[\mathcal{N}] .$$

To illustrate the definition, we consider the CP net in Figure 8 which represents a buffered queue connected to an observer. It transmits received messages in a non-deterministic order.

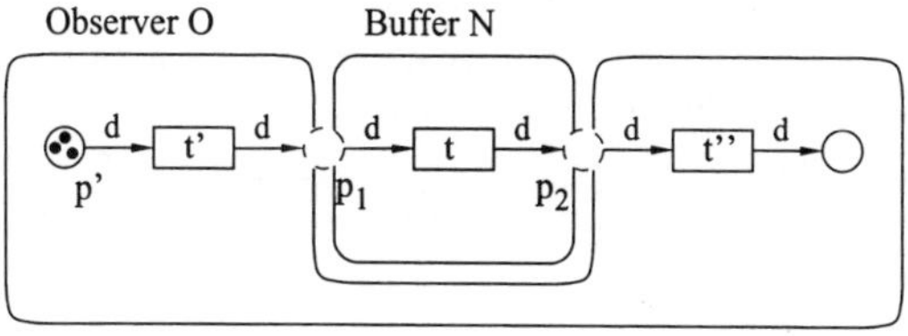

Figure 8: An observer connected to a non-deterministic buffer

Table 1 represents two runs r_1, r_2 of the composed net $\mathcal{O} \circ \mathcal{N}$ assumed that place p' is initialized by multi-set $\{\!|1, 5, 8|\!\}$. Table 2 represents their corresponding traces $tr(r_1)[\mathcal{O} \circ \mathcal{N}]$

	Y_1	Y_2	Y_3	Y_4
r_1 :	$(t', 1)$	$(t', 5) + (t, 1)$	$(t', 8) + (t, 5)$	$(t, 8)$
r_2 :	$(t', 5) + (t', 8)$	$(t', 1)$	$(t, 1) + (t, 8)$	$(t, 5)$

Table 1: Two runs of net $\mathcal{O} \circ \mathcal{N}$

	p'^-	p_1^+	p_1^-	p_2^+
$tr(r_1)$:	$\langle 1, 5, 8, \surd \rangle$	$\langle 1, 5, 8, \surd \rangle$	$\langle \surd, 1, 5, 8 \rangle$	$\langle \surd, 1, 5, 8 \rangle$
$tr(r_2)$:	$\langle 5 + 8, 1, \surd, \surd \rangle$	$\langle 5 + 8, 1, \surd, \surd \rangle$	$\langle \surd, \surd, 1 + 8, 5 \rangle$	$\langle \surd, \surd, 1 + 8, 5 \rangle$

Table 2: Tabular representation of traces of runs r_1 and r_2

and $tr(r_2)[\mathcal{O} \circ \mathcal{N}]$. There, we represent multi-sets by the '+' notation, for example, a multi-set $\{\!| 1, 8 |\!\}$ is represented by $1 + 8$. We also omitted traces that contain exclusively empty messages, i.e., traces according to p'^+ and p_2^-. Since a single variable d occurs in the example net only, we dropped d from the representation of binding elements in Table 1.

We adopt the notion of streams and messages from Section 3 for the behavior of interaction nets. We define a *(net) message* as a multi-set of data elements of the same data type. The intuition behind is that a place may receive or emit several data elements at a single step. Since we use a place-oriented interface, it is possible to send or receive multi-sets of data elements at a time. We apply the definitions of *streams*, *stream relations*, and *operators* on streams from Section 3 to (net) messages. It is straightforward to verify that (i) the trace of a step wrt. an arc is a message, (ii) input and output traces of a step wrt. a place are messages, (iii) input and output traces of runs wrt. a place are streams, (iv) the trace of a net wrt. a run is an element of a stream relation, and (v) the trace of a net is a stream relation. Therefore, we may use the notion of input/output streams as a synonym for input/output traces of nets.

As traces of nets represent stream relations, we may adopt the database perspective from Section 3.2. According to attribute names of relation schemes, we use the following convention: if $P = \{p_1, p_2, \ldots, p_k\}$ is a set of places then $(P)^+ := \{p_1^+, p_2^+, \ldots, p_k^+\}$ are attribute names that denote streams of corresponding input traces, and $(P)^- := \{p_1^-, p_2^-, \ldots, p_k^-\}$ are attribute names that denote streams of corresponding output traces. Attribute domains are defined by the data types of their corresponding places. We define $S_\mathcal{N} := (\mathcal{N}.P)^+ \cup (\mathcal{N}.P)^-$ as the set of stream names of net $\mathcal{N}$. Note: in contrast to Section 3.2, we also consider internal streams. Thereby, each (non-empty) sub-set $S_1 \subseteq S_\mathcal{N}$ represent a relation schema, for example, $S_1 = \{p'^-, p_1^+, p_1^-, p_2^+\}$ as used in Table 2. According elements of a schema S_1, we denote by x_S. Thus, x_S represents a tuple of streams. The type constraint imposed on x_S is represented by '$x_S : S_1$' which reads 'x_S is of type S_1'. We adopted the sub-script '$_S$' from Section 3 to distinguish a tuple of streams x_S from a single stream x. Intuitively the sub-script '$_S$' indicates the existence of an according relation schema.

Commonly, we are not interested in the complete trace of a net $\mathcal{N}$, but in input or output traces of some places only. It corresponds to the projection operation of the relational algebra. For readability, we define the notation:

$$tr(\mathcal{N})[S_1] \;:=\; \pi_{S_1}(tr(\mathcal{N})),$$

if $S_1 \subseteq S_\mathcal{N}$ is a relation schema. The projection operation intuitively applies to traces of runs ('$tr(r)[S_1]$') as well as stream tuples ('$x_S[S_1]$').

Figure 9 motivates that a single observer is usually not able to discover the complete i/o-behavior of an interaction net. Obviously, observer $\mathcal{O}$ provides a restricted view onto the external behavior of net $\mathcal{N}$ only. In particular, it ignores output at place P_3 as well as possible responses to input at place P_4. In addition, neither it tests responses to sending multi-sets of data elements, nor it experiences responses of multi-sets of data elements. Since the external behavior of a net should not depend on the particular abilities of a specific observer $\mathcal{O}$, it has to comprise input/output relations recorded by *any* observer. In the following behavior definition, we use a slightly adapted trace $tr'()$ which will be explained below.

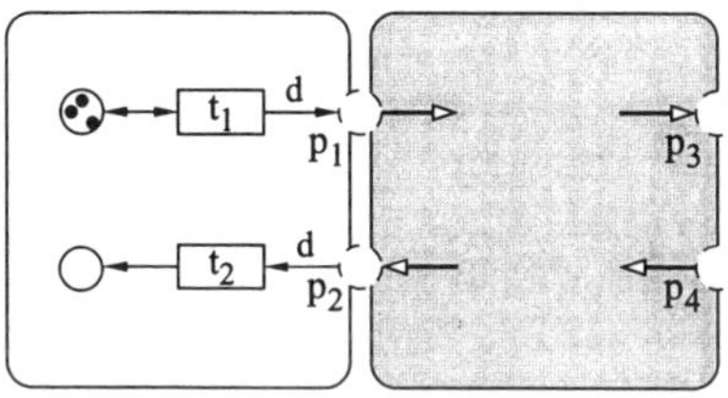

Figure 9: Observer $\mathcal{O}$ initiates input streams and records responses

Definition 4.3 *The* i/o-behavior $io(\mathcal{N})$ of an interaction net $\mathcal{N}$ *is defined as the union of traces of the compositions $\mathcal{N} \circ \mathcal{O}$ over all observers $\mathcal{O}$ of $\mathcal{N}$ projected to the interface streams, i.e.,*

$$io(\mathcal{N}) := \bigcup_{\mathcal{O} \in ob(\mathcal{N})} tr'(\mathcal{N} \circ \mathcal{O})[(\mathcal{N}.P^i)^+ \cup (\mathcal{N}.P^o)^-]$$

$$= \bigcup_{\mathcal{O} \in ob(\mathcal{N})} \bigcup_{r \in run(\mathcal{N} \circ \mathcal{O})} tr'(r)[(\mathcal{N}.P^i)^+ \cup (\mathcal{N}.P^o)^-] .$$

Definition 4.4 *Given a CP net $\mathcal{N}$, a sequence r of steps wrt. net $\mathcal{N}$, and a place $p \in \mathcal{N}.P$. The* shifted traces $tr'(r)[p^+]$ and $tr'(r)[p^-]$ *are defined as*

$$tr'(r)[p^+] := tr(r)[p^+]|_{\#r-1} ,$$
$$tr'(r)[p^-] := rt.tr(r)[p^-] ,$$

if $\#r$ represents the length of sequence r. Shifted traces extend to schemes and nets by attribute-wise application.

The shifted trace $tr'(r)[\mathcal{N}]$ equals trace $tr(r)[\mathcal{N}]$, but (i) the last message of its input streams is removed (if finite), and (ii) the first message of its output streams is removed. According to internal streams of net $\mathcal{N}$, shifted traces obviously carry less information than the usual traces, since some messages are removed. However according to external streams of net $\mathcal{N}$, the shifted traces carry the same information, since we assumed that i/o-places are initially empty. This rather technical transformation yields a natural behavior composition.

4.2 Behavior Composition

In this section, we investigate if the composition model of interaction nets coincides with the component framework introduced in Section 3. Therefore, we have to prove that the characterization of the composition recognized in Section 3.2 is applicable to interaction nets as well. In analogy to Figure 6, we have to confirm the question: *Does behavior function io() represent a (partial) homomorphism from (Interaction nets,* $\circ$*) to (Stream Relations,* $\bowtie$ *)?* The homomorphism is partial, since the net composition $\circ$ is not defined for all pairs of interaction nets. A positive answer to this question would permit to infer the i/o-behavior of composed nets from the i/o-behavior of its sub-nets.

To be precise, we need to comment the join operation $io(\mathcal{N}_1) \bowtie io(\mathcal{N}_2)$. Its intention is to join input streams with connected output streams. By definition 4.3, a connected pair of output/input streams corresponds to attribute names p^- and p^+ respectively. Thus, they actually differ, and thus, the join operator would not combine them. However, as a relaxed notation we may safely ignore superscripts '+' and '−' in any relation schema of $io(\mathcal{N})$. Thereby, the join computes as intended.

Before we state the homomorphism theorem, we will illustrate a motivating example. Figure 10 (left) represents two nets $\mathcal{N}_1$ and $\mathcal{N}_2$. While $\mathcal{N}_1$ duplicates its input, $\mathcal{N}_2$ either eliminates duplicates or replaces its input by constant 'nul'. The sample composition in Figure 10 (right) $\mathcal{N}_1 \circ \mathcal{N}_2$ possesses a unidirectional interaction from $\mathcal{N}_1$ to $\mathcal{N}_2$ realized by a single interface. It is straightforward to verify that Table 3 represents sub-sets of the i/o-behavior relations $io(\mathcal{N}_1)$, $io(\mathcal{N}_2)$, and $io(\mathcal{N}_1 \circ \mathcal{N}_2)$ respectively. Consider, for example, run $r_{1/3}$ of the composed net $\mathcal{N}_1 \circ \mathcal{N}_2$. It corresponds to a parallel execution of runs r_1 and r_3 of the elementary nets $\mathcal{N}_1$ and $\mathcal{N}_2$. In particular, output stream o of net $\mathcal{N}_1$ equals input stream i of net $\mathcal{N}_2$. The same behavior can be observed for runs $r_{1/4}, \dots, r_{2/7}$. These examples indicate a condition according to behavior composition: If there exists elements $(i_1, o_1) \in io(\mathcal{N}_1)$ and $(i_2, o_2) \in io(\mathcal{N}_2)$ with $i_2 = o_1$, then there exists an element $(i_1, o_2) \in io(\mathcal{N}_1 \circ \mathcal{N}_2)$.

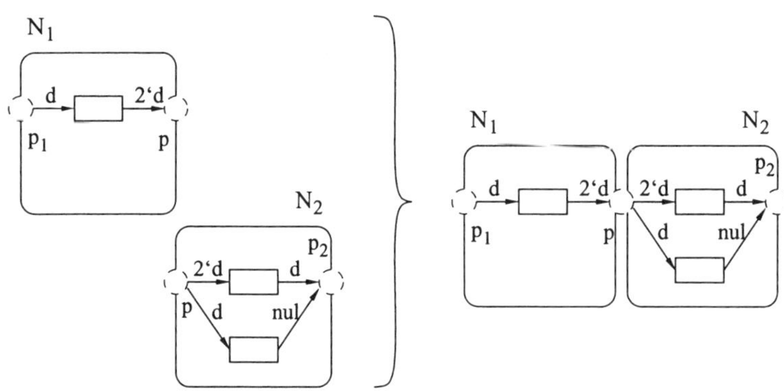

Figure 10: An uni-directional interaction between two interaction nets

The following homomorphism theorem generalizes this example by considering (i) stream tuples instead of single streams, and (ii) bidirectional interaction instead of unidirectional. It provides a positive answer to the question posed above.

Theorem 4.1 *Given two interaction nets* $\mathcal{N}_1$, $\mathcal{N}_2$. *If the net composition* $\mathcal{N}_1 \circ \mathcal{N}_2$ *exists, then the following equality is valid:*

$$io(\mathcal{N}_1 \circ \mathcal{N}_2) \;=\; io(\mathcal{N}_1) \bowtie io(\mathcal{N}_2).$$

The complete proof of the theorem is rather technical and lengthy. Therefore, we decided to omit it from the paper.

Net	Run	Input stream i	Output stream o
$\mathcal{N}_1$	r_1	$\langle 1,2,3,4,\surd\rangle$	$\langle \surd,1+1,2+2,3+3,4+4\rangle$
	r_2	$\langle 1,2,3,4,\surd\rangle$	$\langle \surd,1+1,\surd,3+3,2+2\rangle$
$\mathcal{N}_2$	r_3	$\langle \surd,1+1,2+2,3+3,4+4\rangle$	$\langle \surd,\surd,1,2,3\rangle$
	r_4	$\langle \surd,1+1,2+2,3+3,4+4\rangle$	$\langle \surd,\surd,nul,nul,nul\rangle$
	r_5	$\langle \surd,1+1,2+2,3+3,4+4\rangle$	$\langle \surd,\surd,nul,2,3\rangle$
	r_6	$\langle \surd,1+1,\surd,3+3,2+2\rangle$	$\langle \surd,\surd,nul,nul,3\rangle$
	r_7	$\langle \surd,1+1,\surd,3+3,2+2\rangle$	$\langle \surd,\surd,\surd,1,3\rangle$
$\mathcal{N}_1 \circ \mathcal{N}_2$	$r_{1/3}$	$\langle 1,2,3,4,\surd\rangle$	$\langle \surd,\surd,\surd,1,2,3\rangle$
	$r_{1/4}$	$\langle 1,2,3,4,\surd\rangle$	$\langle \surd,\surd,nul,nul,nul\rangle$
	$r_{1/5}$	$\langle 1,2,3,4,\surd\rangle$	$\langle \surd,\surd,nul,2,3\rangle$
	$r_{2/6}$	$\langle 1,2,3,4,\surd\rangle$	$\langle \surd,\surd,nul,nul,3\rangle$
	$r_{2/7}$	$\langle 1,2,3,4,\surd\rangle$	$\langle \surd,\surd,\surd,1,3\rangle$

Table 3: Sub-sets of the i/o-behavior of nets $\mathcal{N}_1$, $\mathcal{N}_2$, and $\mathcal{N}_1 \circ \mathcal{N}_2$

5 Discussion and Future Work

Component semantics of interaction nets can be applied to ensure interface policies. For example, a hand-shake protocol assumes that both interacting parties satisfy some dynamic properties. One party sends a message and temporarily stops sending further messages, until it receives an acknowledgment. The other party receives a messages and eventually acknowledges it. These interface properties can be expressed by assertions on the i/o-behavior relations of interaction nets. If an assertion is verified according to an interaction net, it will exhibit this property in any composition. The motivation for this statement is that the i/o-behavior comprises input/output histories of *any* net composition, and thus, for each specific composition in particular. A detailed treatment of interface policies is one area of future work.

Besides the aspect of reuse, verification was a major motivation to use a formal model. It permits to answer the following exemplary questions which are useful to ensure quality of interactive components: (i) Which user scenarios are supported? (ii) Which goals can be achieved? (iii) Do there exist goals which cannot be achieved effectively — by means of interactive paths that exceed a given threshold? (iv) Does the context changes of the net coincide with the context changes of the user mental model? In particular, do database views coincide with user's context? We will investigate at some examples to what extent these questions can be analyzed. For this reason, we are currently formalizing an appropriate set of interactive components whose compositions support different kinds of interactive search opportunities.

The component framework of Broy et. al. provides a semantic characterization, whether a component $\mathcal{C}'$ is a specialization of a component $\mathcal{C}$: $\mathcal{C}'$ is a specialization of $\mathcal{C}$, if any input/output history of $\mathcal{C}'$ is also an input/output history of $\mathcal{C}$, i.e.,

$$\mathcal{R}' \subseteq \mathcal{R},$$

if $\mathcal{R}'$ and $\mathcal{R}$ represent the stream relations of $\mathcal{C}'$ and $\mathcal{C}$ respectively. Thereby, a specialization usually reduces non-determinism. Through the component semantics of interaction nets, we can directly apply this definition to deduce or verify the specialization relation on interaction nets.

6 Conclusion

The paper introduced a system independent approach to model, verify, and compose interaction specifications. It supports the reuse of interactive structures of information services. Besides the standard net semantics, a component semantics of the external behavior is introduced. It is well-founded in the sense that the composition of the component semantics coincides with the introduced net composition. The result of the paper can be utilized by the following approach: (1) identify meaningful interaction patterns, (2) design a formal model by an interaction net, (3) verify behavioral properties of the interaction net by analyzing its component semantics, and (4) compose components to compile an application or to design complex components.

References

[1] R. Bastide and P. A. Palanque. A petri net based environment for the design of event-driven interfaces. In *16th Int. Conf. on Application and Theory of Petri Nets*, pages 66 – 83, Turin, Italy, June 1995.

[2] B. Baumgarten. *Petri-Netze: Grundlagen und Anwendungen.* Spektrum Akademischer Verlag, 1996.

[3] J. Borchers. *A Pattern Approach to Interaction Design.* John Wiley & Sons, New York, 2001.

[4] M. Broy and K. Stølen. *Specification and Development of Interactive System.* Springer, New York, 2001.

[5] H. Bunt. Context representation for dialog management. In *2nd Int. and Interdisciplinary Conf. on Modeling and Using Context*, LNCS 1688, pages 77–90, Trento, Italy, Sept. 1999. Springer.

[6] W. Clauss and J. Lewerenz. Abstract interaction specification for information services. In *Int. Conf. On Managing Information Technology Resources in Organizations*, Hershey, Pennsylvania, May 1999.

[7] E. F. Codd. A relational model for large shared data banks. *Commun. ACM*, 13(6), 1970.

[8] T. Feyer, K.-D. Schewe, and B. Thalheim. Conceptual design and development of information services. In *17th Int. Conf. on Conceptual Modeling*, LNCS 1507, Singapore, Nov. 1998. Springer, Berlin.

[9] T. Feyer and B. Thalheim. A model for defining and composing interaction patterns. In *Proc. of the 12th European-Japanese Conference on Information Modelling and Knowledge Bases - EJC'2002*, Krippen, Germany, May 2002.

[10] M. Gaedke and G. Gräf. Development and evolution of web-applications using the webcomposition process model. In *Int. Workshop on Web Engineering at the 9th Int. World-Wide Web Conf.*, Amsterdam, The Netherlands, May 2000. Springer.

[11] F. Garzotto, P. Paolini, D. Bolchini, and S. Valenti. "Modeling-by-patterns" of Web applications. In *Int. Workshop on the World-Wide Web and Conceptual Modeling*, LNCS 1727, Paris, France, Nov. 1999. Springer, Berlin.

[12] K. Jensen. *Coloured Petri Nets. Basic Concepts, Analysis Methods and Practical Use, Volume I.* Springer, 1992.

[13] J. Lewerenz. *Human-Computer Interaction in Heterogeneous and Dynamic Environments: A Framework for its Conceptual and Automatic Customisation.* Dissertation, Brandenburg Technical Universtity at Cottbus, Germany, 2000.

[14] J. McCarthy. Notes on formalizing context. In *International Joint Conference on Artificial Intelligence*, Chambéry, France, Jan. 1993.

[15] D. Schwabe, G. Rossi, Luiselena, and F. Lyardet. Web design frameworks: An approach to improve reuse in web applications. In *Int. Workshop on Web Engineering at the 9th Int. World-Wide Web Conf.*, Amsterdam, The Netherlands, May 2000. Springer.

[16] B. Thalheim. *Entity-Relationship Modeling – Foundations of Database Technology.* Springer, Heidelberg, 2000.

[17] J. van Benthem. Shifting contexts and changing assertions. In *Computing Natural Language*, pages 51 – 65. C S L I Publications, Apr. 1998.

A Dynamic Semantics of CP Nets

Dynamic semantics of CP nets concerns the flow of data elements. Transitions generate, remove, or transform data elements. It basis on the notion of a step which transforms the current net state into a new one. Thereby, the state of a net is defined by its marking.

Definition A.1 *A* binding b *of a transition* t *is a function that associates all variables* $v \in var(t)$ *with data elements in* $type(v)$ *which guarantees that the guard condition* $G(t) < b >$ *is true. Thereby,*

$G(t) < b >$ *denotes an evaluation function which computes the guard expression* $G(t)$ *by substituting its free variables* $var(G(t))$ *corresponding to binding* b *— where binding* b *is interpreted as a variable substitution,*

var(t) *denotes the set of free variables that occur in guard expression* $G(t)$ *or in an arc expression* $E(a)$ *of an arc* a *attached to transition* t*, i.e.,*

$$\forall t \in T.\ var(t) := \{v | v \in var(G(t)) \vee \exists a \in A(t).\, v \in var(E(a))\},$$

where $A(t)$ *denotes the set of arcs attached to* t*.*

A binding element $be = (t, b)$ *is a pair of a transition* t *and a binding* b*.*

A step Y *is a (non-empty) multi-set of binding elements.*

Definition A.2 *A* token element (p, c) *is a pair of a place* p *and a data element* $c \in C(p)$*. The set of all token elements is denoted by* TE*.*

A marking m *is a multi-set over* TE*. The* initial marking m_0 *is the marking obtained by evaluating the initialization expressions, i.e.,*

$$\forall p \in P.\ m_0(p) := I(p) <> .$$

We denote the multi-set of data elements associated with a place p *in a marking* m *by* $m(p)$*.*

Note that there is a slight difference between $I(p)$ and $I(p) <>$. While $I(p)$ denotes a closed expression, $I(p) <>$ denotes the evaluation of this expression, i.e., a multi-set.

Definition A.3 *A step Y is* enabled *in marking M, iff the following condition is satisfied:*

$$\forall p \in P. \sum_{(t,b)\in Y} E(p,t) < b > \leq m(p)\,,$$

where the summation symbol represents the multi-set union.

The occurrence (or execution) of an enabled step Y transforms the marking of the net m_1 to a marking m_2. Roughly, each binding element $(t, b) \in Y$ yields a transformation of marking m_1. More precisely, data elements determined by arc expressions and binding b are consumed from/produced into corresponding places attached to transition t.

Definition A.4 *When a step Y is enabled in a marking m_1, it may* occur. *The* occurrence of Y in m_1 *transforms marking m_1 into marking m_2 by*

$$\forall p \in P.\ m_2(p) := \left(m_1(p) - \sum_{(t,b)\in Y} E(p,t) < b > \right) + \sum_{(t,b)\in Y} E(t,p) < b > .$$

We say that m_2 is directly reachable *from m_1 by the occurrence of step Y, denoted by: $m_1[Y\rangle m_2$.*

The sequence in which transitions are executed does not affect the resulting net marking m_2. Thus, we may think of a parallel execution. The definition exclusively defines the dynamic semantics of the occurrence of a single step. We extend this definition to sequences.

Definition A.5 *A* finite (infinite) occurrence sequence *is a finite (infinite) sequence of markings and steps:*

$$m[Y_1\rangle m_1[Y_2\rangle m_2[Y_2\rangle m_3 \ldots\,,$$

such that $n \in I\!N \cup \{\infty\}$, $m[Y_1\rangle m_1$, and $m_i[Y_{i+1}\rangle m_{i+1}$ for all $1 \leq i < n+1$.

We call the corresponding sequence of steps $r = \langle Y_1, Y_2, \ldots\rangle$ a run, *if the occurrence sequence starts with the initial marking m_0.*

Thereby, we assume the common arithmetic laws on $I\!N \cup \infty$. In particular, $\infty + k = \infty$ and $\infty - k = \infty$ for each constant $k \in I\!N$.

Information Modelling and Knowledge Bases XV
Y. Kiyoki et al. (Eds.)
IOS Press, 2004

A Query-Meaning Recognition Method with a Learning Mechanism for Document Information Retrieval

Xing CHEN* and Yasushi KIYOKI**

**Department of Information & Computer Sciences*
Kanagawa Institute of Technology
1030 Simo-Ogino, Atsugi-shi, Kanagawa 243-0292, Japan
chen@ic.kanagawa-it.ac.jp

***Department of Environmental Information*
Keio University
Fujisawa, Kanagawa 252-8520, Japan
kiyoki@sfc.keio.ac.jp

Abstract Queries including a small number of keywords are usually used in the information retrieval. In order to improve the quality of retrieval results for those kinds of queries, it is important to recognize the meaning of queries correctly. In the retrieval process, if feedbacks for retrieval results are given by users to indicate which retrieval candidates in the retrieval result are appropriate as the desired objects, it is possible to obtain the meaning of queries correctly. If the meaning of a query is dynamically recognized by user's feedback during the retrieval process, it becomes possible to improve the quality of retrieval results obtained by the subsequent information retrieval.

In this paper, we present a query-meaning recognition method with a learning mechanism for document retrieval. In this method, we create a vector space and vectors representing the meaning of queries. Retrieval candidates (documents) are also vectorized based on the words appearing in themselves. The most important feature of our method is that a vector space for representing and mapping a query and retrieval candidates is defined as a set of vectors whose components are defined as words. This feature makes it possible to realize dynamic query-meaning recognition by the vector computations for reflecting user's feedback. Our method improves the quality of information retrieval results obtained by the subsequent information retrieval process. In our method, query vectors are modified based on the user's feedback as a learning process. The norms of the vectors of retrieval candidates are calculated by reflecting the modification. In the retrieval results, retrieval candidates are ranked according to the values of their norms. The retrieval candidate with the largest value of norm is retrieved as the top ranking.

1. Introduction

It is common that keywords are used to access information resources. As word-based pattern-matching retrieval methods do not support semantic retrieval, several retrieval methods based on the semantics have been proposed [3,4,7]. Those methods are efficient to perform semantic retrieval with a certain number of keywords. However, users often use a small number of keywords. This motivates us to design and realize a new method for performing information retrieval with a recognition mechanism for the meaning of query consisting of a small number of keywords. Another motivation is in the cross-language information retrieval [1,2,12,13]. We found that the problem of the translation accuracy between languages must be resolved.

A basic issue is how to recognize the meaning of query. To recognize the meaning of query, we consider that the meaning of query can be recognized by using user's feedback. If a user selects the retrieval candidates that are closely related to the user's requirement, we can use the selection results to recognize the meaning of query and modify the query to be issued in the subsequent retrieval process.

In this paper, we present a new query-meaning recognition method for information retrieval. This method uses user's feedback in the information retrieval process to realize dynamic query-meaning recognition and information retrieval based on the recognized meaning. This method performs the dynamic meaning recognition efficiently in the information retrieval process. In our method, a vector space is created to compute correlations between a query and each retrieval candidate document. The components of vectors for representing a query and retrieval candidates are directly expressed by words. By expressing the components of vectors directly by words, our method makes it possible to determine which words sharply give the meaning of query. In our method, a query and retrieval candidates are vectorized based on the words, and a query vector is modified by the user's feedback to adjust it to the query-meaning sharply. We refer this user's feedback and adjusting process to as "learning mechanism". By applying the learning mechanism to the query vector, we can obtain new query results with the ranking reflecting the query-meaning recognition. Our method improves the quality of information retrieval results obtained by the subsequent information retrieval.

In this paper, we discuss the related work, and then introduce a query-meaning recognition method. We show several experimental results to explain the processes for realizing our method.

2. Related work

Our work is based on the study of MMM (Mathematical Model of Meaning)[4,5,6,7,8] and LSI (Latent Semantic Indexing)[3,10,11]. Both of those research results provide fundamental frameworks for semantic information retrieval using orthogonal vector spaces. MMM uses dictionaries to obtain the semantic definitions of words and create a semantic vector space. LSI finds the semantics of words latent in documents. Retrieval candidates and queries are vectorized in those methods. Information retrieval is performed by calculating correlations between the vector of the query and the vectors of retrieval candidates.

(1)MMM[4,6,7,8]

MMM realizes fundamental semantic associative search for extracting semantically related data resources according to contexts. In MMM, it is basically declared that a word and each retrieval candidate (word and media data) include various meanings. That is, the meaning of a word (or each retrieval candidate) is not fixed statically, but it is fixed only when the context is given. In MMM, machinery for computing contexts is realized by creating an orthogonal knowledge space. Each word and retrieval candidate is placed as a single coordinate point in the knowledge space and dynamically extracted by semantic associative search. In the knowledge space, each context corresponds to one of the subspaces. Given a context, a semantic subspace corresponding to the context is selected. Each word and retrieval candidate is mapped onto the semantic subspace selected according to a given context, and the relationships between data items are dynamically computed by using the metric in the selected semantic subspace reflecting the context. Semantic associative search might not always select appropriate data from databases because the judgment of accuracy is sometimes dependent on individual variation. In [9], a learning mechanism for MMM has been presented for adapting retrieval results according to individual variation and improving accuracy of the retrieval results. The learning is a significant mechanism for semantic associative search because the judgment of accuracy for the retrieval results is dependent on individuals who request semantic associative search. In the learning process of MMM, if inappropriate retrieval results for a request are obtained by the semantic associative search, appropriate data items, which must be the retrieval results, are specified as suggestions. Then, the learning mechanism is applied to the semantic associative search system to obtain the appropriate retrieval results in subsequent requests.

(2) LSI[3,10,11]

In LSI, a mathematical method called SVD is applied for mapping documents and computing correlations on an orthogonal vector space. Associating documents are expected to locate closely to one another. If the vector of a query is close to some document vectors, those documents are selected as the retrieval results. In LSI, queries are represented as pseudo-documents and mapped onto the vector space. If the query contains common words to the target retrieval candidates (target documents), it locates closely to those target documents. And, those documents can be obtained as the retrieval results.

In comparing to MMM and LSI, our method focuses the case that a small number of keywords are given as a query. In MMM and LSI, it is assumed that an appropriate query is given in the information retrieval processes. Our method is practically used for constructing an appropriate query by using the user's feedback for recognizing the query-meaning sharply.

3. Creating the retrieval space based on the documents' clustering

We create the retrieval space by first clustering a sample document set. Each of the clusters has a characteristic that some common terms frequently appear among the documents of the same cluster but rarely appear in the documents of the other clusters. The common terms which frequently appear in a cluster C_i are referred to as C_i's keyword terms. We use a term set k_i to represent the keyword terms. We illustrate this in Fig. 1. In Fig. 1, sample documents are clustered into q clusters. Each cluster contains several documents. For example, cluster C_1 contains documents d_1, d_2... d_i. Terms, t_1... t_a, frequently appear in the documents of d_1, d_2... d_i. They rarely appear in the documents clustered into the other clusters. Therefore, the C_1's keyword terms are those t_1... t_a which are in the set K_1:

$$K_1 = \{t_1, t_2 \cdots t_a\}.$$

	C_1	C_2	...	C_q
t_1 ... t_a	d_1, d_2 ... d_i			
t_{a+1} ... t_b		d_{i+1}... d_{i+j}		
...			...	
t_{n-f} ... t_n				d_{m-s}... d_m

Fig. 1: Document clustering.

Sample documents are clustered into q clusters. Each cluster contains several documents. For example, cluster C_1 contains documents d_1, d_2... d_i. Terms, t_1... t_a, frequently appear in the documents of d_1, d_2... d_i. They rarely appear in the documents clustered into the other clusters.

	d_1	d_2	...	d_m
C_1	$e_{1,1}$	$e_{1,2}$	...	$e_{1,m}$
C_2	$e_{2,1}$	$e_{2,2}$	...	$e_{2,m}$
...	...	...	...	...
C_q	$e_{q,1}$	$e_{q,2}$	...	$e_{q,m}$

Fig. 2: The matrix D.

In the matrix D, each of the rows corresponds to a cluster C_i, each of the columns corresponds to a document d_j, and the ij^{th} entry of D, $e_{i,j}$, is the count of the occurrences of the Ci's keyword terms in the jth document.

The retrieval space is constructed by a matrix D as shown in Fig. 2. In the matrix D, each of the rows corresponds to a cluster C_i, each of the columns corresponds to a document d_j, and the ij^{th} entry of D, $e_{i,j}$, is the count of the occurrences of the C_i's keyword terms in the jth document. Based on our experiment experience, we set the value of $e_{i,j}$ based on the following rule: *when a term appears in a document, it is counted only once no matter how many times it appears*. We use v_t to represent the counted value of a term t.

In the following, we give an example to explain the rule. Suppose the C_1's keyword term set K_1 contains three terms, t_1, t_2 and t_3,

$$K_1=\{ t_1, t_2, t_3\}.$$

If the document d_1 contains the terms t_1 and t_2, but does not contain the term t_3, it is expressed as

$$t_1 \in d_1,\ t_2 \in d_1,\ t_3 \notin d_1.$$

Because both K_1 and d_1 contain the terms t_1, v_{t_1} is set to 1, $v_{t_1}=1$. Same as that, v_{t_2} is set to 1, $v_{t_2}=1$. Because d_1 does not contain t_3, v_{t_3} is set to 0, v_{t_3}=0. The count of the occurrences of the C_1's keyword terms in the document d_1 is calculated as

$$\begin{aligned} e_{1,1} &= v_{t_1} + v_{t_2} + v_{t_3} \\ &= 1+1+0 \\ &= 2\ . \end{aligned}$$

In the following, we use the expression $\sum\{v_{t_1}, v_{t_2}, v_{t_3}\}$ to represent the sum of $v_{t_1} + v_{t_2} + v_{t_3}$. Because t_1, t_2 and t_3 are the elements of the set K_1, the set $\{v_{t_1}, v_{t_2}, v_{t_3}\}$ can be represented as $\{v_t | t \in K_1\}$. Therefore, we use $\sum_{t\in K_1}\{v_t\}$ to represent $\sum\{v_{t_1}, v_{t_2}, v_{t_3}\}$. That is, the sum of $v_{t_1} + v_{t_2} + v_{t_3}$ are represented as

$$v_{t_1} + v_{t_2} + v_{t_3} = \sum_{t\in K_1}\{v_t\}.$$

In this way, the calculation for $e_{i,j}$ is represented by the following formula:

$$e_{i,j} = \sum_{t\in K_i}\{v_t \mid if\ t \in d_j\ v_t = 1\ else\ v_t = 0\ \}.$$

Where, K_i is the set of the C_i's keyword terms and v_t is the counted value of one of the C_i's keyword term *t*. If the document d_j contains the keyword term *t*, v_t is set to 1. If the document d_j does not contain the keyword term *t*, v_t is set to 0.

Based on the matrix D, we use a q dimensional vector $\mathbf{d}_i$ to present the document d_i.

$$\mathbf{d}_i = \begin{bmatrix} e_{1,i} \\ e_{2,i} \\ \vdots \\ e_{q,i} \end{bmatrix}.$$

Each cluster represents a dimension of the vector $\mathbf{d}_i$. We refer it to as the document vector. If the document d_i contains the keyword terms of one cluster, the vector $\mathbf{d}_i$ is a single dimension vector. If the document d_i contains the keyword terms of more than one cluster, it is a multi-dimensional vector. Fig. 3 shows an example of the distribution of the document vectors on a two-dimensional space. From the figure, it can be found that documents are distributed between the two clusters C_1 and C_2. They are divided into 2 groups. One group of documents cluster around C_1 and the other group of documents cluster around C_2.

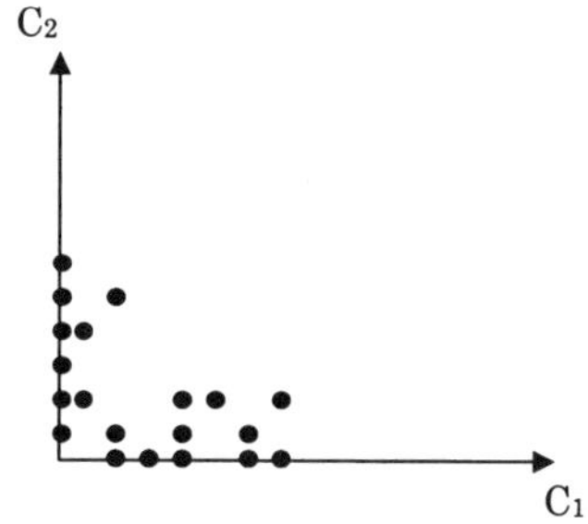

Fig. 3: An example of the distribution of the document vectors on a two –dimensional space.

In the figure, it can be found that documents are distributed between the two clusters C_1 and C_2. They are divided into 2 groups. One group of documents cluster around C_1 and the other group of documents cluster around C_2.

4. Retrieval subspace selection based on query

In our method, document retrieval is performed on a retrieval subspaces. The subspaces are selected from the retrieval space based on queries. The subspace is a v-dimensional space which is a part of the q-dimensional retrieval space, where v is smaller than q. The v-dimensional subspace has v clusters. We use a unit vector $\mathbf{c}_i$, the norm of it is 1, $|\mathbf{c}_i|=1$, to represent the cluster C_i. With the definition of the cluster vector $\mathbf{c}_i$, we express the document vector $\mathbf{d}_j$ as

$$\mathbf{d}_j = \sum_{i=1}^{q} e_{i,j}\mathbf{c}_i .$$

Documents are clustered on the retrieval space. If the document d_j is in the cluster C_i, the component item of $\mathbf{d}_j$ related to the cluster C_i has the maximum value,

$$\left|e_{i,j}\mathbf{c}_i\right| = MAX\left(e_{1,j}, e_{2,j}, \cdots, e_{q,j}\right).$$

The subspace is selected by the following steps.

(1) When a query Q is given, the pattern matching method is used to search the documents which contain the same terms in the query. Documents that have the same terms as those in the query are extracted.
(2) From all the component items of the selected document vector, we extract the cluster vector $\mathbf{c}_i$ of which the related component item $|e_{i,j}\mathbf{c}_i|$ has the maximum value. We use a vector $\mathbf{q}$ referred as the query vector to represent the extracted clusters. We add the extracted cluster vector $\mathbf{c}_i$ to the vector $\mathbf{q}$,

$$\mathbf{q}=\mathbf{q}+\mathbf{c}_i; \text{ where the initial value of } \mathbf{q} \text{ is } 0.$$

(3) We define a retrieval subspace set S containing all the cluster vectors on the retrieval subspace. We calculate the inner product of $\mathbf{c}_i$ and $\mathbf{q}$. If the value of the inner product $\mathbf{c}_i \cdot \mathbf{q}$ is greater than or equal to a threshold ε, $\mathbf{c}_i$ is added to the set S.

When a subspace is selected, the document vector on the subspace is represented as

$$\mathbf{d}_j = \sum_{i=1}^{q} \left\{e_{i,j}\mathbf{c}_i \middle| \mathbf{c}_i \in S\right\}.$$

Following is an example to illustrate the subspace selection.

Example-1:
In this example, we suppose that there are two documents d_1, d_2 and a query Q. The document vectors are represented as follows:

$$\mathbf{d}_1=5\mathbf{c}_1+2\mathbf{c}_2,$$
$$\mathbf{d}_2=3\mathbf{c}_2.$$

We also suppose that the query Q contains the terms that also exist in d_1 and d_2. The subspace selection is performed under the following steps:

1. Document extracting:

For the given query Q, because it contains the terms existing in the two documents, d_1 and d_2 are extracted.

2. Cluster extracting:

The component item $5\mathbf{c}_1$ of d_1 is the maximum value item, $|5\mathbf{c}_1|$=MAX ($5\mathbf{c}_1$, $2\mathbf{c}_2$), so the cluster C_1 is extracted. Similarly, $3\mathbf{c}_2$ of $\mathbf{d}_2$ is the maximum value item, so the cluster C_2 is extracted. As two clusters are extracted, we get the query vector $\mathbf{q}$ as

$$\mathbf{q}=\mathbf{c}_1+\mathbf{c}_2.$$

3. Subspace selecting

The values of the inner products of the cluster vectors $\mathbf{c}_1$ and $\mathbf{c}_2$ with the query vector $\mathbf{q}$ are $1(=\mathbf{c}_1 \cdot \mathbf{q})$ and $1(=\mathbf{c}_2 \cdot \mathbf{q})$, respectively. When the threshold ε is set to 1, both $\mathbf{c}_1$ and $\mathbf{c}_2$ are added to the set S:

$$S=\{\ \mathbf{c}_1, \mathbf{c}_2\ \}.$$

5. Document retrieval

Document retrieval is performed through two steps. The first step is to select a subspace by a given query. That is, the clusters on the selected subspace reflect the meaning of the given query. Therefore, all the documents on the subspace should appear in the retrieval result. The second step is to rank the documents on the subspace. The documents are ranked based on the keyword terms that they contain on the subspace. The document which contains the most keyword terms is ranked at the top. The number of the keyword terms contained in the document d_j is obtained by calculating the norm of the document vector:

$$|\mathbf{d}_j| = \left| \sum_{i=1}^{q} \{ e_{i,j}\mathbf{c}_i | \mathbf{c}_i \in S \} \right|.$$

Where, S is the set containing all the cluster vectors on the selected subspace.

6. The learning mechanism

Based on the document retrieval method mentioned in the Section 5, the documents which do not have the same word patterns as the word pattern in the query can be extracted. We reached the purpose to extract documents which do not contain the same word patterns as the word pattern in the query but have the same meaning with the term in the query.

In our model, the meaning of a query is defined to be reflected in the retrieval result. If the retrieval result is close to the user's requirement, we say the meaning of the query is correctly reflected. If the retrieval result is not close to the user's requirement, we say the meaning of the query is not correctly reflected. In this case, we use a learning mechanism to learn the meaning by user's feedback.

In our model, the document retrieval is performed on the selected subspace based on the query. If the meaning of the query is not correctly reflected, the retrieval subspace should be re-selected. We modify the query vector $\mathbf{q}$ to realize the subspace re-selection.

In our learning mechanism, we require users to indicate the documents which are close to their retrieval requirements from the retrieval results. When documents are indicated, the query vector **q** is modified under the following steps:

(1) From all the component items of an indicated document vector, we extract the cluster vector $\mathbf{c}_i$ of which the related component item $|e_{i,j}\mathbf{c}_i|$ has the maximum value. We add the extracted cluster vector $\mathbf{c}_i$ to the vector **q** to modify it as

$$\mathbf{q}=\mathbf{q}+\mathbf{c}_i.$$

It is worth to notify that the vector **q** which is calculated in the step-2 of Section4 is used as the initial vector in this step.

(2) We set the retrieval subspace set S to an empty set. Then, we calculate the inner product $(\mathbf{c}_i \cdot \mathbf{q})$ of $\mathbf{c}_i$ and **q**. After the inner product of the total extracted cluster vectors is calculated, the cluster vectors, whose inner product values are greater or equal than a threshold ε, are added to the subspace set *S*.

Based on the above steps, when a cluster is repeatedly selected, the query vector becomes closer and closer to the cluster. By setting a suitable threshold, we can obtain the subspace that is closest to the meaning of the query. An example is illustrated in the following.

Example-2:

Based on the Example-1, the query vector **q** is obtained as

$$\mathbf{q}=\mathbf{c}_1+\mathbf{c}_2.$$

If d_1 is indicated in the feedback, $\mathbf{c}_1$ is selected, because its related item has the maximum value, $|5\mathbf{c}_1|$=MAX $(5\mathbf{c}_1, 2\mathbf{c}_2)$. Therefore, the query vector **q** is modified as

$$\mathbf{q}=2\mathbf{c}_1+\mathbf{c}_2.$$

If the threshold ε is set to as 2, $\mathbf{c}_1$ is extracted and added into the subspace set S:

$$S=\{\mathbf{c}_1\}.$$

7. Adding new documents to the retrieval space

The retrieval space is created by clustering the given sample documents. The sample documents have the characteristic that some common terms appear frequently in the documents of the same cluster but rarely appear in the documents of other clusters. These terms are called as clusters' keyword terms. New documents do not exist in the sample documents. We assume that the new documents have the same characteristic as the sample documents. That is, some cluster's keyword terms frequently appear in a new document but the other keyword terms rarely appear.

Based on this characteristic, terms in a new document are classified based on the cluster's keyword terms. We define a term feature set $f_{i,j}$ for a new document d_j. The elements of the set $f_{i,j}$ are the terms of document d_j, which are classified into C_i's cluster.

$$f_{i,j} = \{ t \mid t \in K_i \text{ and } t \in d_j \}.$$

Where, d_j is the new document, t is the term of the document d_j and K_i is the keyword term set of cluster C_i. If there is not a term in the document d_j to be classified into C_i's cluster, $f_{i,j}$ is an empty set. Because sample documents are classified into q clusters, there are q term feature sets, $f_{1,j}$, $f_{2,j}$, ..., $f_{q,j}$ defined for each the document d_j.

A new document is vectorized based on the term feature sets. Because there are q feature sets for each new document, we use a q dimensional vector $\mathbf{d}_i$ to represent a new document d_i. Each feature set represents a dimension of the vector $\mathbf{d}_i$.

$$\mathbf{d}_i = \begin{bmatrix} e_{1,i} \\ e_{2,i} \\ \vdots \\ e_{q,i} \end{bmatrix}.$$

The number of the elements of the set $f_{k,i}$ is enumerated as the component value $e_{k,i}$ of the vector d_i.

$$\begin{aligned} e_{k,i} &= |f_{k,i}| \\ &= \sum_{t \in f_{k,i}} \{ v_t \mid v_t = 1 \}. \end{aligned}$$

Where, $f_{k,i}$ is the term feature set and v_t is the enumerated value of one of the term t in the set $f_{k,i}$. The value v_t is set to 1 for each term in the feature set $f_{k,i}$. Therefore, if there are n elements in the feature set $f_{k,i}$, the value $e_{k,i}$ is n.

With the definition of the cluster vector c_i, $|\mathbf{c}_i|=1$, the vectorized new document is represented as

$$\mathbf{d}_j = \sum_{i=1}^{q} e_{i,j} \mathbf{c}_i$$

When all the components of the new document are calculated, the new document is added onto the retrieval space.

The processes which automatically add a new document on the retrieval space are summarized as follows.

(1) Terms in a new document d_j are sorted.
(2) Duplicated terms are deleted.
(3) For each cluster's keyword term set K_i, i=1, 2, ..., q, repeat step-4 and step-5.
(4) For each term in the set K_i, search the same term from the sorted terms of the new document. If there is a same term is found, copy the term into the feature set $f_{i,j}$.

(5) Enumerate the elements in the set $f_{i,j}$ and copy the enumerated value to $e_{i,j}$, the component value of the document d_j.

In the following, we use an example to explain the above-mentioned processing steps. Suppose that the sample documents are classified into two clusters, C_1 and C_2. The C_1's keyword term set K_1 contains three terms, t_{11}, t_{12} and t_{13}, and the C_2's keyword term set K_2 contains two terms t_{21} and t_{22}.

$$K_1=\{ t_{11}, t_{12}, t_{13}\},$$
$$K_2=\{ t_{21}, t_{22} \}.$$

Suppose that a new document d_i contains the terms t_{11}, t_{12} and t_{22}, but it does not contain the term t_{13} and t_{21}. That is,

$$t_{11}, t_{12}, t_{22} \in d_1, \quad t_{13}, t_{21} \notin d_1.$$

In the step-1 and step-2, terms in the document are sorted and the duplicated terms are deleted. Thus, we get a sorted term set of d_i.

$$d_i=\{..., t_{11}, t_{12}, t_{22}, ...\}.$$

Because there are two clusters in this example, step-4, 5 and 6 are executed twice. During the first execution, it searches whether the set d_i has the same terms as that in the set K_1 or not. Because the terms t_{11}, t_{12} are in the set d_i, these two terms are copied into the feature set $f_{1,i}$.

$$f_{1,i}=\{t_{11}, t_{12}\}.$$

As there are two elements in the set $f_{1,i}$, the value $e_{1,i}$ is set to 2.

$$\begin{aligned} e_{1,i} &= |f_{1,i}| \\ &= 2 \end{aligned}.$$

During the second execution, it searches whether the set d_i has the same terms as that in the set K_2 or not. Because the term t_{22} is in the set d_i, this term is copied into the feature set f_{12}.

$$f_{2,i}=\{t_{22} \}.$$

As there is only one element in the set $f_{2,i}$, the value $e_{2,i}$ is set to 1.

$$e_{2,i} = |f_{2,i}| \\ = 1 .$$

The new document d_i is vectorized as

$$d_i = \begin{bmatrix} 2 \\ 1 \end{bmatrix}.$$

8. Experiment

We have used 100 sample documents, $d_1, d_2, ..., d_{100}$, extracted from ten topics, Topic-1, Topic-2, ..., Topic-10 for experiments. Ten documents are extracted from each topic. The documents $d_1, d_2, ..., d_{10}$ are extracted from Topic-1. The documents $d_{11}, d_{12}, ..., d_{20}$ are extracted from Topic-2. All the other documents are extracted in the same way. The documents extracted from Topic-10 are $d_{91}, d_{92}, ..., d_{100}$. As documents are classified according to each topic, we obtained 10 clusters with 10 documents in each of them. Each cluster corresponds to a topic. Cluster C_i corresponds to Topic-*I*, that is, Cluster C_1 corresponds to Topic-1, cluster C_2 corresponds to Topic-2, and so on.

The keyword terms are extracted from the sample documents. The keyword terms extracted from the documents in a same topic do not appear in the documents of the other topics. Fig. 4 shows the keyword terms extracted from the documents in Topic-2. These keyword terms only appear in the documents $d_{11}, d_{12}, ..., d_{20}$. They do not appear in the other documents. As there are 10 clusters, we obtained 10 keyword term sets, $K_1, K_2, ..., K_{10}$. The keyword terms in the set K_i are extracted from the documents in Topic-*i*.

Keyword terms extracted from the documents $d_{11}, d_{12}, ..., d_{20}$:

accommodate, bestseller, broadband, command, LAN, specifications, TCP

Fig. 4 The keyword terms extracted from the documents under Topic-2
These keyword terms only appears in the documents $d_{11}, d_{12}, ..., d_{20}$. They do not appear in the other documents.

A keyword term-document matrix is created for generating the retrieval space. Each row of the matrix corresponds to a keyword term and each column of the matrix corresponds to a document. Each value of the entry of the matrix is set by using the method as mentioned in Section 3. We divided this matrix into 10 sub-matrixes. Each sub-matrix is constructed by the keyword terms and the documents belonging to the same topic. Fig. 5 shows one of the sub-matrixes constructed by the keyword terms and the documents belonging to Topic-1. In Fig. 5, the keyword terms 'administratively', 'advocates', 'aide', etc. are extracted from the documents $d_1, d_2, d_3, d_4, d_5, d_6, d_7, d_8, d_9$ and d_{10}. Each row of the sub-matrix corresponds to an extracted keyword term, and each column corresponds to a document d_j, here, dj is one of the documents in Topic-1. The ij^{th} entry is generated as follows: If the term in the ith row appears in the document in the jth column, the ij^{th} entry is set to '1'. If the term in the ith row does not appear in the document in the jth column, the

ij^{th} entry is set to '0'.

For example, in Fig. 5, as the keyword term 'administratively' appears in the document d_3, the entry corresponds to 'administratively' and d_3 is set to '1'. As the keyword term 'aide' does not appear in the document d_3, the entry corresponds to 'aide' and d_3 is set to '0'.

topic/document \ keyword term	Topic-1									
	d_1	d_2	d_3	d_4	d_5	d_6	d_7	d_8	d_9	d_{10}
administratively	0	0	1	0	0	0	0	0	0	0
advocates	0	0	0	0	0	0	0	0	1	0
aide	0	0	0	0	1	0	0	0	0	0
...		...								
creditors	0	0	0	0	0	0	0	1	0	0
darrow	0	0	0	0	0	0	0	0	0	1
disbursed	0	1	0	0	0	0	0	0	0	0
...		...								
inspection	1	0	0	0	0	0	0	0	0	0
...	...									
presses	0	0	0	1	0	0	0	0	0	0

Fig. 5 The sub-matrix of the keyword terms and documents under Topic-1

The keyword terms are extracted from the documents d_1, d_2, d_3, d_4, d_5, d_6, d_7, d_8, d_9 and d_{10} in Topic-1. Each row of the sub-matrix corresponds to a keyword term, and each column corresponds to a document d_j, $1 \le i \le 10$. The ij^{th} entry is set as the follows: If the term in the ith row appears in the document in the jth column, the ij^{th} entry is set to '1'. If the term in the ith row does not appear in the document in the jth column, the ij^{th} entry is set to '0'. For example, as the keyword term 'administratively' appears in the document d_3, the entry corresponds to 'administratively' and d_3 is set to '1'. As the keyword term 'aide' does not appear in the document d_3, the entry corresponds to 'aide' and d_3 is set to '0'.

Fig. 6 shows the keyword term-document matrix constructed by the keyword terms and the 100 sample documents. As there are 10 topics, 10 sub-matrixes of keyword terms and documents are created.

In Fig. 6, the entry of the keyword term-document matrix is set to '0' under different topics. Fig. 6 shows that if the ith row's keyword term and the jth column's document are under different topics, the value of the ij^{th} entry is '0'. For example, as the keyword term 'administratively' and the document d_{11} are under different topics, the entry at the row of the keyword term 'administratively' and the column of d_{11} is set to '0'.

As documents are classified into 10 clusters under the 10 topics, a ten-dimensional retrieval space is constructed. The sample documents are vectorized on the ten-dimensional retrieval space.

	Topic-1				...		Topic-10		
	d_1	d_2	...	d_{10}	d_{11}	...	d_{91}	...	d_{100}
administratively	The sub-matrix of the keyword terms and the documents under Topic-1				0	...	0	...	0
advocates					0	...	0	...	0
...					...	...	...	...	
presses					0	...	0	...	0
...	0	0	...	0		...	The sub-matrix of the keyword terms and the documents under Topic-10		
philosophical	0	0	...	0	0	...			

Fig. 6: The keyword term-document matrix

The keyword term-document matrix is constructed by the keyword terms and the 100 sample documents. As there are 10 topics, there are 10 sub-matrixes of keyword terms and documents under the 10 topics. The entry of the keyword term-document matrix is set to '0' under different topics. For example, the keyword term 'administratively' and the document d_{11} are under different topics, therefore the entry at the row of the keyword term 'administratively' and the column of d_{11} is set to '0'.

The document vectors of the sample documents are represented as

$$\mathbf{d}_s = e_{i,s}\mathbf{c}_i ,$$

where $\mathbf{d}_s$ is the sample document vector and $\mathbf{c}_i$ is the cluster vector. The value of $e_{i,s}$ is calculated by the method mentioned in Section 3. Some of the vectors of the sample documents are shown in the following:

$$d_{24}=[0\ 0\ 1\ 0\ 0\ 0\ 0\ 0\ 0\ 0]^T,$$
$$d_{25}=[0\ 0\ 2\ 0\ 0\ 0\ 0\ 0\ 0\ 0]^T,$$
$$d_{26}=[0\ 0\ 8\ 0\ 0\ 0\ 0\ 0\ 0\ 0]^T,$$
$$d_{28}=[0\ 0\ 5\ 0\ 0\ 0\ 0\ 0\ 0\ 0]^T.$$

It can be found that the values of the document vectors on the cluster vector $\mathbf{c}_3$ are not zero. The values on the other cluster vectors are all zero.

After the retrieval space is created, we add other 100 documents, d_{101}, d_{102}, ..., d_{200}, onto the retrieval space. The documents d_{101}, d_{102}, ..., d_{110} are extracted from Topic-1. The documents d_{111}, d_{112}, ..., d_{120} are extracted from Topic-2. The other documents are extracted from Topic-3, Topic-4, ..., Topic-10. The documents d_{191}, d_{192}, ..., d_{200} are extracted from Topic-10. The document vectors of the new added documents are represented as

$$\mathbf{d}_j = \sum_{i=1}^{q} e_{i,j}\mathbf{c}_i ,$$

where $\mathbf{d}_j$ is the new added document vector and $\mathbf{c}_i$ is the cluster vector.

When the new documents are added onto the retrieval space, some of the keyword terms under different topics appear in a same document. Thus, some documents have non-zero values on different cluster vectors. For example, the document d_{127} is vectorized as

$$d_{127}=[1\ 0\ 2\ 1\ 0\ 0\ 0\ 0\ 0\ 0]^T.$$

In Fig. 7, a subspace with two cluster vectors, $\mathbf{c}_2$ and $\mathbf{c}_3$, are taken as an example to show the documents distribution. Fig.7 (a) shows the distribution of sample documents on the retrieval space. Fig. 7 (b) shows the distribution of sample and new added documents on the retrieval space. Documents d_{137} and d_{200} are the noise on $\mathbf{c}_2$ and $\mathbf{c}_3$, respectively. That is, they are not expected to appear on the subspace.

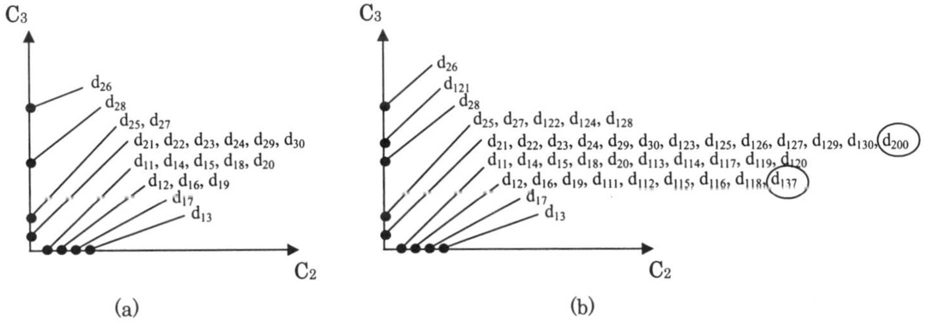

Fig. 7: The documents distribution on the retrieval space.

Fig.7 (a) shows the distribution of sample documents on the retrieval space. Fig. 7 (b) shows the distribution of sample and new added documents on the retrieval space. Documents d_{137} and d_{200} are the noise on $\mathbf{c}_2$ and $\mathbf{c}_3$, respectively.

We have performed retrieval experiments in the following two steps. In the first step, we search sample documents when no new documents are added onto the retrieval space. A. In the second step, we search the documents when the new documents are added onto the retrieval space.

In the first step, we test the efficiency of the learning mechanism. If new documents are not added onto the retrieval space, each document is vectorized on a definite cluster. For a given query, those documents are extracted which contain the same terms as that in the query. If the extracted documents are in a same cluster, all the documents in the cluster are ranked as the retrieval result. In this case, both the recall rate and the precision rate are 1.0. If no document is extracted, a new query is needed.

If the non-keyword terms are used in the query, the documents in different clusters may be extracted. The learning mechanism is used in this case. From the extracted documents, the documents which are required by the user are indicated as the user's feedback. Based on the feedback, the query vector is modified and the required cluster is selected. Fig.8 shows the learning result. In the figure, documents in three clusters are extracted. The documents in one of the three clusters are the user's required documents. Before the feedback is performed, the recall rate is 1.0 and the precision rate is 0.33. When one of the documents in the required cluster is indicated as the feedback, only the documents in the required cluster are extracted and the precision rate is improved to 1.0.

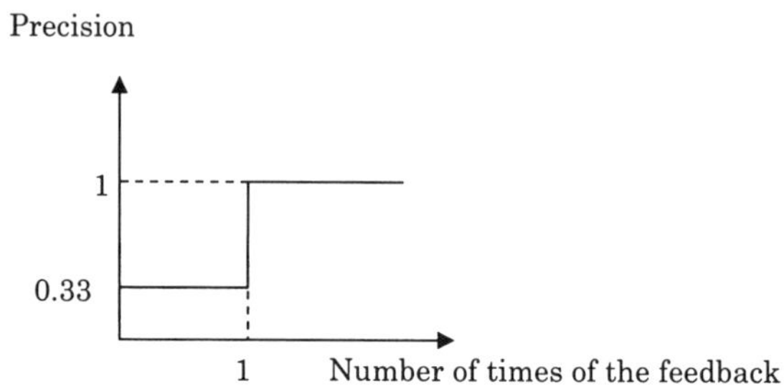

Fig. 8: The learning result.

In the figure, documents in three clusters are extracted. The documents in one of the three clusters are the user's required documents. Before the feedback is performed, the recall rate is 1.0 and the precision rate is 0.33. When one of the documents in the required cluster is indicated as the feedback, only the documents in the required cluster are extracted and the precision rate is improved to 1.0.

When the new documents are added onto the retrieval space, some of the new added documents are vectorized on the different cluster vectors at the same time. 12 new added documents are vectorized on more than two cluster vectors. Among them, 6 documents are vectorized on two cluster vectors, 5 documents are vectorized on three cluster vectors and one document is vectorized on six cluster vectors. The document d_{123} is vectorized on six cluster vectors as the worst case:

$$d_{123}=[3\ 0\ 2\ 0\ 1\ 1\ 2\ 0\ 0\ 1]^T.$$

When a query is given and the documents extracted by the query are in the required cluster, all the documents in the cluster are selected as the retrieval result. In this case, the recall rate is 1.0 but the precision rate goes down. The reason is that some unexpected documents are distributed in the cluster. As the worst retrieval result, 5 unexpected documents are in the retrieval result with the 20 desired documents. In this case, the precision rate goes down to 0.25. But even in the worst cast, most desired documents are ranked in the top-10.

When new keyword terms are extracted from the new added documents and added to the retrieval space, the precision rate is improved. By adding 12 new extracted keyword terms to the retrieval space, the precision rate is improved to 1.0.

If the extracted documents are distributed in more than one cluster, the user's feedback is needed to indicate the required documents. In the most case, the required cluster is selected with only one time (a single) feedback. The number of documents indicated in one feedback influences the number of times of the feedbacks which are needed to select the required cluster. Fig. 9 shows a query example. In the example, if only one document is indicated in each feedback, feedbacks are performed three times before the required cluster is selected. If three documents are indicated in the feedback, the feedback is needed to be performed only once. Fig. 9 also shows that the relationship between the number of documents in a feedback and the number of times of the feedbacks for selecting the required clusters is not liner.

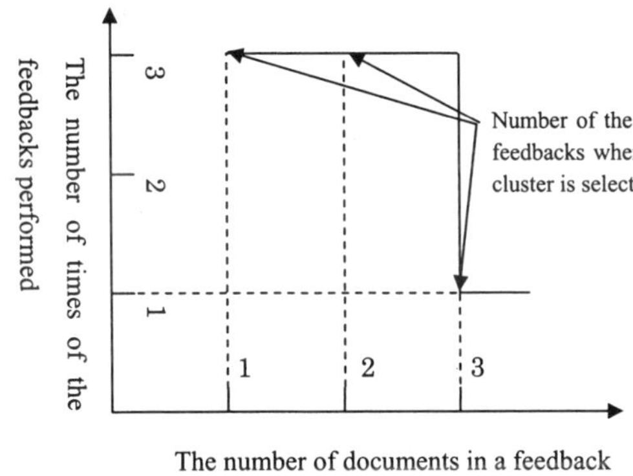

Fig. 9: Relationship between the number of the times of the feedbacks to be performed and the number of documents in each feedback.

If only one document is indicated in each feedback, the feedbacks are performed three times when the desired cluster is selected. If three documents are indicated in the feedback, the feedback is performed only once when the desired cluster is selected.

9. Conclusion

In this paper, we have presented a query-meaning recognition method with a learning mechanism for document retrieval. This method is used for improving the quality of retrieval results obtained by the subsequent information retrieval. The meaning of the query is recognized through user's feedback by selecting appropriate retrieval candidates from the query result. Our method is advantageous for short queries, which contain a small number of keywords for information retrieval. In order to realize information retrieval based on the query-meaning recognized by the user's feedback, we have introduced the methodology for creating a vector space. We have also shown several experiments to explain the processes for adjusting a query vector and clarify the feasibility and effectiveness of our method.

In our future work, we will apply our method to semantic search models, such as MMM and LSI, for constructing appropriate queries in their retrieval processes. Furthermore, we will design a WWW information retrieval system based on our query-meaning recognition method. In this system, we will deal with more complicated situations in which same words are used in different contexts as various topics.

References

[1] Chen, X., Kiyoki, Y. and Kitagawa, T., "*A multi-language oriented intelligent information retrieval system utilizing a semantic associative search method,*" Proceedings of the 17th IASTED International Conference on Applied Informatics, pp.135-140, 1999.

[2] Chen, X., Kiyoki, Y. and Kitagawa, T., "*A semantic metadata-translation method for multilingual cross-language information retrieval,*" Information Modelling and Knowledge Bases XII, Vol. 67, pp.299-315, 2001.

[3] Deerwester, S., Dumais, S., Furnas, G.W., Landauer, T.K. and Harshman, R., "*Indexing by Latent Semantic Analysis*," Journal of the American Society for Information Science, Vol. 41, No. 6, pp.391-407, 1990.

[4] Kitagawa, T. and Kiyoki, Y., "*A mathematical model of meaning and its application to multidatabase systems*," Proc. 3rd IEEE International Workshop on Research Issues on Data Engineering: Interoperability in Multidatabase Systems, pp.130-135, April 1993.

[5] Kiyoki, Y. and Kitagawa, T., "*A metadatabase system for supporting semantic interoperability in multidatabases*," Information Modelling and Knowledge Bases, Vol. V, IOS Press, 1993.

[6] Kiyoki, Y. and Kitagawa, T., "*A semantic associative search method for knowledge acquisition*," Information Modelling and Knowledge Bases (IOS Press), Vol. VI, pp.121-130, 1995.

[7] Kiyoki, Y., Kitagawa, T. and Hitomi, Y., "*A fundamental framework for realizing semantic interoperability in a multidatabase environment*, " International Journal of Integrated Computer-Aided Engineering, Vol.2, No.1(Special Issue on Multidatabase and Interoperable Systems), pp.3-20, John Wiley & Sons, Jan. 1995.

[8] Kiyoki, Y., Kitagawa, T. and Hayama, T., "*A metadatabase system for semantic image search by a mathematical model of meaning*, " ACM SIGMOD Record, Vol.23, No. 4, pp.34-41, Dec. 1994.

[9] Kiyoki, Y., Kitagawa, T. and Kurata, K., "An Adaptive Learning Mechanism for Semantic Associative Search in Databases and Knowledge Bases," Information Modelling and Knowledge Bases (IOS Press), Vol. VIII, May 1996.

[10] Kolda, T. and O'Leary, D.P., "*A semi-discrete matrix decomposition for latent semantic indexing in information retrieval*," ACM Transactions on Information Systems, Vol. 16, pp.322-346, 1998.

[11] Dumais S. D, "Using Latent Semantic Indexing(LSI) for Information Retrieval, Information Filtering and Other Things," Cognitive Technology Workshop, April 1997.

[12] Mori T., Kokubu T. and Tanaka T., "Cross-Lingual Information Retrieval based on LSI with Multiple Word Spaces, "Proc. NTCIR Workshop 2 Meeting on Evaluation of Chinese & Japanese Text Retrieval and Text Summarization, pp.5-67-5-74, Tokyo, Japan, March. 2001.

[13] Susan T. Dumais, Michael L. Littman, Thomas K. Landauer, "Automatic Cross-Language Retrieval Using Latent Semantic Indexing, "AAAI Spring Symposium Technical Report, pp.15-21, March. 1997.

Information Modelling and Knowledge Bases XV
Y. Kiyoki et al. (Eds.)
IOS Press, 2004

A Framework for a Simple Sentence Paraphrase using Concept Hierarchy in SD-Form Semantics Model

Michiharu Niimi, Sayaka Minewaki, Hideki Noda and Eiji Kawaguchi
Kyushu Institute of Technology
1-1 Sensui-cho, Tobata, Kitakyushu, 804-8550 Japan
E-Mail : {niimi,minewaki,noda,kawaguch}@know.comp.kyutech.ac.jp

Abstract. This paper proposes a method for a simple sentence paraphrase based on the meanings of sentences and a method for the evaluation of a paraphrased sentence. To deal with the meanings of sentences, SD-Form Semantics Model that has been developed by the authors is used. In the model, sentences are described by the form named SD-Form. The paraphrase here is defined as SD-Form to SD-Form transformations, which is based on concept hierarchy in the model. In the evaluation, paraphrased concepts are categorized into simplify, elaborate and synonymous concepts. In this paper, we show a concrete way to paraphrase and some examples.

1 Introduction

Paraphrasing is a part of the language ability in human. Its purpose is to find out different expressions which meanings are the same. Human can not only transform one expression to another expressions with the same or nearly the same meaning but also simplify or elaborate it in both spoken and written language.

Paraphrasing has been used as the pre-processing and/or post-processing in natural language processing[1]. In machine translation, for example, paraphrase can be used for rewriting sentences so that it is easier for machines to deal with natural language or correcting unnatural expressions transformed by the machines at pre-processing or post-processing[2]. Automatic abstraction is regarded as another one that leaves important information and reduces the number of characters from original texts. A method for the information retrieval using paraphrase has been proposed[3]. Furthermore, paraphrase can be applied to the information hiding technology of texts data[4][5].

According to Sato [6], the methods for paraphrasing can be categorized into three types : grammatical, semantical and pragmatic methods. Practically, the grammatical paraphrase is useful and almost researchers is approaching to paraphrase from this view. It looks an easy way to realize paraphrasing because it is realized only grammatical knowledge without using knowledge data and dealing with meanings of sentences. However, human being can paraphrase not only grammatically but also semantically. In order to achieve human like computer systems, it is absolute necessity to make use of semantic information for paraphrasing.

In this paper, we propose a scheme for paraphrasing a simple sentence using SD-Form (Semantic-structure Description Form) Semantics Model [7]. SD-Form is a kind of middle language to describe the semantic structure of a natural language expression including statement, conversational expression, emotion expression, etc. It can describe knowledge data, which is used in the operations defined in the model. A sentence in natural language can be described by an SD-Form. SD-Form Semantics Model makes possible to deal with the meaning information of natural language by processing SD-Forms. One of the characteristics of the model is to deal with the semantic difference between two SD-Forms in quantity.

We formalize paraphrasing in natural language as an SD-Form to SD-Form transformation. It is a transformation of a given SD-Form to another Form that is either simpler or more elaborated than the original. A simpler Form corresponds to a simpler meaning, while an elaborated Form corresponds to a more detailed meaning. An actual transformation uses a knowledge hierarchy on the system. We call it a hierarchical knowledge data, or a concept hierarchy in terms of SD-Form. The term "a concept" here is equivalent to "a piece of knowledge data" which is available in the system.

To transform one SD-Form to another SD-forms means to transform its concepts to the simpler concepts or the more elaborate concepts. To transform one concept to the simpler one means to simplify it, on the other hand, to transform one concept to the elaborate one means to elaborate it. It is useful for the applications using the paraphrase to determine that concepts are paraphrased in simplify , elaborate or synonymous concepts. By SD-Form Semantics Model, we can determine whether concepts are paraphrased with simplification or not. This process is termed an "evaluation of the paraphrasing."

The rest of this paper is organized as follows. First, we review the SD-Form Semantics Model briefly in **2**. Next we propose a method to paraphrase a simple sentence using the SD-Form Semantics Model and the evaluation of paraphrased concepts in **3**. Then, we show an example to paraphrase using the proposed method in **4**. Lastly, in **5** we present some concluding remarks.

2 SD-Form Semantics Model

SD-Form Semantics Model is a framework for analyzing concepts in quantitatively. A "concept" in the model is equivalent to an "idea" in a human mind or the "meaning" of a message. It is not limited to the meaning of a single word, but it is used for an independent unit of the meaning of a message in one sentence, in one relation or in one rule. The forms compromised 6 symbols defined in the model are called SD-Form (Semantic Description-Form). SD-Form can describe each concept in natural language, the statement expression and the emotion expression. The model can deal with the semantic difference of two concepts quantitatively.

2.1 Examples of SD-Form

The syntax of SD-Form is regulated by a context-free grammar. SD-Form is composed of 6 symbols which are called 1) concept label, 2) prescriptor, 3) connector, 4) modifier, 5) functional item and 6) delimiter. These symbols are called "SD-Form symbols." An existing word (Japanese or English) can be used as for concept labels, which are categorized into variable labels and simple labels. A functional item means a function in meanings. For example, the subject item is described by $s(D)$ and the predicate item is described by $v(D)$. In each functional item, D is called the contents of the function item.

By combining those 6 symbols under the context-free grammar, SD-Forms describe the concepts of natural language. SD-Forms can be divided into 8 types in syntactic structure. A sentence in natural languages can be described by statement SD-Form or emotion SD-Form. For example, "I play tennis every day." can be described as a statement SD-Form : "$[s(\text{I}), v(\text{TENNIS/TIME/EVERYDAY})]$" and "John!" can be described as an emotion SD-Form : "$[a(\text{JOHN})]$." Knowledge data stored in the system can also be described in the SD-Form. For example, "Fruits includes apples." can be described as "$(\text{APPLE})kdof(\text{FRUITS})$."

Table 1: Examples of primary score

SD-Form symbols	examples	primary score [semit]
variable label	"X, Y, Z, ..."	1
simple label	"CAR, BUY, ..."	10
modifier	"/"	1
prescriptor	"$nega, only, \ldots$"	2
connector	"$para, equa, \ldots$"	1
functional item	"$s, v, o, \ldots$"	1
delimiters	"[ ]"	1
delimiters	"( )"	0

2.2 *Semantic Information of SD-Form*

In order to deal with the meanings of concepts quantitatively, a value called a primary score is given to each SD-Form symbol. In the model, the primary score is not fixed. Every user can define different primary scores to the SD-Form symbols. In [7], the primary scores shown in Table1 are assigned to the SD-Form symbols.

We define the semantic information, which is denoted by n, of an SD-Form as the amount of the sum of primary scores in the SD-Form. Let D be an SD-Form, the semantic information score of D is represented by

$$si(D) = n.$$

The unit of the n is called *semit.*

Let D be "[s(YOU), v(READ/PAST), o(BOOK/THIS)]." When we use the primary scores in Table1, the semantic information score of D is calculated as follows.

$$\begin{aligned} si(D) &= 1 + (1+10) + (1+10+1+10) + (1+10+1+10) \\ &= 56 \end{aligned}$$

The first "1" in the right side means the primary score of "[ ]." The first parenthesis, the second one and last one in the right side means the information score of "s(YOU)", "v(READ/PAST)" and "o(BOOK/THIS)" respectively. In the D, "YOU", "READ", "PAST", "BOOK" and "THIS" represent simple label.

2.3 *Elaboration relation between two concepts*

2.3.1 *Definition of elaboration relation*

Let D_1 and D_2 be two SD-Forms. When D_2 has a meaning elaborated from D_1 and D_1 has a meaning simplified from D_2, We call this relation as "There is an elaboration relation between D_1 and D_2." At this time, D_1 is called the ancestor of D_2 and this D_2 is called the descendant of D_1. We represent the elaboration relation between D_1 and D_2 as

$$elab(D_1, D_2) = n.$$

In the above formula, n ($0 \leq n < \infty$) is called an elaboration score. The n shows the degree of the elaboration quantitatively.

The elaboration relation are categorized into "syntactic elaboration relation" and "knowledge based elaboration relation." Those relations are denoted by

$$elab_{synt}(D_1, D_2) = n,$$

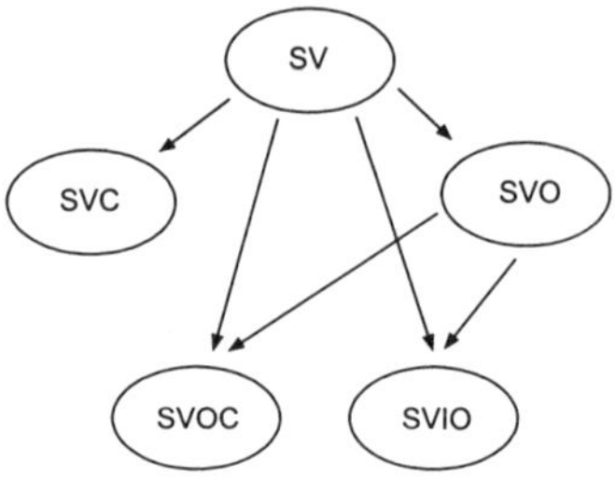

Figure 1: Elaboration relation between two statement SD-Forms

$$elab_{know}(D_1, D_2) = n.$$

By considering those two elaboration relations, the elaboration relation in the model is defined by the following.

$$elab(D_1, D_2) = \min\{elab_{synt}(D_1, D_2), elab_{know}(D_1, D_2)\}$$

2.3.2 *Syntactic elaboration relation*

If we can relate D_1 and D_2 in structure, this relation is called syntactic elaboration relation. The elaboration score of syntactic elaboration relation is defined as follows.

$$elab_{synt}(D_1, D_2) = si(D_2) - si(D_1)$$

Figure 1 shows elaboration relations between two statement SD-Forms.

We show a simple example to calculate $elab_{synt}$. Let D_1 be "CLOCK" and D_2 be "CLOCK/(OLD)*para*(BIG)". In this case, the $elabsynt(D_1, D_2)$ is calculated as follows.

$$\begin{aligned} elab_{synt}(D_1, D_2) &= si(D_2) - si(D_1) \\ &= 32 - 10 \\ &= 10 \end{aligned}$$

In this calculation, the primary score shown in *2.2* was used.

2.3.3 *Knowledge based elaboration relation*

We can relate two concepts, which have no syntactic elaboration relation, by knowledge data. We call it a knowledge based elaboration relation. Knowledge based elaboration relations are categorized into "Specific-Knowledge Based Elaboration Relation" and "General-Knowledge Based Elaboration Relation."

(1) Specific-Knowledge Based Elaboration Relation

Specific-Knowledge Based Elaboration Relation depends on the knowledge data given to the system. Examples are shown in the following.

$$
\begin{aligned}
(D_1)equa(D_2) &\rightarrow elab_{know}(D_1, D_2) = 0 \\
(D_1)defi(D_2) &\rightarrow elab_{know}(D_1, D_2) = 0 \\
(D_1)incl(D_2) &\rightarrow elab_{know}(D_1, D_2) = 3 \\
(D_1)ptof(D_2) &\rightarrow elab_{know}(D_1, D_2) = 3 \\
(D_1)kdof(D_2) &\rightarrow elab_{know}(D_1, D_2) = 3
\end{aligned}
$$

For example, "(SYUTO/JAPAN)*equa*(TOKYO) " is given to the system, the knowledge based elaboration relation, "$elab_{know}$(SYUTO/JAPAN, TOKYO) = 0" is derived.

(2) General-Knowledge Based Elaboration Relation

General-Knowledge Based Elaboration Relation is defined by the rules registered in the system, which is alway true.

$$
\begin{aligned}
elab_{know}(D, nega(nega(D))) &= 2 \\
elab_{know}(D/\mathrm{X}, D/\mathrm{SOME}) &= 1
\end{aligned}
$$

2.4 Semantic difference measure

We calculate semantic difference measure between two concepts using elaboration relation. All common ancestors of D_1 and D_2 are denoted by $D_{0i}(i = 1, 2, \ldots)$. The closest SD-Form to D_1 and D_2 among D_{0i} is called "the nearest common ancestor" and we denote it by D_0. This relations is formalized as follows.

$$
\begin{aligned}
ncoa(D_1, D_0, D_2) &= elab(D_0, D_1) + elab(D_0, D_2) \\
&= \min_i\{elab(D_{0i}, D_1) + elab(D_{0i}, D_2)\} \\
&= n_0
\end{aligned}
$$

The n_0 in the above formula is the semantic difference between D_1 and D_2. Those D_1, D_2 and n_0 relation is represented as

$$diff(D_1, D_2) = n_0.$$

This is to say that the semantic difference can be calculated by finding the nearest common ancestor of D_1 and D_2 within the system.

2.5 Concept hierarchy

The term "concept hierarchy" is a set of concept that is connected according to elaboration relations among knowledge data. We call an operation to organize the knowledge data into a hierarchical structure "concept hierachization." A concept hierarchy consists of nodes and branches where nodes correspond to knowledge pieces, and branches correspond to elaboration relations among the concepts. This concept hierarchy can be regarded as the meaning network.

Let the knowledge data shown in Table 2 be given to the system. In this situation, the illustration of hierarchization of those concepts is shown in Figure 2. Ω in Figure 2 means a set of concepts, that is,

$$\Omega = \{X, F, F_1, F_2, F_3\}.$$

Table 2: Examples of Knowledge data

symbols	SD-Forms	natural language
F_1	SASHIMI	sliced raw fish
F_2	FISHMEAL	fish meals
F_3	(SASHIMI)$kdof$(FISHMEAL)	sliced raw fish is a kind of fish meals.

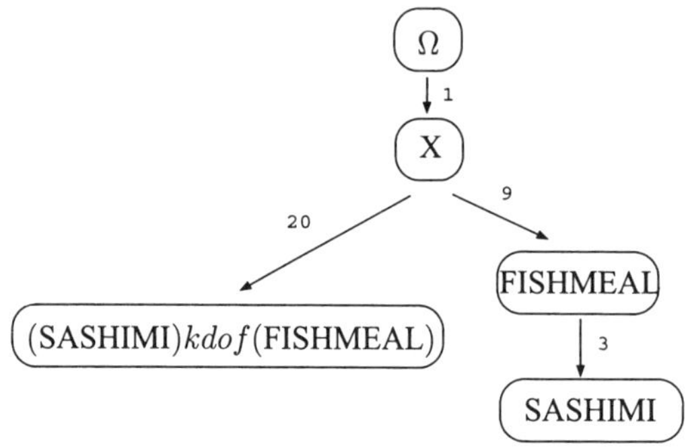

Figure 2: Illustration of a hierarchy of concepts

2.6 Recognition

A framework for intelligent operations like recognition, understanding and interpretation is provided in the SD-Form Semantics Model. In this paper, we show a recognition operation only.

The recognition operation is defined to determine whether the input concept already exits in the concepts hierarchy or not.

Let D_{in} be given to the system, the recognition of D_{in} means to find the closest ancestor in the concept hierarchy. The operation can be formalized by the following.

$$\min_{D}\{elab(D, D_{in})|D \in \Omega\}$$

Note that Ω is a set of concepts. In this case, the relations between D_{in} and D_{rec} are described as follows.

$$recog(D_{in}, D_{rec})$$

3 A simple sentence paraphrase using concept hierarchy in SD-Form Semantics Model

3.1 System overview

In this section we describe the scheme how to transform one SD-Form to another. We also show how to evaluate the transformed SD-Form. In most reported works in the past[6], natural language sentences are paraphrased directly from the original without using deep structure of the sentence. While, our paraphrasing system is based on the semantic information of the

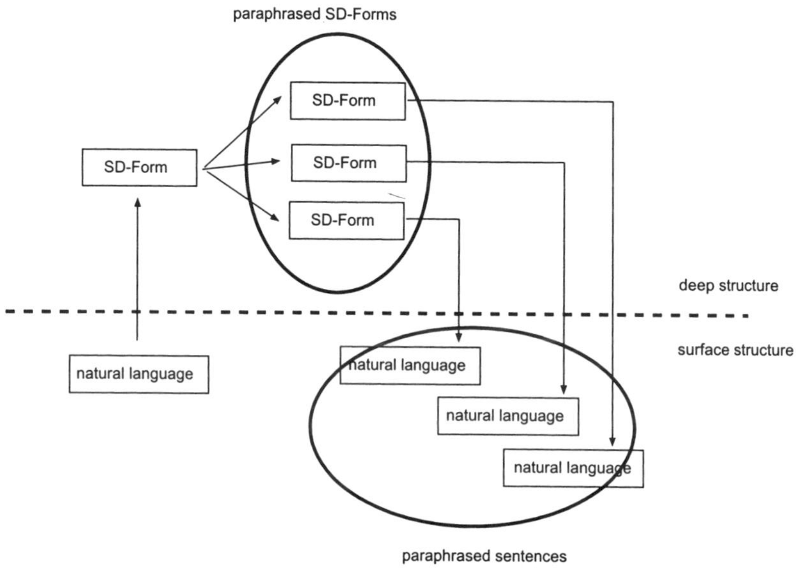

Figure 3: Paraphrase system

sentence. It is shown in Figure3. Firstly, a sentence is translated to an SD-Form that describes the meaning. Then that SD-Form is transformed to another SD-Form with equivalent meaning. Finally, the SD-Forms are translated to natural language sentences.

The paraphrasing method here is achieved by modifying the original SD-Form into another that has a different structure. One SD-Form is paraphrased by using upward/downward relations in the concept hierarchy. A given SD-Form is first recognized as one of the already-known concepts in the hierarchy. Then the recognized concept is paraphrased to a upward node or a downward node along the hierarchy branch. The paraphrasing in this scheme produces three classes of concepts; "simplified concept", "synonymous concepts", and "elaborated concept." These categories are called evaluation results.

3.2 Detailed scheme of the paraphrasing

We now show the detailed way of paraphrasing using concept hierarchy in the systems.

Step-1 Recognition

Let the target SD-Form we want to paraphrase be D_{in}. D_{in} is recognized in the concept hierarchy and the recognized concept is represented by D_{rec}. Where we assume $D_{rec} \neq X$ is satisfied.

Step-2 Substitution of variable labels.

If D_{rec} contains variable labels, the variable labels are substituted with the SD-Form in D_{in} which has the elaboration relation to the label of D_{rec}. The SD-Forms is called a substituted label.

Step-3 generate paraphrased SD-Forms

- All the ancestors of D_{rec} are represented by $HC_p(p = 1, 2, \cdots, n_h)$, and all descendants of D_{rec} are represented by $LC_q(q = 1, 2, \cdots, n_l)$. Where we suppose $HC_p \neq X$ is satisfied.
- We denote the SD-Forms:D_{rec}, HC_p and LC_q, as $Q_m(m = 1, 2, \ldots, 1+n_h+n_l)$. That is,

$$Q_1 = D_{rec}, \quad Q_2 = HC_1, \quad Q_3 = HC_2, \ldots, Q_{1+n_h} = HC_{n_h},$$

$$Q_{1+n_h+1} = LC_1, \quad Q_{1+n_h+2} = LC_2, \ldots.$$

  We call Q_m template concept.
- Let Q_m be Q_{m0}.
- The contents of functional item in the template concepts are denoted by $D_i(i = 1, 2, \cdots)$. All ancestors of D_i and all descendants of D_i in the concept hierarchy are denoted by $D_{ij}(j = 1, 2, \ldots)$ where we assume $D_{ij} \neq X$.
- We produce SD-Forms by substituting D_i with D_{ij}. Those produced SD-Forms are denoted by Q_{mj}.
- If Q_{mj} contains variable labels and the labels are replaceable with the substituted label, we substitute the variable labels with the substituted label. After this operation, if Q_{mj} contains variable labels, then the Q_{mj} does not be considered as a paraphrased concept.
- If Q_{mj} is not the same as D_{rec}, D_{mj} is regarded as a paraphrased SD-Form.

3.3 Evaluation process

As we described earlier, we categorize paraphrased concepts into synonymous concepts, simplified concepts and elaborated concepts. Paraphrased concepts are evaluated using semantic information, semantic difference and elaboration score. The evaluation process is shown in the following.

Step-1 The semantic information of P_k and D_{in} is used for the evaluation. We evaluate paraphrased concepts as

(a) simplified concept if $si(P_k) < si(D_{in})$ is satisfied,

(b) elaborated concept if $si(P_k) > si(D_{in})$ is satisfied.

Otherwise, that means $si(P_k) = si(D_{in})$, we proceed to Step-2.

Step-2 The semantic difference between P_k and D_{in} is used for the evaluation. We evaluate paraphrased concepts as

(a) synonymous concepts if $diff(P_k, D_{in}) = 0$ is satisfied.

Otherwise, that means $diff(P_k, D_{in}) \neq 0$, we proceed to Step-3.

Step-3 The elaboration score between P_k, D_{in} and the nearest common ancestor D_0 is used for the evaluation. We evaluate paraphrased concepts as

Table 3: Knowledge data stored in the system

symbols	SD-Forms	natural language expression
F_1	PLACE	place
F_2	PLACE/X1	the place of X1
F_3	PLACE/[s(X1),c(EXIST)]	the place where X1 is
F_4	(PLACE/X1)incl(PLACE/[s(X1),v(EXIST)])	the place of X1 includes the place where X1 is
F_5	[s(I),v(ASK),o(YOU), c([s(X1),v(EXIST/PLACE/WHERE)])]	Where is X1?
F_6	[s(I),v(ASK),o(YOU($1)), c[s($1),v(KNOW),o(PLACE/X1)]]	Do you know the place of X1?
F_7	$(F_5)incl(F_6)$	F_5 includes F_6.
F_8	[s(I($1)),v(ASK),o(YOU($2)), c[s($2),v(TELL),i($1),o(PLACE/X1)]]	Please tell me the place of X1.
F_9	$(F_6)incl(F_8)$	F_6 includes F_8.

(a) simplified concepts if $elab(D_0, P_k) < elab(D_0, D_{in})$ is satisfied.

(b) elaborated concepts if $elab(D_0, P_k) > elab(D_0, D_{in})$ is satisfied.

Otherwise, that means $elab(D_0, D_{in}) = elab(D_0, P_k)$, we cannot evaluate paraphrased concepts.

In the evaluation process, we use the properties showed in the following.

(1) Semantic information

Semantic information depends on the structure of SD-Forms. The semantic information of the SD-Forms whose structure are complex is large. On the other hand, the semantic information of the SD-Forms which structure are simple is small. In general, the SD-Forms in complex structure provide elaborated concepts and that in simple structure provide simplified concepts.

(2) Semantic difference

Semantic difference is defined as a quantitative difference between two concepts. Hence, if the semantic difference between two concepts is 0, those two concepts are regarded as synonymous concepts.

4 An example of paraphrasing and the evaluation using the proposed method

We now show an example of paraphrasing according to the proposed method and make an evaluation of the paraphrased results. knowledge data shown in Table 3 are registered in the system. The illustration of making a concept hierarchy is shown in Figure 4. As the result of the hierarchization, the new concepts: (X)$incl$(Y), which means X includes Y, are produced. In this example,

$$D_{in} = [s(\mathrm{I}), v(\mathrm{ASK}), o(\mathrm{YOU}(\$1))c(s(\$1), v(\mathrm{KNOW}), o(\mathrm{PLACE/GCCSOURCE}))].$$

is the target concept we make a paraphrase. The D_{in} represents the meaning structure of "Do you know the place of gcc source codes?."

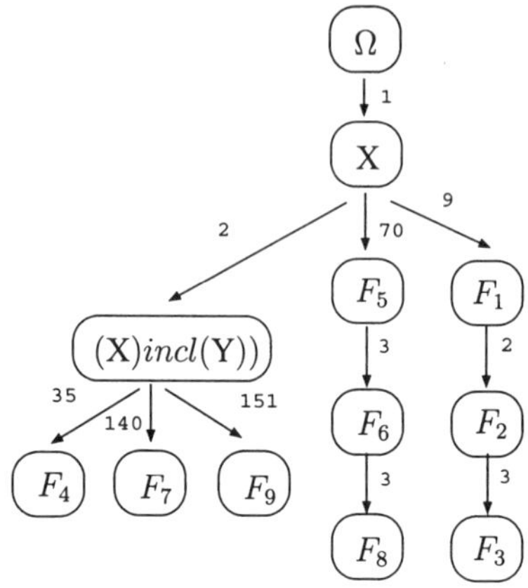

Figure 4: Illustration of systematization of concepts in the system

Step-1 D_{in} is recognized. As the result, we found that F_6 is the closet ancestor to D_{in} in the hierarchy shown in Fig4.

Step-2 We replace the variable label X1 in F_6 with the SD-Form in D_{rec} which has the elaboration relation to the label. The new D_{rec} is,

$$D_{rec} = [s(\text{I}, v(\text{ASK}), o(\text{YOU}(\$1)))c(s(\$1), v(\text{KNOW}), o(\text{PLACE/GCCSOURCE}))].$$

The substituted label is given as

GCCSOURCE.

Step-3 The ancestor HC_p of D_{rec} and a descendant LC_q is $HC_1 = F_5$ and $LC_1 = F_8$. Therefore, Q_m are given by the following.

$$\begin{aligned} Q_1 &= D_{rec} \\ Q_2 &= F_5 \\ Q_3 &= F_8 \end{aligned}$$

Firstly, we use Q_1 as a template concept. Therefore, a paraphrase candidate is produced as

$$Q_{10} = [s(\text{I}), v(\text{ASK}), o(\text{YOU}(\$1))c(s(\$1), v(\text{KNOW}), o(\text{PLACE/GCCSOURCE}))].$$

The function items D_i of template concept (Q_1) are $D_1 = \text{I}$, $D_2 = \text{ASK}$, $D_3 = \text{YOU}$, $D_4 = \text{KNOW}$ and $D_5 = place/X1$. Among D_i, only D_5 has a relation to an ancestor or to a descendant in the hierarchy. The ancestor of D_5 and the descendant of D_5 is $D_{51} = F_1 = \text{PLACE}$, and $D_{52} = F_7 = \text{PLACE}/[s(\text{X1}), v(\text{EXIST})]$, respectively. We can produce the following SD-Forms by substituting D_5 with D_{51} and D_{52}.

$$\begin{aligned} Q_{11} &= [s(\text{I}), v(\text{ASK}), o(\text{YOU}(\$1)), c(s(\$1), v(\text{KNOW}), o(\text{PLACE}))] \\ Q_{12} &= [s(\text{I}), v(\text{ASK}), o(\text{YOU}(\$1)), c(s(\$1), v(\text{KNOW}), \\ &\qquad o(\text{PLACE}/[(\text{GCCSOURCE}), (\text{EXISTENCE})]))] \end{aligned}$$

Table 4: Natural language sentences corresponding to D_{in} and P_k

symbols	natural language expression
D_{in}	Do you know the place of gcc source code?
P_1	Do you know the place?
P_2	Do you know the place where gcc source code is?
P_3	Where is gcc source code?
P_4	Please tell me the place of gcc source code.
P_5	Please tell me the place.
P_6	Please tell me the place where gcc source code is.

Then, we set Q_2 as a template SD-Form. So we can produce a paraphrase concept.

$$Q_{20} = [s(\text{I}), v(\text{ASK}), o(\text{YOU}), c(s(\text{GCCSOURCE}), v(\text{EXISTENCE/PLACE/WHERE}))]$$

Because there is no relationship to the contents of the functional item of Q_2 in the hierarchy, we proceed to the next step.

Finally, we set Q_3 as a template SD-Form.

$$Q_{30} = [s(\text{I}(\$1)), v(\text{ASK}), o(\text{YOU}(\$2)), c(s(\$2), v(\text{TELL}), i(\$1), o(\text{PLACE}/X1)]$$

In Q_3, "PLACE/X1" has SD-Forms in the concept hierarchy which has a elaboration relation. The new SD-Form produced are:

$$\begin{aligned} Q_{31} &= [s(\text{I}(\$1)), v(\text{ASK}), o(\text{YOU}(\$2)), c([s(\$2), v(\text{TELL}), i(\$1), o(\text{PLACE})])] \\ Q_{32} &= [s(\text{I}(\$1)), v(\text{ASK}), o(\text{YOU}(\$2)), c([s(\$2), v(\text{TELL}), i(\$1), o(\text{WHERE} \\ &\qquad /[s(\text{GCCSOURCE}), v(\text{EXIST})])])]. \end{aligned}$$

The variable label X1 in Q_{30} was replaced with the substituted label. After this replacement, no Q_{mj} contain variable labels.

From the steps above, 7 paraphrased candidates are produced. In the candidates, Q_{10} is the same as D_{in}. Therefore we got 6 paraphrased concepts. Table 4 shows the natural language expressions corresponding to the 6 SD-Forms and D_{in}.

We evaluated P_i and the result are shown in Table 5. $si(D_{in})$ was 80 *semit*. The nearest common ancestors used in the evaluation was as follows.

$$\begin{array}{ll} ncoa(P_1, P_1, D_{in}) & (D_0 = P_1) \\ ncoa(P_3, P_3, D_{in}) & (D_0 = P_3) \\ ncoa(P_5, \text{X}, D_{in}) & (D_0 = \text{X}) \end{array}$$

5 Conclusion

We have proposed a scheme to paraphrase a simple sentence using SD-Form Semantics Model and defined the evaluation of the paraphrasing. In this paper, we have shown an example of the processing and evaluation. In the example, natural language sentences are produced by the proposed method. In the future, we will build a prototype system and collect paraphrased sentences then check the proposed method.

Table 5: Evaluation of paraphrased concepts

symbols	$si(P_i)$	semantic difference	elaboration score	evaluation
P_1	69	-	-	simplification
P_2	93	-	-	elaboration
P_3	80	$\neq 0$	$elab(D_0, P_3) < elab(D_0, D_{in})$	simplification
P_4	91	-	-	elaboration
P_5	80	$\neq 0$	$elab(D_0, P_5) > elab(D_0, D_{in})$	elaboration
P_6	104	-		elaboration

References

[1] Keiko Kondo, et al. "Paraphrasing by Case Alternation," Trans. IPSJ, Vol.42, No.30, pp.465-477, 2001.

[2] Kentaro Inui, "paraphrase language representation," NLP, 2002.

[3] P. Wallis, "Information Retrieval based on Paraphrase," PACLING, 1993.

[4] Hiroshi Nakagawa, et al. "Meaning Preserving Information Hiding -Japanese Text Case," Trans. IPSJ, Vol.42, No.9, pp.2339-2350, 2001.

[5] Sayaka Minewaki et al. "Linguistic Steganography using SD-Form Semantic Model," IPSJ SIG Notes, Vol.2002, No.68, 2002-CSEC-18, pp.137-144, 2002.

[6] Satoshi Sato, "Automatic Paraphrase of Technical Papers' Titles," Trans. IPSJ, Vol.40, No.7, pp2937-2945, 1999.

[7] Masahiro Wakiyama, et al. "Computation Algorithm of Semantic Difference Measure in the SD-form Semantics Model," Trans IPSJ, Vol.40, No.3, pp.1065-1079, 1999.

Information Modelling and Knowledge Bases XV
Y. Kiyoki et al. (Eds.)
IOS Press, 2004

An Algebraic Approach for Specifying Compound Terms in Faceted Taxonomies

Yannis Tzitzikas [1,5], Anastasia Analyti[2], Nicolas Spyratos[3], Panos Constantopoulos[2,4]

[1] *Istituto di Scienza e Tecnologie dell' Informazione, CNR-ISTI, Italy*
[2] *Institute of Computer Science, ICS-FORTH, Greece*
[3] *Laboratoire de Recherche en Informatique, Universite de Paris-Sud, France*
[4] *Department of Computer Science, University of Crete, Greece*

Email : tzitzik@isti.cnr.it, {analyti, panos}@ics.forth.gr, spyratos@lri.fr

Abstract. A faceted taxonomy is a set of taxonomies, each describing a given domain from a different aspect, or facet. The indexing of domain objects is done through conjunctive combinations of terms from the facets, called compound terms. A faceted taxonomy has several advantages over a single hierarchy of terms, including conceptual clarity, compactness and scalability. A drawback, however, is the cost of avoiding invalid combinations, i.e. compound terms that do not apply to any object in the domain. This need arises in both indexing and retrieval, and typically involves human effort for specifying the valid compound terms one by one. We here propose a compound term composition algebra which can be used to generate valid compound terms in a given faceted taxonomy in an efficient and flexible manner. It works on the basis of the original simple terms of the facets and a small set of positive and/or negative statements. In each algebraic operation, we adopt a closed-world assumption with respect to the declared positive or negative statements. The taxonomy algebra can be exploited in dynamically generating navigation trees, a significant browsing aid.

1 Introduction

There are several application areas where a *taxonomy* is used for indexing the objects of a knowledge domain (e.g. documents, books, product descriptions, Web pages). For instance, Web catalogs, such as Yahoo! or Open Directory, use taxonomies, for indexing the pages of the Web. These catalogs turn out to be very useful for browsing and querying the Web. Although they index only a fraction of the pages that are indexed by search engines using statistical methods (e.g. Google, AltaVista), they are hand-crafted by domain experts and are therefore of high quality. Recently, the various search engines have begun to exploit these catalogs in order to enhance the quality of retrieval and also to offer new functionalities. Specifically, search engines now employ catalogs for computing "better" degrees of relevance, and for determining (and presenting to the user) a set of relevant pages for each page in the answer set. In addition, some search engines (e.g. Google) now employ taxonomies in order to enable

[5]Work done during the postdoctoral studies of the author at CNR-ISTI as an ERCIM fellow. The first part of this work was done when the author was at ICS-FORTH.

limiting the scope (or defining the context) of search. For example, using Google, one can first select a category, e.g. `Sciences/CS/DataStructures`, from the taxonomy of Open Directory and then submit a natural language query, e.g. "`Tree`". The search engine will compute the degree of relevance, with respect to the natural language query, "`Tree`", only of those pages that fall in the category `Sciences/CS/DataStructures` in the catalog of Open Directory. Clearly, this enhances the precision of retrieval and reduces the computational cost (e.g. see [8], [5]).

A taxonomy is a hierarchically-organized set of terms. In designing a taxonomy, one has to define (a priori) appropriate terms and their subterms, according to various criteria. One basic criterion is that each term must be *valid*, in the sense that it applies to, or *indexes*, at least one object of the underlying domain. However, as pointed out long ago [7], the design of a taxonomy can be done in a more convenient and a more systematic manner, if we first identify a number of different aspects, or facets, of the domain and then design one taxonomy per aspect. This process results in a *faceted taxonomy*, i.e. a *set* of taxonomies, called *facets*.

For example, assume that the domain of interest is a set of hotel Web pages in Greece, and suppose that we want to provide access to these pages according to the *Location* of the hotels and the *Sports* facilities they offer. Figure 1 shows these two facets. Each object is described using a *compound term*, i.e., a set of terms containing one or more terms from each facet. For example, a hotel in Crete providing sea ski and wind-surfing facilities would be described by the compound term $\{Crete, SeaSki, Windsurfing\}$.

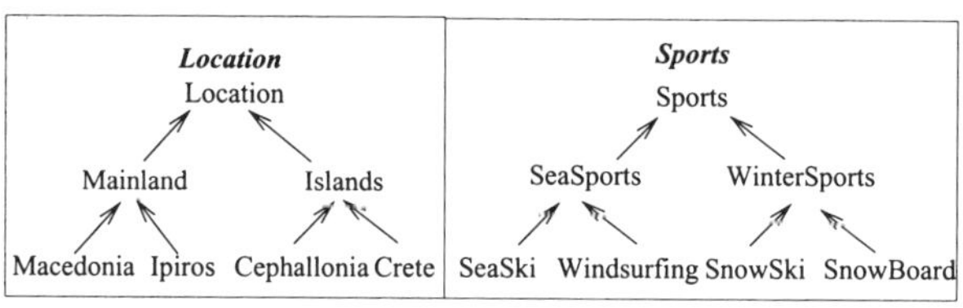

Figure 1: Two facets

The use of a faceted taxonomy, i.e. of a set of taxonomies, instead of a single taxonomy, for indexing the objects of interest, has several consequences. For example, consider two schemes for describing the objects of a domain, one using a single taxonomy consisting of 100 terms, and the other using a faceted taxonomy consisting of 10 facets each having 10 terms. The first scheme has 100 indexing terms while the second has 10^{10}, i.e. 10 billion, compound indexing terms! Although both schemes have the same storage requirements, i.e. each one requires storing 100 terms, the indexing terms of the second scheme are tremendously more than the indexing terms of the first.

Overall, a faceted taxonomy has several advantages by comparison to a single hierarchical taxonomy, such as conceptual clarity, compactness and scalability (e.g. see [6]). Unfortunately, faceted taxonomies also have a serious drawback. Indeed, assuming that each facet has been designed correctly, every single term will be valid. However, even if this assumption holds for every term in every facet, it may not hold for every conceivable compound term. That is, there may exist invalid compound terms, in the sense that there is no object of the underlying domain indexed by all of their terms. For example, it may very well be that the terms *Crete* (from *Location*) and *SnowBoard* (from *Sports*) are each valid, i.e., there are hotels located in Crete and there are hotels that offer snow-board facilities. However, this does not guarantee that the compound term $\{Crete, SnowBoard\}$ is valid. In fact, there is no hotel in Crete offering snowboard facilities. It follows that not all compound terms of a faceted taxonomy are valid, even if each term of every facet is valid.

Invalid compound terms cause serious problems in indexing and browsing that prevent the design and deployment of faceted taxonomies for real and large scale applications. Being able to infer the valid compound terms of a faceted taxonomy would be very useful. It could be exploited in the indexing process in order to aid the indexer and prevent indexing errors. Such an aid is especially important in cases where the indexing is done by many people who are not domain experts. For example, the indexing of Web pages in the Open Directory (which is used by Netscape, Lycos, HotBot and several other search engines) is done by more than 20.000 volunteer human editors (indexers). On the other hand, the inability to infer valid compound terms may give rise to problems in browsing, as an invalid term will yield no objects. However, if we could infer the valid compound terms in a faceted taxonomy then we would be able to generate navigation trees *on the fly*, having only valid compound terms as nodes.

The main goal of this paper is precisely to propose an algebra whose operators allow the efficient and flexible specification of compound terms, thus alleviating the main drawback of faceted taxonomies. Following our approach, given a faceted taxonomy, one can use an *algebraic expression* to define the desired set of compound terms. In each algebraic operation, the designer has to declare either a small set of valid compound terms from which other valid compound terms are inferred, or a small set of invalid compound terms from which other invalid compound terms are inferred. Then, a closed-world assumption is adopted for the rest of the compound terms. In our example, this means that the designer can specify the large number of valid compound terms of a faceted taxonomy by providing a relatively small number of (valid or invalid) compound terms. This is an important feature as it minimizes the effort needed by the designer. A distinctive feature of our approach is that there is no need to store the set of compound terms defined by the expression. We only have to store the defining expression as we provide an inference mechanism which can check whether a compound term belongs to the result of an expression. Thus the compound taxonomies defined by our algebra have low storage space requirements.

The remaining of this paper is organized as follows: Section 2 describes formally taxonomies, compound taxonomies and facets. Section 3 describes the proposed algebra, and Section 4 illustrates its application by an example. Section 5 provides an inference mechanism for checking whether a compound term belongs to the compound taxonomy defined by an algebraic expression. Section 6 describes a mechanism for generating navigation trees. Finally, Section 7 discusses applications and concludes the paper. All proofs are given in the extended version of this paper ([10]).

2 Taxonomies, Compound Taxonomies and Facets

Def 2.1 A *terminology* is a finite set of names, called *terms*.

Def 2.2 A *taxonomy* is a pair $(\mathcal{T}, \leq)$, where $\mathcal{T}$ is a *terminology* and $\leq$ is a reflexive and transitive relation over $\mathcal{T}$, called *subsumption*.

If a and b are terms of $\mathcal{T}$ and $a \leq b$ then we say that a is *subsumed* by b, or that b *subsumes* a. We also say that a is *narrower than* b, or that b is *broader* than a. For example, `Databases` $\leq$ `Informatics`. We say that two terms a and b are *equivalent*, and write $a \sim b$, if both $a \leq b$ and $b \leq a$ hold, e.g., `Computer Science` $\sim$ `Informatics`.

Note that the subsumption relation is a preorder over $\mathcal{T}$ and that $\sim$ is an equivalence relation over the terms of $\mathcal{T}$. Moreover $\leq$ is a partial order over the equivalence classes of terms.

When using diagrams to depict a taxonomy, such as the ones of Figure 1, term subsumption is indicated by a continuous-line arrow from the narrower term to the broader term. Note that we do not represent the entire subsumption relation but only a subset sufficient for generating it. In particular, we do not represent the reflexive nor the transitive arrows of the subsumption relation. Equivalence of terms is indicated by a continuous non-oriented line segment. In what follows, we shall often write $\mathcal{T}$ instead of $(\mathcal{T}, \leq)$, whenever no ambiguity is possible.

We now introduce the concept of compound taxonomy, a basic concept for the rest of this paper. First, we define compound terms over a given taxonomy and their ordering. In all definitions that follow, we assume an underlying taxonomy $(\mathcal{T}, \leq)$.

Def 2.3 A *compound term* over $\mathcal{T}$ is any subset of $\mathcal{T}$.

For example, the following sets of terms are compound terms over the taxonomy *Sports* of Figure 1: $s_1 = \{SeaSki, Windsurfing\}$, $s_2 = \{SeaSports, WinterSports\}$, $s_3 = \{Sports\}$, and $s_4 = \emptyset$.

We denote by $P(\mathcal{T})$ the set of all compound terms over $\mathcal{T}$ (i.e. the powerset of $\mathcal{T}$).

Def 2.4 A *compound terminology* S over $\mathcal{T}$ is any set of compound terms that contains the compound term $\emptyset$.

Clearly, $P(\mathcal{T})$ is a compound terminology over $\mathcal{T}$. The set of all compound terms over $\mathcal{T}$ can be ordered using the following ordering derived from $\leq$.

Def 2.5 Let s, s' be two compound terms over $\mathcal{T}$. The *compound ordering* over $\mathcal{T}$ is defined as follows: $s \preceq s'$ iff $\forall t' \in s'\ \exists t \in s$ such that $t \leq t'$

That is, $s \preceq s'$ iff s contains a narrower term for every term of s'. In addition, s may contain terms not present in s'. Roughly, $s \preceq s'$ means that s carries more specific information than s'. Figure 2.(a) shows the compound ordering over the compound terms of our previous example. Note that $s_1 \preceq s_3$, as s_1 contains *SeaSki* which is a term narrower than the unique term *Sports* of s_3. On the other hand, $s_1 \not\preceq s_2$, as s_1 does not contain a term narrower than *WinterSports*. Finally, $s_2 \preceq s_3$ and $s_3 \preceq \emptyset$. In fact, $s \preceq \emptyset$, for every compound term s.

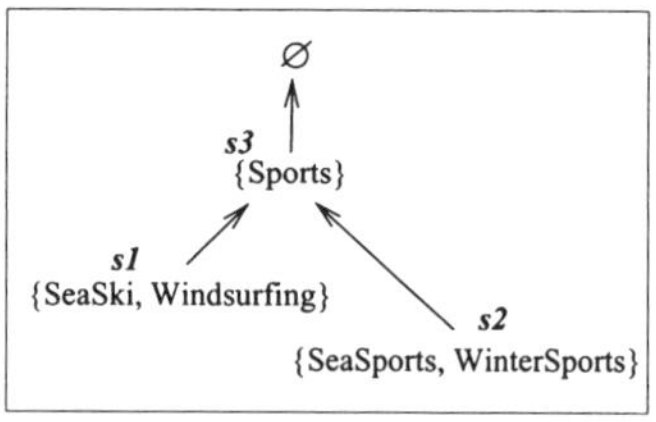

(a)

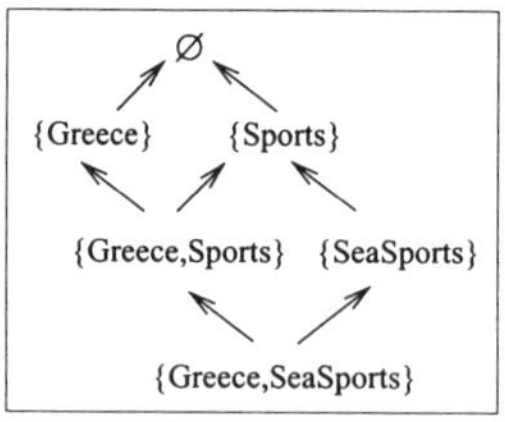

(b)

Figure 2: Two examples of compound taxonomies

Clearly, $\preceq$ is a reflexive and transitive relation over S. Also note that while the relation $\leq$ is provided explicitly by the designer of the taxonomy $\mathcal{T}$, the relation $\preceq$ is *derived* from $\leq$ according to the previous definition.

We say that two compound terms s, s' are *equivalent* iff $s \preceq s'$ and $s' \preceq s$. For example, $\{SeaSki, SeaSports\}$ and $\{SeaSki\}$ are equivalent. Intuitively, equivalent compound terms carry the same information.

Def 2.6 A *compound taxonomy* over $\mathcal{T}$ is a pair $(S, \preceq)$, where S is a compound terminology over $\mathcal{T}$, and $\preceq$ is the compound ordering over $\mathcal{T}$ restricted to S.

Figure 2 shows two example compound taxonomies.

Clearly, $(P(\mathcal{T}), \preceq)$ is a compound taxonomy over $\mathcal{T}$. Let s be a compound term. The broader and the narrower compound terms of s are defined as follows:

$$\begin{aligned} \mathrm{Br}(s) &= \{s' \in P(\mathcal{T}) \mid s \preceq s'\} \\ \mathrm{Nr}(s) &= \{s' \in P(\mathcal{T}) \mid s' \preceq s\} \end{aligned}$$

Let S be a compound terminology over $\mathcal{T}$. The broader and the narrower compound terms of S are defined as follows:

$$\begin{aligned} Br(S) &= \cup\{\mathrm{Br}(s) \mid s \in S\} \\ Nr(S) &= \cup\{\mathrm{Nr}(s) \mid s \in S\} \end{aligned}$$

As already mentioned, one way of designing a taxonomy is by identifying a number of different aspects of the domain of interest and then designing one taxonomy per aspect. As a result we obtain a set of taxonomies called *facets*. Given a set of facets we can define a *faceted taxonomy*.

Def 2.7 Let $\{F_1, ..., F_k\}$ be a finite set of taxonomies, where $F_i = (\mathcal{T}_i, \leq_i)$, and assume that the terminologies $\mathcal{T}_1$, ... ,$\mathcal{T}_k$ are pairwise disjoint. Then the pair $\mathcal{F} = (\mathcal{T}, \leq)$, where $\mathcal{T} = \bigcup_{i=1}^{k} \mathcal{T}_i$ and $\leq \; = \bigcup_{i=1}^{k} \leq_i$, is a taxonomy which we shall call the *faceted taxonomy generated* by $\{F_1, ..., F_k\}$. We shall call the taxonomies $F_1, ..., F_k$ the *facets* of $\mathcal{F}$.

It is common practice to refer to a facet through its top term. For example, we refer to the facets of Figure 1 as *Location* and *Sports*. Clearly, all definitions introduced so far apply also to faceted taxonomies. In particular, compound terms can be derived from a faceted taxonomy. For example, the set $S = \{\{Greece\}, \{Sports\}, \{SeaSports\}, \{Greece, Sports\}, \{Greece, SeaSports\}, \emptyset\}$, is a compound terminology over the terminology $\mathcal{T}$ of the faceted taxonomy shown in Figure 1. The set S together with the compound ordering of $\mathcal{T}$ (restricted to S) is a compound taxonomy over $\mathcal{T}$. This compound taxonomy is shown in Figure 2.(b). For reasons of brevity, hereafter we shall omit the term $\emptyset$ from the compound terminologies of our examples and figures.

We say that a compound term s is *valid* (resp. *invalid*), if there is at least one (resp. no) object of the underlying domain indexed by all terms in s. We assume that every term of $\mathcal{T}$ is valid. However, a compound term over $\mathcal{T}$ may be invalid. Obviously, if s is a valid compound term, all compound terms in $\mathrm{Br}(s)$ are valid. Additionally, if s is an invalid compound term, all compound terms in $\mathrm{Nr}(s)$ are invalid. The formal definition of validity is given in [10].

3 The Compound Term Composition Algebra

Let $\mathcal{F}= (\mathcal{T}, \leq)$ be the faceted taxonomy generated by a given set of facets $\{F_1, ..., F_k\}$. The problem is that $\mathcal{F}$ does not itself specify which compound terms, i.e. which elements of $P(\mathcal{T})$, are valid and which are not. To alleviate this problem, we introduce a method for defining a compound terminology over $\mathcal{T}$ (i.e. a subset of $P(\mathcal{T})$) which consists of the desired compound terms, i.e. those that the designer considers as valid.

The main tool for accomplishing this task is an algebra that we now define. To begin with we associate the terminology $\mathcal{T}_i$ of every facet with a compound terminology T_i that we call the *basic compound terminology* of $\mathcal{T}_i$.

Def 3.1 Let $F_i = (\mathcal{T}_i, \leq)$ be a facet. The *basic compound terminology* of $\mathcal{T}_i$ is the compound terminology:

$$T_i = \cup\{\ \mathrm{Br}(\{t\}) \mid t \in \mathcal{T}_i\}$$

As every term t of a facet is considered valid, all compound terms in $\mathrm{Br}(\{t\})$ are valid. Thus, T_i is the set of compound terms over $\mathcal{T}_i$ that are initially known to be valid. We use the basic compound terminologies as the "building blocks" of our algebra.

Let $\mathcal{S}$ denote the set of all compound terminologies over $\mathcal{T}$. We define an algebra over S, which includes four operations and compound terminologies as operands. Compound terms can be formed by combining terms from different facets, but also terms from the same facet. A binary product operation and a unary self-product operation are defined to generate term combinations respectively. Since not all term combinations are valid, the issue is how to employ available domain knowledge in order to specify only valid compound terms. Such knowledge may be available in positive or negative form: combinations known to be valid or invalid. The issue is dealt by defining more general operations that include positive or negative modifiers, which are sets of known valid or known invalid compound terms. The unmodified product and self-product operations turn out to be special cases with the modifiers at certain extreme values. Thus, the four operations of the algebra are: *plus-product, minus-product, plus-self-product* and *minus-self product.*

For defining the desired compound taxonomy the designer has to formulate an algebraic expression e, using these operations and initial operands the basic compound terminologies $\{T_1, .., T_k\}$.

Before we describe each operation in detail, we define the auxiliary binary operation $\oplus$ over $\mathcal{S}$, i.e. $\oplus : \mathcal{S} \times \mathcal{S} \rightarrow \mathcal{S}$, called *product.*

Def 3.2 Let S and S' be two compound terminologies ($S, S' \in \mathcal{S}$). The *product* of S and S', denoted by $S \oplus S'$, is defined as follows:

$$S \oplus S' = \{s \cup s' \mid s \in S,\ s' \in S'\}$$

This operation results in an "unqualified" compound terminology whose compound terms are all possible unions of compound terms from its arguments. The compound terms of the result are ordered according to the compound ordering (see Definition 2.5). For example, consider the compound terminologies $S = \{\{Greece\}, \{Islands\}\}$ and $S' = \{\{Sports\}, \{SeaSports\}\}$. The compound taxonomy corresponding to $S \oplus S'$ is shown in Figure 3, and consists of 8 terms. Recall that for reasons of brevity, we omit the term $\emptyset$ from the compound terminologies of our examples ($\emptyset$ is an element of

S, S' and $S \oplus S'$). It can be easily seen that the product operation is commutative and associative and that it can be easily extended to an n-ary operation: $S_1 \oplus ... \oplus S_n = \{ s_1 \cup ... \cup s_n \mid s_i \in S_i\}$. Additionally, as $\emptyset \in S, S'$, it holds that $S, S' \subseteq S \oplus S'$.

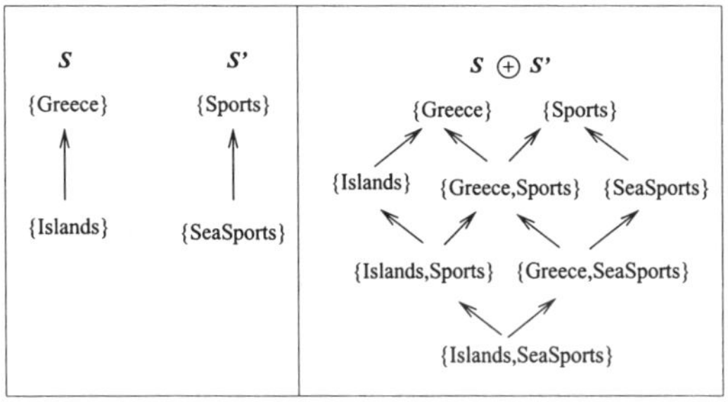

Figure 3: An example of a product $\oplus$ operation

Below we describe each operation of our algebra in detail.

3.1 The *plus-product* and the *minus-product* operations

Consider the compound terminologies S and S' shown in the upper part of Figure 4, and suppose we want to define a compound terminology that does not contain the compound terms $\{Islands, WinterSports\}$ and $\{Islands, SnowSki\}$, because they are invalid. For this purpose we introduce two "variations" of the $\oplus$ operation, namely the *plus-product* and the *minus-product*. Each of these two operations has an extra parameter denoted by P and N, respectively. The set P is a set of compound terms that we certainly want to appear in the result of the operation, i.e. they are valid. On the other hand, the set N is a set of compound terms that we certainly do not want to appear in the result of the operation, i.e. they are invalid.

To proceed we need to distinguish what we shall call *genuine compound terms*. Intuitively, a genuine compound term combines non-empty compound terms from more that one compound terminologies.

Def 3.3 The set of *genuine* compound terms over a set of compound terminologies $S_1, ..., S_n$, denoted by $G_{S_1,...,S_n}$, is defined as follows:

$$G_{S_1,...,S_n} = S_1 \oplus ... \oplus S_n - \bigcup_{i=1}^{n} S_i$$

For example if $S_1 = \{\{Greece\}, \{Islands\}\}$, $S_2 = \{\{Sports\}, \{WinterSports\}\}$, and $S_3 = \{\{Pensions\}, \{Hotels\}\}$ then

$$\begin{aligned} \{Greece, WinterSports, Hotels\} &\in G_{S_1,S_2,S_3}, \\ \{WinterSports, Hotels\} &\in G_{S_1,S_2,S_3} \text{ , but} \\ \{Hotels\} &\notin G_{S_1,S_2,S_3} \end{aligned}$$

Assume that the compound terms of $S_1, ..., S_n$ are valid. We are interested in characterizing the validity of all combinations of compound terms of $S_1, ..., S_n$. As we already know the validity of the compound terms of $S_1, ..., S_n$, we are basically interested in characterizing the validity of the compound terms in $G_{S_1,...,S_n}$. This is done through the following operations, plus-product and minus-product.

We can now define the *plus-product* operation, $\oplus_P$, an n-ary operation over $\mathcal{S}$ ($\oplus_P : \mathcal{S} \times ... \times \mathcal{S} \to \mathcal{S}$), where the parameter P is a set of valid compound terms from the product of the input compound terminologies. The set P is a subset of $G_{S_1,...,S_n}$ (i.e., $P \subseteq G_{S_1,...,S_n}$), as we already know that all compound terms in $\bigcup_{i=1}^{n} S_i$ are valid.

Def 3.4 Let $S_1, ..., S_n$ be compound terminologies and $P \subseteq G_{S_1,...,S_n}$. The *plus-product* of $S_1, ..., S_n$ with respect to P, denoted by $\oplus_P(S_1, ..., S_n)$, is defined as follows:

$$\oplus_P(S_1, ...S_n) = S_1 \cup ... \cup S_n \ \cup \ Br(P)$$

This operation results in a compound terminology consisting of the compound terms of the initial compound terminologies, *plus* the compound terms which are broader than an element of P. This is because, all compound terms in $S_1 \cup ... \cup S_n \ \cup \ Br(P)$ are valid. By adopting a closed-world assumption, all compound terms in $S_1 \oplus ... \oplus S_n - \oplus_P(S_1, ...S_n) = G_{S_1,...,S_n} - Br(P)$ are invalid.

For example, consider the compound terminologies S and S' of Figure 4 and suppose that $P = \{\{Islands, Seasports\}, \{Greece, SnowSki\}\}$. The compound taxonomy of the operation $\oplus_P(S, S')$ is shown in Figure 4. In this figure we enclose in squares the elements of P. We see that the compound terminology $\oplus_P(S, S')$ contains the compound term $s = \{Greece, Sports\}$, as $s \in Br(\{Islands, SeaSports\})$. However, it does not contain the compound terms $\{Islands, WinterSports\}$ and $\{Islands, SnowSki\}$ as they do not belong to $S \cup S' \cup Br(P)$.

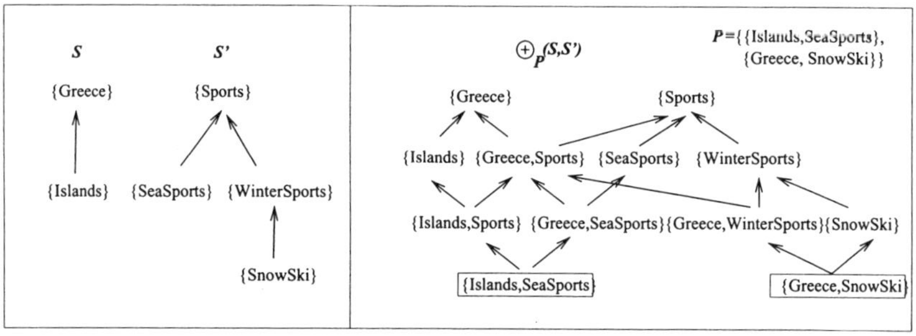

Figure 4: An example of a *plus-product*, $\oplus_P$, operation

The following proposition gives two simplifications of the operation for the two extreme values of the P parameter. The first property says that the product is a special case of the plus-product, while the second property says that if $P = \emptyset$ then the plus-product operation defines a compound terminology that contains only the compound terms of the operands.

Prop. 3.1 Given compound terminologies S_i, $i = 1, ..., n$,

(1) If $P = G_{S_1,...,S_n}$ then $\oplus_P(S_1, ..., S_n) = S_1 \oplus ... \oplus S_n$, and

(2) if $P = \emptyset$ then $\oplus_P(S_1, ..., S_n) = \bigcup_{i=1}^{n} S_i$.

Now we define the *minus-product* operation, $\ominus_N$, an n-ary operation over $\mathcal{S}$ ($\ominus_N : \mathcal{S} \times ... \times \mathcal{S} \to \mathcal{S}$), where the parameter N is a set of invalid compound terms from the product of the input compound terminologies. The set N is a subset of $G_{S_1,...,S_n}$ (i.e., $N \subseteq G_{S_1,...,S_n}$), as all compound terms in $\bigcup_{i=1}^{n} S_i$ are valid.

Def 3.5 Let $S_1, ..., S_n$ be compound taxonomies and $N \subseteq G_{S_1,...,S_n}$. The *minus-product* of $S_1, ..., S_n$ with respect to N, denoted by $\ominus_N(S_1, ..., S_n)$, is defined as follows:

$$\ominus_N(S_1, ...S_n) = S_1 \oplus ... \oplus S_n - Nr(N)$$

This operation results in a compound terminology consisting of all compound terms in the product of the initial compound terminologies, *minus* all compound terms which are narrower than an element of N. This is because, all compound terms in $Nr(N)$ are invalid. By adopting a closed-world assumption, all compound terms in $\ominus_N(S_1, ...S_n) = S_1 \oplus ... \oplus S_n - Nr(N)$ are valid.

For example, consider the compound terminologies S and S' of the previous example and suppose that $N = \{\{Islands, WinterSports\}\}$. The result of the operation $\ominus_N(S, S')$ is shown in Figure 5. We see that the compound terminology $\ominus_N(S, S')$ does not contain the compound terms $\{Islands, WinterSports\}$ and $\{Islands, SnowSki\}$, as they are elements of $Nr(N)$. Notice that the compound taxonomies of figures 4 and 5 coincide. These examples demonstrate two alternative ways of defining the desired compound taxonomy.

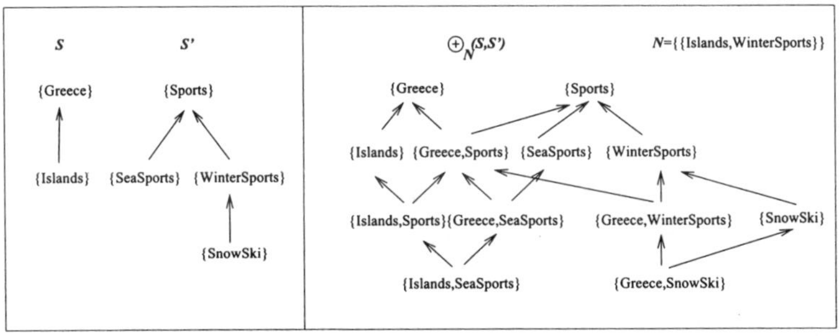

Figure 5: An example of a *minus-product*, $\ominus_N$, operation

The following proposition gives two simplifications of the operation for the two extreme values of the N parameter. Note that these two simplifications are the opposite of these of the $\oplus_P$ operation, given in Proposition 3.1.

Prop. 3.2 Given the compound terminologies S_i, $i = 1, ..., n$,

(1) If $N = G_{S_1,...,S_n}$ then $\ominus_N(S_1, ..., S_n) = \bigcup_{i=1}^{n} S_i$, and

(2) if $N = \emptyset$ then $\ominus_N(S_1, ..., S_n) = S_1 \oplus ... \oplus S_n$.

3.2 The *Self-product* operations

The operators introduced so far allow defining a compound terminology which consists of compound terms that contain at most one compound term from each basic compound terminology. However, a valid compound term may contain any set of terms of the same facet (multiple classification). To capture such cases, we define the *self-product*, $\overset{*}{\oplus}$, a

unary operation which gives all possible compound terms of one facet. Subsequently, we shall modify this operation with the parameters P and N.
Let $\mathcal{BS}$ be the set of basic compound terminologies, that is $\mathcal{BS}= \{T_1, ..., T_k\}$.

Def 3.6 Let T_i be a basic compound terminology. The *self-product* of T_i, denoted by $\overset{*}{\oplus}(T_i)$, is defined as: $\overset{*}{\oplus}(T_i) = P(T_i)$.

In the above definition, $P(T_i)$ denotes the powerset of the terminology T_i, not the powerset of the basic compound terminology T_i.
For example, consider the facet *Sports* of Figure 1. The compound terms $\{SeaSports, WinterSports\}$
and $\{SeaSki, Windsurfing, WinterSports\}$ are elements of $\overset{*}{\oplus}(Sports)$.
The notion of genuine compound terms is also necessary here.

Def 3.7 The set of *genuine* compound terms over a basic compound terminology T_i, denoted by G_{T_i}, is defined as follows: $G_{T_i} = \overset{*}{\oplus}(T_i) - T_i$

Now we define the *plus-self-product* operation, $\overset{*}{\oplus}_P$, a unary operation ($\overset{*}{\oplus}_P$: $\mathcal{BS} \rightarrow \mathcal{S}$) where the parameter P is a set of compound terms that we want to appear in the result of the operation. The set P is a subset of G_{T_i}.

Def 3.8 Let T_i be a basic compound terminology and $P \subseteq G_{T_i}$. The *plus-self-product* of T_i with respect to P, denoted by $\overset{*}{\oplus}_P(T_i)$, is defined as follows:

$$\overset{*}{\oplus}_P(T_i) = T_i \cup Br(P)$$

This operation results in a compound terminology consisting of the compound terms of the initial basic compound terminology, *plus* all compound terms which are broader than an element of P. For example, the result of the operation $\overset{*}{\oplus}_P(Sports)$, where $P = \{\{SeaSki, Windsurfing\}, \{SnowSki, SkiBoard\}\}$ is shown in Figure 6. The analogous of Prop. 3.1 with regard to the extreme cases of P holds, namely, $\overset{*}{\oplus}_{G_{T_i}}(T_i) = \overset{*}{\oplus} T_i$ and $\overset{*}{\oplus}_{\emptyset} = T_i$.

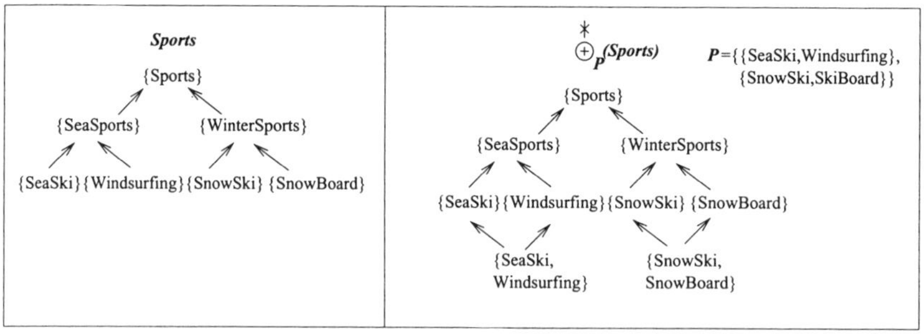

Figure 6: An example of a *plus-self-product*,$\overset{*}{\oplus}_P$, operation

The following definition introduces the *minus-self-product* operation, $\overset{*}{\oplus}_N$, a unary operation ($\overset{*}{\ominus}_N$: $\mathcal{BS} \rightarrow \mathcal{S}$) where the parameter N is a set of compound terms that we do not want to appear in the result of the operation. The set N is a subset of G_{T_i}.

Def 3.9 Let T_i be a basic compound terminology and $N \subseteq G_{T_i}$. The *minus-self-product* of T_i with respect to N, denoted by $\overset{*}{\ominus}_N (T_i)$, is defined as follows:

$$\overset{*}{\ominus}_N (T_i) = \overset{*}{\oplus} (T_i) - Nr(N)$$

This operation results in a compound terminology consisting of all compound terms in the self-product of T_i, *minus* the compound terms which are narrower than an element in N. For example, we can obtain the compound terminology of Figure 6 by the operation $\overset{*}{\ominus}_N (Sports)$, where $N = \{\{SeaSports, WinterSports\}\}$. Concerning the extreme cases of N, the analogous of Prop. 3.2 holds: $\overset{*}{\ominus}_{G_{T_i}} (T_i) = T_i$, and $\overset{*}{\ominus}_{\emptyset} (T_i) = \overset{*}{\oplus} T_i$.

3.3 Algebraic Expressions

For defining the desired compound taxonomy, the designer has to formulate an expression e, where an expression is defined as follows:

Def 3.10 An expression over a set of facets $\{F_1, ..., F_k\}$ is defined according to the following grammar:

$$e ::= \oplus_P(e, ..., e) \mid \ominus_N (e, ..., e) \mid \overset{*}{\oplus}_P T_i \mid \overset{*}{\ominus}_N T_i \mid T_i$$

The outcome of the evaluation of an expression e is denoted by S_e and is called the *compound terminology* of e, and any element of S_e is called *compound term* of e. In addition, $(S_e, \preceq)$ is called the *compound taxonomy* of e.

All compound terms in S_e are *valid*, and the rest in $P(\mathcal{T}_e) - S_e$ are *invalid*, where $\mathcal{T}_e$ is the union of the terminologies of the facets appearing in e.

We are interested only in *well-formed* expressions, defined as follows:

Def 3.11 An expression e is *well-formed* iff:

(i) each basic compound terminology T_i appears at most once in e,

(ii) each parameter P that appears in e, is a subset of the associated set of genuine compound terms, and

(iii) each parameter N that appears in e, is a subset of the associated set of genuine compound terms.

For example, the expression $(T_1 \oplus_P T_2) \ominus_N T_1$ is not well-formed as T_1 appears twice in the expression.

Constraints (i), (ii), and (iii) ensure that we have *no conflicts*, meaning that that the valid and invalid compound terms of an expression e increase as the length of e increases[6]. For example, if we omit constraint (i) then an invalid compound term according to an expression $T_1 \oplus_P T_2$ could be valid according to a larger expression $(T_1 \oplus_{P_1} T_2) \ominus_{P_2} T_1$. If we omit constraint (ii) then an invalid compound term according to an expression $T_1 \oplus_{P_1} T_2$ could be valid according to a larger expression $(T_1 \oplus_{P_1} T_2) \oplus_{P_2} T_3$. Additionally, if we omit constraint (iii) then a valid compound term according to an expression $T_1 \oplus_P T_2$ could be invalid according to a larger expression $(T_1 \oplus_P T_2) \ominus_N T_3$.

[6]Proof of this property is given in [10].

This monotonic behaviour in the evaluation of a well-formed expression results in a number of useful properties, found in [10]. In addition, due to their monotonicity, well-formed expressions can be formulated in a systematic, gradual manner (intermediate results of subexpressions are not invalidated by larger expressions).

In this paper, we consider only well-formed expressions. The algorithm needed for checking whether an expression is well-formed, and the model-theoretic semantics of well-formed algebraic expressions are given in [10].

4 Example

Suppose that the domain of interest is a set of hotel Web pages and that we want to index these pages using a faceted taxonomy. First, we must define the taxonomy. Suppose it is decided to do the indexing according to three facets, namely the *location* of the hotels, the kind of *accommodation*, and the *facilities* they offer. Specifically, assume that the designer employs (or designs from scratch) the facets shown in Figure 7.

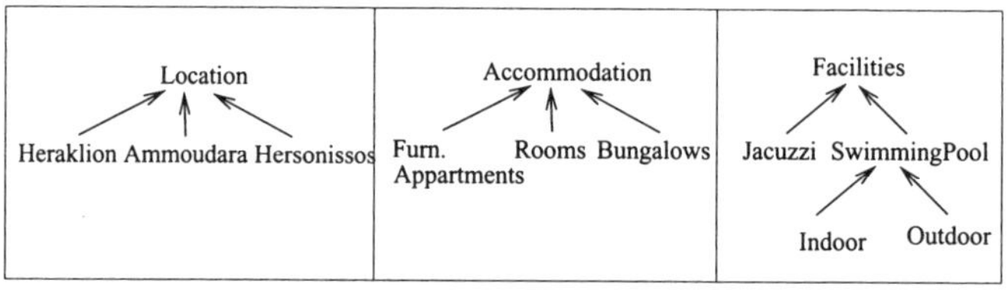

Figure 7: Three-facets

The faceted taxonomy has 13 terms ($|\mathcal{T}|$=13) and $P(\mathcal{T})$ has 890 compound terms[7]. However, available domain knowledge suggests that only 96 compound terms are valid. Omitting the compound terms which are singletons or contain top terms of the facets, the following 23 valid compound terms remain:

$$\{Heraklion, Furn.Appartments, \}, \{Heraklion, Rooms\},$$
$$\{Ammoudara, Furn.Appartments\}, \{Ammoudara, Rooms\},$$
$$\{Ammoudara, Bungalows\}, \{Hersonissos, Furn.Appartments\},$$
$$\{Hersonissos, Rooms\}, \{Hersonissos, Bungalows\},$$
$$\{Hersonissos, SwimmingPool\}, \{Hersonissos, Indoor\},$$
$$\{Hersonissos, Outdoor\}, \{Ammoudara, Jacuzzi\},$$
$$\{Rooms, SwimmingPool\}, \{Rooms, Indoor\},$$
$$\{Bungalows, SwimmingPool\}, \{Bungalows, Outdoor\},$$
$$\{Bungalows, Jacuzzi\}, \{Hersonissos, Rooms, SwimmingPool\},$$
$$\{Hersonissos, Rooms, Indoor\}, \{Hersonissos, Bungalows, SwimmingPool\},$$
$$\{Hersonissos, Bungalows, Outdoor\}, \ \{Ammoudara, Bungalows, Jacuzzi\}.$$

[7]Recall that equivalent compound terms are considered the same. Thus, $|P(\mathcal{T})|$ is not 2^{13} but 890. This is computed as follows: It holds that $|\overset{*}{\oplus}(Location)|$=8, $|\overset{*}{\oplus}(Accomodation)| = 8$, and $|\overset{*}{\oplus}(Facilities)| = 10$. Thus, $|P(\mathcal{T})| = |(\overset{*}{\oplus}(Location)) \oplus (\overset{*}{\oplus}(Accomodation)) \oplus (\overset{*}{\oplus}(Facilities)|\,| = (8 + 8*8 + 8*10 + 8*8*10) + (8 + 8*10) + 10 = 890$.

Rather than being explicitly enumerated, the 96 valid compound terms can be algebraically specified. In this way, the specification of the desired compound terms can be done in a systematic, gradual, and easy manner. For example, the following plus-product operation can be used:

$$\oplus_P(Location, Accommodation, Facilities), \text{ where}$$

$$\begin{aligned} P = \; & \{\{Heraklion, Furn.Appartments\}, \\ & \{Heraklion, Rooms\}, \\ & \{Ammoudara, Furn.Appartments\}, \\ & \{Ammoudara, Rooms\}, \\ & \{Hersonissos, Furn.Appartments\}, \\ & \{Ammoudara, Bungalows, Jacuzzi\}, \\ & \{Hersonissos, Rooms, Indoor\}, \\ & \{Hersonissos, Bungalows, Outdoor\}\} \end{aligned}$$

Note that the compound terms in P are only 8. Alternatively, the same result can be obtained more efficiently through the expression:

$$(Location \ominus_N Accommodation) \oplus_P Facilities,$$
where

$$\begin{aligned} N = \; & \{\{Heraklion, Bungalows\}\}, \text{ and} \\ P = \; & \{\{Hersonissos, Rooms, Indoor\}, \\ & \{Hersonissos, Bungalows, Outdoor\}, \\ & \{Ammoudara, Bungalows, Jacuzzi\}\} \end{aligned}$$

Note that now the total number of compound terms in P and N is just 4. In summary, the faceted taxonomy of our example, includes 13 terms, 890 compound terms, and 96 valid compound terms which can be specified by providing only 4 (carefully selected) compound terms and an appropriate algebraic expression.

Let us now discuss the methodology for formulating the expression e and the corresponding parameters P and N. Consider two facets F and F'. If the majority of the compound terms over these two facets are valid then it is better to use a *minus-product* operation so as to specify only the invalid compound terms. Concerning the defining of the set N, it is more efficient to put in N "short" compound terms that consist of "broad" terms. The reason is that from such compound terms a large number of new invalid compound terms can be inferred. Conversely, if the majority of compound terms are invalid, then it is better to employ a *plus-product* operation so as to specify only the valid compound terms. Concerning the definition of the set P, it is more efficient to put in P "long" compound terms that consist of "narrow" terms, since from such compound terms a large number of new valid compound terms can be inferred.

5 Checking the Validity of a Compound Term

We now turn to the problem of checking whether an arbitrary compound term s ($s \in P(\mathcal{T})$) belongs to the compound terminology S_e of a given expression e. The straightforward way to achieve this is to first compute and store the compound terminology S_e and then to check whether $s \in S_e$. However, the number of computations needed for computing S_e, as well as the storage requirements, may be very large. An alternative which we choose is to develop an algorithm which can check whether $s \in S_e$ *without* having to compute S_e. Consequently, only the expression e must be stored.

Below we present the algorithm $IsValid(e, s)$ which takes as arguments a (well-formed) expression e and a compound term s, and returns TRUE if $s \in S_e$ and FALSE otherwise (i.e. if $s \notin S_e$). This algorithm has polynomial time complexity, specifically $O(|\mathcal{T}|^3 * |\mathcal{P} \cup \mathcal{N}|)$, where $\mathcal{P}$ denotes the union of all P parameters and $\mathcal{N}$ denotes the union of all N parameters appearing in e (for more see [10]).

To present the algorithm we need some more notations. Let e be an expression over a facet set $\{F_1, ..., F_k\}$. The *facets* of e, denoted by $F(e)$, are defined as: $F(e) = \{F_i \mid F_i \text{ appears in } e\}$. Clearly, $F(e) \subseteq \{F_1, ..., F_k\}$. We shall denote by $F(t)$ the facet to which a term $t \in \mathcal{T}$ belongs, e.g. in Figure 1, we have $F(Crete) = Location$ and $F(SeaSki) = Sports$.

Algorithm 5.1 $IsValid(e, s)$
Input: An expression e and a compound term $s \subseteq \mathcal{T}$
Ouptut: TRUE if s belongs to S_e, or
FALSE, otherwise

```
if s = ∅ then return (TRUE)
If ∃ t ∈ s such that F(t) ∉ F(e),  then return(FALSE)
if s is singleton then return(TRUE)
case(e)  {
⊕P(e1, ..., en):
                    if ∃ p ∈ P such that p ≼ s then return(TRUE)
                    For i = 1, ..., n
                       if IsValid(ei, s) then return(TRUE)
                    return(FALSE)
⊖N(e1, ..., en):    if ∃n ∈ N such that s ≼ n
                    then return(FALSE)
                    For i = 1, ..., n
                       Let si = {t ∈ s | F(t) ∈ F(ei)}
                       if IsValid(ei, si)=FALSE then return(FALSE)
                    return(TRUE)
⊕*P (Ti):           if ∃p ∈ P such that p ≼ s then return(TRUE)
                    if s ∈ Ti then return(TRUE)
                    else return(FALSE)
⊖*N (Ti):           if ∃n ∈ N such that s ≼ n then return(FALSE)
                    else return(TRUE)
Ti:                 If s ∈ Ti then return(TRUE)
                    else return(FALSE)
}
```

The algorithm is based on the parse tree of the expression e. For example, consider the faceted taxonomy of Figure 7 and assume that the desired compound taxonomy is defined by the expression $e = (Location \ominus_N Accommodation) \oplus_P Facilities$, where

$$\begin{aligned} N = \quad & \{\{Heraklion, Bungalows\}\} \\ P = \quad & \{\{Hersonissos, Rooms, Indoor\}, \\ & \{Hersonissos, Bungalows, Outdoor\}, \\ & \{Ammoudara, Bungalows, Jacuzzi\}\} \end{aligned}$$

Figure 8 shows the parse tree of this expression.

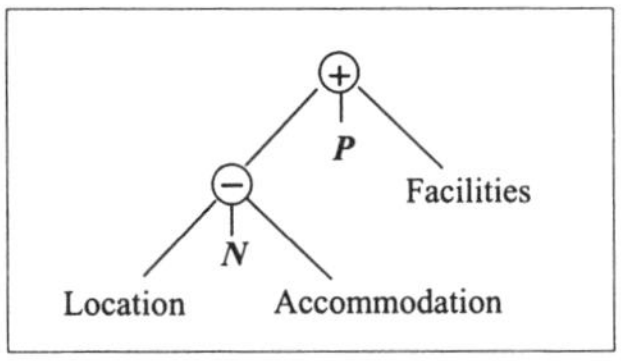

Figure 8: The parse tree of an expression

Then, it holds:
$IsValid(e, \{Hersonissos, Bungalows, SwimmingPool\})$=TRUE
$IsValid(e, \{Heraklion, Furn.Appartments\})$=TRUE

The trace of the execution of the call
$IsValid(e, \{Hersonissos, Bungalows, SwimmingPool\})$ is:

call $IsValid(e, \{Hersonissos, Bungalows, SwimmingPool\})$
/* $\exists p \in P$ s.t. $p \preceq \{Hersonissos, Bungalows, SwimmingPool\}$ */
  return(TRUE)

The trace of the execution of the call $IsValid(e, \{Heraklion, Furn.Appartments\})$ is:

call $IsValid((Location \ominus_N Accommodation) \oplus_P Facilities, \{Heraklion, Furn.Appartments\})$
/* $\nexists p \in P$ s.t. $p \preceq \{Heraklion, Furn.Appartments\}$ */
  call $IsValid((Location \ominus_N Accommodation), \{Heraklion, Furn.Appartments\})$
    call $IsValid(Location, \{Heraklion\})$
      return(TRUE)
    call $IsValid(Accommodation, \{Furn.Appartments\})$
      return(TRUE)
    return(TRUE)
  return(TRUE)

Additionally, we give the trace of the execution of the call
$IsValid(e, \{Hersonnissos, Bungalows, Jacuzzi\})$.

call $IsValid((Location \ominus_N Accommodation) \oplus_P Facilities, \{Hersonnissos, Bungalows, Jacuzzi\})$
/* $\nexists p \in P$ s.t. $p \preceq \{Hersonnissos, Bungalows, Jacuzzi\}$ */
  call $IsValid((Location \ominus_N Accommodation), \{Hersonnissos, Bungalows, Jacuzzi\})$
    return(FALSE)
  call $IsValid(Facilities, \{Hersonnissos, Bungalows, Jacuzzi\})$
    return(FALSE)
  return(FALSE)

6 Generating Navigation Trees

Let e be the expression that defines a desired compound taxonomy $(S_e, \preceq)$. In this section we describe a method for deriving a *navigation tree* for $(S_e, \preceq)$, that can be used during the following activities:

- *Indexing* the objects of the domain. This tree can speed up the indexing process and prevent indexing errors.

- *Browsing.* This tree can aid the user to reach the objects that satisfy a given information need.
- *Testing* whether the compound taxonomy contains only the desired set of compound terms.

A *navigation tree* is a directed acyclic graph (N, R) where N is the set of *nodes* and R is the set of *edges*. The nodes in N correspond to valid compound terms. Moreover, N contains nodes that enable the user to start browsing in one facet and then cross to another, and so on, until reaching the desired level of specificity.

Let us now introduce some notations. Given a term t, we denote by $\mathrm{Brd}(t)$ the set of all terms that are broader than t, i.e. $\mathrm{Brd}(t) = \{t' \mid t \leq t'\}$. Given a compound term $s = \{t_1, ..., t_k\}$, let $Brd(s)$ be the set of all terms t such that t is broader than some term t_i, $i = 1, ..., k$, i.e. $Brd(s) = \mathrm{Brd}(t_1) \cup ... \cup \mathrm{Brd}(t_k)$. By $Brd(s)/\sim$ we denote the set of equivalence classes of the terms[8] in $Brd(s)$. For brevity hereafter we shall use $Brd(s)$ to denote $Brd(s)/\sim$.

The navigation tree (N, R) that we construct has the following property:

> for each compound term $s \in S_e$, the navigation tree has a path (starting from the root) for each *topological sort*[9] of the terms of the directed acyclic graph $(Brd(s), \leq)$.

For example consider the faceted taxonomy shown in Figure 1, and suppose that $\{Crete, SeaSports\} \in S$. The navigation tree in this case will include the following paths:

Location.Islands.Crete.Sports.SeaSports
Location.Islands.Sports.Crete.SeaSports
Location.Islands.Sports.SeaSports.Crete
Location.Sports.Islands.SeaSports.Crete
...
...
Sports.SeaSports.Location.Islands.Crete

As a further user aid whenever facet crossing occurs, a new node is created which presents the name of the facet (specifically its top term prefixed by the string "by") that we are crossing to. This facet crossing mechanism corresponds to the use of so-called "guide terms" for thesaurus expansion.

There are two approaches to deriving the navigation tree. The first approach is to generate a "complete" static navigation tree through an algorithm that takes e as input and returns a navigation tree. The second approach is to design a mechanism that generates the navigation tree dynamically during browsing.

Without loss of generality below we assume that each facet F_i has a greatest term with respect to subsumption which we denote by $top(F_i)$. Each node n of the navigation tree (N, R) is associated with a triple $(s(n), Fc(n), Nm(n))$ where:

- $s(n)$ is a *compound term*.
  As we shall see below, we construct navigation trees with nodes whose compound terms are valid.

---

[8] Equivalence of terms was defined at the beginning of Section 2.

[9] *Topological sort* of a set of terms is a sort that respects the partial order of the terms. That is, if $t, t' \in Brd(s)$ and $t \leq t'$, then t should always appear to the left of t' in the topological sort.

- $Fc(n)$ is a so-called *focus term*.
  The focus term of a node n is a distinguished term among those that appear in $s(n)$ such that the children of n that are not used for facet-crossing are immediate children of $Fc(n)$. This means that from n, we either proceed to a different facet or we expand $Fc(n)$.

- $Nm(n)$ is a *name* for n.
  The name of a node is used for presenting the node at the user interface. It coincides with the focus term of n, unless n is a node for facet crossing. In the latter case the name of n is the name of the top term of the facet we are crossing to, prefixed by the string "by".

Below we describe an algorithm which takes as input the expression e that defines the compound taxonomy and returns a navigation tree (N, R). Roughly, the navigation tree is constructed as follows: At first we create a node for the top term of each facet that appears in e. Specifically, for each facet F_i we create a node whose compound term is the top term of F_i i.e. $top(F_i)$; we set as name and focus term of each such node the term $top(F_i)$. Now, for each node n we create *two* groups of children. The compound terms of the nodes in the first group are the results of replacing the focus term of n (i.e. $Fc(n)$) by an immediately narrower term of $Fc(n)$, while the second group consists of nodes for facet crossing.

Instead of presenting the algorithm for constructing the entire navigation tree, in Algorithm $NavTreeInit(e)$, we present the initialization step, i.e. the creation of a top node for each facet appearing in e and, in Algorithm $CreateChildren(n)$, we present the steps for creating the children of a node n of the navigation tree. These steps can be synthesized (in a depth-first-search manner) to get an algorithm that constructs the entire navigation tree. The algorithms use the function `IsValid`(e, s) which returns `True` if s is a valid compound term according to e and `False` otherwise. The procedure `createNode` $(Nm(n), s(n), Fc(n))$ creates a node with the given parameters. The function $Nar(t)$ returns the immediately narrower terms of t. The procedure `AddChild` (n, n') makes n' child of n.

Algorithm 6.1 $NavTreeInit(e)$
Input: An algebraic expression e
Output: An initial top node for each facet in e

```
// Initialization: Creation of a top node for each facet
For each F ∈ F(e)
   createNode( top(F), {top(F)}, top(F))
```

Algorithm 6.2 $CreateChildren(n)$
Input: A node n of the navigation tree
Output: The children of n

```
B.1   // Creating the children of a node on the basis of the focus term
      For each t ∈ Nar(Fc(n))
         Let s' := (s(n) − Fc(n)) ∪ {t}
         If IsValid(e, s') then
            n':=createNode(t, s', t)
            AddChild(n, n')
```

```
B.2   // Creating the children of a node for "facet crossing"
      For each F_i ∈ F(e) − F(Fc(n))
         Let t_i := s(n)∩T_i
         If t_i = ∅ then
            Let s' := s(n) ∪ {top(F_i)}
            If IsValid(e, s') then
               n':=createNode("by" + top(F_i), s', top(F_i) )
               AddChild(n, n')
         else
            If ∃t' ∈ Nar(t_i) such that
            IsValid( (s(n) − {t_i}) ∪ {t'}) then
               n':=createNode("by"+top(F_i), s(n), t_i)
               AddChild(n, n')
```

Figure 9 shows a part of the navigation tree that is generated by this algorithm for the taxonomy shown in that Figure and expression e = *Sports* $\oplus_N$ *Location*, where $N = \{\{WinterSports, Islands\}, \{SeaSports, Olympus\}\}$. In the navigation tree, each node n is presented by its name, $Nm(n)$. For example, the node n_{22} has $Nm(n_{22})$ = `Mainland`, $s(n_{22}) = \{\{\texttt{Sports}, \texttt{Mainland}\}\}$, $Fc(n_{22})$ = `Mainland`. The nodes n_{23} and n_{27} are generated by part B.1 of the algorithm, while node n_{30} is generated by part B.2.

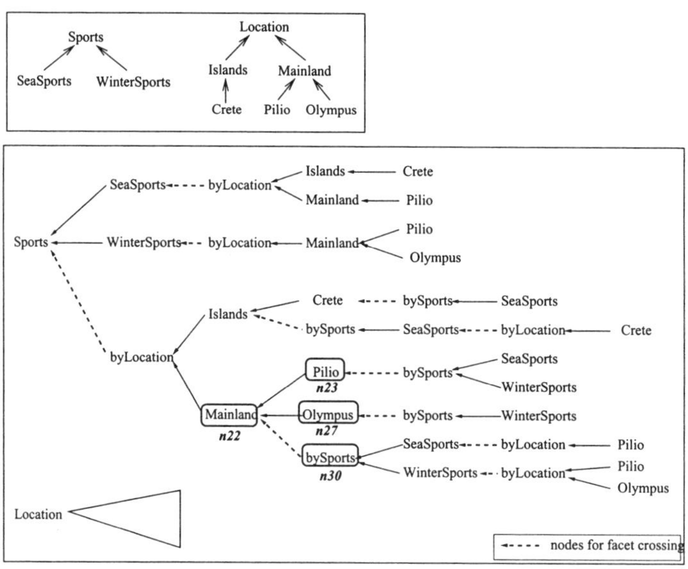

Figure 9: Example of a navigation tree

7 Concluding Remarks

The novelty of our approach lies in enriching a faceted scheme with an algebra for specifying the valid compound terms. This method can be used in order to construct taxonomies or thesauri, which unlike existing thesauri, do not present the problem of missing terms or missing relationships (for more about this problem see [1]). We have not elaborated facet analysis, i.e. which facets should be selected and how they should be constructed. This process can be carried out either formally (see for example [4], [13], or [2]), or informally, as it is usually done by the designers of Web catalogs. Moreover, and in order to avoid misunderstanding we have to note here that our algebra is not related with the algebras that have been proposed for ontology engineering (e.g. [14, 3]). Our algebra is the only one that focuses on the problem of compound terms. It actually combines into a unified theory the extensions presented in [12]. There, the ideas of the plus and minus-product operations are called $PEFT$ and $NEFT$ respectively and they could be applied once on all facets. That is, $PEFT$ and $NEFT$ could not be synthesized. In the current work we presented an algebra which allows combining these two operations. In addition the algebra provides operators for capturing the cases of multiple classification within a facet, i.e. the self-product operations.

The advantages of our approach are the following:

- The algebra that we propose is quite *flexible* and quite *easy* to use. The designer does not have to write a program or to be familiar with logic-based languages. He just decides the order by which the facets appear in the expression and sets the parameters P and N which are just sets of compound terms. The simplicity of the compound terms considered (conjunctions of terms only) apart from allowing a very efficient inference mechanism, makes our approach easy to use and scalable. We believe that it can be adopted by catalog designers (librarians, etc) who are not familiar with logic-based representation languages.

- The operations are defined in a way that ensures that *no consistency problems* arise. This means that when the designer adds a new facet to the expression and defines the parameters P or N, he does not have to worry about inconsistencies.

- The compound terminologies defined by our algebra have *low storage space* requirements. There is no need to store the compound terminology of an expression. Only the expression has to be stored, as we provided an *efficient* inference mechanism which can check whether a compound term belongs to the compound terminology of the expression.

Our algebra can be used in any application that indexes objects using a controlled structured vocabulary, i.e. a taxonomy. For example it can be used for designing taxonomies for products, for fields of knowledge (e.g. for indexing the books of a library), etc. Moreover, we demonstrated how we can generate dynamically *navigation trees* which are suitable for browsing and can be also exploited during the indexing process (to aid the indexer and prevent indexing errors).

Currently, our algebra is been used for building the taxonomy of a tourist portal. The results that the designers report to us, concerning flexibility and ease of use, are so far very encouraging. An interesting application that we are going to investigate and implement in the near future, is to employ this algebra in order to design compound taxonomies for Web portals. Suppose that we want to create indexing terms that allow partitioning of 10^6 Web pages, in blocks of 10 pages. For doing this, we need at least 100 thousand (10^5) different terms, if we assume that each page is indexed by one term. If we want these terms to be the leaves of a complete balanced decimal tree, then this tree would have: $10^5 + 10^4 + ... + 10 + 1 =$ 111,111 terms in total. By adopting a faceted taxonomy, we can obtain the same discrimination capability with much fewer terms. For example, with 5 facets each one having 10 leaves, the number of compound terms is greater that $10 \times 10 \times 10 \times 10 \times 10 = 10^5$. Assume that each facet is a complete balanced decimal tree, then the entire faceted taxonomy would have: $(10 + 1) \times 5 = 55$ terms in total. Notice the tremendous difference between 111,111 and 44. However, it is probably impossible to find 88 terms such that all of their combinations are valid. The faceted taxonomy is expected to have many more terms and many combinations of these terms are expected to be invalid. However, our algebra offers a powerful means for specifying the valid compound terms. Returning back to our example, we believe that using our algebra we can obtain the desired discrimination capability with a relatively smaller number of terms and stored descriptions in P and N, by comparison to the 111,111 terms of a single hierarchical taxonomy.

Summarizing, instead of building huge hierarchical taxonomies we propose the employment of faceted taxonomies plus the usage of our algebra. In this way the designer can obtain taxonomies consisting of big numbers of valid indexing terms with less effort. Moreover the resulting compound taxonomies have low storage space requirements. Finally we have to note that the advantages of the compound faceted taxonomies that we propose (compactness, conceptual clarity, scalability, valid compound terms) can facilitate several other associated tasks. Specifically, they can certainly facilitate the design of *mediators* over several taxonomy-based sources (using the approach presented in [11]), and the *personalization* of Web catalogs (using the approach presented in [9]).

References

[1] Peter Clark, John Thompson, Heather Holmback, and Lisbeth Duncan. "Exploiting a Thesaurus-based Semantic Net for Knowledge-based Search". In *Procs of 12th Conf. on Innovative Applications of AI (AAAI/IAAI'00)*, pages 988–995, 2000.

[2] Elizabeth B. Duncan. "A Faceted Approach to Hypertext". In Ray McAleese, editor, *HYPERTEXT: theory into practice, BSP*, 1989.

[3] J. Jannink, S. Pichai, D. Verheijen, and G. Wiederhold. "Encapsulation and composition of ontologies". In *Proceedings of 1998 AAAI Workshop on AI & Information Integration*, 1998.

[4] P. H. Lindsay and D. A. Norman. *Human Information Processing.* Academic press, New York, 1977.

[5] Deborah L. McGuinness. "Ontological Issues for Knowledge-Enhanced Search". In *Proceedings of FOIS'98*, Trento, Italy, June 1998. Amsterdam, IOS Press.

[6] Ruben Prieto-Diaz. "Implementing Faceted Classification for Software Reuse". *Communications of the ACM*, page 88, 1991.

[7] S. R. Ranganathan. "The Colon Classification". In Susan Artandi, editor, *Vol IV of the Rutgers Series on Systems for the Intellectual Organization of Information.* New Brunswick, NJ: Graduate School of Library Science, Rutgers University, 1965.

[8] G. Salton. *"Introduction to Modern Information Retrieval"*. McGraw-Hill, 1983.

[9] Nicolas Spyratos, Yannis Tzitzikas, and Vassilis Christophides. "On Personalizing the Catalogs of Web Portals". In *15th International FLAIRS Conference, FLAIRS'02*, pages 430–434, Pensacola, Florida, May 2002.

[10] Yannis Tzitzikas, Anastasia Analyti, Nicolas Spyratos, and Panos Constantopoulos. "An Algebra for Specifying Compound Terms for Faceted Taxonomies". Technical Report TR-314, Institute of Computer Science-FORTH, October 2002.

[11] Yannis Tzitzikas, Nicolas Spyratos, and Panos Constantopoulos. "Mediators over Ontology-based Information Sources". In *Proceedings of the 2nd International Conference on Web Information Systems Engineering, WISE 2001*, pages 31–40, Kyoto, Japan, December 2001.

[12] Yannis Tzitzikas, Nicolas Spyratos, Panos Constantopoulos, and Anastasia Analyti. "Extended Faceted Taxonomies for Web Catalogs". In *Proceedings of the 3rd International Conference on Web Information Systems Engineering, WISE 2002*, pages 192–204, Singapore, December 2002.

[13] B. C. Vickery. "Knowledge Representation: A Brief Review". *Journal of Documentation*, 42(3):145–159, 1986.

[14] Gio Wiederhold. "An Algebra for Ontology Composition". In *Proceedings of 1994 Monterey Workshop on Formal Methods*, pages 56–61, September 1994.

Information Modelling and Knowledge Bases XV
Y. Kiyoki et al. (Eds.)
IOS Press, 2004

A new Normal Form for Conceptual Databases

Sven Hartmann, Sebastian Link, Klaus-Dieter Schewe

Information Science Research Centre
Massey University, New Zealand
e-mail: [s.hartmann|s.link|k.d.schewe]@massey.ac.nz

Abstract. Functional dependencies have recently been generalized to conceptual schemata, i.e., to higher-order entity-relationship (HERM) schemata. As in the relational data model (RDM), functional dependencies in the HERM also cause redundancies in the representation of data and abnormal update behaviour. It is investigated whether a generalization of the Boyce-Codd Normal Form (BCNF) to database types in the HERM yields a suitable normal form which avoids redundancies and abnormal update behaviour. It turns out that BCNF is too strong. Therefore, the Higher Level Normal Form (HLNF) is proposed as a weaker normal form for database types. It is demonstrated that database types are in HLNF if and only if they are non-redundant with respect to a given set of functional dependencies on that database type. Furthermore, HLNF is equivalent to the absence of insertion and replacement anomalies. Since relation schemata are a special case of database types, the results in this paper generalize well-known results from the RDM.

1 Introduction

Relational database systems have evolved to an industry standard since their invention by Codd in 1970 ([10]). This is a result of the simplicity and the sound theoretical basis of the relational data model (RDM). One important issue associated with the use of relational databases is the correct structure or design of data to be used. Several criteria, referred to as *normal forms*, have been proposed as conditions for relation schemata that a database design should satisfy to ensure an absence of processing difficulties with the database. Such normal forms have already been introduced in [11] by Codd himself. In general, they are dependent on the type of integrity constraints or rules which apply to data items within the database. The most important class of integrity constraints are *functional dependencies* which have been intensely studied since their introduction in [11]. Functional dependencies cause difficulties such as redundancy in the representation of data or update anomalies. Codd proposed the Boyce-Codd normal form (BCNF) in [12] to overcome these difficulties. He conjectured that BCNF is an exact condition on a relation schema that avoids redundancies and update anomalies. Later on, after the notions of redundancy and update anomaly had been clarified and formalized, it was shown in [6], [13] and [24] that this is indeed the case. Thus, BCNF is a completely justified normal form in that sense.

In recent years many new and different data models have been proposed. One important class are conceptual data models with its most prominent representative being the Entity-Relationship model, introduced by Chen in [8]. It is widely accepted now that databases are best designed first on a conceptual level ([3]). Entity-Relationship diagrams are on one hand a suitable abstraction tool to capture specification requirements in a first schema. Moreoever, they are an exceptionally good communication tool with the users and allow a step-by-step refinement. Chen [9] pointed out that English sentences can be mapped to entity-relationship schemata in a natural way. The same observation holds for most other languages, see [23]. Many extensions of the Entity-Relationship model have been proposed. The Higher-Order Entity-Relationship model (HERM), introduced by Thalheim in [21], is such an interesting extension, that is well-founded in theory. For a comprehensive study see also [22]. The HERM is not only an intuitive tool for conceptual design, but may serve as a mathematical model upon which database management systems are built. In [15] functional dependencies have been defined in the context of the HERM, and a sound and complete set of inference rules for the implication of functional dependencies has been proposed which naturally extends the Armstrong Axioms from the RDM ([2]).

The present article continues this line of research. It is observed that functional dependencies in the HERM also cause redundancies in the representation of data. Therefore, the formal notion of redundancy from the RDM is taken up in the context of the HERM. It turns out that this notion is too strong and therefore has to be adopted. Moreover, insertion and replacement anomalies of three different types are formally defined on the conceptual level. It is then investigated whether the notion of BCNF in the HERM is a justified normal form with respect to the absence of redundancy and update anomalies. In fact, BCNF is too strong and a new normal form, the Higher-Level Normal Form (HLNF), is introduced. It is demonstrated that database types are in HLNF if and only if they do not have redundancies. Surprisingly, non-redundancy of database types does not avoid *all* update anomalies. However, HLNF is an exact condition on database types for the absence of *strong* insertion and replacement anomalies.

2 Preliminaries

We assume familarity with fundamental definitions of the RDM and functional dependencies in the RDM. Any of [1, 20] provide more than we need.

The setting of this paper is the Higher-Order Entity-Relationship Model, introduced in [21]. For a comprehensive study see also [22]. We briefly repeat the most fundamental definitions that are needed for the sequel of the paper.

One key feature of the HERM is the nesting of attributes. Starting point, however, is a set $\mathbb{B}$ of *base types* such as *STRING, INTEGER, BOOL, DATE* etc., a set $\mathcal{D}$ of domains and a domain assignment $dom : \mathbb{B} \to \mathcal{D}$. A *type assignment* takes a given countable set $\mathcal{U}$ of attribute names and assigns a base type to each of these attribute names, i.e., $type : \mathcal{U} \to \mathbb{B}$.

New types over $\mathbb{B}$ can be obtained by the application of *type constructors* such as records, finite sets, lists, multisets etc. Throughout the paper we will use the type system $t := b \mid (a_1 : t_1, \ldots, a_n : t_n) \mid \{t\}$, i.e., a type $t \in \mathbb{T}$ over $\mathbb{B}$ is a base type b, a record type $(a_1 : t_1, \ldots, a_n : t_n)$ with disjoint labels $a_i \in L$ for $i = 1, \ldots, n$ and a countable set L, or a finite set type $\{t\}$.

The domain assignment *dom* for base types can then be extended to a domain assignment *Dom* for all types in $\mathbb{T}$, i.e., $Dom(b) = dom(b)$ for all $b \in \mathbb{B}$, $Dom((a_1 : t_1, \ldots, a_n : t_n)) = \prod_{i=1}^{n} Dom(t_i)$ and $Dom(\{t\}) = \mathcal{P}_0(Dom(t))$ where $\mathcal{P}_0(D)$ denotes the set of all finite subsets of D. Herein, we make the assumption that every domain of a base type has at least cardinality two.

Given countable disjoint sets $\mathcal{U}$ and L of flat attribute names and labels, respectively, the set $\mathcal{N}\mathrm{A} = \mathcal{N}\mathrm{A}(\mathcal{U}, L)$ of *nested attributes* is the smallest set that contains $\mathcal{U}$, the null attribute λ, a tuple-valued attribute $X(A_1, \dots, A_n)$ whenever $X \in L$ and $A_1, \dots, A_n \in \mathcal{N}\mathrm{A}$ such that no flat attribute names and no labels are used twice in $X(A_1, \dots, A_n)$, and a set-valued attribute $X\{A\}$ whenever $X \in L$ and $A \in \mathcal{N}\mathrm{A}$ such that X is not used twice in $X\{A\}$.

The type assignment $type : \mathcal{U} \to \mathbb{B}$ is extended to a type assignment $Type : \mathcal{N}\mathrm{A} \to \mathbb{T}$ by $Type(\lambda) = OK$, $Type(A) = type(A)$ for every $A \in \mathcal{U}$, $Type(X(A_1, \dots, A_n)) = (A_1 : Type(A_1), \dots, A_n : Type(A_n))$ and $Type(X\{A\}) = \{Type(A)\}$. This induces a domain assignment Dom on nested attributes with $Dom(X) = Dom(Type(X))$. Note that the domain of OK is some singleton set, for instance $\{ok\}$.

In the following, we identify nested attributes up to occurences of λ and up to the order of the attributes within a record-valued attribute. Define $\equiv \subseteq \mathcal{N}\mathrm{A} \times \mathcal{N}\mathrm{A}$ as the smallest equivalence relation on $\mathcal{N}\mathrm{A}$ with

- $A(A_1, \dots, A_n, \lambda) \equiv A(A_1, \dots, A_n)$, $A(\lambda) \equiv \lambda$,
- $A(A_1, \dots, A_n) \equiv A(A_{\pi(1)}, \dots, A_{\pi(n)})$ for all $\pi \in \mathcal{S}_n$,
- $A(B_1, \dots, B_n) \equiv A(C_1, \dots, C_n)$ if $B_i \equiv C_i$ for $i = 1, \dots, n$,
- $A\{B\} \equiv A\{C\}$ if $B \equiv C$.

The nested attribute $A(B(C, \lambda, D), E\{\lambda\}, F(\lambda), \lambda, G(H\{K\}, L))$ is, for instance, equivalent to $A(E\{\lambda\}, B(C, D), G(H\{K\}, L))$. For the sake of simplicity, we write $\mathcal{N}\mathrm{A}$ instead of $\mathcal{N}\mathrm{A}/\equiv$.

The nesting of attributes induces an ordering on nested attributes. Informally, $A \leq B$ for $A, B \in \mathcal{N}\mathrm{A}$ if and only if A comprises at most as much information as B does. We call A a *subattribute* of B if and only if $A \leq B$ holds. More formally, $\leq \subseteq \mathcal{N}\mathrm{A} \times \mathcal{N}\mathrm{A}$ is defined as the smallest partial order with

- $\lambda \leq A$ for all $A \in \mathcal{N}\mathrm{A}$,
- $A(A_1, \dots, A_n) \leq A(B_1, \dots, B_n)$ whenever $A_i \leq B_i$ for all $i = 1, \dots, n$, and
- $A\{B\} \leq A\{C\}$ whenever $B \leq C$.

We write $A \not\leq B$ whenever A is not a subattribute of B. The informal description of a subattribute is formally documented by the existence of a projection function $\pi_B^A : Dom(A) \to Dom(B)$ in case $B \leq A$ holds.The partial order $\leq$ on nested attributes allows to generalise the concept of a subset. A subset $\mathcal{Y} \subseteq \mathcal{N}\mathrm{A}$ is called a *generalised subset* of a finite set $\mathcal{X} \subseteq \mathcal{N}\mathrm{A}$, denoted by $\mathcal{Y} \subseteq_{\mathrm{gen}} \mathcal{X}$, if and only if for all $Y \in \mathcal{Y}$ there is some $X \in \mathcal{X}$ with $Y \leq X$.

A *database type* $R = (comp(R), attr(R), id(R))$ *of order* i consists of a name R, a finite set $comp(R) = \{r_1 : R_1, \dots, r_n : R_n\}$ with pairwise distinct role names $r_1, \dots, r_n$ and names of database types $R_1, \dots, R_n$ of order $j < i$ and at least one R_i is the name of a database type of order $i - 1$, a finite set $attr(R) \subseteq \mathcal{N}\mathrm{A}$ of nested attributes and a key $id(R)$ of the form $id(R) = comp'(R) \cup X$ where $comp'(R) \subseteq comp(R)$ and X is a generalised subset of $attr(R)$. Database types E of order 0 satisfy $comp(E) = \emptyset$ and are called *entity types*. Database types of order $i > 0$ are called *relationship types*. Given an entity type $E = (\emptyset, \{A_1, \dots, A_n\}, \{B_1, \dots, B_m\})$ we define the *corresponding nested attribute of* E as $N_E = E(A_1, \dots, A_n) \in \mathcal{N}\mathrm{A}$ and the primary key of N_E as $N_E^P = \{E(B_1), \dots, E(B_m)\} \subseteq_{\mathrm{gen}} \{N_E\}$. Given a relationship type $R = (\{r_1 : R_1, \dots, r_k : R_k\}, \{A_1, \dots, A_u\}, \{s_1 : S_1, \dots, s_l : S_l, B_1, \dots, B_v\})$, the *corresponding nested attribute of* R is $N_R = R(r_1(N_{R_1}), \dots, r_k(N_{R_k}), A_1, \dots, A_u) \in \mathcal{N}\mathrm{A}$ and the primary key of N_R is $N_R^P = \bigcup_{i=1}^{l} \{R(s_i(X)) : X \in N_{S_i}^P\} \cup \{R(B_1), \dots, R(B_v)\} \subseteq_{\text{gen}} \{N_R\}$. A *HERM Schema* is a finite and non-empty set $\mathcal{S}$ of database types such that for all relationship types $R \in \mathcal{S}$ and for all $(r : R') \in comp(R)$ also $R' \in \mathcal{S}$ holds. An *instance* $\mathcal{I}$ of $\mathcal{S}$ assigns to every database type $R \in \mathcal{S}$ a finite set $\mathcal{I}(R) \subseteq Dom(N_R)$ such that for all $(r : R') \in comp(R)$ and for all $t \in \mathcal{I}(R)$ we have $\pi^{N_R}_{R(r(N_{R'}))}(t) \in \mathcal{I}(R')$, and the projection functions $\pi^{N_R}_X |_{\mathcal{I}(R)}$ are injective for all $X \in N_R^P$.

EXAMPLE 1. Imagine we would like to keep track of Sumo matches in different tournaments[1]. More precisely, two fighters (*rikishi*) have a match (*bout*) in a tournament (*basho*). We define a HERM schema OZUMO={RIKISHI,BASHO,BOUT} as follows[2].

RIKISHI = ({Person(Heya, Name, Shikona, Birthday(Date, Place),Height, Weight), Won{Yusho},Awards(Shukon-Sho,Kanto-Sho,Gino-Sho)},{Person(Shikona, Weight), Won{Yusho}, Awards(Shukon-Sho, Kanto-Sho, Gino-Sho)})
BASHO = ({Name, Year, Participating{Rikishis}}; {Name, Year})
BOUT = ({Winner:RIKISHI, Loser:RIKISHI, at:BASHO}, {Win(Rank, Yokozuna-since{Date}), Stats(Day, Kimarite, Bout-Time)}; {Winner:RIKISHI, Loser:RIKISHI, at:BASHO}).

Figure 1 shows the corresponding illustration of OZUMO by an HERM diagram. Key attributes are underlined, key components have a dot on the corresponding arc.

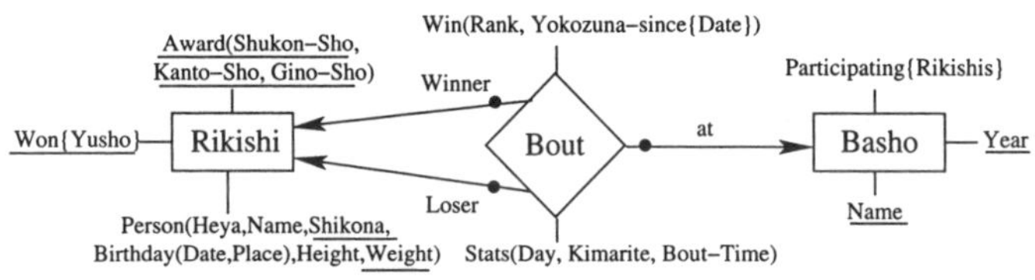

Fig. 1. HERM Diagram for OZUMO

Let

- $t_{\text{Musashimaru}}$ = ((Musashiwaga, Koyo Musashimaru, Musashimaru, (02.05.1971, USA), 191 cm, 231 kg),{Nagoya 94, Kyushu 96, Hatsu 98, Haru 99, Aki 99, Kyushu 99},(1,1,1)),
- $t_{\text{Takanohana}}$ = ((Futagoyama, Koji Hanada, Takanohana, (12.08.1972, Tokyo), 184 cm, 149 kg),{Hatsu 92, Aki 92, Natsu 93, Hatsu 94, Natsu 94, Aki 94, Kyushu 94, Hatsu 95, Natsu 95, Nagoya 95, Aki 95, Haru 96, Natsu 96, Nagoya 96, Aki 96, Haru 97, Nagoya 97, Aki 97, Nagoya 98, Aki 98},(4,2,3)), and
- $t_{\text{Chiyotaikai}}$ = ((Kokonoe, Ryuji Hiroshima, Chiyotaikai, (29. 04. 1976, Oita), 181 cm, 158 kg),{Hatsu 99},(1,1,3)).

Define an OZUMA instance $\mathcal{I}$ as follows:

- $\mathcal{I}$(RIKISHI) = $\{t_{\text{Musashimaru}}, t_{\text{Takanohana}}, t_{\text{Chiyotaikai}}\}$,

[1] This running example may serve the cultural exchange between Japan and Europe

[2] We recommend *http://www.chijanofuji.com/* for an introduction to Sumo wrestling.

- $\mathcal{I}$(BASHO)=$\{t_{\text{Kyushu00}}$=(Kyushu, 2000, {Musashimaru, Takanohana, Chiyotaikai})} and
- $\mathcal{I}$(BOUT) = $\{t_1, t_2, t_3\}$ with
  - $t_1 = (t_{\text{Chiyotaikai}}, t_{\text{Takanohana}}, t_{\text{Kyushu00}},$ (Ozeki, $\emptyset$), (10, Tsukiotoshi, 18 sec.)),
  - $t_2 = (t_{\text{Musashimaru}}, t_{\text{Chiyotaikai}}, t_{\text{Kyushu00}},$ (Yokozuna, {May 99}), (12, Oshidashi, 13 sec.)) and
  - $t_3 = (t_{\text{Musashimaru}}, t_{\text{Takanohana}}, t_{\text{Kyushu00}},$ (Yokozuna, {May 99}), (13, Sukuinage, 94 sec.)). □

Fix a set $\mathcal{U}$ of attribute names, a set L of labels, and a set $\mathbb{B}$ of base types together with a type assignment $type : \mathcal{U} \to \mathbb{B}$.

Definition 1. Let $X \in \mathcal{N}A$ be a nested attribute. The set $Sub(X)$ of *subattributes of* X is $Sub(X) = \{Y \mid Y \leq X\}$. □

The notion of a subattribute corresponds to the notion of a subset of attributes in the RDM. It has been proven in [15] that $Sub(X)/\equiv$ carries the structure of a so-called *Brouwerian Algebra*. See for instance [17] for a definition. Take for example the corresponding nested attribute X = BASHO(Name, Year, Participating{Rikishis}) for the database type BASHO from Example 1. Then the structure of $Sub(X)$ is illustrated in Figure 2.

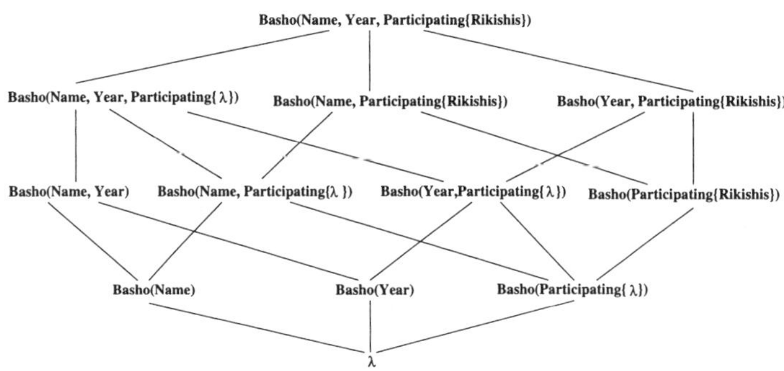

Fig. 2. The Brouwerian Algebra of N_{BASHO}

In particular, two subattributes $Y, Z \in Sub(X)$ always have a least upper bound (join) $Y \sqcup_X Z$ in $Sub(X)$. The index X in $\sqcup_X$ is usually omitted. For instance, if Y = BASHO(Name, Participating{λ}) and Z = BASHO(Participating{Rikishis}), then $Y \sqcup Z$ = BASHO(Name, Participating{Rikishis}).

Take a closer look at the subattributes BASHO(Participating{λ}), RIKISHI(Won{λ}) and BOUT(Win(Yokozuna-since{λ})) with domain $\{\emptyset, \{ok\}\}$. Intuitively, the first attribute tells us whether there are any participants in a basho at all. If there are no participants, then the corresponding value is $\emptyset$. Is the value {ok}, then we know that there are some participants. The second attribute reveals whether a rikishi has ever won a tournament ($\{ok\}$) or not ($\emptyset$). Finally, the last attribute says whether a winner of a bout has the rank of a yokozuna ($\{ok\}$) or not ($\emptyset$). These kind of attributes have therefore a neat impact on conceptual modeling and do not occur in any other approaches to normalization of nested relations. Therefore, the HERM-approach to nested attributes is already different from other approaches to nested attributes such as [18],[19] when we restrict the type system to base, record and finite set types.

3 Functional Dependencies in HERM

This section repeats the definition of functional dependencies in the HERM and mentions some results from [15].

Definition 2. Let $N \in \mathcal{N}A$ be a nested attribute. A *functional dependency on* N is an expression of the form $\mathcal{X} \to \mathcal{Y}$ where $\mathcal{X}, \mathcal{Y} \subseteq Sub(N)$ are non-empty. A finite set $r \subseteq Dom(N)$ *satisfies* a functional dependency $\mathcal{X} \to \mathcal{Y}$ on N ($\models_r \mathcal{X} \to \mathcal{Y}$) if and only if $\pi_Y^N(t_1) = \pi_Y^N(t_2)$ holds for all $Y \in \mathcal{Y}$ whenever $\pi_X^N(t_1) = \pi_X^N(t_2)$ holds for all $X \in \mathcal{X}$ and any $t_1, t_2 \in r$. A functional dependency on a database type R is a functional dependency on the corresponding nested attribute N_R of R. □

If $\mathcal{X} \to \mathcal{Y}$ is a functional dependency on some nested attribute N and $\mathcal{X} = \{X\}$ and $\mathcal{Y} = \{Y\}$ are singletons, then we write $X \to Y$ instead of $\{X\} \to \{Y\}$.

EXAMPLE 2. Consider the HERM schema OZUMO from Example 1. We define a set Σ of functional dependencies on the database type BOUT. The first dependency represents the key on N_{BOUT}:

$$\text{BOUT}(\text{Winner}(N_{\text{RIKISHI}}), \text{Loser}(N_{\text{RIKISHI}}), \text{at}(N_{\text{BASHO}})) \to N_{\text{BOUT}}. \quad (1)$$

The *shikona* (ringname) of a rikishi determines all the static information of that rikishi, i.e., everything but his weight, the tournaments he has won (*yusho*) and the numbers of different awards he has been given.

$$\text{BOUT}(\text{Winner}(\text{RIKISHI}(\text{Person}(\text{Shikona})))) \to \text{BOUT}(\text{Winner}(\text{RIKISHI}(\text{Person}(\text{Heya}, \text{Name}, \text{Shikona}, \text{Birthday}(\text{Date},\text{Place}), \text{height})))) \quad (2)$$

Recall that during a single basho, every rikishi has only one bout a day. Furthermore, the winner of a bout in a basho determines also the tournaments and awards won by the winner at that time, i.e.,

$$\text{BOUT}(\text{Winner}(\text{RIKISHI}(\text{Person}(\text{Shikona}))), \text{Stats}(\text{Day}), \text{at}(N_{\text{BASHO}})) \to N_{\text{BOUT}}. \quad (3)$$

The rank of a rikishi depends on his performance in the tournaments. However, once he has been awarded the highest rank of a *yokozuna*, he will remain yokozuna until he retires. That is, the rank already determines whether the rank of a yokozuna has been awarded or not, but it does not determine the date when this rank was awarded.

$$\text{BOUT}(\text{Win}(\text{Rank})) \to \text{BOUT}(\text{Win}(\text{Yokozuna-since}\{\lambda\})) \quad (4)$$

The shikona and tournament determine the current rank of the shikona and also the date when the shikona was awarded the rank of a yokozuna (if he is not a yokozuna, then the set of this date is empty).

$$\text{BOUT}(\text{Winner}(\text{RIKISHI}(\text{Person}(\text{Shikona}))), \text{at}(N_{\text{Basho}})) \to \text{BOUT}(\text{Win}(\text{Rank},\text{Yokozuna-since}\{\text{Date}\})) \quad (5)$$

The functional dependencies

$$\text{BOUT}(\text{at}(\text{BASHO}(\text{Name}, \text{Year}))) \to \text{BOUT}(\text{at}(N_{\text{BASHO}})) \quad (6)$$

$$\text{BOUT}(\text{Winner}(\text{RIKISHI}(\text{Person}(\text{Shikona}, \text{Weight}), \text{Won}\{\text{Yusho}\}, \text{Awards}(\text{Shukon-Sho}, \text{Kanto-Sho}, \text{Gino-Sho})))) \to \text{BOUT}(\text{Winner}(N_{\text{RIKISHI}})) \quad (7)$$

$$\text{BOUT}(\text{Loser}(\text{RIKISHI}(\text{Person}(\text{Shikona}, \text{Weight}), \text{Won}\{\text{Yusho}\}, \text{Awards}(\text{Shukon-Sho}, \text{Kanto-Sho}, \text{Gino-Sho})))) \to \text{BOUT}(\text{Loser}(N_{\text{RIKISHI}})) \quad (8)$$

describe what the keys on N_{RIKISHI} and N_{BASHO} are. □

The notions of implication ($\models$) and derivability ($\vdash_{\mathfrak{R}}$) with respect to a rule system $\mathfrak{R}$ for functional dependencies on a nested attribute can be defined analogously to the notions in the RDM (see for instance [1, p. 164-168]). Let Σ be a set of functional dependencies on some nested attribute N. We are interested in the set of all functional dependencies implied by Σ, i.e., $\Sigma^* = \{\varphi \mid \Sigma \models \varphi\}$. Our aim is finding a set $\mathfrak{R}$ of inference rules which is *sound* ($\Sigma^+ \subseteq \Sigma^*$) and *complete* ($\Sigma^* \subseteq \Sigma^+$), where $\Sigma^+ = \{\varphi \mid \Sigma \vdash_{\mathfrak{R}} \varphi\}$ is the set of functional dependencies derivable from Σ using only inference rules from $\mathfrak{R}$.

In general, values on subattributes X and Y do not determine values on $X \sqcup Y$. A sufficient condition when values on subattributes X and Y determine the values on $X \sqcup Y$ is the following.

Definition 3. Let $N \in \mathcal{N}A$. The subattributes $X, Y \in Sub(N)$ are *semi-disjoint* if and only if there are subattributes $X' \leq X$ and $Y' \leq Y$ with $X' \sqcap Y' = \lambda$ and $X \sqcup Y = X' \sqcup Y'$. □

Semi-disjointness of two subattributes is in fact an exact condition. The following result was proven in [15].

Theorem 4. *The generalised Armstrong Axioms for functional dependencies, i.e.*

$$\frac{}{\mathcal{X} \to \mathcal{Y}}\ \mathcal{Y} \subseteq \mathcal{X}, \quad \frac{}{\{X\} \to \{Y\}}\ Y \leq X, \quad \frac{\mathcal{X} \to \mathcal{Y}}{\mathcal{X} \to \mathcal{X} \cup \mathcal{Y}},$$

$$\frac{}{\{X, Y\} \to \{X \sqcup Y\}}\ X, Y\ \textit{semi-disjoint}, \quad \frac{\mathcal{X} \to \mathcal{Y},\ \mathcal{Y} \to \mathcal{Z}}{\mathcal{X} \to \mathcal{Z}},$$

reflexivity axiom, subattribute axiom, extension rule, restricted join axiom and transitivity rule, are sound and complete for the implication of functional dependencies in the HERM. □

The key result in proving Theorem 4 is the following lemma which is also proven in [15]. The lemma will also prove to be very useful in further investigations in this paper.

Lemma 5. *Let $N \in \mathcal{N}A$, and $\emptyset \neq \mathcal{X} \subseteq Sub(N)$ an ideal with respect to $\leq$ with the property that $X, Y \in \mathcal{X}$ and $X \sqcap Y = \lambda$ implies $X \sqcup Y \in \mathcal{X}$. Then there are $t_N, t'_N \in Dom(N)$ with $\pi^N_W(t_N) = \pi^N_W(t'_N)$ iff $W \in \mathcal{X}$.* □

4 Redundancy and Normal Forms in HERM

This section investigates how the notion of redundancy in terms of functional dependencies in the RDM has to be adopted to the HERM. In order to characterize non-redundant database types, a new normal form is proposed which is weaker than BCNF.

4.1 Preparations

Some further preliminary definitions are given which will be needed later on.

Definition 6. Let $N \in \mathcal{N}A$. The *subattribute basis* $SubB(N)$ *of* N is the smallest set $SubB(N) \subseteq Sub(N)$ such that for all $X \in Sub(N)$ we have $X = \sqcup Z$ for some $Z \subseteq SubB(N)$. Every $X \in SubB(N)$ is called a *basis attribute* for N. A basis attribute $X \in SubB(N)$ is called *maximal* if and only if $X \leq Y$ for some basis attribute $Y \in SubB(N)$ implies that $X = Y$ holds. Basis attributes that are not maximal are called *non-maximal*. □

It is immediate that $\lambda \notin SubB(N)$ since $\lambda = \sqcup\emptyset$. Furthermore, $SubB(N)$ is, in general, not an anti-chain with respect to $\leq$.

EXAMPLE 3. Let $N = A(B, C\{D(E, F\{G\})\})$. The subattribute basis is then

$$SubB(N) = \{A(B), A(C\{\lambda\}), A(C\{D(F\{\lambda\})\}), A(C\{D(E)\}), A(C\{D(F\{G\})\})\}.$$

The maximal basis attributes are $A(B), A(C\{D(E)\})$ and $A(C\{D(F\{G\})\})$. The non-maximal basis attributes are $A(C\{\lambda\})$ and $A(C\{D(F\{\lambda\})\})$. □

The concept of keys is very important in relational databases. We will therefore define what keys are in the HERM.

Definition 7. Let $N \in \mathcal{N}A$ be a nested attribute and Σ a set of functional dependencies on N. A set of subattributes $\mathcal{X} \subseteq Sub(N)$ is called a *superkey for* N if and only if $\Sigma \models \mathcal{X} \to N$ holds. A superkey $\mathcal{X}$ is called a *minimal key for* N if and only if $\mathcal{X}$ is an anti-chain with respect to $\leq$ and there is no superkey $\mathcal{X}'$ of N with $\mathcal{X}' \subseteq_{\text{gen}} \mathcal{X}$ and $\mathcal{X}' \neq \mathcal{X}$. □

Obviously, $\mathcal{X} \subseteq Sub(N)$ is a superkey if and only if $\mathcal{X} \to N \in \Sigma^+$ by Theorem 4. Moreover, $\mathcal{X}$ is a superkey for N if and only if $N \in \mathcal{X}^+ = \{Z : \mathcal{X} \to \{Z\} \in \Sigma^+\}$. If $\models_r \Sigma^*$ for some $r \subseteq Dom(N)$ and $\mathcal{X}$ is a superkey for N, then $t_1 = t_2$ whenever $\pi_X^N(t_1) = \pi_X^N(t_2)$ for all $X \in \mathcal{X}$ and some $t_1, t_2 \in r$. A functional dependency $\mathcal{X} \to \mathcal{Y} \in \Sigma^*$ is called a *key dependency* on N if and only if $\mathcal{X}$ is a superkey for N.

EXAMPLE 4. The functional dependencies (1) and (3) in Example 2 are both key dependencies on N_{BOUT}, i.e.,

BOUT(Winner(N_{RIKISHI}), Loser(N_{RIKISHI}), at(N_{BASHO})) and
BOUT(Winner(RIKISHI(Person(Shikona))), Stats(Day), at(N_{BASHO}))

are superkeys on N_{BOUT}. They are, however, not minimal due to the functional dependencies (6) to (8). The set

{BOUT(Winner(RIKISHI(Person(Shikona)))),BOUT(Stats(Day)),
BOUT(at(BASHO(Name))), BOUT(at(BASHO(Year)))}

is a minimal key for N_{BOUT}. □

Take another look at Example 2, in particular at the dependencies (6) to (8). The left-hand sides of these dependencies represent superkeys for N_{RIKISHI} and N_{BASHO} within the context of the database type BOUT. They are not, however, key dependencies on N_{BOUT}. This motivates the following definition.

Definition 8. Let R be a database type and Σ a set of functional dependencies on R. A functional dependency $\mathcal{X} \to \mathcal{Y} \in \Sigma^+$ is called a *key dependency on a subcomponent of* R if and only if $\mathcal{Y} = \{R(r_1(R_1(\cdots(r_n(N_{R_n}))\cdots)))\}$ with $r_i : R_i \in comp(R_{i-1})$ for $i = 1, \ldots, n$ and $R_0 = R$ and $\mathcal{X} \subseteq_{\text{gen}} \mathcal{Y}$. In this case, $\mathcal{X}$ is called a superkey for the subcomponent R_n of R. □

EXAMPLE 5. The functional dependencies (6) to (8) from Example 2 are key dependencies on subcomponents of BOUT. In particular, BOUT(at(BASHO(Name, Year))) is a superkey for the component BASHO of BOUT and

BOUT(Winner(RIKISHI(Person(Shikona, Weight), Won{Yusho}, Awards(Shukon-Sho, Kanto-Sho, Gino-Sho)))) and
BOUT(Loser(RIKISHI(Person(Shikona, Weight), Won{Yusho}, Awards(Shukon-Sho, Kanto-Sho, Gino-Sho))))

are superkeys for the component RIKISHI of BOUT. □

Suppose we are given a nested attribute N. As in the RDM, there are functional dependencies on N which are satisfied by any $r \subseteq Dom(N)$. We call these functional dependencies *trivial*. How can we characterise trivial functional dependencies $\mathcal{X} \rightarrow \mathcal{Y}$? Intuitively, $\mathcal{X} \rightarrow \mathcal{Y}$ is trivial if it can be derived from the empty set of functional dependencies.

Lemma 9. *A functional dependency $\mathcal{X} \rightarrow \mathcal{Y}$ on some nested attribute $N \in \mathcal{N}A$ is trivial if and only if $\mathcal{Y} \subseteq \mathcal{X}^{triv}$ holds where $\mathcal{X}^{triv} = \{Z : \mathcal{X} \rightarrow \{Z\} \in \emptyset^+\}$.*

Proof. Let $\mathcal{Y} \subseteq \mathcal{X}^{\text{triv}}$. We show that $\mathcal{X} \rightarrow \mathcal{Y}$ is satisfied by every $r \subseteq Dom(N)$. Let $t_1, t_2 \in r$ be such $\pi_X^N(t_1) = \pi_X^N(t_2)$ for all $X \in \mathcal{X}$. Since it is immediate that $\mathcal{X} \rightarrow \mathcal{X}^{\text{triv}} \in \emptyset^+$ holds, it follows from the soundness of the generalised Armstrong Axioms from Theorem 4 that $\pi_Z^N(t_1) = \pi_Z^N(t_2)$ for all $Z \in \mathcal{X}^{\text{triv}}$ holds. Consequently, $\pi_Y^N(t_1) = \pi_Y^N(t_2)$ holds for all $Y \in \mathcal{Y}$ as well since $\mathcal{Y} \subseteq \mathcal{X}^{\text{triv}}$. Therefore, $\models_r \mathcal{X} \rightarrow \mathcal{Y}$.

We show that $\mathcal{Y} \subseteq \mathcal{X}^{\text{triv}}$ is also a necessary condition for the triviality of $\mathcal{X} \rightarrow \mathcal{Y}$. Suppose $\mathcal{Y} \subseteq \mathcal{X}^{\text{triv}}$ does not hold, i.e., there is some $Y \in \mathcal{Y}$ with $Y \notin \mathcal{X}^{\text{triv}}$. Note that for $X_1, X_2 \in \mathcal{X}^{\text{triv}}$ with $X_1 \sqcap X_2 = \lambda$ we also have $X_1 \sqcup X_2 \in \mathcal{X}^{\text{triv}}$ by the restricted join axiom. It follows that $\mathcal{X}^{\text{triv}}$ is an ideal with respect to $\leq$ that meets the properties of Lemma 5. Note that we can always assume that $\lambda \in \mathcal{X}^{\text{triv}}$ holds as $\mathcal{X} \rightarrow \lambda$ is a trivial functional dependency for any $\mathcal{X}$. Hence, there are $t_1, t_2 \in Dom(N)$ with $\pi_W^N(t_1) = \pi_W^N(t_2)$ iff $W \in \mathcal{X}^{\text{triv}}$. Let $r = \{t_1, t_2\}$. As $\mathcal{X} \subseteq \mathcal{X}^{\text{triv}}$ we have $\pi_X^N(t_1) = \pi_X^N(t_2)$ for all $X \in \mathcal{X}$. Moreover, $Y \notin \mathcal{X}^{\text{triv}}$ for some $Y \in \mathcal{Y}$, i.e., $\pi_Y^N(t_1) \neq \pi_Y^N(t_2)$ and therefore $\not\models_r \mathcal{X} \rightarrow \mathcal{Y}$. □

EXAMPLE 6. All functional dependencies in Example 2 are non-trivial. A trivial dependency on N_{BOUT} is for instance

$$\text{BOUT(Win(Yokozuna-since\{Date\}))} \rightarrow \text{BOUT(Win(Yokozuna-since}\{\lambda\}))\ .$$ □

4.2 The Notion of Redundancy in the HERM

In the RDM, the definition of redundancy is based on viewing functional dependencies not only as integrity constraints on a relation, but also as representing the fundamental units of information for retrieving and updating the data in a relation. This interpretation of the semantics of the information stored in a relation was implicit in the original study of normalization by Codd [11], and has since been used in many aspects of database theory. A relation schema is defined to be redundant with respect to a given set of functional dependencies if there exists a relation over the schema which satisfies all these functional dependencies and which has at least two tuples which are identical on a fact. If we formalize this notion of redundancy from the RDM, which goes back to [4], in the HERM, then we obtain the following definition. Let R be a database type and Σ a set of functional dependencies on R. We call R *redundant with respect to* Σ if and only if there is some $r \subseteq Dom(N_R)$ with $\models_r \Sigma$ and there are some $t_1, t_2 \in r$ with $t_1 \neq t_2$ and $\pi_Z^{N_R}(t_1) = \pi_Z^{N_R}(t_2)$ for all $Z \in \mathcal{X} \cup \mathcal{Y}$ and some non-trivial functional dependency $\mathcal{X} \rightarrow \mathcal{Y} \in \Sigma$. Intuitively, this notion of redundancy seems to make perfect sense.

EXAMPLE 7. Consider the functional dependency (4)

$$\text{BOUT}(\text{Win}(\text{Rank})) \rightarrow \text{BOUT}(\text{Win}(\text{Yokozuna-since}\{\lambda\}))$$

from Example 2. Obviously, this is a *non-trivial* functional dependency and, according to our current definition, the database type BOUT is redundant. That is, the elements $t_2, t_3 \in \mathcal{I}(\text{BOUT})$ from Example 1 have the same value on BOUT(Win(Rank, Yokozuna-since$\{\lambda\}$)). □

The last example shows that our current definition of redundancy is not really appropriate anymore. That is, the functional dependency

$$\text{BOUT}(\text{Win}(\text{Rank})) \rightarrow \text{BOUT}(\text{Win}(\text{Yokozuna-since}\{\text{Date}\}))$$

is not satisfied and, consequently, redundancy would need to be defined in terms of the non-maximal basis attribute BOUT(Win(Yokozuna-since$\{\lambda\}$)) of N_{BOUT}. This, however, appears to be impossible as the information in BOUT(Win(Yokozuna-since$\{\lambda\}$)) will always be contained in BOUT(Win(Yokozuna-since{Date})). The point here is that the information in a non-maximal basis attribute Y cannot be separated from the information in the maximal basis attribute Z with $Y \leq Z$.

Furthermore, we have seen in Example 5 that the functional dependencies (6) to (8) from Example 2 are key dependencies for subcomponents of the database type BOUT. Those dependencies do not cause redundancies, but only identify values of subcomponent types. This motivates the following definition.

Definition 10. Let $N \in \mathcal{N}\text{A}$ be a nested attribute of some database type R and Σ a set of functional dependencies on N. Let $\Sigma_{\text{nasty}} \subseteq \Sigma^+$ denote the set of all $\mathcal{X} \rightarrow \mathcal{Y} \in \Sigma^+$ where

- $\mathcal{Y} \subseteq \mathcal{X}^{\text{triv}}$ holds or
- $\mathcal{Y} = \{Y\}$ with a non-maximal basis attribute Y of N or
- $\mathcal{X} \rightarrow \mathcal{Y}$ is a key dependency on a subcomponent of N.

The elements of the closure Σ^+_{nasty} of Σ_{nasty} under derivation with respect to the generalized Armstrong Axioms from Theorem 4 are called *nasty functional dependencies* on N with respect to Σ. □

We are now ready to introduce a better notion of redundancy for database types *in terms of functional dependencies.*

Definition 11. Let R be a database type and Σ a set of functional dependencies on R. We call R *redundant with respect to* Σ if and only if there is some $r \subseteq Dom(N_R)$ with $\models_r \Sigma$ and there are some $t_1, t_2 \in r$ with $t_1 \neq t_2$ and $\pi_Z^{N_R}(t_1) = \pi_Z^{N_R}(t_2)$ for all $Z \in \mathcal{X} \cup \mathcal{Y}$ and some functional dependency $\mathcal{X} \rightarrow \mathcal{Y} \in \Sigma$ which is not nasty on N_R with respect to Σ. □

EXAMPLE 8. The database type BOUT from Example 1 is redundant with respect to the set Σ of functional dependencies from Example 2. Even the artificially small instance $\mathcal{I}$ from Example 1 contains redundant information. That is, tuples t_2 and t_3 are different, but have the same values on $\mathcal{X} \cup \mathcal{Y}$ where $\mathcal{X} \rightarrow \mathcal{Y}$ is the functional dependency (5) from Example 2 which is not nasty. □

As in the RDM, one might define redundancy with respect to all *implied* functional dependencies, i.e., Σ^*. That is, R is called *redundant with respect to* Σ^* if and only if there is some $r \subseteq Dom(N_R)$ with $\models_r \Sigma^*$ and there are some $t_1, t_2 \in r$ with $t_1 \neq t_2$ and $\pi_Z^{N_R}(t_1) = \pi_Z^{N_R}(t_2)$ for all $Z \in \mathcal{X} \cup \mathcal{Y}$ and some functional dependency $\mathcal{X} \to \mathcal{Y} \in \Sigma^*$ which is not nasty on N_R with respect to Σ^*. Note that $\mathcal{X} \to \mathcal{Y}$ is nasty with respect to Σ if and only if it is nasty with respect to $\Sigma^* = \Sigma^+$ according to Definition 10.

Proposition 12. *Let R be a database type and Σ a set of functional dependencies on R. Then R is redundant with respect to Σ if and only if R is redundant with respect to Σ^*.*

Proof. It is easy to see that redundancy of R with respect to Σ is sufficient for the redundancy of R with respect to Σ^+ since $\models_r \Sigma$ implies $\models_r \Sigma^+$ and $\Sigma \subseteq \Sigma^+$. It remains to show that redundancy of R with respect to Σ is also a necessary condition for R to be redundant with respect to Σ^*. Therefore, we assume that R is *non-redundant* with respect to Σ. This means that for all $r \subseteq Dom(N_R)$ with $\models_r \Sigma$ and for all $t_1, t_2 \in r$ with $\pi_Z^{N_R}(t_1) = \pi_Z^{N_R}(t_2)$ for all $Z \in \mathcal{X} \cup \mathcal{Y}$ and some $\mathcal{X} \to \mathcal{Y} \in \Sigma$, which is not nasty, follows $t_1 = t_2$. We will show that R is non-redundant with respect to Σ^+. Let therefore

$$\Sigma = \Sigma_0 \subset \Sigma_1 \subset \ldots \subset \Sigma^+$$

be a chain where Σ_j results from Σ_{j-1} by a single application of one of the Armstrong Axioms from Theorem 4, i.e., $\Sigma_j - \Sigma_{j-1}$ consists of exactly one dependency $\mathcal{X} \to \mathcal{Y}$ when $j > 0$. What we show, in fact, is that Σ can be replaced by Σ_j. We proceed by induction on j. For $j = 0$ there is nothing to show. Let $j > 0$.

If $\mathcal{X} \to \mathcal{Y}$ has been infered using the *reflexivity axiom*, then $\mathcal{Y} \subseteq \mathcal{X}$ which means that $\mathcal{X} \to \mathcal{Y}$ is trivial and, therefore, also nasty. The non-redundancy of R with respect to Σ_j follows therefore from the hypothesis that R is non-redundant with respect to Σ_{j-1}.

In the case where $\mathcal{X} \to \mathcal{Y}$ has been infered using the *subattribute axiom* we have $\mathcal{X} = \{X\}, \mathcal{Y} = \{Y\}$ and $Y \leq X$. Obviously, $\mathcal{X} \to \mathcal{Y}$ is trivial and, therefore, also nasty.

Consider the case where $\mathcal{X} \to \mathcal{Y}$ has been infered using the *extension rule*, i.e., $\mathcal{Y} = \mathcal{X} \cup \mathcal{Y}'$ with $\mathcal{X} \to \mathcal{Y}' \in \Sigma_{j-1}$. If $\mathcal{X} \to \mathcal{Y}$ is nasty, the statement follows from the hypothesis. Assume therefore that $\mathcal{X} \to \mathcal{Y}$ is not nasty and $\pi_Z^{N_R}(t_1) = \pi_Z^{N_R}(t_2)$ holds for all $Z \in \mathcal{X} \cup \mathcal{Y}$ and some $t_1, t_2 \in r$ with $r \subseteq Dom(N_R)$ with $\models_r \Sigma_j$. It follows that $\pi_X^{N_R}(t_1) = \pi_X^{N_R}(t_2)$ for all $X \in \mathcal{X}$ and since $\models_r \mathcal{X} \to \mathcal{Y}'$ holds, we obtain that $\pi_{Z'}^{N_R}(t_1) = \pi_{Z'}^{N_R}(t_2)$ for all $Z' \in \mathcal{X} \cup \mathcal{Y}'$ holds. If $\mathcal{X} \to \mathcal{Y}'$ was nasty, then $\mathcal{X} \to \mathcal{Y}$ would be nasty, too. Assume therefore that $\mathcal{X} \to \mathcal{Y}'$ is not nasty. Then apply hypothesis and conclude that $t_1 = t_2$ holds. It follows that R is non-redundant with respect to Σ_j.

Suppose $\mathcal{X} \to \mathcal{Y}$ has been derived using the *restricted join axiom* with $\mathcal{X} = \{X, Y\}, \mathcal{Y} = \{X \sqcup Y\}$ and X, Y semi-disjoint. It follows that $\mathcal{Y} \subseteq \mathcal{X}^{\text{triv}}$, i.e., $\mathcal{X} \to \mathcal{Y}$ is trivial and, in particular, nasty.

Finally, consider the case where $\mathcal{X} \to \mathcal{Y}$ has been derived using the *transitivity rule* with $\mathcal{X} \to \mathcal{W}$, $\mathcal{W} \to \mathcal{Y} \in \Sigma_{j-1}$. Again, we assume that $\models_r \Sigma_j$ for some $r \subseteq Dom(N_R)$ and $\pi_Z^{N_R}(t_1) = \pi_Z^{N_R}(t_2)$ holds for all $Z \in \mathcal{X} \cup \mathcal{Y}$ with $\mathcal{X} \to \mathcal{Y}$ not being nasty. Since $\models_r \Sigma_{j-1}$, we conclude that $\pi_{W'}^{N_R}(t_1) = \pi_{W'}^{N_R}(t_2)$ for all $W' \in \mathcal{X} \cup \mathcal{W}$ and $\pi_{W'}^{N_R}(t_1) = \pi_{W'}^{N_R}(t_2)$ holds for all $W' \in \mathcal{W} \cup \mathcal{Y}$ as well. If $\mathcal{X} \to \mathcal{W}$ and $\mathcal{W} \to \mathcal{Y}$ were both nasty, then $\mathcal{X} \to \mathcal{Y}$ would be nasty, too. It follows that at least one of $\mathcal{X} \to \mathcal{W}$ or $\mathcal{W} \to \mathcal{Y}$ is not nasty. In either case we can apply the hypothesis, and consequently $t_1 = t_2$. This concludes the proof. □

4.3 The Higher-Level Normal Form

The Boyce-Codd Normal Form has been introduced in [12] and intensively studied since then. A relation schema R is in BCNF if and only if it is non-redundant with respect to the set of functional dependencies on R. One might therefore say that a well-designed schema should be in BCNF. If R is some database type and Σ a set of functional dependencies on R, then we say that R is in *Boyce-Codd Normal Form (BCNF)* if and only if every $\mathcal{X} \to \mathcal{Y} \in \Sigma^*$ is trivial or a key dependency on N_R. We might now ask whether BCNF for a database type is a sufficient and necessary condition for the non-redundance of R. Clearly, a database type in BCNF is non-redundant in the sense of Definition 11. The converse, however, is false.

EXAMPLE 9. Let BANZUKE={RIKISHI′,BASHO′,PARTICIPANT} be a HERM schema with

- RIKISHI′ =({Shikona, Name, Birthday(Date, Place), Height}, {Shikona}),
- BASHO′ =({Name, Year},{Name, Year}) and
- PARTICIPANT = ({is : RIKISHI′, in : BASHO′}, {Rank, Yokozuna-since{Date}, {is : RIKISHI′, in : BASHO′}).

Functional dependencies on PARTICIPANT are

$$\text{PARTICIPANT}(\text{is}(\text{RIKISHI}'(\text{Shikona}))) \to \text{PARTICIPANT}(\text{is}(N_{\text{RIKISHI}'}) \qquad (9)$$

$$\text{PARTICIPANT}(\text{in}(\text{BASHO}'(\text{Name, Year}))) \to \text{PARTICIPANT}(\text{in}(N_{\text{BASHO}'}) \qquad (10)$$

$$\text{PARTICIPANT}(\text{Rank}) \to \text{PARTICIPANT}(\text{Yokozuna-since}\{\lambda\}) \qquad (11)$$

$$\text{PARTICIPANT}(\text{is}(\text{RIKISHI}'(\text{Shikona})), \text{in}(\text{BASHO}'(\text{Name, Year}))) \to N_{\text{PARTICIPANT}} \qquad (12)$$

where (9) is a key dependency for the component RIKISHI′ of PARTICIPANT, (10) is a trivial key dependency for the component BASHO′ of PARTICIPANT, (11) is a nasty dependency and (12) is a key dependency on PARTICIPANT. Thus, (12) is the only dependency on PARTICIPANT which is not nasty. Since it is a key dependency, however, PARTICIPANT is a non-redundant database type with respect to Definition 11. As the dependencies (9) and (11) are not trivial, PARTICIPANT is a non-redundant database type which is *not* in BCNF. □

Example 9 shows that BCNF is not a necessary property for non-redundant database types. Thus, BCNF is too strong to characterise non-redundant database types and, therefore, we would like to find a weaker normal form.

Definition 13. Let R be some database type and Σ a set of functional dependencies on R. We say that R is in *Higher Level Normal Form (HLNF)* if and only if every $\mathcal{X} \to \mathcal{Y} \in \Sigma^*$ is a key dependency on N_R or a nasty dependency on N_R with respect to Σ. □

Note that BCNF for database types implies HLNF. We show now that HLNF captures exactly those database types which are non-redundant in the sense of Definition 11.

Theorem 14. *Let R be a database type and Σ a set of functional dependencies on R. Then R is non-redundant with respect to Σ if and only if R is in HLNF.*

Proof. Assume that R is in HLNF. If R was redundant with respect to Σ^*, then there would be some $r \subseteq Dom(N_R)$ with $\models_r \Sigma^*$ and $t_1, t_2 \in r$, $t_1 \neq t_2$ with $\pi_Z^{N_R}(t_1) = \pi_Z^{N_R}(t_2)$ for all $Z \in \mathcal{X} \cup \mathcal{Y}$ and some functional dependency $\mathcal{X} \to \mathcal{Y} \in \Sigma^*$ which is not nasty. In particular, $\pi_X^{N_R}(t_1) = \pi_X^{N_R}(t_2)$ holds for all $X \in \mathcal{X}$. Since R is in HLNF and $\mathcal{X} \to \mathcal{Y}$ is not nasty it follows that $\mathcal{X}$ is a superkey for N_R. This implies $t_1 = t_2$ which is a contradication. Therefore, R must be non-redundant with respect to Σ^*.

Assume R is non-redundant with respect to Σ^*. Let $\mathcal{X} \to \mathcal{Y} \in \Sigma^*$ be a functional dependency which is not nasty. Non-redundance of R with respect to Σ^* implies that $t_1 = t_2$ for all $t_1, t_2 \in r \subseteq Dom(N_R)$ with $\models_r \Sigma^*$ and $\pi_Z^{N_R}(t_1) = \pi_Z^{N_R}(t_2)$ for all $Z \in \mathcal{X} \cup \mathcal{Y}$. This means that $\mathcal{X} \cup \mathcal{Y}$ is a superkey for N_R. If $\pi_X^{N_R}(t_1) = \pi_X^{N_R}(t_2)$ holds for all $X \in \mathcal{X}$ for some $t_1, t_2 \in r$, then $\pi_Y^{N_R}(t_1) = \pi_Y^{N_R}(t_2)$ also holds for all $Y \in \mathcal{Y}$ since $\models_r \mathcal{X} \to \mathcal{Y}$. This implies $\pi_Z^{N_R}(t_1) = \pi_Z^{N_R}(t_2)$ for all $Z \in \mathcal{X} \cup \mathcal{Y}$ and $t_1 = t_2$ follows. In other words, $\mathcal{X}$ is already a superkey for N_R. Since this is true for every $\mathcal{X} \to \mathcal{Y} \in \Sigma^*$ which is not nasty we conclude that R is in HLNF. □

EXAMPLE 10. The database type BOUT from Example 1 is not in HLNF with respect to the set Σ from Example 2. In particular, the functional dependencies (2) and (5) are not key dependencies and not nasty on BOUT. □

Finally, we present an equivalent HERM schema for OZUMO from Example 1 where every database type is in HLNF.

EXAMPLE 11. Define a HERM schema OZUMO′={RIKISHI, BASHO, STATISTICS, PARTICIPANT, BOUT} with

- RIKISHI = ({Heya, Name, Shikona, Birthday(Date, Place), Height}, {Shikona}),
- BASHO = ({Name, Year, Part{Rikishis}}, {Namc, Year}),
- STATISTICS = ({of : RIKISHI}, {Weight, Won{Yusho}, Awards(Shukon-Sho, Kanto-Sho, Gino-Sho)}, {of : RIKISHI, Weight, Won{Yusho}, Awards(Shukon-Sho, Kanto-Sho, Gino-Sho)}),
- PARTICIPANT = ({is : RIKISHI, in : BASHO}, {Rank, Yokozuna-since{Date}}, {is : RIKISHI, in : BASHO}}), and
- BOUT = ({Winner : PARTICIPANT, Loser : RIKISHI},{Day, Kimarite, Bout-Time}, {Winner : PARTICIPANT, Loser : RIKISHI}).

Figure 3 illustrates the HERM schema OZUMO′.

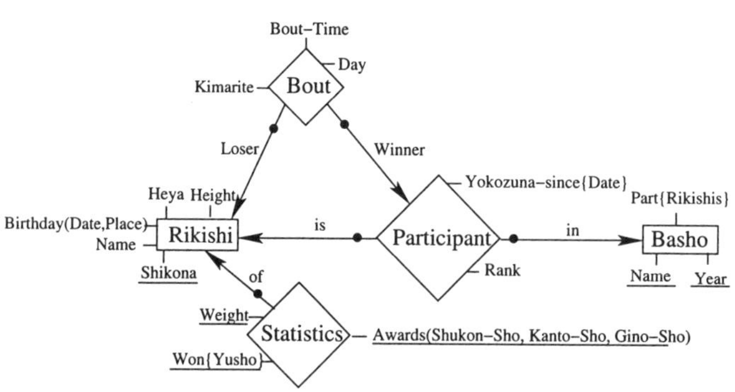

Fig. 3. The corresponding HERM diagram for OZUMO′

We will now define functional dependencies on BOUT and STATISTICS. First we have the key dependency

$$\text{BOUT}(\text{Winner}(N_{\text{PARTICIPANT}}), \text{Loser}(N_{\text{RIKISHI}})) \rightarrow N_{\text{BOUT}}$$

on BOUT. Moreover, the winner of a bout in a tournament and the day of the bout determine the loser, i.e.,

$$\text{BOUT}(\text{Winner}(\text{PARTICIPANT}(\text{is}(N_{\text{RIKISHI}}), \text{in}(N_{\text{BASHO}}))), \text{Day}) \rightarrow N_{\text{BOUT}}.$$

Next, we have two key dependencies on the subcomponent RIKISHI of BOUT, namely

$$\text{BOUT}(\text{Winner}(\text{PARTICIPANT}(\text{is}(\text{RIKISHI}(\text{Shikona}))))) \rightarrow \text{BOUT}(\text{Winner}(\text{PARTICIPANT}(\text{is}(N_{\text{RIKISHI}}))))$$

and

$$\text{BOUT}(\text{Loser}(\text{RIKISHI}(\text{Shikona}))) \rightarrow \text{BOUT}(\text{Loser}(N_{\text{RIKISHI}})).$$

Furthermore, a key dependencies on the subcomponent PARTICIPANT of BOUT is

$$\text{BOUT}(\text{Winner}(\text{PARTICIPANT}(\text{is}(N_{\text{RIKISHI}}), \text{in}(N_{\text{BASHO}})))) \rightarrow \text{BOUT}(\text{Winner}(N_{\text{PARTICIPANT}})).$$

A key dependency on the subcomponent BASHO of BOUT is

$$\text{BOUT}(\text{Winner}(\text{PARTICIPANT}(\text{in}(\text{BASHO}(\text{Name}, \text{Year}))))) \rightarrow \text{BOUT}(\text{Winner}(\text{PARTICIPANT}(\text{in}(N_{\text{BASHO}})))).$$

A key dependency on the component RIKISHI of STATISTICS is

$$\text{STATISTICS}(\text{of}(\text{RIKISHI}(\text{Shikona}))) \rightarrow \text{STATISTICS}(\text{of}(N_{\text{RIKISHI}})).$$

The key dependency for STATISTICS itself is trivial

$$\text{STATISTICS}(\text{of}(N_{\text{RIKISHI}}), \text{Weight}, \text{Won}\{\text{Yusho}\}, \text{Award}(\text{Shukon-Sho}, \text{Kanto-Sho}, \text{Gino-Sho})) \rightarrow N_{\text{STATISTICS}}.$$

Finally, we have the nasty dependency

$$\text{BOUT}(\text{Winner}(\text{PARTICIPANT}(\text{Rank}))) \rightarrow \text{BOUT}(\text{Winner}(\text{PARTICIPANT}(\text{Yokozuna-since}\{\lambda\}))).$$

Since all dependencies are key dependencies or nasty functional dependencies, BOUT and STATISTICS are both in HLNF. The functional dependencies on RIKISHI, BASHO and PARTICIPANT are already implicitely given. All are key dependencies or nasty, as well. Therefore, all database types of OZUMO′ are in HLNF. □

5 Update Anomalies

In the RDM, a relation schema in BCNF does not have any update anomalies. This is another justification why relation schemata should be in BCNF (see [6]). In fact, Fagin proves in [13] that BCNF is equivalent to the fact that there are no insertion anomalies. Moreover, Vincent defines replacement anomalies of three different types and shows that BCNF is equivalent to the absence of replacement anomalies of type 1 and 2 (see [24]). The next example reveals a surprising fact.

EXAMPLE 12. Take again a look at the HERM schema BANZUKE from Example 9 together with the set Σ of functional dependencies (9) to (12). Recall that the database type PARTICIPANT was non-redundant with respect to Σ. Assume now that there is an instance $\mathcal{I}$ over PARTICIPANT with exactly one element

((Musashimaru, Koyo Musashimaru, (02. 05. 1971, America), 191cm), (Kyushu, 2000), Yokozuna, {May 99}).

Suppose now that one would like to insert the element

((Takanohna, Koyi Hanada, (12. 08. 1972, Tokyo), 184cm), (Kyushu, 2000), Yokozuna, $\emptyset$)

into $\mathcal{I}$. Then still, after the insertion, all key dependencies on PARTICIPANT and all key dependencies on subcomponents of PARTICIPANT are satisfied. The functional dependency (11), however, does not hold anymore. Clearly, this defines an insertion anomaly. □

Example 12 shows that, in general, the absence of redundancy for a database type does not imply the absence of insertion anomalies. Therefore, it cannot be expected that database types in HLNF do not have update anomalies. We define, however, strong update anomalies in the context of the HERM. The main difference to the RDM is that updated relations which have any strong anomaly do not only satisfy all key dependencies on a database type, but also all nasty functional dependencies on this database type. As in the RDM, deletion anomalies cannot occur with functional dependencies and are therefore not defined.

Definition 15. Let R be a database type and Σ a set of functional dependencies on R. Let $\Sigma_{\text{key}} \subseteq \Sigma^*$ be the set of key dependencies on R.

(i) We say that R has a *strong insertion anomaly* if and only if there is some $r \subseteq Dom(N_R)$ with $\models_r \Sigma$ and some $t \notin r$ with $\models_{r\cup\{t\}} \Sigma_{\text{key}} \cup \Sigma^+_{\text{nasty}}$, but $\not\models_{r\cup\{t\}} \Sigma$.

(ii) We say that R has a *strong replacement anomaly*

- *of type 1* if and only if there is some $r \subseteq Dom(N_R)$ with $\models_r \Sigma$ and some $t \in r$ and $t' \in Dom(N_R)$ with $\pi_K^{N_R}(t) = \pi_K^{N_R}(t')$ for all $K \in \mathcal{K}$ of some superkey $\mathcal{K}$ on R and $\models_{r-\{t\}\cup\{t'\}} \Sigma_{\text{key}} \cup \Sigma^+_{\text{nasty}}$ and $\not\models_{r-\{t\}\cup\{t'\}} \Sigma$ hold.
- *of type 2* if and only if there is some $r \subseteq Dom(N_R)$ with $\models_r \Sigma$ and some $t \in r$ and $t' \in Dom(N_R)$ with $\pi_K^{N_R}(t) = \pi_K^{N_R}(t')$ for all $K \in \mathcal{K}$ of some primary key $\mathcal{K}$ on R and $\models_{r-\{t\}\cup\{t'\}} \Sigma_{\text{key}} \cup \Sigma^+_{\text{nasty}}$ and $\not\models_{r-\{t\}\cup\{t'\}} \Sigma$ hold.
- *of type 3* if and only if there is some $r \subseteq Dom(N_R)$ with $\models_r \Sigma$ and some $t \in r$ and $t' \in Dom(N_R)$ with $\pi_K^{N_R}(t) = \pi_K^{N_R}(t')$ for all $K \in \mathcal{K}$ of all minimal keys $\mathcal{K}$ on R and $\models_{r-\{t\}\cup\{t'\}} \Sigma_{\text{key}} \cup \Sigma^+_{\text{nasty}}$ and $\not\models_{r-\{t\}\cup\{t'\}} \Sigma$ hold.

We say that R has a *strong update anomaly* if and only if R has a strong insertion or a strong replacement anomaly of some type. □

In general, strong replacement anomalies of type 3 are also strong replacement anomalies of type 2, and strong replacement anomalies of type 2 are also strong replacement anomalies of type 1. We will see later on that strong replacement anomalies of type 1 coincide with strong replacement anomalies of type 2, but strong replacement anomalies of type 2 are, in general, not strong replacement anomalies of type 3.

EXAMPLE 13. Consider again the database type BOUT from Example 1 together with the set Σ of functional dependencies from Example 2. Then, BOUT has a strong insertion anomaly. If one inserts for instance the value $t_4=(t_{\text{Chiyotaikai}}, t_{\text{Takanohana}}, t_{\text{Kyushu00}},$ (Yokozuna, {November 2000}), (15, Kawazugake, 22 sec.)) into $\mathcal{I}(\text{BOUT})$, then all dependencies from Example 2 are satisfied apart from (5). BOUT has also a strong replacement anomaly of type 1. If we replace t_2 in $\mathcal{I}(\text{BOUT})$ by $t_2'=(t_{\text{Musashimaru}}, t_{\text{Chiyotaikai}},$ $t_{\text{Kyushu00}},$ (Ozeki, $\emptyset$), (12, Oshidashi, 13 sec.)), then again all functional dependencies apart from (5) are satisfied. It is easy to see that BOUT has even strong replacement anomalies of type 2 and 3. □

The next result generalizes results from [13] and [24].

Theorem 16. *Let R be a database type and Σ a set of functional dependencies on R. Then*

(i) R is in HLNF if and only if R does not have any strong insertion anomaly.
(ii) R is in HLNF if and only if R does not have any strong replacement anomaly of type 1 and 2.
(iii) If R is in HLNF, then R does not have a strong replacement anomaly of type 3. □

Proof. (**Sketch**) We show only the statement for strong insertion anomalies. Proofs for the remaining statements are similar.

We show first that the HLNF is a sufficient condition for the absence of insertion anomalies. If R is not in HLNF, then there is some functional dependency $\mathcal{X} \to \mathcal{Y} \in \Sigma^*$ which is not nasty and where $\mathcal{X}$ is not a superkey. We define the closure $\mathcal{X}^{\text{nasty}} = \{Z : \mathcal{X} \to \{Z\} \in \Sigma^+_{\text{nasty}}\}$ of $\mathcal{X}$ with respect to nasty functional dependencies. Note that $\mathcal{X} \to \mathcal{U} \in \Sigma^+_{\text{nasty}}$ holds for all $\mathcal{U} \subseteq \mathcal{X}^{\text{nasty}}$. The set $\mathcal{X}^{\text{nasty}}$ is obviously again an ideal which meets the properties of Lemma 5. Note that we can always assume that $\mathcal{X}^{\text{nasty}}$ contains at least λ as $\mathcal{X} \to \lambda$ is a trivial dependency. Therefore, we define some $\{t', t\} \subseteq Dom(N_R)$ by

$$\pi^{N_R}_W(t') = \pi^{N_R}_W(t) \quad \text{if and only if} \quad W \in \mathcal{X}^{\text{nasty}} \quad .$$

Obviously, the singleton set $r = \{t'\}$ satisfies $\models_r \Sigma$. We show first that $\models_{r\cup\{t\}} \Sigma_{\text{key}}$. Let $\mathcal{K}$ be an arbitrary superkey for N_R. Since $\mathcal{X}$ is not a superkey for R we have $N \notin \mathcal{X}^+ = \{Z : \mathcal{X} \to \{Z\} \in \Sigma^+\}$. From $\mathcal{X}^{\text{nasty}} \subseteq \mathcal{X}^+$ follows now that $N \notin \mathcal{X}^{\text{nasty}}$. This implies that $\mathcal{X}^{\text{nasty}}$ cannot be a superkey neither. Consequently, $\mathcal{K} \not\subseteq \mathcal{X}^{\text{nasty}}$, and there is some $K \in \mathcal{K}$ with $K \notin \mathcal{X}^{\text{nasty}}$. We conclude that $\pi^{N_R}_K(t') \neq \pi^{N_R}_K(t)$ holds.

We show that $\models_{r\cup\{t\}} \Sigma^+_{\text{nasty}}$ holds. Let $\mathcal{U} \to \mathcal{V} \in \Sigma^+_{\text{nasty}}$. If $\mathcal{U} \not\subseteq \mathcal{X}^{\text{nasty}}$, then $\pi^{N_R}_U(t') \neq \pi^{N_R}_U(t)$ for some $U \in \mathcal{U}$ and $\models_{r\cup\{t\}} \mathcal{U} \to \mathcal{V}$ holds. Suppose $\mathcal{U} \subseteq \mathcal{X}^{\text{nasty}}$ and, therefore, $\pi^{N_R}_U(t') = \pi^{N_R}_U(t)$ for all $U \in \mathcal{U}$. It follows $\mathcal{X} \to \mathcal{U} \in \Sigma^+_{\text{nasty}}$. Since $\mathcal{U} \to \mathcal{V} \in \Sigma^+_{\text{nasty}}$, we derive $\mathcal{X} \to \mathcal{V} \in \Sigma^+_{\text{nasty}}$ as well. This means $\mathcal{V} \subseteq \mathcal{X}^{\text{nasty}}$ and we conclude $\pi^{N_R}_V(t') = \pi^{N_R}_V(t)$ for all $V \in \mathcal{V}$. Hence, $\models_{r\cup\{t\}} \mathcal{U} \to \mathcal{V}$.

Finally, we show that $\not\models_{r\cup\{t\}} \Sigma$ holds. If $\mathcal{Y} \subseteq \mathcal{X}^{\text{nasty}}$ held we would infer that $\mathcal{X} \to \mathcal{Y} \in \Sigma^+_{\text{nasty}}$ holds as well. This, however, is a contradiction to our assumption that $\mathcal{X} \to \mathcal{Y}$ is not nasty. Therefore, $\mathcal{Y} \not\subseteq \mathcal{X}^{\text{nasty}}$ and as $\mathcal{X} \subseteq \mathcal{X}^{\text{nasty}}$ holds as well, it follows that $\pi^{N_R}_X(t') = \pi^{N_R}_X(t)$ holds for all $X \in \mathcal{X}$ and $\pi^{N_R}_Y(t') \neq \pi^{N_R}_Y(t)$ for at least some $Y \in \mathcal{Y}$ holds. We conclude $\not\models_{r\cup\{t\}} \Sigma^*$ and consequently $\not\models_{r\cup\{t\}} \Sigma$.

Vice versa, if R has an insertion anomaly, then there is some dependency $\mathcal{X} \to \mathcal{Y} \in \Sigma$ which is not nasty and where $\mathcal{X}$ is not a superkey. Hence, R cannot be in HLNF. □

6 Conclusion and Future Work

Normalization is one of the most deeply studied topics in relational database design, and relational database systems have benefited a lot from this research. The present article is the starting point for normalization in conceptual data models. It has taken up the notion of redundancy caused by the presence of functional dependencies in the RDM, and adapted it to the context of conceptual schemata. It has been demonstrated that Boyce-Codd normal form is too strong to exactly describe non-redundant database types on the conceptual level. For this reason, the higher level normal form (HLNF) has been proposed which exactly identifies the absence of redundancy. The HLNF is also justified by the fact that it exactly describes database types that do not have any strong insertion nor replacement anomalies. Moreover, BCNF always implies HLNF and in the case of the RDM, both notions coincide. The results suggest that normalization should be studied more deeply on the conceptual level.

There are some approaches to normalization in the nested relational model such as partition normal form and nested normal form in [18],[19]. However, HLNF already deviates from those normal forms when we restrict the underlying type system to base, record and finite set types, since nested attributes such as RIKISHI(Won$\{\lambda\}$) cannot be expressed in the nested relational model. A detailed comparison, however, is beyond the scope of this paper and will be studied in the near future.

Many interesting questions are brought up by the results of this article. It is well-known that relational database schemata can be always decomposed into BCNF in a lossless manner. This is due to the fact, that a relation is the natural join of some of its projections whenever it satisfies a functional dependency. A similar result holds in the context of the HERM which rises the question whether a lossless HLNF-decomposition algorithm exists. It may also turn out that *pivoting* is a much more natural approach to decomposing database types (see [7] and [14]). Example 11 shows a database schema in HLNF. Can we obtain such a normal form for any database schema and for any set of functional dependencies? If the answer is negative, then a generalization of the third normal form to conceptual database schemata might be helpful. The study of *multi-valued dependencies* in the context of conceptual databases is planned next. It is well-known that multi-valued dependencies also cause redundancies and update anomalies in the RDM, and that *fourth normal form* exactly identifies relation schemata that are non-redundant and do not have update anomalies (see [24]). A generalization of this fourth normal form is therefore also desirable on the conceptual level.

References

1. S. Abiteboul, R. Hull, V. Vianu: Foundations of Databases, *Addison-Wesley*, 1995.
2. W.W. Armstrong: Dependency structures of database relationships, *Inform. Process. 74*, 1974, 580-583.
3. C. Batini, S. Ceri, S.B. Navathe: Conceptual Database Design: An Entity-Relationship Approach, *Benjamin Cummings*, 1992.
4. C. Beeri, P.A. Bernstein, N. Goodman: A sophisticate's introduction to database normalization theory. *Proceedings of the 4th International Conference on Very Large Databases*, pp. 113-124, 1978.
5. C. Beeri, P.A. Bernstein: Computational problems related to the design of normal form relational schemata. *ACM Transactions on Database Systems*, 4, 1, 30-59, 1979.

6. P.A. Bernstein, N. Goodman: What Does Boyce-Codd Normal Form Do?, *Proc. VLDB 1980*, pp. 245-259, 1980.
7. J. Biskup, R. Menzel, T. Polle, Y. Sagiv: Decomposition of relationships through pivoting, in: B. Thalheim (Ed.) *Conceptual Modeling*, vol. 823, LNCS, Springer, Berlin, pp. 28-41, 1996.
8. P.P. Chen: The Entity-Relationship Model: Towards a unified View of Data, *ACM Transactions Database Systems 1*, pp. 9-36, 1976.
9. P.P. Chen: English sentence structure and entity-relationship diagrams, *Information Science 29*, pp. 127-149, 1983.
10. E.F. Codd: A relational model of data for large shared data banks. *Communications of the ACM*, 13, 6, pp. 377-387, 1970.
11. E.F. Codd: Further normalization of the database relational model. In *Courant Computer Science Symposia 6: Data Base Systems*, R. Rustin (Ed.), Prentice-Hall, Englewood Cliffs, N.J., pp. 33-64, 1972.
12. E.F. Codd: Recent investigations in relational database system, *Proceedings of the IFIP Conference*, Stockholm, Sweden, 1017-1021, 1974.
13. R. Fagin: A Normal Form for Relational Databases that is based on domains and keys. *ACM Transactions on Database Systems*, 6, 3, 387-415, 1981.
14. S. Hartmann: Decomposing relationship types by pivoting and schema equivalence. *Data & Knowledge Engineering*, Vol. 39, pp. 75-99, 2001.
15. S. Hartmann, A. Hoffmann, S. Link, K. D. Schewe: Axiomatizing Functional Dependencies in the Higher-Order Entity-Relationship Model, to appear in *Information Processing Letters*, 2003.
16. M. Kirchberg, S. Link: On the Implication Problem of Functional Dependencies in the Higher-Order Entity-Relationship Model, in Proceedings of *The Australasian Database Conference*, Volume 17, pp. 115-124, 2003.
17. J.C.C McKinsey, A. Tarski: On closed elements in closure algebras, Annals of Mathematics ,Volume 47, pp. 122-146, 1946.
18. W.Y. Mok, Y.K. Ng, D.W. Embley: A normal form for precisely charachterizing redundancy in nested relations, *ACM Transactions on Database Systems*, Vol. 21, 77-106, 1996
19. Z.M. Özsoyoglu, L.Y. Yuan: A new normal form for nested relations, *ACM Transactions on Database Systems*, Vol. 12, 111-136, 1987.
20. J. Paredaens, P. De Bra, M. Gyssens, D. Van Gucht: The Structure of the Relational Database Model, *EATCS Monographs on Theoretical Computer Science*, Springer-Verlag, 1989.
21. B. Thalheim: Foundations of entity-relationship modeling, *Ann.Math.Artificial Intelligence 6*, 1992, 197-256.
22. B. Thalheim: Entity-Relationship Modeling: Foundations of Database Technology, *Springer*, 2000.
23. A.M. Tjoa, L. Berger: Transformation of requirement specifications expressed in natural language into an EER model, in R.A. Elmasri, V. Kouramajian, B. Thalheim (Eds.): *Entity-Relationship Approach*, vol. 823, LNCS, Springer, Berlin, 1993.
24. M. W. Vincent: The semantic justification for normal forms in relational database design, *PhD-thesis*, Department of Computer Science, Monash University, 1994.

Information Modelling and Knowledge Bases XV
Y. Kiyoki et al. (Eds.)
IOS Press, 2004

An Ontological Approach to Unified Contract Management

Vandana Kabilan, Paul Johannesson, Dickson Rugaimukamu
{vandana, pajo, si-dmr}@dsv.su.se

Department of Computer and Systems Sciences
Stockholm University and Royal Institute of Technology
Forum 100, SE-164 40 Kista, Sweden

Easy access of Internet has revolutionized the concept of electronic commerce. As the bulk of business transactions shifts to electronic media, we have business collaborations being negotiated between previously unknown partners. Thus a Contract is the key to a successful business relationship. We foresee a need for a unified contract management in order to achieve coherent business operations. Interoperability and integration of business processes with the '*agreed upon*' business, economic and legal terms and conditions as stated in a Contract is one of our primary goals. We aim at building conceptual models to capture the semantics of a Contract. An ontological approach enable us to analyze the same contract from different perspectives – the legal and social behavioral centric, the business and process centric, as well as the document centric 'contract document' view. This results in a basis for a Unified Contract Management framework supporting all the phases of a Contract life cycle including conception, formation, negotiation, monitoring and fulfillment.

1 Introduction

Contract management is not a novel concept. Contract Management tools and techniques have been around for quite some time. One of the pioneers in the field of Contracting was Ronald M Lee [6]. He has proposed methods to monitor and automate contracts using Logic models and Artificial Intelligence agents. The advent of EDI made the vision of electronic commerce possible but still remains elusive and expensive. The backbone of the Internet is drastically changing this situation. Business partnerships are discovered and negotiated on the Internet. Most business and trade relations are based on trust, competency and understanding, which is of paramount importance between parties who are relatively unknown to each other. This trust and understanding are recorded and captured in the form of Agreements and Contracts and all the Obligations, responsibilities and duties of each of the contracting parties are all captured in a contract.

2 Related Research

Contracts have been a topic for research in diverse areas and for different purposes. Frameworks for e-Contracts, have focused on different aspects, some of the key aspects being:

Document Centric, in which case a contract is an archived document that is subject to negotiations, signed and circulated among parties involved. After that, processes are determined by rules and conditions that are defined in the contract. Most contract management tools available in the market today, deal with the structural composition of a contract and they extract the relevant Meta data content.

Process Centric, in which case a contract is an interpretation of *activity* states of business processes as well as constraints on the business events. There exist constraint based business rules courteous logic programming approach, which enables automated agents to understand the rules of a contract as proposed by B. Grosof [3]. The COSMOS project (Common Open Service Market for SMEs) has tried to model an Internet based e-Contracting service to facilitate the business transaction process by providing tools for automated contract negotiation and execution. They have a good conceptual model for a contract but then have concentrated on the actual process centric and support infrastructure.

Responsibility/Obligation Centric, in which case a contract is an establishment of various jurisdiction and contract laws and clauses. This has a special legal textual implication. We find advances in the realm of Artificial Intelligence and logic programming. Works of Asspassia Daskalopolu [1,2] have focused on the legal aspects of contracts like logic-based tools for the analysis and representation of legal contracts, using Artificial Intelligence, information retrieval from large corpora of legal texts and cases, (Rissland et al., 1995;Hafner, 1987), interpretation of legal text, (Allen et al., 1993), argumentation, (Prakken, 1997; Sartor, 1994), and legislative drafting, (Allen, 1982). Daskalopolu has also been involved in a project to formalize the obligations and utterances of a business contract in a Formal Language for Business Communication (FLBC), which is based on the speech act theory developed by Austin, Searle and others. Yao-Hua Tan [4] has used both speech act fundamentals and event semantics to analyze European Contract Law. He has handled the concept of promises made by party and their prepositional content in an appropriate manner. Currently there are legal groups like LegalXML are working on developing Legal Ontologies for contracting within the ebXML Technical Committee Group.

3 Current Approach

We find that any of the above perspectives alone is not sufficient to represent and manage a contract in its entirety. One or all of the aspects play a vital role in different phases of the contract life cycle. An Ontology provides a means to define an intermediate open layer that enables translation and integration of all the facets involved in a contract management scenario. A semantic ontology of contractual terms along with a conceptual modeling of the understanding of the obligations, responsibilities and duties of each counterpart of a contract, will aid in every phase of contract management, staring with contract monitoring and execution. We are working on modeling a multi-layered approach for a conceptual model along similar lines as proposed by Nicola Guarino [7].

A global upper level layer, Figure 1, could consist of fundamental concepts for any contract, like their common terminology or their interrelationships. It is generic but outlines the concepts and the inherent relations, constraints, which are inherited by domain

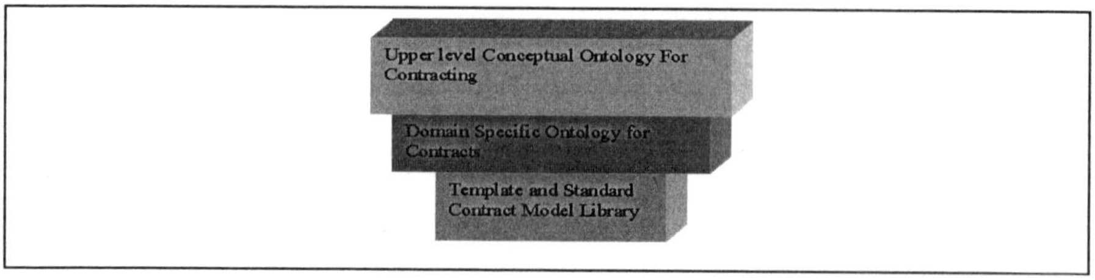

Figure 1: Multi Layered Approach for Contracting

specific contracts. Some of the main concepts include Actors (parties to the agreement), their Roles, their Obligations (responsibilities, duties), Consideration (purpose behind the contract) etc. (See Figure 2: the figure is an illustration of some of the main concepts which could be included). We introduce a classification of Commitment and Commitment types along with commitment states and their transition in accordance with business actions.

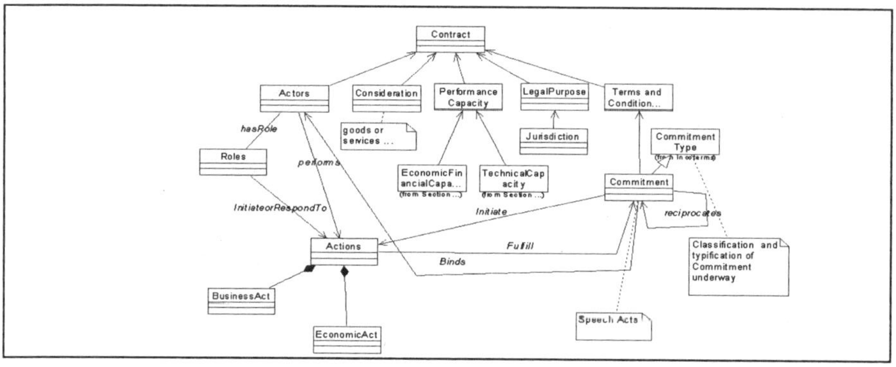

Figure 2: Example for an Upper Level Conceptual Ontology

A domain specific ontology could be a secondary layer, which comprises of terminology and concepts pertaining to a specific type or domain of contracting, like say Sale of Goods Contract [10] (refer to Figure 3 given below, a sample sketch for a Sale of Goods contract ontology). This inherits and builds on the concepts from the upper level ontology. For example we can define a Seller as a principal Actor in the Sale of Goods Contract Model whose primary role is to sell goods to a Buyer (who is an Actor with an obligation to buy and pay for the goods received). This layer identifies concepts, which are specific to the particular contract domain and can outline all allowable choices for this level. For example ICC's INCOTERMS could be shared ontology for Delivery Patterns for International Commercial Sale of Goods.

At the lowest level we propose a library or catalogue of templates modeled or implemented on the basis of the shared domain ontology. They could be ready to use pluggable versions of standard contract models and guidelines, which can be readily instantiated as a factual contract. For example the model for sale of motorboats or sale of vehicle or a template for software licensing may all be modeled as template ontology. The template ontology differs from the shared ontology in that it has a specific usage.

In order to have Unified Contract Management we need to have a methodology to cover every phase of a contract life cycle from conception, negotiation, and storage, call off, fulfillment. To have an effective contract management we need to have a seamless

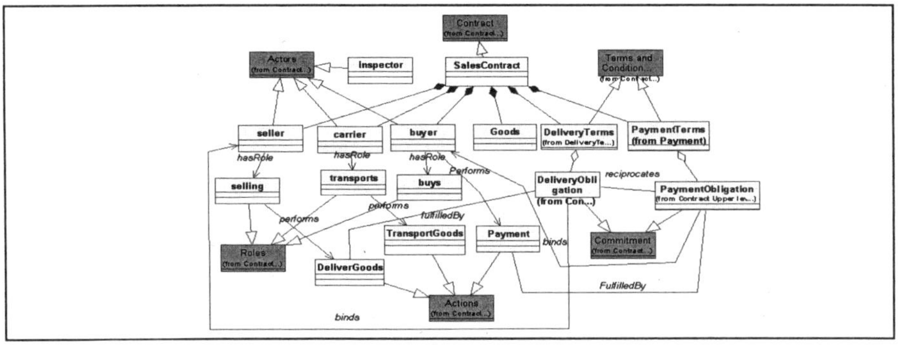

Figure 3: Example for a Domain Specific Shared Ontology

integration and interoperability with the actual business process (the purpose behind the contracting). Hence we also intend to have a semantic mapping in between our model and existing ontology like the REA ontology [8] and other Business Process Models. As a first exercise we model the knowledge embedded in the INCOTERMS [9].

4 *Ongoing Case Study*

In our quest to model the concepts behind contracts, we chose INCOTERMS as a first case study to evaluate as well as to test our theories and models. INCOTERMS are standard and widely accepted trade definitions most commonly used in international sales contracts. Devised and published by the International Chamber of Commerce, they are at the heart of world trade. This makes the INCOTERMS an ideal candidate for a case study. For example, a delivery pattern like EX-Works (EXW) outlines the obligations and duties of a seller and a buyer. It also apportions the division of risks and costs in between them. The obligation of a seller is fulfilled once he has marked the goods for delivery prior to the agreed delivery date and accordingly informs the buyer so. Henceforth it's the buyer's responsibility and cost to arrange for the transport, customs clearance and all other risks and damage liabilities. We can see business activities like purchase order placement, packaging, shipment, customs clearance, delivery, invoicing in the contract delivery pattern. We also see that there is an agreed sequence and choreography of these activities. On the legal perspective, we need to be aware of the extent of the seller's obligation and the buyers and the time and point of transfer of risk, responsibility, division of costs etc. We link each action to its direct and implied commitments and their possible consequences and counter actions. Since all these agreed terms have an existence in the form of an agreement (whether as a physical document or an electronic archived document) we also analyze the structural composition of the agreement or contract instance.

5 *Uniqueness of Approach*

We summarize the salient features of our ongoing work as:

- Three Tiered Architecture for a Contracts Conceptual Model
- Modeling the different nature and types of Commitments and obligations stipulated in a Contract using Speech Acts

- Multi-faceted approach to interpret every aspect of a contract.
- Easy interoperability with business process models and other Ontologies like REA [8]
- Covers the whole contract life cycle from the pre-planning phase through the negotiation phase to the actual contract signing to the actual fulfillment and monitoring of the contract. This is the foundation for our Unified Contract Management framework.

6 Advantages

Most frameworks have concentrated on a single aspect of a contract and have proceeded on their chosen track. In contrast our approach takes into consideration all the major aspects and also has the key advantages of any ontology like sharing of domain knowledge, reusability of knowledge, portability etc. In addition to these obvious advantages, some specific advantages are

- Classification and definition of Commitment Types, their relationships to Business Processes, Actions.
- Semantic mappings to other existing enterprise Ontology
- Our conceptual model is an integrated framework analysis of the context, contents and business model interoperability of a contract. Integrated approach for Unified Contract Management from conception to fulfillment.

7 References

[1] A. Daskalopulu. Logic Based Tools for Legal Contract Drafting: Prospects and Problems. Proceedings of the 1st Logic Symposium 1997. University of Cyprus Press, pp.213-222

[2] A. Daskalopulu & MJ Sergot (1997). The Representation of Legal Contracts, AI and Society 11(Nos. ½), pp 6-17

[3] B. N. Grosof, Yannis Labrou, Hoi Y Chan. A Declarative Approach to Business Rules in Contracts: Couteous Logic Programs in XML, Proceedings of 1st ACM Conference on Electronic Commerce (EC99).

[4] Yao-Hua Tan, Walter Thoen. Using Event Semantics for Modeling Contracts. Proceedings of 35th Hawaii International Conference on System Sciences –2002.

[5] A. Goodchild, Charles Herring, Z. Milosevic. Business Contracts for B2B. Proceedings of the CAISE00 Workshop on Infrastructure for Dynamic Business-to-Business Service Outsourcing, 2000

[6] Lee, R.M., A logic Model for Electronic Contracting, 1988

[7] Works of N. Guarino Available Online at Publications on Formal Ontologies, Conceptual Modeling and Knowledge Engineering. (http://www.ladseb.pd.cnr.it/infor/Ontology/Papers/FormOntKR.pdf)

[8] William E. McCarthy, Guido L. Geerts; The Ontological Foundation of REA Enterprise Ontology; Michigan State University; USA; 2000

[9] Jan Ramberg; ICC Guide to Incoterms 2000. Understanding and Practical Use; International Chamber ofCommerce 2000

[10] ICC International contract for sale of goods, published by ICC books, 2002. Also see International Chamber of Commerce, http://www.iccwbo.org/

Information Modelling and Knowledge Bases XV
Y. Kiyoki et al. (Eds.)
IOS Press, 2004

Towards Implicit Invocation of Web Services Functions

Takehiro Tokuda, Tetsuya Suzuki, and Hideki Nakayama
{tokuda, tetsuya, nakayama}@tt.cs.titech.ac.jp
Department of Computer Science
Tokyo Institute of Technology
Meguro, Tokyo 152-8552, Japan

Abstract. We present an approach to implicit invocation of Web services functions. Currently Web services functions must be invoked by explicitly mentioning function names. By giving the set of semantic tags to a small set of Web services functions, we may implicitly invoke all the necessary Web services functions automatically.

1 Introduction

The purpose of this paper is to invite information modelling and knowledge bases research people to take a closer look at current problems of the idea of Web services and hopefully give better solutions. Our proposal here is essentially to use a small set of semantic tags for Web services functions. Currently Web services functions must be invoked by explicitly mentioning function names. By giving a set of semantic tags to a small set of Web services functions, we may implicitly invoke all the necessary Web services functions automatically.

The idea of Web services [1] is the realistic successor of Web applications we have now and the predecessor of Semantic web [2, 3] expected to come in a future.

Now the clients of Web applications are human beings. Human beings manually extract all the necessary semantic contents from the given HTML data. For example, if we have a text "The temperature of Boston, Massachusetts on December 1st is 30 degrees." in some HTML page, then we understand that Boston is a US city and 30 degree temperature is described in Fahrenheit.

On the other hand, the clients of Web services are programs. Programs perform explicit invocations of Web services functions according to the specified interface given by a language called WSDL (Web Services Description Language). Client programs can receive the resulting data in spite of the differences of operating systems and programming languages. For example, a function converting the integer value representing Fahrenheit temperature into the integer value representing the Celsius temperature is a typical Web services function.

Finally, the clients of Semantic Web are programs and human beings. Programs may automatically recognize semantic contents from XML data with semantic tags and RDF (Resource Description Framework) relations. Programs may have dialogues and negotiations with other programs based on the large scale Web ontologies of semantic tags automatically. For example, if we have a statement "The temperature of Boston, Massachusetts on December 1st is 30 degrees" in some XML page, Boston may have a semantic tag "US city" and 30 degrees may have a semantic tag "Fahrenheit temperature". Hence the program may recognize that the temperature of this US city is below the freezing point of water.

2 Implicit Invocation

Our approach to achieve implicit invocation of Web services functions is as follows.

[Our Approach]

1. For a given small set of Web services functions we introduce semantic tags for parameters of functions. We record the correspondence from semantic tags to actual data structures of parameters of functions.

2. We allow users to implicitly invoke Web services functions by mentioning the given input data with semantic tags and the semantic tag of the necessary output data.

3. From the given input data with semantic tags and the semantic tag of the necessary output data, we determine the necessary ordering of explicit invocations.

We give one example of implicit invocation of Web services functions. In Fig.1, we assume that we have two functions `get_flight_list` and `get_first_flight` in one Web service. Then we introduce semantic tags, `flight`, `date`, `flight_no`, `from_city`, `to_city`, `departure_time`, `arrival_time`, `flight_set`, and `first_flight`. As described in relations among semantic tags, one data with semantic tag flight is a structure whose component data are respectively data with semantic tags, `date`, `flight_no`, `from_city`, `to_city`, `departure_time` and `arrival_time`. One data with semantic tag `flight_set` is a set of data with semantic tag `flight`. The set of data with semantic tag `first_flight` is a subset of the set of data with semantic tag `flight`. (We say that the semantic tag `first_flight` is a subclass of the semantic tag `flight`.) The function `get_flight_list` has three input data with semantic tags `date`, `from_city`, and `to_city`, and one output data with semantic tag `flight_set`. The function `get_first_flight` has one input data with semantic tag `flight_set` and one output data with semantic tag `first_flight`.

An example of implicit invocation of these Web services functions is shown in Fig.2. Here we would like to know the first flight from Tokyo to Sapporo on April 1st, 2003.

The process of constructing explicit invocations of functions from the given input data with semantic tags and the output semantic tag can be informally described in Fig.3.

Here we explain guidelines of semantic tags used for describing Web services functions. Traditionally semantic tags may have subclass relations, synonym relations and antonym relations. For our purpose, we have following guidelines.

[Guidelines]

1. Each parameter of Web services functions has a semantic tag.

2. Semantic tag `tag1` may have a precise definition of testing if any given data is an instance of `tag1` or not.

Relations among semantic tags:

```
flight = [date,flight_no,from_city,to_city, departure_time,arrival_time]
flight_set = set flight
flight - first_flight
```

The set of functions:

```
get_flight_list(in date,in from_city,
in to_city, out flight_set)
get_first_flight(in flight_set, out first_flight)
```

Figure 1: Functions and semantic tags

```
in date 04-01-2003
in from_city TOKYO
in to_city SAPPORO
out first_flight
```

Figure 2: Implicit invocation of functions

3. Semantic tags `tag1` and `tag2` may have a subclass relation, a component relation, a set relation and a sequence relation.

4. The relations of semantic tags `tag1` and `tag2` must be compatible with corresponding data structures of parameters. Corresponding data structures have same subclass relations, component relations, set relations or sequence relations.

For example, if we introduce semantic tags, `zipdata`, `zipcode`, `prefecture`, `city`, `town`, and `postcard_pdfdata`, then ZIP code functions may be stated as shown in Fig. 4.

An implicit invocation of Fig.5 causes invocations of functions `getAddressFromZipcode` and `getPDFData`. Eventually we get a postcard layout PDF data representing the postal address of ZIP code 1930045.

3 Mechanisms for Implicit Invocation

In order to achieve implicit invocations of a wider class of sets of Web services functions, we need to perform following steps.

We first check if the set of functions with semantic tags have uniqueness (uniqueness checking). Then we construct explicit invocations to achieve the given implicit invocation (planning). Finally we actually invoke functions according to the result of the planning.

We construct a directed hypergraph. We check if, from any set of input semantic tags to any output semantic tag, there exists at most one directed path of hyperedges. In implicit invocation, we provide at most one instance of data for one input semantic tag.

The necessary functions and their appropriate ordering of invocations are computed. This computation can be done by forward computation and backward computation.

In forward computation, we initially start from the set of semantic tags, which is the set of given input semantic tags. Then we repeatedly increase the set of computable semantic tags by using the set of functions until no new semantic tags can be added further. Then we check if the set has given output semantic tag.

1. The output semantic tag is `first_flight`. Given input semantic tags are `date`, `from_city`, and to_city.
2. We take a look at output `first_flight` tag in `get_first_flight` function.
3. The input semantic tag of this function is `flight_set`. If the value of `flight_set` tag is known, then we may invoke the `get_first_flight` function.
4. We search for a function where `flight_set` tag is output. We find the `get_flight_list` function.
5. We have all values of input semantic tags of the `get_flight_list` function.
6. Hence, we first invoke `get_flight_list` function to get the value of `flight_set`. Then, we invoke `get_first_flight` function to get the value with tag `first_flight`.

Figure 3: Actual explicit invocations

Relations among semantic tags:

```
zipdata=[zipcode,prefecture,city,town]
```

The set of functions:

```
getAddressFromZipcode(in zipcode, out zipdata)
getPDFData(in zipdata, out postcard_pdfdata)
```

Figure 4: ZIP code functions with semantic tags

```
in zipcode 1930045
out postcard_pdfdata
```

Figure 5: Implicit invocation with semantic tags

In backward computation, we initially start from the set of semantic tags, which is the set of given output semantic tag. Then we repeatedly compute the set of sets of necessary input semantic tags by using the set of functions until all the necessary input semantic tags of some set are in the set of given input semantic tags.

4 Conclusion

We have presented the idea of Web services functions with semantic tags and an application to implicit invocation of web services functions. A small set of semantic tags may allow us to invoke a number of necessary functions implicitly and automatically.

Web services functions with semantic tags may have other types of applications. For example, we may convert one XML document having the semantic tag of Fahrenheit temperature into another XML document having the semantic tag of Celsius temperature with corresponding values automatically.

References

[1] E. Christensen et al.: Web Services Description Language 1.1, http://www.w3.org/TR/wsdl, W3 Consortium, 2001.

[2] T. Berners-Lee et al.: The Semantic Web, Scientific American, May 2001.

[3] M. Dean et al.: Web Ontology Language OWL Reference Version 1.0 http://www.w3.org/TR/owl-ref/, W3 Consortium, 2002.

Information Modelling and Knowledge Bases XV
Y. Kiyoki et al. (Eds.)
IOS Press, 2004

Treecube: 3D Visualization Tool for Hierarchical Information

Yoichi Tanaka, Yoshihiro Okada and Koichi Niijima
Graduate School of Information Science and Electrical Engineering, Kyushu University
6-1 Kasuga-koen, Kasuga, Fukuoka 816-8580, Japan
Phone +81-92-583-7633, Fax +81-92-583-7635
e-mail: {y-tanaka, okada, niijima}@i.kyushu-u.ac.jp

Abstract. This paper proposes a new 3D visualization tool for hierarchical information. A 2D visualization tool for hierarchical information called treemap [1] has already been proposed by Ben Shneiderman, et al. in 1992. In general, hierarchical information is represented as a tree structure. Treemap hierarchically lays out each node as a bounding box, whose size is the same as the specific weight or attribute value of the node. After the original treemap algorithm called slice-and-dice, some extentions to it have been proposed: squarified treemap [2], ordered treemap [3] and quantum treemap [4]. In this paper, authors propose a new 3D visualization tool for hierarchical information called treecube that can be taken as a 3D extension of treemap. This tool seems very convenient for layouts of 3D objects in a specified, restricted 3D space. This paper explains the layout algorithm of treecube and shows its prospective application examples.

1. Introduction

This paper proposes a new 3D visualization tool for hierarchical information. A 2D visualization tool for hierarchical information called treemap [1] has already been proposed by Ben Shneiderman, et al in 1992. Generally, hierarchical information is represented as a tree structure. Treemap hierarchically lays out each node as a bounding box, whose size is the same as the specific weight or attribute value given to the node. Practically, a lot of tree-structured data exist and the size of such data is going to be greater and greater. Such a huge size of tree-structured data needs efficient visualization tool. As a result, the treemap has become one of the very useful visualization tools. Furthermore, some extensions to the original treemap called slice-and-dice have been proposed, for instance, squarified treemap [2], ordered treemap [3] and quantum treemap [4]. However, all of them are 2D layout algorithms. Recent advances in hardware technologies have made it possible to render 3D images in real time even using a standard PC. As a result, 3D graphics visualization tools have become in great demand. This fact motivated us to propose a new 3D visualization tool called treecube that can be assumed as a 3D extension of treemap. To be precise, in this paper, we have extended 2D versions of slice-and-dice and ordered treemap algorithms to their 3D counterparts. This tool seems to be very convenient for layout of 3D objects in a specified, restricted 3D space. This paper explains the layout algorithm of treecube and shows its prospective application examples.

The remainder of this paper is organized as follows: First of all, Section 2 introduces our treecube and explains its 3D layout algorithms, i.e., slice-and-dice and ordered treecube algorithms. Following that, Section 3 discusses prospective application examples of treecube. Finally Section 4 concludes the paper.

2. Treecube Algorithms

Treecube lays out hierarchically structured information into a specified, restricted 3D space. This uses, in fact, 3D versions of the treemap algorithms. Next two subsections explain them.

2.1 Slice-and-dice treecube algorithm

2D slice-and-dice algorithm creates a layout where the bounding box of each item (node/leaf) is located by the simple linear order. However, the aspect ratio of each bounding box does not satisfy the requirement that the aspect ratio should be one in visual efficiency. In this 2D slice-and-dice algorithm, a basic operation is applied to each intermediate node. It lays out all the child nodes of this node. Each of them is placed sequentially and vertically if their level is an even number, and horizontally if it is an odd number. In order to extend the 2D slice-and-dice algorithm to 3D, we modified it as follows:

Like treemap algorithm, treecube algorithm also visualizes tree structural data consisting of several nodes. At first, the user has to fix a rectangular solid. In 3D slice-and-dice algorithm, each node is represented as a rectangular solid whose space corresponds to the weight value. All the child nodes of a parent node should be placed filling the space of this parent node space. So the rectangular solid space of a parent node is divided into the same number of sub-rectangular solids as the number of child nodes of the parent node. This is an essential operation. Actually, this operation cuts the given rectangular solid space along the direction determined by the level of the tree, i.e., along x-direction if the level is i*3, along y-diection if the level is i*3+1, and along z-direction if the level is i*3+2, where i is a non-negative integer.

For example, hierarchical information shown in Fig. 1(a) is laid out as shown in Fig. 1(b).

Implementation

Figure 2 shows a screen shot of treecube visualization tool. In this case, the tool visualizes files and subdirectories structure of a certain directory of a file system using the slice-and-dice treecube algorithm. This visualization tool is implemented using OpenGL 3D graphics library. Because of the availability of transparent rendering mode in OpenGL, the user can see inside as well as outside.

From figure 2, we see that there are many slender rectangular solids in this layout. That is, these rectangular solids have high aspect ratio.

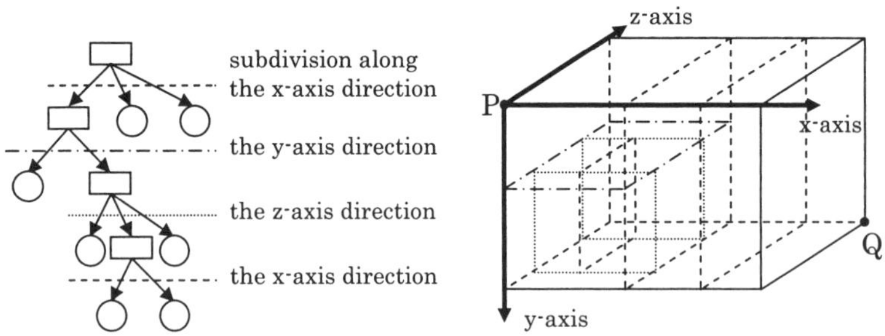

(a) Hierarchical information and the direction of the subdivision operation in its each level.

(b) 3-dimensional slice-and-dice layout of the hirarchical information shown in Fig. 1. (a)

Fig. 1: Layout example of hierarchical informatio by the slice-and-dice treecube algorithm.

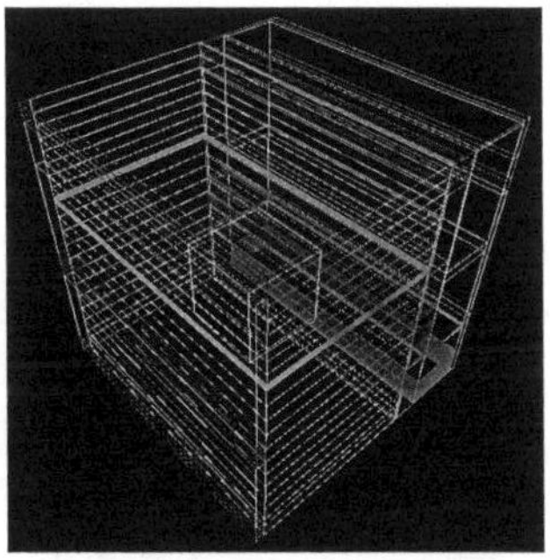

Fig. 2: Treecube: slice-and-dice algorithm.

2.2 Ordered treecube algorithm

The main difference from the ordered treemap is that a rectangular solid (bounding box) is divided into five volumes as shown in Fig. 3. There are four sub-bounding boxes R_1, R_{2-1}, R_{2-2} and R_3 adjacent to R_p. One of the inputs given to the ordered treecube algorithm is a rectangular solid R. It represents a parent node. Another input is an ordered list of children of this parent node. First of all, a pivot R_p has to be determined. Similar to ordered treemap, there are three ways to choose a pivot. After selecting R_p using one of the three methods, the remaining items of the list are assigned to the four sub-bounding boxes other than R_p. Fathermore, this process is applied to each sub-bounding box recursively.

Concrete Algorithm

The ordered treecube algorithm using pivot-by-size is described below.

1. The item of the largest space in the list is chosen as pivot *P*.
2. If the width of R is greater than or equal to its height as well as its depth, then divide R into five rectangular solids, i.e., R_1, R_p, R_{2-1}, R_{2-2} and R_3, as shown in Fig. 3. If the height is greater than the width as well as the depth, use the same basic arrangement but rotate 90 degrees along the diagonal line. If the depth is greater than the other two dimensions, rotate -90 degrees.
3. *P* is placed in the R_p, whose exact position will be determined by Step 4.
4. Distribute the items of the list (except *P*) into four lists *L1, L2-1, L2-2, L3* laid out to R_1, R_{2-1}, R_{2-2} and R_3 respectively. Let *L1* consist of all items whose indices are smaller than that of *P* in the ordering. Let *L2-1, L2-2*, and *L3* consist of all items whose indices are greater than that of *P*, and let *L2-1* consist of all items whose indices are smaller than those of the items in *L2-2*, which are smaller than those of the items in *L3*.
5. Recursively layout *L1, L2-1, L2-2* and *L3* (if any are non-empty) in R_1, R_{2-1}, R_{2-2} and R_3 by applying step 1 through step 4.

Implementation

Figure 4 shows another screen shot of treecube corresponding to the ordered treecube algorithm. This also visualizes files and subdirectories structure of the same directory shown in Fig. 2. This case uses the extended ordered treecube algorithm. As is easily understood by the color, treecube of Fig. 4 has a lot of bounding boxes of low aspect ratio. This feature is better than that of the extended slice-and-dice algorithm.

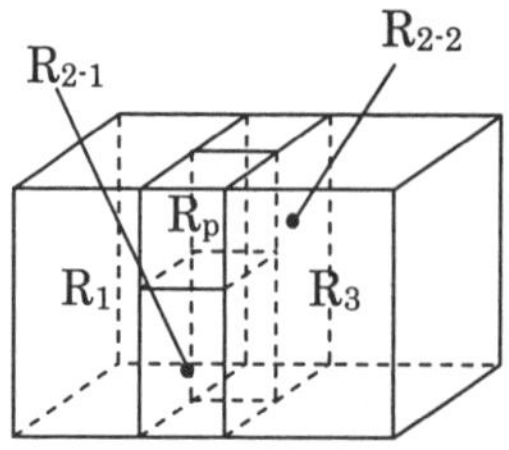

Fig. 3: The pivot configuration of the ordered treecube algorithm.

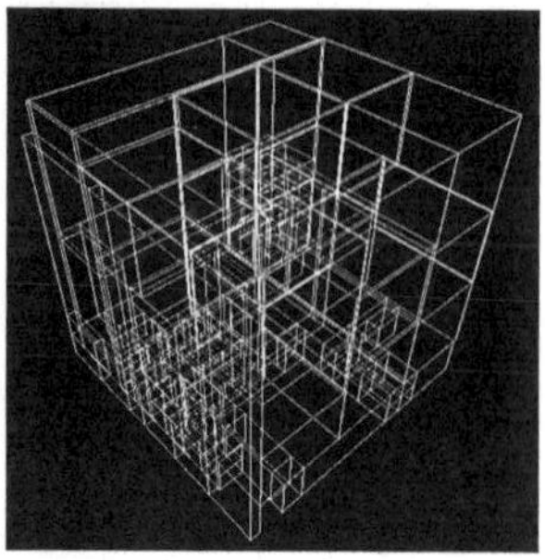

Fig. 4: Treecube: ordered treecube algorithm.

3. Applications

The visualization tools demonstrated in Fig. 2 and Fig. 4 seem to be useful for visualization of various databases, for example, a 3D model database. However, current system provides only an operation of its view direction change. Other operations/manipulations are not supported. So, currently we are implementing the slice-and-dice and ordered treecube algorithm as functions of *IntelligentBox*[5], which is a constructive 3D software development system and provides various functions as software components and allows us various manipulations. Therefore, using *IntelligentBox*, our 3D treecube algorithm is a strong visualization tool for various databases. First of all, we will develop a virtual museum system. It would enable the user to browse and search many kinds of databases represented by a 3D shape model, color, text information as if he/she is located in the real museum.

4. Concluding Remarks

This paper proposed a new 3D visualization tool for hierarchical information. A 2D visualization tool for hierarchical information called treemap has been proposed originally by Ben Shneiderman, et al. in 1992. Treemap layouts hierarchically each node of a tree diagram represented as a bounding box. In this paper, we proposed a 3D visualization tool called treecube that can be taken as a 3D extension of treemap. Especially, we extended slice-and-dice and ordered treemap algorithm to their 3D counterparts. This tool seems to be very convenient for layouts of 3D objects in a specified, restricted 3D space.

References

[1] Shneiderman, B. (1992). Tree Visualization with Treemaps: A 2-D Space-Filling Approach. ACM Transactions on Graphics, 11(1), pp. 92-99.

[2] Buls, M., Huizing, K., & van Wijk, J.J. (2000). Squarified Treemaps. Proc. of Joint Eurographics and IEEE TCVG Symposium on Visualization (TCVG 2000), IEEE Press, pp. 33-42.

[3] Shneiderman, B., & Wattenberg, M. (2001). Ordered Treemap Layouts. Proc. of IEEE Information Visualization (InfoVis 2001), IEEE Press, pp. 73-78..

[4] Bederson, B.B, Shneiderman, B. & Wattenberg, M. (2002). Ordered and Quantum Treemaps: Making Effective Use of 2D Space to Display Hierarchies. ACM Transactions on Graphics, 21(4), pp. 833-854.

[5] Okada, Y. and Tanaka, Y. (1995). IntelligentBox: A Constructive Visual Software Development System for Interactive 3D Graphic Applications, Proc. of Computer Animation '95, IEEE Computer Society Press, pp.114-125.

Information Modelling and Knowledge Bases XV
Y. Kiyoki et al. (Eds.)
IOS Press, 2004

Methodological Tools for Describing Children's Knowledge Construction Process in Multimedia Environment

Marjatta KANGASSALO* Kristiina KUMPULAINEN**

**University of Tampere, Department of Teacher Education*
FIN-33014 University of Tampere, Finland, Email: marjatta.kangassalo@uta.fi
***University of Oulu, Faculty of Education, P.O.Box 2000, FIN-90014 Oulu, Finland,*
Email: kristiina.kumpulainen@oulu.fi

Basis and Aim of the Research

This position paper is one part of an ongoing research project that investigates children's science learning and thinking in a social context of a multimedia environment in an early years classroom. The goal of the research project is to widen theoretical, methodological and pedagogical understanding of children's conceptual development in an activity context based upon tool-mediation and socially shared learning activities, child-initiation and spontaneous exploration. The detailed research questions are seen in the authors' earlier article [6]. In this paper we will be concentrated in methodological questions. *At a methodological level*, the research project develops new analysis tools to capture the situative dynamics of conceptual learning mediated by adult-child and child-child interactions and social activities. [6]

The research project approaches conceptual learning from the perspective of cognitive and sociocultural psychology in order to illuminate the sociocognitive processes of science learning when modern multimedia technological possibilities are in children's use. The theoretical and methodological foundations of the research project are laid by theories and set of concepts derived from cognitive and social psychology, cognitive science, studies of discourse, learning and social practice and from artificial intelligence. The empirical data of this research project is derived from one Finnish day care centre. Twenty-three children aged between six to seven years participated in the study. The data collection was conducted in a four-week period during which the children took part in a learning unit on space and time. The learning activities and tools in the unit consisted of child-initiated, exploratory activities during which children had versatile tools in their use, including a multimedia learning tool, PICCO. The description of the PICCO –simulation program has been seen in the earlier articles [1, 2, 6]. In all, the research project aims at broadening and deepening the authors' existing research which has highlighted some intriguing findings concerning the development of children's conceptual understanding, exploratory learning, social interaction and their meaning in children's conceptual thinking and knowledge construction of natural phenomena when working in an open tool rich learning environment [1, 2, 3, 4, 5, 6].

Requirements for Analysis Methods and Description Techniques

The research methods of this research project include the elicitation of children's conceptual models, as well as micro-level analyses of children's exploration processes and social interactions when working in an open, tool rich learning environment. The data of the research project consist of video-recordings of children's interviews before and after the learning unit as well as of the children's individual and social activities during the learning unit. Children's exploration paths during the use of the multimedia environment have also been recorded. Subsidiary data of the project consist of teacher interviews and parent diaries.

In order to obtain a coherent picture of children's conceptual understanding, exploratory learning, social interaction and their meaning in children's conceptual thinking and knowledge construction, it has been necessary to synthesize the collected empirical data into a coherent form. Specific description techniques have been developed for this purpose. The description techniques aim at describing children's conceptual learning and thinking at different phases by taking into account their social interaction, communication and exploration processes in the situated context. Due to the developmental age of the children as well as due to the tool rich learning context, the analysis techniques do not only rest on verbal data. Instead, the techniques try to capture children's activities from the holistic viewpoint by concentrating on modeling their non-verbal behavior and kinetics.

Earlier Research Methods and Description Techniques as a Starting Point

During earlier research projects, a model was constructed for describing children's conceptual models and the changes that occur in them. The description technique pays attention to the different stages of the formation of children's conceptual models, as well as how the conceptual model concerning a given phenomenon is expressed. This means that the operative, visual and verbal expressions of children that concern with a phenomenon or construction are included in the description and can be differentiated from each other. With the description technique, it is possible to follow the process of children's knowledge construction in its different stages, forms of expression children use, and changes that occur in the conceptual model. The basis for the development of procedures for the elicitation of a conceptual model of the given natural phenomenon has formed the theoretical framework for the concept of a conceptual model, the given natural phenomenon and the children's insufficient ability to express recalled things verbally. In the elicitation of a conceptual model, attention was paid to the order, continuity and regularity of events of the natural phenomenon on the earth, the interconnections of the Earth and the Sun in space, and interrelations of phenomena on the earth and in space. In addition, the description techniques for children's exploration processes have been developed in the earlier research. In this research those techniques will be developed and integrated (e.g. [2, 7]).

The analysis of social interaction follows the framework developed by Kumpulainen and Mutanen [8, 9]. This method of analysis particularly focuses on the mechanisms through which the social and cognitive features of interaction operate in a socially mediated learning activity. The theoretical grounding of the analysis framework is informed by the sociocultural and socio-constructivist perspectives on interaction and learning. In this method, learning is seen to take place as a result of individuals' active participation in the practices of the social environment. Learning is viewed as an interactional process that requires an understanding of language and other semiotic tools as both personal and social resources [10, 11, 12]. Social interaction is treated as a dynamic process in which language and other semiotic tools are used as instruments of communication and learning. Interaction is seen as a complex social phenomenon which is composed of non-verbal and social properties in addition to its verbal characteristics. Discourse itself is not treated as representing a person's inner cognitive world, nor even as descriptive of an outer reality, but rather as a tool-in-action shaped by participants' culturally-based definitions of the situation [13].

In order to advance understanding of children's conceptual learning at the intersection of new technologies and learning cultures, it is necessary to develop new data analyses and presentation techniques. Modern computer technology may provide researchers with new powerful tools for the realization of these challenging goals. One of the researchers of this project, Ohsuga [5] is making research on such an advanced method of modelling and its manipulation. This method may be used effectively in this research project.

Conclusions

The present research project aims at developing computer-based analysis and description techniques in modelling the situated processes of children's conceptual learning in an open, tool rich-learning context mediated by free exploration and social activities. The aim is to develop techniques that will simulate and animate children's individual and collaborative knowledge construction processes in a multimedia environment. The pre-requisites for such developmental work are to describe both knowledge construction processes and their phases. In addition, the analysis tools should allow the researcher to investigate verbal and non-verbal communication and behaviour. Furthermore, the unit of analysis for such a system need to be both the individual child and the collective group. In an ideal situation, the system could analyse and describe children's conceptual learning from multiple dimensions by taking into account the dynamic and situated nature of conceptual learning and knowledge construction.

In this presentation we shall describe the existing description techniques and consider their possibilities in the development of computer-based analyses tools and techniques for modelling children's conceptual learning and knowledge construction processes in contemporary early years classrooms.

References

[1] Kangassalo, Marjatta 1992. The Pictorial Computer-Based Simulation in Natural Sciences for Children's Use. In Ohsuga, S., Kangassalo, H., Jaakkola, H., Hori, K. and Yonezaki, N. (Eds.) Information Modelling and Knowledge Bases III: Foundations, Theory and Applications. Amsterdam: IOS Press, 511-524.

[2] Kangassalo, Marjatta 1997. The Formation of Children's Conceptual Models concerning a Particular Natural Phenomenon Using PICCO, a Pictorial Computer Simulation. Acta Universitatis Tamperensis 559. University of Tampere. Tampere. 188 p.

[3] Kumpulainen, K. & Mutanen, M. 1998. Collaborative practice of science construction in a computer-based multimedia environment. Computers and Education, 30, 75-85.

[4] Kumpulainen, K., Salovaara, H. & Mutanen, M. 2001. The nature of students' sociocognitive activity in handling and processing multimedia-based science material in a small group learning task. Instructional Science, 29, 481-515.

[5] Ohsuga, Setsuo 1996. Aspects of Conceptual Modeling - As Kernel of New Information Technology. In Y. Tanaka, H. Kangassalo, H. Jaakkola and A. Yamamoto (Eds.) Information Modelling and Knowledge Bases VII. Amsterdam: IOS Press, 1-21.

[6] Kangassalo, M and Kumpulainen, K. 2002. The Dynamics of Children's Science Learning and Thinking in a Social Context of a Multimedia Environment. In Information Modelling and Knowledge Bases XIV. 2003 (Eds.) Hannu Kangassalo, Eiji Kawaguchi, Bernhard Thalheim and Hannu Jaakkola. Amsterdam: IOS Press.

[7] Kangassalo, Marjatta 1994. Children's Independent Exploration of a Natural Phenomenon by Using a Pictorial Computer-Based Simulation. Journal of Computing in Childhood Education 5 (3/4), 285-297.

[8] Kumpulainen, K. & Mutanen, M. 1999. Interaktiotutkimus sosiokulturaalisen ja konstruktivistisen oppimisnäkemyksen viitekehyksessä. [Social interaction and learning - Interaction research in the framework of sociocultural and constructivist perspectives to learning]. Kasvatus, 1, 5-17.

[9] Kumpulainen, K. & Mutanen, M. 1999. The situated dynamics of peer group interaction: An introduction to an analytic framework. Learning and Instruction, 9, 449-474.

[10] Wertsch, J. V. 1991. Voices of the mind: Sociocultural approach to mediated action. Cambridge, MA: Harvard University Press.

[11] Cole, M. 1996. Cultural psychology: A once and future discipline. Cambridge, MA: Harvard University Press.

[12] Halliday and Hasan 1989. Language, context, and text. London: Oxford University Press.

[13] Edwards, D. & Potter, J. 1992. Discursive psychology. Newbury Park, CA: Sage.

Information Modelling and Knowledge Bases XV
Y. Kiyoki et al. (Eds.)
IOS Press, 2004

Coherent Enterprise Information Modelling in practice

Koenraad Vandenborre
Peter Heinckiens
Ghislain Hoffman
Herman Tromp

Inno.com, Heiststeenweg 131, 2580 Beerzel, Belgium,
Koenraad.Vandenborre@inno.com
TMME, Bourgetlaan 60, 1140 Brussel, Belgium,
Peter.Heinckiens@toyota-europe.com
Ghent University, Intec, Sint-Pietersnieuwstraat 41, 9000 Gent, Belgium,
Ghislain.Hoffman@rug.ac.be, Herman.Tromp@rug.ac.be

Abstract

In large-scale organizations, the need for enterprise information modelling originates from new business opportunities like B2C and B2B and new cross-domain business demands. This paper sketches why enterprise information modelling is important in this context and where it should be situated in the software engineering process. We further stress the importance of coherent modelling. The content of this position paper is the result of the application of academic ideas in the real-life context of Toyota Motor Europe.

1. Introduction

Currently large-scale organizations are facing huge challenges in IT. Within the organization, newly demanded business functionality crosscuts legacy system borders. On the other hand the internet and its related technologies offer new business opportunities, forcing the organization to externalize some of its IT-systems. The newly demanded functionality and the externalization however, were both out of the scope of the design of the systems and applications currently executing company critical tasks; they are said to be monolithic, designed to execute their task and not designed to deliver services to other systems. In every-day practice this means that every one of these systems has been constructed with its own view on the business model, its own design model, and its own implementation model. The effort to filter out commonalities, model and implement them separately and make them reusable was, if not at all inexistent, too small to be useful today. The reasons for this, although mostly valuable, are for instance the scope of the project, the available technology, the complexity of the system, the deadlines and costs… The major concern at this point is to fulfil the new needs with the resources available at this moment.

We are convinced that Enterprise Information Modelling is of crucial importance to the organization and its needs, in order to be able to adequately answer the new challenges it

faces. We're also convinced that coherence with other steps of the software engineering process is crucial in order to introduce Enterprise Information Modelling successfully.
The ideas presented in this paper follow from and elaborate further on former work from some of the authors [3], on well known work from others, nowadays considered as standard works - we mention [1], [6], [7] – and on related new publications in the field (see e.g. [4], [5]).
The structure of this paper is as follows: first, we present our understanding of Enterprise Information Modelling; thereafter we situate it within other modelling efforts and within the software engineering process. This is followed by a discussion of important implementation issues that have to be tackled.

2. Enterprise Information Modelling

2.1. Information Domains

The concept of Enterprise Information Modelling, as defined in the next paragraph, followed from our work regarding Information Domains. Information Domains, in our lines of thought, are certain areas within an organization that deal with concepts that are of importance to at least that area and possibly other areas. The concepts herein must be made persistent under a certain form, mostly a database and more general a data-store. Whereas we consider the data-store to contain the raw data, we consider information to be the service-based delivery of that data through a well-defined interface into a format that is independent on the format of the underlying data and that has the correct semantics for the client(s) requesting that information. We consider a domain to be a higher structure containing a set of concepts, the higher structure often being referred to as a package. It is obvious that different approaches can be taken; we tried packaging by starting from an organizational point of view, defining different domains from the organization chart, an application / systems point of view, defining the domains from the existing logical grouping of applications within the organization and a business process point of view whereby domains are identified from looking to and organizing the concepts used within the business processes. In our experience it turned out that a new view, orthogonal to the ones formerly mentioned, gives the most natural classification of domains.

2.2. Definition

To our understanding, enterprise information modelling is that part of modelling that is situated between the modelling of business processes and the modelling of any single system or application. Its main objective is to define and model assets which are of common use to different domains within the organization. In this way, Enterprise Information Modelling presents an added value to the organization as a whole through its reusability and its common semantics to different interested parties within the organization. Where formerly the same concepts were modelled many times, often in different forms and each time for the sake of one particular application, this effort can be done once. The result of this reusability is a reduction in the overall cost. Furthermore Enterprise Information Models do augment the understanding of the concepts modelled herein.

2.3. Positioning Enterprise Information Modelling

Modelling efforts on the highest level in an organization chart the business processes of the organization. These business processes form the heart of the organization;

they are its reason of existence. Applications are built to automate tasks or activities extracted from the business processes. In that context they're a form of specification of the task at hand: requirements are gathered, the task gets analysed, and a design and an implementation are made. A crucial part that's often lost, while automating a task, is preserving an overview of how that task is interrelated with other tasks originating from the same business process, how this task gets influenced and influences other tasks possibly operating on the same information.

Things get even worse if another task in the business process is to be automated. More often than not, the formerly automated task is not taken into account while designing the automation of the new task, and even if it is, the conclusion is often that the former cannot be reused. This should not astonish us as the first automated task was never designed for reuse.

The conclusion to make here is that apparently an important step is overlooked; the analysis of the task under hand should consider how previous efforts can be reused and how the automation of this task can be achieved with possible reuse in mind. This exactly is what Enterprise Information Modelling aims at and leads to the generalized modelling overview in Figure 1.

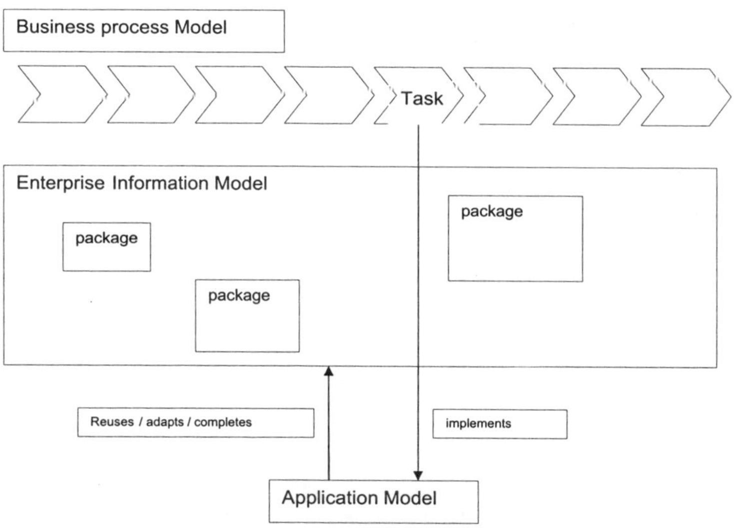

Figure 1 : Interrelation between different models

As we will describe further (see the section on "2.5: Coherence"), the Enterprise Information Model must be based on the Business Process Model. It is interesting to note that Figure 1 also indicates that Business Process Modelling and Enterprise Information Modelling can be looked upon as a horizontal cut through the organisation as where Application Modelling is a vertical cut.

2.4. Using Enterprise Information Modelling in the software engineering process

Whatever software engineering process is chosen, RUP, a tailored UP or extreme programming, it is important to note that a consistent build-up and use of an Enterprise Information Model will have a profound impact on the process itself. As described in the previous paragraph, mining for existing assets and mining for new assets must become part of the process.

The mining for new assets must be done as soon as possible in the software engineering process and the outcome of this effort will clearly affect the overall cost for building the application. An application that is responsible for the construction of a company-wide reusable information asset clearly will have a higher price than the same application solely built to serve its own purposes. The ROI for building this asset will only be achieved through reuse, the initial cost is higher, see [2]. Furthermore, the actual construction of the asset must be closely followed and guarded, to preserve its integrity and future reuse. When using RUP e.g. yhis clearly has an impact on the inception, elaboration and construction phase.

A possibly reusable information asset must be assessed for its reuse for the application to be built in the first phase of the software engineering process.

2.5. Coherence

Whatever the correctness and the validity of every separate model in the modelling chain may be, if there is no coherence between the different models, much of their intrinsic value will be lost. Non-coherent models don't lead to a common understanding of the business and the problem at hand; they even cause more misunderstandings and misinterpretations. This in turn causes a decreased reusability and an increased resistance to use the models.

Furthermore, it's not only important to guard coherence between different models, but it's as important to keep coherence between the models and the implementations made. The ultimate goal is always to build a running system that not only meets the business requirements but also the requirements imposed by the ideas behind Enterprise Information Modelling. If this cannot be achieved, the reusability of the system will decrease to a level comparable with the reusability of the older systems and the effort put in the modelling will be lost.

An important feature to achieve coherence between different models is traceability between different models. Traceability is necessary to be able to point out the repercussion of a change in one model on other related models. Traceability as an extra requirement for coherence allows for instance to check if all requirements are met and, in its ultimate form, a traceable change in implementation shows the repercussion on the business process model which offers an opportunity to formulate a business case and perform a cost-benefit analysis.

Achieving coherence between models and the implementation is not only a technical matter; organizational structures also play an important role. When looking at the path from the business process model up to the actual information delivering service, build upon a data-source, different profiles of people are involved. We mention for instance business analysts, business modellers, project managers, application architects, implementers... Ideally, every effort should be streamlined but every-day experience learns that, for a plethora of possible reasons, involvement in other projects, deadlines, and available resources... focus gets lost. It therefore is important to have a mediator role within the organization. Within the Toyota Motor Europe context this role is, amongst others, performed by the Information Systems Architecture team.

3. Work in progress

Enterprise Information Modelling can be considered as a centralization effort within an organization. Centralization efforts are always somehow squeezed between their intrinsic long-time character and the needed quick-wins to maintain sponsorship from management and business users. Applying lessons learned from the past, as well within Toyota Motor Europe as outside, we set for an incremental strategy, wherein we mined for small, rapid and easy to implement company assets. The mining and the development of the basic strategy started as a small Architecture-internal project, preparing us to jump in at the moment a new project needed the asset. This bought us visibility and credibility. We now are on the verge of mining for more elaborate company assets stimulated by our business users.

The mining for other assets, modelling them and implementing them from within the context of a business-driven project, is a technical matter we will have to deal with in the future. From an organizational viewpoint it's important that, building on the first success, awareness and buy-in is further created for the way of working described in this paper throughout the organization. The matrix-based organization model of Toyota Motor Europe is very helpful at this point. The awareness creation and buy-in is not only essential to get the needed sponsorship but is a seed in the brains of those involved to look at IT from a company-wide perspective instead of a one-application perspective.

In trying to preserve inter-model and model-implementation coherence, certainly in a start-up phase, it is important to maintain an overview of what is going on at all different levels, the business process modelling, the enterprise information modelling, the application modelling and to support and motivate every participant in the process.

One of the most interesting challenges we met was the concern about information-ownership. The question who is the owner of certain information has to be answered. The main problem in this area is to define who has the right to create, update or delete information. Again the answer was found by looking at the business process and by determining where the information entered this process. Starting from there, a conceptual owner can be defined and a set of guidelines on information ownership was created. This now serves as a working document that gets fine-tuned from experiences with and feedback from projects under construction.

4. Conclusions

Our conclusions so far are the following:

1. There is a need for a central team to keep a view on the complete process, from Business Process Modeling over Enterprise Information Modeling to Application Modeling and the actual implementation in the systems. This requires highly skilled people with different competences and specializations but who are able to keep an eye on the overall effort.
2. It is not sufficient to create a technical sound solution; the organizational structure at hand must be taken into account and must be used to set out a strategy for realization.

3. Every effort made must be related to a business context or a business case, the models under construction must adhere to the business and the actual implementations must follow from projects realizing business needs.
4. Buy-in from management and from business users is a crucial factor. This long term buy-in can only be achieved through successfully delivering projects.

5. Future work

To preserve the usability of the Enterprise Information Model it is of the uttermost importance to have a structure to consult the information base. This must be done as well on the modeling level as on the implementation level. On the modeling level we have a first realization of a "city map", showing the different assets, their packaging and their interrelation. It will be very important to keep this "city map" synchronized with new realizations from projects under construction. On the implementation level, standards and guidelines have to be set for component and data-store development and maintenance. This for instance must include guidelines for replication of information and guidelines for coupling between different information assets.

The academic partners follow closely the efforts around modeling undertaken in the Aspect Oriented Software Development community. By its very nature of describing crosscutting concerns, this new paradigm may bring a tremendous advantage to Enterprise Information Modeling once it becomes mature.

While modeling and implementing more and more company assets, the importance of traceability will become greater and greater. How this can be achieved must be part of future investigations and / or product selection.

How Enterprise Information Modeling and other modeling efforts within the organization relate to the Model Driven Architecture proposed by the OMG – at whose core is the gradually refinement of models - is also a topic which must be addressed by future research.

Acknowledgements

This research would not have been possible without the co-operation and support of Inno.com and Toyota Motor Europe.

References

[1] Martin Fowler, Analysis Patterns: Reusable Object Models, ISBN: 0201895420, Addison-Wesley, 1997
[2] Ivar Jacobson et al: Software Reuse: Architecture Process and Organization for Business Success, ISBN: 0201924765 Addison-Wesley, 1997
[3] Peter Heinckiens: Building Scalable Database Applications: Object-Oriented Design, Architectures, and Implementations, ISBN: 0201310139, Addison-Wesley, 1998
[4] Stuart Madnick, Richard Wang, Wei Zhang: A Framework for Corporate Householding, Proceedings of the Seventh International Conference on Information Quality, pp 36-46, 2002
[5] Hans Diepstraten: (Multi-) Enterprise Architecture: A Business Process Governance Approach, white paper, Atos Origin, 2002

[6] Paul Clements, Linda Northrop: Software Product Lines: Practices and Patterns, ISBN: 0201703327, Addison-Wesley, 2001
[7] Len Bass, Paul Clements, Rick Kazman: Software Architectures in Practice: ISBN: 0201199300, Addison-Wesley, 1997

Information Modelling and Knowledge Bases XV
Y. Kiyoki et al. (Eds.)
IOS Press, 2004

Modelling a Process Repository for Enterprise Application Integration Based on Business Knowledge and Semantics

Sebamalai Jeronious PAHEERATHAN
Department of Computer and System Sciences, Stockholm University, Forum 100, SE 164 40 Kista, Sweden

Abstract. Enterprise Application Integration (EAI), in association with Business Process Management (BPM) has become a more appreciated and attractive approach in meeting information system challenges of enterprises specially operating in competitive business environments. Managing business processes in EAI is a wider capability increasingly becoming a business requirement than technical.

Business Process Management is a capability to discover, design, deploy, execute, interact with, operate, and optimise and analyse end-to-end processes, and to do it at the level of business design, not technical implementation [1]

Therefore, tools enabling BPM should evolve to bridge the gap between the technological and business aspects of managing business processes. Furthermore, future BPM tools should allow business analysts to undertake business process management at the level of business design while also ensuring the value created by the business process to its stakeholders and the profitability to the business enterprise that operate it. Strictly enforcing business ontology in the modelling of business processes, and associating various parameters that can help capturing the business process related requirements at different levels of abstraction of a business process could lead to the attainment of the above goal. Along with this, the utilisation of a process repository can help providing the required support to business analysts during BPM activities. This requires the process repository is to be modelled based on business knowledge and semantics in addition to the process knowledge.

1. Introducing the Problem

Business Process Management (BPM) is becoming increasingly popular at enterprises, especially at those operating in competitive business environments as it provides the means and ways of setting up business processes required by different business activities using Enterprise Application Integration (EAI). But, business processes required by modern business enterprises, appears to be fluid and dynamic, mostly due to the reason that they require varying levels of customisation in meeting different service levels demanded by different stakeholders.

At the same time, there are opportunities to reuse business processes as business scenarios that lead to the selection and enactment of a business process repeat during business activities. Furthermore, the BPM responsibility is becoming more a business requirement than a technical requirement. As a result the business analysts at enterprises are required to handle BPM at the level of business design by identifying and compiling business processes required by specific business scenarios.

Addressing the demands for specifying and modelling business processes by business analysts at the level of business design is the core problem to be addressed in this paper. The solution proposed is about improving the "status of readiness" of enterprises to exercise variants of business processes required to meet different business requirements by storing the process knowledge in a process repository. In addition it is also proposed to capture different business knowledge related to business processes enabling the specification and modelling of business processes at the level of business design.

2. Business Process Modeling Fundamentals

A business process is a persistent unit of work started by a Business Event such as an invoice, request for proposal or a request for funds transfer and driven by business rules that trigger tasks and sub-processes, with each state transition is executed within a transaction and audited for business reasons when required [3]. At the higher levels a business processes represents the exchange of different real world resources/commodities between different real world agents with respect to specific business contexts. In practice business processes are modelled as a combination of scripts and rules, where scripts defines the process flow at a high level, and rules are the branch logic used to dynamically determine the flow at the execution time. Tasks and sub-processes in the business process are assigned to agents, which are either human possibly belonging to organisational units or software, which are capable and authorised to play specific roles in the business process. Rules can help determine the next step to be executed or binds the next step to a specific agent and their evaluation is based on the workflow context and execution state, workflow history, availability of agents, data retrieved from databases or passed in messages and business policies.

Business processes are case based and a business process is often designed to handle similar cases. Every piece of work is a business process is executed for a specific case, while BPM requires handing cases efficient and effective as possible. Cases are handled by executing tasks and/or sub-processes in a specific order, and the routing specifies which task need to be executed and in which order [4].

At the bottom-most level a business process can be considered as a set of message exchanges between the different information agents and activities mainly involving in the preparation and conversion of information to be exchanged (See Figure 1).

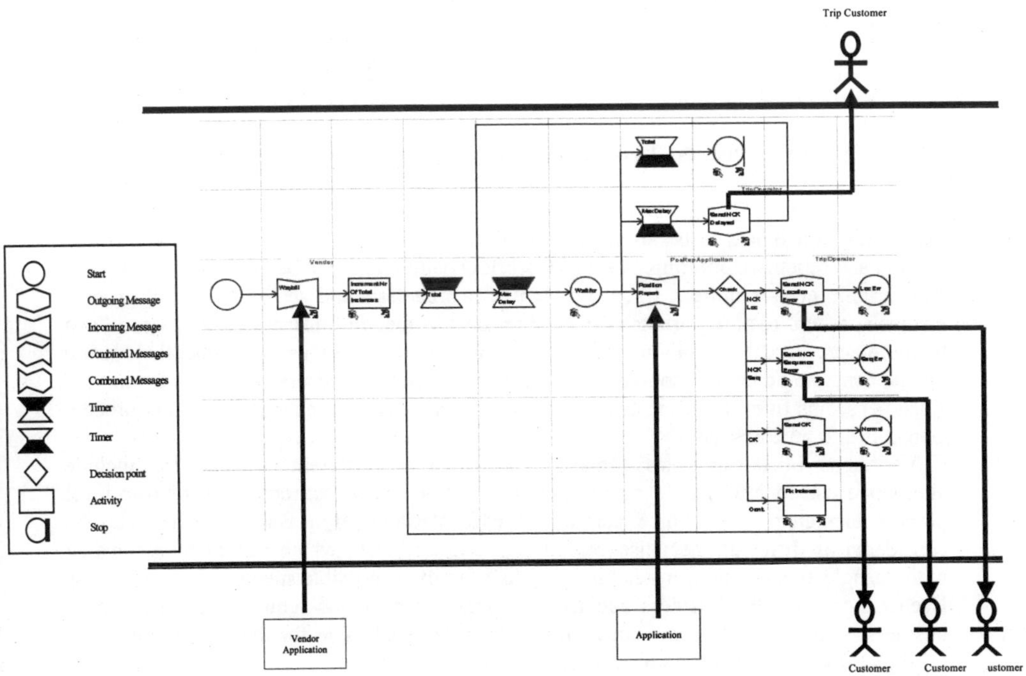

Figure 1: A Business Process at Bottom Level Representation

Detail level messages are considered as information resources and used in two types of exchanges namely input and output types involving information agents. Information agents involved at low-level message exchanges are of two types, the applications/application components, which participate at automated activities and human actors who participate over manual activities of the business process.

Message exchanges and other elements at the bottom level can be grouped to form Business Tasks, which can be associated to specific Business Events in particular business domains (See Figure 2).

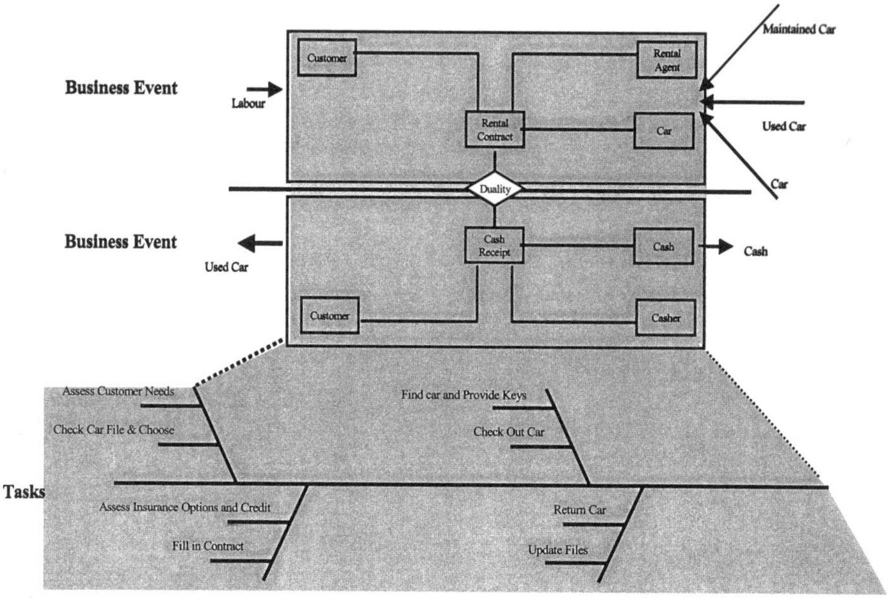

Figure 2: Business Tasks and Business Events in a Duality Relationship

Business tasks requires the bottom-most level process elements such as the message exchanges, and others to be arranged in a particular order using all required sequential, parallel and repetitive ordering. A set of workflow patterns [5] can be used for this purpose. While some tasks require a fixed ordering of a predetermined set of root level process elements, others require variations depending on the specific business circumstances and requirements. A categorisation scheme proposed for business process modelling using atomic concrete processes, non-atomic concrete processes and generic processes by van der Aalst [4] seems fit even for the ordering of root level message exchanges and other process elements into business tasks.

Variations of business tasks may be achieved by different means. This include alternative use of information agents and information resources, reordering of root level process elements to introduce parallelism etc.. Variants of a Business Task can be considered as different specialisations of a generalised task, which cannot be associated with a single specification, instead it refers to a family of possible specifications. Business Events represents the business actions at a larger context and requires the ordering of business tasks using the same conventions and rules applicable for the ordering of root-level process elements at the business tasks.

3. Modelling of Business Process at the Level of Business Design

Business processes are executed to help achieving business goals. Business goals are liable to change over time due to changing business conditions such as the demand for customisation and pressures imposed by competition, thereby also the business processes. The value created by each business process to its stakeholders and the profitability to organisation that operates the business process also requires measurement and assessment.

Considering the above, it is proposed to model a business process at four different levels of abstraction namely the Business Process Scenarios, Contracts, Commitment and Consent levels (See Figure 3).

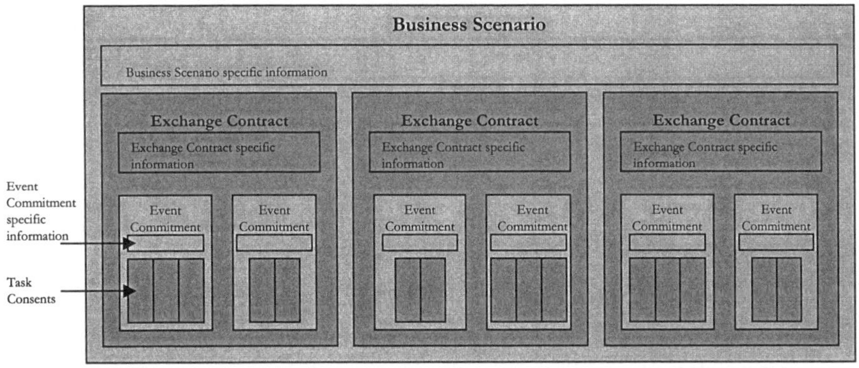

Figure 3: Business Process Scenario, Contract, Commitments and Consents

The Business Process Scenario refers to the circumstances that demand for the execution of a particular business process instance or case, where such a scenario or case can be associated with a serial, selective, parallel and repetitive organisation of a set of Economic Exchanges. A Scenario can refer to a set of Business Process Contracts, where each such Contract is proposed to be associated with a value chain activity, as proposed by Michael Porter [6] and corresponds to an Economic Exchange, which can be represented by a duality relationship between one or more inflow and one or more outflow Economic Events as proposed in the REA ontology by McCarthy and Geerts [7]. (see Figure 4).

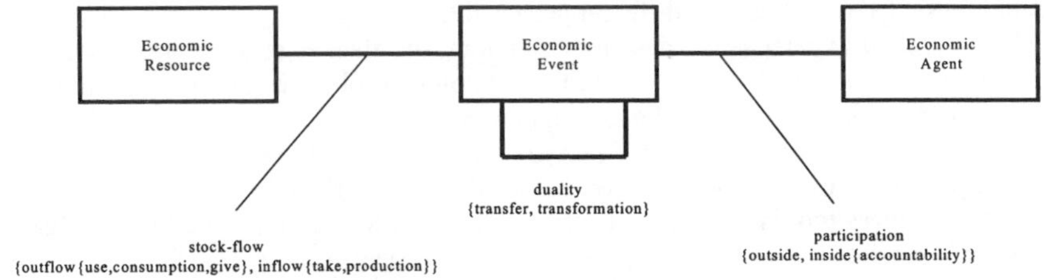

Figure 4: An Economic Exchange

A Contract will also refer to the ordering of Economic Events in the Economic Exchange. Representing a business process as a set of Economic Exchanges gives an opportunity to assess the economic and stakeholder values of a business process as each Economic Exchange in a business process comprises a set of Economic Events, which can be associated with a set of real world resources and agents (See Figure 5).

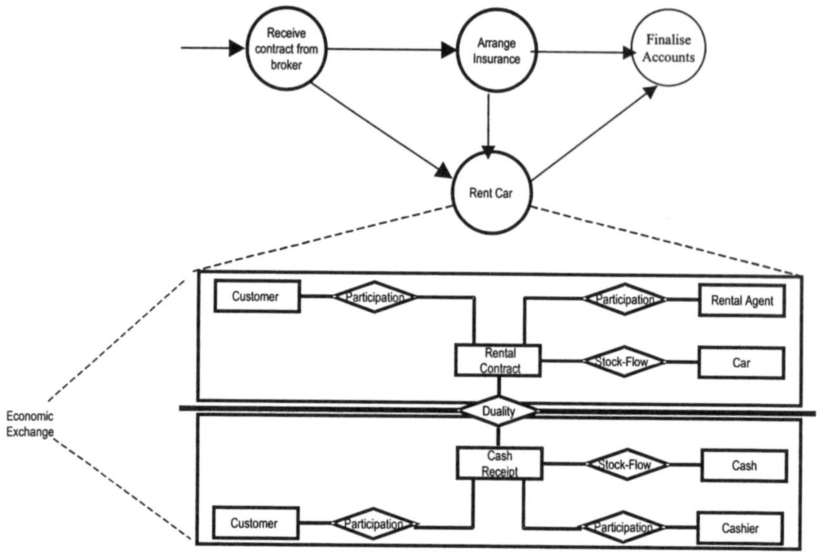

Figure 5: Business Process, a Collection of Business Exchanges

As an Event is represented by a set of Tasks, which in turn can be represented by a set of root-level process elements, an Event can also be associated with a set of information agents and resources. Real world agents and resources are not necessarily the same as the information agents and resources of an Event, and real world agents and resources may not involve in any information exchange with the business process concerned. But a set of relationships and associations that can be defined within and between the real world entities can be used to specify a business process at its different levels of abstractions.

A Business Process Commitment will be used to define an Event and the circumstances that will lead to the enactment of an Event in a Business Process Contract of a Business Process Scenario. It will also define the order of tasks in an Event. Similarly Business Process Consent will be used to define a Task in full.

Complying with the trends and results of the continuous research in the area of workflow and business process modelling, this paper proposes to describe business processes in a broader sense, from a number of different perspectives.

The control flow perspective describes activities and their execution ordering through different constructs, which permit flow of execution control by incorporating the options for sequencing, selection, and parallelism and join synchronisation of activities.

A second perspective, the resource perspective refers to both real world resources and information resources as defined above. While the real world resources will be used to define the business processes and their elements through the declaration and identification of a set of associations the business process and its elements can have with the real world resources such as commercial and other commodities, the information resources will be used to lay the business and processing data on the control flow where business documents and other objects, which flow between activities, and the local variables of the business process, qualify in effect pre- and post- conditions of activity execution [4].

The third perspective is an agent perspective, which provides both an organisational structure anchor and interaction and control properties of business processes in the form of human and device or software roles. As the agents refers to both real world agents and information agents, this perspective can be used to define both the context related to the business process and the interaction and service consumption properties of business processes.

Finally a fourth perspective is the operational perspective describes the elementary actions executed by activities, where the action map into underlying applications also referring to business and process data passed into and out of applications through activity to application interfaces, permitting manipulation of data within applications. In defining a business process further perspectives are possible, by combining the above perspectives.

Referring to the three levels of process abstraction, a Business Process Scenario is proposed to be at the highest possible level, and needed to be associated with a set of business level parameters, which can be used to identify a business process instance, which required to be enacted in order to meet a particular business circumstance. Exploding a business scenario will lead to the identification and organisation of Economic Exchange instances that make up the business process instance. A Business Process Contract will define the organisation of Business Event instances in a Economic Exchange instance and a set of business level parameters that will justify the selection of particular instances of Business Events in a particular Exchange instance. Similarly, Business Process Commitment and Consents too defined to reflect business requirements at their appropriate levels of abstraction.

Based on the above, it is possible to consider a business process as a composition of Economic Exchanges, Economic Events and/or Business Tasks. In compatible with REA, an Economic Exchange is made out of at least two Economic Events, where an Economic Event is defined to be a composition of a set of Business Tasks. (See Figure 6).

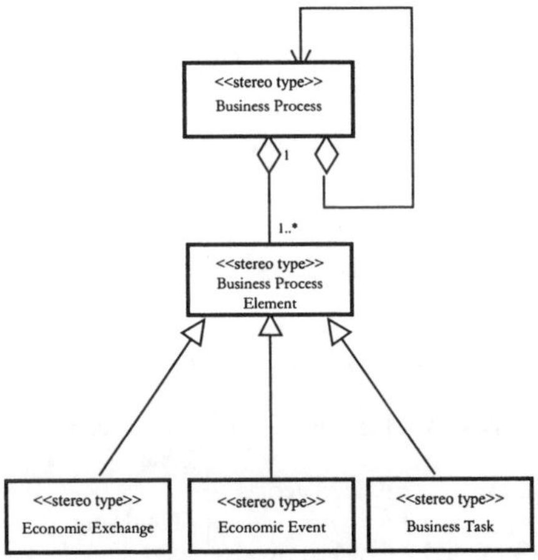

Figure 6: Compositions of a Business Process

4. Categorisation of Business Process Elements

Considering the fact that a Business Event participating in a Business Exchange is a Value Chain activity, it is now possible to position an organisational business process and its elements in specific business domains. Within the business domains selected, the business processes elements at levels below the Business Events can be assigned to specific normative sub categories of the Porter Value Chain. This proposal to model business processes at the level of business design proposes extensions to this categorisation in order to accommodate the categorisations of resources and agents.

Table 1: Porter Value Chain and Extensions

Normative Category	Normative Sub-Category	Resource Inflows and Outflow	Major Types of Events	Economic Agents and Roles
Procurement	Bid Submission Contract Negotiation Purchase Order Preparation Receiving	Money Raw Materials Facilities Services Technology	Payments Purchase Purchase Orders Price Quotes Contract Negotiation	Buyer Seller Vendor Cashier
Human Resources	Hiring Training Payroll Management Personnel Deployment	Money Purchased Training Materials Purchased Benefit Packages	Cash Payments Acquisition Of Labour Training	Employee Student Beneficiary
Transportation	Loading Shipping Packaging	Raw Materials Delivered Raw Materials Manufactured Goods Delivered Manufactured Goods	Shipment Warehousing Tasks Material Handling Trucking	Buyer Vendor Logistics Worker Trucker
Manufacturing	Product Development Product Design Assembly Quality Control	Facilities And Technology Labour Raw Materials Finished Goods	Manufacturing Operation Raw Material Issue Manufacturing Job	Factory Worker Supervisor QC Inspector

Normative Category	Normative Sub-Category	Business Events	Business Tasks	Real world Resource inflow and outflow	Information Resource inflow and outflow	Real world Agents and Roles	Information Agents and Roles

Accordingly, a further column to list the different possible tasks for each Business Event and a split to both the resource and agent columns currently listing the economic agents and resources in the Porter's Value Chain to list the real world and information resources and agents separately are proposed.

5. Associations and Relationships

Considering the possible associations and relationships that can be exploited to define business processes and its elements at the level of business design, it is proposed to look at some of the early work by both William McCarthy & Geerts [7], and Eric Yu & John Mylopoulos [8], [9]. While capitalising on these works, this paper is proposing to refine the associations and relationships so that further relationships can be established to define the business process and its elements (content) and the context they operate using the semiotic relations the business processes can have with its environment namely the resources and agents. It is also proposed to establish relationships so that business processes and its elements can be described unambiguously at four levels of abstractions proposed, thereby business processes and their elements required to meet specific business conditions can be identified and enacted with the help of a process repository. To facilitate this, a process repository should be designed to accommodate both the process knowledge and their associated business knowledge involving these semiotic relationships. It is also proposed to organise this process and business knowledge in such a way, that the knowledge can be used incrementally during the identification of a specific business process so that more detail level knowledge is required only when tracing for more ambiguous processes.

The strategic actor dependency relationship as defined by Yu & Mylopoulos proposes to model the business process with respect to its goals and rules. Yu and Mylopoulos proposes four kinds of dependency relationships namely the goal dependency, task dependency, resource dependency and soft-goal dependency

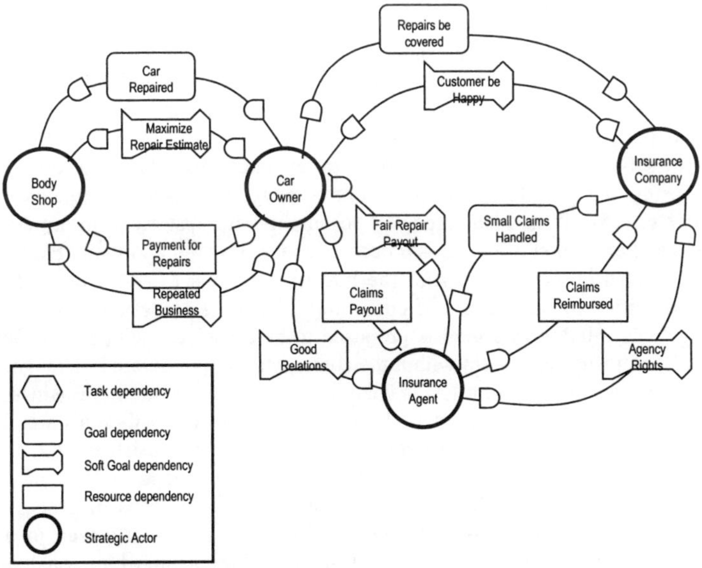

Figure 7: Actor Dependency Relationships [8]

Using a vehicle accident insurance claim example, they propose a goal dependency between each pair of actors, and a set of soft-goal dependencies to strengthen the properties of the goal. "Repairs be covered" a goal set between the "Car owner" and "Insurance company" has a soft-goal "Customer be happy" probably can be used to define a set of properties with which the customer can be made happy. These properties possibly interpreted as a set of non-functional requirements associated with the functions involved in providing the cover to repairs after an accident. They also propose a workflow model representing the different activities and flows of information resources between the activities [10].

As an extension of these thoughts, this paper insists the need to model a business process as a control flow of activities represented at different levels of abstractions as suggested in the early parts of this paper and a set of background models, which will capture different business related semantics in terms of different business parameters at each level of abstraction. For this purpose it is proposed to restrict the representation of information entities to the modelling of control flow and the real world entities in the background models. This means while the information agents and information resources will be modelled with process activities in control flow, a set of background models will be produced based on the relationships between the process elements and real world agents and real world resources. This approach will help precise definition of business processes with respect to specific business circumstances.

Starting with background models, a business process can be defined at its highest level of abstraction as a set of business goals to be achieved, where each such business goal can be associated with an Economic Exchange as proposed by this paper, thereby enabling a rough assessment of economic and stakeholder value of a business process at its initial states of definition. Each such goal is proposed to be set between a collection of real world agents and resources unlike the case in the strategic actor dependency relationships as proposed by YU and Mylopoulos, where it is associated with a pair of agents participating in a Depender and Dependee relationship [8].

Economic Exchanges that will make up a business process need to be categorised by different business domains under which they will be assigned to sub-categories of normative categories of the value Chain [6]. A repository of process and related business knowledge can help business analysts in the identification of a set of Economic Exchanges associated with a required business case. This knowledge needs to be fed to the repository by domain experts. The process repository is also expected to accommodate the information that help organise the Economic Exchanges by business analysts in the desired business processes using the possible workflow control structures such as sequence, selection, repetition, etc., [5]. It is also expected to incorporate historical information on the compilation and execution of business processes concerning the Economic Exchanges.

This paper also proposes to permit the business analysts to associate each Economic Exchange identified in the process of compiling a business process to a set of sub-goals. Each sub-goal in relation to a goal is proposed to be associated with a workflow activity and to represent a Business Event within the corresponding Economic Exchange. Sub-goals need to be expressed in different levels enabling their mapping against Business Events at their higher levels down to Business Tasks at their lower levels. Sub-goals are also need to be traced with a set of real world agents and resources in consistent with the goal. In addition it is also to be associated with a set of information agents and resources enabling the construction of a control flow of the business process in terms of process activities, information agents and information resources. Each sub-goal is proposed to be possibly associated with a set of soft-goals, each defining a different non-functional requirement associated with the Business Event or Task. The process repository proposed is expected to contain information required in the selection of specific Business Events for an Economic Exchange selected and the ordering of such Events in it.

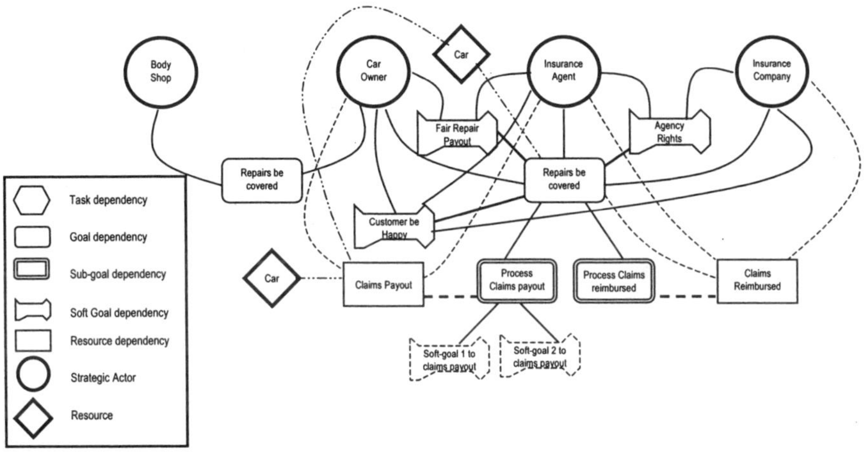

Figure 8: Proposal for Extensions to Dependency Relationships

It is also possible to formulate a set of relationships representing the semiotic associations between the information entities namely the information agents and information resources and the process elements to formulate a control flow of the business process.

6. Business Scenarios, Contracts, Commitments and Consents

The Business Scenario is proposed to define the context that requires the execution of a specific business process to meet a specific business case. The different parameters required in defining the Scenario are to be selected from the different relationships the economic primitives namely the real world agents and resources will have with the specific instance of a business process and the associations within themselves with respect to a particular business process instance. Therefore the process repository is to be designed to accommodate these details.

This requires a Scenario to be considered as an aggregation of information pertaining the relationships and associations between three types of constructs namely a business process instance, one or more real world/information agents involved, and one or more real world/information resources exchanged over the different Economic Exchanges, Events, and/or process activities included in the Business Process (See Figure 9). In addition information on sequencing process activities in the business process and any goal specific information that cannot be directly associated to the relationships and associations proposed, need to be attached to business scenarios.

A set of business process instances referring to different Scenarios may belongs to a Business Process Type, which is a criteria that can be used to group business processes in the process repository. The different Business Process instances of a Business Process Type are the different customisations, which need be instantiated with respect to different business cases.

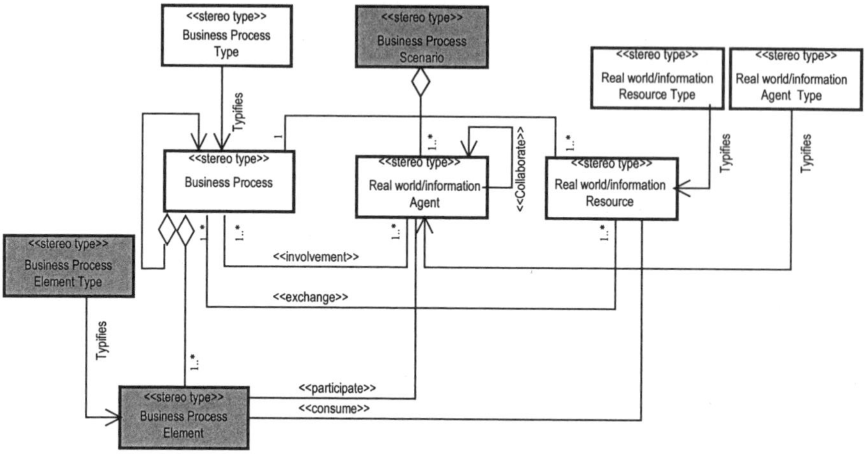

Figure 9: Business Process Scenario (Semantics)

A set of parameters that can be used to define the circumstances that demand for the selection of a particular Economic Exchange instance within a particular Business Process instance is named as a Contract (See Figure 10). The different parameters required in defining the Contract are to be selected from the different relationships the real world/information primitives such as agents and resources will have with respect to an Economic Exchange instance and the associations of such primitives within and between themselves with respect to the instance concerned.

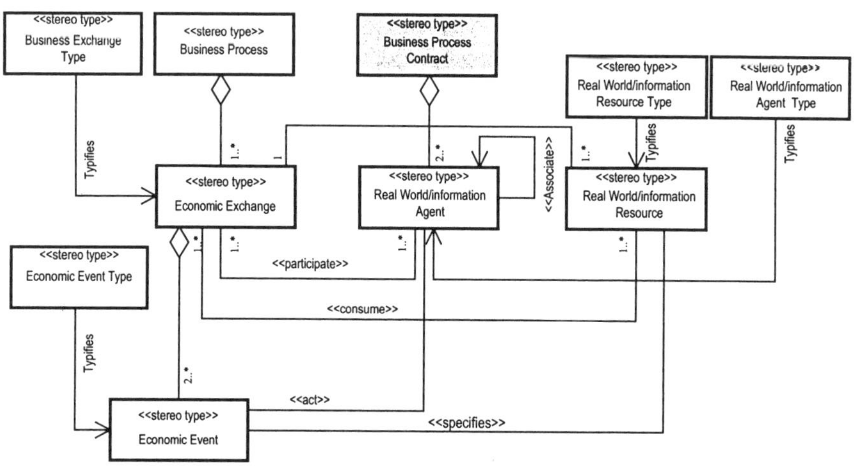

Figure 10: Business Process Contract (Semantics)

This requires the process repository is to be structured to capture the set of associations and relationships the real world/information resources and real world/information agents will have with economic exchanges and their values with respect to specific Economic Exchange instances. As in the case of business processes, it is necessary to have information pertaining to Exchanges and Exchange types to be captured and retained in the repository for this purpose. Semantics pertaining to associated sub-goals will be represented in terms associations and relationships between the process elements and real world/information primitives.

Similarly, a set of parameters that can be used to define the circumstances that demand for the selection of a particular Economic Event to be used within an Economic Exchange is named as an Event Commitment (See Figure 11) and those that can be used to define the context of a Task are defined by a Consent (See Figure 12).

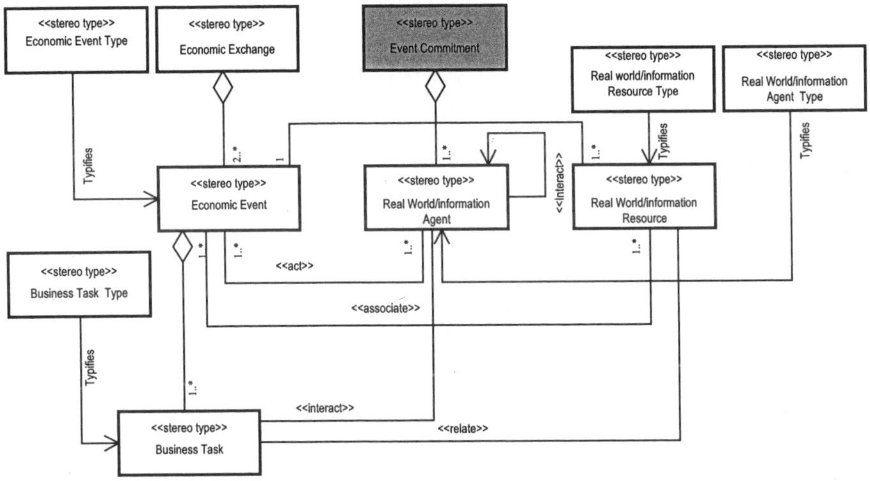

Figure 11: Business Process Event Commitment (Semantics)

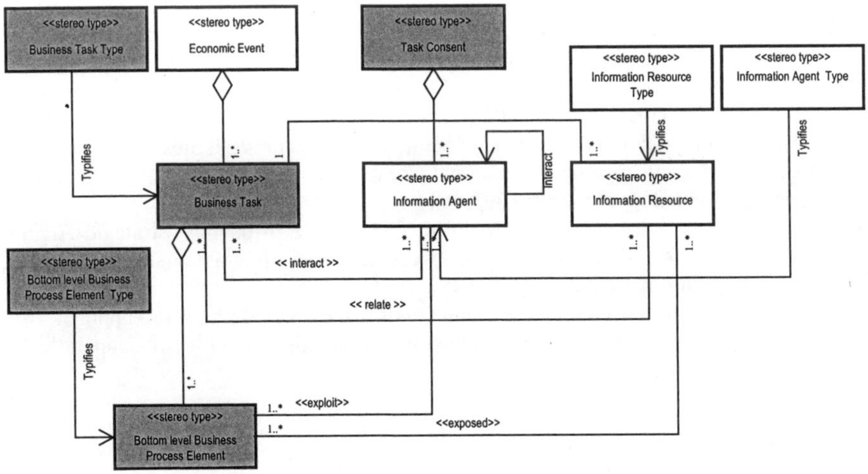

Figure 12: Business Process Task Consent (Semantics)

7. Conclusion

It is appealing to engage business analysts in business process management as the people who can understand the language of the business can effectively engage in the management of business processes at enterprises. In making this goal a reality, the business processes needs to be represented at the level of business design, and the facilities should be made available to support the activities of business analysts at the level of business design. This necessitates the application of a process repository at which, the business and process knowledge from domain experts can be captured and retained for use by business analysts during the BPM. When a business process repository is modelled in the manner presented above, to capture business process semantics at four different levels of abstractions, it is possible to associate the requirements pertaining to the enactment of a business process with a set of business level semantics. What is required is the identification and definition of a set of parameters, which can comprehensively define the business process at these levels of abstractions. This will enable the business analysts to compile the business processes required to specific business requirements instantly using the constructs in the process repository, and pave the way to the BPM in future BPM support tools.

References

[1] H. Smith, D.Neal, L. Ferrara, and F. Hayden, The Emergence of Business Process Management, CSC Research Services, January 2002.

[2] H. Smith, P. Fingar Business Process Management: The Third Wave, Meghan-Kiffer Press. December 2002

[3] U. Dayal, M. Hsu, R. Ladin, R., Business Process Coordination: State of the Art, trends, and Open Issues, Proceedings of the 27th VLDB Conference, Roma, 2001.

[4] W. M. P. van der Aalst, How to handle dynamic change and capture management information? An approach based on generic workflow models.

[5] W. M. P. van der Aalst, A. H. M ter Hofstede, B. Kiepuszewski, A. P. Barros, Workflow Patterns, 2000.

[6] M. E. Porter, Competitive advantages, Creating and Sustaining Superior Performance, The Free Press, 1998.

[7] G. L. Geerts, and W. E. McCarthy,The Ontological Foundation of REA Enterprise Information Systems, November 1999, March, August 2000.

[8] S. K. Eric Yu, and J. Mylopoulos, Modeling Organizational Issues for Enterprise Integration, Proceedings of International Conference on Enterprise Integration and Modeling Technology, October 1997, Italy.

[9] S. K. Eric Yu, and J. Mylopoulos, From E-R to A-R Modeling Strategic Actor Relationships for Business Process Reengineering, International Journal of Cooperative Information Systems (IJCIS), 1995

[10] S. K. Eric Yu, and J. Mylopoulos, Using Goals, Rules, and Methods to Support Reasoning in Business Process Reengineering, International Journal of Cooperative Information Systems (IJCIS), 1995

Information Modelling and Knowledge Bases XV
Y. Kiyoki et al. (Eds.)
IOS Press, 2004

A Meta-Level Active Multidatabase System Architecture for Heterogeneous Information Resources

Shuichi KURABAYASHI[†] and Yasushi KIYOKI[‡]
[†] *Graduate School of Media and Governance, Keio University*
[‡] *Faculty of Environmental Information, Keio University*
Endo 5322, Fujisawa, Kanagawa, 252-8520, Japan
{kurabaya, kiyoki}@sfc.keio.ac.jp

Abstract. With the rapid progress of global network and database technology, various information resources, such as relational databases, document databases and web contents, have become accessible over networks. The integration among those information resources adds new values to themselves. An active multidatabase system is essential to provide dynamic access and integration functions for those information resources. This paper presents a principled architecture of a meta-level active multidatabase system that provides active database functionalities for accessing and integrating heterogeneous information resources. The meta-level active multidatabase system realizes active rules that check and react to changes of contents in different information resources on the global-area network. The essence of our method is that active database functionalities and database integration mechanisms are realized in the meta-level system over local information resources. Our method applies the active database functionalities to heterogeneous information resources to access and integrate them in a dynamic way. In this paper, we clarify feasibility and effectiveness of our system architecture by showing several experimental results.

1 Introduction

In global-area network environments, we have opportunities to access various information resources, but database management systems, access methods and data models of those information resources are extremely heterogeneous. Providing an integration mechanism for various information resources makes it possible to add new values to those information resources [4].

Most of those databases in the global-area network are passive databases, and they are triggered in response to requests given by users. Active database systems realize new searching/modifying operations in response to changes of contents and situation in databases [5, 18]. Active databases also realize automatic provision of information in their application phases. Conventional active database systems can push up-to-date information in specific information resources to users. However, users must manually compare, examine and integrate different information resources to obtain objective information, because it is difficult for the conventional systems to support such comparison and examination automatically among different information resources.

In the current situation of the global development and evolution of WWW, people are publishing and sharing information in lightweight data repositories, such as spreadsheets, HTML files or text files, rather than traditional heavyweight databases, such as relational databases. Users can easily write and upload HTML files, and quickly link them from/to other files. Because those lightweight data repositories support incremental and ad-hoc authoring, tasks for authoring information are easily facilitated. However, when lightweight repositories grow larger in scale and become more semantically complex, it is difficult to automatically check and react to changes of contents in those data repositories. The Internet is still a passive infrastructure, because methodology for activating a variety of such ad-hoc repositories does not exist. Evolution of the Internet and WWW to the "active " infrastructure is important to realize an advanced information system environment.

Semantic interoperability of heterogeneous information resources on WWW is also an important issue to be solved. It is difficult to statically describe semantic relationships among information resources on WWW, which are dynamically changing. Therefore, we focus on the system design for dynamically computing the semantic relationships among heterogeneous information resources.

Currently, a large legacy information systems, such as web servers and RDB servers, have been already running on the Internet. When we try to make those legacy servers "active", it is desirable to minimize the change to their system configuration for the active integration.

To realize those new objectives, we propose a system architecture for active integration of heterogeneous information resources. This paper presents a meta-level active multidatabase system architecture, called *Active and Dynamic Meta-level Integration System (ADMIS)*, that realizes active database functionalities for accessing and integrating heterogeneous information resources, such as relational databases, document databases or web services. The design of ADMIS is motivated by the current situation of the global development and evolution of WWW. To retrieve up-to-date information through information servers on the Internet, we have designed and implemented both an integration mechanism and an active database framework for heterogeneous information resources. ADMIS dynamically applies **reactive actions** to information resources according to changes of contents and situation on the Internet. Four distinguishing features of ADMIS are as follows:

Feature 1: ADMIS makes it possible to deal with heterogeneous information resources as a single active database, because ADMIS provides the active database functionalities over those information resources. **Even if those information resources are manipulated in passive systems, such as plain text files or web search engines**, ADMIS actively integrates those information resources in the framework of active database, because ADMIS provides the capability of accessing and integrating passive systems with the processes of condition evaluation or action execution.

Feature 2: ADMIS is a meta-level system, that is designed in an abstract and higher level layer of local information systems, and it is constructed independently of the local information systems. We do not take an approach to directly integrate legacy databases, but an approach that connects those databases to the meta-level system to indirectly integrate them [13]. To realize semantic interoperability of heterogeneous information resources, we have designed *relationship computation functions* that dynamically compute relationships between data values of heterogeneous information resources. We have already proposed methods for spatial and temporal database computations [8] and the framework for computing verbal context recognition [10, 13] for the relationship computational method.

Feature 3: ADMIS manages and executes active rules, called **Meta-Active rules** in the meta-level system. Meta-Active rules are triggered upon events on heterogeneous information resources. ADMIS provides event algebra in the meta-level layer to specify meta-level composite events which consist of local-level primitive events. Meta-Active rules need to react every local event and map it to the meta-level system. The meta-level system detects various meta-level events by applying meta-level event algebra to those events. ADMIS semantically evaluates conditions among heterogeneous information resources by applying the relationship computation functions to heterogeneous information resources in the meta-level layer. The most important feature of ADMIS is to realize both active database functionalities and database integration mechanisms in the meta-level system.

Feature 4: To achieve architecture independence and applicability of Meta-Active rules, we have designed a basic operation set (primitive set) of Meta-Active rules. Users can define Meta-Active rules with these primitive operators and the relationship computation functions. The system architecture of ADMIS reduces the implementation overhead to integrate heterogeneous information resources, even if information resources dynamically change.

Several active database systems for heterogeneous databases have been studied. For example, the paper [15] presented active database functionalities in the CORBA services, and this system realizes unified utilization for active database functionalities in the distributed and heterogeneous database environment. This system also includes the active database framework in information systems. The paper [9] presented a method to use heterogeneous legacy OODBs as active databases by implementing middlewares which interpret active rules. It defines data types and operations for spatial databases in the CORBA framework. This method also provides spatial database functionalities to the active databases. In those systems, active database functionalities are defined and implemented within a single database system. Therefore, those systems do not support the active rules, such as the meta-level composite events, the meta-level condition evaluation and the meta-level action execution, among heterogeneous databases. Although these systems provide the active database functionalities for individual databases, it is difficult to detect the events which occur among heterogeneous databases. It is also difficult to implement condition evaluation and action execution mechanisms among heterogeneous databases.

In the paper [16], we have proposed the active meta-level system that connects relational database systems as local information resources. In this paper, we present a system architecture of a meta-level active multidatabase system, that provides active database functionalities for accessing and integrating heterogeneous information resources.

2 An Example Application of ADMIS

To explain how ADMIS manages and executes the Meta-Active rules, we consider the situation that someone who wants to know the lowest price of a laptop PC writes a Meta-Active rule. This Meta-Active rule monitors the update of different on-line shopping sites, and integrates the price information of the laptop PC to retrieve the lowest and most recent price. When ADMIS accepts this Meta-Active rule, the event monitoring daemons required by the Meta-Active rule are invoked. If the price information is updated, the event monitoring daemons signal to the event manager of ADMIS server as shown in (1) of Figure 1. The event manager detects composite events from event log written by the event monitoring daemons ((2) of Figure 1). In order to retrieve the lowest price of the laptop PC, the condition evaluator integrates price information in the different on-line shopping sites ((3) of Figure 1). When the condition evaluator detects that the lowest price is updated, the action handler invokes the e-mail client to notify users that the lowest price of the laptop PC is updated ((4) of Figure 1). In this example, the database of Shop3 is passive, but ADMIS successfully integrates all three databases in an active database framework. We show the Meta-Active rule script for this application as follows:

```
DEFINE META RULE exprule
  ON update_on_shop1 OR update_on_shop2
  WHERE shop1.item == 'Laptop PC'
    OR shop2.item == 'Laptop PC'
    OR shop3.item == 'Laptop PC'
  DO select item, min(price)
    FROM
     (SELECT * FROM shop1
        UNION SELECT * FROM shop2
        UNION SELECT * FROM shop3)
    AS pricelist;
```

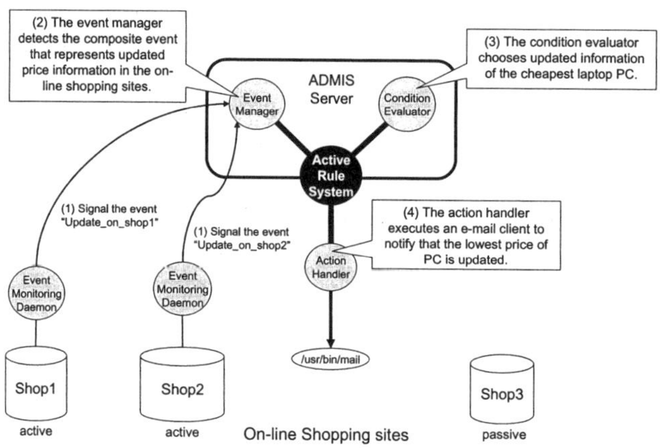

Figure 1: An Application for On-line shopping

3 Meta-Level Active Rule System

In order to realize an active rule system for the multidatabase environment, we have designed a Meta-Active rule language. The Meta-Active rule language is need to define rules which evaluates conditions among different legacy databases. The important feature of Meta-Active rules is that they specify events, conditions and actions in a meta-level, which corresponds to the higher level of local information resources, independently of the implementation of legacy information resources. In the meta-level layer, the events of rules are composed from different local events on heterogeneous information resources. The conditions of the Meta-Active rules are evaluated with semantic relationships between data values from heterogeneous information resources. The actions are executed as multidatabase commands over those heterogeneous information resources. The general form of Meta-Active rules is described in the following:

define meta rule *rule-name*
on event-expression
where condition
do action

The **on** clause specifies composite events that trigger rules. ADMIS provides a highly configurable event structure. Table 1 shows the basic event structure of Meta-Active rules. The **primitive event** is a fundamental element in Meta-Active rules, that simply represents the change of contents and situation in local information resources. To preserve architecture independency and extensibility of the event structure, we have designed an **abstract event** in event types, that is not related to any particular information resources. ADMIS accepts arbitrary events as abstract events defined by users or applications, because the abstract event structure provides capabilities to define/detect composite events which consists of various events in local information resources. **Composite event** consists of the primitive events. ADMIS applies the *event algebra* [18] to the primitive events in the meta-level layer to create a new composite event as shown in Figure 2. ADMIS provides five operators: *And, Or, Not, Repeat* and *Cycle*. The most important point of this approach is that all events, which occur in different information systems, are mapped to the meta-level system, which detects the meta-level events by applying meta-level event algebra to those mapped events. This approach makes it possible to detect various composite events independently of implementation of heterogeneous information resources.

Table 1: Summary of Event Structure

Category	Instantiation	illustration
Primitive Event	Abstract	External Event, Application Defined Event
Composite Event	Abstract	Composite of Abstract Primitive Event
Event Algebra	And	When two events occur.
	Or	When one of events occur.
	Not	When an event does not occur.
	Repeat	When an event repeatedly occurs.
	Cycle	When an event periodically occurs.

The **where** clause specifies conditions among legacy information resources. To realize semantic interoperability among those heterogeneous information resources, ADMIS provides *relationship computational functions*. Users can specify relationships among those heterogeneous information resources by using various relationship computational functions and their parameters. For example, a spacial condition *"A distance_less_than(r) B"* represents that a distance between A and B is less than *"r"*. In this case, *"distance_less_than()"* is the relationship computation function, and *"r"* is its relationship parameter. By applying those relationship computation functions dynamically to heterogeneous information resources, ADMIS semantically evaluate conditions among those information resources.

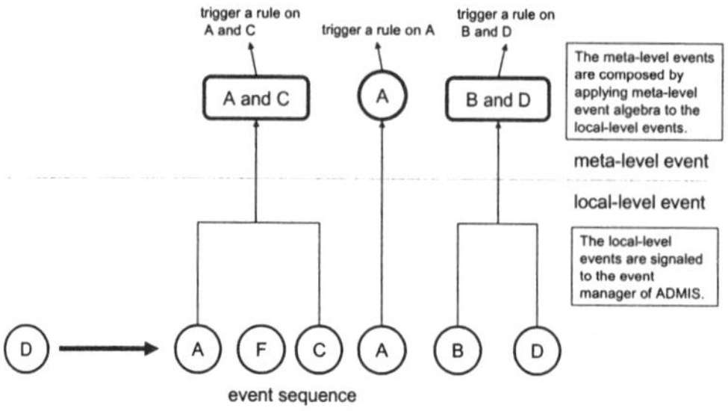

Figure 2: Meta-level Event Detection

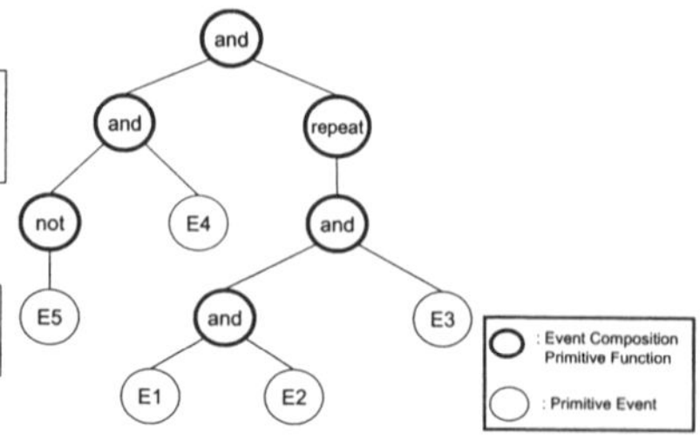

Figure 3: Tree Structure Representation of Composite Event "repeat((E1 and E2) or E3) and ((not E5) and E4)"

The **do** clause specifies an action to be performed when a rule fires. The action corresponds to a multidatabase query or information notification commands. ADMIS provides the primitive operators to specify actions.

The important feature of the Meta-Active rule is that ADMIS supports three different opportunities to integrate information resources: the integration of event detection using the meta-level event algebra, the integration of semantic condition evaluation using relationship computation functions, and the integration of action execution with multidatabase queries. This feature makes ADMIS feasible and flexible, which integrates heterogeneous information resources in the framework of an active database.

3.1 Knowledge Model of Meta-Active Rule

Table 2 shows the knowledge model of Meta Active rules, based on the fundamental knowledge model of active database systems [18]. We extend the conventional knowledge model to create a knowledge model for adjusting it to a multidatabase environment. By this extension, our knowledge model can be applied to a multidatabase environment that the conventional knowledge model does not support.

Table 2: Summary of the Knowledge Model

Category	Feature	Instantiation
Event	Type	{Primitive, Composite}
	Source	Abstract
	Granularity	Arbitrary
	Role	Mandatory
Conditions	Role	Optional
	Context	DB_C
Action	Options	External, Structure Operation
	Context	DB_A

We have designed the **abstract event** in the event type, that is not related to any particular information resources. Users and applications can define their own events as abstract events.

ADMIS provides the capability to evaluate conditions among heterogeneous information resources. ADMIS deal with the DB_C database context without supporting transaction processing in a multidatabase environment. DB_C means the state of database in a condition evaluation phase.

As an action, ADMIS executes multidatabase queries or external programs, such as /usr/bin/perl, /usr/bin/mail and /bin/sh to push required information to users. DB_A means the state of database in an action execution phase.

3.2 Primitive Operators for the Meta-Level Active Rule System

As a basic operation set of the proposed multidatabase system, we define a primitive set in the meta-level system. The primitive operation set is independent of legacy information systems implementation. We implement each primitive operation as a function, and these primitives are called *primitive functions*. The Meta-Active rule is described in a high-level declarative language. A rule processor of the system transforms it into an equivalent sequence of low-level primitive functions. Since the system interprets those primitive functions in a framework of functional computation [7], the meta-level multidatabase query is easily evaluated in a distributed and parallel processing environment. We have designed and implemented the primitive functions for meta-level active database functionalities as follows:

AP1: $composite\_event(EV_1^{in}, EV_2^{in}, q) \rightarrow EV^{out}$

AP1 is a primitive function for defining composite events in the meta-level system. This function accepts two meta-level event definitions "EV_1^{in}" and "EV_2^{in}", and the meta-level event algebra "q" which represents a relationship between "EV_1^{in}" and "EV_2^{in}". As shown in Figure 3, ADMIS defines a meta-level event as a tree structure. This function returns a tree structured meta-level event "EV^{out}". By recursively applying the *composite_event* function to this structure, we can define various composite events in the meta-level. We show an example of this function call is shown as follows:

```
composite_event('update_on_d1', 'clicked_on_d2' AND) -> EV1;
composite_event(EV1, 'error_on_d3', OR) -> EV2;
```

This example uses the event algebra AND and OR to describe a composite event.

AP2: $detect\_event(EV, ES) \rightarrow boolean$

AP2 is a primitive function to detect a primitive or composite meta-level event. "EV" is a tree structured meta-level event definition which is composed by the function *composite_event*. As shown in Figure 2, "ES" is the history data of primitive events notified to the meta-level system. By comparing "EV" and "ES" in the meta-level system, ADMIS can detect various composite events that are composed from events in different information resources independently of the implementation of those information resources.

AP3: $notify\_event(EV)$

AP3 notifies an event "EV" to the meta-level system when the specified event occurs. The event monitoring daemons use this function, but users do not directly use this function. Every event used in ADMIS is mapped to the meta-level system by this function. We show an example of this function call is shown as follows:

```
notify_event('update_on_r1')
```

This example notifies the event 'update_on_r1'. Any Meta-Active rule that requires this event can be fired.

AP4: $register\_event(EV)$

AP4 is a primitive function for registering events to be monitored. If this function is called, the specified event monitoring daemon starts the monitoring session. When the event occurs, the event monitoring daemon calls the $notify\_event$ function.

AP5: $semantic\_eval\_cond(V_1^{in}, V_2^{in}, F(r)) \rightarrow boolean$

AP5 is a primitive function for evaluating conditions. By applying a relationship computation function "$F()$" and its semantic parameter "r", the *semantic_eval_cond* function computes relationships between two data sets "V_1^{in}" and "V_2^{in}". This function returns the true value if the condition of "$F(r)$" is satisfied with the relationship between "V_1^{in}" and "V_2^{in}". For example, the function call "$semantic\_eval\_cond(R_1, R_2, distance\_lt(10))$" means that the data sets "R_1" and "R_2" are spatial data, and the distance between "R_1" and "R_2" is less than 10 meters. To realize semantic interoperability among heterogeneous information resources, **ADMIS dynamically computes relationships among those information resources, by applying various relationship computation functions**. This is the most important feature of the mechanism for evaluating conditions in ADMIS.

AP6: $exec\_action(handler, args) \rightarrow Integer$

AP6 is a primitive function for action execution. This function executes external programs with several arguments. This function accepts a file system path of "$handler$" and arguments for its "$args$". This function returns a return value of the executed program. An example of this function call is shown as follows:

```
exec_action('/usr/bin/perl',
  '/home/bob/scripts/mailto kurabaya@sfc.keio.ac.jp')
```

This example executes /usr/bin/perl to send an e-mail.

3.3 Rule Execution

This section explains semantics of rule execution in ADMIS. We have designed ADMIS for applying it to the retrieval operations on multiple and heterogeneous information resources. The primitive operators for accessing databases are designed for retrieving. Any updating operation is not supported. The Meta-Active rules, given as a set of primitive operations, do not include updating operations and do not cause any updating conflicts among themselves. The knowledge model does not cause any updating conflicts among the Meta-Active rules.

As shown in Figure 4, the rule system of ADMIS is composed of four modules: a rule parser, an event manager, a rule manager, and a primitive interpreter manager. The rule parser analyzes a Meta-Active rule and register the parsed rule to the rule manager. The rule parser transforms an event expression specified in the "on" clause into primitive functions. For example, the event expression "(E1 and E2) or E3" is transformed as follows:

```
composite_event(E1, E2, and)->ME1;
composite_event(ME1, E3, or)->ME2;
```

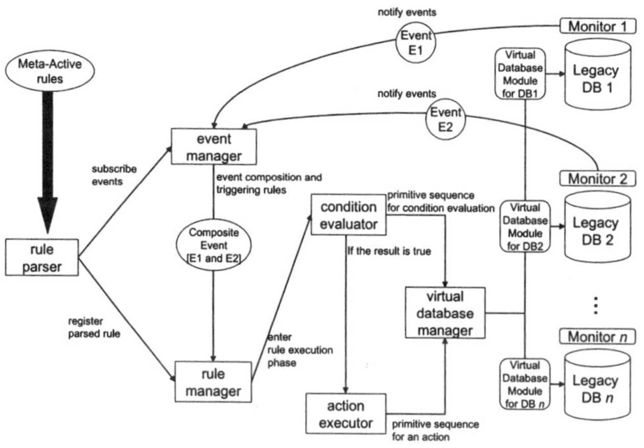

Figure 4: Rule System Architecture

The rule parser also registers events that trigger the rule to the event manager. The primitive sequence created by the above translation process is registered to the event manager. The rule parser also transforms a condition expression and an action command into primitive sequences.

To detect meta-level events, the event manager calls the function "$detect\_event(EV, ES)$". When it detects meta-level events, the event manager notifies the rule manager to trigger Meta-Active rules. The rule manager evaluates conditions among heterogeneous information resources by using the condition evaluator and the action executor. To evaluate conditions semantically, the condition evaluator uses the function "$semantic\_eval\_cond(V_1^{in}, V_2^{in}, F(r))$". If the result of condition evaluation is "true", the action executor executes the function "$exec\_action(handler, args)$".

4 The Design and Concept of ADMIS System Architecture

The main feature of ADMIS is that ADMIS provides both information integration mechanisms and active database functionalities in the meta-level system. In this section, we present the meta-level architecture for active integration of heterogeneous information resources.

4.1 The System Architecture

Figure 5 shows the system overview of the ADMIS architecture. As shown in Figure 5, ADMIS consists of four components:

Event Manager: The event manager records an event-log and detects a composite event among heterogeneous information resources. ADMIS provides a reactive event detection mechanism where each event source notifies occurrences of events to the event manager. The event manager has capability of detecting composite events that are composed with primitive

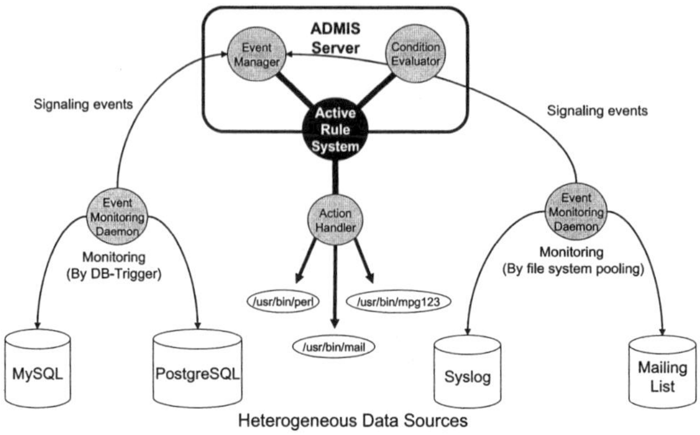

Figure 5: ADMIS System Architecture

events of different information resources. To detect various composite events, ADMIS provides primitive operators and *the meta-level event algebra*. Users can describe the composite events with the event algebra.

Condition Evaluator: This subsystem evaluates conditions among the integrated information resources. ADMIS dynamically integrates heterogeneous information resources, in according with active rules given by users.

Action Handler: The action handler executes multidatabase queries, external programs or internal special commands with a specific security policy. In the design of ADMIS, we assumed that the applications of ADMIS are related to the provisions of up-to-date information, such as the example shown earlier to find the lowest price or an intelligent navigation system in the mobile computing environment. We did not intend to develop conventional applications of active databases, such as maintenance of integrity constraints. By this design principle, ADMIS provides flexibility to execute actions with invocation of the external programs for the information provision.

Event Monitoring Daemons: ADMIS provides a reactive event detection mechanism. When an event occurs in legacy databases, the event monitoring daemons signal to the event manager as shown in Figure 6. The event manager adds the signaled events to the event log. ADMIS can accept any information system that is capable of signaling to the event manager, even if the information system has poor computation resources, such as GPS, PDA or a cellular phone. To realize such a flexible architecture of the event monitoring daemons, we have implemented a three-layer model of the event monitoring daemons as shown in Figure 6. The bottom layer of the event monitoring daemons represents a mechanism for monitoring a specific information resource, such as a database trigger or a file system monitoring mechanisms provided by an operating system kernel. The middle layer represents an access method to the bottom layer, such as database connection libraries or file I/O libraries. The top layer represents an event notification module provided by ADMIS. This layer is common to all event monitoring daemons.

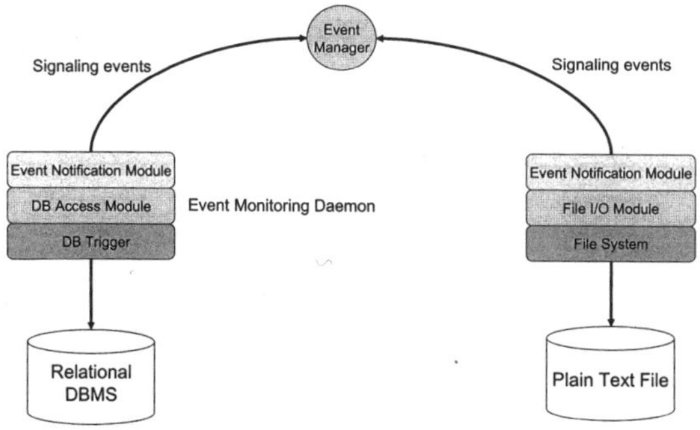

Figure 6: A Three Layer Architecture of Event Monitoring Daemons

One of the important advantages of this architecture is to reduce I/O overhead between the meta-level system and the event monitoring daemons. We can reduce the I/O overhead, by tightly coupling the bottom layer of the event monitoring daemon onto a legacy information system. And, we can construct flexible and reusable event monitoring daemons by loosely coupling event monitoring daemons. Naturally, flexibility and performance are under the trade-off relationship. We should choose s tight or loose coupling carefully, depending on the frequency of updating or scale of information resources. This three-layer model makes the event monitoring daemons flexible and portable.

5 System Implementation

In this section, we describe the system implementation of ADMIS. As shown in Figure 7, we have implemented ADMIS by using the PostgreSQL server [19], which is currently one of the typical open source ORDBMS's. The reason for using PostgreSQL is that the implementation for source codes of ADMIS can be supported by using the relational algebra and triggers provided by PostgreSQL. We have implemented our system in C language. The amount of source codes for the system proposed as a multidatabase system in the paper [16] is approximately 6,500 lines in the Java language. The mechanisms of the extensible SQL are useful to implement ADMIS.

5.1 Semantic Interoperability in Virtual Database

To realize transparent data accesses to remote information resources in the conventional ORDBMS, we propose a concept of **virtual database**, that is used for giving a view for remote and heterogeneous information resources. The virtual database gives abstraction of access methods to remote information resources by view mechanisms provided by the conventional ORDBMS. As shown in Figure 10, an integrated schema is available and accessible as views that are defined as virtual databases. When a user gives a query to those virtual databases, the query is rewritten as a new query that contains connection/retrieval procedures to remote information resources. ADMIS provides capability for extension of local information resources by using the pluggable modules called *access drivers* which include the access/retrieval pro-

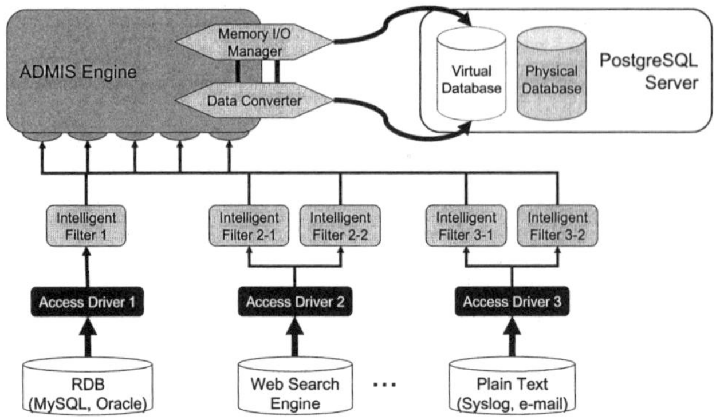

Figure 7: Implemented System

cedures to information resources. To integrate schema-less information resources, such as plain texts or HTML files, we have designed *an intelligent filter* that organizes local data into a relation in the conventional ORDBMS. The intelligent filter also converts data types. To realize flexible and portable conversion of data types, the access drivers create local data as an ASCII text form, not as a binary form. Users can apply various data formatting/converting functions to those ASCII text data to convert those data into complex objects, such as a 2D Point type or a Box Region type. Users can also apply aggregation functions in SQL to the virtual databases. In addition, users can apply existing database applications, such as SQL clients, OLAP engines and database visualization utilities, to the virtual databases. Figure 8 shows the relationship among the three components in a manner of traditional three-level schema architecture of DBMS. By these virtual database mechanisms, we realize transparent accesses to remote and heterogeneous information resources in conventional ORDBMS.

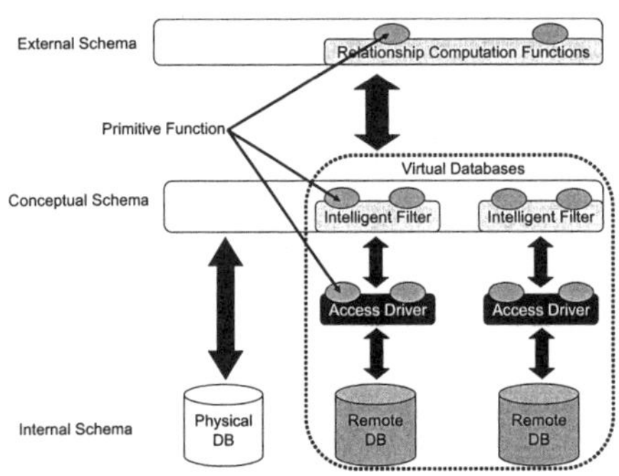

Figure 8: Three Level Schema Architecture

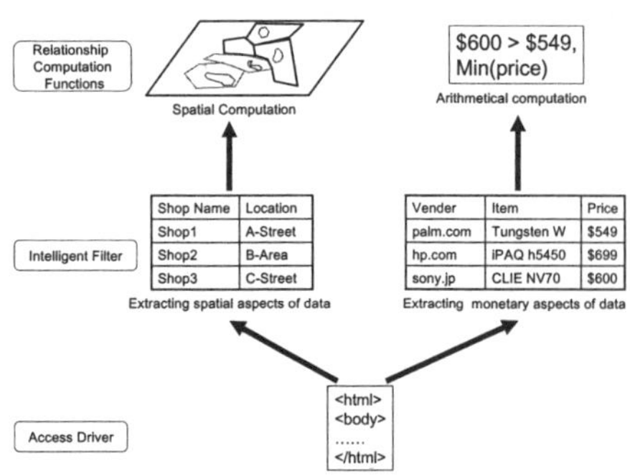

Figure 9: Data Flow

5.2 Access Driver Mechanism

To integrate heterogeneous information resources, we have designed an abstract access driver mechanism that is specialized for a multidatabase environment. This driver mechanism provides a highly abstract interface to heterogeneous information resources. ADMIS loads an appropriate access driver according to a database URL given by users. For example, when a user connects to PostgreSQL server on 192.168.0.1, the user gives the database URL "virtualdb:postgresql://192.168.0.1/sampledb". We define the format of database URL as follows:

```
protocol:sub protocol://{host name | IP address}/database name
```

To connect to different databases, a user changes a sub protocol name. When a user connects to the Google web search engine, the database URL is given as "virtualdb:google:// www.google.com/". When a user connects to a CSV file, the database URL is given as "virtualdb:csv:// localhost/home/foo/data.csv".

5.3 Intelligent Filter

ADMIS provides an intelligent filter to integrate information resources that are created based on heterogeneous data models. The intelligent filter creates a schema of the virtual database with the access driver and formatting/converting functions. To realize transparency with the relational model in PostgreSQL, we have implemented the intelligent filter with the view mechanism and the query rewriting system of PostgreSQL. In a multidatabase environment, it is difficult for access drivers to provide the unified data conversion mechanism, because those access drivers are commonly used by all applications that require different data conversion mechanisms. The intelligent filter provides customizable data conversion mechanisms for each application. We show example of data mapping as follows:

```
select  vdb_attr(shadow.ptr, 0)::text as rname,
   vdb_attr(shadow.ptr, 1)::text as outflow,
   vdb_attr(shadow.ptr, 2)::integer as len,
   vdb_attr(shadow.ptr, 3)::integer as basin,
   vdb_attr(shadow.ptr, 4)::integer as rate
from (select
  virtualdb('virtualdb:mysql://localhost/dbc', 'shuichi', 'mysql',
      'select rname, outflow, len, basin, rate from river')
as ptr) as shadow;
```

The implementation of functions used in the example is as follows:

ICP1: *virtualdb(URL, USER, PASS, QUERY, FILTER) → ConnectionHandle*

This function connects to remote information resources by using an appropriate connection driver, and returns a pointer to the connected object. We show an example for connecting to the Google web search engine and submitting a query "Multidatabase and Active" as follows:

```
virtualdb('virtualdb:google://www.google.com', '', '',
    'Multidatabase+Active', 'Google2Table')
```

ICP2: *vdb_attr(ConnectionHandle, Index) → Value*

This function retrieves a value through *ConnectionHandle* using a value index. We show an example that retrieves a value, named "outflow," from ConnectionHandle shadow.ptr, and converts the value as a text.

```
vdb_attr(shadow.ptr, 1)::text as outflow,
```

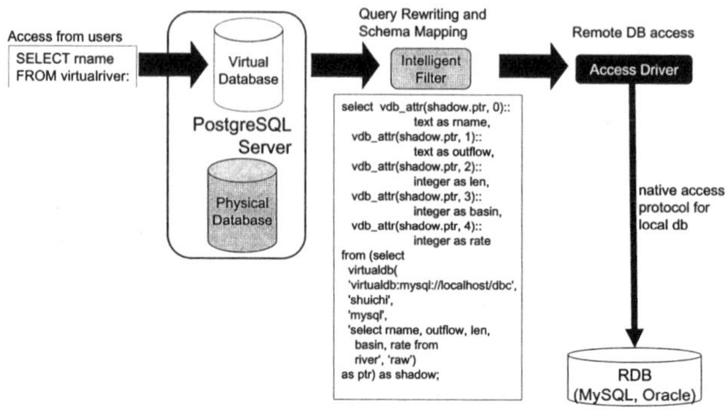

Figure 10: Query Rewriting for Remote Information Resources

6 Experiments

We have performed two experiments to clarify feasibility and effectiveness of our meta-level system. We have designed an experimental environment to show the execution process of Meta-Active rules by ADMIS.

6.1 Experiment-1

We have performed the experiment for executing an actual Meta-Active rule in ADMIS. The aim of this experiment is to clarify the feasibility and availability of ADMIS by showing the detail of our system processes. We have implemented three local information resources and an active rule in the experimental environment.

- **Local Information Resources**

  We have connected the following two relational database systems and a web search engine to ADMIS.

  (LDB_1) PostgreSQL V7.2.1

  (LDB_2) MySQL V3.23.49

  (LDB_3) Google (www.google.com)

  We have generated sample data, and stored them into LDB_1 and LDB_2. These data consist of two text string attributes, and those attributes are named "title" and "location". The "title" attribute represents a location name, and the "location" attribute represents a geographical place with x and y axis values. The followings are sample data of those local databases.

name	location
KEIO UNIVERSITY SHONAN-FUJISAWA CAMPUS	(50, 10)
The Tokyo City Kanasogi elementary school	(100, 200)
Ota-City Syosen Elementary School	(20, 10)

LDB_3 is one of the most famous web search engines. We have implemented the access driver for Google to connect it into ADMIS. By applying the intelligent filter shown in Section 5, LDB_3 will have a relational schema as follows:

title	URL
European Japanese Conference on Information Modeling and ...	www.pori.tut.fi/ hj/ejc/

- **Meta-Active rule**

  We have applied the following Meta-Active rule to ADMIS. This rule detects the composite event "insert_on_ldb1 AND delete_on_ldb2" which means that the update operation occurred in LDB_1 and the delete operation occurred in LDB_2. When the composite event is detected, ADMIS checks conditions "ldb1.location distance_lt(10) ldb2.location AND ldb1.name == ldb3.title ". These conditions mean that the distance between the locations of LDB_1 and LDB_2 is less than 10 meters. The location of LDB_1 is restricted by the result obtained from LDB_3.

```
DEFINE META RULE exprule
  ON update_on_ldb1 AND insert_on_ldb2
  WHERE ldb1.location distance_lt(10) ldb2.location
    AND ldb1.name == ldb3.title
  DO 'benchmark';
```

As shown in Section 3, ADMIS executes Meta-Active rules by the six steps. All the active database operations of ADMIS are implemented as primitive functions. To process the Meta-Active rules, ADMIS interprets those primitive functions.

Step-1 Parsing Rule: If the Meta-Active rule is submitted for execution, ADMIS parses the Meta-Active rule. The parser module generates the primitive sequence shown in Section 3.2. The Meta-Active rule is parsed into three primitive sequences: event detection sequence, condition evaluation sequence and action sequence.

Step-2 Register Monitoring Events: The following event detection sequence is registered in the event manager.

```
register_event(update_on_ldb1);
register_event(insert_on_ldb2);
composite_event(update_on_ldb1, insert_on_ldb2, and)->E1;
```

The event manager interprets the primitive sequence and invokes event monitoring daemons for each local information resource.

Step-3 Event Signaling: If events occur, the event monitoring daemons signal to the event manager by using the primitive function $notify\_event()$ as follows:

```
notify_event(update_on_ldb1);
notify_event(insert_on_ldb2);
```

Step-4 Event Detection: The event manager detects meta-level composite events by applying the *detect_event* primitive function to event sequence which is signaled by the event monitoring daemons. When the *detect_event* primitive function returns "true", the event manager triggers the Meta-Active rule.

Step-5 Condition Evaluation: When the Meta-Active rule is triggered, the condition evaluator executes the condition evaluation primitive sequence. In the process of condition evaluation, ADMIS integrates heterogeneous information resources by applying the relationship computation function to those information resources. In this case, "*distance_lt*()" is the relationship computation function, which evaluates whether the distance between "ldb1.location" and "ldb2.location" is less than 10km. The primitive sequence for condition evaluation is described as follows:

```
open(ldb1, place1)->DB1;
open(ldb2, place2)->DB2;
open(ldb3, web)->DB3;

join(place1, location, place2, location, distance_lt(10))->R1;
join(R1, name, DB3, title, =)->R2;
```

The primitive function *open*() is used to establish a connection to local information resources, and to retrieve the required data. The implementation of this function is provided by each access driver for local information resources.

Step-6 Action Execution: As an action, the action handler executes multidatabase queries, external programs and internal special commands. In this case, the action handler executes the internal special command "*benchmark*" to record the benchmark of this rule.

6.2 Experiment-2

We have performed an experiment to clarify feasibility and effectiveness of our meta-level system in the view point of system performance. In this experiment, we have used ADMIS and the Meta-Active rule used in Experiment-1, and have measured the system performance in processing the Meta-Active rule. We examine the time when the last event is notified to the meta-level system and the corresponding action is executed. The aim of the study is to show that ADMIS actively integrates heterogeneous information resources with practical performance for realizing the active multidatabase environment. We have implemented ADMIS on a PC/AT compatible machine whose specification is as follows:

Category	Instantiation
CPU	Intel Mobile Pentium4 1.6GHz
Main Memory	512MB
Hard Disk	IDE 40GB (5,400rpm, UltraATA100, 16MB Cache)
NIC	100Base-TX
OS	Linux Kernel version 2.4.18
File System	ext3

Figure 11 shows the average elapsed time for processing the Meta-Active rule. In this graph, the horizontal axis represents the number of tuples in each local information resource, and the vertical axis represents the average elapsed time for processing the Meta-Active rule. Our system processed the Meta-Active rule for 100,000 tuples in 2.2 seconds per each local DB. This experimental result shows feasibility and effectiveness of ADMIS for integrating heterogeneous information resources.

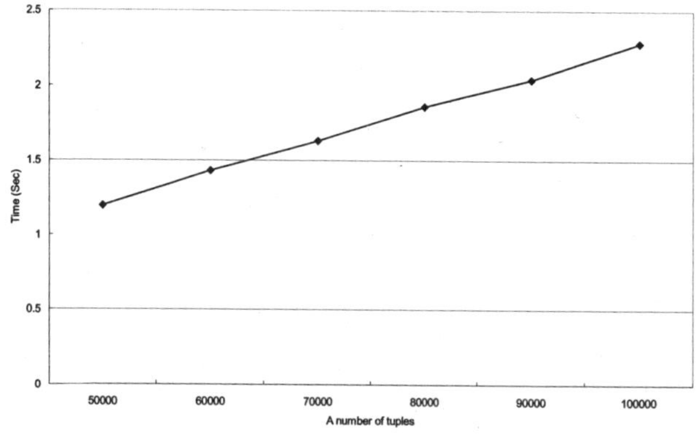

Figure 11: System Performance

7 Conclusion

In this paper, we have presented the active multidatabase system architecture which realizes the meta-level database retrieval and integration mechanisms, called ADMIS. ADMIS provides an execution framework of active rules in the meta-level system. The most important feature of ADMIS is to realize the active database functionalities for heterogeneous information resources, even if the information resources are manipulated by passive systems.

We have implemented the ADMIS architecture, and clarified feasibility and effectiveness of meta-level active database functionalities through the experimental study in the view point of processing time. As the future work, we will develop actual applications related to mobile computing or ad-hoc network environment and we will analyze the system performance on practical application environments.

Acknowledgments
We acknowledge with the gratitude contribution of Naoki Ishibashi (Graduate School of Media and Governance, Keio University) for his valuable and helpful comments for this study.

References

[1] J. F. Allen, "Maintaining Knowledge about Temporal Intervals", *Communications of the ACM*, No. 26, 1983, 832–843.

[2] C. Batini, M. Lenzerini and S.B. Navathe, "A comparative analysis of methodologies for database schema integration", *ACM Computing Surveys*, Vol. 18, No. 4, 1986, 324–364.

[3] A. Bouguettaya, B. Benatallah and A. Elgermid, "An Overview of Multidatabase Systems: Past and Present", In A. Elgermid, M. Rukinkiewiez, and A. Sheth (Ed.), *Management of Heterogeneous and Autonomous Database Systems*, Morgan Kaufmann, 1998, 1–27.

[4] M. W. Bright, A. R. Hurson and S. Pakzad, A Taxonomy and Current Issues in Multidatabase Systems, *Computer*, Vol. 25, No. 3, 1992, 50–60.

[5] K. R. Dittrich, S. Gatziu and A. Geppert, "The Active Database Management System Manifesto: A Rule-base of ADBMS Features", *Proc. 2nd International Workshop on Rules in Databases (RIDS)*, Athens, September 1995, 101–115. Springer-Verlag LNCS-985.

[6] M. J. Egenhofer, "Spatial Relations: Models, Inferences, and their Future Application", *Proceedings of Advanced Database Symposium, Tokyo, Japan, December 2-4*, 1996.

[7] Y. Hosokawa and Y. Kiyoki, "Functional and parallel query processing and query optimization for multidatabase systems", *Proc. the 17 the IASTED International Conference on Applied Informatics*, Austria, 1999, 101–106.

[8] N. Ishibashi, Y. Hosokawa and Y. Kiyoki, "A Spatial and Temporal Data Integration Method for Heterogeneous Database Environments", *Proceedings of the IASTED International Conference on APPLIED INFORMATICS Symposium 2. Networks, Parallel and Distributed Processing, and Applications*, 2001, 323–330.

[9] K. C. Kim, S. B. Yoo, K. W. Ko and S. K. Cha, "Active System for Heterogeneous ODBMS Using Mobile Rule Codes", *ADBIS-DASFAA 2000*, Prague, Czech Republic, September 5-8, 2000, 93–106.

[10] T. Kitagawa and Y. Kiyoki, "The mathematical model of meaning and its application to multidatabase systems", *Proc. 3rd IEEE Int. Workshop on Research Issues on Data Engineering: Interoperability in Multidatabase Systems*, 1993, 130–135.

[11] Y. Kiyoki and T. Kitagawa, "Application of a Semantic Associative Search Method to Multidatabases for Environmental Information," Information Modelling and Knowledge Bases (IOS Press), Vol. XI, May, 1999.

[12] Y. Kiyoki, T. Kitagawa and T. Hayama, "A metadatabase system for semantic image search by a mathematical model of meaning", *ACM SIGMOD Record*, Vol.23, No.4, pp.34–41, Dec. 1994.

[13] Y. Kiyoki, T. Kitagawa and Y. Hitomi, "A fundamental framework for realizing semantic interoperability in a multidatabase environment", *Journal of Integrated Computer-Aided Engineering*, Vol. 2, No. 1(Special Issue on Multidatabase and Interoperable Systems), John Wiley & Sons, Jan. 1995, 3–20.

[14] Y. Kiyoki, A. Miyagawa and T. Kitagawa, "A multiple view mechanism with semantic learning for multidatabase environments," Information Modelling and Knowledge Bases (IOS Press), Vol. IX, May, 1997.

[15] A. Koschel, R. Kramer, G. V. Bultzingsloewen, T. Bleibel, P. Krumlinde, S. Schmuck and C. Weinand, "Configurable Active Functionality for CORBA", *11th ECOOP'97 Workshop #7: CORBA: Implementation, Use, and Evaluation.* Jyvaskyla, Finland, June 10th, 1997.

[16] S. Kurabayashi, N. Ishibashi and Y. Kiyoki, "A Multidatabase System Architecture for Integrating Heterogeneous Databases with Meta-Level Active Rule Primitives", Proceedings of the 20th IASTED International Conference on Applied Informatics, 2002, 378–387.

[17] L.V.S. Lakshmanan, F. Sadri and S.N. Subramanian: "SchemaSQL–An Extension to SQL for Multidatabase Interoperability", *ACM Transactions on Database Systems*, Vol. 26, No. 4, December 2001, 476–519.

[18] N. W. Paton, and O. Diaz, "Active Database System", *ACM Computing Surveys*, Vol. 31, No. 1, 1999, 63–103.

[19] PostgreSQL, PostgreSQL Global Development Group, http://www.postgresql.org.

Information Modelling and Knowledge Bases XV
Y. Kiyoki et al. (Eds.)
IOS Press, 2004

A Computational Method for Spatial and Temporal Equivalence with Context Recognition Functions for Document Databases

YOSHIHIDE HOSOKAWA † and YASUSHI KIYOKI ‡
† Department of Electrical & Computer Engineering, Nagoya Institute of Technology
‡ Faculty of Environmental Information, KEIO University

Abstract. In this paper, we present a new computational method for spatial and temporal equivalence with context recognition functions for document databases.

There are two types of spatial and temporal representations: (type-1) a coordinate representation (C) like (x, y), and (type-2) a pair of a context and a coordinate representation (CX, C). The type-2 representation points out a region where the boundary is dynamically defined by a context 'CX'. The feature of the type-2 representation is to include the context information for computing spatial and temporal equivalence in a context-dependent way. By introducing context information, type-2 representations are more expressive than type-1 representations.

In our method, spatial and temporal equivalence is computed between the type-2 'A' and the type-2 'B' when A.CX = B.CX $\wedge$ A.C = B.C. We define the process for computing A.CX = B.CX, as 'context recognition'. Our method makes it possible to extend the applicable scope of existing databases to that with spatial and temporal contexts.

We clarify the feasibility and effectiveness of our method by showing several experimental results.

1 Introduction

Information resources with spatial and temporal representations are increasing in a wide area computer network. Spatial and temporal computation technology can be applied to information retrieval for those resources from spatial and temporal viewpoints.

In this paper, we present a new computational method for spatial and temporal equivalence between spatial and temporal representations in the information resources.

We classify spatial and temporal representations into the following two types, and propose a new computational method for spatial and temporal equivalence between type-2 representations.

Type-1 (C)

This type is used to describe a region in a spatial or temporal space. The region is defined as a finite set of boundaries. The region is also described as a set of coordinate values 'C'. We define 'C' as 'a coordinate representation'.

Type-2 (CX, C)

This type is used to describe a region where the boundary is dynamically defined by a context 'CX'. The feature of this type is to include the context information for computing spatial and temporal equivalence in a context-dependent way.

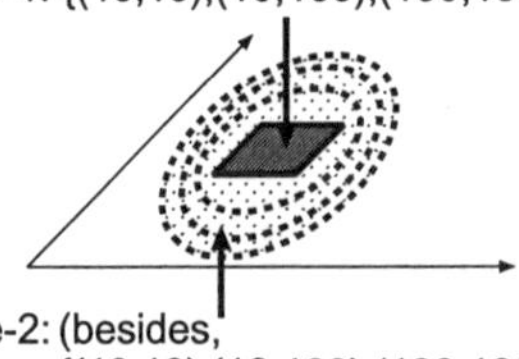

Figure 1: Type-2 and its location

Figure 1 shows type-1 and type-2 representations in a 2-dimensional space. In this figure, the type-1 representation strictly defines a rectangle by the boundary. The type-2 representation defines a area around the rectangle. It is difficult to define the area by using a finite set of boundaries (the broken lines in the figure). By using various contexts, we can fix the boundary of the area around the rectangle. By introducing context information, type-2 representations are more expressive than type-1 representations.

In our method, spatial and temporal equivalence is computed between the type-2 'A' and the type-2 'B' when A.CX = B.CX $\wedge$ A.C = B.C. We define a process for recognizing A.CX = B.CX, as 'context recognition'.

Temporal relationships for type-1 representations have been described in [1, 10]. Spatial relationships for type-1 representations have been described in [2]. A spatial and temporal data integration method among heterogeneous legacy databases has been presented in [5]. Those conventional computational methods mainly use type-1 representations for spatial and temporal relationships[1, 2, 5, 10].

Our method makes it possible to extend the applicable scope of existing databases to that with spatial and temporal contexts.

The main features of our method are summarized as follows.

(1) A practical context recognition

Our method is used for practical context recognition with type-2 representations. This method realizes 'prepositional-phrase-based context recognition' for type-2 representations.

We focus on contexts related to prepositional phrases. The location (the meaning) of a type-2 representation changes according to interpretations for the prepositional phrases.

As shown in Figure 2, our method recognizes that (Document-A) and (Document-B) give the same meaning about the park, and (Document-C) gives the different meaning about the park from (Document-A) and (Document-B).

We show availability and effectiveness of our method by several experiments.

(2) A semantic recognition on equivalence between contexts without describing explicit semantic equivalence

Our method is used for computing semantic equivalence between contexts without describing explicit semantic equivalence.

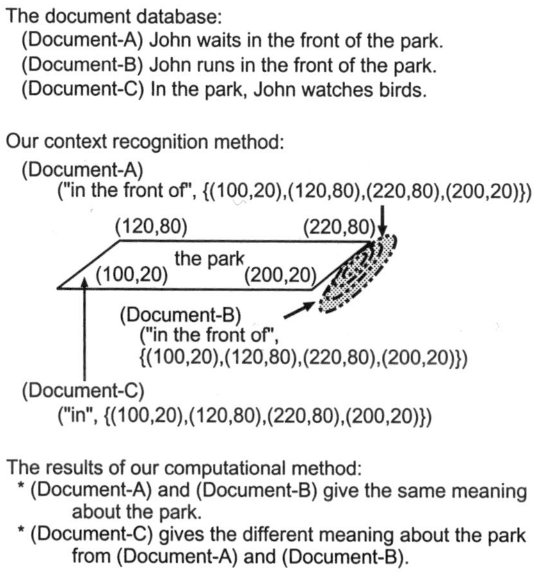

Figure 2: Our approach for computing spatial equivalence in a document database

Many methods for computing semantic equivalence have been proposed. Thesaurus, Ontology and the Mathematical Model of Meaning [7, 8] have been designed as computational methods for semantic equivalence.

By cooperating with those methods, our method can compute semantic equivalence between contexts without describing explicit semantic equivalence.

(3) A language-independent context recognition

Our method can be applied to type-2 representations described in any language, because our method uses conventional methods for computing semantic equivalence.

2 Related Work

A computational method for spatial predicates by using a natural language has been designed in [3]. This method has contributed to simple manipulation for geographic information systems by using a natural language. Our method is designed to compute semantic equivalence for type-2 representations. Our method makes it possible to extend the applicable scope of existing databases to that with spatial and temporal contexts.

Some spatial and temporal information retrieval systems for document data have been developed in [9, 11]. Those systems have been developed to compute similarity among document data by spatial and temporal terms of the document data. Our method can compute spatial and temporal equivalence between document data by supporting the type-2 representations appearing in the document data.

In terms of context recognition, the Mathematical Model of Meaning[7, 8] has been developed to compute semantic equivalence and similarity among words dynamically, according to a given context. Our method is designed to identify the same type-2 representations with different context representations.

3 A computational method for spatial and temporal equivalence for type-2 representations

Our method computes spatial and temporal equivalence between type-2 representations by the following procedure.

(Step-1) Context recognition for type-2 representations

This step evaluates A.CX = B.CX by A.CX ∈ X, and it computes A.CX ∈ X by using a simple pattern matching technique, where X is a set of contexts with the same meaning as B.CX.

In this step, our method recognizes semantic equivalence between contexts with different representations.

Figure 3 shows that our method identifies type-2 representations with the same context.

Thesaurus, Ontology and the Mathematical Model of Meaning [7, 8] have been designed as computational methods for semantic equivalence. By computing A.CX ∈ X by using those methods, our method can compute semantic equivalence between contexts automatically.

(Step-2) Location recognition for type-2 representations

In this step, our method computes A.C = B.C by using the spatial and temporal boolean operator f_c(A.C,u_c) described in [1, 2].

The spatial and temporal relationships between type-1 representations can define a set of the coordinate representations with the same meaning as B.C in a continuous space.

In Figure 3, there are infinite points in the given rectangle, and the user describes all of the points by using the spatial operator 'contains' for type-1 representations. Our method can select only correct locations in the given rectangle, from the results of (Step-1).

By applying the conventional spatial operator to 'Type-2' in Figure 3, four locations in the rectangle are selected. Two of the four locations are not suited to the context. Our method makes it possible to select type-2 representations only corresponding to a user's context.

3.1 The data structure of a type-2 representation

Our method represents 'CX' in a variable-length array of characters.

Our method also represents 'C' in the data structures of the spatial and temporal operators described in [1, 2].

This figure shows the procedure for recognizing an area around the buildings in a given rectangle.
The conditions of the recognition are as follows:
(1) Type-2.CX is one of the following contexts: 'in the front of', 'besides' and 'behind'.
(2) contains({S2dVr,(10,10),(50,50)},Type-2.C) = true.
'Type-2' shows a set of locations on the 2D space.
'Contains' shows a spatial operator for type-1 representations in [2], and returns 'true' when the second input is the interior of the first input.
The given rectange {S2dVr,(10,10),(50,50)} is defined by a diagonal line {(10,10),(50,50)}.
'S2dVr' represents that the coordinate representation is a rectangle on the 2D space.
'S2dVs' represents that the coordinate representation is a point on the 2D space.

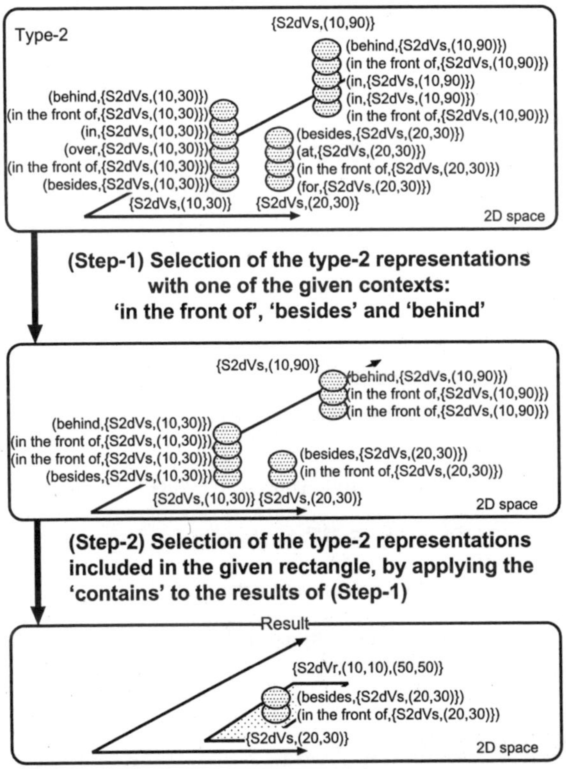

Figure 3: The computation of spatial equivalence for type-2 representations by our method

3.2 The primitive operators for computing spatial and temporal equivalence for type-2 representations

Our method computes spatial and temporal equivalence for type-2 representations by the following primitive operators.

(F-1) $recognize\_context(D^{in}, U_l) \rightarrow D^{out}$

This operator performs (Step-1).

D^{in} shows a set of type-2 representations. U_l shows a set of representations of the same context.

The result D^{out} is defined as the following set of type-2 representations :

$$D^{out} = \{d|(^{\exists}u_l)(u_l \in U_l \wedge d \in D^{in} \wedge d.CX = u_l)\},$$

where u_l shows an element of U_l, d shows an element of D^{in}, and $d.CX$ shows the context of d.

In our method, equivalence between $d.CX$ and u_l ($d.CX = u_l$) is computed by the simple pattern matching technique.

(F-2) $recognize\_location(D^{in}, \{f_c, u_c\}) \rightarrow D^{out}$

This operator performs (Step-2).

D^{in} shows a set of type-2 representations. Here, f_c shows a spatial and temporal operator for type-1 representations, and u_c shows a coordinate representation.

The result D^{out} is defined as the following set of type-2 representations :

$$D^{out} = \{d|d \in D^{in} \wedge f_c(d.C, u_c) = true\},$$

where $d.C$ shows the coordinate representation of d.

In our method, the set operators are defined as follows:

(F-3) $union(D_1^{in}, D_2^{in}) \rightarrow D^{out}$

(F-4) $difference(D_1^{in}, D_2^{in}) \rightarrow D^{out}$

(F-5) $intersection(D_1^{in}, D_2^{in}) \rightarrow D^{out}$.

3.3 The procedure for computing spatial and temporal equivalence for type-2 representations

The procedure for computing spatial and temporal equivalence for type-2 representations is expressed as follows.

$$recognize\_location(recognize\_context(D^{in}, U_l), \{f_c, u_c\})$$

Table 1: All contexts of the temporal type-2 representations in the articles

Context	Number
on	61
in	29
during	18
since	10
of	4
after	2
from	2
at the end of	1
late in	1
later	1
before	1
through	1
to	1
for about	1
earlier	1
until	1

Table 2: All contexts of the spatial type-2 representations in the articles

Context	Number
in	58
at	7
from	2

4 Experiments

We have performed several experiments to clarify feasibility and effectiveness for our computational method.

Experiment-1: Feasibility of our method for recognizing semantic equivalence between contexts

Experiment-2: Extension of the applicable scope of existing databases to that with spatial and temporal contexts by our method

4.1 The experimental data

In these experiments, we used 44 English articles of The Japan Times [6] as the experimental data. These articles describe the results of the baseball games in which a baseball pitcher 'Nomo' pitched from Jan. 1st, 2000 to May 31st, 2001.

There were also some temporal and adverbial phrases such as 'last year' and 'last week', in the articles. We converted those phrases to the type-2 representations with the preposition 'during'.

Table 1 and Table 2 show all contexts and the number of contexts in each article.

Table 3 shows the operators used in the experiments. The operators with the prefix 'tld_' are temporal operators in [1]. The operators with the prefix 's2d_' are some spatial operators in [2].

Table 3: Boolean operators for type-1 representations used in the experiments

Operators	True conditions
$t1d\_contain(t1, t2)$	$t1$ is during $t2$.
$t1d\_before(t1, t2)$	$t1$ is before $t2$.
$t1d\_disjoint(t1, t2)$	$t1$ and $t2$ are not joined.
$s2d\_inside(s1, s2)$	$s1$ is inside of $s2$.
$s2d\_equal(s1, s2)$	$s1$ is the same location as $s2$.

4.2 Experiment-1

To clarify feasibility of our method for recognizing semantic equivalence between contexts, we compare our method and a comparative method, in terms of accuracy of computational results.

We have implemented our method and the comparative method which was designed so as to deal with just a single context representation, unlike our method.

We have used the following three context sets as queries.

Context Set-1 {on, in, during} for temporal type-2 representations

These contexts give the same meaning for temporal type-2 representations, because any type-2 representation represents when an event (a fact) happened. In this experiment, for dealing with this set, several queries have been executed for retrieving articles describing events (facts) happened at the time.

Context Set-2 {late in, at the end of} for temporal type-2 representations

These contexts give the same meaning for temporal type-2 representations, because any type-2 representation represents the end of time. In this experiment, for dealing with this set, some queries have been executed for retrieving articles describing an events (a fact) happened at the end of indicated time.

Context Set-3 {in, at} for spatial type-2 representations

These contexts give the same meaning for spatial type-2 representations, because any type-2 representation represents a location where an event (a fact) happened. In this experiment, for dealing with this set, some queries have been executed for retrieving the articles describing an event (a fact) happened in a given location.

We have used three pairs of $\{f_c, u_c\}$. Table 4 shows all queries for both methods.

We compare the results of both methods by using the following indicators which are often used to evaluate information retrieval systems.

$$Recall = \frac{CorrectBySystem}{CorrectArticles}$$

$$Precision = \frac{CorrectBySystem}{ArticlesBySystem}$$

$CorrectBySystem$ shows the number of the correct articles retrieved by a system. $CorrectArticles$ shows the number of the correct articles. $ArticlesBySystem$ shows the number of the articles retrieved by the system.

Table 4: The queries used in the Experiment-1

	The queries for our method	The queries for the comparative method
Context Set-1 {on, in, during }	recognize_location(recognize_context(D^{in}, {on, in, during}), {t1d_before, {T1dVp,(20010501)}})	recognize_location(recognize_context(D^{in}, {on}), {t1d_before, {T1dVp,(20010501)}})
		recognize_location(recognize_context(D^{in}, {in}), {t1d_before, {T1dVp,(20010501)}})
		recognize_location(recognize_context(D^{in}, {during}), {t1d_before, {T1dVp,(20010501)}})
Context Set-2 {late in, at the end of}	union(union(union(recognize_location(recognize_context(D^{in}, {late in, at the end of}), {!t1d_disjoint, {T1dVi,(19990901,20000101)}}), recognize_location(recognize_context(D^{in}, {late in, at the end of}), {!t1d_disjoint, {T1dVi,(20000901,20010101)}})), recognize_location(D^{in}, {t1d_contain, {T1dVi,(19990901,20000101)}})), recognize_location(D^{in}, {t1d_contain, {T1dVi,(20000901,20010101)}}))	union(recognize_location(recognize_context(D^{in},{late in}), {!t1d_disjoint, {T1dVi,(19990901,20000101)}}), recognize_location(recognize_context(D^{in},{late in}), {!t1d_disjoint, {T1dVi,(20000901,20010101)}}))
		union(recognize_location(recognize_context(D^{in},{at the end of}), {!t1d_disjoint, {T1dVi,(19990901,20000101)}}), recognize_location(recognize_context(D^{in},{at the end of}), {!t1d_disjoint, {T1dVi, (20000901,20010101)}}))
Context Set-3 {in, at}	recognize_location(recognize_context(D^{in},{in, at}), {s2d_inside, {S2dVr,(100,100),(350,200)}})	recognize_location(recognize_context(D^{in},{in}), {s2d_inside, {S2dVr,(100,100),(350,200)}})
		recognize_location(recognize_context(D^{in},{at}), {s2d_inside,{S2dVr,(100,100),(350,200)}})

4.2.1 The experimental results and consideration

Figure 4 shows the recalls and precisions of the queries in Table 4.

The white diamonds show the recalls and the precisions of our method. The black diamond shows the average in our method. The white triangles show the recalls and the precisions of the comparative method. The black triangle shows the average in the comparative method.

By those results, we have clarified that our method could recognize semantic equivalence between contexts without describing explicit semantic equivalence.

4.3 Experiment-2

This experiment has been performed to show the new applicable scope of our method for spatial and temporal databases. We compare the accuracy of the retrieval results of four document retrieval systems statistically.

System-1 The spatial and temporal document retrieval system by our method (Our system)

In this system, an article is represented as a set of tuples. Each tuple is composed of the following items: **(AID)** the identifier of an article, **(Article)** a set of all words in the article, and **(Type-2)** a type-2 representations included in the article.

Table 5 shows the representations of an article including four type-2 representations.

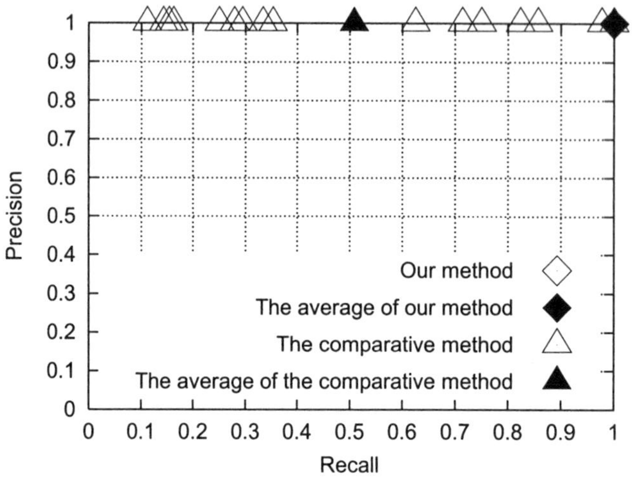

Figure 4: The results of the Experiment-1

This system returns the following set of articles:

$$\{t.\mathrm{AID}|t \in T^{in} \wedge U_k \subseteq t.\mathrm{Article}$$
$$\wedge t.\mathrm{Type\text{-}2} \in \mathit{recognize\_location}(\mathit{recognize\_context}(T^{in}.\mathrm{Type\text{-}2}, U_l), \{f_c, u_c\})\},$$

where 'T^{in}' shows a set of articles, 't.AID' shows 'AID' of the article 't', 't.Article' shows 'Article' of 't', 'T^{in}.Type-2' shows a set of the type-2 representations in 'T^{in}', 'U_l' shows prepositions given as queries, and 'U_k' shows keywords given as queries.

This system also evaluates '$U_k \subseteq t$.Article' by a conventional document retrieval method based on the pattern matching technique.

System-2-1 A spatial and temporal document retrieval system by the conventional methods in [1, 2]

In this system, an article is represented as a set of tuples. Each tuple is composed of the following items: **(AID)** the identifier of an article, **(Article)** a set of all words in the article, and **(Type-1)** a type-1 included in the article.

This system returns the following set of articles:

$$\{t.\mathrm{AID}|t \in T^{in} \wedge U_k \subseteq t.\mathrm{Article}$$
$$\wedge t.\mathrm{Type\text{-}1} \in \mathit{recognize\_location}(T^{in}.\mathrm{Type\text{-}1}, \{f_c, u_c\})\},$$

where 'T^{in}' shows a set of articles, 't.AID' shows 'AID' of the article 't', 't.Article' shows 'Article' of 't', 'T^{in}.Type-1' shows the set of all type-1 representations in 'T^{in}', 'U_l' shows prepositions given as queries, and 'U_k' shows keywords given as queries.

This system also evaluates '$U_k \subseteq t$.Article' by using a conventional document retrieval method based on the pattern matching technique.

Table 5: An example of the experimental data for the System-1 in the Experiment-2

AID	Article	Type-2	
		CX	C
20000602	In Chicago, ... walked two.	in	{S2dVs,(256,162)}
20000602	In Chicago, ... walked two.	on	{T1dVp,(20000602)}
20000602	In Chicago, ... walked two.	since	{T1dVi,(19451001),(19451101)}
20000602	In Chicago, ... walked two.	during	{T1dVi,(19451001),(19451101)}

System-2-2 Another spatial and temporal document retrieval system by the conventional methods in [1, 2]

This system is designed to realize another context recognition for type-2 representations by selecting articles including one of given prepositions.

The data structure of this system is the same as System2-1. This system returns the following set of articles:

$$\{t.\text{AID}|(t \in T^{in} \wedge (^{\exists}u_l \in U_l)(u_l \in t.\text{Article} \\ \wedge U_k \subseteq t.\text{Article} \wedge t.\text{Type-1} \in \textit{recognize\_location}(T^{in}.\text{Type-1}, \{f_c, u_c\})\},$$

where 'T^{in}' shows a set of articles, 't.AID' shows 'AID' of the article 't', 't.Article' shows 'Article' of 't', 'T^{in}.Type-1' shows a set of the type-1 representations in 'T^{in}', 'U_l' shows prepositions given as queries, and 'U_k' shows keywords given as queries.

This system also evaluates '$U_k \subseteq t$.Article' by using a conventional document retrieval method based on the pattern matching technique.

System-3 A conventional document retrieval system based on a pattern matching technique.

In this system, an article is represented in a set of tuples. Each tuple is composed of the following items: **(AID)** the identifier of an article, and **(Article)** a set of all words in the article.

This system returns the following set of articles:

$$\{t.\text{AID}|t \in T^{in} \wedge U_k \subseteq t.\text{Article}\},$$

where 'T' shows a set of articles, and 'U_k' shows keywords given as queries.

We have used several conditions for document retrieval. Table 6 shows the six groups of retrieval conditions and the number of the correct articles.

We evaluate accuracy of the results of the four methods by using the same indicators used in the Experiment-1.

4.3.1 The experimental results and consideration

Figure 5, Figure 6, Figure 7, Figure 8, Figure 9 and Figure 10 show the averages of precisions and recalls in query execution in the four systems.

The precision of the System-1 (our system) was higher than that of the System-2-1. The gap between the precisions was larger, when U_l was composed of rare prepositions in the articles (Figure 5 and Figure 7).

Table 6: The query groups used in Experiment-2

Query Group	U_k	U_l	$\{f_c, u_c\}$	the number of the correct articles
Condition-1	Nomo, win, won	{since}	{t1d_contain, {T1dVi,(20000101),(20010601)}}	3
			{t1d_contain, {T1dVi,(20000101),(20010101)}}	3
			{t1d_contain, {T1dVi,(20000401),(20000701)}}	3
			{t1d_before, {T1dVp,(19990101)}}	3
			{t1d_before, {T1dVp,(19900101)}}	2
			{t1d_before, {T1dVp,(19800101)}}	2
Condition-2	Nomo, win, won	{on,in, during}	{t1d_contain, {T1dVi,(20000401),(20000430)}}	1
			{t1d_contain, {T1dVi,(20000401),(20000531)}}	2
			{t1d_contain, {T1dVi,(20000401),(20000630)}}	2
			{t1d_contain, {T1dVi,(20000401),(20001101)}}	8
			{t1d_contain, {T1dVi,(20000101),(20010101)}}	8
			{t1d_contain, {T1dVi,(20000101),(20010601)}}	13
Condition-3	no-hitter, complete game	{since}	{t1d_before, {T1dVp,(20000101)}}	3
			{t1d_before, {T1dVp,(19980101)}}	3
			{t1d_before, {T1dVp,(19960101)}}	3
Condition-4	Orioles	{in, at}	{s2d_inside, {S2dVr, (100,100),(350,200)}}	3
			{s2d_inside, {S2dVr, (100,100),(350,200)}}	3
			{s2d_equal, {S2dVs, (310,156)}}	2
Condition-5	Tigers	{on,in, during}	{t1d_contain, {T1dVi,(20000401),(20000701)}}	14
			{t1d_contain, {T1dVi,(20000401),(20001101)}}	28
			{t1d_contain, {T1dVi,(20000401),(20010601)}}	28
Condition-6	Tigers	{since}	{t1d_before, {T1dVp,(20020101)}}	3
			{t1d_before, {T1dVp,(20010101)}}	3
			{t1d_before, {T1dVp,(20000101)}}	3
			{t1d_before, {T1dVp,(19990101)}}	3
			{t1d_before, {T1dVp,(19900101)}}	2

In Figure 6 (the Condition-2), the precision of the System-1 was very low. This result shows that the conventional document retrieval method could not distinguish the following articles: (A-1) the articles of Nomo's victory, and (A-2) the articles of the opposing teams' victory in the game when Nomo pitched.

The System-1 marked the same recall as the System-2-1 in Figure 5, Figure 6, Figure 7, Figure 8 and Figure 9, and it showed the lower recall than the System-2-1 in Figure10. This result shows that our method could not identify the same time represented by different context representations and different coordinate representations. In this experiment, though 'since 1950' and 'in 50 years' were equivalent in the articles described in 2000, our system retrieved only 'since 1950'. However, our method is more effective than the conventional methods in most cases.

The System-1 always led to higher precision than the System-2-2. This result shows that the System-2-2 could not recognize the connection between a context representation and a coordinate representation. Our context recognition process for type-2 representations is important to improve the accuracy of document retrieval results. Our method has also contributed to the extension of the applicable scope of existing databases to spatial and temporal databases.

In comparison with the System-3, our method has contributed to the improvement of the precision of document retrieval results drastically. It is available to apply our method to a filtering function for document databases.

By those experimental results and the considerations for document retrieval, we have clarified that our method gives higher feasibility than conventional spatial and temporal computational methods, and contributes to the extension of the applicable scope of spatial and temporal databases.

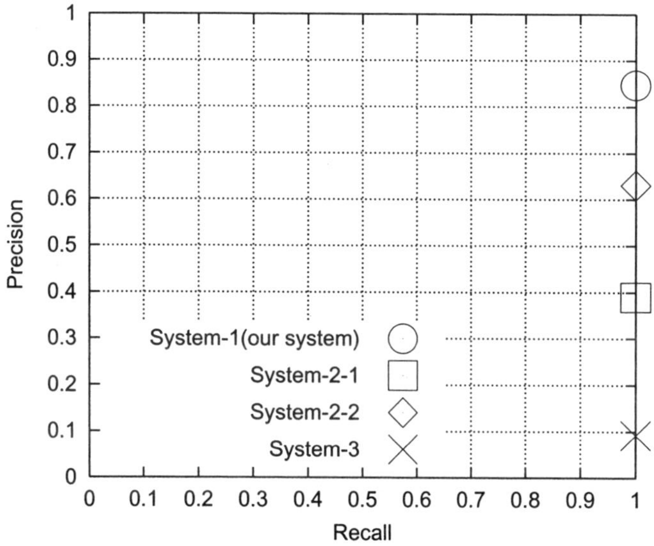

Figure 5: The results for the Condition-1 in the Experiment-2

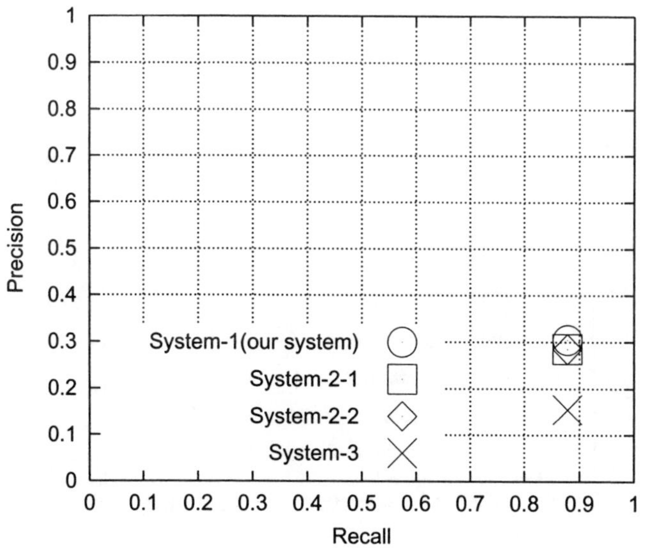

Figure 6: The results for the Condition-2 in the Experiment-2

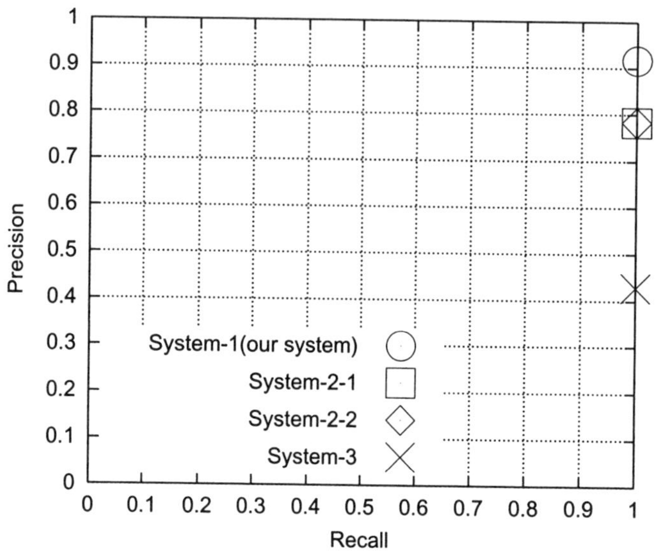

Figure 7: The results for the Condition-3 in the Experiment-2

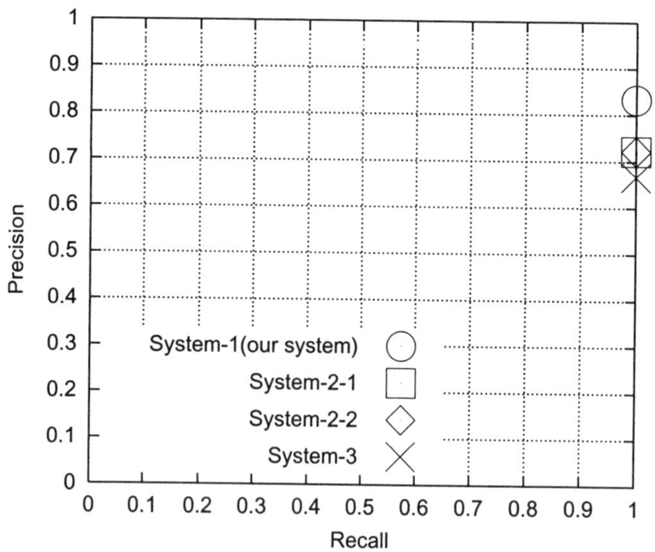

Figure 8: The results for the Condition-4 in the Experiment-2

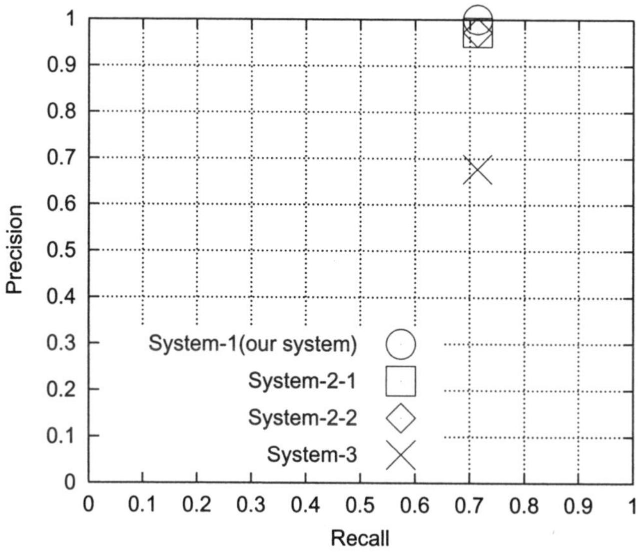

Figure 9: The results for the Condition-5 in the Experiment-2

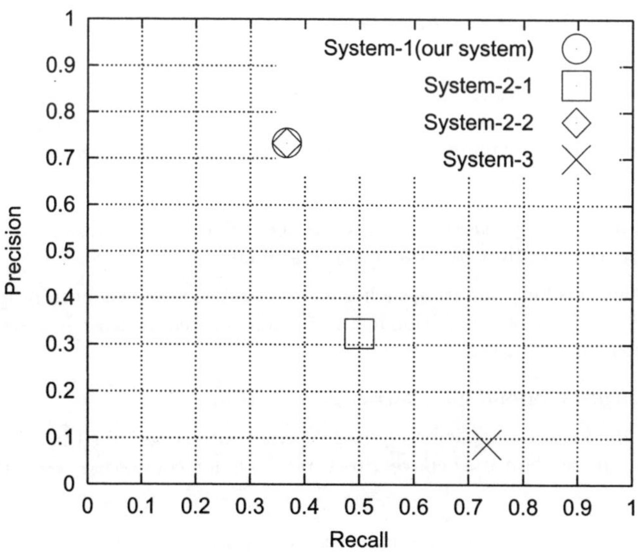

Figure 10: The results for the Condition-6 in the Experiment-2

4.4 Consideration for effective processing of our method

There are several effective processing mechanisms for the conventional pattern matching technique and the spatial and temporal computing techniques. Those mechanisms, such as hashing, B-tree, R-tree[4] and so on, contribute to high performance processing by our method.

It is also possible to optimize processing of application programs including our functions on the basis of the optimization scheme for functional programming.

5 Conclusion

In this paper, we have presented a new computational method for spatial and temporal equivalence in database retrieving.

There are two types of spatial and temporal representations: (type-1) a coordinate representation (C) like (x, y), and (type-2) a pair of a context and a coordinate representation (CX, C). The type-2 representation points out a region where the boundary is dynamically defined by a context 'CX'. The feature of the type-2 representation is to include the context information for computing spatial and temporal equivalence in a context-dependent way.

In our method, spatial and temporal equivalence is computed between the type-2 'A' and the type-2 'B' when A.CX = B.CX $\wedge$ A.C = B.C. We have defined a process for recognizing A.CX = B.CX, as 'context recognition'.

Our method makes it possible to extend the applicable scope of existing databases to that with spatial and temporal contexts.

The main features of our method are as follows.

(1) A practical context recognition

Our method is used for practical context recognition for type-2 representations. This method realizes 'prepositional-phrase-based context recognition' for type-2 representations. We focus on contexts related to prepositional phrases because the location (the meaning) of a type-2 representation changes according to interpretations for the prepositional phrases.

(2) A semantic recognition on equivalence between contexts without describing the explicit semantic equivalence

Many methods for computing such semantic equivalence have been proposed. We have also proposed a recognition method of semantic equivalence between contexts by cooperating with those methods.

(3) A language-independent context recognition

Our method can be applied to type-2 representations described in any language, because our method uses conventional methods for computing semantic equivalence.

We have clarified that our method is very attractive in comparison with the conventional spatial and temporal computational methods for document retrieval, and contributes to extending the applicable scope of existing databases to that with spatial and temporal contexts.

As the future work, we will design and implement a method for recognizing the same type-2 representations with different contexts and different coordinate representations.

We will also realize a computational model for the other relationships between type-2 representations, like 'part-of', similarity and so on. We will realize a method for automatically extracting type-2 representations from document databases.

References

[1] Allen, J.F.: "Maintaining Knowledge about Temporal Intervals", *Comm. of the ACM*, No.26, pp.832–843 (1983)

[2] Egenhofer, M.J.: "Spatial Relations: Models, Inferences, and their Future Application", *Proc. Advanced Database Symposium '96*, separate volume, Japan (1996)

[3] Egenhofer, M.J., Rashid, A. and Shariff, B.M.: "Metric Details for Natural-Language Spatial-Relations", *ACM Transaction on Information System*, Vol.16, No.4, pp.295–321 (1998)

[4] Guttman, A. "R-Trees: A Dynamic Index Structure for Spatial Searching", *Proc of the 1984 ACM SIGMOD Int'l Conf on Mgmt of Data*, pp.45–57 (1984)

[5] Ishibashi, N., Hosokawa, Y. and Kiyoki, Y.: "A Spatial and Temporal Data Integration Method for Heterogeneous Database Environments", *Proc. the IASTED International Conference APPLIED INFORMATICS Symposium 2. Networks, Parallel and Distributed Processing, and Applications*, pp.323–330 (2001)

[6] "The Japan Times Monthly Bound Volume", The Japan Times, Ltd.

[7] Kitagawa, T. and Kiyoki, Y.: "The mathematical model of meaning and its application to multidatabase systems", *Proc. the 3rd IEEE Int. Workshop on Research Issues on Data Engineering: Interoperability in Multidatabase Systems*, pp.130–135 (1993)

[8] Kiyoki, Y., Kitagawa, T. and Hitomi, Y.: "A fundamental framework for realizing semantic interoperability in a multidatabase environment", *Journal of Integrated Computer-Aided Engineering*, Vol.2, No.1, pp.3–20, John Wiley & Sons (1995)

[9] Liu, G. Z.: Semantic vector space model: Implementation and evaluation, *J. the American Society for Information Science*, Vol. 48, No. 5, pp.395–417 (1997)

[10] Masunaga, Y.: "A temporal expansion to the multimedia object model in OMEGA", *Proc. the 4th International Conference on Database Systems for Advanced Applications (DASFAA'95)*, pp.430–440 (1995)

[11] Wendlandt, E. B., and Driscoll, J. R.: Incorporating a semantic analysis into a document retrieval strategy, *Proc. the Annual International ACM SIGIR Conference on Research and Development in Information Retrieval*, pp.1–14 (1991)

Information Modelling and Knowledge Bases XV
Y. Kiyoki et al. (Eds.)
IOS Press, 2004

Document Similarities in Web Based Collaborative Environments

Michael Gindonis, Tapio Niemi, and Marko Niinimäki
Michael.Gindonis@cern.ch, tapio@cs.uta.fi, Marko.Niinimaki@cern.ch
Helsinki Institute of Physics at CERN, CH-1211 Geneva, Switzerland

Abstract.

Collaborative editing of documents online in organizations helps the collaborators keep up to date with rapidly changing information, especially in technical fields. Because of its speed, editing documents on-line can have disadvantages, too: the repository of documents (document space) can grow large and redundant.

To enforce coherence and reduce redundancy, a strong (hierarchical) structure of the document space can be imposed. In this case, each document has a strictly defined slot in the document space, it can be located by navigation and altered or extended. It has been our experience, however, that users do not like hierarchical structures and find the navigation cumbersome. Another possibility, more liked by the users, is to have a loosely structured document space, and support the users with tools for document retrieval and intelligent linking between documents.

In this paper, we present a tool with which the user can see which other documents are related to his documents. The intended use for the tool is that the user edits a document to insert a query variable and after editing saves it. Saving a document automatically launches a query, whose results are a set of links to the most similar documents in the work space.

In order to measure similarity, we have evaluated several methods, including Myers' O(ND) method (string comparson by edit distance) and a method based on Salton's Vector Model. In our reference document server (that contains about 1000 technical documents entered by the users) it was found that both methods worked quite well.

The users of the document server have found our implementation useful, since they can (i) see if someone has already considered the topic that they are working with (ii) find information that is otherwise interesting to them.

1 Introduction

Collaborative environments for sharing information in organizations have been around since the introduction of Local Area Networks (LANs). Most collaborative environments feature "pages" of information and hyperlinks that link these pages with each other. Simple links can easily lead to badly structured information. To prevent that, intelligent linking [13] and hierarchical structures in the collaborative environment user interface (as with Tuovi/Kronodoc document management system, [16]) have been proposed and implemented.

In this paper, we concentrate on an Open Source collaborative environment called TWiki. TWiki is a World Wide Web (WWW) based "collaboration platform" [20] that enables editing pages of the collaborative environment using a normal WWW browser. TWiki's flexible software structure makes it easy to write additional modules to extend TWiki's functionality.

We present a prototype of an additional TWiki plug in module called SimilarityPlugin. It focuses on the problem of badly structured information by finding similar pages in the collaborative environment. The intended use of the plug in is as follows: the user types a page and checks if there are some related one already in which case he makes links to them.

The benefits of this module are making the users aware of related information that is already there, discouraging redundant work.

2 Background and Terminology

Bielawski and Boyle [2] define document management as creation, management and distribution of document-based information. Here, we define a collaborative environment simply as a computer program that facilitates document management, typically within one organization. We call the collection of documents within one collaborative environment a document space.

The World Wide Web (Web) is a network of information resources [4]. The Web relies on three mechanisms to make these resources readily available to the widest possible audience: 1. A uniform naming scheme for locating resources on the Web (e.g., Universal Resource Identifiers, URIs). 2. Protocols, for access to named resources over the Web (e.g., HyperText Transfer Protocol, HTTP). 3. Hypertext, for easy navigation among resources (e.g., HyperText Markup Language HTML).

A server is "an application program that accepts connections in order to service requests by sending back responses." [7] Thus, a world wide web server is a server that accepts HTTP requests and as responses send information in the form of HTML.

A web based collaborative environment in the world wide web context is a collaborative environment implemented by means of a web server. Documents are HTML pages and contain links to other documents in the same document space.

3 Related Work

Knowledge management in organizations is a widely studied area (e.g. [1]). There are also many works focused in knowledge management in WWW environment (e.g. [14]).

In information retrival, methods of recovering documents based on keywords are well known. In a typical application, the user enters a query, i.e. a keyword or a set of keywords. The system tries to find documents that match the user's query. The system's response is a group of documents such that for each of them there is a "rank", a similarity index often based on the amount of matched words compared to the total number of words in the document (see e.g. [6]).

To evaluate how well the resulting documents correspond to the given query, Kent et al. [10] have defined two measurements for information retrieval: Precision, that is, how large portion of the retrieved documents were relevant and recall, that is, how large portion of all relevant documents were retrieved. These measures serve well as a theoretical background; studies in information retrieval discuss how to design and implement systems that find a good balance of precision and recall (see e.g. [9]). The problem with these measures is, however, that it is very difficult to evaluate them in practice.

We can generalise the notion of document - query similarity to document - document similarity. There, maybe the best known of document - document similarity measurements is the traditional Salton Vector Model [19]. The idea behind the vector model is to present the documents as vectors and then compute the similarity of these vectors. The vectors are constructed based on the words in the document. It is possible to use only some (human) defined key words or process the whole document using computer. Salton [18] shows that automated method works as well as manual one. Common words, like articles and prepositions, should be removed before constructing the vector. Other possible methods to compare similarities are, for example, string comparison methods, like O(ND) of Myers [12] based on edit distances. In our case, the string comparison method gave similar kinds of result as the Vector Model. Most of the methods return a decimal value that indicates how similar the documents are. This enables us to rank the relevant documents. The ranking is useful since in large databases the number of relevant documents can be too much to display for the user [8].

Among the more recent approaches, semantic networks and structural similarity have gained attention.

Ruge has used semantic networks in information retrieval in order to find alternative query terms [17]. This study shows that a spreading activation network [3] can easily find alternative terms that are more than just synonyms. Our method can be seen as a application of semantic networks. The documents are nodes in the networks and the connections between the nodes represent the similarity of the nodes. The activation of the document at hand is increased and the increased activation spread via the connections to other nodes. The activation level of the node detones the nodes' relevance for the user.

Cruz et al. [5] have studied how structural similarity of web pages can be detected. Their idea is to give the user a possibility to retrieve information from web pages based on the structure of the pages. They use three different distance functions for measuring the similarity of documents. The functions are based on tag frequencies, parametric functions, and edit distances.

An obvious application of similarity measurements is detecting plagiarism. We have tested an algorithm primary designed for this purpose ("Sherlock" discussed in [11]) in our implementation, too.

4 Wiki, TWiki Basics, and use at the Helsinki Institute of Physics Technology Programme

"TWiki is a leading-edge, web-based collaboration platform targeting the corporate intranet world. TWiki fosters information flow within an organization; lets distributed teams work together seamlessly and productively; and eliminates the one-webmaster syndrome of outdated intranet content." [20]

TWiki is a enhanced implementation of Cunningham's "WikiWikiWeb" (http://c2.com /cgi/wiki), software that allows users to create, edit and hyperlink web pages using only a web browser. The first Wiki implementation used at Cunningham's website consisted of about 500 lines of Perl code interfaced to a database manager, in this case Gnu DBM (gdbm) the GNU database manager.

A basic Wiki installation consists of the following features: (i) A simple syntax for formatting headings, bold, italic, fixed font text, creating internal and external links. (ii) Possibility to create internal hyperlinks to pages within the wiki installation using a "WikiWord" syntax and external links with by embedding a traditional "http://" link within the text. (iii) A simple search facility that will provide links to pages containing the search text.

A WikiWord is any word consisting of one upper case character followed by one or more lower case characters followed by one upper case character followed by one one or more lower case characters. If a page with the name WikiName exists, the test WikiName will link to the page called WikiName. Otherwise, a question mark following WikiName ('WikiName?') will link to a page allowing one to create a page named WikiName.

The Helsinki Institute of Physics, Technology Programme started to use Cunningham's Wiki in February 2001 to maintain a non-hierarchical and easy to update set of web pages for internal and external use.

The following TWiki Enhancements influenced our decision to adopt TWiki in November 2001: (i) Version control and ability to look at changes between different versions of a page. One of the uses of the TWiki was to keep track of configuration information. The version control allowed us to see by whom and when changes were made to documents. (ii) Flexible access control (Read/Write/Change by a user or a group of users, editable by users via a browser interface). (iii) "Webs", i.e. separate document spaces of interest to a limited audience.

From a user's perspective, the following features have been most useful:

(i) The ability to upload files from a browser. (ii) More flexible WikiWord syntax allowing use of multiple upper case letters as well as numbers. (iii) Possibility to subscribe to daily notifications via email of changes to pages in a web. (iv) Signing up and password setting via a simple web form. (v) Syntax for including tables in a page, and (vi) The ability to put HTML tags into the text.

TWiki does not enforce a strict hierarchy of documents: within one web, all documents are on the same level. It is up to the user to provide links between them. Naturally, this can lead to redundancy. The SimilarityPlugin has been developed as a solution to this problem.

5 Description and Implementation of the Similarity Search

5.1 Description

Before creating a new document, users regularly use the basic search function to see if there are related documents (e.g. same words in their subjects) in the document space already. However, since the documents can be edited by dozens of users, any two documents may end up having lots of related contents, even if the phrasing of their subject is different. The users find this annoying especially in the cases when the documents describe solutions to technical problems: the user writes his solution and discovers later that someone else had already produced a similar solution.

In order to overcome the difficulties of redundant documents in Wikihip (available on: http://wikihip.cern.ch), a similarity search function was proposed. The users envisaged that the system should function in a following way:

- The user either enters a new document or edits an existing one;
- When saving his documents he would have an option of checking if there is already a similar document in the document space.
- If this option is selected, the software should output links to the most similar documents.
- The user can follow the links and study the related documents.

5.2 Implementation

The algorithm employed by default is that of O(ND) of Myers [12]. We have tested an algorithm based on Salton's Vector Model (outlined in [15]), too, but its implementation was slower and there was no apparent differences in the results. The algorithm can be changed, since the interface supports any function that compares two strings or files and outputs their relative similarity.

The function was implemented using TWiki's "plugin API", and can be described as follows:

```
store the current page in variable CURRENT
initialize a list LIST of pairs <page,similarity-value>
for each page PAGE in document space
  compare similarity with CURRENT
  push PAGE and similarity value into LIST
sort LIST according to similarity values
```

The plugin in action (while editing and after saving the document) can be seen in Figure 1.

6 Conclusions and Discussion

In this paper, we presented a practical method to reduce redundancy in collaborative document management environment, an automated similarity search.

As a possibility to extend the system, a thesaurus can be introduced as a part of it. in other words, we would use a controlled vocabulary to find documents that are about the same subject but can use different terminology.

As a prototype environment, we used TWiki, a web based document management program. Our instance of TWiki (used at CERN), currently contains about 1000 documents and serves ca. 50 users. User feedback has been positive; the users especially appreciate the possibility to find technical (trouble shooting) documents similar to theirs.

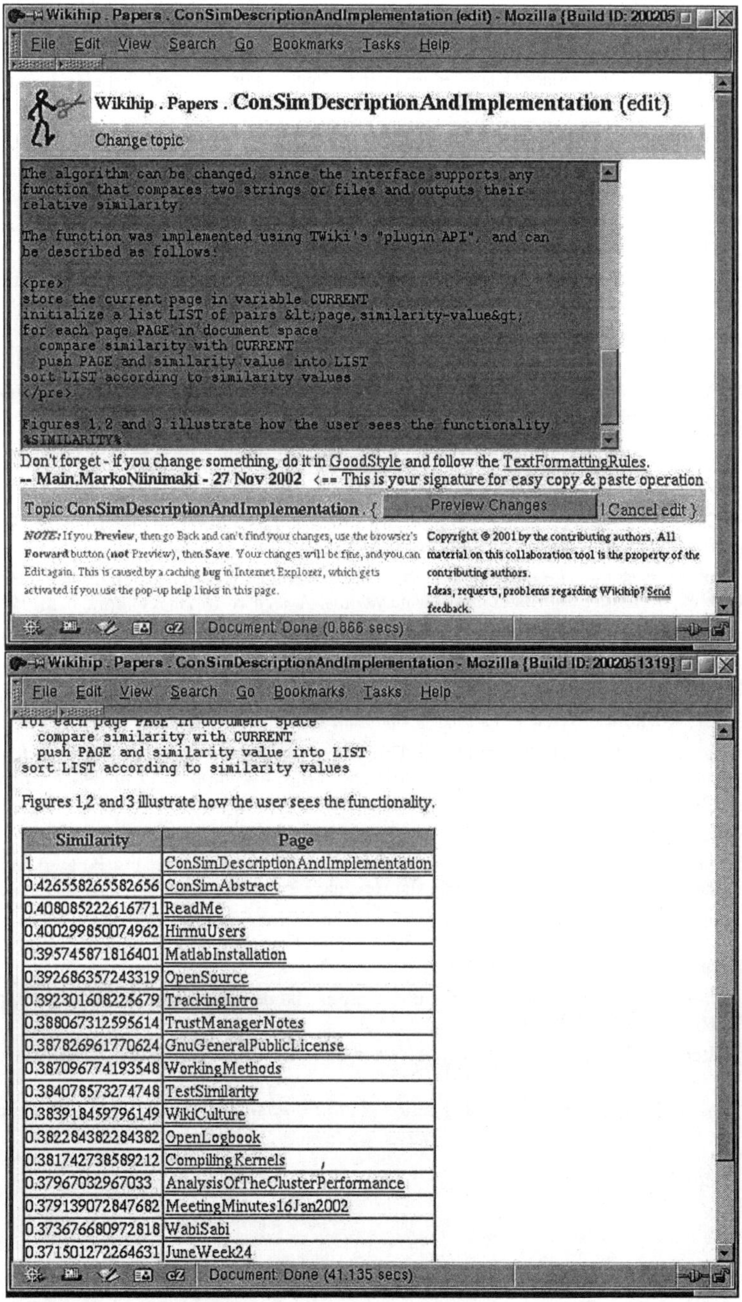

Figure 1: The similarity plugin and its user interface.

References

[1] M. Alavi and D. E. Leidner. Knowledge management systems: issues, challenges, and benefits. *Communications of the AIS*, 1(2es):1, 1999.

[2] L. Bielawski and J. Boyle. *Electronic Document Management Systems*. Prentice Hall, 1997.

[3] A. Collins and E. Loftus. spreading activation theory of semantic memory. *Psychological Review*, 6(82), 1975.

[4] The World Wide Web Consortium. Html 4.01 specification. Available on: http://www.w3.org/TR/html401/, 1999.

[5] I. F. Cruz, S. Borisov, M. A. Marks, and T. R. Webb. Measuring structural similarity among Web documents: Preliminary results. *Lecture Notes in Computer Science*, 1375, 1998.

[6] C. Faloutsos and D. W. Oard. A survey of information retrieval and filtering methods. Technical report, 1995.

[7] Network Working Group. Hypertext transfer protocol HTTP/1.1 – rfc 2616. Available on: ftp://ftp.rfc-editor.org/in-notes/rfc2616.txt, 1999.

[8] K. Järvelin and J. Kekäläinen. IR evaluation methods for retrieving highly relevant documents. In *Proceedings of the 23rd Annual International ACM SIGIR Conference on Research and Development in Information Retrieval, Athens, Greece, 24.-28.7.2000*, 2000.

[9] J. Kekäläinen. *The effects of query complexity, expansion and structure on retrieval performance in probabilistic text retrieval*. PhD thesis, University of Tampere, 1999.

[10] A. Kent, M. Berry, F. U. Leuhrs, and J. W. Perry. Machine literature searching viii: Operational criteria for designing information retrieval systems. *American Documentation*, 6(2), 1955.

[11] M. Luck and M. Joy. A secure on-line submission system. *Software - Practice and Experience*, 29(8):721–740, 1999.

[12] E. Myers. An O (ND) difference algorithm and its variations. *Algorithmica*, 1(2):251–266, 1986.

[13] H. Oinas-Kukkonen. What's in a link? *Communications of the ACM*, 41(1), 1998.

[14] H. Ong, A. Tan, J. Ng, H. Pan, and Q. Li. Foci: flexible organizer for competitive intelligence. In *Proceedings of the tenth international conference on Information and knowledge management*, pages 523–525. ACM Press, 2001.

[15] U. Pfeifer. Information retrieval, and what pack 'w' is for. *The Perl Journal*, Summer 1997.

[16] M. Puittinen. Implementing project management tools in a world wide web based engineering data management system. Master's thesis, Helsinki University of Technology, 2000.

[17] G. Ruge. Human memory models and term association cognition and association. In *Proceedings of the Eighteenth Annual International ACM SIGIR Conference on Research and Development in Information Retrieval*. ACM, 1995.

[18] G. Salton. Recent studies in automatic text analysis and document retrieval. *Journal of the ACM (JACM)*, 20(2):258–278, 1973.

[19] G. Salton, A. Wong, and C. S. Yang. A vector space model for automatic indexing. *Communications of the ACM*, 18(11):613–620, 1975.

[20] P. Thoeny. Twiki, a web based collaboration platform. Available on: http://www.twiki.org, 2002.

Information Modelling and Knowledge Bases XV
Y. Kiyoki et al. (Eds.)
IOS Press, 2004

A Prototype of Semantic Retrieval for Video Data Using SD-Form

Masahiro Wakiyama†, Shota Yoshihara††, Koichi Nozaki††† and Eiji Kawaguchi††††

†*Kitakyushu National College of Technology*
5-20-1 Shii Kokura-Minami-ku Kitakyushu-shi 802-0985, Japan
E-Mail : wakiyama@kct.ac.jp

††*Nagasaki Junshin Catholic University*
Faculty of Humanities

†††*Nagasaki University*

††††*Kyushu Institute of Technology*

Abstract.
The SD-Form Semantics Model, developed by the authors, is a framework to deal with semantic processing of natural language. We made the new retrieval system based on web-based system. The new system use video movie, text data, and the SD-Form as their semantic description. The System used HTML (Hyper Text Markup Language) for the video database and use common gateway interface scripts are written in perl and the system worked well.

1. Introduction

Recently, the number of web-based applications is increasing at very fast rate with the exponential increase in the number of people using the World Wide Web (WWW). So it is very important to utilize efficiently the available application on network. In this paper we apply the semantic retrieval for video data on a network. This scheme differs in implementation with respect to the semantic processing on WWW.

Previously, the authors proposed a new semantics model using SD-Forms as a meaning description language.[1), 2), 6), 14), 17)] They termed it the SD-Form Semantics Model. The authors have already reported several feasibility studies on applications.[5), 7), 9), 12), 15), 16)] The most important point of the model is that it is equipped with a scheme for semantic metric computation in terms of a semantic difference measure.

This paper presents our new attempts to video database system. The most important point is that each video scene and dialogues is described semantically by using SD-Form. Each scene is retrieved by an SD-Form. In other words, similarity of two gives scenes is computed by using attached SD-Form in conjunction with the system knowledge that are episode knowledge, scene knowledge and general knowledge.

In Section 2 we review the SD-Form Semantics Model. In section 3 we will explain our system. Finally in Section 4, we summarize our present work and show the problems for our future work.

2. The SD-Form Semantics Model

The SD-Form Semantics Model defines the SD-Form as a meaning description language.

An SD-Form is a well-formed symbol string which we use to describe concept structures. "A concept" in English generally refers to "word meaning." While, in this paper, it refers to a piece of an idea contained in a word, sentence, greeting phrase, fact, rule, or emotional utterance.

2.1 The syntax of the SD-Form

The syntax of the SD-Form is regulated by a context-free grammar named SDG (SD-Form derivative Grammar.) [1), 10)] Symbols of the SD-Form include the following.

SD-Forms are categorized into the 8 types of syntactic structures which follow. "D, D_1, D_2,..." in the following description take one of 8 types.

Type 1) Variable label
X, X1, Y (something)

Type 2) Simple label
FOREST, SNOWHITE, HUMAN, RUN, SOME, 21, $1

Type 3) Parameterized label : g(f)
AGE(40), PAGE(3), DOLLAR(25) (age 40, page 3, 25 dollars)

Type 4) Modified SD-Form : D/D_1
APPLE/(PRETTY)*para*(RED) (a pretty red apple)

Type 5) Prescribed SD-Form : P_i(D)
nega(AWAKE/MOOD/ABILITY) (can not awake)

Type 6) Connected SD-Form: (D_1)C_i(D_2)
(SNOWHITE)*kdof*(HUMAN) (Snow-White is a kind of human.)

Type 7) Statement SD-Form : [*s*(D_1),*v*(D_2), ...]
[*s*(QUEEN/SOME),*v*(BE),*c*(MOTHER/SNOWHITE)]
(Some Queen is the mother of Snow-White.)

Type 8) Emotion SD-Form : [*a*(D)], [*r*(D)] or [*e*(D)]
[*a*([*s*(1STPSN),*v*(SURPRISE)])] (Oh!)

The usage of each SD-Form type is standardized by a usage manual[4)]. Each SD-Form(D) has a "semantic information score" described by *SI*(D). The reason we associate each SD-Form with such a score is so we can evaluate the amount of semantic information of each concept by a number .

2.2 Semantic information of an SD-Form

Each SD-Form (D) carries a certain amount of semantic information. This amount depends on the syntactic structure of D. We designate it by *SI*(D) and call it the semantic information score of D. Although the score-assignment details are left open to each model user, we have some general ideas about it.

2.3 Elaboration in the SD-Form Semantics Model

An elaboration relation in the SD-Form Semantics Model is a generalized idea of the traditional "IS-A", "PART-OF" or "IF-THEN" relations. This is because all the "IS-A", "PART-OF" and "IF-THEN" relations describe the inheritance of a true property, and the elaboration relation in the SD-Form Semantics Model also refers to the inheritance of a true concept property. It has two types. One is $ELAB_{synt}$(D_1,D_2) and the other is $ELAB_{know}$(D_1,D_2).

When D_1 and D_2 are related in one of the following cases, D_2 is called "syntactically elaborated" from D_1 by the score *n*.

We designate it by, $ELAB_{synt}$(D_1,D_2) = *n*, or $ELAB_{synt}$(D_1,D_2,*n*).

We introduce the "specific-knowledge based" elaboration relation.

We designate it by,$ELAB_{know}$(D_1,D_2) = *n*, or $ELAB_{know}$(D_1, D_2, *n*) Let a system be equipped with specific knowledge, then the corresponding $ELAB_{know}$(D_1,D_2) relations on the right side hold true. Specific knowledge must be explicitly given to the system by users. Therefore, different systems have different specific-knowledge based elaboration scores depending on the knowledge difference.

2.4 Definition of *ELAB* relation

In the SD-Form Semantics Model, an elaboration relation between D_1 and D_2 is denoted by

$$ELAB(D_1,D_2)=n, \quad \text{or} \quad ELAB(D_1,D_2,n)$$

where, n is the elaboration score given by

$$n = min\ \{ELAB_{synt}(D_1,D_2), ELAB_{know}(D_1,D_2)\}.$$

(i.e., n is the minimum value of $ELAB_{synt}(D_1,D_2)$ and $ELAB_{know}(D_1,D_2)$).

$ELAB_{synt}$ and $ELAB_{know}$ are syntactic and knowledge based elaborations, respectively. The unit of both scores is "semit."

2.5 Nearest common ancestor and the semantic difference measure

The nearest common ancestor (D_0) of D_1 and D_2 is a common ancestor which is the nearest to both D_1 and D_2 among all common ancestors.

We describe this relation as follows.

$$NCOA(D_1,D_0,D_2,n)$$

$$(n = \{ELAB(D_0,D_1)+ ELAB(D_0,D_2)\} = min_D\ \{ELAB(D,D_1)+ ELAB(D,D_2)\})$$

We define the semantic difference measure between D_1 and D_2 as;

$$DIFF(D_1,D_2)=n.$$

3. Video database

3.1 Video data

A video movie data is a time series of motion picture associated with speech sound and other sounds. A video movie sequel is a segmented story. Each segment, in some case, is a short story on video movie which is called "Episode." An episode forms a substory of a whole story. An episode consists of time series of "Scenes", and a scene is a series of "Shots" (cf. Fig.1).

When we talk about a motion picture with speech sound included, we phrase it as "video" like in "video scene" and "video shot."

We picked up a video movie, as our source data for our system, which was for 122 minutes. This story was not only in Japan as an entertainment program on video movie, but also as a study material for people who are eager to learn conversational English. The most special point about this story is that it is bilingual (English and Japanese). A typical episode in this story has a statistics like the following.

1. A video movie data has 10 episode.
2. One episode has 5-15 scenes.
3. One scene (lasting for about 2 minutes) has 10-40 shots.
4. Number of speech utterances in one scene is 5-50.

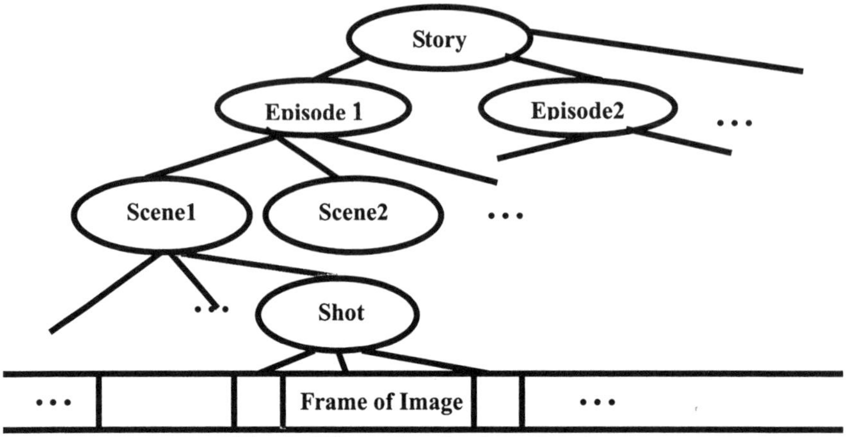

Fig. 1 Hierarchy of a story structure

3.2 Definition of Scene

Most scenes include some people, and they converse on some topic. The conversation topic, as well as the place of conversation, will last or continuously shift within a scene, but will not go beyond the scene. We assume that one scene has only one conversation topic and one place. A "place" in this context is not necessarily a geographical place. We also assume that every scene includes at least one utterance of speech sound. A shot is an interval of motion picture, which is a series of still picture frames, during which the picture was taken without interruption. Fig.1 illustrates this hierarchy.

3.3 Description of Video data

We are filing each video scene (motion picture with speech sound) of a video movie in our PC system. The sampling features are as follows.

Image Sampling

1 Frame	: 320 × 240 pixel
Pixel Color	: 24 bit/pixel (Full colors)
Number of Frames	: 30 Frame /second

Speech Sampling

Data Bits	: 8 bit
Sampling Frequency	: 32 KHz
Number of Channels	: 2 (English and Japanese)

At the moment, we do not use any image compression technique in filing. All data are directly stored in the hard disk of the server. The amount of necessary memory for one minute sampling is about 70 MBytes. This means one episode of video movie data needs more than 3 GBytes. We found that almost half part of a whole episode is silent, or voiceless, i.e., we need not file it as a part of video scene. Therefore, we need about 1.5 GBytes or more for one episode.

3.4 Description of meaning data

In our new system we are implementing a new operation which retrieves a specific scene through semantic data. For instance, we want to find out such an explosive scene.

In order to make such a retrieval possible, each scene (identified by Scene-Id) in system must be associated with (or linked to) the following.

1. Keywords of the scene
2. Structural information of the scene
3. Scene description (Scenario) by SD-Form
4. Scene-Specific Knowledge by SD-Form

Information in categories 1, 2 and 3 is the semantic description of the scene. In scene retrieval operation, the system searches for a specific scene firstly by Keywords, secondly by Structural information, and finally by the Scene description by SD-Form. Information in category 4 works as the Knowledge when the system searches for a scene. An illustrative example is shown below.

<Example>

This example illustrates the way we gave semantic information to a specific scene in video movie data. In this scene, the terrorists were making escape with 747 airplane. The leader of terrorist is Colonel Stuart. McClane, police lieutenant, attaches fire to fuel that is overflowing from an airplane to impede it, and explodes and checked the escape of a terrorist.

Scene Id :

DH2: EP10: 084

1. Scene Keywords:

(Airplane, Cargo bay, Cockpit, Explosion, Flame, Lieutenant, Plane, Runway, Terrorist)

2. Scene Structure:

Participant-Type	(Lieutenant, Terrorist)
Number of Participants	(3)
Names of Participants	(McClane, Stuart, Terrorist)
Focused Participants	(McClane, Stuart)
Scene Atmosphere	(Joy, Despair)

3. Scene Description (Scenario) by SD-Form

S-1. [*s*(747($1)),*v*(MOVE/(CONTINUE)*para*(PLACE/RUNWAY))*para*
(CONCUR/[*s*($1),*v*(SPILL/(CONTINUE)),*o*(FUEL)])]
(The 747 continues to move along the runway, spilling a trail of fuel.)

A-1. [*s*(MCCLANE),*v*(LIGHT),*o*(TRAIL/FUEL)]
(McClane lights the trail of fuel.)
(Speech-11), (Speech-12)

S-2. [*s*(FLAME),*v*(RACE/(TO/PLANE)*para*(TIME/[*s*(PLANE),*v*(TAKE-OFF)]))]
(The flame races toward the plane as it begins to lift off the ground.)

S-3. [*s*(FLAME),*v*(SHOOT/(PLACE/REAR/747))]
(Flames shoot through the rear of the 747.)

S-4. [*s*(COCKPIT),*v*(*pass*(DESTROY),*b*(FLAME)]
(The cockpit is engulfed in flames.)

S-5. [*s*(747),*v*(EXPLODE/(TOOL/FLAME))]]
(The 747 explodes into flames.)

A-2. ([*s*(MCCLANE),*v*(LIE/PLACE/GROUND)])*pseq*([*s*(HE),*v*(LAUGH)])
(Mclane lies on the ground and laughs.)
(Speech-21), (Speech-22)

Speech-11: Yippee-ki-yea, motherfucker.
Speech-12: Yeah. All right.
Speech-21: Holly!
Speech-22: There's your fuckin'landing lights!

As we see in this example, "Scene Description" consists of three types of information, e.g.;

Scene Setup (S-1, S-2, ..., S-5),

Action Description (A-1, A-2),
Sequence of Speech Utterance (Speech-11, Speech-12, ..., Speech-22).

The Scene Setup describes the setup of the present visual scene, Action Description explains the movement of the participants in the scene, and Sequence of Speech Utterance designates the timing of respective speech in the scene. It is linked to speech text in English and Japanese Text base.

3.5 Description of Knowledge data

We experience daily, human conversation stands on knowledge which speaker and listener share in common. Such knowledge in our system is categorized into three classes. The example below is taken from video movie data again.

A. General Knowledge

Story-independent knowledge is categorized as General Knowledge. It is pre-installed in the system. It is utilized independent of each story.

<Example>

[*s*(AIRPLANE),*v*(POSSESS),*o*((COCKPIT)*plus*(REAR))]
(There are the cockpit and the rear in airplane.)
((*assu*([*s*(X),*v*(BE),*c*(WIFE/Z)]))*caus*([s(Z),*v*(BE),*c*(HUSBAND/X)]))
(If X is a wife of Z, Z is a husband of X.)
((*assu*([*s*(X),*v*(EXPLODE)]))*caus*([*s*(CREW/X),*v*(DIE)]))
(If X explodes, then the crew die.)

B. Story-Specific Knowledge

This gives us the background information about the story. In some case it can be subcategorized into Episode-Specific Knowledge. Knowledge data in this category must be associated with Story-Name.

<Example>

[*s*(STUART/COLONEL),*v*(BE),*c*(LIEUTENANT)]
(Colonel Stuart is a terrorist.)
[*s*(HOLLY),*v*(BE),*c*(WIFE/ MCCLANE)])
(Holly is a wife of McClane.)
[s(LORENZO/CAPTAIN),*v*(BE),*c*(POLICE/AIRPORT))]
(Captain Lorenzo is an airport police.)

In retrieving operation, the system utilizes the knowledge in this category independent of scene. It must be replaced every time the system seeks around different stories.

C. Scene-Specific Knowledge

Special knowledge about a specific scene is categorized as Scene-Specific Knowledge. A piece of knowledge which is true in one scene is not always true in another scene. However, there is no strict distinction between Story-Specific and Scene-Specific knowledge. Scene-Specific Knowledge is assigned to respective Scene Id. When scene changes, it must be replaced.

<Example>

[*s*(747),*v*(BE),*c*(AIRPLANE)]
(The 747 is a plane.)
[*s*(CREW /747),*v*(BE),*c*(TERRORIST)]
(The 747 crew are terrorist.)

Those knowledge are categorized as a set of facts, some of which are unified with general rules (i.e., the General Knowledge in the system).

3.6 Video data retrieval system[16)]

Our mechanism of the video data retrieval system is a client/server model. It uses a standard http to load the HTML from the web server. The client is independent of any platform, it must have access to the Internet. The Web clients can be located anywhere in the network. Our system with common gateway interface (cgi) scripts are written in perl language. The data in the server host is accessed by internet using world wide web.
Our system operation is as follows.

1. We input the input-data which is retrieving scene.
2. The system compute the semantic difference between input-data and scene-data which is semantic data of scene (cf. section 3.4.)
   DIFF(input-data, scene-data).
3. The system creates new pages and the user view such desired scenes by web-browser.

The details are beyond the scope of this paper.

4. Conclusion

In this paper we described web-based video data retrieval system. The system worked well. The system is experimental research level. We must make more video scene data and knowledge data. Presently, we are working on the following projects in conjunction with SD-Form Semantics Model.

1. Question answering system [11)]
2. Story understanding system [5), 12)]
3. Self organization process of concept hierarchy [2), 8)]
4. English and Japanese sentence generation [9), 15)]
5. Retrieval of multimedia data [16)]

All these projects are more experimental than theoretical. We will soon become more explicit about soundness and usefulness of the SD-Form Semantics Model through these research projects.

The merits of the SD-Form Semantics Model are the following.

(1) It gives a well-formed syntactic structure for meaning description.
(2) The syntactic difference of two SD-Forms expresses the semantic difference.
(3) It is an interlingua reflecting the basic structure of natural language such as English and Japanese.
(4) It is easy to learn SD-Form usage in the meaning description.

The algorithm of the semantic difference computation will open many ways to the meaning processing of natural language, such as in recognition, understanding and learning.

Some of the problems we should work on in the near future are the following.

(1) Testing the model in a more realistic world, even if it is small.
(2) An abstracting algorithm of story data written by SD-Forms.
(3) To make our SDENV-3 a faster system.

References

[1] Kawaguchi, E., Wakiyama, M. and Nozaki, K.: A Semantic Structure Description Model of General Concepts in a Natural Language World, *Proc.* of *PRICAI*, pp.298-303 (1990)
[2] Kawaguchi, E., Kamata, S. and Wakiyama, M.: Elaboration Relation and the Nearest Common Ancestor of a Concept Pair in the SD-Form Semantics Model, *Proc. of 2nd PRICAI*, pp.426-432 (1992)
[3] Kawaguchi, E., Lee, M. and Nozaki, K.: Meaning description by SD-Forms and a prototype of a conversational-text retrieval system, *Proc. of TAI93*, pp.306-310 (1993)

[4] Kawaguchi, E., Wakiyama, M., Nozaki, K. and Shao, G.: How to describe the Meaning of Natural-Language Sentences and System Knowledge by Using SD-Forms, Proc. of the NLPRS'93, pp.380-386 (1993)

[5] Kawaguchi, E., Wakiyama, M., Lee, M. and Shao, G.: A Framework of Story Understanding in the SD-Form Semantics Model, *Information Modeling and Knowledge Bases V*, ed. by H.Kangassalo, et al, IOS (1994)

[6] Kawaguchi, E., Kamata, S.and Wakiyama, M..: The Semantic Metric Computation Scheme in the SD-Form Semantics Model, *Proc. of 3rd PRICAI*, pp.623-629 (1994)

[7] Kawaguchi, E., Wakiyama, M.: Some Topics on the SD-Form Semantics Model, *Proc. of NLPRS'95*, Poster Session China (1995)

[8] Shao, G. and Kawaguchi, E.: A Self Organization Process of Concept Hierarchy in the SD-Form Semantics Model, *Proc. of 5th International Symposium on Artificial Intelligence*, pp.393-400 (1992)

[9] Shao, G.,Wakiyama, M. and Kawaguchi, E.: A Prototype of English Sentence Generation System Based on SD-form Semantics Model, *Proc. of 1st PACLING*, pp.261-268 (1993)

[10] Shao, G., Nozaki, K., Kamata, S., and Kawaguchi, E.: SD-Forms as interlingua and a prototype of a conversational-text retrieving system, *J. of Japanese Society for Artificial Intelligence*, Vol. 9, No. 5, pp.684-693 (1994)

[11] Wakiyama, M., Nozaki, K. and Kawaguchi, E.: Semantic processing of story data by the SD-Form model approach, *Proc. of NLPRS'91*, pp.288-295 (1991)

[12] Wakiyama, M., Shao,G., Nozaki, K. and Kawaguchi, E.: Anaphora Processing of Story Data by the SD-Form Semantics Model Approach, *Proc. PRICAI*, pp.1169-1175 (1992)

[13] Wakiyama, M., Shao,G., Nozaki, K. and Kawaguchi, E.: Anaphora Resolution by Machine in the SD-Form Semantics Model, *Proc. of 2nd NLPRS'93*, pp.256-263(1993)

[14] Wakiyama, M., Shao,G., Nozaki, K. and Kawaguchi, E.: The Toward Generalization of the Semantic Metric in the SD-Form Semantics Model, *Proc. of 4th PRICAI'96 Poster*, pp.61-68(1996)

[15] Wakiyama, M. , Yoshihara, S. and Kawaguchi, E.: A Prototype of Japanese Sentence Generation System from SD-Formed Meaning Data, *Proc. of the PACLING'97*, pp333-344 (1997)

[16] Wakiyama, M. and Kawaguchi, E.: Retrieval of Multimedia Data for Natural Language in the Network, *Proc. of 4th NLPRS'97 Poster*, pp605-608 (1997)

[17] Wakiyama, M., Noda, H. and Kawaguchi, E.: Computation Algorithm of Semantic Difference Measure in the SD-Form Semantics Model, *Transaction of IPSJ*, pp1065-1079 (1999)

Information Modelling and Knowledge Bases XV
Y. Kiyoki et al. (Eds.)
IOS Press, 2004

Concepts, Language and Ontologies (from a Logical Point of View)

Marie Duží
VSB-Technical University of Ostrava
17. listopadu 15, Ostrava, 708 33, Czech Republic
marie.duzi@vsb.cz

Motto: Es gibt eine und nur eine vollstaendige Analyse des Satzes.
Wittgenstein, Tractatus, 3.25

Abstract. Traditional, intuitive conceptions of concepts and their shortcomings are summarised first. We pose five worrisome questions, answering which becomes extremely important when we want to build ontologies of particular domains of interest, to "conceptualise" them and to perform a terminological classification, which should be used for an intelligent search in the huge amount of data on web pages. Since traditional, set-theoretical concept theories do not answer these questions in a satisfactory way, we introduce a new non-traditional theory of concepts. A concept is explicated by the key notion of Transparent intensional logic – *logical construction*, i.e. *structured* procedure. We show that between an expression (of any language) and the denoted object beyond the language (*denotatum*) there is just the meaning of the expression, i.e., the respective concept, which identifies (or fails to identify – in case of empty concepts) the denotatum. Whereas the denotatum is a "flat" set-theoretical entity (intension in case of empirical expressions), the meaning (concept) is *structured* procedure consisting of parts – constituents. This conception enables to adequately solve the problem of the so-called hyper-intensional contexts of *knowledge, beliefs* and *hypotheses.* Thus our theory not only provides a precise explication of intuitively used notions like *concept, ontology, meaning*, etc., but it also provides an essential extension of traditional theories including Kauppi's axiomatic theory and Ganter-Wille conception.

Key words. Concept, structured meaning, construction, ontology, conceptual lattice.

1. Introduction

Ontology is a notion borrowed from philosophy where it stands for handling possibilities and conditions of *being*, so that it is closely related to *epistemology*, which envisages the possibilities and limits of human perceiving and knowledge. Answering the fundamental ontological question "What is there?" is in no way as trivial as it may seem, since (quoting from [16]):

a) our perception of reality by our organs is filtered, so that we cannot be sure that the world so is and behaves as we perceive it
b) answering has necessarily to use linguistic means, so that we possibly digress from the properly 'being' when choosing our concepts and using special words.

And we add:

c) There are also many abstract objects the acquisition of which by our 'mind eyes' is limited by our mind capabilities.

In many areas of informatics we meet the task of representing *what is known, believed,* inferring other pieces of deduced knowledge and hypotheses, and communicating such *knowledge.* Hence knowledge is inherently endowed and connected with *concepts.* Men can obtain, save and exploit concepts intuitively, using their mind capabilities. If, on the other hand, *automata* take over the search, inference and communication, they need the *representation* of the respective concepts (and their interrelations). Thus in the recent years we can notice a proliferation of the term 'ontology', since some branches of informatics have for the above purpose coined the notion *ontology*. T. Gruber [15] has defined ontology as "an explicit formal specification of a *shared conceptualisation*". In this sense ontology describes a *knowledge domain* by means of a standardised terminology, concepts and inference rules. Since there are many knowledge domains – using specific or even competing vocabularies – it is meaningful to use (unlike in philosophy) also plural "*ontologies*". The use of ontologies in informatics is very broad, in particular in those domains that concern saving, combination and derivation of knowledge, i.e. in artificial intelligence, (deductive) databases and (global) information systems ("the web").

Building ontologies (and semantic search methods in particular) is, in general, based on a traditional conception of concepts: *Concept* is generally understood as a 'universal', which is expressed by a meaningful expression and is determined by its *content (intension)* and *extent (extension)*. Further, the extension of a concept is understood as a set of objects that 'fall under' the concept; the intension of a concept is the set of attributes (aspects) that characterise these objects. Thus, for instance, '*municipalities of the Czech republic*' and '*cities and districts of the Czech Republic*' have the same extension (the set of cities, towns, etc.), but different intensions, which means that these are distinct concepts. Classically it is affirmed that between an intension and extension of a concept there is an inverse relation: Increasing the content of a concept decreases its extent, and vice versa. Thus, for instance '*university student*' has a greater content than '*student*', but smaller extent.

This might seem to be a satisfactory theory, but accepting it, we meet many problems and questions. First, it was already Bernard Bolzano [2] who realised that it does not answer a fundamental ontological question, namely:

a) *What* kind of entity *is a concept*?

It only says that a concept consists of content and extent; but what is the content and what is the extent? If these are not defined independently of a "concept", we have a case of a circular "definition". If, on the other hand, content and extent are conceived in a naïve way, just "syntactically" as a set of sub-expressions, we meet serious problems. Thus, e.g., the concept of '*prime*(numbers)' has a content distinct from that of the concept of '*numbers that have exactly two factors*', and yet these are evidently identical concepts, what else might the expression 'prime' *mean* than the latter?

The inverse relation between content and extent of a concept is also not precisely specified: For instance the concept '*student of a Prague university*' has smaller content but *also smaller extent* than the concept '*student of a university in Prague or in Brno*'. (B. Bolzano adduced a similar well-known example: '*Man who understands all European languages*' vs. '*Man who understands all living European languages*'.) Moreover, it is obvious that concepts are not independent. For instance, the concept '*cities and districts of the Czech republic*' has content distinct from (greater than?) the content of '*cities and districts in Moravia*', but the extension of the latter is *necessarily* a subset of the extension of the former. There is also a problem of adjectives, which modify a property to form another (possibly independent of the original) property: '*Wooden horse*' has a greater content than '*horse*', but the extent of the former is never a subset of the latter (wooden horse is not a horse!). Is the concept of 'horse' contained in the concept of 'wooden horse'? We can formulate two further questions:

b) *What* kind of entity *is the content and extent of a concept*?

c) *What can be deduced from ("follows from") a concept*?

Still, there are other worry-some questions: The extent (as "defined" above) of a concept C keeps changing! For instance, the extent of the concept '*university student*' varies with each newly accepted student or a student who graduates. Hence this concept keeps changing? But it is all the same concept! Yet, it is often said that "concepts change, evolve, arise, cease, etc.". Did the concept of 'ontology' evolve? Or did the concept of a computer exist before people invented computers? The other question to answer is:

d) ***Do concepts "change"?***

If we want to build ontologies of particular domains of interest, to "conceptualise" them and to perform a terminological classification, which should be used for an intelligent search in the huge amount of data on web pages, these questions are extremely important. For instance, using the *Law of inverse proportion of extension E and intension I,* a partial ordering on a set of 'concepts' is defined: $<I_1, E_1> \leq <I_2, E_2>$ iff $I_1 \subseteq I_2$ (or $E_2 \subseteq E_1$, which is said to be the same as the former). If correctly defined (e.g. on the basis of Galois connections [14]), the poset of 'concepts' forms a lattice, and a theory of *conceptual lattices* has been developed, which is broadly used just for the intelligent 'semantic' search. In order that the theory can be used properly, the above partial ordering should be based on the relation of "what follows" from a concept, which is trivially fulfilled by the traditional *conjunctive conception.* However, it is just a special case, not exhausting all the possibilities. For instance, if somebody is a university student, than he certainly is a student (concept 'student' is contained in the concept 'university student'), but not only that. We can also deduce that he is tax sheltered, etc. Moreover, there are important concepts which cannot even be defined using conjunction of some attributes, e.g., '*ancestors of an entity*'.

It might seem, that *concept* can be identified with a meaningful expression, which is actually the case in traditional conceptions. But how would we then answer the question

e) What does it mean that some ***expressions are synonymous*****?**

Well, they are expressions with the same *meaning,* but then there is another question ***what* the *meaning is*.** Denotational semantic theories answer that meaning of an expression is the entity that is '*talked about*', i.e. the entity denoted by the expression, its *denotatum.* Leaving aside for a moment the question 'what the *denotatum* is[1]', let us contemplate whether denotational semantics is fine-grained enough. Consider the classical example 'equilateral triangle' vs 'equiangular triangle'. These expressions denote exactly the same set of geometrical figures; does it mean that they are synonymous, have the same meaning? But these are evidently distinct concepts (with different contents), and if they had the same meaning we would not have to study geometry so as to know that they have the same denotation, linguistic competence would do. Or, our students would not have to learn logic, they would know immediately that sentences like 'It is not true that if A then B' and 'A and not B' are equivalent, i.e. denoting the same proposition (and up to logical symbols they have the same "content"), knowledge of mother tongue would suffice. How would we perform translation into another language? On the basis of identical denotations? But then it would not matter whether we translated a sentence of the former type or of the latter, which again is obviously not true. Moreover, some *meaningful* mathematical expressions, like 'the greatest prime', do not denote any object; does it mean that they do not have any meaning? But we can reasonably claim and prove that 'the greatest prime does not exist'; how then could we compose a non-reasonable expression into a reasonable true sentence? What are we talking about? According to Parmenides, we cannot talk about anything that does not exist!

An attempt at a more sophisticated theory of concepts is presented by Ganter & Wille in [14], and Kauppi in [18] introduces perhaps the best work out of axiomatic set-theoretical concept theories. K.D. Schewe presented in [26] a very good survey of these traditional

[1] If, e.g., the denotatum=meaning of 'the mayor of Dunedin' were the extension of this concept, then we would not understand it till we'd perform some empirical investigation, e.g., visiting New Zealand and finding out who happens to hold the office of the mayor, but how could we perform such an investigation when not understanding the term?

conceptions, including the intuitionistic approach. Summarising briefly, all these set-theoretical conceptions could be in general characterised as follows: a concept is a logical theory, axioms of which form the intension of the concept, and a set of models of the theory is the extension of the concept. These axiomatic conceptions are more adequate in solving the problems as stated above, still do not answer all the questions we pose. In particular, they do not distinguish between identical and equivalent concepts. In the concluding Chapter 5 we summarise particular items in which the theory of *structured* meaning proposed in this paper form an essential extension of these traditional theories.

In this paper we answer the above questions, exploiting modern theory of concepts, first proposed by Materna in [20]. This theory conceives concepts as *structured, "hyper-intensional" entities, i.e., as logical constructions.* The origins of the theory can be found already at B. Bolzano [2] and in part also at G. Frege [13], and B. Russell [25], but its full development has been made possible by a new paradigm of Transparent Intensional Logic (TIL), the author of which is late Prof. Pavel Tichý [29]; his follower Pavel Materna [20] and others [6], [7], [8], [9] explicated concept by the key notion of TIL, namely logical *construction.* Chapter 2 is a brief introduction into the philosophy and basic notions of TIL. The exposition of the theory of concepts can be found in Chapter 3, and in Chapter 4 we deal with the problem of analyzing natural language. The concluding Chapter 5 contains an outline of possible applications. The goal of this brief study cannot be a detailed recapitulation and exhibition of the entire theory and its applications, we would rather like to motivate the reader so as to find the theory interesting, worth studying, and to stimulate further discussion on its possible promising use.

2. Transparent Intensional Logic

Due to the sensitivity of a meaning to the logical *structure* of an expression, the analysis of 'what is known, believed' and other attitudes has become a stumbling block for all the denotational (set-theoretical) semantic theories that take into account just the denoted entity. Our knowledge and inferential capabilities are inherently connected with the *sense (meaning)* of an expression. Since Frege's times, many leading logicians strived after logically handling *structured meanings,* to name at least Russell's structured propositions, Carnap's [4] attempts at the formulation of a stronger criterion for the identity of belief, i.e. *intensional isomorphism* between substituted expressions, Cresswell's tuples [5], etc., etc. B. Russell's results were perhaps the closest to a satisfactory solution: The world consists of "complexes" that are to be understood as "logical constructions" formed from the immediately given entities of sensation, viz., "sensibilia". (Russell 1918, [25]). Still, none of these attempts carries conviction of a full adequacy and correctness (see, e.g., Tichy [29], Materna [20]).

Frege's contextualist approach inherited by most of current logicians (including Montague [22]) has been criticised by Pavel Tichý who presented a fundamental revision of Frege's (sense-reference) semantic scheme, which makes it possible to adequately explicate the "behaviour" of expressions even in hyper-intensional belief/knowledge contexts. Tichý's solution respects the distinction between the meaning (sense) of an expression and the object denoted by the expression; but it differs from most current conceptions (incl. Montague's) in at least two points:

a) it logically handles the hyperintensional structure of the meaning, sense is explicated as a hyperintensional entity (construction)

b) No contextualism is present; expressions simply denote *either* an extension *or* an intension via its *sense*. Empirical expressions always denote intensions, and where it seems that they denote extensions they only possess *de re* supposition.

In contrast to a model theory, which starts with a naked syntax and only subsequently proceeds to a semantic interpretation in a model, TIL is 'transparent' not only that it is anti-contextualistic but also not formalistic. Notion of a naked formal expression as a pure graphic shape can be arrived at only through abstracting its sense from it. In terms of conceptual priority, TIL starts with sense-endowed expressions, which is to say that the "formal language" of TIL-constructions constitutes an "interpreted formalism". Every factor that is semantically salient is explicitly present in the respective formalism. This is evident, for instance, in the explicit typing of the theory, the types of TIL being exclusively objectual. So what qualifies the formal language of TIL as transparent, inherently interpreted, is that a naked shape can be introduced as an expression only if it is paired off with a construction constructing an object of a particular type.

Definition 1 (Simple types of order 1):
(An objectual) base is a collection of mutually disjoint nonempty sets.

i) Every member of the base is a *type over base.*
ii) Let $\alpha, \beta_1,..., \beta_m$ be *types over base,* then $(\alpha\ \beta_1... \beta_m)$, i.e. the set of all *m*-ary (total and partial) functions with an argument (a tuple) $\langle b_1,...,b_m\rangle$, where b_i $(1 \leq i \leq m)$ is a member of the type β_i, and at most one value of type α, is a *type over base.*
iii) Nothing is a *type over base* unless it so follows from i) - ii).

An object O (that is a member) of a type α will be called an α-object, denoted O/α.

An objectual base is a special kind of base, over which (an infinite) hierarchy of functions and constructions can be built up, and our conceptual scheme can be adequately modelled within this system. This base consists of sets of objects of four basic categories: ι, o, ω, τ, where ι is a type (set) of **individuals**. The objectual base together with the interpretation of other elements constitutes an *epistemic frame.* Interpretation of its other elements is as follows: o is the type (set) of **truth-values** {T, F}; ω is the type (set) of **possible worlds,** and τ is the type (set) of **time points** (or **real numbers**). The collection of pre-theoretically given (basic) features (traits), by the usage of which all the other notions are defined, constitutes the *intensional base* of the given system.[2]

Empirical expressions denote *intensions*, i.e. functions from possible worlds to chronologies of members of a type α. Hence α-intensions are functions of type $((\alpha\tau)\omega)$, which will be abbreviated by $\alpha_{\tau\omega}$. *Extensions* are objects of other types (α-objects), namely they are *not* functions from possible worlds ...

Note: Intention (extension) in the above sense, viz., $\alpha_{\tau\omega}$-object (α-object) must not be confused with 'intention of a concept' ('extension of a concept'). We will better use the terms 'content/intent' and 'extent' for the latter.

Examples of intensions:
Individual concepts (*offices*), like 'the Pope', 'the richest man', are objects of type $\iota_{\tau\omega}$;
properties of individuals, like (being a) 'student', are objects of type $(o\iota)_{\tau\omega}$;
binary *relations-in-intensions* between individuals, like 'kicking', are objects of type $(o\iota\iota)_{\tau\omega}$;
propositions, like 'The Pope is in danger', are objects of type $o_{\tau\omega}$.

According to Zalta [30], Russellian 'structured propositions' play the desired role of *complexes* that result by 'plugging' objects into the gaps of properties and relations. In our opinion, properties, relations, i.e. functions in general, have no 'gaps'; particular objects simply are members of (the arguments of) these flat functions. But we can accept the possible-world semantics of propositions, while the demand of *structured meanings* is met by

[2] For details, see [Tichý 1988, 201ff].

another entity: Between an expression and the denoted flat object there is a structured *mode of presentation* (*construction* in our terminology) of the object, i.e. meaning (perhaps the Fregean sense) of the expression. It is a complex, a (declaration of a) *procedure* that consists in a *creation of a function* by abstracting over objects and/or in *applying the function* to its arguments. But particular (physical/abstract) objects cannot be "plugged" into such a (conceptual) procedure; they must always be presented in an (albeit primitive) way, i.e., their concepts are constituents of the procedure. There are two such primitive modes of presentations that fill in the objects into the construction: *variables* and *trivialisations*. The other two kinds of constructions working over these ones are more complex; they are *closure* (creating a function by abstraction) and *composition* (applying a function to an argument).

The TIL language of constructions can be viewed as a typed λ-calculus whose terms are names of (denote) constructions. They might be conceived as Montague's λ-terms with fixed (intended) interpretation of components, which denote *not* the function (or its value), but *the way of arriving at* it. Due to the perfect correspondence between terms and constructions it is idle to mention the terms, and we transparently talk about the constructions. Thus, e.g., instead of claiming that '$\lambda x\ [^0\!> x\ ^0 0]$' denotes the construction $\lambda x\ [^0\!> x\ ^0 0]$ which constructs the class of positive numbers, we simply say $\lambda x\ [^0\!> x\ ^0 0]$ is the construction.

Definition 2 (Constructions):

i) *Variables* are ***constructions.*** Variables and constructions involving variables construct objects dependently on a valuation v, they v-construct.

ii) If X is an entity whatsoever, even a construction, then ^{0}X is a ***construction*** called *trivialisation.* Trivialisation ^{0}X constructs X without any change.

iii) If X_0 is a construction that v-constructs a function (mapping) F, i.e. an $(\alpha\ \beta_1...\beta_n)$-object, and $X_1,...,X_n$ are constructions that v-construct β_1-,...,β_n-objects $b_1,...,b_n$, respectively, then $[X_0\ X_1\ ...\ X_n]$ is a ***construction*** called *composition.* If F is defined on the argument $\langle b_1,...,b_n\rangle$, then the composition $[X_0\ X_1...X_n]$ v-constructs the value of F on $\langle b_1,...,b_n\rangle$; otherwise it does not construct anything, it is *v-improper.*

iv) Let $x_1,...,x_n$ be pairwise distinct variables that range over types $\beta_1,...,\beta_n$, and let X be a construction that v-constructs an α-object for some type α. Then $[\lambda x_1...x_n\ X]$ is a ***construction*** called *closure* (abstraction). It v-constructs the following function F (of the type $(\alpha\ \beta_1...\beta_n)$)**:** Let v' be a valuation that differs from v at most by assigning objects $b_1,...,b_n$, (of the respective types) to variables $x_1,...,x_n$, respectively. Then the value of the function F on the argument $\langle b_1,...,b_n\rangle$ is the object v'-constructed by X. If X is v'-improper, then F is *undefined* on the given argument.

v) Nothing is a ***construction*** unless it follows from i) - iv).

Notes:

1. The simplest constructions are variables; they are open constructions that construct objects dependently on valuation (they v-construct). They are no letters, characters, 'x', 'y', 'z', ... are *names* of variables.

2. Trivialisation consists in grasping an object and its "delivering" without any change. If X is an entity, then ^{0}X is a presentation of X without a "perspective". The term '^{0}X' might be likened to a constant of a formal language; but unlike such a formal constant, which can be interpreted in many ways so as to denote different entities and thus actually not being a constant but a "variable construction", '^{0}X' rigidly denotes construction ^{0}X that constantly constructs the X. A possible objection against such a conception might be: Well, your transparent approach is punctilious, but you lose the expressive power of model theories that enable us to examine common features of properties and relations

between objects of all the particular models. Our answer is: Not at all; TIL transparent approach is more precise without losing anything; due to the infinite hierarchy of types we have at our disposal variables ranging over objects at any level, which makes it possible to render particular "models" by valuations of (higher-level) variables.

3. A composition corresponds to the traditional operation of *application* (of a function to an argument). (Only) composition may fail to construct anything, it may be (v-)improper, namely in two cases: *First,* the component X_0 constructs a function F and components $X_1,...,X_n$ construct $\langle b_1,...,b_n \rangle$, but F is not defined at this argument. *Second,* some of the components X_0, X_1, ..., X_n fail to construct an object (they are v-improper). (In case $X_1,...,X_n$ do not construct objects of proper types to create an argument of F, the expression '$[X_0\ X_1\ ...\ X_n]$' is meaningless, it does not denote a construction.)
4. Closure (λ-abstraction) enables us to construct a function, and thus to analyse talking about the whole function (to "mention" it), not only talking about a particular value at a given argument (to "use" the function). Closure can never be improper, even if it constructs a (degenerated) function that is undefined at any of its arguments, like, e.g., $\lambda x[^0\!:\ x\ ^0 0]$.

We commonly use variable w as ranging over ω, and variable t as ranging over τ. If X is a construction that constructs an intension of type $\alpha_{\tau\omega}$, then instead of $[[Xw]t]$ we write X_{wt}.

Quantifiers – general $\forall_\alpha$ and existential $\exists_\alpha$ – are functional objects of type $(o(o\alpha))$. We will write $\forall x$A, $\exists x$A instead of $[^0\forall_\alpha\ \lambda x\ A]$, $[^0\exists_\alpha\ \lambda x\ A]$, respectively. Quantifiers are "totalising", i.e., they always return a truth value when being applied to a class (even if the characteristic function of the class were undefined at some arguments), namely $[^0\forall_\alpha\ \lambda x\ A]$ returns True iff $[\lambda x\ A]$ constructs the whole type α (A v-constructs True for all x ranging over α), otherwise False, $[^0\exists_\alpha\ \lambda x\ A]$ constructs True iff $[\lambda x\ A]$ constructs a non-empty subset of α (A v-constructs True for some x), otherwise False. Singulariser ι_α is an object of type $(\alpha(o\alpha))$, and instead of $[^0\iota_\alpha \lambda x\ A]$ we will use ιxA (*the only x such that A)*; $[^0\iota_\alpha \lambda x\ A]$ constructs the only member of the class constructed by $[\lambda x\ A]$ iff $[\lambda x\ A]$ constructs a singleton, otherwise it is an improper construction. We will use a standard infix notation without trivialisation in case of using truth-value functions ($\wedge$, $\vee$, …), less-than, greater-than and identity functions ($\geq$, $\leq$, $=$, …), but we have to keep in mind that these are just abbreviations that conceal the self-contained intrinsic meaning of the respective 'logical symbols'.

The bridge between an expression and a construction (logical analysis of the expression) is provided by a *principle of subject-matter,* which says, roughly, that an expression is about all and only those objects, incl. *constructions,* which receive mention in the expression (see [10]). Constructions are mentioned, e.g., in *hyper-intensional* contexts of knowledge, belief, etc., where the meaning, i.e. the expressed construction plays a crucial role. Thus a construction/meaning is a 'full-right' object to talk about, and has to be of a definite (higher-order) type, which is not possible within the simple hierarchy of types. What follows is a modification of Russell's ramified hierarchy of types:

Definition 3 (*Ramified hierarchy of types*)
Let B be an objectual base, i.e. a collection of mutually disjoint non-empty sets.
1. ***Types of order 1 over B***
defined according to Definition 1.
2. ***Constructions of order n*** *over B.*
(C_ni) Let α be a *type of order n over* B. If ξ is a variable that ranges over α, then ξ is a *construction of order n over B.*

($C_n$ii) If X is a member of a type of order n, then ^{0}X is a *construction of order n over B.*

($C_n$iii) If X_0, X_1,..., X_m are *constructions of order n over B,* then $[X_0\ X_1...X_m]$ is a *construction of order n over B.*

($C_n$iv) If distinct variables x_1, ..., x_m, as well as X, are *constructions of order n over B,* then $[\lambda x_1...x_m X]$ is a *construction of order n over B.*

Let $*_n$ be the collection of all constructions of order n over B. Types of order n+1 over B are defined as follow:

3. *Types of order n+1 over B.*

(T_{n+1} i) $*_n$ and all the types of order n are *types of order n+1 over* B.

(T_{n+1} ii) If α, β_1, ..., β_m are *types of order n+1,* then the set $(\alpha\ \beta_1...\beta_m)$ of all m-ary (total and partial) functions from $\beta_1 \times ... \times \beta_m$ to α is also a *type of order n+1 over B.*

(T_{n+1} iii) Nothing is a *type of order n+1 over B* unless it so follows from (T_{n+1}i) or (T_{n+1}ii).

Since the terminology in the area of logical analysis of natural language is vague and ambiguous, we exploit the results of Tichy's followers, as they have been presented, e.g., in [20], [21]. Just a brief summary: An expression expresses its *sense (=meaning, concept)* that identifies (non-fregean) *denotation.* Hence an expression denotes (talks about) its denotation via its meaning-sense.[3] The sense of an expression is in principle a (structured) 'procedure' – a closed construction (the concept specified by the expression). A construction identifies (constructs) the denoted object that is (in case of a "successful" constructing, i.e. construction not being improper) an intension or extension (a first-order, set-theoretical object), or even a higher-order object (involving a lower-order construction). Empirical expressions always denote an intension, and in this case we also speak about a referent or *reference* of an expression, which is the value of the denoted intension in a given world/time. The relation between the first-order object (intension) and that what is in most semantic theories considered to be a reference of an expression (for instance an individual in space and time, a set of individuals, etc.) *does not have a semantic character*; it is influenced by an empirical factor – state of affairs, and thus it is not directly a subject of a semantic-theory investigation. Hence a co-reference of expressions is from the TIL viewpoint a contingent, empirical matter. Expressions can be *equivalent* when they denote one and the same object, but do not have (even in this case) to have the same sense, i.e. *do not have to be synonymous.*

Definition 4

(From the TIL viewpoint) *logical analysis* of an (empirical) expression E consists in specifying a construction expressed by E, which (v-)constructs the object denoted by E.

Note: Correct analysis of an expression E has to respect the *principle of subject matter.* It means that *the* very perfect *analysis* of E (the concept expressed by E) has to be composed of only and just the constructions of all the entities E talks about.

Example: We will analyse the sentence
The assets of the richest (i.e. "the most rich") man are greater than $10 000 000.

a) Type-theoretical analysis of subexpressions:

Assets → Ass / $(\tau\iota)_{\tau\omega}$	Empirical function that assigns a number to an individual
Most → Most / $(\iota(o\iota))$	Function *that picks up an individual from a set of individuals*

[3] This is the most significant divergence from Tichý's original proposal, according to which an expression denotes its referent that is the respective construction. [Tichý 1988, 224].

Rich → Rich / $((o\iota)(o\iota)_{\tau\omega})_{\tau\omega}$	Adjective modifier creates a new property from a property
Man → Man / $(o\iota)_{\tau\omega}$	Property of individuals
Greater than → > / $(o(\tau\tau))$	Relation between numbers; (10 000 000 / τ)

b) Synthesis (into the construction)

Rich man denotes a property of individuals / $(o\iota)_{\tau\omega}$, which is constructed by:

$\lambda w\lambda t\ [^0\text{Rich}_{wt}\ ^0\text{Man}]$ – concept of a rich man

The richest man denotes an individual office / $\iota_{\tau\omega}$, which is constructed by:

$\lambda w\lambda t\ [^0\text{Most}\ [\lambda w\lambda t\ [^0\text{Rich}_{wt}\ ^0\text{Man}]]_{wt}\ ]$ – concept of the richest man

Assets of the richest man denotes a magnitude / $\tau_{\tau\omega}$, which is constructed by:

$\lambda w\lambda t\ [^0\text{Ass}_{wt}\ [\lambda w\lambda t\ [^0\text{Most}\ [\lambda w\lambda t\ [^0\text{Rich}_{wt}\ ^0\text{Man}]]_{wt}\ ]]_{wt}\ ]$ –
concept of the assets of the richest man

The whole sentence claims:

The value of this magnitude (in a world/time) is greater than 10 000 000:

$\lambda w\lambda t\ [\lambda w\lambda t\ [^0\text{Ass}_{wt}\ [\lambda w\lambda t\ [^0\text{Most}\ [\lambda w\lambda t\ [^0\text{Rich}_{wt}\ ^0\text{Man}]]_{wt}\ ]]_{wt}\ ]]_{wt} > 10\,000\,000]$

This is the very analysis of our sentence, which can be "hominized" by performing equivalent β-reductions:

$\lambda w\lambda t\ [\ [\ ^0\text{Ass}_{wt}\ [\ ^0\text{Most}\ [^0\text{Rich}_{wt}\ ^0\text{Man}]]\ ] > 10\,000\,000\ ]$

c) Type-theoretical checking:

$\lambda w\lambda t\ [\ [\ ^0\text{Ass}_{wt}\ [\ ^0\text{Most}\ [^0\text{Rich}_{wt}\ ^0\text{Man}]]\ ] > 10\,000\,000\ ]$

$(o\iota)(o\iota)_{\tau\omega}\quad (o\iota)_{\tau\omega}$

$\iota(o\iota)\quad (o\iota)$

$\tau\iota\quad \iota$

$\tau\quad o(\tau\tau)\quad \tau$

$o_{\tau\omega}\quad o$

Note: Such a correct analysis is a *necessary condition* of performing adequate inferences. Now, using inferential rules of the system (Gentzen's natural deduction in our case) we can deduce that, e.g.:

The richest man exists

Some rich man possesses more than $10 000 000

Some man possesses more than $10 000 000, etc.

But oůr sentence does not talk about any particular individual; in particular, it does not talk about Bill Gates (the office of the richest man serves here only as a 'pointer' to an unspecified individual). If we perform an *empirical investigation* (for instance the search in the database), and find out that Bill Gates happens to play the role of the richest man, then only by using this *additional premise* we can deduce that Bill gates possesses more than $10 000 000.

3. Theory of concepts

Now you can ask: Did we answer the fundamental ontological *question **a)*** What is a concept? Not yet. We just provided a preliminary characterization: It is the meaning of an expression, i.e. the logical construction specifying the way, in which particular entities the expression talks about are composed, so as to identify the resulting denotation of the expression.

For instance, the meaning of the expression 'primes' is a concept of primes, i.e. the construction: $\lambda x\ (\ [^0\text{Nat}\ x] \wedge [^0\text{Card}\ \lambda y\ ([^0\text{Nat}\ y] \wedge [^0\text{Div}\ x\ y])] = {}^0 2\ )$, which constructs the class of natural numbers that have exactly two factors. Meaning of the expression 'the greatest natural number' is the concept: $\iota x\ (\ [^0\text{Nat}\ x] \wedge \forall y\ ([^0\text{Nat}\ y] \supset [x \geq y])\ )$, which does not identify anything, it is an empty concept.

Concepts, logical constructions, are abstract objects (like numbers, algorithms, procedures – but not their recording or performing); therefore it is not reasonable to ask whether they *exist*, or *where* and *when* they are. They are beyond time and space [3]. Hence concepts are entities beyond the language, we do *not create* them, and we just *discover* some useful "needed" procedures and coin them by expressions. Conceivng concepts as constructions might answer the question a), but we still have to perform a slight correction of our conception. First, concepts are only *closed constructions* (without free variables). But constructions are in a way too fine-grained entities to specify (conceptual) procedures. Thus constructions that are almost ('quasi-') identical up to using bound variables, like $\lambda x[x > {}^0 0]$, $\lambda y[y > {}^0 0]$, $\lambda z[z > {}^0 0]$, etc., are, from the conceptual point of view, almost indiscernible. Hence we say that *concept* is the first (in lexicographic ordering) of them, the other point at the concept. Moreover, concept is not that construction which is "unreasonably η-expanded". For instance, (primitive) concept of adding is ${}^0+$, but not $\lambda xy\ [{}^0+\ x\ y]$ (which just points at the former). (For details see [17].) The following definition provides an answer to the *question **a)***:

Definition 5. *Concept* is a closed construction C such that C is the first one from the ordered set of quasi-identical constructions that point at C.

Neglecting, for the sake of simplicity, the slight distinction between quasi-identical constructions, we answer another *question **b)***:

Definition 6 *(content and extent of a concept).*

A concept C_1 is *(intensionally) contained in a concept* C_2, iff C_1 is a sub-construction of C_2.

Content (intension) of a concept C is the set of concepts that are contained in C.

Extent (extension) of a concept C is the object E, which is constructed by C.

An empirical concept is such a concept C_E, the extent of which is an α-intension I ($/\ \alpha_{\tau\omega}$).

The *extent of an empirical concept C_E in a world/time w,t* is the value of its extent in w,t (I_{wt}).

An empty concept is a concept the extent of which is an empty set.

A strictly empty concept is a concept that does not have an extent (does not construct anything, the construction is improper).

A simple concept (primitive with respect to a given conceptual system) of an object X is ${}^0X$ (it cannot be strictly empty).

Relation of intensional containment, as defined above, is the relation of partial ordering on the set of concepts; it is evidently reflexive, anti-symmetric and transitive. Still, in general, it cannot be used for a correct definition of a semantic conceptual lattice, because it does not have to be in accordance with the relation of 'deducing from a concept', which will be defined in the next chapter. Just an enumeration of the set of contained concepts *does not suffice*. We also have to specify *the way* in which these contained concepts are composed together to form a complex (see [9]). Otherwise we might obtain such absurd consequences, as have been presented, e.g., in [23].

4. Language and concepts

As has been stated in Chapter 2, analysis of an expression consists in specifying a construction expressed by the expression that identifies its denotation. But each expression can be usually analysed in more correct ways, less or more fine-grained. A correct analysis follows the principle of subject matter, i.e., *only* constructions of the objects mentioned by the expression are composed together. This principle has been first formulated by Frege [12]:

> *Ueberhaupt ist es unmöglich, von einem Gegenstande zu sprechen, ohne ihn irgendwie zu bezeichnen oder zu benennen.*

Such a correct analysis enables us to perform *adequate* inferences. To be able to perform *all* the correct inferences, our deduction has to be based on *the* most fine-grained correct analysis, which takes into account all the objects mentioned or used by the expression. The proof of the claim that to each meaningful expression E the unique best analysis C exists has been adduced in [10]. This analysis C is the ***concept expressed by expression*** E, the meaning of E.

Example: Expression 'assets of the richest man' might be analysed by ^{0}ARM, where ARM / $\tau_{\tau\omega}$ is the denoted magnitude. Obviously, such an "analysis" would not enable us to perform any reasonable inferences. But meaning of the expression is the concept

$\lambda w\lambda t\ [^0Ass_{wt}\ [\lambda w\lambda t\ [^0Most\ [\lambda w\lambda t\ [^0Rich_{wt}\ ^0Man]]_{wt}\ ]]_{wt}\ ]$,

β-reduced equivalent analysis $\lambda w\lambda t\ [^0Ass_{wt}\ [^0Most\ [^0Rich_{wt}\ ^0Man]]]$ is easier to read, it points at the concept. The extent of this concept is the magnitude ARM / $\tau_{\tau\omega}$, the extent in w,t is a number / τ, i.e. the value of the assets in w,t (the world/time is usually 'mirrored by' a knowledge base).

The concept contains (besides the simple concepts ^{0}Ass, ^{0}Most, ^{0}Rich, ^{0}Man) compound empirical concepts:

$\lambda w\lambda t\ [^0Rich_{wt}\ ^0Man]$ – concept of a rich man

$\lambda w\lambda t\ [^0Most\ [\lambda w\lambda t\ [^0Rich_{wt}\ ^0Man]]_{wt}\ ]$ – concept of the richest man

The extent of the former is a property of individuals RM / $(o\iota)_{\tau\omega}$, the extent in w,t is a set of rich men. The extent of the latter is an individual office MRM / $\iota_{\tau\omega}$, the extent in w,t is the individual who plays the role of the richest man (in w, t).

But the assignment 'expression → concept (=meaning)' is given by a linguistic convention, it is an empirical relation. Thus an answer to another introductory *question **d)** Do concepts change*? is *no*; just the above assignment of concepts to expressions can change, meaning of an expression changes, we even invent new expressions to name some 'newly discovered' concepts, and some old expressions cease to be used. Hence a (living) language develops, and moreover, each domain of interest uses actually its own "jargon". (We have to take into account a certain fixed, say current, standard, official language of a domain.)

Now we can answer the remaining introductory *questions **c)*** and ***e)***. We first define synonymy, homonymy and equivalence of expressions, and then explicate a vernacular "what follows from a concept".

Definition 7.

An expression E is *homonymous*, if E has more meanings, i.e., E expresses distinct concepts.

Expressions E_1, E_2 are *synonymous*, if they have the same meaning, i.e., E_1 and E_2 express one and the same concept C.

Expressions E_1, E_2 are *equivalent*, if they denote one and the same object O, i.e., concept C_1 – meaning of E_1, and concept C_2 – meaning of E_2 have the same extent, they construct O.

Empirical expressions E_1 and E_2 are *coincident (co-referential)*, if they currently refer to the same object (in the actual world/time), i.e., Concepts C_1 and C_2 happen to have the same extent in the actual, current world/time.

Examples:

- Coincident (but not equivalent) expressions: *Morning Star, Evening Star.*
  They denote distinct offices / $\iota_{\tau\omega}$
- Equivalent (but not synonymous) expressions:
  E_1 – Charles likes only football fans
  E_2 – Charles does not like anybody who is not a football fan.
  E_3 – There is nobody such that Charles likes him and he is not a football fan.
  E_1, E_2 and E_3 are equivalent, they denote the same proposition P / $o_{\tau\omega}$, constructed by:

E_1' – $\lambda w \lambda t\ \forall x\ ([{}^0\text{Like}_{wt}\ {}^0\text{Ch}\ x] \supset [\text{FootFan}_{wt}\ x])$
E_2' – $\lambda w \lambda t\ \forall x\ (\neg[\text{FootFan}_{wt}\ x] \supset \neg[{}^0\text{Like}_{wt}\ {}^0\text{Ch}\ x])$
E_3' – $\lambda w \lambda t\ \neg\exists x\ ([{}^0\text{Like}_{wt}\ {}^0\text{Ch}\ x] \wedge \neg[\text{FootFan}_{wt}\ x])$

Definition 8.
Each complex nonempty concept C is an *ontological definition* of its extent, i.e., *concept C defines the object O* constructed by C.

***Example*:** Ontological definition of (the class of) prime numbers (/οτ) is:

$$\lambda x\ (\ [{}^0\text{Nat}\ x] \wedge [{}^0\text{Card}\ \lambda y\ ([{}^0\text{Nat}\ y] \wedge [{}^0\text{Div}\ x\ y])] = {}^0 2\ )$$

This is not a common way of using the term 'definition'; there is no *definiendum* and *definiens*! By a 'definition' we usually understand the following schema:

Expression E_1 (*definiendum*) $=_{df}$ expression E_2 (*definiens*).

From the logical point of view this is a *linguistic definition.* It associates the expression E_1 (which is usually, but not necessarily, a simple expression that has not been used in the language till now) with the meaning of the expression E_2. In other words, linguistic definition assigns a new meaning to E_1, namely the ontological definition of the object denoted by E_2, i.e., it makes the two expressions synonymous on the basis of linguistic convention. Thus simple expressions often do not express primitive simple concepts (trivialisation of a denoted object), but *complex concepts,* see also [21].

Example: Primes $=_{df}$ Numbers that have exactly two factors
Cat $=_{df}$ Domestic carnivorous animal, a feline, …

To answer the last question c), which means to explicate vernacular "what follows from a concept", we need to define the so-called requisites of a property (/of an office) and properties typical for a property (/for an office):

Definition 9. Let P, Q, G be any properties and U an office. We define:

$[\text{Req}^{pr}\ \text{P Q}] = \forall wt\ \forall x\ [[\text{Q}_{wt}\ x] \supset [\text{P}_{wt}\ x]]$ (*P is a requisite of Q*)

$[\text{Req}^{of}\ \text{P U}] = \forall wt\ [[{}^0\text{E}_{wt}\ \text{U}] \supset \forall x\ [[\text{U}_{wt} = x] \supset [\text{P}_{wt}\ x]]]$
(P *is a requisite of* U, where E is the property (of an office) of existence)

$[\text{TP}^{pr}\ \text{P Q G}] = \forall wt\ \forall x\ [\neg[\text{G}_{wt}\ x] \supset [[\text{Q}_{wt}\ x] \supset [\text{P}_{wt}\ x]]]$
(*P is typical for Q, unless G*)

$[\text{TP}^{of}\ \text{P U G}] = \forall wt\ [[{}^0\text{E}_{wt}\ \text{U}] \supset \forall x\ [\neg[\text{G}_{wt}\ x] \supset [[\text{U}_{wt} = x] \supset [\text{P}_{wt}\ x]]]\ ]$
(*P is typical for U, unless G)*

Note: In artificial intelligence the condition G in the definition of a typical property is called *the guard* of a rule. The existential E / $(o\ \iota_{\tau\omega})_{\tau\omega}$ is a property of an office, returning True (in w,t) when the office is occupied (in this w,t). Generally, existential presupposition concerning the 'office rules' can be also conceived as a guard of the rule. Such an existential guard is indispensable in case of offices, because if the office U is vacant in some world/time w,t, then the composition U_{wt}, and thus the whole composition $[[\text{U}_{wt} = x] \supset [\text{P}_{wt}\ x]]$, are *v*-improper, see Definition 2.

For instance, sentence *The King of France is a ruler of France* is ambiguous. It can be read as a true sentence claiming that *being a ruler of France* is a requisite of *the King of France* (which does not imply the existence of the King), or as a sentence claiming that *the (current occupant of the office of the) King of France is a ruler of France*, which does not have *any* truth value, because its existential presupposition is not met. If it were true or false, then it would imply that the King of France exists (see [28]).

Examples of typical properties are, e.g.:
A typical property of a bird is flying, unless it is a penguin or an ostrich.
A typical property of a swan is being white, unless it has been born in Australia or New Zealand.

Now we can answer *question **c)**:*

Definition 10.
Let C be an empirical concept, the extent of which is an intension I, and let the "population" of I in a world/time be I_{wt}. Then it *follows from the concept C* that:
Any member of the population I_{wt} has any property R such that R is a requisite of I, and has any property T such that T is typical for I, if the guard is satisfied.

Hence we can say that it follows from the concept of cat that my "Minka" is a feline, or, it follows from the concept of spider that any spider has eight limbs, etc.

Finally, we define a semantic partial ordering on the set of (equivalence classes of) concepts that can induce a *conceptual lattice.*

Definition 11.
Let C_1 and C_2 be empirical concepts such that C_1 constructs a requisite R of the extent I constructed by C_2. Then *C_1 is weaker than or equivalent to C_2,* denoted $C_1 \leq C_2$.

***Claim*:**
Let properties EC_1, EC_2 be extents of concepts C_1, C_2, respectively, such that $C_1 \leq C_2$. Then necessarily, i.e., in all world/times w,t, $EC_{2wt} \subseteq EC_{1wt}$.

Proof: Follows from the definition of requisites.

As a special case, if the number of *all* the requisites R^i of an intension I is *finite*, a concept C can construct I by means of "conjuncting" R^i:

$$\lambda w \lambda t\, \lambda x\, ([R^1{}_{wt}\, x] \wedge \ldots \wedge [R^n{}_{wt}\, x]).$$

Then, obviously, for any C_j such that
$C_j = \lambda w \lambda t\, \lambda x\, ([R^{i1}{}_{wt}\, x] \wedge \ldots \wedge [R^{ik}{}_{wt}\, x])$, where $\{i_1,\ldots,i_k\} \subseteq \{1,\ldots,n\}$ it holds that $C_j \leq C$ and in any world/time the extent of C is a subset of the extent of C_j ($EC_{wt} \subseteq EC_{jwt}$), i.e., the *law of inverse proportion* is valid.

We have explicated and obtained the classical *conjunctive conception* of Galois ordering, which is just a special case of our general definition.

Another *"weaker semantic" ordering* on the set of concepts can be defined on the basis of typical properties: Let C_1 and C_2 be empirical concepts such that C_1 constructs a property T typical for the extent I constructed by C_2. Then $C_1 \leq_G C_2$;

Now the inverse relation between the extents in world/times holds only on the condition that the respective guards are satisfied (which can be formulated as some non-intrinsic integrity constraints, and their validity will be checked by the program):

***Claim*:**
Let intensions EC_1, EC_2 be extents of concepts C_1, C_2, respectively, such that $C_1 \leq_G C_2$. Then a *guarded rule* is valid on the assumption that the respective guard G is satisfied (in world/time w,t): $EC_{2wt} \subseteq EC_{1wt}$ (in case EC_2 is an office and the office is not vacant, then $EC_{2wt} \in EC_{1wt}$).

Proof: Follows from the definition of requisites and typical properties.

5. Conclusion

We presented logical apparatus together with the philosophical background of a new *modern theory of concepts*, and proved that this theory not only provides an exact explication of frequently used but vaguely "defined" traditional terms like 'concept', 'ontologies', 'conceptual lattice', 'semantic search', etc., but that this theory is an *essential extension* of the traditional conception. Thus the simplest case, when the definition of the denoted 'sought' object is given in the form of a conjunction of basic traits (requisites in our terminology, or perhaps Bolzano's "*Merkmale*") is just a special case of our general theory. Since such a conjunctive definition (though frequently used) is not the only possible one, and it is often the case that the object which is sought cannot be even defined in this way, our general theory may lead to a substantial qualitative extension of the methods of building particular domain ontologies, and provide a powerful tool supporting semantic search in the huge amount of data spread in web files. Last but not least, the TIL method of finding *the* analysis of an expression serves as a common unique tool for *knowledge representation* and *acquisition*. Knowledge can be not only described and specified in this language, but also particular *queries* on both explicit and implicit (deduced) knowledge can be specified (see [11]).

You may wonder, which of the logical features provided by TIL are not covered by traditional systems. What follows is a brief summary specifying the essence of TIL extension as compared with particular traditional logics. Since Ganter-Wille and Kauppian theories are based on a classical predicate logic, this survey provides a comparison of a set-theoretical classical theory of concept vs. TIL-like procedural theory of concepts as well.

a) *Extensional systems* of predicate logics (of any order) do not make it possible to distinguish between analytical and empirical expressions, i.e., *empirical expressions* the reference of which changes dependently on states of affairs (i.e. dependent on *modal* and/or *temporal* parameters) are not properly analysed.

   Possible recovery: Using some system of modal and/or temporal logic, or (preferably) intensional logic, e.g. Montagues's system or TIL.

   However, most of these systems (unlike TIL) do not distinguish between *temporal* and *modal* parameters.

b) First order predicate logic does not make it possible to analyse *mentioning* of functions, propositions, properties and relations, which is to say, the distinction between using an expression (and its respective meaning - construction) in the *de dicto* vs. *de re* supposition is not rendered.

   Possible recovery: Using some system of higher order logic.

c) *Denotational approach* to semantics (the meaning of an expression is conceived as a denoted object) does not take into account the *mode of the presentation* of the denoted object, and *synonymous* expressions are not distinguished from *equivalent* expressions. Therefore, the proper analysis of the so-called hyper-intensional contexts (of *knowledge, beliefs, hypotheses*) is a stumbling block for all the denotational semantics, including Montague's systems. Since Frege's times, logicians strive for logically treating *structured meanings* (to mention at least Russell's structured propositions, Carnap's intensional isomorphism – critised by Church and Tichý, Cresswell's structured meanings, i.e. tuples – critised by Tichý and Jespersen, etc., etc.).

   Possible recovery: Using *procedural declarative semantics* that enables us not only to use concepts – constructions, but also to mention them.

d) *Formalistic approach* to semantics does not make it possible to handle a rather fine-grained distinction between a representation of a construction and the construction itself.

Possible recovery: Using a transparent (formal but anti-formalistic) approach.
Note: Items ad c) and d) are closely interrelated. The need to mention particular constructions can be (to some extend) met even in a formalistic logic using Gödel's system of numbering formulas. However, a loyal knowledge representation should take into account attitudes to constructions.

e) Classical systems of predicate logics do not make it possible to handle *partial functions.* This feature is particularly restrictive when analysing definite descriptions (like *the* greatest prime, *the* King of France, etc.) when we have to deal with value gaps ('holes in reality'). The problems of (non-)existence and sentences with *existential presuppositions* become a stumbling block of classical logics.
Possible recovery: Using a system that can properly handle partial functions and 'empty concepts'. There are many of them[4]; the question is which of these is a proper one (from a mathematical point of view, computer scientist's point of view, analytical-philosophy point of view, etc.). From the viewpoint of analysing natural language, perhaps the most promising are the systems that use the method of 'partiality being propagated up', which is adopted by TIL as well.

We can see that from classical 1st-order predicate logic we would need to proceed to more and more expressive systems, which less or more still lack some expressiveness. An ideal apparatus should cover all the features mentioned above so to say "under one hat" and without the necessity to use a meta-language. Such an ideal logic that would enable us to cover all the peculiarities of natural language is of course just a dream. Logic can hardly involve, e.g., pragmatic features of a language, particular emotional attitudes, poetic metaphors, context dependent anaphors and situation dependent indexicals, etc. Yet, under some simplification, considering a standard form of current language, we can claim that TIL is the system that meets all the needs we have stated above. In other words, TIL is an ideal system for logical analysis of a language. When performing logical analysis of a language, we also abstract of the 'evolutionary features' of the language and of the way in which the concept acquisition is performed. In cognitive disciplines these features are important, and a form of Quine's approach ("don't ask for meaning, ask for using") might be justified.

Still, one of the problems that have to be solved is a practical applicability of the method in the web environment comprising a huge amount of *heterogeneous documents.* Adequate logical analysis of a natural language is only a *necessary* condition to meet the problem. But we also have to deal with reducing the 'dimension of the problem', which is usually not a subject of a logical theory. Anyway, a promising idea of using lattice theory promoting building ontologies in the area of 'Information retrieval' has been presented already in the work of Arents and Bogaerts [1]. In the Department of Computer Science of our university the Amphora Research Group (ARG) was founded in 2001, the intention of which is to form an organized research unit specialized in topics of Information Retrieval (IR) and other related disciplines. A software tool has been built up here, which exploits a generalized theory of 'conceptual lattices' [14], SVD (singular value decomposition) and other methods [27], [19], to explore web pages so as to "quarry", extract particular interesting domains together with their (limited) vocabularies.

The next step to be done now is a linguistic one: it consists in a disambiguation of the obtained vocabulary, and creation of the so-called 'intelligent thesaurus', viz., a semantic dictionary in which each important term is provided with the ontological definition of the denoted object, i.e., the concept (logical construction) expressed by the expression is assigned to it. Using inference rules of the logical system (Gentzen's natural deduction in case of TIL,

[4] A good survey of particular approaches to partiality within the Simple Theory of Types can be found in [31]

or logical programming tools of resolution and unification), we can define a semantic partial ordering on the obtained set of concepts and create the respective conceptual lattice, which will make it possible to conduct a really semantic and at the same time effective 'web-search'.

Another promising area of future theoretical research is using soft-computing methods of reasoning and inferring implicit knowledge. TIL, being a higher-order logic, is not and cannot be, of course, complete. But Henkin's completeness can be obtained in a 'TIL-like (limited) theory', and the first theoretical results obtained so far in the area of 'designing fuzzy TIL' are presented by V. Novák in [24].

This work has been supported by the grant project of GAČR No. 401/03/1403 – Principles of Logical Analysis

References

[1] Arents H.C., Bogaerts W.F.L.:Concept-based indexing and retrieval of hypermedia information.In Encyclopedia of Library and Information Science, Vol 58, Academic Press, New York 1996, 1-29.
[2] Bolzano, B.: *Wissenschaftslehre I, II.* Sulzbach, 1837.
[3] Brown, J.R.: *Philosophy of Mathematics.* Routledge, London, New York, 1999.
[4] Carnap, R.: *Meaning and Necessity.* Chicago UP, 1947.
[5] Cresswell, M.J.: *Structured meanings.* MIT Press, Cambridge, Mass., 1985.
[6] Duží, M.: Logical Foundations of Conceptual Modelling using HIT Data Model. In: *Information Modelling and Knowledge Bases XII,* IOS Press 2000, pp. 65-80.
[7] Duží, M.: A Contribution to the Discussion on Concept Theory. *Information Modelling and Knowledge Bases* XII, IOS Press 2000, pp. 346-351.
[8] Duží, M.: Two approaches to conceptual data modelling. Prague International Colloquium on Conceptual Representation, Prague, 1999. In: *Topics in Conceptual Analysis and Modelling*, Institute of Philosophy, Czech Academy of Sciences, Prague 2000, pp. 305-340.
[9] Duží, M.: *Logical Foundations of Conceptual Modelling.* Thesis, VŠB-Technical University of Ostrava, 2002, http://www.cs.vsb.cz/duzi/.
[10] Duží, M., Materna, P.: Parmenides Principle (An analysis of aboutness). In: *The Logica Yearbook 2002,* FILOSOFIA, ed. by T.Childers, Institute of Philosophy, Academy of Sciences of the Czech Republic, Prague, pp. 159-178.
[11] Duží, M., Materna, P.: Intensional Logic as a Medium of Knowledge Representation and Acquisition in the HIT Conceptual Model. In: Proc. of the *12th European-Japanese Conference on Information Modelling and Knowledge Bases*, Germany, 2002, pp.62-76.
[12] Frege, G.: *Die Grundlagen der Arithmetik.* W. Koebner, Breslau, 1884.
[13] Frege, G.: "Über Sinn and Bedeutung". *Zeitschrift f. Philosophie und philosophische Kritik 100,* 1892, pp.25-50.
[14] Ganter B., Wille R.: *Formal Concept Analysis, Mathematical Foundation.* Springer-Verlag, 1999.
[15] Gruber, T.: A Translation approach to portable ontologies. *Knowledge Acquisition,* 5(2), 1993, pp. 199-220.
[16] Hesse, W.: Ontologie(n). Das aktuelle Schlagwort. In: *Informatik-Spektrum* 25.6, pp. 477-480 (2002).
[17] Horák, A.: *The Normal Translational Algorithm in Transparent Intensional Logic for Czech.* PhD thesis, Masaryk University of Brno, 2001.
[18] Kauppi, R.: *Einfuhrung in die Theorie der Begriffsysteme.* Acta Universitatis Temperensis, Ser.A, Vol.15, Tampere 1967.
[19] M.Krátký, J. Pokorný, T.Skopal, V.Snášel, Geometric framework for indexing and querying XML documents. *EurAsia ICT 2002*, LNCS 2510, Springer-Verlag, Shiraz, Iran, to appear.
[20] Materna, P.: *Concepts and Objects.* Acta Philosophica Fenica, vol. 63, 1998.
[21] Materna, P.: Simple concepts and simple expressions. *Logica'99*, FILOSOFIA, Prague 2000, 245-257.
[22] Montague, R.: *Formal Philosophy.* In: Thomason, New Haven and London, Yale University Press, 1974.
[23] Niemi, T.: New Approaches to Intensional Concept Theory. University of Tampere, 1998.

[24] Novák, V.: *On Fuzzy Type Theory.* Manuscript, 2002.
[25] Russell, B.: The Philosophy of Logical Atomism. In: *Logic and Knowledge*, London 1956, 177-281.
[26] Schewe, K.,D.: A Logical Treatment of Concept Theories. In: *Proceedings of the 12th European-Japanese Conference on Information Modelling and Knowledge Bases,* ed. by H. Kangassalo, E. Kawaguchi, Krippen, Germany, 2002, pp. 1-13.
[27] Snášel, V., Skopal, T., Ďuráková, D.: Navigation Through Query Result Using Concept Order. *ADBIS 2002*, Bratislava, Slovakia, to appear.
[28] Strawson, P.F.: On Referring. *Mind* 59, 1950, pp.320-344.
[29] Tichý, P.: *The Foundations of Frege's Logic.* De Gruyter, 1988.
[30] Zalta, E.N.: "Singular Propositions, Abstract Constituents, and Propositional Attitudes", Themes from Kaplan, J. Almog, J. Perry, and H. Wettstein (eds.), Oxford: Oxford University Press, 1989, 455-478.
[31] Farmer, W.M.: A partial Functions version of Church's Simple Theory of Types. *Journal of Symbolic Logic*, Vol. 55, Issue 3 (1990), pp. 1269-1291.

Information Modelling and Knowledge Bases XV
Y. Kiyoki et al. (Eds.)
IOS Press, 2004

A dialogue manager for accessing databases

Salvador Abreu, Paulo Quaresma, Luis Quintano, Irene Rodrigues
Departamento de Informática,
Universidade de Évora,
7000 Évora, Portugal
`spa|pq|ljcq|ipr@di.uevora.pt`,
Tel: 351 266 745300; Fax: 351 266 745360

Abstract.

We present a logic programming based dialogue system that enables the access in natural language to the heterogeneous external relational databases of the Évora University.

The proposed system has the capability of inferring user attitudes and uses ISCO in order to view the University relational databases as a part of a declarative/deductive object-oriented (with inheritance) database allowing the mapping of relational tables to classes – which may be used as logic (Prolog) predicates.

Keywords: dialogue managers, natural language processing, logic programming, knowledge bases.

1 Introduction

Over the last couple of years Universidade de Évora has committed itself to the development of an Integrated Information System (SIIUE) [2]. SIIUE is not just a set of databases which have information about several aspects of the University (Academic, Research, etc.) but also a group of applications built to give that information an easy (read/write) access in conjunction with the ISCO development tool [2, 1].

The main purpose of the dialogue system presented in this article is to enable the users – eg. the administration – that are not aware of the University information structure to obtain the information they need. For instance, in the context of the University degrees evaluation the following question could be posed by the administrative staff in order to evaluate the performance of computer science professors that teach in the mathematics degree.

Que docentes de informática leccionam matemática?

(Which computer science professors teach mathematics?)

This information could be obtained in the University web pages (or with an SQL or ISCO query) if the staff knows the internal structure of the university information. The above natural language query will allow the staff to obtain the answer even when they do not know the information structure.

This query has some ambiguities that our system must resolve before it answers the user. The system is able to dialogue with the user to resolve ambiguities such as the one introduced by the noun phrase "computer science professors". In the context of the University of Évora information system this phrase may refer to[1]:

- professors that teach computer science courses
- professors that teach courses from the computer science degree
- professors that belong to the computer science department

The phrase "mathematics" in this context may refer to:

- applied mathematic curriculum
- mathematic teachers curriculum
- mathematic courses

Note that the administrative staff may not be aware of all the possible interpretations of their query. They may not know that the university has two degrees with the word 'mathematics' in their name but when they are confronted with those options they are able to choose the right one.

The remainder of this article is structured as follows: in section 2, the ISCO language is described. In section 3, the LUPS language is briefly described. In section 4 the overall structure of the system is presented; section 5 deals with the semantic/ pragmatic interpretation. In section 6 the dialogue manager is presented more extensive example is presented and, finally, in section 7 we discuss some current limitations of the system and lay out possible lines of future work.

2 ISCO

ISCO is a new Logic-Based development language implemented over GNU Prolog that gives the developer several distinct possibilities, useful for the development of applications such as SIIUE:

- It gives a simple database structure description language that can help in database schema analysis. Tools are available to create an ISCO database description from an existing relational database schema and also the opposite action.
- View relational databases as a part of a declarative/deductive object-oriented (with inheritance) database. Among other things, the system maps relational tables to classes – which may be used as Prolog predicates.
- Gives simple access to arbitrary relational data through ODBC using a GNU Prolog interface with unixODBC, which has been developed within the SIIUE project. Whenever appropriate, native interfaces to specific databases have been developed; such is the case for PostgreSQL.

[1]This example will be detailed in the following sections where we show how is that our system deals with the problems of this question.

- By virtue of the GNU Prolog implementation base, ISCO applications may resort to Constraint Logic Programming techniques. More specifically, finite domain constraints are supported in ISCO queries.

The dialogue modules use ISCO's capability to establish connections from Prolog to the relational databases in an efficient way. For example, the following SQL table:

```
CREATE TABLE "student" (
 "number" int4 NOT NULL,
 "name" text,
 "id_card" text,
 Constraint "number_pkey" Primary Key ("number")
);
```

Maps into the following ISCO class definition, which can be automatically generated by a support tool:

```
external(sac,student) class student.
  number: int. key.
  name: text.
  id_card: text.
```

Class `student` is mapped into clauses for a set of Prolog predicates that implement the four basic operations: query, insert, update and delete.

Variables occurring in queries are mapped to SQL and may carry CLP(FD) constraints, which will be expressed in SQL, whenever possible. For example, suppose variable `X` is an FD variable whose domain is `(1..1000)`, the query `student(number = X, name = Y)` will return all pairs `(X, Y)` where `X` is a student registration number and `Y` is the student's name. `X` is subject to the constraints that were valid upon execution of the query, ie. in the range 1 to 1000.

ISCO class declarations feature inheritance, simple domain integrity constraints, global integrity constraints and a comprehensive and simple to express access-control mechanism.

3 Dynamic LP and LUPS

LUPS ("Language of UPdateS" [3]) is a declarative language for knowledge updates that describes transitions between consecutive knowledge states. It consists of commands, which specify what updates should be applied to any given knowledge state in order to obtain the next knowledge state.

The simplest update command consists of adding a rule to the current knowledge state and has the form: $assert\ (L \leftarrow L_1, \ldots, L_k)$. In general, the addition of a rule to a knowledge state may depend upon some preconditions being true in the current state. To allow for that, the assert command in LUPS has a more general form:

$$assert\ (L \leftarrow L_1, \ldots, L_k)\ when\ (L_{k+1}, \ldots, L_m) \tag{1}$$

The meaning of this assert command is that if the preconditions $L_{k+1}, \ldots, L_m$ are true in the current knowledge state, then the rule $L \leftarrow L_1, \ldots, L_k$ should hold true in the successor knowledge state. The added rules are *inertial,* i.e., they remain in force from then on by inertia, until possibly defeated by some future update or until retracted.

However, in some cases the persistence of rules by inertia should not be assumed. Take, for instance, an user utterance. This is a *one-time event* that should not persist by inertia after the successor state. Accordingly, the assert command allows for the keyword *event*, indicating that the added *rule* is *non-inertial.*

$$assert\ event\ (L \leftarrow L_1, \ldots, L_k)\ when\ (L_{k+1}, \ldots, L_m) \quad (2)$$

In order to specify *persistent update commands* (which are called *update laws*) it exists the syntax:

$$always\ [event]\ (L \leftarrow L_1, \ldots, L_k)\ when\ (L_{k+1}, \ldots, L_m) \quad (3)$$

4 Natural Language Dialogue System

As was already stated the main goal of this work was to build a system that could get a Portuguese natural language sentence sent by a user through a web interface and respond accordingly.

To answer the question/sentence the system has to pass it from a web-based interface to a GNU Prolog/ISCO active process (A), the process must analyze the sentence accessing the relational database(s) when needed to get or check any information (B) and finally when acquiring all needed information, it has to build a comprehensive answer and pass it to the web-based interface (C).

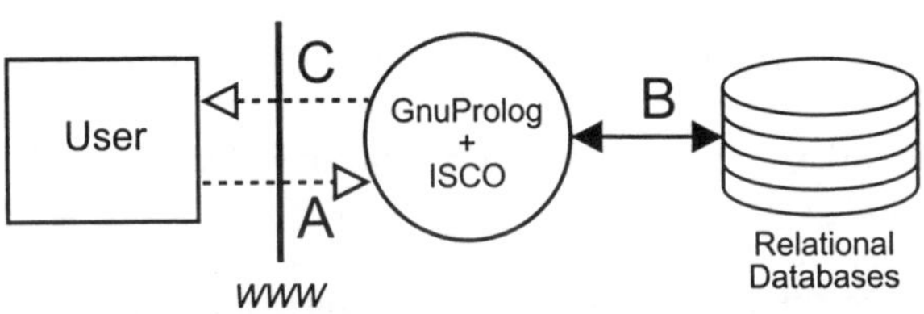

Figure 1: Simplifi ed SIIUE-NL system architecture

The processement of a natural language sentence is split in four subprocesses: Syntax, Semantics, Pragmatics, Dialogue manager

The user sends the question about the information that exists in the SIIUE. For that he/she uses a web-based interface using the scripting language PHP and the tools available by the php module of ISCO.

The question is then sent to an active Prolog process that already knows all the relational database structure to be used. ISCO manages the conversion of that structure to Prolog predicates that can access the relational databases through SQL primitives as selects, inserts, updates or deletes. In our case, as we're facing a querying system we only need to use selects.

Besides all database structures, this Prolog process does all syntactic, semantic and pragmatic analysis. After analyzing the sentence received, the process has to generate an adequate answer, which will be shown to the user through the web interface.

Syntax Analysis The syntactic interpreter was built using *Chart Parsers*[4]. This is one of many techniques to build syntactic interpreters. The decision of developing the interpreter using this technique was mainly because chart parsers can parse incomplete sentences. The user can place complete or incomplete questions and the system must be able to answer them accordingly, so the need to parse incomplete sentences is essential.

The interpreter also uses a lexicon to identify the syntactic properties of the words in the sentences. For that the interpreter is connected with a relational database (Polaris) which has syntactic (and semantic) information about Portuguese words. This integration is possible through ISCO because this tool already knows the Polaris database structure and can access it through ODBC.

This module will produce an output that consists in a list with all possible syntactic representations of the sentence placed by the user. As an example, if the user placed the following sentence as input to the system:

"Que docentes de informática leccionam à matemática?"

("Which computer science professors teach mathematics?")

The syntax module will return a list with the sentences' syntactic parse:

```
phrase([np([det(que,_+_+_), n('docente',3+p+m),
            pp(de,np([name('informática',3+s+f)]))]),
        vp(v('leccionar',3+p+_)),
        args_v([np([name('matemática',3+s+f)])])]).
%(phrase([np([det(which,_+p+_), n('professor',_+p+m),
%            pp(of,np([name('computer science',_+s+m)]))]),
%        vp(v('teach',3+p+_)),
%        args_v([np([name('mathematic',_+p+m)])])]).)
```

Semantic Interpretation The syntactic parsing output will be sent to the semantic module. This module will get the syntactic structure and rewrite it in a First-Order Logic. The technique used for this parsing is based on DRS's (Discourse Representation Structures)[6].

This technique identifies triggering syntactic configurations on the global sentence structure, which activates the rewriting rules. We always rewrite the pp's by the relation 'rel(A,B)' postponing its interpretation to the semantic pragmatic module.

This module returns a DRS build with two lists, one with the new sentence rewritten and the other with information about the referents that were created in this analysis.

For instance, if this module receives the syntax module output presented in the previous sections it will return as semantic representation of the sentence the expression:

```
professor(A), name(B, 'computer science'),
name(C,'mathematics'),
rel(A,B), teaches(A,C).
```

and the list with the discourse referents:

```
[ref(A,p+_+_,which),ref(B,s+_+_,undef),ref(C,p+_+_,undef)]
```

5 Semantic/Pragmatic Interpretation

The semantic/pragmatic module receives the sentence rewritten (into a First Order Logic form) and tries to interpret it in the context of the SIIUE databases information.

In order to achieve this behavior the system tries to find the best explanations for the sentence logic form to be true in the knowledge base for the semantic/pragmatic interpretation. This strategie for interpretation is known as "interpretation as abduction" [5].

The knowledge base for the semantic/pragmatic interpretation is built from the ISCO description of the SIIUE databases. The Kb rules are generated from the databases descriptions. This process was described in detail in [9].

From the description of the relation *si_teaches* the KB has rules for the interpretation of the predicates: *teaches(A,B)* and *rel(A,B)*.

```
class si_teaches.
  lecture: si_individual.id.
  degree: si_degree.code.
  course: si_course.code.
  year: int.
```

The rules in semantic/pragmatic Knowledge base are like the one below and they enable the interpretation of a sentence like "lecture teaches course" as the ISCO expression:
si_teaches(course = B, lecturer = A).

```
  rel(A,B) <-
    si_lecturer(A),
    si_course(B),
    abduct(si_teaches(course = B, lecturer = A)).
```

In the semantic/pragmatic interpretation the evaluation of a predicate like "si_course(A)" is done by an access to the relational databases through ISCO. The result of such an evaluation is the constraint of variable A to database identifiers of objects from class course.

The interpretation of names (eg. name(A,mathematics)) is done by accessing the SIIUE in order to collect in (constraint) A all entity identifiers that have in their name the word 'mathematics'.

The result of interpreting the sentence represented by:

```
professor(A), name(B, 'computer science'),
name(C,'mathematics'),
rel(A,B), teaches(A,C).

[ref(A,p+_+_,which),ref(B,s+_+_,undef),ref(C,p+_+_,undef)]
```

is the following ISCO expressions:

1. teaches(lecturer=A,course=B,degree=C)
   - `A=_#(7001...7852)` – A is constraint to all lectures
   - `B=_#(1046..1049:1345:1456..1457)` – B is constraint to the courses that have in their name the expression 'computer science'

- `C=_#(3046:3123)` – C is constraint to degrees with the word 'mathematics' in their name.

2. teaches(lecturer=A:,course=C:,degree=B:)

   - `A=_#(7001...7852)` – A is constraint to all lectures
   - `B=_#(3012)` – B is constraint to degrees with the word 'computer science' in their name.
   - `C=_#(1265..1281:1431:1454..1455:1784:1791)` – is constraint to the courses that have in their name the word 'mathematics'.

3. department(key=B:, lecturer=A:), teaches(lecturer=A:,degree=C:)

   - `A=_#(7001...7852)` – A is constraint to all lectures
   - `B=_#(101)` – B is constraint to departments with the word 'computer science' in their name.
   - `C=_#(3046:3123)` – C is constraint to degrees that have in their name the word 'mathematics'.

4. department(key=B:, lecturer=A:), teaches(lecturer=A:,course=C:)

   - `A=_#(7001...7852)` – A is constraint to all lectures
   - `B=_#(101)` – B is constraint to departments with the word 'computer science' in their name.
   - `C=_#(1265..1281:1431:1454..1455:1784:1791)` – C is constraint to courses that have in their name the word 'mathematics'.

The above ISCO expression contains the possible interpretations of the sentence in the context of the University information.

6 Dialogue Manager

The Dialogue Manager must disambiguate the sentence possible semantic pragmatic interpretations. It has to recognize the speech act associated with the sentence (in this domain it can be an $inform$, a $request$, or a $askif$ speech act), to model the user attitudes (intentions and beliefs), and to represent and to make inferences over the dialogue domain.

This task is achieved through the use of a logic programming framework rules and the LUPS language (see [8, 7] for a more detailed description of these rules).

For instance, the rules which describe the effect of an inform, a request, and a ask-if speech act from the point of view of the receptor are:

always bel(A,bel(B,P)) *when* inform(B,A,P)

always bel(A,int(B,Action)) *when* request(B,A,Action)

always bel(A,int(B,inform-if(A,B,P))) *when* ask-if(B,A,P)

In order to represent collaborative behavior it is necessary to model how information is transferred between the different agents:

always bel(A,P) *when* bel(A,bel(B,P))

always int(A,Action) *when* bel(A,int(B,Action))

These two rules allow beliefs and intentions to be transferred between agents if they are not inconsistent with their previous mental state.

There is also the need for rules that link the system intentions and the databases accesses:

always yes(P) ← query(P), one-sol(P) *when* int(A, inform-if(A, B, P))

always no(P) ← query(P), no-sol(P) *when* int(A, inform-if(A, B, P))

always clarif(P) ← query(P), n-sol(P) *when* int(A, inform-if(A, B, P))

These three rules update the system's mental state with the result of accessing the knowledge bases: yes, if there is only one solution; no, if there are no solutions; and clarification, if there are many solutions (the predicates that determine the cardinality of the solution are not presented here due to space problems, but there implementation is quite simple).

After accessing the databases, the system should answer the user:

always confirm(A,B,P) *when* yes, int(A, inform-if(A, B, P))

always reject(A,B,P) *when* no, int(A, inform-if(A, B, P))

always ask-select(A,B,C) ← cluster(P,C) *when* clarif(P), int(A, inform-if(A, B, P))

The first rule defines that, after a unique solution query, the system confirms the answer. The next rule defines that, after a no solution query, the system rejects the question. The last rule defines that, after a multiple solution query, the system starts a clarification answer, asking the user to select one of the possible solutions. In order to collaborate with the user we have defined a cluster predicate that tries to aggregate the solutions into coherent sets, but its complete definition is outside the scope of this paper.

Considering the question:

Which computer science professors teach mathematics?

As we presented in the previous section the semantic/pragmatic interpretation will give rise to the following expression:

```
R=[ref(A,p+_+f_,which),ref(B,s+_+_,undef),ref(C,p+_+_,undef)]

V=[(A1,B1,C1),(A2,B2,C3),(A3,B3,C3),(A4,B4,C4)]

I=[si_teaches(lecturer=A1, course=B1, degree=C1),
   si_teaches(lecturer=A2, course=C2, degree=B2),
   (si_department(key=B3, lecturer=A3),
        si_teaches(lecturer=A3, degree=C3)),
   (si_department(key=B4, lecturer=A4),
        si_teaches(lecturer=A4, course=C4))]
```

After having the sentence re-written into its semantic representation form, the speech act is recognized and we'll have:

```
ask-if(user, system, [R,V,I])
```

Using the "ask-if" and the transference of intentions rules we'll have:

```
int(system,inform-if(system, user, [R,V,I])).
```

Now, using the rules presented in the previous section, the system may access the knowledge bases (using the ISCO modules). The first step is to decide what is the meaning of the user sentence since there are four possible interpretations for each discourse referent (the V list has four elements). Using the following rule, the system is able to detect if there are many possible interpretations, and to obtain, for each referent variable, its respective classes. Then, it will ask the user to disambiguate the question:

> *always* ask-select(A,B,[VC,R,V,I]) ← int(A, inform-if(A, B, [R,V,I])), cardinality(V,N), N > 1, get_classes(V, VC).

get_classes is a predicate that obtains the set of possible classes for each variable referent. For instance, in our example we have:

> get_classes([(A1,B1,C1),(A2,B2,C2),(A3,B3,C3),(A4,B4,C4)], [([lecturer], [course, degree, department], [degree, course])])

The *ask_select* predicate chooses the first referent variable which has more than one possible class (B in the example) and, as a consequence, the dialogue system is able to ask if the user wants 'computer science' to refer to:

- course
- degree
- department

Suppose the user selects the option *department*. In this situation, there are two possible options for variable C: degree and course. The system will ask again the user to select the class of variable C. Suppose the user selects *degree*. Now, there is only one possible interpretation.

```
I = [teaches(lecturer=A, degree=C),
     department(key=B, lecturer=A)]
```

After having disambiguated the question interpretation, the system will use the rule presented previously and it will access the databases: $query(I)$

Suppose there are two possible solutions for the variable referent C: one for the degree of "Applied Mathematics" and another for "Mathematic Teachers". In this situation the *n_sol* predicate holds and the system will start a clarify interaction (using the *ask_select* rule and the cluster predicate):

```
ask-select(system, user, ["Applied Mathematics",
                          "Mathematic Teachers"]).
```

Now, suppose the user answers "Applied Mathematics". Using the inform and the transference rules, the system is able to add the information to the constraints of the current question and to, finally, answer the user question.

7 Conclusions and Future Work

The dialogue system described in this paper is still in an experimental stage and it has not been tested in "real" situations. We intend to have it available to all users using the University's internal web interface, via Universidade de Évora's web page (`http://www.uevora.pt/`) in a short period of time.

Clearly, and due to its complexity, all modules have aspects that may be improved:

- The syntactical coverage of the Portuguese grammar
- The coverage of the semantic analyzer (plurals, quantifiers, ...)
- The capability of the dialogue manager to take into account previous interactions and the user models

References

[1] Salvador Abreu. Isco: A practical language for heterogeneous information system construction. In *Proceedings of INAP'01*, Tokyo, Japan, October 2001. INAP.

[2] Salvador Pinto Abreu. A Logic-based Information System. In Enrico Pontelli and Vitor Santos-Costa, editors, *2nd International Workshop on Practical Aspects of Declarative Languages (PADL'2000)*, volume 1753 of *Lecture Notes in Computer Science*, pages 141–153, Boston, MA, USA, January 2000. Springer-Verlag.

[3] J. J. Alferes, L. M. Pereira, H. Przymusinska, T. C. Przymusinski, and P. Quaresma. Preliminary exploration on actions as updates. In M. C. Meo and M. Vilares-Ferro, editors, *Procs. of the 1999 Joint Conference on Declarative Programming (AGP'99)*, pages 259–271, L'Aquila, Italy, September 1999.

[4] Gerald Gazdar and Chris Mellish. *Natural Language Processing in PROLOG*. Addison-Wesley, 1989.

[5] Jerry Hobbs, Mark Stickel, Douglas Appelt, and Paul Martin. Interpretation as abduction. Technical Report SRI Technical Note 499, 333 Ravenswood Ave., Menlo Park, CA 94025, 1990.

[6] H. Kamp and U. Reyle. *From Discourse to Logic*. Kluwer, Dordrecht, 1993.

[7] P. Quaresma and J. G. Lopes. Unifi ed logic programming approach to the abduction of plans and intentions in information-seeking dialogues. *Journal of Logic Programming*, 54, 1995.

[8] Paulo Quaresma and Irene Rodrigues. Using logic programming to model multi-agent web legal systems – an application report. In *Proceedings of the ICAIL'01 - International Conference on Artificial Intelligence and Law*, St. Louis, USA, May 2001. ACM. 10 pages.

[9] Luis Quintano, Irene Rodrigues, and Salvador Abreu. Relational information retrieval through natural lanaguage analysis. In *Proceedings of INAP'01*, Tokyo, Japan, October 2001. INAP.

Information Modelling and Knowledge Bases XV
Y. Kiyoki et al. (Eds.)
IOS Press, 2004

A Theory of Signs for Database Semantics

Roland Hausser

Universität Erlangen-Nürnberg
Abteilung Computerlinguistik (CLUE)
rrh@linguistik.uni-erlangen.de

Abstract

The goal of this paper is to build a bridge from a certain intuitive conception of natural language communication, called the SLIM theory of language, to a technical approach, called database semantics (cf. Hausser 1999/2001). The intuitive approach proceeds from the interfaces of a cognitive agent's recognition and action, the levels of language and context, the nature of concepts, and the reconstruction of reference based on internal matching between the two levels, including an intuitive theory of signs. The technical software approach begins with a data structure suitable for the indexing and retrieval of content, an algorithm operating on the data structure, and a procedure for modeling language interpretation, inferencing, and production based on this algorithm.

Both approaches have coexisted for years, illuminating each other in suggestive ways, but without a systematic transition from one to the other. When it comes to the details of handling individual words in language interpretation and production, however, the intuitive theory of signs must be reconciled with the structural details required by the technical approach. The solution presented in this paper reconstructs the language and context components of the intuitive approach by refining the data structure of database semantics. For this, the different sign types are integrated into the basic information units of proplets as the values of certain attributes. Furthermore, different language proplets and context proplets are distinguished, and stored in different areas of the database.

1 Interfaces and Basic Components of a Cognitive Agent

Up to now, scientific analyses of natural language have been mostly limited to structural objects, fixed on paper or magnetic tape. Such objects are exemplified by a single word form, a sentence, or a text. By concentrating on the structure of the signs, one has attempted to abstract away from the aspect of communication.

The purpose of producing and interpreting language in the first place, however, is interaction between cognitive agents. Therefore, a scientific analysis of natural language cannot fail to be inadequate if it does not include the production and interpretation procedures inside the cognitive agents. The question should not be what a sign of language *is*, but rather what it *does*, and how it does it by virtue of the way it is.

In order to have artificial agents which can tell what they see and do what we tell them, they must be designed to have vision, hearing, articulation, locomotion, and an arm to handle things. And they must have a central control which integrates cognitive input and output as well as physical interaction with the world into a smooth routine.

Such a functional model must be verified in the form of a hardware realization which interacts with the real world. This is an engineering task consisting of a hardware part and a software part. In order for the various parts to interact smoothly, there should be a *declarative specification*. A declarative specification may be written as a design plan before starting to program or as a design explanation after the implementation. Often the two interact in a sequence of development cycles.

The crucial aspect of a declarative description is its level of abstraction. The need for such a level is shown by computer source code, which runs perfectly but is very hard to read. Moreover, source code fails to specify which properties are accidental (e.g., programming style including choice of programming language) and which are necessary. Therefore, a declarative specification is needed not only to guide the implementation of the system, but also to provide a wider public with a clear understanding of the theoretical solution instantiated by the implementation.

A declarative specification should be like an algebraic definition in logic: it should list the basic elements and specify the rules of combination. However, unlike an algebraic definition, a declarative specification is not restricted to set theory. Also unlike an algebraic definition, a declarative specification must take care of many additional aspects related to computational modeling such as the input-output conditions, the procedures of recognition and action, the data structure, the method of indexing and retrieval, inferencing, control structure, spatio-temporal orientation, interpretation and production of language, etc.

Let us begin the design of the declarative specification of our functional model by determining the input-output conditions of a talking cognitive agent. They are based on (i) sign recognition and synthesis and (ii) context recognition and action.

1.1 INTERFACES OF A COGNITIVE AGENT

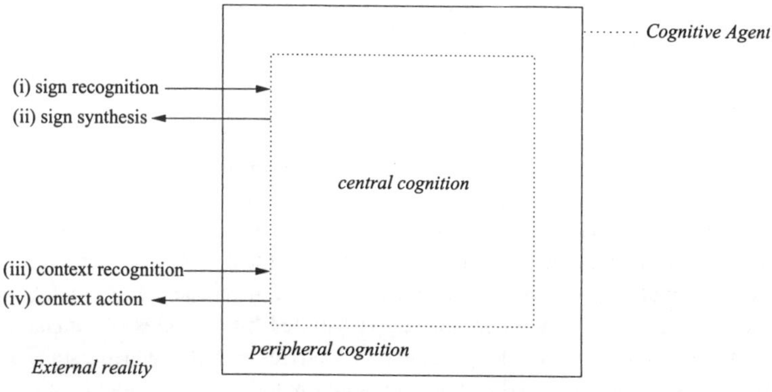

Peripheral cognition handles the agent's interaction with the external world. This interaction may be viewed as the processes of transporting agent-external aspects of the world into agent-internal cognition (recognition and language interpretation) and of transporting agent-internal aspects of cognition into the world (action and language production).

Central cognition handles storage and retrieval of content provided originally by peripheral cognition. We may assume that the processing of this content in central cognition is based on a homogenous coding, such as neural activity in humans or electronic operations in a computer. This coding may be described in an abstract manner which is independent of its realization in brain or computer.

Next we turn to the basic functional principles of cognition. The first, obvious requirement is that these functions combine to connect the input and the output of the agent.

That is, sign recognition must be connected to context action and context recognition must be connected to sign synthesis. These connections are not just a reflex between a stimulus and a response, but based on a memory with associated inferencing. This is the basis for sign and context recognition with processing but without external action, for context interaction without language, and for language interaction without input-output activity at the context level.

These structural properties of communication and cognition are best handled by complementing the distinction between peripheral and central cognition, indicated in 1.1 above, with the distinction between the levels of language and context, shown below:

1.2 COMPONENTS OF CENTRAL COGNITION

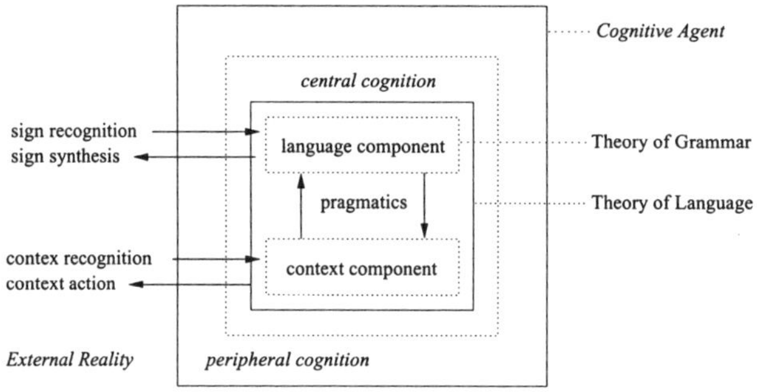

The distinction between the levels of language and context is motivated by the evolutionary fact that there are cognitive agents which resemble humans in many respect, yet don't have the capability of language. Thus, language may be viewed as an additional component, built upon the earlier developed context component.

The distinction between the two levels is also motivated functionally in that the context provides the content which is expressed in language by the speaker and stored in the context by the hearer. The context component stores what the agent recognizes, and provides algorithms for drawing inferences on this content and for deriving actions. The language level, in contrast, has the task of encoding a certain content of the context level (speaker mode) and of decoding a given language sign for storage in the contextual database (hearer mode).

The interaction between the two components is handled by the rules of language pragmatics. Language pragmatics may be analyzed as a phylo- and ontogenetic specialization of nonlinguistic pragmatics, just as language recognition and synthesis may be analyzed as phylo- and ontogenetic specializations of contextual recognition and action, respectively.

2 A First Step: Designing a Context Component

The structural analyses presented in 1.1 and 1.2 raise the question of whether they could be agreed upon by a wider range of sciences. After all, the basic structure of cognition is being studied in several fields, each taking its own point of view. Consider the following examples.

Evolutionary psychology studies higher primates in order to construct a model of communication which explains how human communication evolved from this higher primates. Thereby it finds that these animals have skill teaching, highly evolved social structures, and some surprisingly language-like forms of communication (Marc D. Hauser 1997).

Cognitive psychology wrestles with the question of how to present the concept of, e.g., a car, given that we can see only one side of a car but are able to imagine the whole shape, and even add structural and functional information such as where the engine is and what it does (Barsalou 1999). Others study the emergence of language from embodiment (MacWhinney 1999), which has also become a topic in philosophy, as witnessed by a recent boom in Merleau-Ponty (Dreyfus 2002).

Artificial intelligences is spearheaded by the MIT robotic lab. Its wellknown effort is the building of COG (Brooks et al. 1998), a metallic robot resembling a human from the waiste up, with a face consisting of video cameras, but also eye brows to signal emotions, with arms and hands to perform acts of holding and moving, and an elaborate mechanism to model 'shared attention', i.e., the following of the other's gaze during communication, especially important in early child-mother interaction.

As the cognitive models mentioned above do not form a coherent, explicit theoretical whole, we do not know whether our model of input-output conditions, peripheral and central cognition, and language and context level would be acceptable to them. To enhance compatibility, however, we pay heed to the other sciences' credos. Thus, we would certainly want our model to be in concord with the basic principles of evolution. It should also be compatible with the findings of cognitive psychology. And it should be verified in the form of computational hard ware models functioning in the real world.

Given the difficulty of our task, we would like to begin with the most basic component in its most basic form. This component is what we call the *context*. In animals without language, the context is the only component of cognition. In humans, it is one of two cognitive components, the other being the language component.

The construction of a cognitive agent with a context but without language, as exemplified by a dog, is a good starting point[1] for the following reasons. First, when we come to modeling language interpretation and production, we will need a context component anyway. Second, if we assume that there is a natural relation between the cognition of dogs and humans, there is a good chance that there is a natural upscaling from a model of a dog's cognition to that of a human. Third, the comparison of what the cognition of a dog and a human have in common, i.e. the context component, provides heuristics for finding abstract representations behind a multitude of variants.[2]

3 Level of Abstraction

To increase the chances of success, we must simplify the design of a context. For this, we take a lesson from modern ecology by controlling the robot's environment – and thus the conditions of its recognition. For the purpose of modeling recognition and action in principle, we use the simplified world of colored geometric objects such as triangles, squares, etc.

The cognitive building blocks of the context are called *concepts*. They are used to classify bitmap outlines for recognizing squares and triangles as well as intervalls of the color spectrum to recognize red, green, etc. They are also used for storing content in memory, as the data on which inferences are run, as the input to context action and language production, etc.

Concepts come in two varieties, types and tokens. This distinction, introduced by Peirce, is illustrated in the following example of the type and the token of the concept *square*:

[1] We are using dogs as our example because higher primates are currently subject of a debate as to whether or not they exhibit rudimentary language and culture.

[2] For example, we take the liberty to omit smell in our model, even though it is important for dogs (and for non-verbal communication in humans).

3.1 THE TYPE AND A TOKEN OF THE CONCEPT *square*

type *token*

$$\begin{bmatrix} \text{edge 1: } \alpha \\ \text{angle 1/2: } 90^o \\ \text{edge 2: } \alpha \\ \text{angle 2/3: } 90^o \\ \text{edge 3: } \alpha \\ \text{angle 3/4: } 90^o \\ \text{edge 4: } \alpha \\ \text{angle 4/1: } 90^o \end{bmatrix} \qquad \begin{bmatrix} \text{edge 1: 2cm} \\ \text{angle 1/2: } 90^o \\ \text{edge 2: 2cm} \\ \text{angle 2/3: } 90^o \\ \text{edge 3: 2cm} \\ \text{angle 3/4: } 90^o \\ \text{edge 4: 2cm} \\ \text{angle 4/1: } 90^o \end{bmatrix}$$

The type defines the necessary properties of a concept by means of constants and the accidental properties by means of variables. In the above example, the necessary properties of the concept type *square* are four angles of 90 degrees and four edges of equal length. The accidental property is the edge length, represented by the variable α. The variable makes the concept type applicable to squares of any size.

In recognition, concept types and concept tokens function together as follows:

3.2 CONCEPT TYPES AND TOKENS IN CONTEXTUAL RECOGNITION

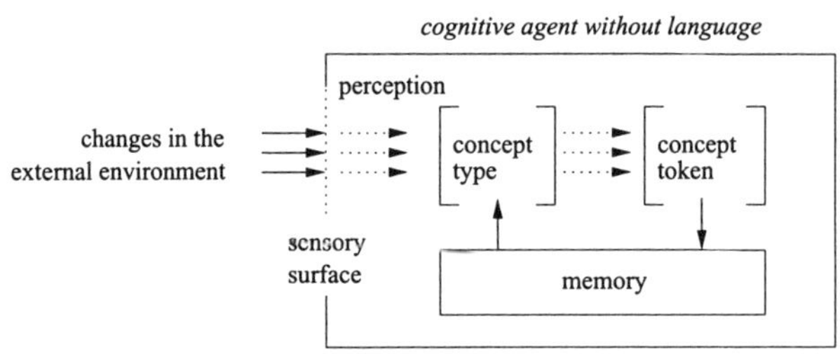

The incoming parameter values are matched by a concept type, which is instantiated as concept token: The concept type is provided by memory. The resulting context token is stored in memory. The matching process involving a concept type and and a concept token is illustrated below with the recognition of a square:

3.3 CONCEPT TYPES AND CONCEPT TOKENS IN RECOGNIZING A SQUARE

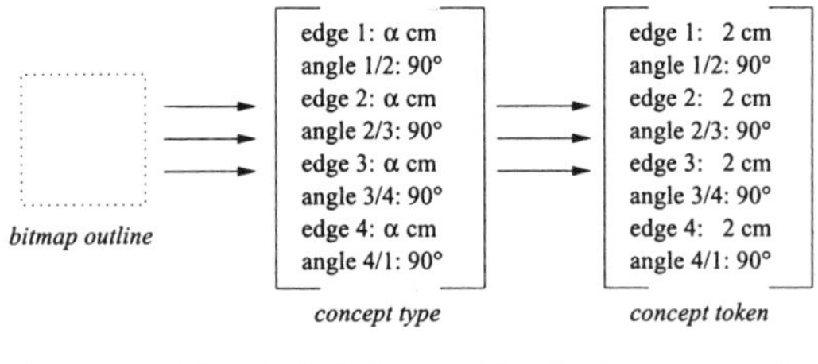

It would be no problem to build a machine that can recognize colored geometric objects using concepts like those illustrated above. This is because the notions used in the definitions have procedural counterparts which can be implemented relatively easily. Incidentally, they also correspond to the line, edge, and angle detectors discovered by Hubel and Wiesel 1962 in the visual cortex of cats.

Next consider the inverse direction. The inverse of perception and recognition is intention and action. Intention is the process of developing an action cognitively, while action is the mechanism of realizing an intention by changing the external environment.

3.4 CONCEPT TYPES AND CONCEPT TOKENS IN ACTION

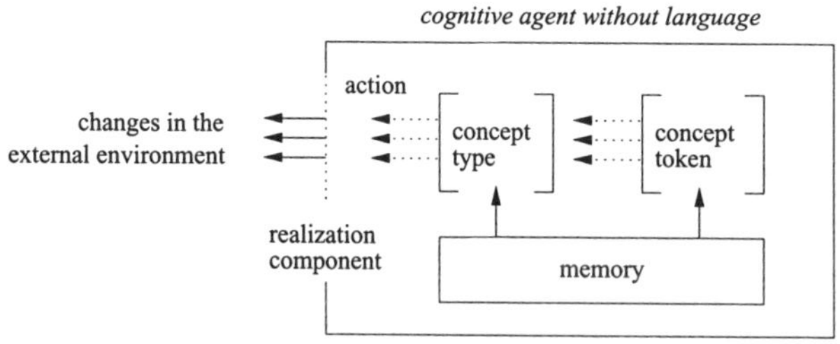

Intentions are represented as constellations of concept tokens and realized as actions by means of corresponding types. The formation of intentions is based on the agent's control structure, current situation, and inferences over content stored in memory.

4 Adding Language: Basic Reference

In cognitive agents with language, the concept types acquire a secondary function as the meanings of words. This is the basis of reference, which comes about by matching the concept types of language meaning with the concept tokens at the level of context:

4.1 SYMBOLIC REFERENCE BASED ON INTERNAL MATCHING

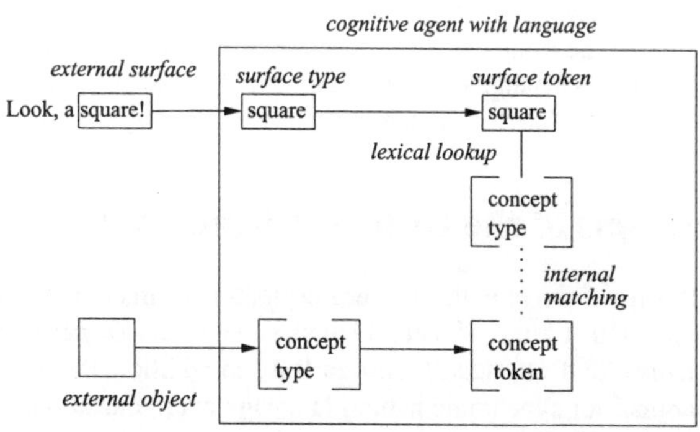

In this example, the cognitive agent recognizes a square at the level of context and the sign Look, a square! at the level of language (immediate reference).

Sign recognition and synthesis at the level of language are analyzed as specializations of context recognition and action, respectively. Just as the recognition of a square at the level context is based on parameter values in a certain modality (here vision) which are matched by a concept type and instantiated as a concept token, the recognition of the word surface square is based on parameter values in a certain modality (e.g., hearing) which are matched by a surface type and instantiated as a surface token. And similarly for contextual action (cf. 3.4) and sign synthesis.

The recognized surface of the sign is passed to lexical lookup, which assigns a literal meaning defined as a concept type. Reference comes about by matching the language concept type with the context concept token, as illustrated below:

4.2 INTERNAL MATCHING BASED ON THE TYPE-TOKEN CORRELATION

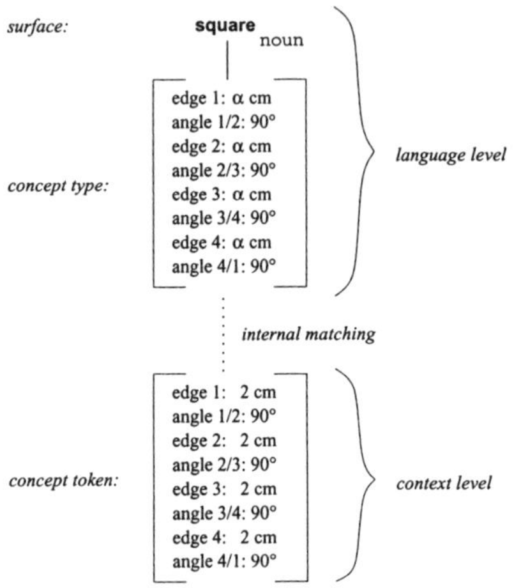

In this example, the concept type used in 3.3 for contextual recognition is reused in a secondary function as a literal meaning which is lexically attached to the English surface square. Furthermore, the type/token relation used in 3.3 for recognition is reused in the secondary function of *internal matching*.

The principle of internal matching between concept types and concept tokens models the flexibility of reference which distinguishes the natural languages from the logical and programming languages. It allows use of the same analyzed sign to refer to an open number of different referents at the level of context – in language interpretation and language production, and in immediate reference as well as mediated reference.

5 Reference Mechanisms of the Different Kinds of Signs

The mechanism of reference illustrated above with the word square is characteristic for a certain kind of sign, called *symbol*. Other kinds of natural language signs are *proper names* like John or R2D2, and *indexicals* like here, now, I, you, or this. In addition, there is the sign type of *icons*, which is marginal for synchronic natural language communication,[3] but important for explaining the evolution of symbols.

In modern times, the theory of signs was founded by Peirce, who analyzes the sign kinds symbol, indexical, and icon, but omits names. Symbols are defined as follows:

> A symbol is a sign which would lose the character which renders it a sign if there were no interpretant. Such is any utterance of speech which signifies what it does only by virtue of its being understood to have signification.
>
> Peirce 1940, p. 104.

[3] As pointed out by de Saussure 1967, pp. 81, 82. See Hausser 1999/2001, pp. 114 f.

Similarly, an index is defined by Peirce as a sign which would lose the character which renders it a sign as soon as the object it is pointing at is removed; an icon is defined as a sign which retains its character as a sign even if there is no object to refer to, and no interpretant.

The disadvantage of Peirce's definitions is that they are unsuitable for computational implementation. For the purpose of modeling natural language communication computationally, the functioning of the different sign types, i.e., their respective mechanisms of reference, must be explained in terms of their meaning structures instead.

The different reference mechanisms of symbols, indexicals, and names, based on their different kinds of meanings, is illustrated in the following schematic comparison of the three sign types, used to refer to the same contextual object, i.e., a blue square.

5.1 COMPARING ICONIC, NAME-BASED, AND INDEXICAL REFERENCE

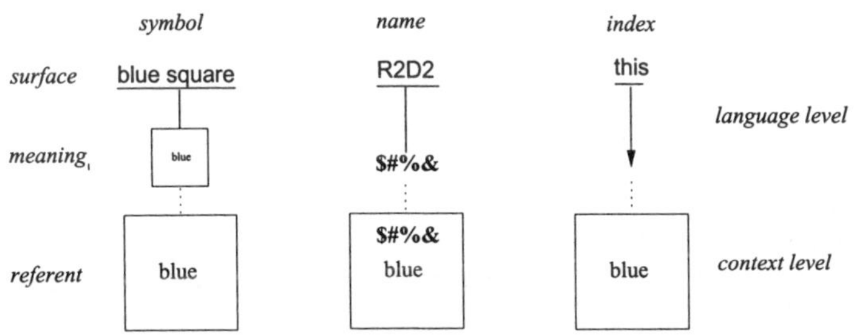

At the language level, each sign type consists of a surface and a lexically attached meaning$_1$. At the context level, the referential object is a blue square in a simplified representation of a concept token.

The meaning$_1$ of a *symbol* is a concept type. As explained in the previous section, reference with the sign type of symbol is based on matching the concept type at the level of language with a corresponding concept token at the level of context.

In the sign type *name*, the role of the meaning$_1$ is taken up by private identity markers. They originate at the level of context in order to indicate that different appearances of the referential object are being recognized as the same individual.[4]

In cognitive agents with language, (copies of) the private markers are reused by attaching them to public surfaces in an act of naming. Thereafter, reference with a name uses the public surface to call up each agent's private marker to match the corresponding marker in each agent's cognitive representation of the referential object.

Acts of naming may be explicit, as in a ceremony of baptism, or implicit, as in the following example: Agent A observes an unfamiliar dog running around, appearing and disappearing in the bushes. For continuity, the private identity marker $#%& is inserted into the cognitive structures representing the different appearances of the dog in A's context. Later, the owner calls the dog Fido. Agent A adopts the name by attaching $#%& to the public surface Fido. Henceforth, the name Fido refers for A to the dog in question by matching the private marker attached to the name with the corresponding marker inserted into (the cognitive representations of) the referent.

The sign type *indexical*, finally, has a meaning$_1$ defined as one of two characteristic pointers. The first points into the agent's context and is called the context pointer or C. The second points at the agent and is called the agent pointer or A. Consider the following examples:

---

[4]The marker used in 5.1 is $#%&, because the cognitive ability of recognizing identity may be present in agents without language and without a competence of numbering.

5.2 Indexicals as Nouns and Adjectives with A and C Pointers

noun A	*noun C*	*adj A*	*adj C*
I, we	you he, she, it this, they	here now	there then

Indexicals sharing the same pointer differ in terms of additional symbolic-grammatical distinctions. For example, the context pointer of the word this is restricted to single, non-animate referential objects, while they is restricted to a plurality of referential objects which may be animate or inanimate. Similarly, you is restricted to referential objects of any number and gender which are potential partners of communication, while he is restricted to a single referential object of male gender which is currently is not regarded as a partner of communication.

All three mechanisms of reference must be analyzed as internal, cognitive procedures. This is because it would be ontologically unjustifiable to locate the fixed connections between surface and meaning$_1$ in the external reality.

The distinction between the different *kinds of signs*, i.e., symbol, name, and indexical is orthogonal to the distinction between the main *parts of speech*, i.e., noun, verb, and adjective, as well as to the corresponding distinction between the basic *elements of propositions*, i.e., argument, functor, and modifier. *Symbols* occur as noun, verb, and adjective. *Indexicals* occur as noun and adjective. *Name* occur only as noun.

The orthogonal correlation between the kinds of signs and the parts of speech may be represented graphically as follows:

5.3 Relation between the Kinds of Sign and the Parts of Speech

name	Fido		
indexical	this	here	
symbol	dog	black	see
	noun	*adj.*	*verb*

The kind of sign which is the most general with respect to the parts of speech is the symbol, while the name is the most restricted. Conversely, the part of speech (and, correspondingly, the propositional element) which is the most general with respect to different kinds of sign is the noun (object), while the verb (relation) is the most restricted.

6 Database Metaphor of Successful Communication

The theory of language outlined above is modeled computationally in database semantics (dbs). Dbs is based on the assumption that the knowledge of the speaker and the hearer are represented in the form of databases. Furthermore, communication is successful if the speaker encodes a certain part of his or her database into language, and the hearer reconstructs this part *analogously* in his or her database – in terms of (i) a correct decoding and (ii) a correct storage at a corresponding location.

It is a crucial property of natural language that a sign's storage location in the speaker's database can be reconstructed by the hearer without any need for special indexing information. Achieving this kind of automatic indexing and retrieval is not trivial.

Consider robot A coding current observations in the following form:

Field contains triangle. Field contains square.

These are two elementary propositions[5] concatenated in terms of their adjacent position in the sequence. The elements of the propositions are the words.

Intrapropositonally, the words are related by a functor-argument structure. The functors are two instances of *contain*, which have the arguments *field* and *triangle* in the first proposition, and the arguments *field* and *square* in the second.

Extrapropositionally, the two propositions are related by their concatenation in terms of adjacency. They are also related in terms of the identity between the referents of the two occurrences of the noun *field* – assuming that the triangle and the square are observed in the same field.

Robot A's reporting his findings to robot B using a language raises the question of where robot B should store the propositions in its database:

6.1 ILLUSTRATION OF THE HEARER'S STORAGE PROBLEM

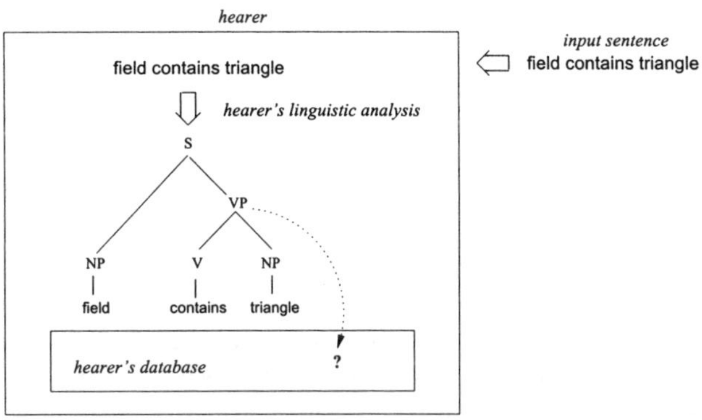

The external sign (input sentence) is represented inside the hearer and linguistically analyzed. For the sake of the argument, the analysis is a familiar phrase structure tree.

Storing this analysis in the hearer's memory (database) requires a *primary key*. Which property of the tree should be selected? The S node is not suitable as a primary key because it is shared by all phrase structure trees. The structure of the tree[6] is not be suitable either because it is shared by many different contents.

Furthermore, when the hearer turns into a speaker, the hearer's problem of storage turns into the speaker's problem of retrieval. Assume, for example, that the speaker has just the uttered the proposition field contained triangle. This raises the question: Which key should allow the robot to retrieve the closely related content of field contained square in order to arrive at a coherent sequence of utterances?

7 Data Structure of a Word Bank

The solution of database semantics to the indexing and retrieval problem of successful communication is based on following principles:

[5]For an explanation of the classic notion of a proposition see Hausser 1999/2001, Section 3.4, pp. 61–63.

[6]Assuming that the tree structure is coded into a compressed form, e.g. (S(NP VP (V NP))).

7.1 BASIC PRINCIPLES OF DATABASE SEMANTICS

1. The primary key is the content words. Content words are the nouns (including names), verbs, and adjectives, in contradistinction to function words, which include determiners, auxiliaries, and prepositions.

2. Content words may be connected by two kinds of relations: intrapropositional and extrapropositional. The intrapropositional relations are the functor-argument structure between verbs, nouns and adjectives within the same elementary proposition. The extrapropositional relations are the identity between nouns and the conjunction between verbs of different propositions.

3. The intra- and extrapropositional relations are not represented by graphical means. Instead, the content words are analyzed as feature structures called *proplets*[7] such that all intra- and extrapropositional relations are coded by means of attributes.

These principles are realized as the data structure of a word bank, consisting of proplet types and proplet tokens.

7.2 DATA STRUCTURE OF A WORD BANK

type_a	token_{a1} token_{a2} token_{a3} token_{a4}, etc.
type_b	token_{b1} token_{b2} token_{b3} token_{b4}, etc.
type_c	token_{c1} token_{c2} token_{c3} token_{c4}, etc.
etc.	

The proplet types are like the *owner records*, and the proplet tokens are like the *member records* of a classic *network database*. Like a network database, a word bank can be simulated in a relational database system.

In a word bank, the two concatenated propositions of 6 are represented as follows:

7.3 REPRESENTATING THE PROPOSITIONS OF 1.2.1 IN A WORD BANK

PROPLET TYPES PROPLET TOKENS

$$\begin{bmatrix}\text{verb: }\textit{contain}\\ \text{arg:}\\ \text{ctn:}\\ \text{ctp:}\\ \text{prn:}\end{bmatrix} \qquad \begin{bmatrix}\text{verb: }\textit{contain}\\ \text{arg:fi eld triangle}\\ \text{ctn: 2 contain}\\ \text{ctp:}\\ \text{prn: 1}\end{bmatrix} \begin{bmatrix}\text{verb: }\textit{contain}\\ \text{arg:fi eld square}\\ \text{ctn:}\\ \text{ctp: 1 contain}\\ \text{prn: 2}\end{bmatrix}$$

$$\begin{bmatrix}\text{noun: }\textit{fi eld}\\ \text{fnc:}\\ \text{idy:}\\ \text{prn:}\end{bmatrix} \qquad \begin{bmatrix}\text{noun: }\textit{fi eld}\\ \text{fnc: contain}\\ \text{idy: 1}\\ \text{prn: 1}\end{bmatrix} \begin{bmatrix}\text{noun: }\textit{fi eld}\\ \text{fnc: contain}\\ \text{idy:1}\\ \text{prn: 2}\end{bmatrix}$$

$$\begin{bmatrix}\text{noun: }\textit{square}\\ \text{fnc:}\\ \text{idy:}\\ \text{prn:}\end{bmatrix} \qquad \begin{bmatrix}\text{noun: }\textit{square}\\ \text{fnc: contain}\\ \text{idy: 2}\\ \text{prn: 2}\end{bmatrix}$$

[7] The term *proplet* is coined by analogy to *droplet* and refers to a basic part of an elementary proposition.

$$\begin{bmatrix} \text{noun: } \textit{triangle} \\ \text{fnc:} \\ \text{idy:} \\ \text{prn:} \end{bmatrix} \quad \begin{bmatrix} \text{noun: } \textit{triangle} \\ \text{fnc: contain} \\ \text{idy: 3} \\ \text{prn: 1} \end{bmatrix}$$

This word bank is based on two kinds of proplets, verbs and nouns, the attributes of which are defined as follows:

7.4 Definition of Attributes in Verbal and Nominal Proplets

verb:	= part of speech
arg:	= argument(s) of a verb
ctn:	= connection to next
ctp:	= connection to previous
prn:	= proposition number

noun:	= part of speech
fnc:	= functor of noun
idy:	= identity number
prn:	= proposition number

In proplet types, all attributes except for the part of speech (pos) have the value NIL (represented by empty space). As shown in 7.3, the types are ordered alphabetically in a column. Each type is followed by a *token line*. All proplets in a token line have the same pos value. The number of proplets in a token line is open.

Proplet tokens belonging to the same proposition share a common proposition number prn. The arg attribute in verbs and the fnc attributes in nouns are the intrapropositional continuation predicates. They code the functor- argument structure. For example, the proplet[8]

$$\begin{bmatrix} \text{verb: } \textit{contain} \\ \text{arg:fi eld triangle} \\ \text{ctn: 2 contain} \\ \text{ctp:} \\ \text{prn: 1} \end{bmatrix}$$

of proposition 1 specifies field and triangle as its arguments. The proplets

$$\begin{bmatrix} \text{noun: } \textit{fi eld} \\ \text{fnc: contain} \\ \text{idy: 1} \\ \text{prn: 1} \end{bmatrix} \text{ and } \begin{bmatrix} \text{noun: } \textit{triangle} \\ \text{fnc: contain} \\ \text{idy: 3} \\ \text{prn: 1} \end{bmatrix},$$

also belonging to proposition 1, specify contain as their functor.

The extraprositional relation of *conjunction* is coded in the ctn and ctp attributes of the two verb proplets in the word bank 7.3 :

$$\begin{bmatrix} \text{verb: } \textit{contain} \\ \text{arg:fi eld triangle} \\ \text{ctn: 2 contain} \\ \text{ctp:} \\ \text{prn: 1} \end{bmatrix} \quad \begin{bmatrix} \text{verb: } \textit{contain} \\ \text{arg:fi eld square} \\ \text{ctn:} \\ \text{ctp: 1 contain} \\ \text{prn: 2} \end{bmatrix}$$

As shown by their different proposition numbers, these two proplets belong to two different propositions. However, the ctn attribute of the verb of proposition 1 specifies the proplet

[8]Superfi cially, proplets may seem to resemble the feature structures of HPSG. The latter, however, are intended to be part of a phrase structure tree rather than a database, do not encode the functor-argument structure in terms of *bidirectional* pointers, do not concatenate propositions in terms of extrapropositional relations, and thus do not provide a suitable basis for time-linear navigation.

contain of proposition 2 as its successor, while the ctp attribute of the verb of proposition 2 specifies the proplet contain of proposition 1 as its predecessor.

The extrapropositional relation of *identity* is coded in the idy attributes of the following two noun proplets in the word bank 7.3:

noun: *fi eld* fnc: contain idy: 1 prn: 1	noun: *fi eld* fnc: contain idy:1 prn: 2

Again, the different proposition numbers indicate that these two proplets belong to different propositions. They are asserted to be coreferential, however, as indicated by their idy attributes having the same value, namely 1.

8 Autonomous Navigation

By coding all intra- and extrapropositional relations of concatenated propositions into the proplets of their content words, database semantics achieves complete freedom from the constraints of graphical representations. This provides for easy storage and powerful retrieval.

The continuous retrieval of successor or predecessor proplets in a word bank constitutes a kind of operation which conventional databases do not provide, namely an autonomous time-linear navigation through the concatenated propositions of the database. Navigation plays a crucial role in the modeling of successful communication in database semantics: it is used for the *conceptualization* and basic *serialization* of language production by the speaker.

Consider the following example of language production from a word bank:

8.1 PRODUCTION OF fi eld contains triangle

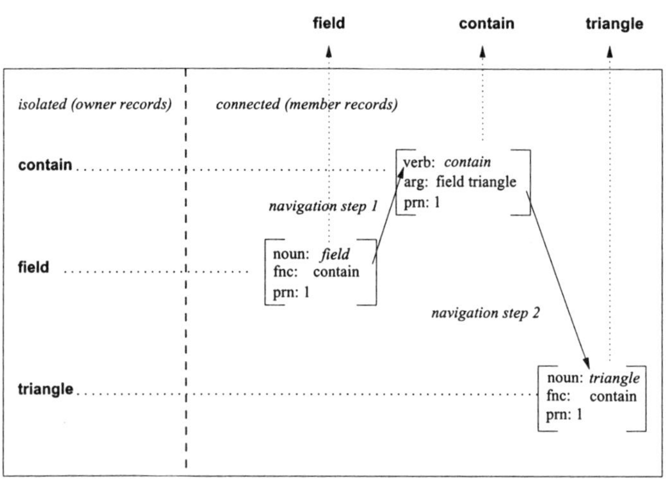

The navigation happens to begin at the proplet *field* with the proposition number 1. Based on the proplet's continuation predicate, i.e., [fnc: contain], the navigation algorithm looks for the token line of contain and proceeds from the owner record to the member record with the prn value 1. The proplet *contain* has the continuation predicate [arg: field triangle]. The first value, field, confirms the previous navigation. The second value triangle is the new 'next'

proplet. Again, it is found by going to the token line of **triangle** and proceeding from the owner record to the member record with the prn value 1.

The content traversed may be read out automatically by matching the value of its pos attributes (here *field, contain*, and *triangle*) with corresponding language-dependent surfaces – as indicated in the top line of 8.1. The hearer receives the surfaces and assigns suitable language proplets to them via lexical look-up, resulting in a sequence of lexical types. Time-linear parsing of this sequence completes the lexical types into proplet tokens.

8.2 INTERPRETATION OF field contains triangle

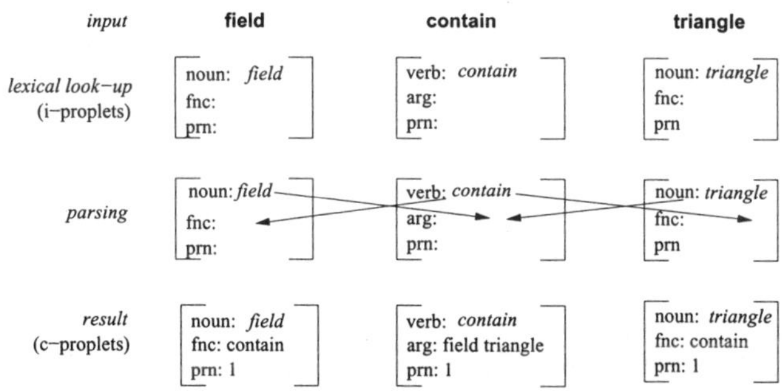

The completion consists in copying the pos value of one proplet into a suitable continuation attribute of another, and vice versa. The result is a(n unordered) set of the three co-indexed proplets *field*, *contain*, and *triangle*. The hearer may store the resulting proplets in accordance with the principles of the data structure in question, eliminating the time-linear order:

8.3 TRANSMISSION OF CONTENT BY MEANS OF NATURAL LANGUAGE

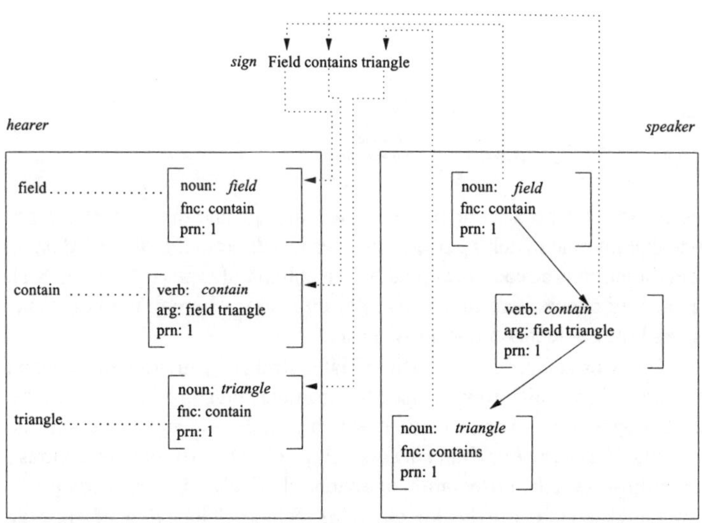

When the hearer turns into the speaker, however, the time-linear structure of language is reintroduced by means of navigation.

9 Reconstructing Internal Matching in a Word Bank

Next, the theory of signs presented informally in Section 5 must be reconciled with the data structure and communication mechanism of a word bank. This is accomplished by means of the following extensions of the data structure:

9.1 EXTENSIONS OF WORD BANK TO ACCOMMODATE THEORY OF SIGNS

1. The levels of language and context must be distinguished in the data structure of a word bank.

2. The different kinds of signs must be integrated into the proplets representing the language level.

The first requirement is fulfilled by introducing a general distinction between language proplets and context proplets in a word bank. This distinction is realized (i) by introducing characteristic differences between proplets and (ii) by storing different kinds of proplets in different areas in the word bank.

The distinction between areas in a word bank is shown in the following example in comparison to our intuitive correlation of the language and the context level:

9.2 ADAPTING INTUITIVE APPROACH TO WORD BANK DATA STRUCTURE

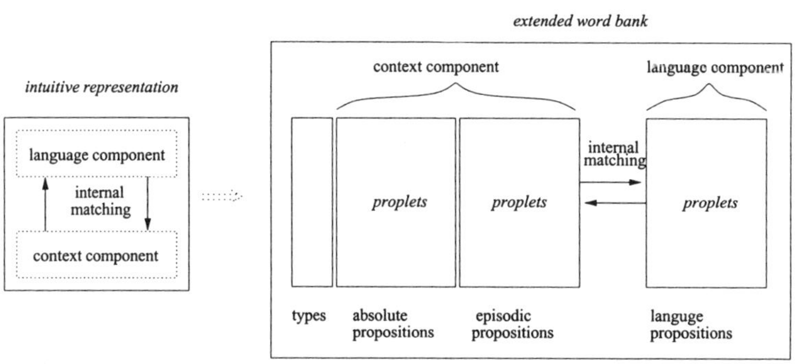

In the intuitive representation, the border line between the language and the context component is horizontal, such that internal matching occurs in a vertical direction. In the word bank, in contrast, the vertical direction is already occupied by the column of types (cf 7.3 and 8.1). Therefore, internal matching occurs here in a horizontal direction, whereby the borderline between the language and the context component is vertical.

The horizontal axis of the word bank in 9.2 is differentiated further by dividing the context into the areas for absolute and episodic proplets, used for absolute and episodic propositions, respectively. Absolute propositions express content which is independent of any specific spatio-temporal event, like *A square has four corners*. Episodic propositions, in contrast, express content representing a specific observation or action, like *Field contains a square*.

In addition, the horizontal axis is utilized for the spatio-temporal indexing of episodic propositions. This is shown by the following example of a word bank, containing an absolute, two episodic, and one language proposition.

9.3 HORIZONTAL MATCHING OF LANGUAGE AND CONTEXT PROPLETS

context type	*absolute context token*	*episodic context token*			*language token*
sur: noun: *apple* cat: NP sem: mdr: fnc: idy: prn:	sur: noun: *apple* cat: NP sem: sg def mdr: fnc: be idy: 2 prn: a4	sur: noun: *apple* cat: NP sem: sg def mdr: fnc: buy idy: 2 prn: e14	sur: noun: *apple* cat: NP sem: sg def mdr: fnc: eat idy: 2 prn: e15	⇒	sur: this noun: C cat: SNP sem: -animate sg mdr: fnc: eat idy: 1 prn: 1
sur: verb: *be* cat: V sem: mdr: fnc: ctn: ctp: prn:	sur: verb: *be* cat: V sem: pres mdr: arg: apple fruit ctn: ctp: prn: a4				
sur: verb: *buy* cat: V sem: mdr: fnc: ctn: ctp: prn:		sur: verb: *buy* cat: V sem: pres mdr: arg: $person^z$ apple ctn: e15 eat ctp: prn: e14			
sur: verb: *eat* cat: V sem: mdr: fnc: ctn: ctp: prn:			sur: verb: *eat* cat: V sem: pres mdr: arg: $person^z$ apple ctn: ctp: e14 buy prn: e15	⇒	sur: ate verb: *eat* cat: V sem: pres mdr: arg: $person^z$ C ctn: ctp: prn: 1
sur: noun: *fruit* cat: NP sem: mdr: fnc: idy: prn:	sur: noun: *fruit* cat: NP sem: sg def mdr: fnc: be idy: 2 prn: a4				
sur: noun: *$person^z$* cat: NM sem: sg def mdr: fnc: idy: *&%# prn:		sur: noun: *$person^z$* cat: NM sem: sg def mdr: fnc: buy idy: *&%# prn: e14	sur: noun: *$person^z$* cat: NM sem: sg def mdr: fnc: eat idy: *&%# prn: e15	⇒	sur: John noun: *$person^z$* cat: NM sem: sg def mdr: fnc: eat idy: *&%# prn: 1

The first column shows the proplet types serving as owner records. The second column presents the absolute proposition *an apple is a fruit* with the proposition number a4. The third and fourth column present the episodic propositions *John buys an apple* and *John eats the apple* with the proposition numbers e14 and e15, respectively. The fifth and last column shows the language proposition John ate this with the prn 1, containing the symbol ate, the name John and the indexical this. It is produced from proposition e15 by matching its episodic proplets with corresponding language proplets.

The spatio-temporal indexing is based on the linear sequence of content coming into (recognition) and going out of (action) the agent's database, illustrated by the propositions e14 and e15 in 9.3. The sequence is established by adding episodic propositions representing the agent's incoming recognitions and outgoing actions in the natural order of their occurrence.

For spatio-temporal orientation, the agent uses propositions which relate to temporal or spatial *landmarks*. Temporal landmarks are cyclical events such as the change of day and night, the phases of the moon, the changing seasons, the daily round of the milkman, etc.[9] Spatial landmarks are familiar objects fixed in the agent's environment.[10]

10 Integrating Different Kinds of Signs into Proplets

To complete the reconstruction of our intuitive theory of signs in database semantics, it remains to realize the second requirement of 9.1. It is fulfilled by replacing the values of the noun, verb, and adj attributes in language proplets – represented so far by English words for simplicity – by corresponding concepts in the case of symbols, identity markers in the case of names, and pointers in the case of indexicals.

As an example consider the following language proplets representing a symbol:

10.1 LEXICAL PROPLET TYPE AND LANGUAGE PROPLET TOKEN OF square

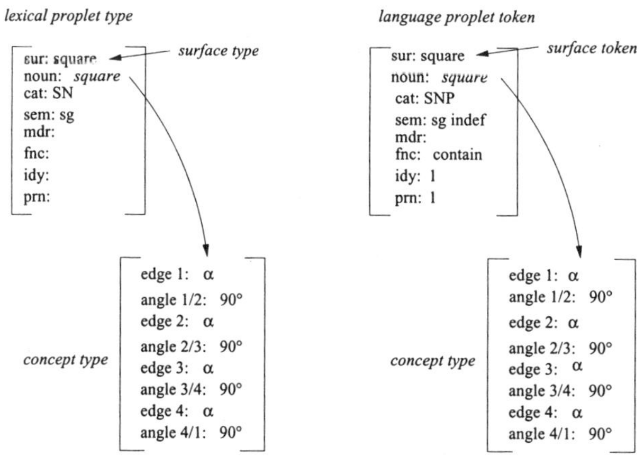

In language interpretation, the parameter values of the incoming sign surface, here square, are matched by the surface type[11] of a matching lexical proplet. Thereby, the surface is in-

[9]Cyclical events are also used for structuring the future, as when telling a child: *You have to sleep three more nights and then it will be your birthday.* Applying temporal inferencing learned from analyzing the past, the child can extrapolate into the future.

[10]Our approach to spatio-temporal indexing corresponds to the A-series of MacTaggert 1908. His distinction between the A- and the B-series reflects two basic approaches found from antiquity to present, called here the subjective and the objective approach. Simply speaking, we say that on the subjective approach time and space are moving through the agent, while on the objective approach the agent is moving through time and space.

[11]The difference between surface types and tokens resembles that between concept types and tokens in that surface types specify accidental properties by means of variables while surface tokens specify them by means of constants.

stantiated as a token and provided with a lexical analysis (lexical lookup). Syntactic-semantic parsing of the preceding and following proplets (cf. 8.2) results in a language token of square by supplying values to various attributes. Both kinds of language proplets use lexically provided concept *types* as the value of their noun attribute.

The corresponding context proplets differ from language proplets in that the value of their sur attribute is NIL. There are context proplet *types*, which serve as the owner records of the word bank, and context proplet *tokens*. The tokens are divided further into absolute and episodic proplet tokens for representing absolute and episodic propositions, respectively.

The three kinds of proplets at the context level are illustrated below with explicit concepts:

10.2 CONTEXT TYPE AND ABSOLUTE AND EPISODIC CONTEXT TOKENS

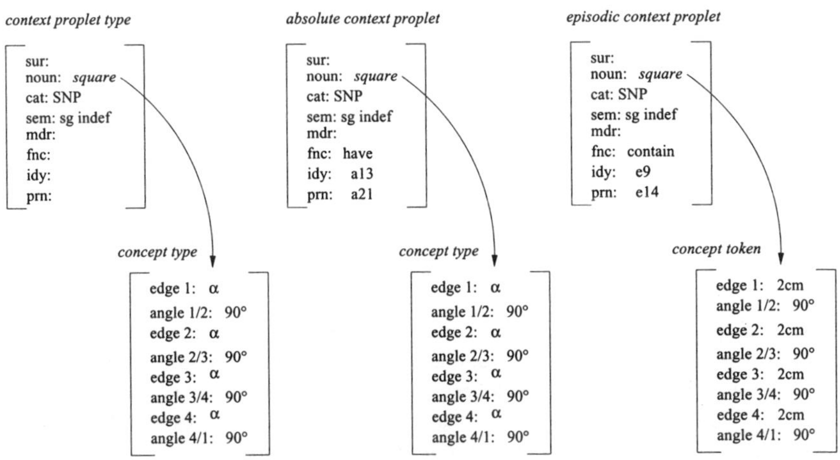

Context types and absolute context tokens take concept types as the value of their part of speech attribute (here noun), while episodic context tokens take concept tokens. Absolute and episodic proplets are further distinguished in terms of their identity and propositions numbers, which are prefixed by a and e, respectively (cf. 9.3). Context proplet types are like absolute context proplet tokens except that most of their attributes have the value NIL.

The five kinds of proplets used in dbs may be represented as the following hierarchy:

10.3 HIERARCHY OF THE FIVE KINDS OF PROPLETS USED IN DBS

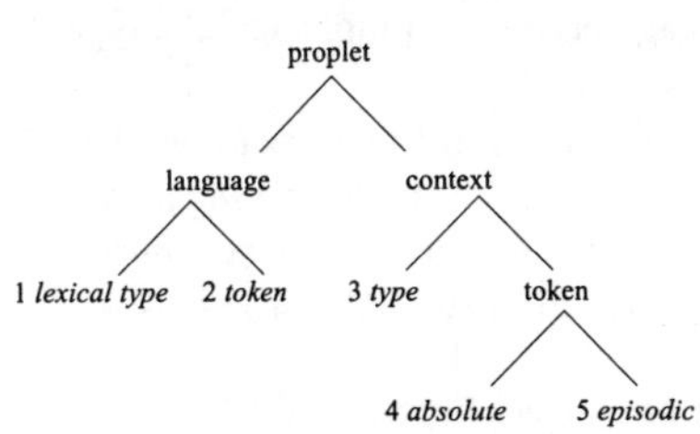

The different proplet kinds have the same attributes for nouns, verbs, and adjectives, respectively. They differ only in whether certain values are types, tokens, or NIL.

Just as the sign type of symbols is based on the prior existence of concept types[12] as their literal meanings, the sign type of *names* is based on the prior existence of private markers. Consider the following illustration of the five kinds proplets of a proper name, corresponding to those of a symbol in 10.1 and 10.2:

10.4 FIVE KINDS OF PROPLETS RELATED TO A NAME

lexical type	*language token*	*context type*	*absolute token*	*episodic token*
sur: Fido	sur: Fido	sur:	sur:	sur:
noun: dog^z	noun: dog^z	noun: dog^z	noun: dog^z	noun: dog^z
cat: NM	cat: NM	cat: NP	cat: NP	cat: NP
sem: sg def	sem: sg def	sem:	sem: sg def	sem: sg def
mdr:	mdr: black	mdr:	mdr:	mdr:
fnc:	fnc: run	fnc:	fnc: have	fnc: run
idy: *&%#	idy: *&%#	idy: *&%#	idy: *&%#	idy: *&%#
prn:	prn: 32	prn:	prn: a21	prn: e14

The identity marker characteristic of a proper name is the value *&%# of the regular idy attribute of nouns. For simplicity, we will use numbers prefixed by n, e.g., n1, n2, n3, etc., to represent the idy value of names.

In addition to the idy value, the referent of a name is characterized by a concept, here dog^z, which serves as the value of the noun attribute. In the name proplet of a person like Aristotle, the concept would be $person^y$, in the name proplet of ship like Missouri, the concept would be $ship^x$, and similarly with cities, countries, cars, pet animals, etc.[13]

The concept dog^z in the lexical type, the context type, and the absolute token of 10.4 is the type of a particular dog, which is instantiated by corresponding concept tokens in the proplets of language tokens and episodic tokens. For example, the concept type of Fido may characterize it as a dog of medium size, black shaggy hair, etc., while a corresponding concept token may instantiate the hair at a particular moment as wet and dirty.

The general concept *dog* of a symbolic context type and the particular concept dog^z of a named context type may interact as follows: first, the agent recognizes a dog, using a symbolic context proplet type; then the agent recognizes the dog as Fido using a named context proplet type, and instantiating it as a named episodic proplet token. Assuming that Fido is familiar, the agent has a lexical type as well as a context type already available, both containing the same specialized dog^z concept type and the same identity marker *&%#.

A symbolic language proplet can refer to a symbolic token as well as a named token. For example, the name-based context token *Fido* may be referred to with the language proplet dog. A name-based language proplet, however, cannot refer to a symbolic context token. For example, one cannot normally use Fido to refer to a generic dog. This is because the particular concept dog^z in the name-based language proplet is a more specific type than the concept *dog* in the corresponding symbolic episodic token.

Finally consider the reconstruction of *indexicals* in the word bank example 9.3: the language proplet this is positioned opposite the episodic proplet apple serving as referent, the characteristic pointer into the context is represented by the value C, and the values SNP (singular noun phrase), -animate and eat provide additional referential restrictions.

[12]In the sense that the concept types evolve already in agents without language. Cf. 3.2 and 3.4.

[13]On the on hand, our analysis follows Frege 1896 in that name proplets contain a concept which may be regarded as providing a sense ('Kennzeichnung'). On the other hand, our analysis differs from Frege in that the reference of names depends not only on the concept, but also on the private identity marker.

Thus, the formal reconstruction of indexicals as proplets provides at least as many structural details as the intuitive approach illustrated in 5.1. A systematic analysis, however, requires more space than that remaining in this paper.

Conclusion

This paper reconstructed the language and context components of an intuitive approach to natural language communication by refining the data structure of a word bank. The motivation for this refinement was the introduction of different kinds of signs, i.e., symbols, names, and indexicals, into database semantics.

This leads naturally to the question of how exactly the mechanisms of reference characteristic of each kind of sign function in language interpretation and production. In the case of symbols and names, the storage of language and context proplets in the same token line, and the compatibility or incompatibility of their attribute values, provides for a fairly straightforward implementation, at least for literal uses. The inferences[14] needed for non-literal uses, based in part on absolute propositions, and the spatio-temporal indexing[15] needed for indexicals, however, lead into areas beyond the scope of our present topic. Apparently, the questions raised by a paper are sometimes more interesting than those it set out to answer.

References

Brooks, R., C. Breazeal, M. Marjanovic, B. Scassellati, & M. Williamson (1998) "The Cog Project: Building a Humanoid Robot," in C. Nehaniv, ed., *Computation for Metaphors, Analogy and Agents*, Vol. 1562 of Springer Lecture Notes in Artificial Intelligence, Springer-Verlag.

Dreyfus, H. (2002) "Intelligence without representation – Merleau Ponty's critique of mental representation," in *Phenomenology and the Cognitive Sciences*, Vol. 1: 367–383, Kluwer.

Frege, G. (1967) *Kleine Schriften*, ed. by Ignacio Angelelli, Wiss. Buchgesellschaft, Darmstadt.

Hauser, M.D. (1997) *The Evolution of Communication*, MIT Press.

Hausser, R. (1999/2001) *Foundations of Computational Linguistics: Human-Computer Communication in Natural Language*, Springer-Verlag, Berlin-New York.

Hausser, Roland (2001a): "Spatio-Temporal Indexing in Database Semantics," in A. Gelbukh (ed). *Computational Linguistics and Intelligent Text Processing*, Vol. 2004 of Springer Lecture Notes in Computer Science, Springer-Verlag.

Hausser, R. (2001b) "Database Semantics for Natural Language," *Artifi cial Intelligence*, Vol. 130.1:27–74, Elsevier, Dordrecht.

Hubel, D.H. & Wiesel, T.N. (1962) "Receptive Fields, Binocular Interaction, and Functional Architecture in the Cat's Visual Cortex", *Journal of Physiology*, 160: 106–154

MacWhinney, B. (1999) "The Emergence of Language from Embodiment,'' in B. MacWhinney (ed.).

MacWhinney, B. (ed.) (1999) *The Emergence of Language*. Lawrence Erlbaum, Mahwah, NJ.

Peirce, W.S. (1931 – 1958) *Collected Papers of Charles Sanders Peirce*, edited by C. Hartshorne and P. Weiss, 6 vols. Harvard U. Press, Cambridge, Mass.

Saussure, F. de (1972) *Cours de linguistique générale*, Édition critique préparée par Tullio de Mauro, Éditions Payot, Paris.

---

[14]Cf. Hausser 2001b.

[15]For a more detailed analysis of spatio-temporal indexing in database semantics see Hausser 2001a as well as work in progress.

Information Modelling and Knowledge Bases XV
Y. Kiyoki et al. (Eds.)
IOS Press, 2004

3D Model Database System by Hand Sketch Query and Its Intuitive Interface

Yoshihiro Okada
Graduate School of Information Science and Electrical Engineering, Kyushu University
6-1 Kasuga-koen, Kasuga, Fukuoka 816-8580, Japan
Phone +81-92-583-7632, Fax +81-92-583-7632
e-mail: okada@i.kyushu-u.ac.jp

Abstract. This paper treats a 3D model database system that accepts a hand sketch image as its query. To develop 3D model database systems, two main questions arise: what is the best feature as the similarity measure among 3D models and what is the best way to specify the query. In this paper, the author proposes the hand sketch image as the answer of the second question. Then the author has already developed a 3D model database system [1, 2] that accepts a hand sketch image as the query. This system employs the silhouette image matching as similarity measure. This is the answer of the first question. Furthermore, the author has developed more intuitive interface for entering the query as hand sketch images using *IntelligentBox* [3]. This paper proposes such a database system and describes its usefulness showing its experimental results.

1. Introduction

This paper treats a 3D model database system. The development of 3D model database system poses two main questions: which feature can be assumed to be the best similarity measure among 3D models, and what is the best way to specify the query. We have already proposed the hand sketch image as the answer of the second question and the silhouette image matching as the answer of the first question. Then we developed such a 3D model database system [1, 2]. Furthermore, we have developed more intuitive interface for entering the query as hand sketch images using *IntelligentBox* [3]. In this interface, the user specifies the bounding box of his/her required 3D model in a 3D space, and does painting silhouette images of the model on the three orthogonal faces of that bounding box using a mouse-device. In this paper, we propose such a 3D model database system and describe the usefulness of the system with experimental results.

Some works on 3D model matching have already been done. Paquet and Rioux [4] proposed a 3D model database system. This system manages colored 3D models because it employs the color distribution in addition to the scale and the shape distribution as similarity measure. Osada et al [5] proposed 3D model matching, called *D2*, using distribution of distances between any two random points on the surface of a 3D model. This paper reported good search results in comparison with the other same typed similarity measures based on rough (global) features of shapes. As a similarity measure based on local features of shapes, Hiraga et al [6] proposed a new topology matching technique using Multiresolutional Reeb Graphs (MRGs). Bandlow et al proposed recognition method of objects using their silhouette [7]. In this case, objects are not 3D models but 2D images. We have not met any research on 3D model matching using a hand sketch image as the query, and any 3D model database system that has such an intuitive interface for entering the query as proposed in this paper.

The remainder of this paper is organized as follows: Section 2 describes overview of the 3D model database system and explains the silhouette image matching. Section 3 describes how the system works by showing its screen images. In Section 4, we show experimental results to clarify usefulness of the system. Finally Section 5 concludes the paper.

2. Matching algorithms

Basic idea is very simple as shown in Figure 1. First of all, the system automatically generates silhouette images of each 3D model in a 3D model database and stores them as their feature information. Next, the user enters hand sketch images as the query to search his/her required models. After that, the system retrieves and shows the best match models according to the silhouette image matching result.

2.1. Principal axes

Silhouette image generation needs a 3D model to be rendered on a computer screen, and its image to be captured and stored. For rendering a 3D model, it is necessary to determine its view direction from the eye-position. A very common way is to use the principal axes of the tensor of inertia of a model [4][8]. The tensor of inertia of a model is defined as a matrix I, where

$$I = \begin{bmatrix} I_{xx} & I_{xy} & I_{xz} \\ I_{yx} & I_{yy} & I_{yz} \\ I_{zx} & I_{zy} & I_{zz} \end{bmatrix}. \qquad (1)$$

Here, each element I_{qr}, $q,r \in \{x,y,z\}$ is calculated by the following equation:

$$I_{qr} = \left[\frac{1}{n}\sum_{i=1}^{n}\left[S_i \times (q_i - q_{CM}) \times (r_i - r_{CM})\right]\right], \qquad (2)$$

where n is the number of triangular faces of a model, S_i is the area of i-th face, q_{CM}, r_{CM} are q,r elements of the center of mass of the model, and q_i, r_i are q,r elements of the center of i-th face.

Finally, the principal axes are obtained by computing the eigen vectors of the tensor as follows:

$$I\vec{a_i} = \lambda_i \vec{a_i}, \quad i \in \{1,2,3\} \qquad (3)$$

The eigen vector having the biggest eigen value is the first principal axis and the eigen vector having the second biggest eigen value is the second principal axis. The remainder is the third principal axis. Their positive or negative directions are determined by distribution of amount of surface area.

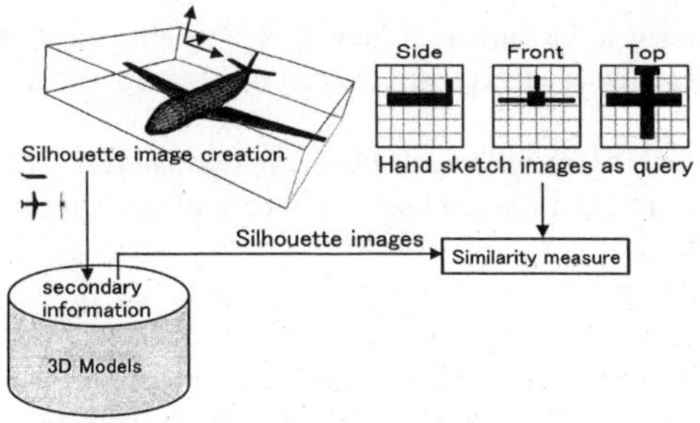

Figure 1: System overview.

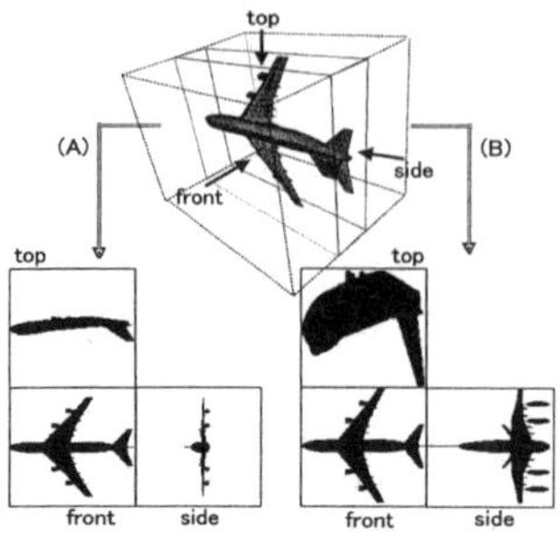

Figure 2: Two sets of normalized images.

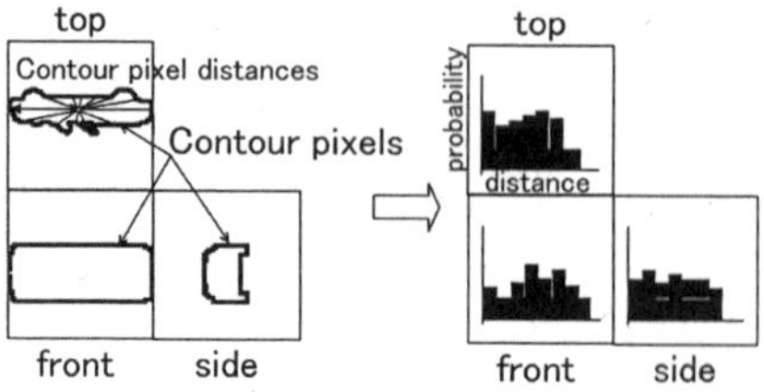

Figure 3: Histogram of contour pixel distances.

2.2. Silhouette image generation

As shown in Figure 2, the system generates three black and white silhouette images by rendering 3D scenes on a computer screen, e.g., a background color is set to white and a 3D model color is set to black. The calculation cost is very small because the most part of the rendering process is supported by the hardware. After rendering one scene, its image is captured as a square shape in specified resolution, e.g., eight by eight, 16×16, 32×32 (pixels) ···, and then is stored into a storage device. As will be described in **2.3.1**, the square shape of a silhouette image is convenient because each model has three silhouette images and there are some combination patterns of image comparing, e.g., the system compares the top image of a model with the front image of another model.

There are two kinds of normalizations, (A) and (B), as shown in Figure 2. The (A) uses the maximum length of the width, height and depth of the bounding box of a 3D model as a size of the square. The ratio among the depth, width and height of the bounding box of a model is one of important similarity measures, and is preserved in this case. On the other hand, the case (B), the bounding box of a 3D model is normalized into a cube shape and the 3D model is also normalized. Then three silhouette images are generated and stored. In this case, information of the ratio among the width, height and depth size of a 3D model is lost. To compensate this, scaling information is used as another part of similarity measure as will be explained in **2.3.2**. Furthermore, as will be described in **2.3.1**, while calculating similarity between three silhouette images of a model and three hand sketch images entered by the user, we use their contour pixel distribution as shown in Figure 3. Such information, which is a set of three histograms of the contour pixel distributions, is also stored besides the silhouette images.

2.3. Silhouette image matching

Two 3D models are assumed to be similar if they have a smaller error between their three silhouette images. In the following subsections, we describe how to calculate the error.

2.3.1 Error between the two set of the silhouette images of two models

Simply, error between two images is determined as the ratio of the number of different pixels to the total pixels as follows.

$$Error_{\text{image}} = \frac{different\ pixels}{total\ pixels} \tag{4}$$

However this is very sensitive to their scale and position. Therefore, we decided to use an error value as difference between the contours of two silhouette images. Namely, we use distribution of contour pixel distances as shown in Figure 3. Contour pixel distances are represented as the following set.

$$D = \{D_1, D_2, \cdots, D_i, \cdots, D_{n-1}, D_n\}, \qquad (5)$$

where D is a set of all contour pixel distances from their center, and D_i is i-th contour pixel distance calculated by the following equation.

$$D_i = \sqrt{(x_i - X)^2 + (y_i - Y)^2} \qquad (6)$$

where X and Y are coordinates of the contour center.

Three histograms of three contour pixel distributions are generated as shown on the right part of Fig. 3. Finally, we obtain the error value between two images as the Euclidean distance between the two histograms, F and G, calculated by the following equation.

$$Error_{\text{image}} = D(F,G) = \sqrt{\sum_i (f_i - g_i)^2} \qquad (7)$$

where f_i and g_i are the i-th rank value of a histogram F and a histogram G respectively. Each 3D model has its three silhouette images. Total error is determined as mean value of three image match errors as follows:

$$Error = \frac{Error_{\text{top\_image}} + Error_{\text{front\_image}} + Error_{\text{side\_image}}}{3} \qquad (8)$$

However, even if the shape of one 3D model is very similar to that of the other model to be compared, their three principal axes may be different. Therefore, we have to calculate equation (8) for all combination patterns as shown in Table 1. There are six combination patterns. The error $PError_k$ of each combination pattern is calculated by the following equation:

$$PError_k = \frac{\sum_{j=1}^{3} Error_j}{3}. \qquad (9)$$

For example, in the case of $PError_1$ between a model A and a model B, $Error_1$ is an error value between the front image of model A and the front image of model B, $Error_2$ is an error value between the top image of model A and the top image of model B, and $Error_3$ is an error value between the side image of model A and the top image of model B.

Then we obtain the final error value between two 3D models as the minimum of error values, i.e., six combination patterns.

$$Error_{\text{image}} = \min(PError_1, PError_2, \cdots, PError_6) \qquad (10)$$

2.3.2 Error for scaling factor between two models

As previously mentioned, there are two sets of normalized silhouette images (A) and (B) as shown in Figure 2. As will be described in Sec. **3**, our intuitive interface generates hand sketch images falling in the category of the set (B). In this case, the scaling factor of a 3D model is lost due to the reason already described in **2.2**. To compensate this defect, information of ratio among the width, height and depth size of a 3D model should be used because this information is important to distinguish the 3D model from others. We employ

Table 1: Six combination patterns between model A's three images and model B's three images.

	k=	1	2	3	4	5	6
j=	modelA's	modelB's	modelB's	modelB's	modelB's	modelB's	modelB's
1	Front	Front	Front	Top	Top	Side	Side
2	Top	Top	Side	Front	Side	Top	Front
3	Side	Side	Top	Side	Front	Front	Top

two scaling values, i.e., the ratio of the length of the second principal axis to that of the first principal axis and the ratio of the length of the third principal axis to that of the first principal axis. Next equation (11) defines the error between two 3D models concerning their scaling factor. Mean square root value is used because it is popular measure.

$$Error_{\text{scale}} = \sqrt{(l_2 - m_2)^2 + (l_3 - m_3)^2} \qquad (11)$$

Here l_2 is the ratio of the length of the second principal axis to that of the first principal axis and l_3 is the ratio of the length of the third principal axis to that of the first principal axis for one of the two 3D models to be compared. Similarly, m_2, m_3 are the two ratios for the other 3D model.

2.3.3 Total error between two models

Finally, we calculate the total error value using the next equation.

$$Error = \frac{Weight_{\text{image}} \times Error_{\text{image}} + Weight_{\text{scale}} \times Error_{\text{scale}}}{Weight_{\text{image}} + Weight_{\text{scale}}} \qquad (12)$$

Here $Weight_{\text{image}}$ and $Weight_{\text{scale}}$ are weight values, which are specified arbitrarily by the user. If the user thinks the shape of his/her required model is significant, the user should make $Weight_{\text{image}}$ larger than $Weight_{\text{scale}}$. If the user thinks the scale of his/her required model is significant, the user should make them opposite.

3. 3D Model database system and its intuitive interface

Figure 4 shows a screen image of the previous prototype system. The system automatically generates three silhouette images for each 3D model by actually rendering them on a computer screen. Then the user enters the query as his/her hand sketch images on the computer screen and retrieves required 3D models interactively. Three right lower small windows are query windows for entering three hand sketch images. The main window on the left upper corner shows the *camaro* model that is actually retrieved from the 3D model database as the first match of the three hand sketch images shown in each of the three query windows.

As you see Fig. 4 and understand, the three query windows are not intuitive interface. Although these windows correspond to top, side and front silhouette images, it is difficult to understand, for example, which side of the front silhouette window is top or bottom, and left or right. To overcome this problem, we developed more intuitive interface using *IntelligentBox* [3]. Figure 5 shows four screen images of the interface. The upper-left, lower-left and upper-right screen image correspond to front, side and top silhouette images respectively. The lower-right screen image depicts components of the interface.

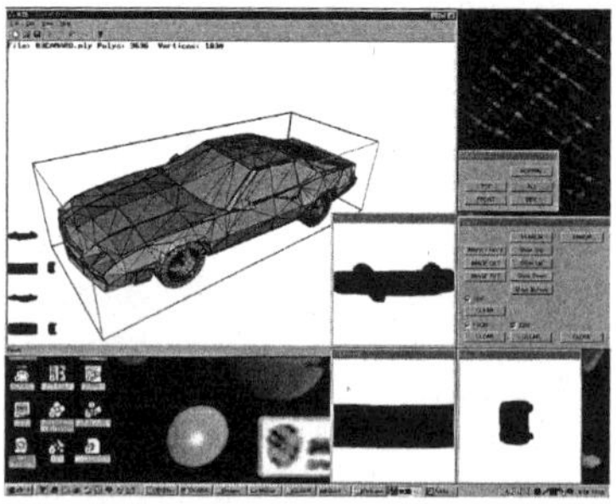

Figure 4: Screen image of the prototype system.

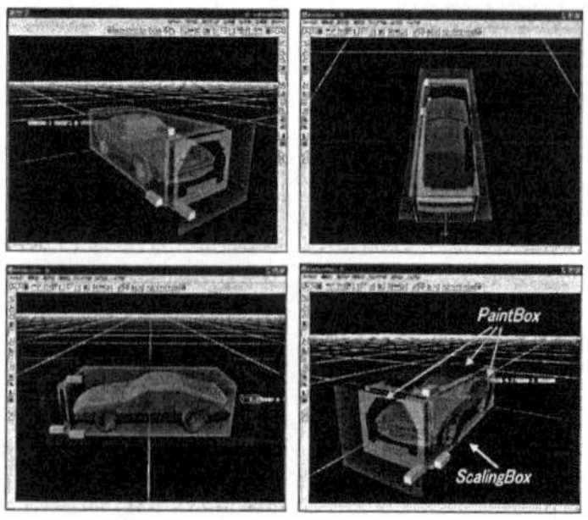

Figure 5: Intuitive interface for entering silhouette images by hand sketches.

IntelligentBox is a constructive visual 3D software development system. It provides various 3D visual components called *boxes*. This interface is realized as the composition of several *boxes*, i.e., mainly *PaintBox* and *ScalingBox*. *PaintBox* uses a texture mapping mechanism and provides a canvas on which the user does painting using a mouse-device. Indeed, three *PaintBoxes* are used in the interface. *ScalingBox* changes the size of itself by the mouse-device operation. Three *PaintBoxes* are assigned as children of the *ScalingBox,* and then, the user can decide the size of front, top and side silhouette images by manipulating the *ScalingBox* interactively. In this case, the shape of a *PaintBox* changes visually. However, the shape of its texture image does not change due to the ease of implementation. Therefore, each *PaintBox* has a fixed texture image, i.e., a square image, and its hand sketch image becomes a normalized image like one of the set (B) of Figure 2.

4. Experiments

This section presents experimental results of 3D model search using hand sketch images as the query and using a 3D model as the query. First of all, we introduce our 3D model database in the following subsection.

4.1. Preparation

We made a 3D model database by collecting 3D models from Internet. It consists of 150 models. We classified 150 models into 30 classes so that each class consists of five same kinds of models. Our prototype system generated three silhouette images of each model and totally 450 silhouette images of all the models. Its generation time for one set of three silhouette images, 32×32 pixels resolution, and three histograms of their contour pixel distributions, is about 0.3 second on a standard PC (Pentium IV 2GHz CPU, 512MB memory, GeForce3 Graphics).

4.2. Search by hand sketch images and its results

We performed experiments of 3D model search using hand sketch images as the query [1]. For example, if the same three orthogonal hand sketch images, as shown in Figure 4, are entered, the system outputs 3D models illustrated in Figure 6. Top 12 models include all the five car models. Figure 7 shows jet-plane search result. In this case, top 15 match models include all the five jet-plane models. Execution time for one search is less than one second

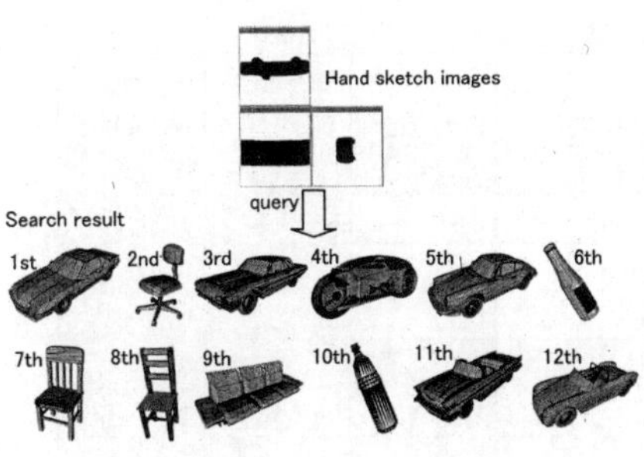

Figure 6: Result of automobile search.

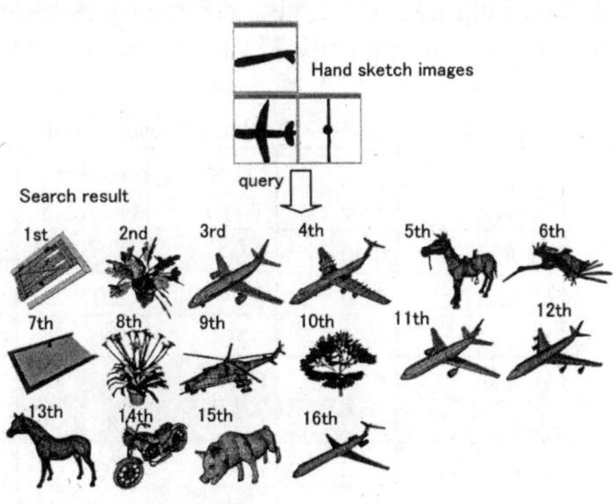

Figure 7: Result of jet-plane search.

when silhouette image resolution is 32 × 32 pixels. More accurate time appears in **4.3.2**.

4.3. Similarity search and its results

Furthermore, we performed experiments of 3D model search using a 3D model as the query. First of all, the following subsection explains evaluation measures and, then subsection **4.3.2** shows experimental results and discusses them.

4.3.1 Evaluation measures

We use the same three evaluation measures described in [5]. They are "First Tier", "Second Tier" and "Nearest Neighbor" as follows.

First Tier : This criteria means the percentage of top $(k-1)$ matches (excluding the query) from the query's class, where k is the size of the class. This criteria is stringent, since each model in the class has only one chance to be in the first tier.

Second Tier : This criteria is the same type of result, but for the top $2(k-1)$ matches.

$$FirstTier = \frac{Top(k-1)matches}{k-1} \quad (13), \qquad SecondTier = \frac{Top2(k-1)matches}{k-1} \quad (14)$$

Nearest Neighbor : This criteria means the percentage of test in which the top match was from the query's class.

4.3.2 Results and discussion

Table 2 shows experimental results. *First tier*, *Second tier* and *Nearest neighbor* results are 0.390, 0.528 and 0.533 respectively. Each of these three values is the mean of the corresponding values for all models. These values are better than the corresponding values of *D2* applied on the same 3D database because they are 0.317, 0.418 and 0.447. Osada et al present their own evaluation results in their paper. These values are 0.49, 0.66 and 0.66 for their own 3D model database. These values depend on a 3D model database. Any way, our results are very close to them. Our total search time for 150 model queries is 12 seconds using the same PC (Pentium IV 2GHz CPU, 512MB memory) so that one search time is 0.08 second. This value is not bad because *D2* takes more time. Therefore, it can be said that our silhouette image matching is efficient as similarity measure for 3D model search. In Table 2, deep color columns are classes that have larger value than 0.5, i.e., a better value rather than others. These classes apt to have three principal axes those are independently distinguished. So our methods are especially efficient for models belong to such classes.

Table 3 shows evaluation results with silhouette images of varying resolution. As you see this table, at most 32×32 resolution is enough. Of course, search time is also better than that in cases of higher resolutions. All the cases use the same PC (Pentium IV2GHz CPU, 512MB memory). Consequently 32×32 resolution is the best for our method.

Table 2: Evaluation result 1 (silhouette image resolution: 32×32 pixels)

Classes	First Tier	Second Tier	Nearest Neighbor	Classes	First Tier	Second Tier	Nearest Neighbor
Jet Plane	0.40	0.80	0.80	Air Force	0.55	0.85	0.80
Helicopter	0.30	0.55	0.20	Missile	0.35	0.55	1.00
Space Ship	0.15	0.20	0.00	Guitar	0.45	0.50	0.80
Human	0.35	0.65	0.60	Tree	0.30	0.50	0.60
Head	0.65	0.70	0.80	Flower	0.80	1.00	0.80
Fish	0.30	0.35	0.00	Ball	1.00	1.00	1.00
Bird	0.45	0.50	0.60	Car	0.95	1.00	0.80
4 legs animal	0.15	0.30	0.20	Motor Bike	0.10	0.15	0.20

Computer	0.20	0.25	0.60	Submarine	0.05	0.15	0.00
Chair	0.60	0.95	0.80	Hand Gun	0.65	0.85	0.80
Sofa	0.30	0.35	0.40	Rifle	0.15	0.20	0.20
Bed	0.15	0.20	0.20	Knife	0.30	0.40	0.60
Cup	0.20	0.30	0.40	Sword	0.25	0.25	0.60
Glass	0.40	0.45	0.60	Door	0.20	0.35	0.00
Bottle	0.55	0.65	0.60				
Can	0.45	0.90	1.00	Mean value	0.390	0.528	0.533

Table 3: Evaluation result 2 (various silhouette image resolutions)

Resolution (pixels)	Search time (sec)	First Tier	Second Tier	Nearest Neighbor
8×8	0.05	0.250	0.375	0.407
16×16	0.06	0.350	0.482	0.507
32×32	0.08	0.390	0.528	0.533
64×64	0.09	0.375	0.553	0.533
128×128	0.14	0.363	0.545	0.500

5. Concluding remarks

We proposed a 3D model database system that uses the silhouette image matching as the similarity measure and accepts hand sketch images of 3D models as the query. This paper especially proposed the new interface of the system for entering hand sketch images easily and rapidly. This allows us to enter the query in more intuitive manner rather than our previous system. This paper also presented the experimental results.

As future works, our 3D model matching is based on the 2D image matching. Already many researches on the 2D image matching have been done [9]. Using such more efficient algorithms, we will make our 3D model database system enable to retrieve 3D models more accurately.

References

[1] Okada, Y. : 3D MODEL DATABASE SYSTEM BY HAND SKETCH QUERY, Proc. of 2002 IEEE International Conference on Multimedia and Expo (ICME2002), Vol. I, pp. 889-892, Lausanne, Switzerland, August 2002.

[2] Okada, Y. : 3D Model Matching Based On Silhouette Image Matching, Proc. of CSCC2002 (Recent Advances in Circuits, Systems and Signal Processing), WSEAS Press, pp. 380-385, Rethimno Greece, July 2002.

[3] Okada, Y. and Tanaka, Y.: IntelligentBox: A Constructive Visual Software Development System for Interactive 3D Graphic Applications, Proc. of Computer Animation '95, IEEE Computer Society Press, pp. 114-125, 1995.

[4] Eric Paquet, Marc Rioux: Nefertiti: a query by content system for three-dimensional model and image databases management, Image and Vision Computing 17, 157-166, 1999.

[5] Osada, R, et al: Matching 3D Models with Shape Distributions, Shape Modeling International, May 2001.

[6] M. Hiraga, Y. Shinagawa, T. Kohmura and T. L. Kunii: Topology Matching for Fully Automatic Similarity Estimation of 3D Shapes, Proc. SIGGRAPH2001, pp.203-212, 2001.

[7] Thorsten Bandlow, Alexa Hauck, Tobias Einsele, and Georg Färber: Recognising Objects by their Silhouette. In *IMACS Conf. on Comp. Eng. in Systems Appl. (CESA'98)*, pages 744-749, April 1998.

[8] Gottschalk, S., Lin, M. C. and Manocha, D.: OBBTree: A Hierarchical Structure for Rapid Interference Detection, Computer Graphics (SIGGRAPH '96 Proceedings), pp. 171-180, 1996.

[9] R. C. Veltkamp and M. Hagedoorn: State-of-the-art in Shape Matching, Technical Report UU-CS-1999-27, Utrecht University, the Netherlands, 1999.

Information Modelling and Knowledge Bases XV
Y. Kiyoki et al. (Eds.)
IOS Press, 2004

On modeling conceptual and narrative structure of fairytales

*Shinya Kawakami, *Yoko Sato, *Masaki Nakagawa, **Bipin Indurkhya
*Department of information and communication,
**Department of mechanics,
Tokyo University of Agriculture and Technology
*kawakami@hands.ei.tuat.ac.jp

Abstract. We describe here our ongoing research on modeling conceptual and narrative structure of fairytales by a computer system. In this paper we focus on the variations of fairytales based on Cinderella from all around the world. We analyzed twenty-three Japanese texts of Cinderella tales and modeled their conceptual and narrative structures using the notions of composition elements and motifs. We then incorporated all these structures into a unified structural model of Cinderella story. Finally, we implemented a computer system based on the unified structural model to automatically generate variations of Cinderella tales. The system was able to generate variations that were quite different from any of the original Cinderella tales.

1. Introduction

Humans find it natural to organize information in terms of narrative structures. For example, in ancient times, elders passed their knowledge and wisdom to the new generation by telling stories, which were often augmented or modified slightly with each retelling to incorporate the experiences and interpretations of the narrator. Variously referred to as folktales, fairytales, myths, etc., such stories have played a powerful role as archetypes that influence one's individual perceptions and actions as well as define societies and cultures, and continue to do so even in this modern age of information technology (Campbell [1]).

Several studies have been done to analyze the structure of folktales, fairytales, and stories in general (Bal [2], Chatman [3], Currie [4], Martin [5], Propp [6]). Essentially, two structural components can be identified in a story: one concerned with the relationship among the characters, which we will refer to as *conceptual structure,* and the other concerned with the temporal relationship among the events, which we will refer to as *narrative structure.* Artificial Intelligence researchers have also been quick to recognize the importance of the role played by stories in knowledge representation, and some attempts have been made to model their underlying conceptual and narrative structures and apply it for various purposes (Lang [7], Rumelhart [8], Schank [9]). All this research has been applied to develop narration theory-based information systems that present stories in various mediums such as text, theater, animations, etc., and allow different levels of interactions between the system and the user, who manipulate the system to generate stories (Szilas [10], Riedk *et.al.*[11]).

In all the studies mentioned above, the narrative elements are defined independently of each other, and the task of braiding these elements into a story is relegated to narrative theories. Such approaches do not clarify how a user imagines and plans the conceptual and narrative structures of a generated story, and how the user-system interaction leads to the unfolding of this structure. Of course, in these situations, the system can produce unexpected progressions of events in stories, which can entertain or delight the user. Nonetheless, it reduces the role of the user to an audience or at most to a limited participant. For story-generating systems that are designed to leave the user in the driver's seat, unexpected progressions generated by the system can cause frustration to the user and may lead to ineffectiveness.

The purpose of this research is to extend these ideas and explore more deeply the issues concerning how to represent the conceptual and narrative structures of stories in an information system, and how to manipulate and apply these structures effectively. More concretely, we have focused on variations of the classical fairytale Cinderella found around the world. We refer to these variations as *Cinderella tales* in this paper. In the research presented here, we analyzed twenty-three Japanese texts of Cinderella tales to abstract the conceptual and narrative structures inherent in these stories. Based on this analysis, we created a synthesized structural model of Cinderella tales.

The motivation behind developing this structural model, and the criterion used for evaluating it, is that it can be used to regenerate each of the original stories on the analysis of which the model was based, as well as new variations. As far as the original stories are concerned, they can be generated from the structural information containing definitions of kinds and consequences of actions, sequences of actions, and methods to reason about actions and situations. In generating new variations, however, the following problem occurs. Once an action in a sequence is replaced with another kind of action, the consequence of the new action and the following sequence may become quite different from the original. In this case, the story based on the generated sequence may not always be regarded as a variation of the original. In order to resolve this problem, it is necessary to somehow capture the essence of a story in terms of constraints on its conceptual and narrative structure. But this is difficult to realize in models based on action sequences because a generated action sequence carries a different significance than the original, and the essence of the story, however it may have been characterized, must cover the new action sequence (in being able to decide whether it is a variation of the original or a different story.) Therefore, one must rely on some other method to characterize the essence of a story.

Our approach is to introduce a *motif network model* of narrative structure to resolve this issue. In our analysis, we identified the motifs appearing in each of the stories, looked at their order of appearance, considered which motifs can be unified with each other, and generated groups of mutually compatible motifs. The motif network model incorporates the conceptual and narrative structures of each of the analyzed story, multiplexing parts of the stories where motifs are unified. This characteristic of the structural model makes it easy to regenerate any of the original stories and also to generate new ones. Thus, the motif network model described here is an open-ended synthesized structural model of Cinderella tales.

Finally, we implemented a computer system to automatically generate variations of Cinderella tales. The system can regenerate any of twenty-three original Cinderella tales as well as versions not in the original. We present one such variation generated by our program, and then discuss the implications of our research for information modeling as well as future research directions.

2. Analysis of Cinderella tales

The goal of this analysis is to identify and delineate the conceptual and narrative structures underlying different variations of Cinderella-based fairytales, and identify a common archetype for them. The traditional approaches for analyzing folk and fairy tales often use *motifs* for representing narrative structures. Though we also use motifs to represent abstract structure of a story, our method of analysis is to divide the text of a story into small fragments, and then represent the structure of each fragment as a *composition element.* Thus, in our approach, conceptual and narrative structures are analyzed and composed in terms of compositional elements. This allows us to stay very close to the concrete text, which makes it easier to use the model in the reverse direction, that is, to generate a text based on the structure specified in terms of compositional elements.

In the rest of this section we provide a list of texts used in our analysis, define motif and composition element, describe the factors that affect compositional elements, compatibility among compositional elements, and a method to integrate conceptual and narrative structures of each text.

2.1 Texts for Analysis

We analyzed the following twenty-three texts of fairytales from around the world that can be considered as variations on Cinderella. All the texts used were in Japanese.

Text01: *SANDORIYON or Shoes of small glass, France* [12]
Text02: *HAIKABURI, Germany* [13]
Text03: *RODOPISU NO KUTSU, ancient Egypt*
Text04: *RIAOH NO KODOMOTACHI, Ireland*
Text05: *RAGUNA RODOBUROKU NO SAGA, North Europe*
Text06: *KUNARATAISHI NO HANASHI, ancient India*
Text07: *RARUDAIOH TO HUTARI NO ADOKENAI HIME, India*
Text08: *KIN NO SHOKUDAI, Iran*
Text09: *KEGAWA MUSUME, Turkey*
Text10: *MAMAHAHA TO MAMAMUSUME, Macedonia*
Text11: *YOGEN SURU USHI TO SONO SHUJIN, Hungary*
Text12: *JUUNI NO TSUKI, the Czech Republic*
Text13: *KUCHI WO KIKU ATAMA, England*
Text14: *NAKUSHITA KIN NO KUTSU, Iceland*
Text15: *KIN NO KUTSU, Ukraine*
Text16: *FURISHA TO HUTARI NO MUSUME, North Africa*
Text17: *AOI OUSHI, New México, North America*
Text18: *PAWANGU PUTEE TO PAWANGU MERA, Java island*
Text19: *KONJI PATJI, Korea peninsula*
Text20: *HUTATUME, North China*
Text21: *YANPA TO YANRAN, the Miao tribe, China*
Text22: *PA ERU PU NO SANSHIMAI, Tibet* [14]
Text23: *NUKAHUKU KOMEHUKU, Japan* [15]

Some texts are partially abbreviated and a few others exist only as outlines. The last text is originally mentioned in a separate volume, "Folktale of Ina-mura", of "Notebook of folktale" (Daiichi Hohki and Society of Japanese folktales).

2.2 Motif and narrative structure

Given a portion of text, we define its *motif* as the most significant action described by the text. The representation of a motif contains information about the kind of action, the characters performing the action or affected by the action, the objectives of the action, and so on. Certain motifs may be incidental, whereas others may recur repeatedly and contribute to the narrative structure of the story. Also, in comparing motifs across different stories, we find that some motifs are peculiar to a certain story, but some others are shared by different stories.

Motifs make it possible to compare the structure of two or more stories without having to abstract and standardize objective units such as actions, episodes, etc. that may differ in various texts. Narrative structure of each story is expressed in terms of motifs. Different narrative structures arise from different configurations of motifs. In previous research, Cox [16] and Rooth [17] have examined and compared some common motifs underlying Cinderella tales. Cox classified three hundred forty-five variations of Cinderella tales into five categories, where each category is characterized by its principal motifs as shown below:

Group1	"heroine abused" and "recognition by shoes"
Group2	"unusual father" and "flight of heroine"
Group3	"Judgment of King Rea" and "banishment of heroine"
Group4	Similar but not applicable to those three groups
Group5	The protagonists are male.

Rooth also classified Cinderella tales into five types. Each type and its particular motifs are given in the following table:

Type A	"stepmother", "deceased mother", "spin into yarn" and "cow as an assistance

	person"
Type AB	"garments", "party", "shoes" and "marriage" in addition to type A
Type B	"stepmother", "deceased mother", "tree", "garments", "division grains", "party", "shoes" and "marriage"
Type BI	"father proposes"
Type C	The protagonists are stepsons.

Even though those motifs signify structural differences among the groups, they contain only information that is common among the original stories. In other words, the motifs and other information pertaining to the peculiarities of individual stories are not maintained.

2.3 Composition element

We define a *composition element* to be a small set of actions that comprises an action sequence. A composition element also contains a label pointing to the motif corresponding to it, information about the characters participating in the action and their situational settings, and a template of the original text. Thus, each composition element contains a partial conceptual and narrative structure and also preserves information that is omitted from the original story in motifs.

To divide an original story into composition elements, first we extract principal characters from the story and all actions concerning these characters. Next we identify those actions that make a sequence of actions temporally or spatially dependent. Actions such as speaking are combined with other related significant actions. These sets of actions are now regarded as composition elements. Then the most significant action is extracted from each action set and is regarded as the motif of the composition element. Relationships among the characters that were affected by the actions, as well as their state and setting is also extracted and included in the composition elements.

Composition elements are similar to events, episodes or scripts, which are often used to represent narrative structures. For example, Rumelhart [8] and Schank [9] described narrative grammars that represent narrative structures using these concepts. Based on these representations, some story-generating systems have been implemented by Lang [7], Hosaka *et al.* [18] and Kawakami [19]. However, episodes and scripts (also stories) are eventually represented as a sequence of actions conceptually. Thus, if each action sequence can be identified, narrative structure of a story would be represented by the series of actions without mentioning episodes or scripts. We choose this action-level representation because it has the flexibility and potential for being extended when using the model for generating stories. Fig. 1 shows the conceptual relationship among different levels of representation including composition element and motif.

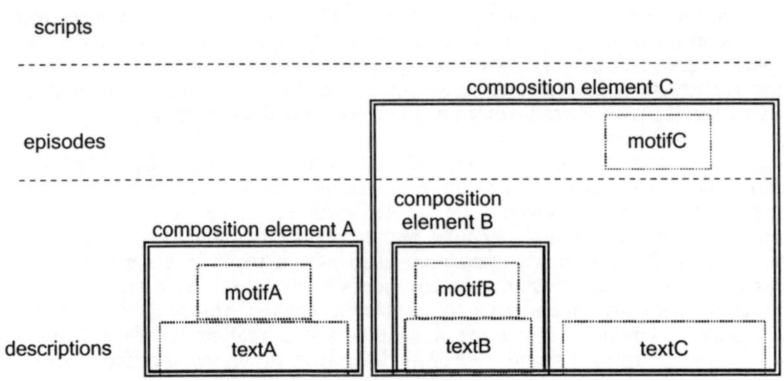

Fig.1 Conceptual level of stories and composition elements

2.4 Narrative structure

Narrative structure of a story is represented by appropriate composition elements ordered linearly. In previous studies that focused on narrative grammars or motifs as mentioned before, narrative structures of folktales were also linear. For example, Propp [6] analyzed Russian folktales and extracted forty-two functional elements in terms of which narrative structures of many of the Russian magical folktales can be represented. In this approach, each functional element is property that relevant part of a folktale signifies that kind of function and the narrative structure of the folktale is constituted by a linear sequence of functional elements. However, in cases when a false hero or heroine appears in a story, its narrative structure becomes partially parallel.

The effectiveness of representing the narrative structure of a story in terms of functional elements is marred by the fact that a sequence of functional elements does not allow sufficient variations in the features. Features are inherently variable in any part of a narrative structure. In functional element-based representation, in order to figure out feature variations allowed within a functional element, it is necessary to refer to the contents of all those parts of the narrative structure that are relevant to that functional element. This problem is also encountered in action-based approaches [7][8][9], where narrative rules define features as 'variation' gathered from all relevant parts of the narrative structure.

Accordingly, our model focuses on narrative structures of variations in 'Cinderella tales'. In particular, we define composition elements and linkages between composition elements to represent detailed information about the contents of a story and allowable feature variations for 'Cinderella tales'. Of course our model is not yet extensible to cover other kinds of fairytales, especially general stories, but we feel that our research constitutes a first step towards this larger goal.

2.5 Conceptual structure

Conceptual structure of a story is composed from information contained in various facts mentioned in the story. This structure includes information about the characters, their attributes and roles, settings, social relationships among them, ownership relation between them and items, and so on. The information contained in the conceptual structure, which is essentially situational, is orthogonal to the structure contained in the narrative structure, which is temporal. However, the situational information also changes in response to the unfolding of the narrative structure. Therefore, we explicitly introduce the concept of time into conceptual structures. Temporal durations, if attached to a fact, determine the time period during which that fact remains valid.

2.6 Compatibility of composition elements and Similarity between narrative structures

We chose to enforce a conceptual compatibility among composition elements that correspond to the same motif. A motif essentially contains an abstracted structure, as explained above in Sec. 2.2, and each composition element contains its own concrete narrative structure, as explained in Sec. 2.3. Therefore, different composition elements that are labeled with the same motif must be conceptually compatible.

However, composition elements labeled with the same motif are not always compatible when narrative structures are reconstituted. It is because, even though different composition elements are labeled with the same motif, each composition element contains different conceptual and narrative structures internally. Furthermore, the number of times each composition element can recur in a narrative structure is restricted. When a composition element needs to be chosen from among the available compatible composition elements, the choice must be determined depending on relevant conceptual and narrative structures. In creating a structural model of Cinderella tales, to be described in the next section, we unified narrative structures of different stories.

It is possible to consider similarity between narrative structures based on motifs. For example, in the area of oral literature, Aarne and Thompson [20] focused on narrative features including motifs to consider similarity between various kinds of folktales in their comparative studies. Seki [21] also classified Japanese folktales by a similar method. Our method of analyzing the similarity between texts focused on composition elements including relevant motifs. This method keeps the potential for comparison, while at the same time maintaining the required information to describe the contents of each part in the structural model of Cinderella tales.

2.7 Temporal points through a story

The concept of temporal point is used to represent the time progression in a story. We divided narrative structure of a story into several composition elements, with all the elements serially ordered. The indices corresponding to the position of each composition element in the sequence of narrative structure is regarded as temporal points of the story. A simple example is shown in Fig. 2.

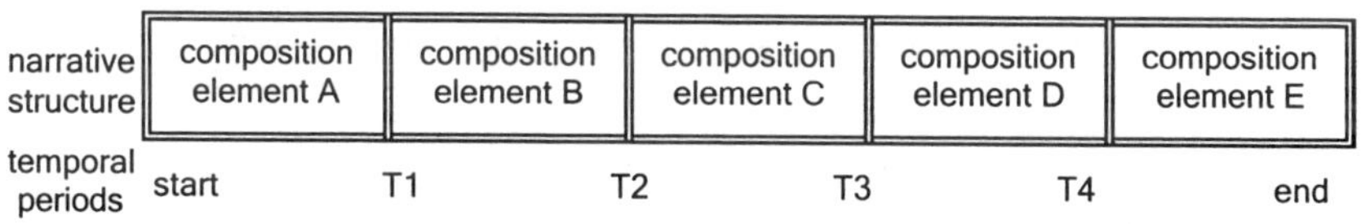

Fig.2 Temporal periods through a narrative structure

Strictly speaking, any action performed by a character requires some time to finish. Under this consideration, a composition element that contains several actions is spread over a period of time. In stories other than fairytales, such as novels and movies, this kind of spread over time is explicitly mentioned or visually presented. For example, a scene is described in more detail and many concrete particulars are provided. However, this kind of spread over time is not common in fairytales. For example, Luthi [22] noted that in fairytales, the time progression does not cause any change in the protagonists. Therefore, we assume that any changes in the protagonists happen suddenly at a particular point in time and are completed immediately. Thus, in our analysis, only the concept of temporal points is considered.

2.8 Unifying composition elements

We unified composition elements extracted from variations of Cinderella tales into an integrated model. In the unification process, each composition element is regarded as a node and each link between two composition elements is represented as an arrow. Nodes of conceptually compatible composition elements are unified into a node and links between the unified node and following composition elements form branches. We performed integration of composition elements following this process:

Step1 Analyze HAIKABURI and SANDORIYON, compare composition elements of each story and unify them. These two stories are quite typical and their variations are well known. They were also written at about the same time. So it is easy to compare them.
Step2 Analyze other texts and unify composition elements extracted from them that are compatible to the composition elements unified at Step1.
Step3 Unify "banishment" and "flight"
Step4 Unify other appropriate composition elements.

2.9 Results of analysis

We obtained five hundred fifty-four composition elements and relation links between pairs of them from analyzing twenty-two stories. We also obtained consistent conceptual structures for these composition elements. From this data, we created a structural model of Cinderella tales as described in the next section.

3. A structural model of Cinderella tales

The structural model of Cinderella tales is composed from composition elements, consistent settings of characters that were mentioned in each story and linkages between pairs of composition elements occurring in a sequence. Composition elements and linkages between pairs of composition elements are combined into a network model of narrative structures. Composition elements which are recognized as compatible are unifiyed in the network model of narrative structure. Conceptual structures are made up of composition elements and settings of characters. Fig. 3 shows the information contained in the structural model.

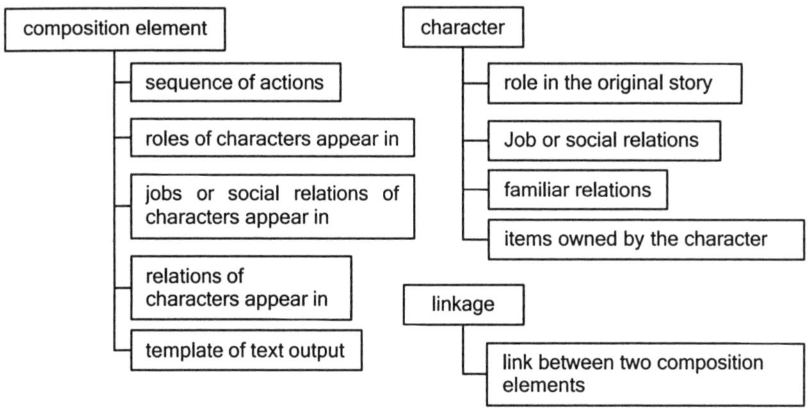

Fig.3 Knowledge stored in structural model

3.1 Setting of characters in each analyzed story

Settings of the characters mentioned in the story in which the characters appeared originally are integrated into the structural model. Each setting is consistently available throughout the story here. There are four items of information contained in the setting of a character as follows:

Role in the original story
Job or social relations
Familial relations
Items owned by the character

3.2 Composition elements

Each composition element has a label to identify its motif. It contains a series of actions where apropriate roles of characters occur as well as conceptual information and restrictions required of those roles. Situational settings are also restricted in the composition elements and defined under temporal points. Five kinds of information and restrictions contained in each composition element are:

Sequence of actions
Roles of characters appearing in this part
Job or social relations of characters appearing in this part
Relations of characters appearing in this part
Template of text output

3.3 Links between pairs of composition elements occurring in a series

Links between pairs of composition elements occurring in a series are integrated into the structural model. The structural model has the characteristic of a network model.

The progression of a story is represented through composition elements from the start to the end. Some composition elements are connected with two or more linkages at the output. Such connections carry the information that the progression of the story has branches here. Fig. 4 shows a part of the structural model containing some composition elements and linkages between them. Each labeled rectangle signifies a composition element. Arrows signify the direction of progression of the story.

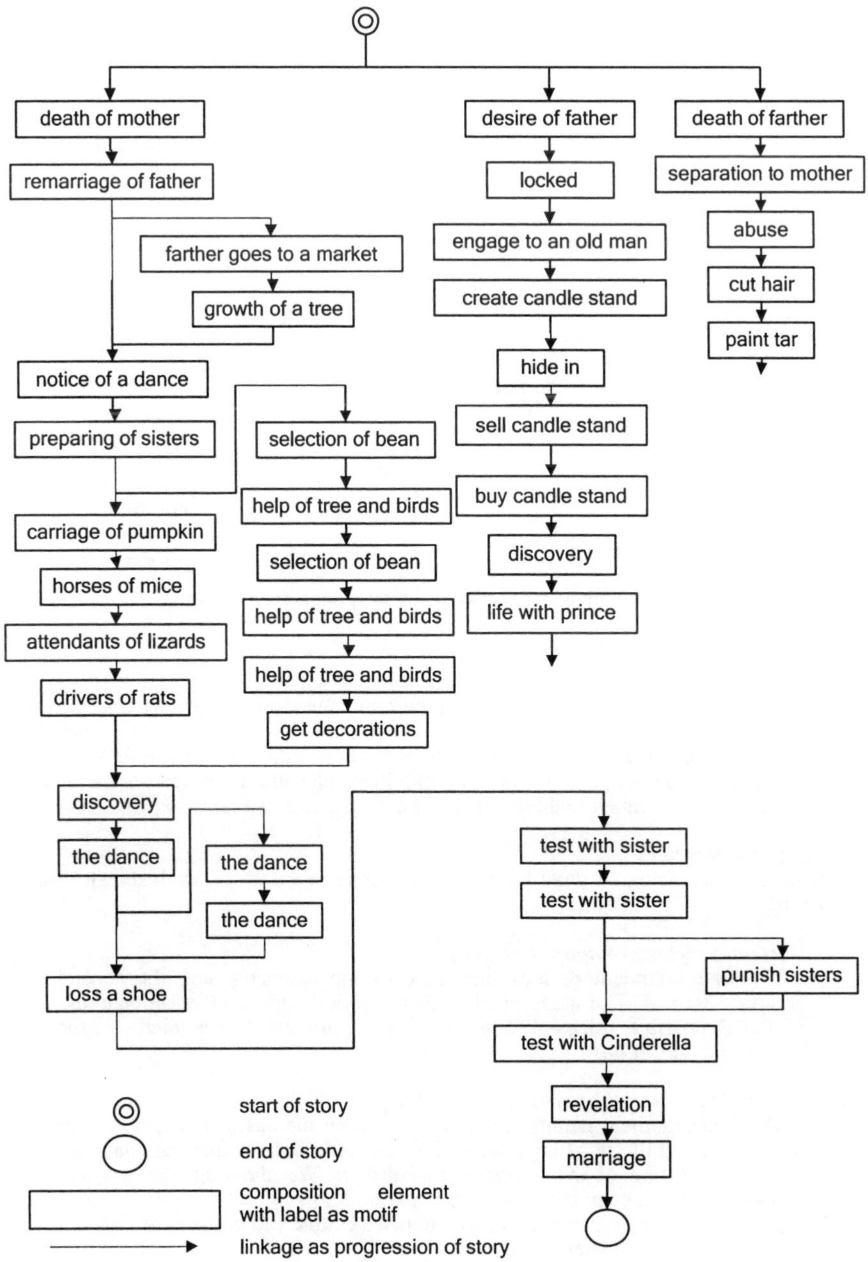

Fig.4 A part of the structural model

4. A story-generation system based on the structural model of Cinderella tales

Based on the structural model of Cinderella tales, we implemented a system to generate variations of Cinderella tales. It contains five kinds of database, including the structural model explained above, and a main module containing four sub-modules. The story-generation system generates variations as 'Cinderella tales' searching the network model. Fig. 5 shows the internal structure of the story-generation system. We briefly describe each database and each module in the rest of this section.

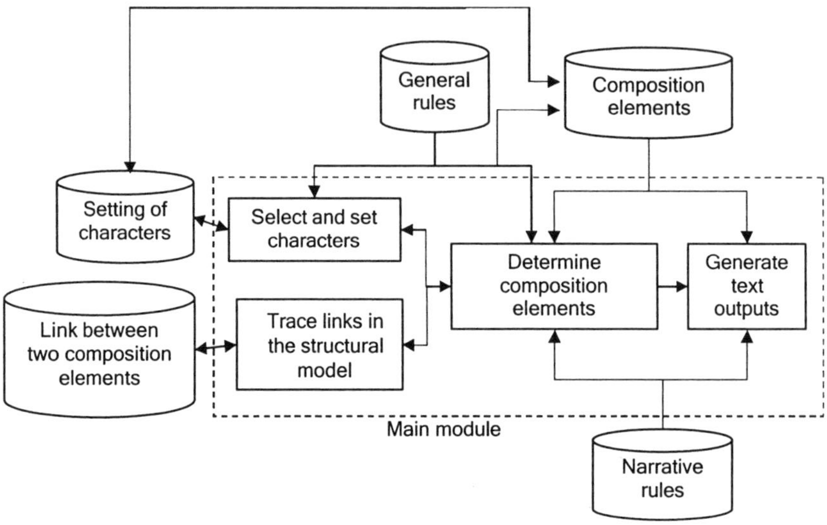

Fig.5 Internal structure of the story generation system

4.1 Databases

Five kinds of databases are used in the system. The database of character settings, composition elements and links between two composition elements corresponds to the three kinds of information contained in the structural model of Cinderella tales. Even though the databases of general rules and narrative rules are not based on the analyzed stories, the rules contained in these databases are generally available in folktales.

Setting of characters

Setting of characters is done based on their appearance in the analyzed stories, for example:

role(sandoriyon, protagonist, 0, 100).

The first argument defines the name of the character, and the second argument its role. The name of each character is unique, and it can take one of the 8 possible roles: *protagonist*, *father*, *mother*, *step-mother*, *villain*, *helper*, *gift*, and *spouse*.

relation(parents, father, sandoriyon, 0, 100).

The first argument names the relation between the characters specified in the second and the third arguments. This example defines that the character *father* is a parent of the character *sandoriyon*. We classified the possible relations between characters into two kinds as follows:

Familial relations: Parent and child, married couple and brothers or sisters

Social relation: Master and servant

own(sandoriyon, pampikin, 0, 100).

It defines that the character specified in the first argument owns the item specified in the second argument.

job(prince, prince, 0, 100).
It defines that the character specified in the first argument has the job named in the second argument.

live-in(king, castle, 0, 100).
It defines that the character specified in the first argument lives at the location or place specified in the second argument.

The last two arguments of each rule signify the initial point and the final point of the time period when the declaration of the rule is valid. A value of 0 means beginning of the story and 100 means its end. By default, each definition is assumed to be valid from the beginning till the end, but it can be set differently depending on how a particular story is progressing.

Additionally, definitions containing two binary functions, *a-kind-of* and *locate-in,* are incorporated in the database. These definitions form an invariant part of the database. In other words, these two functions cannot be invoked in a story.

ako(pumpkin, pumpkin).
It defines the first argument to be a kind of the second argument. Such definitions create a classification hierarchy of characters, items, locations, etc.

locate-in(pen of elephants, castle).
It defines the location or the place corresponding to the first argument to be located at the location or the place named in the second argument. Such definitions declare geographic relations between two locations or places that cannot be moved.

Composition elements
Composition elements are formed as shown in the example below:

element (test with shoe,1,X,T,R,STORY1,STORY2):-
determine character (protagonist, A, X, T),
determine character (spouse, B, X, T),
determine character (sister, D, X, T),
determine character (sister, E, X, T),
relation (elder and younger, D,E,T),
relation (master and servant, B, C, T),
determine character (assistant, C, X, T),
own (A,H,T),
concept (H, shoes),
re-define(DEFINITIONS_OF_CHARACTERS),
define(DEFINITIONS_OF_CHARACTERS),
generate text ([STORY1,Relevant_template, character list], STORY2).

The first argument of a composition element is a label that serves as its identifier. The second argument contains the index of the original story from which the composition element was extracted. The third, fourth, and fifth arguments contain, respectively, a unified list of characters that are related to any action in this composition element, a temporal step indicating the sequential position where this composition element occurs in the current narrative structure, and the number of times the composition elements that have the same label recurs. The last two arguments contain text outputs.

When any composition element is evoked, its corresponding characters are activated to satisfy each role related to its character settings. Some of these characters are examined to see if they hold any appropriate relation or own any item that is required and that appears in this composition element. If any item appears in this composition element, the concept or kind of that item is examined. If any part of a character's definition is added or changed, the corresponding setting is defined or re-defined. These determinations, detections, definitions and re-definitions proceed under the current temporal point in accessing the databases 'Setting of characters' and 'General rules'. Finally, a text output is generated from the unified data and the appropriate text templates.

Links between two composition elements

A link is formed when two composition elements are ordered. For example:

Link elements (propose, give presents).

The order of the arguments corresponds to the order of the composition elements. A link can be defined recursively. For example:

Link elements(imitate king, imitate king).

This information is accessed from the module 'Trace links in the structural model' to explore possible progressions of a story. These definitions are randomly ordered when the story generation system is initialized.

General rules

This database contains concept definitions and declarations of commonsense reasoning. These rules are accessed from the module 'Select and set characters', 'Determine composition elements'. Some examples of these rules are as follows:

Concept definitions (reasoning for conceptualization of characters and items)

These rules are used to conceptualize characters and items when composition elements are activated.

Commonsense reasoning (reasoning about familial relations)

This kind of rules is used to determine familial relations such as parent-child, elder sister-younger sister, and spouses, between two characters. Referring to these rules, it is determined which character takes which part. In Cinderella tales, for example, such relations occur frequently.

Narrative rules

This database contains typical rules used in constructing narratives. We incorporated the analysis of Luthi [22], who found that the same motif or episode is repeated by the protagonist often three times in a fairytale with variations and expansions in the details of the situation or setting, by designing corresponding rules. These rules are used by module 'Determine composition elements' and 'Generate text outputs'. Two examples of such rules are:

Rules for repeating a kind of composition elements

This rule allows a composition element to be repeated in a story that is being generated in the system. The repetition depends on the linkages in the structural model because composition elements or sets of composition elements are connected recursively. These rules permit repetitions at most thrice. However, the composition elements of "marriage", "help of fairy", "discovery" and "revelation" are exceptions (they are not allowed to be repeated) because they typically do not occur twice in a fairytale.

Rules for determining items of the same kind but differing in degree

These rules are used to determine items that are of the same kind, but in differ in the degree of some relevant attribute such as expensiveness, beauty, etc. For example, in variations of Cinderella tales, an event corresponding to the protagonist going to a dance often appears three times. He or she wears a general dress the first time, a more expensive dress the second times then the most expensive dress the last time. These three kinds of dress in different degrees are determined referring to the rule that allows repeating the same kind of composition elements.

Rules for determining items in the same concept and different kinds
These rules are used to determine items which are in the same concept but are of different kinds, for example, a general dress and a robe where each kind is in a concept 'wears' and differ from each other. These rules are often referred to when an assistant who has magical abilities transforms poor items owned by the protagonists into expensive items in certain composition elements.

4.2 Main module

The main module manages all the other modules used in generating stories. The procedure for generating a story proceeds in four main steps: 1) select and set characters, 2) determine composition elements, 3) trace linkages in the structural model and select composition elements, and 4) generate text outputs. The process of selecting and setting characters occurs once at the beginning of generating a story. The process of determining composition elements proceeds by selecting and determining composition elements and forming narrative structure of the story being generated. This process manages the other two processes of tracing linkages in the structural model and process generating text outputs. We designed a module corresponding to each of these four processes. Each of these modules is briefly described below.

Select and set characters
This module selects characters to fill various roles from the database, and makes a list of these characters at the beginning of generating a story. The characters are chosen randomly, or as the original set of any of the analyzed stories. In the case of random selection, the original settings of all the characters in the database are inherited. However, relations between selected characters can change.

While the narration is in progress, this module decides whether a character included in the list of characters and assigned a restricted role under a composition element satisfies the required conditions. Different composition elements often require different arguments to compose consistent components of a story.

Whenever the character settings change, for example if relations between the characters change during the progression of story, this module updates the character settings. This redefinition is processed when an updated definition satisfies the temporal point at which a composition element is currently active.
Fig. 6 shows the internal structure of the module 'Select and set characters'.

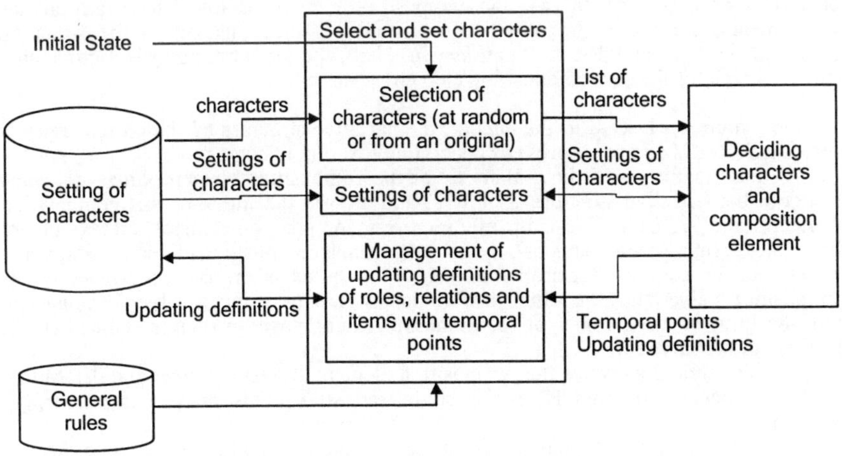

Fig.6 Internal structure of the module 'Select and set characters'

Determine composition elements

This module makes up the narrative structure of the story being generated, determines its composition elements, and indicates sequels of generating story and formation of text data corresponded into the composition elements. These processes are implemented as clauses of the procedure *make_storytrace*:

```
make_storytrace(opening, X, T, List, STRUCT, STORY):-
    link_elements(opening, NextElement),
    make_storytrace(NextElement, X, T, List, STRUCT, STORY).

make_storytrace(ending, X, T, List, List, end):-!.

make_storytrace(CurrentElement, X, T1, List, STRUCT, STORY1):-
    countAppear(CurrentElement, List, 0, R1),
    check_repeat(CurrentElement, R1, RR1),
    element(CurrentElement, ANY, X, T1, RR1, [], BUFF1) ->
            link_elements(CurrentElement, NextElement),
    T2 is T1+1,
    make_storytrace(NextElement, X, T2, [CurrentElement|List], STRUCT,
    STORY2),
    countAppear(CurrentElement, STRUCT, 0, R4)->
    check_repeat(CurrentElement, RR1, R4, R),
    element(CurrentElement, ANY, X, T1, R, [], BUFF4),
    atom_concat(BUFF4,STORY2,STORY1).
```

The first argument corresponds to a composition element that is indicated as a possible candidate. The second argument corresponds to the list of characters set at the beginning of story generation. The third argument corresponds to the temporal point of this step. The fourth and the fifth arguments, respectively, correspond to the list of composition elements that are currently being used to construct the narrative structure, and to the completed structure. The last argument corresponds to the text output of the generated story.

We now briefly describe the process of determining composition elements. First, this module counts how many times the composition element *CurrentElement* occurs in the narrative structure *List* that is being former. Then, it verifies that the number of repetition of this composition element is under the limit specified in the database of narrative rules.

Next, this module activates the composition element *CurrentElement* and determines whether it can occur consistently at this step in the story being generated, referring to the database of general rules and that of narrative rules. This process is repeated recursively as necessary. In case the composition element is found to satisfy all the requirements, the control is passed to the module 'Trace linkages in the structural model' to select a candidate as *NextElement*. Next, the temporal point is incremented and the search for the next composition element is started.

If the search reaches up to the *ending*, the narrative structure of the current story is stored in *STRUCT* and the process of generating text output begins.

First, this module counts how many times the composition element *CurrentElement* occurs in the narrative structure *STRUCT*, and adjusts the index of this composition element in the *STRUCT*. The index of a recurring composition element can take one of three values: first, second, and last. In the case when a composition element occurs once or twice in the completed narrative structure, the index of the last occurrence of the composition value takes the value 'last'. This assignment of index values is consistent with the limit on the number of recurrences of a composition rule as defined in the database of narrative rules.

Next, this module activates the composition element *CurrentElement* and determines whether it occurs consistently in the completed story. This process is repeated if necessary.

Finally, the control is passed to 'Generate text output' module to generate the text corresponding to the sequence of composition elements and the character settings.

Trace linkages in the structural model

This module refers to the database of links between pairs of composition elements and selects composition elements that can possibly occur in the generated story. It also reorders all the link information randomly at the start of each story generation. Finally, it passes a candidate composition element to the module 'Determine composition elements.' Fig. 7 shows the internal structure of this module.

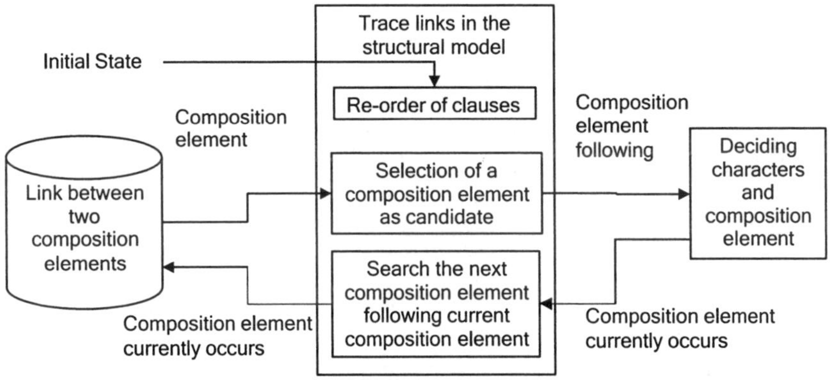

Fig.7 Internal structure of the module 'Trace linkages in the structure model'

Generate text outputs

Depending on the output of the module 'Determine composition elements', this module generates a text containing the relevant parts of the story that are covered by the composition elements. In this process, this module receives information about the characters, items and templates from the module 'Determine composition elements' for generating the text. It also refers to the database of narrative rules for adding narrative characteristics into the text.

4.3 Samples of generated stories

The story-generating system produced variations of Cinderella tales that were not the same as any of the analyzed stories. We provide below two sample stories generated by the system with a sets of characters and an order of composition elements that are combined into each story. Sample story1 is almost the same as one of the original analyzed story (Text08). This story is generated under the restriction that the character settings were the same as in Text08. Sample story2 is a new variation, and is generated with the kinds of roles allowed set to a maximum, and with the characters being selected at random from several analyzed stories.

Sample story1:

The following roles and characters were randomly selected:

[PROTAGONIST, FATHER, MAN, ASSISTANT, ASSISTANT, ASSISTANT, ASSISTANT, SPOUSE, OPPONENT, OPPONENT, OPPONENT].

Set of characters:

[Girl, Trader, Ugly oldman, Oldman, King, Blacksmith, Retainer, Prince, Princess, Queen, Slave]

Order of composition elements:

[desire of fathor, locked, marriage engage to oldman, create candle stand, hide in, sell candle stand, leave from home, buy candle stand, discovery, life with prince, jerous of princess, rent candle stand, burnt, abuse, excile, help of oldman, life with oldman, sick of prince, order to treat, cook gruel, put ring, discovery of ring, revelation, marriage]

Story (Japanese description):
あるしょうばいにんがうつくしいむすめをもっていました。むすめはあまりにもむすめがうつくしいので、よめにやるきになりませんでした。しょうばいにんはむすめをいえにとじこめて、だれにもあわせようとしませんでした。しょうばいにんはむすめをみにくいろうじんとけっこんさせようとかんがえました。むすめはしょうばいにんにかんがえをかえるようにたのみましたが、しょうばいにんはいうことをききませんでした。むすめはあきらめてしょうばいにんに「おおきなきんのしょくだいをつくってください。そうしたらわたしはしょうばいにんのおよめになりましょう」といいました。しょうばいにんはさっそくおおきなきんのしょくだいをつくりました。しょうばいにんがしごとにでかけると、むすめはいどにくつをおいてじぶんはきんのしょくだいのなかにはいって、とびらをかたくしめました。しょうばいにんがかえってくるとむすめのすがたはどこにもみえません。むすめのくつがいどにおいてあるのをみて、むすめがいどにみをなげたのだとおもいました。しょうばいにんはかなしくてきんのしょくだいをかじやにうってしまいました。あるとき、おうじがけらいをとおりかかりました。おうじはきんのしょくだいをとてもきにいり、かってかえりました。そしてじぶんのおしろにおきました。おうじは、そのうつくしいむすめのところへきて、そのてをとっていっしょにダンスをおどりました。ほかのひとがきても、おうじはけしててをはなさず、ぶとうかいのあいだじゅう、ずっとむすめとだけおどりつづけました。おうじはむすめをとてもすきになりました。おうじはつぎのひもまた、むすめがあらわれるのをベッドのなかからみていました。みっかめのよるにむすめがでてくるとおうじははねおきてむすめをつかまえました。おうじは「おまえはまものか、それともようせいか」とたずねると、むすめは「わたしはにんげんのおんなのこです」とこたえ、これまでのことをすべてはなしましたました。そうしておうじとむすめはなかよしになり、むすめは、ひるまはきんのしょくだいにかくれ、よるなるとでてきておうじとたのしくすごしました。ところがあるよる、おうじとむすめがおしろでたのしくはなしているのを、とおりがかったどれいがみみにして、なかをのぞくと、むすめがきんのしょくだいのなかにはいっていくのをみました。そしてどれいはおうじのこんやくしゃであるひめに、このことをつたえました。ひめはとてもおこりました。あるひ、おうじがかりにでかけてきゅうでんをるすにしました。ひめはおうじのははぎみに「きょうはわたしのところにきゃくがあるので、どうかきんのしょくだいをかしてください」とたのみました。ははぎみはおうじがきんのしょくだいにだれもさわらせないことをしっていたので、ことわろうとしましたが、ひめがくりかえしたのむので、ついにきんのしょくだいをかしてあげました。ひめはきんのしょくだいに 40 ほんのろうそくをたて、すべてにひをつけました。ろうそくのほのおできんのしょくだいのなかはだんだんとあつくなり、むすめはがまんしきれずにとびだしました。むすめはからだじゅうにやけどをおって、そのまままきをうしないました。ひめはむすめがしんだとおもい、どれいにめいじて、むすめをきゅうでんのほりにすてさせました。そこへまずしいろうじんがとおりかかると、どこからかかすかなうめきごえがきこえてきました。ろうじんはむすめにきがついて、たすけだしました。そして、いえにつれてかえり、やけどにくすりをぬってあげました。ろうじんはむすめをかわいそうにおもい、やしなうことにしました。おうじがかりからもどってみると、きんのしょくだいはありましたが、なかはからっぽになっていました。おうじはむすめがいなくなったことをとてもかなしみ、とうとうびょうきになってしまいました。おうじは 40 にちのあいだくすりもたべものもとらず、ねたきりになりました。くにじゅうのいしゃがおうじをみましたが、だれもなおすことはできませんでした。あるとき、こまりはてたおうに、けらいが「おうじさまのやまいは、すきなひとのかおをみるまではなおらないでしょう」といいました。おうはそれをきいて「かねもちもまずしいものも、みぶんのたかいものもひくいものも、すべてのものはりょうりをひとしなつくり、おうじのもとへじさんせよ」と、くにじゅうにめいれいしました。そうしてあらゆるひとがりょうりをもってきましたが、おうじはどれひとつとしてたべようとしませんでした。ろうじんがおかゆのおたっしのことをはなすとむすめはおかゆをつくりました。そしてむすめはおかゆをみすぼらしいうつわにいれて、おうじにもらったきんのゆびわをいれると、ろうじんにきゅうでんにもっていかせました。まずしいろうじんがみすぼらしいうつわをもってきたのをみると、みながあざわらいました。しかしおうじは、おかゆをみるとしょくよくがわいてきて、たべはじめました。おかゆはとてもおいしくて、おうじはすべてたいらげました。するとうつわのそこにきんのゆびわがはいっていました。おうじはとたんにげんきになり、すぐさまろうじんをよびよせて「おかゆをつくったのはだれなのか」とといただしました。ろうじんは「うちにいるむすめがつくりました」とこたえ、ろうじんはむすめのことをすべてはなしました。そうして、むすめはおうじとけっこんしました。おしまい

(Abridged translation):

There was a Girl and she was beautiful. Father desired Girl. Father locked Girl in the house and engaged her to an Ugly oldman. Girl asked Father to make a big gold candlestand. Girl hid in the candlestand. Father lost Girl and sold the candlestand to a Blacksmith. A Prince bought the candle stand from Blacksmith. Prince discovered Girl in the candlestand. Girl and Prince lived in the Prince's room. Princess found Girl and asked Prince lend the candlestand. Princess ignited candles and burnt Girl. Princess exiled Girl. An Oldman found Girl and helped her. Girl lived in the house of Oldman. Prince became sick. King ordered people to cook for Prince. Girl cooked gruel and hid the ring Prince gave her into the gruel on the plate. Oldman brought Prince the plate. Prince ate gruel and found the ring. Girl was found by Prince and they were married.

Sample story2:

The following roles and characters were randomly selected:

[PROTAGONIST, STEPMOTHER, WOMAN, FATHER, SISTER, SISTER, ASSISTANT, ASSISTANT, ASSISTANT, SPOUSE, OPPONENT, MAN].

Set of characters:

[*Cinderella, Stepmother, Queen, Father, Younger sister, Elder sister, Kusha-Rakan, Ministor, King Bob, Prince, Pirates, Rich man*]

Order of composition elements:

[*remarriage of father*] [*jealous of stepmother*] [*cut hair*] [*paint tar*] [*harsh work*] [*bathing*] [*discovery*] [*marriage*]

Story (Japanese description):

シンデレラというおんなのこがいました。あるとき、ちちはままははとさいこんしました。ままははとてもこうまんちきなおんなのひとでした。ままははシンデレラがうつくしいのにやきもちをやき、かみをきり、かおにタールをぬって、かちくのせわをさせて、ひどくはたらかせました。シンデレラはかちくにえさをあげたあと、おがわでみずあびをしていました。やがてシンデレラとおうじはけっこんしきをあげました。シンデレラはまた、あねたちもまた、だいきぞくとけっこんさせました。そうしてしあわせにくらしました。おしまい

(Translation):

There was a girl named Cinderella. One day, her Father married a Stepmother. Stepmother was very arrogant. Stepmother feeling jealousy towards Cinderella, cut her hair, painted her face with tar, and ordered harsh work. Cinderella bathed after working. Cinderella married a Prince. Cinderella arranged her sisters to marry with nobles.

5. Discussion

The story generating system produced new variations of Cinderella tales based on the structural model. Depending on the combinations of conceptual structures and narrative structures that the system chose, it produced some stories that were similar to the analyzed stories, but also some that were quiet different. When attempting to generate stories with characters that appeared in an original story, conceptual structures become closely constrained by the characters and by the composition elements from the original story. In the case of random selections, the conceptual structures are not so constrained. As one might expect, we found that more stories similar to the originals were generated in the former case than in the case of random selections.

Given the variety of narrative structures in generated stories, we consider that the number of composition elements and the linkages among the composition elements implemented in the structural model are sufficient for generating variations of Cinderella tales. However, as the character settings and relations among them are inherited from the original stories, relations among the characters and between characters and items are sometimes inconsistent. Thus, the system sometimes produces inconsistent combinations between some kinds of composition elements and sets of characters, and story generation under these conditions fails.

One way to resolve those kinds of inconsistencies is to add a possibility to redefine the settings of characters and relations between them at any activation of composition elements. However, relaxing this constraint may also weaken the cohesiveness of the structural model, thereby making it possible to generate stories that may not be considered a Cinderella tale at all.

Using composition elements has the potential to facilitate regenerating text outputs and expanding the structural model. A complex story can be divided into parts regarded as composition elements. Then the information about the settings of characters and the linkages between composition elements can be determined. Finally, one can incorporate the complex data into the structural model without having to conceptualizations in terms of narrative grammars and theories.

Another problem occuring in the current implementation of the story-generating system is that it sometimes generates strange stories because of juxtaposing unrelated composition elements. For example, a protagonist and the spouse may be married suddnly after their meeting. This problem may be resolved by introducing appropriate rules to constrain the possible places in a sequence that a composition element is able to occupy.

6. Conclusions and Future Research

We created a structural model of Cinderella tales that was composed from three kinds of information: settings of characters, composition elements and linkages between two composition elements. Narrative structures were made from composition elements ordered linearly, and conceptual structures provided settings of characters and composition elements. Based on this structural model, we implemented a story generating system that produces variations of Cinderella tales. Modelling of conceptual and narrative structures focussing on motifs and composition elements allows for ease of implementation and explanation.

We consider the structural model developed in this research is as a network model and also a state transition model. Taking this point of view, we plan to design an interactive system to generate stories between two computational systems or between a computation system and a human. Based on the rules which decide appearance of composition elements, it is also possible to introduce models of objective authoring into the story generating system. Many story-generating systems, including the current version of our system, determine conceptual and narrative structures that compose a new story from subjective characters in the story. However, functions with models of objective authoring cause the story generation task to let the conceptual structures and narrative structures proceed in parallel and influence each other.

References

[1] J. Campbell (with Bill Moyers), *The power of myth.* Doubleday New York,1988.
[2] M. Bal, *Narratology: Introduction to the theory of narrative.* Univ. of Toronto Press, Toronto, 1997.
[3] S. Chatman, *Story and discourse: Narrative structure in fiction and film.* Cornell University Press, Ithaca (NY), 1978.
[4] M. Currie, *Postmodern narrative theory.* St. Martin's Press, New York, 1998.
[5] W. Martin, *Recent theories of narrative.* Cornell University Press, Ithaca (NY), 1986.
[6] V. Propp, *Morphology of the folktales.* University of Texas Press, Austin, 1968.
[7] R. R. Lang, A declarative Model for Simple Narratives. *Narrative Intelligence Symposium: AAAI Fall symposium Series, 1999.*
[8] D. E. Rumelhart, Notes on a Schema for stories. In D.G. Bobrow and A. Collins (eds.), *Representation and Understanding,* Academic Press, New York, 1975, pp.211-236.
[9] R. C. Shank and R. P. Abelson, *Scripts, Plans, Goals and Understanding.* Lawrence Erbaum, Hillsdale (NJ), 1977.
[10] N. Szilas, IDtension: a narrative engine for Interactive Drama, *1st International Conference on Technologies for Interactive Digital Storytelling and Entertainment (TIDSE 2003)*, Darmstadt, Germany, 2003.
[11] M. Riedl, C. J. Saretto, and R. M. Young, Managing interaction between users and agents in a multiagent storytelling environment, *the Proceedings of the Second International Conference on Autonomous Agents and Multi-Agent Systems*, June, 2003.
[12] C. Prrrault, Contes de Perrault, In A. Niikura (translated in Japanese), Perrault's fairy tales, Iwanami, Tokyo, 1982.
[13] J. Grim and W. Grim, Kinder and Hause Marchen, In K. Kaneda (translated in Japanese), Grimm's fairytales, vol.1, Iwanami, Tokyo, 1979
[14] S. Yamamuro, Cinderella tales in the world, Shinchosha, Tokyo, 1979.
[15] Society of a Japanese folktales authored, 100 tales of Japan, Kokudo-Sha, Tokyo, 1986.
[16] M. R. Cox Cinderella: Three Hundred and Forty-five Variants of Cinderella, Catskin, and Cap O'Rushes, Abstracted and Tabulated, with a Discussion of Mediaeval Analogues, and Notes, David Nutt, London, 1893.
[17] A. B. Rooth, The Cinderella Cycle, Greerup, Lund, 1951.
[18] Y. Hosaka and T. Ogata, Generation of Stories and their Visual Representation, *The 16th Annual conference of Japanese Society for Artificial Intelligence*, 2002.
[19] S. Kawakami *et al.*, A Story Making System for Children, Advanced research in computers and communications in education, G.. Cumming *et al.* (eds.), IOS press, Ohmcha, 1999, pp.359-362.
[20] A. Aarne, THE TYPES OF THE FOLKTALE - A CLASSIFICATION AND BIBLIOGRAPHY, translated and enlarged by Stith Thompson A.Aarne's "Verzeichnis der Marchentypen" FF Communication No.3 Second Revision, Helsinki, 1964, FFC No.184.
[21] K. Seki, Japanese folktales, vol. 1, vol12", Kadokawa, Tokyo, 1979.
[22] M. Luthi, Folktales of Europe, In T. Ozawa (translated in Japanese), Iwasaki Bijutsu-sha, Tokyo, 1969.

Information Modelling and Knowledge Bases XV
Y. Kiyoki et al. (Eds.)
IOS Press, 2004

Web Application Wrapping by Demonstration

Kimihito ITO and Yuzuru TANAKA
Meme Media Laboratory, Hokkaido University, Sapporo 060-8628, Japan

Abstract. Recent innovations in Web technologies enable end-users to easily use various services through their Web browsers. Examples of such services include various kinds of database service and various sorts of analysis tools. This evolution in Web applications causes difficulty in reusing functions embedded in Web applications. The purpose of this study is to develop an environment where even an end-user can easily wrap complicated Web applications to reuse their embedded functions. In this paper, we propose a framework that enables end-users to wrap Web applications through instruction by demonstration. IntelligentPad architecture enables end-users to dynamically define functional linkages among wrapped Web applications through drag & drop and paste operations.

1 Introduction

During the last several years, the Web has evolved into a world-wide information pool where people can share intellectual resources. Information publishers represent their intellectual resources in the form of semi-structured documents on the Web. Hyperlinks among documents allow users to navigate from one document to another related document. An input-form in an HTML document enables users to submit data to a server-side program, which is called Web application. A Web application is an application program that has an HTML-based front-end for users to utilize remote services. Today, many companies and researchers provide Web applications, such as various kinds of database services and various sorts of analysis tools.

Recent innovations in Web technologies enable end-users to easily use various services through their Web browsers. CGI(Common Gateway Interface), ASPs (Active Server Pages), Java's Servlet, JSP(JavaServer Pages) and PHP(PHP:Hypertext Preprocessor) are all running at server-sides to dynamically provide HTML-based front-end interfaces to users. Some sites use frames to present documents with multiple embedded document views, or to popup certain information aside. Some sites use cookies to maintain a session.

The evolution of Web application technologies causes various difficulties in reusing embedded functions in Web applications. For example, if a user wants to send an output from one Web application to an input-form of another Web application, he or she needs to repeat complicated and sometimes tedious copy-and-paste operations. Firstly, he must input some data on the first Web application and navigate through result pages to obtain some result data. Secondly, he must copy a part of the result data using his mouse, and paste this copy into the input-form on the second Web application. Finally he must submit the input-form and navigate through the result pages to obtain some result data from the second Web application. The user must repeat these three steps, if he wants to apply the same processing for different inputs. Currently, in order to automate this process, users must write a program called a *wrapper* in a programming

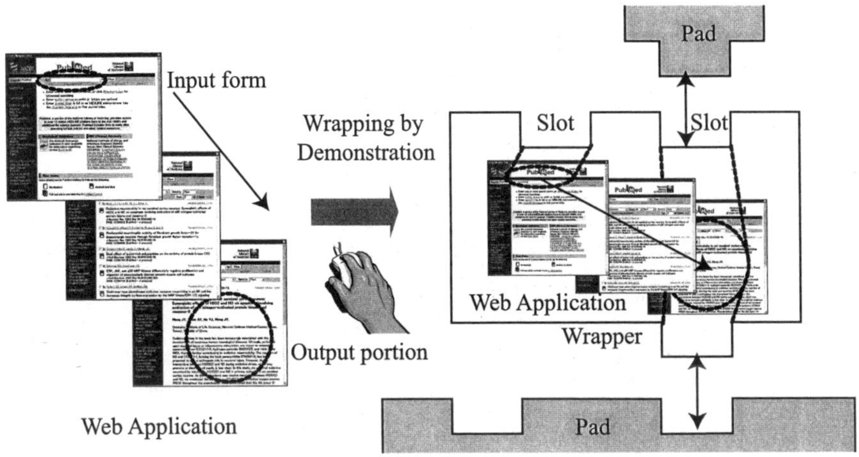

Figure 1: An outline of our approach.

language such as Perl or Java, or based on a specialized framework such as SOAP, to perform the required processing. Maintenance of a large number of wrappers is not easy in practice. It is time consuming to rewrite a wrapper program every time the syntax of the Web application page changes.

From this point of view, we propose a new framework that enables users to wrap arbitrary Web applications through instruction by demonstration. IntelligentPad architecture enables end-users to define functional linkages among wrapped Web applications through drag & drop and paste operations. In our previous works[14, 16], we presented the simplest version of our wrapping method, and discussed its application to mobile computing[16]. In [17], the whole strategy for the wrapping and functional linkage using IntelligentPad architecture was given. In this paper, we focus on Web application wrapping through instruction by demonstration.

This paper is organized as follows. In Section 2, we address some fundamental requirements concerning the end-users' reuse of Web applications. Our methodology for the Web application wrapping through instruction by demonstration is described in Section 3. Details of the IntelligentPad architecture are presented in Section 4. Related work is discussed in Section 5, and we conclude in Section 6 with our future research plan.

2 Reuse of Web Applications : Requirements and Our Approach

In bioinformatics, for example, there are already many different kinds of database services, analysis services, and related reference information services; most of them are available as Web applications. However they are hard to interoperate with each other. This has two reasons. Different Web applications use different data formats. In addition, there is no way on the client side to connect the output of one Web application to the input form of another Web application other than making a copy of the appropriate output text portion on the source page and pasting it in the input form of the target page. While SOAP allows you to write a program to functionally integrate more than one Web service, it is hard to use for non-programmers.

Before we describe our approach to solve this problem, we address some fundamental requirements concerning the end-users' reuse of Web applications.

A framework where end-users can reuse Web applications requires the following capabilities.

1. Easy specification of input and output portions of Web applications to reuse embedded functions in them.

2. Easy definition of functional linkage between Web applications to compose a new integrated application.

For the first requirement, we will propose a Web application wrapping method based on the instruction by demonstrating an example sequence of user operations. IntelligentPad architecture enables end-users to define functional linkage between wrapped Web applications through drag & drop and paste operations. The use of IntelligentPad[28, 29, 27] technologies achieve the second capability.

In figure 1, we summarize our approach of reusing functions embedded in behind Web applications.

Users can create wrapper pads for Web applications based on the programming by demonstration (PBD). A WebNavigationWrapperPad has the facility to record and replay operations that are performed by a user. During its definition phase, WebNavigationWrapperPad records user's operations on the Web browser interface. Users can define data I/O ports called slots on intermediate pages that are returned by Web applications. Parameters in the recorded operations, such as values submitted to forms, can be modified through corresponding input slots. WebNavigationWrapperPad automates navigation using the modified values. Users can also define arbitrary document portions in pages that are returned by the Web application to work as output slots.

Using IntelligentPad architecture, users can functionally combine these wrapped Web applications by connecting slots through the use of drag-and-drop and paste operations. Users can also reuse wrapped Web applications in collaboration with wrapped local legacy applications.

3 Web Application Wrapping by Demonstration

In this section we present our method of the Web application wrapping based on instructions by demonstration. Programming by Demonstration (PBD)[7] enables users to construct a script program by simply performing actions in the user interface. With PBD, the user instructs the system to watch what I do, and a PBD system creates generalized programs from the recorded actions.

3.1 Modeling Navigation within Web Applications

Many Web applications use more than one page to output and input data to and from users. For example, the Web application shown in Figure 2 uses three pages for its input and output. On the first page, this application requests users to input data. The second page displays a list of result items. Users may select one of these items and click its anchor to jump to the third page, where they will get result data from this application.

Figure3 shows a site-specific navigation model for PubMed paper search[23], which answers queries of the form "Search PubMed for words w".

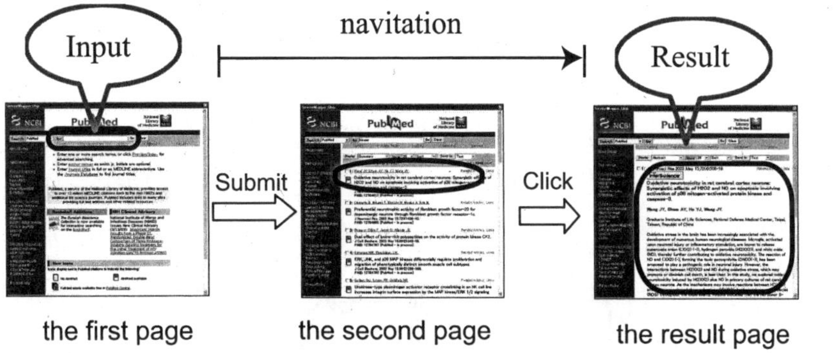

Figure 2: An example of a Web application.

In order to simplify the description of our method, we first model the Web application as a directed graph. We denote a graph of a Web application WA by $G(WA)$. For a Web application WA, graph $G(WA)$ contains a node for each page p in WA. In $G(WA)$, there exists a directed edge (p, q) labeled with an operation op, if and only if op on p causes a jump to the page q in WA. Examples of operations includes opening a page specified by a url, navigation along a hyperlink, and submitting some data to a form.

We denote *a navigation* in a Web application as follows:

$$p_0 \xrightarrow{op_0} p_1 \xrightarrow{op_2} \cdots \xrightarrow{op_{k-1}} p_k,$$

where $p_0, p_1, \ldots, p_k$ are Web pages, and each op_i is a user-operation at page p_i to jump to the next page p_{i+1}. Formally, a navigation in a Web application WA is a path in the graph $G(WA)$.

We call a sequence of user-operations $op_0, \ldots, op_{k-1}$ a *navigation path.* By a navigation path $op_0, \ldots, op_{k-1}$, we identify the Web page p_k in a Web application WA as long as $op_0, \ldots, op_{k-1}$ is a path in $G(WA)$.

$$p_k = op_0.op_1.op_2.\cdots.op_{k-1}.$$

We may fetch the page p_k with a URL directly. In general, however, every pages is not accessible with URLs. For example, Web pages that are returned as a result of POST are not specified by URLs.

By modifying an operator op_i with op'_i, we get another Web page p'_k of WA through the same navigation from p'_{i+1} to p'_k.

$$p_0 \xrightarrow{op_0} p_1 \cdots \xrightarrow{op_{i-1}} p_i \xrightarrow{op'_i} p'_{i+1} \xrightarrow{op_{i+1}} p'_{i+2} \cdots \xrightarrow{op_{k-1}} p'_k,$$

Example of modifications contains substitution of input-value for an input-form on p_{i-1}.

The page p'_k that are obtained by the modified navigation-path is represented by

$$p'_k = op_0.op_1.\cdots.op_{i-1}.op'_i.op_{i+1}.\cdots.op_{k-1}.$$

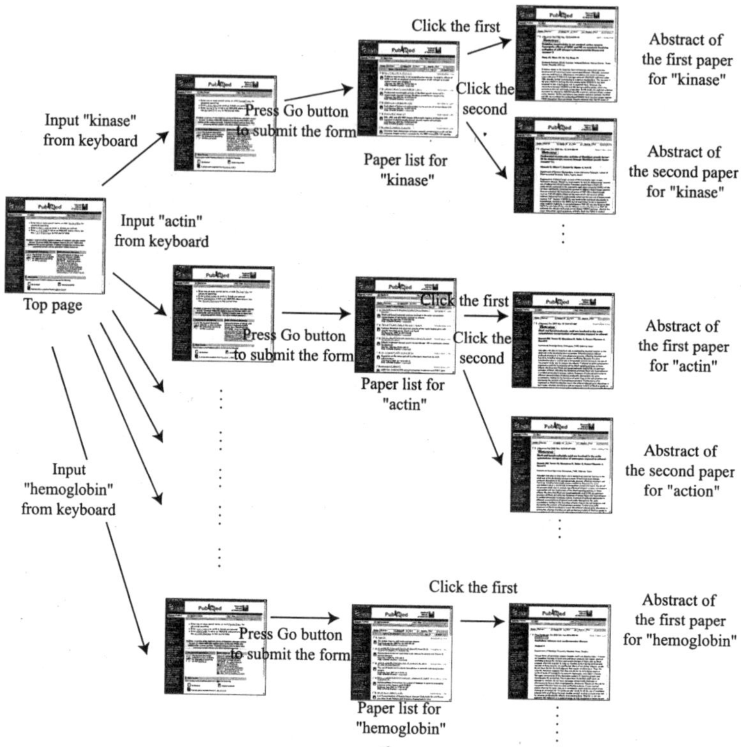

Figure 3: A model of navigations within PubMed service.

3.2 User Operations within Web Pages

A *user-operation op* is an operation that users can perform with ordinary Web browsers such as Netscape Navigator or Internet Explorer. Examples of user operations include open of a specified url, click of an anchor, and submission of some data to a form.

In our framework, we use the following 5 operations.

$$\begin{aligned} \textit{user-operation} ::= \; & \text{Open}(\textit{url}) \\ | \; & \text{Click}(\textit{anchor-elm}) \\ | \; & \text{Set}(\textit{input-elm}, \textit{value}) \\ | \; & \text{Submit}(\textit{form-elm}) \\ | \; & \text{Back}(). \end{aligned}$$

An Open(*url*) operation opens the page specified by given URL. A Click(*anchor-elm*) follows hyperlink with the anchor-element *anchor-elm*. A Set(*input-elm*, *value*) sets the given value to the specified input-form. and a Submit(*form-elm*) operation submits the specified form to the appropriate Web Server to jump to the next page.

A *navigation path* is a sequence of user operations. Using a navigation path, we can represent how to access a Web page.

$$\begin{aligned} \textit{navigation-path} ::= \; & \textit{user-operation} \\ | \; & \textit{user-operation.navigation-path}. \end{aligned}$$

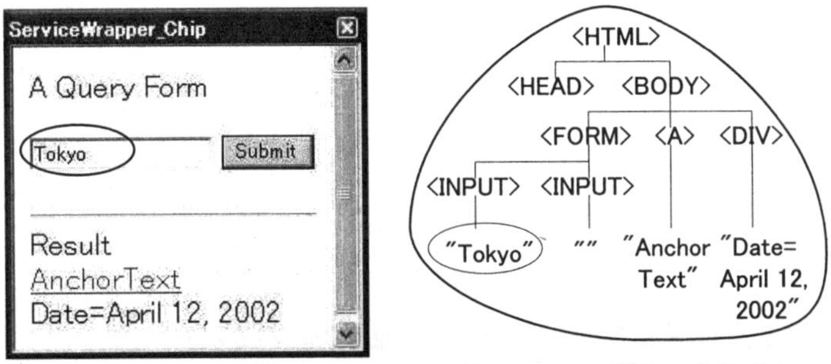

Document View Document Object Model

```
<HTML>
  <HEAD><TITLE>Sample HTML</TITLE></HEAD>
  <BODY>
    A Query Form<BR>
    <FORM method="GET" action=./sample.cgi>
      <INPUT value="Tokyo" name="query">
      <INPUT type="submit">
    </FORM>
    <HR>Result<BR>
    <A href="http://www.meme.hokudai.ac.jp">
      AnchorText</A>
    <DIV>Date=April 12, 2002</DIV>
  </BODY>
</HTML>
```

Figure 4: An HTML document with its DOM tree.

3.3 Identification of HTML-Elements

There are many ways to characterize the position of specific HTML-elements in a DOM tree.

Many researchers have worked on developing robust wrapping method of Web applications[3, 25, 19]. Some wrapping method have robustness for changes in formatting. From the view point of computational learning theory, it is impossible to deal with every kinds of formatting change. We do not focus on such robustness in this paper. We focus on how instantaneously users can create wrappers of Web applications.

We use HTML-paths to specify elements in a DOM tree. The HTML-path expression is the specialization of the XPath expression[30].

An *HTML-path* is a concatenation of node identifiers along a path from the root to the specified element. Each element identifier consists of a tag name and an index i, where this node is the ith sibling that has the same tag name. We define the syntax of HTML-paths as follows:

$$\begin{array}{rl} \textit{HTML-path} ::= & \textit{tagname}[i] \\ | & \textit{HTML-path}/\textit{tagname}[i]. \end{array}$$

Figure 4 shows an HTML document with its DOM tree representation of a Web application. Using HTML-paths, we can access texts in a DOM tree.

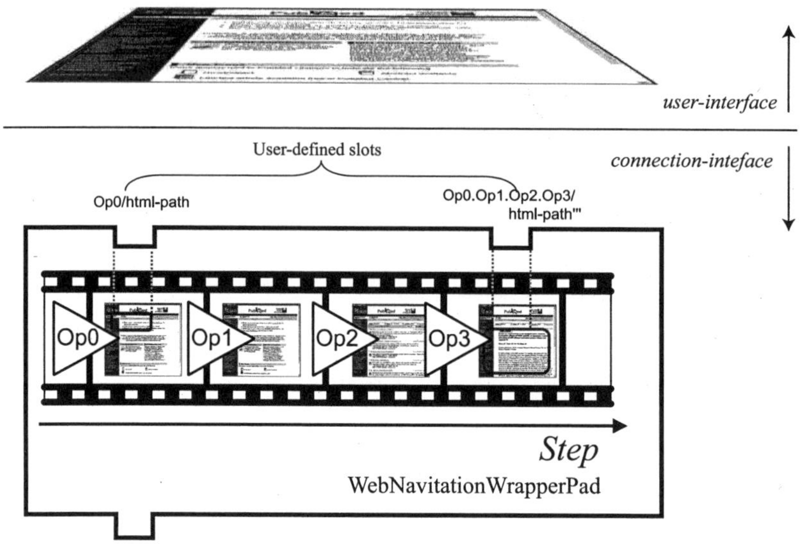

Figure 5: Abstract architecture of WebNavigationWrapperPad.

For example, The circled portion in the document in Figure 4 corresponds to the circled node whose HTML-path is

`HTML[1]/BODY[1]/FORM[1]/INPUT[1].`

This is the HTML-path of an input element of this Web application.

To access the detail of an HTML element, we use the following two extensions added to the path-expression.

- *HTML-path/*`@`*attribute-name*
- *HTML-path/*`text()`

The function @*attribute-name* selects an attribute value named with the specified name. We can set and get the value of the attribute. The function text() selects a text value of the element. For example, consider the DOM tree in Figure 4. The attribute value identified by "HTML[1]/BODY[1]/A[1]/@href" is the string:

"http://www.meme.hokudai.ac.jp".

The text value pointed by "HTML[1]/BODY[1]/A[1]/text()" is the string "Anchor Text".

We will extend HTML-paths with navigation-paths. *Operational HTML-paths* are defined as follows.

Operational HTML-path ::= *navigation-path*/*HTML-path*

Using an operational HTML-path, we can extract data in a Web page that is not specified by a particular url address, and we can wrap Web application into a component.

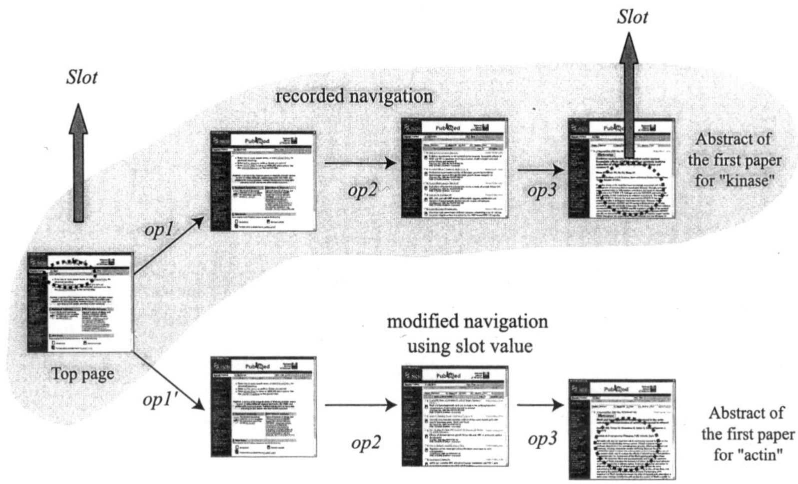

Figure 6: Recorded navigation and modified navigation in replaying phase

3.4 Operation-based Wrapper of a Web Application

WebNavigationWrapperPad is a general wrapper for a Web Application. Figure 5 shows an abstract architecture of a WebNavigationWrapperPad. A WebNavigationWrapper-Pad is a kind of Web browser. Its facility to render Web documents is implemented by wrapping Internet Explorer's API[24].

A WebNavigationWrapperPad has user-defined HTML-node slots as its connection interface. These slots are named with operational HTML-paths. The view of this pad shows current page that is returned by a Web application. The value of an HTML-node slot named with an operational HTML-path p is the text value of the HTML-node at p.

In its recording phase, WebNavigationWrapperPad records user's operations into a navigation-path.

If the value of a slot of an input-form is changed, then the WebNavigationWrapperPad modifies the recorded navigation-path that the user performed previously, and automatically replays it. While the wrapper replays the modified navigation-path, the wrapper updates the values of slots defined within the loaded pages(Figure6).

As we describe in Section 4, IntelligentPad architecture allows users to define functional linkage among wrapped Web applications through slot-connection.

3.5 User Interface for the Wrapping

To define a wrapper of a Web application, users may just open the Web page they want to wrap using a WebNavigationWrapperPad. When a user performs a sequence of operations on a WebNavigationWrapperPad to browse the Web, the WebNavigationWrapperPad records these operations into a navigation-path. If a user defines an HTML-node to work as a slot, the pad associates this slot with the operational HTML-path. The values of the user-specified slots are accessed through navigation-paths and its HTML-paths on the DOM-trees.

To hide HTML-paths from users, the system calculates HTML path expressions

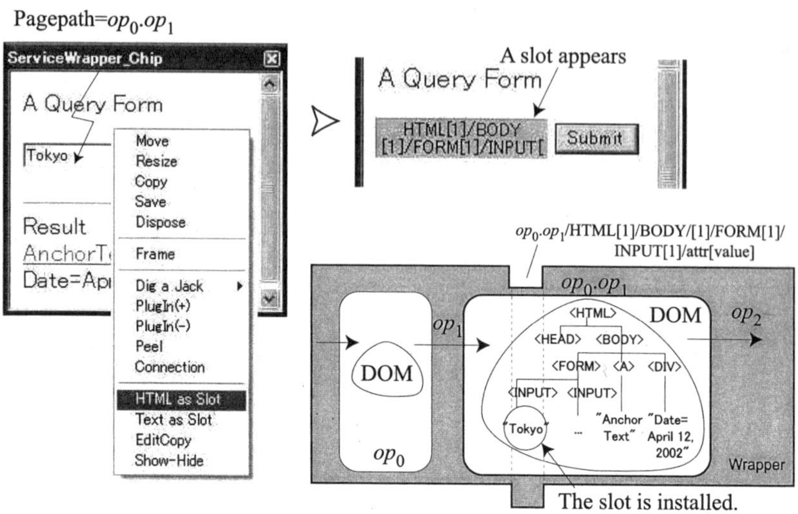

Figure 7: User interface for the slot definition.

from users' operations. Using his mouse, users can directly specify any HTML-node to work as a slot.

There are two ways for users to specify an HTML-node to work as a slot:

- specify an HTML element to work as a slot,
- specify a text portion to work as a slot.

If a user clicks with the right mouse button on a region that he wants to use as a slot, a popup menu will be shown.

Selecting "HTML as Slot" in the popup menu, the user can use the HTML-element at this location as a slot. Let *pagepath* be the navigation-path of the current page, and *htmlpath* be the HTML-path of the element (Figure 7).

1. If the element is a textinput element or textarea element, WebNavigationWrapperPad installs a slot named *pagepath/htmlpath/*@value.
2. If the element is an anchor element, WebNavigationWrapperPad installs a slot named *pagepath/htmlpath/*@href.
3. WebNavigationWrapperPad installs a slot named *pagepath/htmlpath*, otherwise.

Selecting "Text as Slot" in the popup menu, the user can use the text string contained in selected element to work as a slot. Let p be the HTML-path of the selected HTML-element. The WebNavigationWrapperPad installs a slot named with p/text().

In Figure 7, the user selects a text input element to use this as a text input slot. WebNavigationWrapperPad installed the slot named

$op_0.op_1$`/HTML[1]/BODY[1]/FORM[1]/INPUT[1]/@value`,

where $op_0.op_1$ is the current navigation-path of the page shown on this pad.

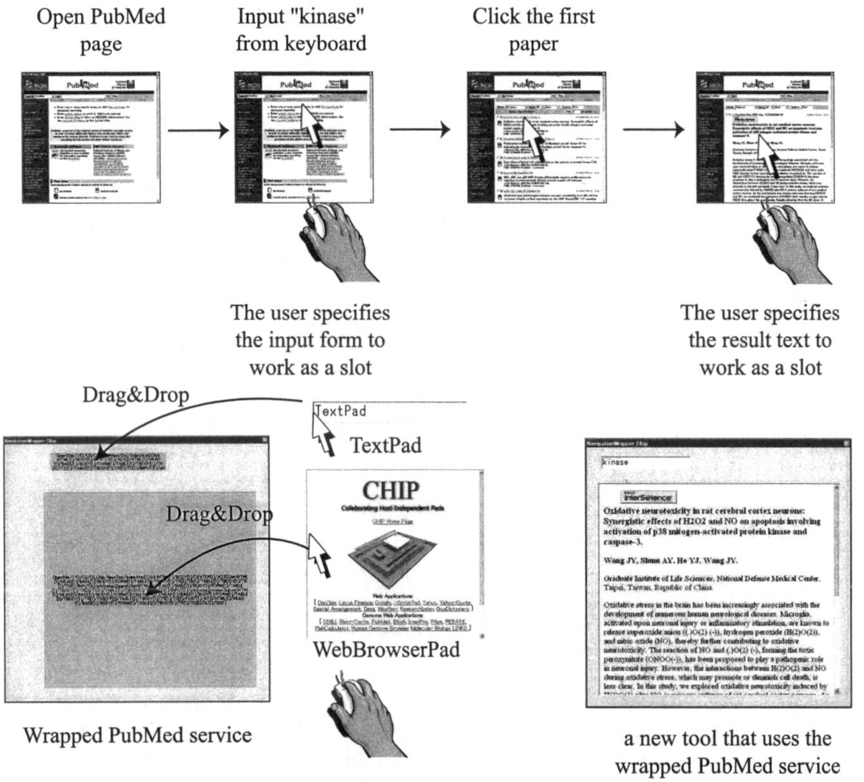

Figure 8: Creation of wrapper of Web applications through mouse operations.

In Figure 8, a user creates a wrapper pad that wraps PubMed service. Firstly, the user may open the target NCBI page on a WebNavigationWrapperPad. Secondly, using his mouse, he may specify regions that he wants to work as slots. Then the slots will appear as sunk shaded regions on this page. The user may keep the background Web page either visible or make it invisible. Thirdly, the user may embed other pads, such as TextPads and WebBrowserPad, into these slots. Finally, the user may arbitrarily relocate and resize the embedded pads to design their layout. If the user inputs some data to the TextPad that is embedded in the input-form slot, then the WebNavigation-WrapperPad will send this form value to the server. As a result, the WebBrowserPad shows a new document that is retrieved by PubMed.

4 Re-using Web Application through Functional Linkage

In this section, we present how to visually define functional linkage among Web Applications. We apply the IntelligentPad architecture to this problem.

IntelligentPad architecture allows users to combine media objects(called *pads*), such as multimedia documents and application programs, through their view integration. Each pad has slots as data I/O ports. Through drag-and-drop and paste operations, users can connect one pad to a slot of another pad. This operation simultaneously creates both a composite view and a functional linkage through a slot connection.

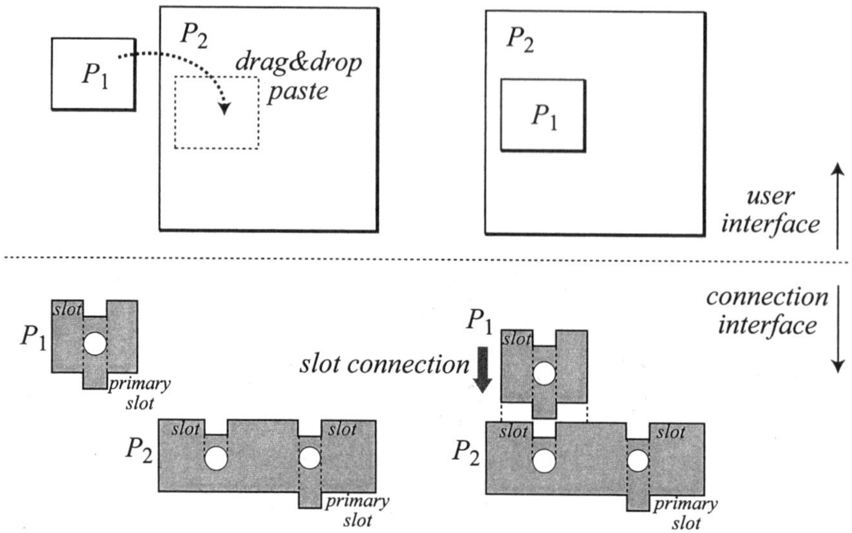

Figure 9: User interface and connection interface. If a user paste P_1 on a slot of P_2, primary slot of P_1 is connected to the slot of P_2.

4.1 IntelligentPad Architecture

IntelligentPad[29] represents each component as a pad, a sheet of paper on the screen. A pad can be pasted on another pad to define both a physical containment relationship and a functional linkage between them. When a pad P_1 is pasted on another pad P_2, the pad P_1 becomes a child of P_2, and P_2 becomes the parent of P_1. No pad may have more than one parent pad. Pads can be pasted together to define various multimedia documents and application tools. Unless otherwise specified, composite pads are always decomposable and re-editable.

Each pad has both a standard user interface and a standard connection interface. The user interface of a pad has a card like view on the screen and a standard set of operations like 'move', 'resize', 'copy', 'paste', and 'peel'. Users can easily replicate any pad, paste a pad onto another, and peel a pad off a composite pad. Pads are decomposable persistent objects. You can easily decompose any composite pad by simply peeling off the primitive or composite pad from its parent pad. As its connection interface, each pad provides a list of slots that work as connection jacks of an AV-system component, and a single connection to a slot of its parent pad(Figure9).

To set up data connection between pads, IntelligentPad uses three standard messages, set, gimme and update. We show an outline of these three messages in Table 1.

Table 1: A summary of three standard messages.

Message	Summary
set slotname value	a child sets the specified value to its parent's slot
gimme slotname	a child requests its parent to return the value of its specified slot
update	a parent notifies its children that some slot value has been changed

Each pad is embedded in one parent at most with its connection to one of the parent

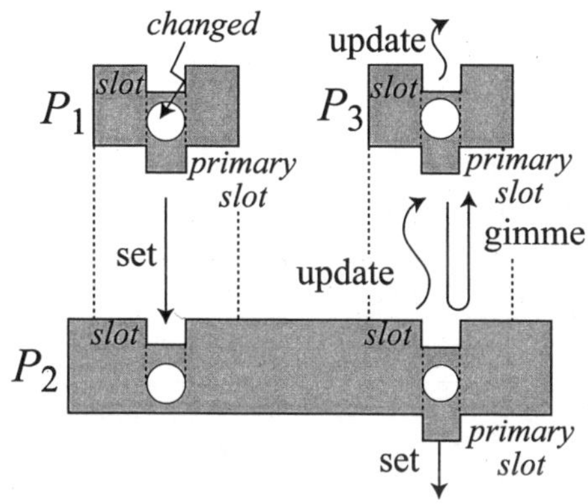

Figure 10: Three standard messages, 'set', 'gimme' and 'update', between pads.

pad slots. Connected pads form a tree structure. We do not restrict the maximum depth of the tree.

Each pad has one primary slot. When the value of the primary slot of a child is changed, the child sends a set message with the new slot value to its parents. Using this value, the parent changes its own slot values. Then, the parent pad notifies all of its children pads of its state change by sending an update message. Each child that has received an update message sends a gimme message to the parent pad, changes its own slot values using the return value of this gimme message, and then sends an update message to each of its children. Using this mechanism, state changes are propagated from one pad to all the pads connected to it through slots (Figure 10).

4.2 Functional Linkage of Wrapped Web Applications through View Integration

A pad that wraps a Web application provides slots for some of the original's input forms and output text strings. Since wrapped Web applications are pads, you may combine wrapped Web applications together through drag&drop paste operations. Through data linkage between slots specified by a user, these wrapped Web applications cooperate with each other (Figure 11).

Figure 12 shows a composite tool that integrates DDBJ's Blast homology search [9], GenBank Report service[8] and PubMed's[23] paper reference service. Blast service allows us to input a sample DNA sequence, and outputs genes with similar DNA sequences. We have specified the input form and the accession number of the first candidate sequence to work as slots. The accession number works as an anchor linking to a GenBank Report Web page containing the detail information about this gene. Its corresponding slot contains the URL to the target GenBank Report page. We have pasted a WebNavigationWrapperPad with its connection to this second slot. As a result, this child WebNavigationWrapperPad shows the corresponding GenBank Report page. This page contains bibliographic information about the related research papers. We have visually specified the title portion of the first research paper to work as a slot of this pad. We have also wrapped the PubMed service with its input form working as a slot. PubMed service returns a list of full documents that contains given keywords. We have made this slot work as the primary slot. By pasting this wrapped PubMed service on the WebNavigationWrapperPad showing a GenBank Report page with its

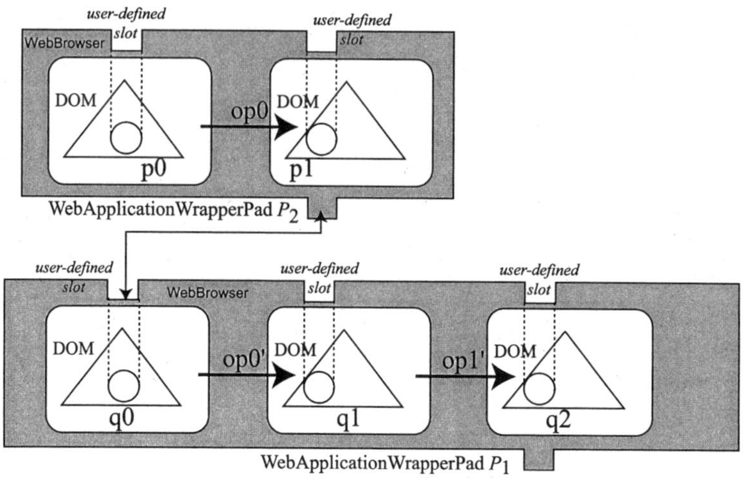

Figure 11: Functional linkage among different Web applications.

connection to the title slot, you will obtain a composite tool that functionally integrates these three services.

The new integrated application in Figure12 was composed within several minutes by a biologist who has no programming expertise.

5 Related Work

There are lots of preceding research studies on wrapping of Web pages by demonstration. However, there are few research studies that allow end-users to wrap Web applications by defining input and output port for them.

WebVCR[1] provides sophisticated interface to record and replay users' actions. It replays a series of browsing steps in "smart bookmarks", which are shortcuts to Web contents that require multiple steps to be retrieved. Creation and update of smart bookmarks is a simple process involving only the usual browsing actions by the user. However, the system does not support the definition of I/O ports for Web applications. For example, end-users could not modify the parameters for an input-form.

Bauer and Dengler[3] have also introduced a PBD(Programming by Demonstrations) method in which even naive users can configure their own Web based information services satisfying their individual information needs. They have implemented the method into InfoBeans [2]. By accessing an InfoBox with an ordinary Web browser, users can wrap Web applications. By connecting channels among InfoBeans on the InfoBox, users can also integrate them functionally together. However, it seems difficult for users to reuse a part of composite Web applications defined by other users.

W4F[26], which is semi-automatic wrapper generator, provides a GUI support tool to define an extraction. The system creates a wrapper class written in Java from user's demonstration. To use this wrapper class, users need to write program codes. DebyE[11] provides more powerful GUI support tool for the wrapping of Web applications. WbyE stores the extracted text portions in XML repository. Users have to use another XML tool to combine extracted data from Web applications. LExIKON[12] learns an underlying relation among objects within a Web page from a user-specified ordered set

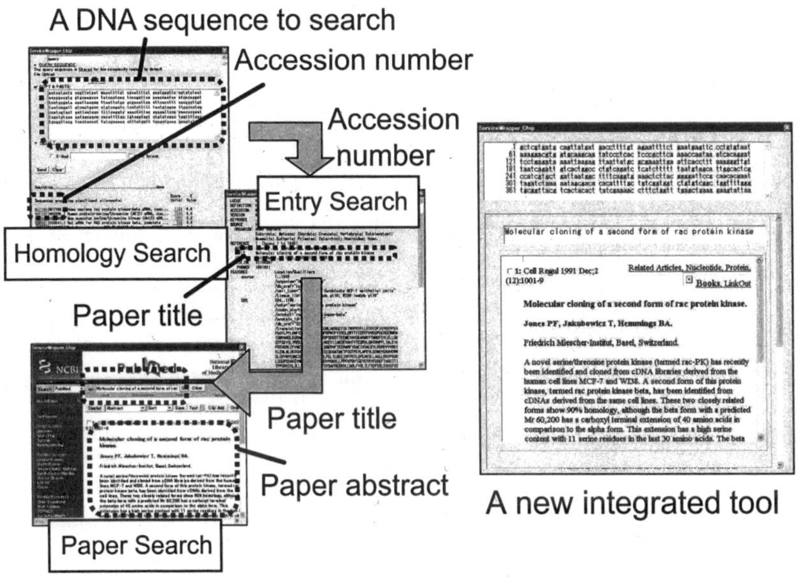

Figure 12: Dynamic gene annotation with visually wrapped Web applications. This was composed within several minutes by a biologist who has no programming expertise.

of text strings. There is no GUI support tool for the join of two extracted relations. WebView[10] allows us to define customized views of Web contents. However it seems difficult for end-users to create a new view that integrates different Web applications.

6 Concluding Remarks

In this paper, we have proposed a Web application wrapping method based on a sequence of user operations on the target Web application. This framework is based on the IntelligentPad architecture. Users can visually wrap Web applications into visual components, and visually combine them together to define functional linkages among them. Users can also visually define functional linkages between wrapped Web applications and such local tools in pad forms as chart drawing and spreadsheet tools to compose a single integrated tool.

For future work, we are planning to introduce facilities to support debugging. We have not implemented debugging tools such as error notification for defined wrappers. WebNavigationWrapperPad may detect format changes when the extraction is failed. Reasonable heuristics can be used to detect format-changes.

We also need to discuss solution to the copyright problem. Copyright policies have been reconsidered and modified every time when people introduced new media technologies. Whenever a new media technology is introduced, the consensus on new copyright policies gradually coevolves with new copyright protection and/or license management technologies. We have been, and are observing such coevolution of new policies with the Web technologies. Some have established closed services on the Web that are exclusive to their members, while others have established a closed network, such as the I-mode cellular phone network in Japan by NTT DoCoMo. Many other types of license and account management are currently tried on the Web. The same situation will occur for our technologies.

References

[1] V. Anupam, J. Freire, B. Kumar, and D. F. Lieuwen. Automating web navigation with the webvcr. *WWW9 / Computer Networks*, 33(1-6):pages 503-517, 2000.

[2] M. Bauer and D. Dengler: InfoBeans -Configuration of Personalized Information Services, In Proc. of IUI99, pages 153-156, 1999.

[3] M. Bauer, D. Dengler, and G. Paul: Instructible Agents for Web Mining, In Proc. of IUI2000, pages 21-28, 2000.

[4] M. Bauer, D. Dengler: TrIAs - An Architecture for Trainable Information Assistants. Proc AAAI'98 Workshop on AI and Information Integration, 1998.

[5] M. Birbeck and etc. *Professional XML.* Wrox Press Ltd., 2000.

[6] L. A. Carr, D. D. Roure, W. Hall, and G. Hill. Implementing an open link service for the world wide web. In *Proc. of World Wide Web 1(2)*, pages 61–71, 1998.

[7] Allen Cypher editor: *Watch What I Do: Programming by Demonstration* MIT Press Cambridge MA, 1993.

[8] DNA Data Bank of Japan. GetEntry. http://ftp2.ddbj.nig.ac.jp:8000/getstart-e.html.

[9] DNA Data Bank of Japan. Search and analysis. http://www.ddbj.nig.ac.jp/E-mail/homology.html.

[10] J. Freire, B. Kumar, and D. F. Lieuwen. Webviews: accessing personalized web content and services. In *Proc. of The tenth international World Wide Web conference on World Wide Web*, pages 576–586, 2001.

[11] P. B. Golgher, A. H. F. Laender, A. S. da Silva, and B. A. Ribeiro-Neto. An example-based environment for wrapper generation. In *Proc. of International Workshop on The World Wide Web and Conceptual Modeling*, pages 152–164, 2000.

[12] G. Grieser, K. P. Jantke, S. Lange, and B. Thomas. A unifying approach to html wrapper representation and learning. In *Proc. of Discovery Science 2000*, pages 50–64, 2000.

[13] K. Ito. CHIP(Collaborating Host-Independent Pads) Homepage. http://ca.meme.hokudai.ac.jp/people/itok/CHIP.

[14] K. Ito and Y. Tanaka. Visual wrapping and composition of web applications for their interoperations, 2002. In CDROM of WWW2002, Poster Tracks 64, 2002.

[15] K. Ito, T. Sugibuchi, Y. Fujita, T. Oda, M. Ohigashi, Y. Tanaka Integrated Visualization and Reification of Database and Web Contents In CDROM of WWW2003, Poster Tracks 129, 2003.

[16] K. Ito and Y. Tanaka. Visual wrapping and Functional Linkage of Web Applications (to appear in) Emerging Applications for Wireless and Mobile Access(MobEA), 2003.

[17] K. Ito and Y. Tanaka. Visual Environment for Web Application Composition. (to appear in) Hypertext'03, 2003.

[18] T. Kistler, H. Marais: WebL - A Programming Language for the Web. WWW7 / ComputerNetworks 30(1-7) pages 259-270 1998.

[19] N. Kushmerick: Wrapper induction: Efficiency and expressiveness. Artificial Intelligence 118(1-2) pages 15-68 2000.

[20] Tessa Lau and Daniel S. Weld: Programming by Demonstration: an Inductive Learning Formulation, IUI '99, Redondo Beach, CA, January 1999.

[21] K. C. Malcolm, S. E. Poltrock, and D. Schuler. Industrial strength hypermedia: Requirements for a large engineering enterprise. In *Proc. of Hypertext*, pages 13–24, 1991.

[22] T. Nelson: Transcopyright, Project Xanadu, http://xanadu.com/tco/

[23] National Center for biotechnology Information. PubMed . http://www.ncbi.nlm.nih.gov/entrez/query.fcgi?CMD=search&DB=PubMed.

[24] Microsoft. MSHTML Reference. MSDN Library.

[25] T.A. Phelps and R. Wilensky: Robust intradocument locations. WWW9 / Computer-Networks 33(1-6) pages 105-118, 2000.

[26] A. Sahuguet and F. Azavant. Building intelligent web applications using lightweight wrappers. *Data & Knowledge Engineering*, 36(3):283–316, 2001.

[27] Y. Tanaka. From augmentation media to meme media: Intelligentpad and the world-wide repository of pads. In *Information Modelling and Knowledge Bases*, volume VI, pages 91–107. IOS Press, 1995.

[28] Y. Tanaka and T. Imataki. Intelligentpad: A hypermedia system allowing functional composition of active media objects through direct manipulations. In *Proc. of IFIP'89*, pages 541–546, 1989.

[29] Y. Tanaka, A. Nagasaki, M. Akaishi, and T. Noguchi. A synthetic media architecture for an object-oriented open platform. In *Proc.IFIP Congress*, volume 3, pages 104–110, 1992.

[30] The World Wide Web Consotium. XML path language(XPath) version 1.0, November 1999. http://www.w3.org/TR/xpath.

[31] The World Wide Web Consotium. Document object model (DOM) level 2 HTML specification version 1.0, December 2001. http://www.w3.org/TR/2001/WD-DOM-Level-2-HTML-20011210/.

Information Modelling and Knowledge Bases XV
Y. Kiyoki et al. (Eds.)
IOS Press, 2004

Database Visualization Framework based on relational data model

Tsuyoshi Sugibuchi and Yuzuru Tanaka

Abstract. This paper proposes a framework for a database visualization system. In this framework, specifications of visualization are expressed based on the relational model, and both query and specification of visualization can be described in SQL statements. We developed a database visualization system based on this framework. This system provides functional components called operator boxes to specify database queries and visualization schemes. Each operator box has a single function to modify an input database query. This system allows users to design database visualizations easily and interactively by manipulating and composing operator boxes in a 3-dimensional virtual space.

1 Introduction

Because of the significant performance improvement of database management systems (DBMS), the typical size of databases has remarkably grown during the last couple of decades and new database applications are developed in various research and business areas. Many new database technologies have been studied to understand global features of retrieval data sets and to discover some useful knowledge from them. Information visualization is one of the major research topics in the 1990s to support user's exploration and analysis of large data sets.

A good visualization may be used to extract meaningful structures or trends from a large data set beyond the manual analysis. For rapid construction of suitable visualizations of a given data set, automated visualization algorithms and visual programming environments have been extensively studied in the last decade. Moreover, dynamic manipulations of visualization have been studied for multivariate data analysis. By using such method, users can dynamically change parameter values for visualizations and find trends in the target data set by observing the change of visualization.

In this paper we focused on trial-and-error data exploration tasks. In such exploration tasks, users try to combine a data set with other probably related data sets, and visualize them from various aspects. Users need to specify arbitrary combinations of data sources, and need to combine data sources with visualizations in arbitrary ways. Therefore, a visualization system must have an internal data model which permits combinations of various data sources and visualizations. Moreover, various direct manipulation techniques of visualizations including zooming, brushing and dragging-and-dropping have been developed. Nevertheless, these direct manipulations are hard-coded in most interactive visualization systems. Hence these manipulations can be applied only to prearranged data sets in a pre defined manner. To apply these manipulations to arbitrary data sets, these manipulations must be formalized based on an internal data model of a visualization system.

This paper propose s a new database visualization framework based on the relational model. The primary idea of this framework is that everything visualized is treated as a view relation. Each visualization is represented as an extended view relation, and any portion of a visualization is also treated as a view relation. Furthermore, user operations on visualizations are treated as relational operations on view relations. We can associate a tabular data with a visualization by projecting source data to a view relation specifying a visualization. We can select regions or graphical elements of visualizations by applying restriction operations to the corresponding view relation. Moreover, deriving a new visualization from other visualizations is equivalent to deriving a new view relation from others by means of relational operations. In the current implementation of our framework, these user operations are associated with direct manipulations in a 3-dimensional virtual space. Users can specify visualizations by interactively manipulating 3D functional components.

2 Related work

In this section we review related works of information visualization systems in term of the following three points.

The first point is the design of a new effective visualization system to understand target data sets. In the beginning of the 1990's, several visualization systems that support automated mechanisms to generate new visualization are developed. These include APT[1], BOZ[2], and SAGE[3]. SAGE has abilities to recognize data characterizations of the source data and a knowledge database to apply effective representation methods. SAGE system can generate effective visualizations from user's completely partial specifications of visualizations. AVS and IBM DataExplore are flexible data visualization systems that can be applied to various data domains. They have visual programming environments and user can develop new visualization by constructing data flow diagrams in these environments. Tioga-2[4] is a database visualization system and it also has a visual programming environment similar to AVS and IBM DataExplore.

The second point is the direct manipulation of visualization. Many visualization systems support such direct manipulation as changing restrictions of visualized data dynamically or moving viewpoints in large data sets. To support direct manipulations effectively, the visualization system can update its display quickly.

The last point is coordinating multiple visualizations. To understand complex and multivariate data, the specification of coordination among multiple visualizations that represent the same information in different viewpoints is more effective than visualization of all the information in a single visualization. In this method when users manipulate one visualization, then other visualizations are updated immediately. This method supports users to explore large data sets. DEVise[5] is one of data visualization systems and it allows users to create multiple coordinated visualizations by specifying links among visualization. DEVise supports several type links and many types of coordinating functions (brushing-and-linkage, drill-down, aggregation, etc.). The snap-together-visualization[6] system is based on SpotFire[7] and it also supports multiple coordinated visualizations. In this system users can specify coordination between two visualizations dynamically.

3 Framework

In this section we describe our database visualization framework. The basic idea of this framework is to specify database visualization schemes based on the relational data model.

3.1 V-Extended View

To specify visualization by using the relational model, a structure of a representation graphics is represented as a relational view. We call this view a v-extended view.

V-Extended View

XCOORD	YCOORD	ZCOORD	TEMPLATE NAME
0.1	0.003	0.1	"BALL"
1.8	0.05	0.1	"BALL"
0.1	0.09	0.2	"BALL"
...	....	...	...

VD (visual deriving) attributes

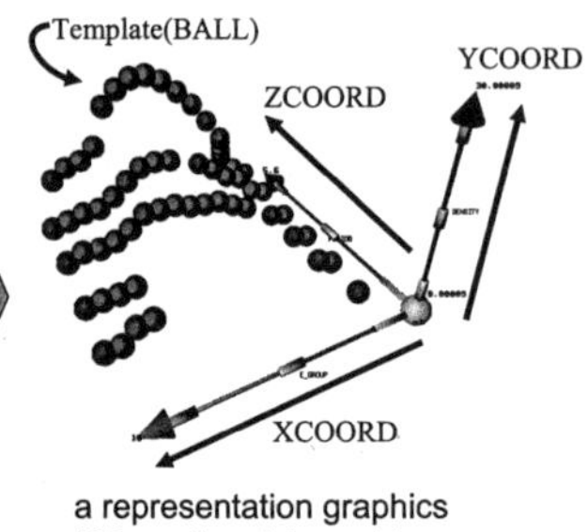

Figure 1: V-Extended View

A v-extended view is a user-defined relational view and it consists of a set of VD (visual deriving) attributes. Each VD attribute corresponds to a property of graphics, like color, position, orientation, size, etc.

The v-extended view example is illustrated in Figure 1. In this example the v-extended view consists of four VD attributes. The attribute `TEMPLATENAME` specify a *template* to represent each retrieved record. A template contains several graphical components including graphical primitives, text, and more functional objects. Users can design a template by combining arbitrary graphical components. We give a detailed description of templates in subsection 4.3. Other attributes `XCOORD`, `YCOORD` and `ZCOORD` specify geometrical location in 3-dimensional space to arrange visualized records. Therefore, this v-extended view described a specification of a 3-dimensional scatter plot.

V-Extended views are defined according as structures of representation graphics. For example, a v-extended view of a 2-dimensional bar chart consists of two VD attributes, `XCOORD`, `LENGTH` (of each bar). When users design a new visualization scheme by composing a new template or a coordinate system, our visualization system modifies the v-extended view according to the new visualization specification.

3.2 Graphics specifications described in SQL

In many visualization systems, visualization methods are defined by mapping source data attributes to visible properties of graphics. Usually these mappings are called *visual mappings*. In our framework, a specification of graphics is expressed as one relational view, and a visual mapping is equivalent to one projection operation on source data schema.

To define visual mappings, source data attributes are associated with VD attributes of a v-extended view. In the example illustrated in figure 2, three source data attributes, `E_GROUP`, `PERIOD`, `DENSITY`, are associated with three VD attributes of the v-extended view, `XCOORD`, `YCOORD`, and `ZCOORD`. To represent each retrieved record as a ball, values of attribute `TEMPLATENAME` are fixed as "BALL". This visual mapping is equivalent to a projection operation on a source data schema to a v-extended view. This projection operation can be described as a query written in SQL.

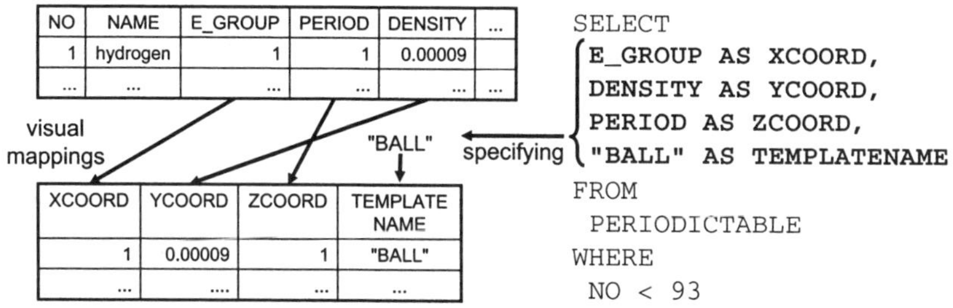

Figure 2: visual mappings described in SQL

In this query, the specification of the visual mapping is described in the "SELECT" list, and the name of the source relation is specified in the "FROM" clause. Moreover, a condition to restrict retrieved records is specified in the "WHERE" clause. In our framework a specification of a visualization and a specification of a query are unified into a specification of a query defining a v-extended view.

When our visualization system tries to display this visualization result, our system executes this SQL query and fetches the retrieved records. Then our system interprets attribute names and the value of each retrieved record to create a visualization result from them.

3.3 Operators

Our framework provides several operators to specify SQL statements. Each operator corresponds to an primitive operation to specify database queries and visualizations.

Operators for specifying queries	
TableBox	to specify a database relation to visualize
SelectBox	to select records it enclosed
RecordFilterBox	to add a new condition to restrict records
JoinBox	to join two relations

Operators for specifying representations	
TemplateManagerBox	to specify a template to represent records
AxisBox, OriginBox	to specify the coordinate system to arrange records
ContainerBox	to evaluate the input query and visualize records
OverlayBox	to overlay more than one visualization result

Table 1: operators and its operations

Operators are classified into two categories, query specifying operators and representation specifying operators. Queries specifying operators specify a base table to visualize (TableBox), add a new condition to restrict retrieved records (RecordFilterBox, SelectBox), and join two relations (JoinBox), etc. Representations specifying operators specify a template to represent each retrieved record (TemplateManagerBox), specify a coordination system to arrange retrieved records (OriginBox, AxisBox), overlay two representations (OverlayBox), and evaluate an SQL statement to visualize retrieved records (ContainerBox). We would like to emphasize that most operators are designed to correspond to user operations, but not to relational operators nor to clauses in SQL. This allows users who are not database expert to design visualizations by themselves.

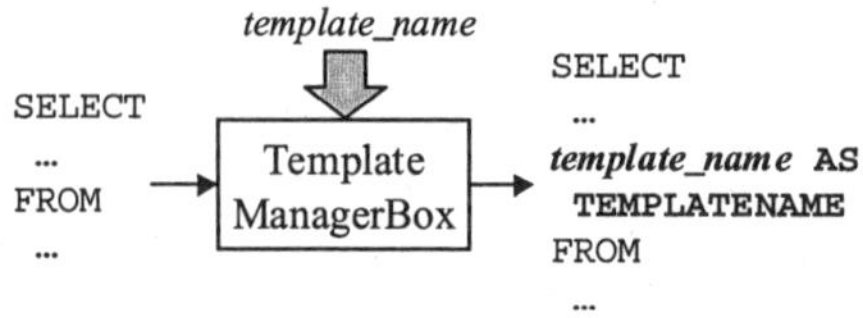

Figure 3: Operator Example

Each operator takes an SQL statement as input and performs its operation by modifying the input SQL statement. Then each operator outputs the modified SQL statement. For example, a TemplateManagerBox is illustrated in Figure 3. To represent each retrieved record, users can select a template named as *template_name*, and this TemplateManagerBox adds a virtual attribute in the `SELECT` clause of the input SQL statement, un such a way as "*template_name* `AS TEMPLATENAME`". Users can create connections among operators, and SQL statements are sent along these connections. An SQL statement to define visualization is specified by a query flow, i.e., a flow diagram consisting of operators and connections among them. The visualization specification is equivalent to the query flow illustrated in Figure 4.

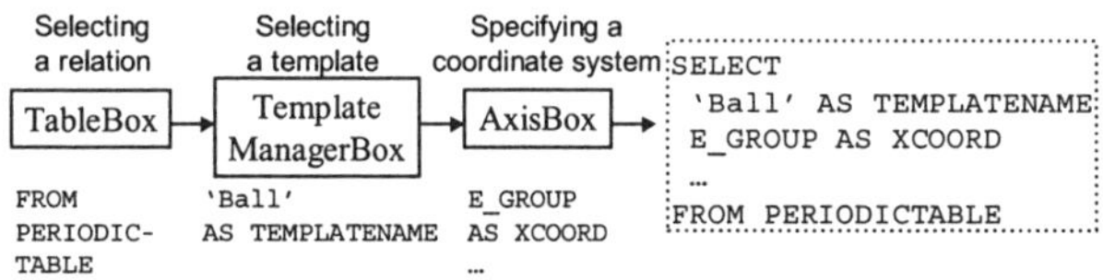

Figure 4: query flow

SQL statements defining v-extended views are modified by each operator when these statements flow through components in this diagram. A ContainerBox evaluates the input SQL statement and retrieves records.

Currently, our DB visualization system based on this framework provides two methods to connect operators interactively. The first method uses visible plugs and visible

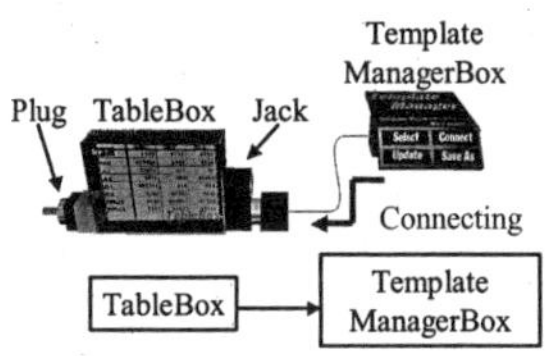

Figure 5: connecing by using jacks and plugs

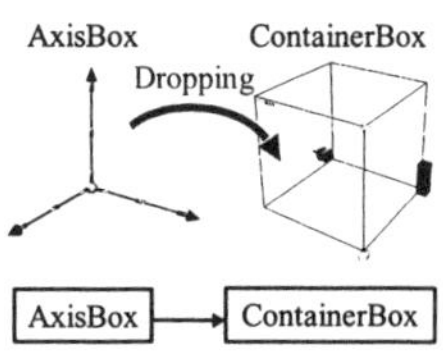

Figure 6: connecing by drag-and-drop action

jacks as illustrated in Figure 5. Some operator may have several plugs as input ports and several jacks as output. Users can interactively connect a plug to a jack to connect one operator to another in such a way as connecting AV equipment with cables. The second method is a drag-and-drop action as illustrated in Figure 6. When an operator is dropped into another operator, our system connects these two operators. For example, when users drop an AxisBox (an operator to specify a coordinate system) into a ContainerBox (an operator to visualize its input view), the coordinate system defined by the AxisBox is applied to the visualization space defined by the ContainerBox.

However, it is difficult for users to perform these manipulations in 3-dimensional virtual space because a mouse can sense only two dimensional movements. Hence, our system supports user's manipulations to connect a plug or to drop an operator by presuming the destination object and automatically adjusting the Z-location of the manipulated object. Furthermore, jacks and plugs reject wrong connections that make loop connections.

3.4 Deriving new visualizations

In our framework users can derive a new visualization from others by modifying v-extended view relations.

To derive new visualizations, users can select a portion of a visualization by modifying a v-extended view. For instance, users can select a rectangular region in a visualization by adding conditions to restrict attributes that are associated with coordinates attributes XCOORD, YCOORD and ZCOORD.

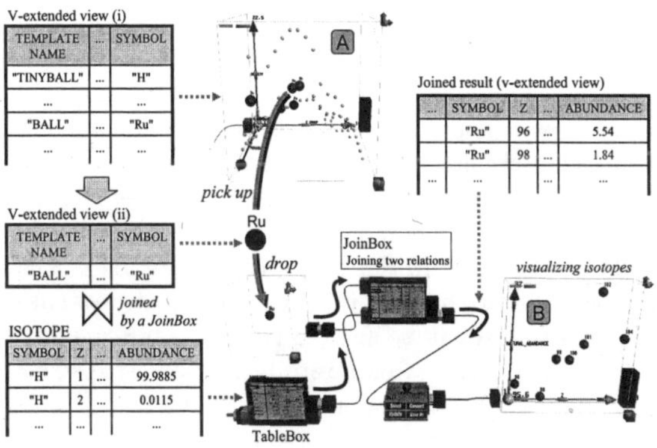

Figure 7: Deriving a visualization from one record

Moreover, we can also derive visualizations from one retrieved record by directly manipulating a visual component representing a record. In our framework each operator is implemented as a visual interactive component, and it outputs some view relations modified by its own function. On the other hand, a visualization result consists of visual objects. In our framework any portions of a visualization correspond to some view relations, therefore a visual object contained in a visualization result also represents a view relation corresponding to it.

As a result, an operator and a visual object contained in a visualization can be generalized to components which output some view relations. By connecting such a visual object to a query flow diagram, users can derive a visualization from a single retrieved record.

In the example illustrated in Figure 7, a ball which represents *ruthenium* is dropped into the SelectBox. A v-extended view which selects ruthenium from the periodic table of elements is associated with this ball. Therefore, users can retrieve information related to ruthenium by modifying this v-extended view. In this example, a list of isotopes is joined to this v-extended view. As its result, all the isotopes of ruthenium are visualized like B.

To perform this operation, a visual object representing a record must be an interactive object which allows direct manipulation. Moreover, such an object must be a functional component which outputs a v-extended view related to a corresponding record.

4 Implementation

We have developed a database visualization system based on this framework. In this section we describe the implementation detail of this visualization system. First, we describe the IntelligentBox[8] architecture we used as a base system.

4.1 IntelligentBox

IntelligentBox is component-ware architecture to develop 3D interactive applications. IntelligentBox system provides 3D visual components which we call boxes. Boxes are interactive and functional component. Boxes allow users to manipulate them by a direct mouse operation, or by using other input devices (data gloves, WAND, etc) in a 3D virtual space. Boxes have internal functions and several slots, i.e., a logical interface to access the internal states of each box. IntelligentBox architecture dynamically supports mechanisms to specify geometrical compositions and functional compositions between two boxes. These mechanisms are box composition and slot connection.

IntelligentBox system allows users to combine two boxes into one composite box. Between two combined boxes a hierarchical relation is defined. One composite box example is illustrated in Figure 8. In this example, the Box B1 is a child box and B2 is a parent box. Inferior boxes are fixed in the local coordinate system spanned by theirs parent boxes. A composite box can be also referred to as boxes, and users can combine a composite box with other boxes. Composite boxes have tree structures that consist of primitive boxes and hierarchical relations among them.

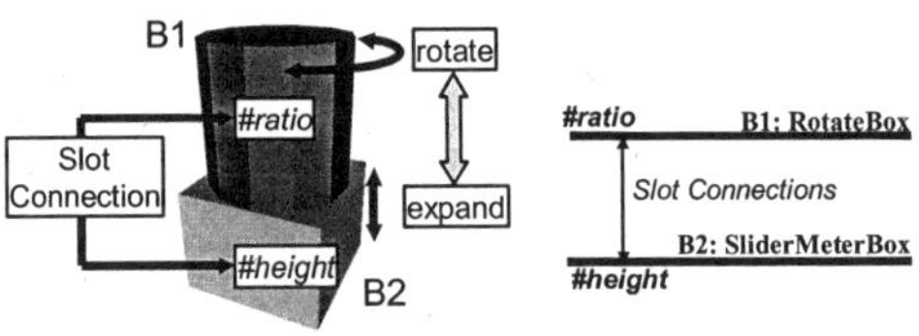

Figure 8: composite box example

IntelligentBox architecture supports the slot connection mechanism to create a functional linkage between two combined boxes. In Figure 8, the slot #ratio of B1 is connected to the slot #height of B2. Each connected slot can read or update the value of the other slot respectively by a *set* message or a *gimme* message. When the slot value of a parent box is updated, an *update* message is broadcasted to child boxes. In this example, if the box B2 changes its height, a value of the slot #height is updated and an update message is broadcasted to child boxes. The box B1 receives this update message, and B1 reads the value of the #height slot by sending a gimme message to B2. Then the box B1 updates the value of its own #ratio slot to the read-out #height slot value, and rotates its own shape according to the value of #ratio slot.

Currently there are several implementations of the IntelligentBox architecture. In this work, we use SGI IRIX version and Linux version IntelligentBox system developed at Hokkaido University.

4.2 System architecture overview

We use the IntelligentBox system as a basis to implement a database visualization system based on our framework. Our visualization system provides components supporting operator functions as boxes. We call these boxes operator boxes. Users can create database visualizations by manipulating and connecting operator boxes. Our system uses composite boxes to represent each retrieved record and its attributes. In the current implementation, our system uses an Oracle8 DBMS as a database server. Our system can access a database server by using a small application implemented in Java. This application uses the JDBC API and has an ability to transport data and queries between a database server and an IntelligentBox system. A summary of this system architecture is illustrated in Figure 9.

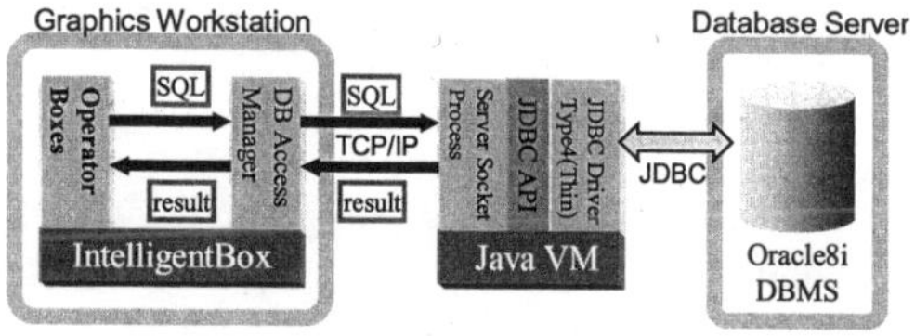

Figure 9: overview of system architecture

4.3 Templates

Our visualization system uses composite boxes to represent retrieved records. We call these boxes templates. IntelligentBox system provides many primitive boxes that can be used to represent data values, and users can design templates by arbitrarily combining these boxes. To represent attributes of retrieved records, visual mappings between source data attributes and a template are required. Our system supports users to define visual mappings by means of a TemplateBaseBoxes and TemplateManagerBoxes.

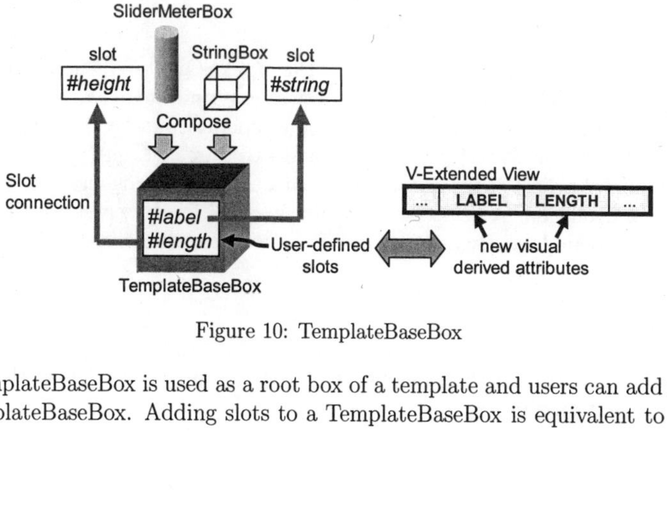

Figure 10: TemplateBaseBox

A TemplateBaseBox is used as a root box of a template and users can add new slots to a TemplateBaseBox. Adding slots to a TemplateBaseBox is equivalent to adding a new VD attribute to a v-extended view. An example is illustrated in Figure 10. In this example the #length slot and the #label slot are added to a TemplateBaseBox. Moreover, a SliderMeterBox and a StringBox are combined and two slot connections are specified to represent values of two slots.

In our system, templates are stored in a template catalog that is an additional relation stored in the database. A template catalog has two attributes, `TEMPLATEBOX` and `TEMPLATENAME`. The first attribute stores registered templates. Registered templates are named, and the second attribute stores a name of each template, as illustrated in Figure 11.

A TemplateManagerBox specifies a template to represent each retrieved record and specifies visual mappings. A TemplateManagerBox allows users to select a template by using a menu dialog of templates stored in a template catalog. When a template is selected, the TemplateManagerBox adds a virtual attribute in the `SELECT` clause of the input SQL statement, in such a way as *template_name* `AS TEMPLATENAME`. A TemplateManagerBox allows users to associate attributes of source data with slots of a TemplateBaseBox to specify visual mappings. If the attribute DENSITY is associated with the #length slot, a TemplateManagerBox adds a new attribute in the input SQL statement, in such a way as `DENSITY AS LENGTH`.

4.4 Operator Boxes

Our system provides operator boxes that support an operator function. Operator boxes have an input slot and an output slot to take SQL statements as input and output modified them.

In later subsections we describe operator boxes supported by our current implementation.

4.4.1 TableBox

A TableBox specifies a relation in the database to visualize. A TableBox supports this function by specifying the `FROM` clause in the SQL statement. A TableBox can access the database DDD and create a relation name list dialog. Users can select a relation by using this dialog. When a relation is selected, a TableBox specifies the `FROM` clause in such a way as `SELECT ... FROM` *relname*.

4.4.2 RecordFilterBox and SelectBox

A RecordFilterBox adds a new condition to the input SQL statement. User can give a new condition to the RecordFilterBox by specifying a conditional expression directly or using select dialogs for selecting an attribute, an operator, and a threshold. To create these dialogs, a RecordFilterBox generates and executes SQL queries to get attribute names lists or value lists of the selected attribute. A SelectBox is another operator box to add a new condition. A SelectBox adds a new condition to select visualized records enclosed by its boundary. By using a SelectBox, users can select visible records directly and interactively.

4.4.3 JoinBox

A JoinBox accepts two queries as inputs, and output a query that defines the relational join of two input queries.

4.4.4 TemplateManagerBox

A TemplateManagerBox specifies a template to represent retrieved records and specify visual mappings to represent attributes of retrieved records.

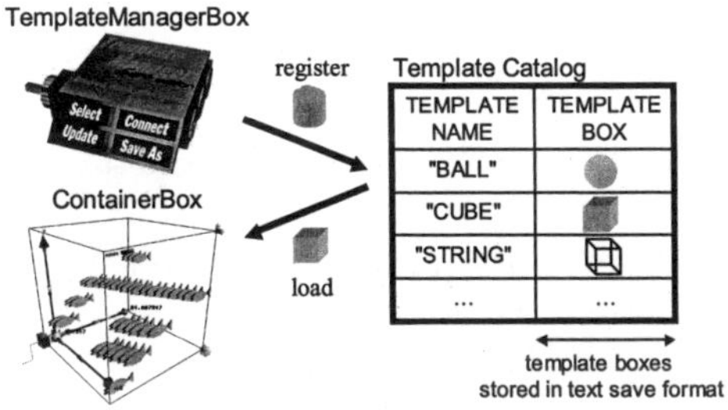

Figure 11: template catalog

Furthermore, a TemplateManagerBox manages templates and template catalogs. All templates used in our system are stored in the template catalog relation as illustrated in Figure 11. Each template is stored in the template catalog relation as a text type column value. A TemplateManagerBox can create a new template catalog and attach one template catalog on itself to use. By using the TemplateManagerBox, users can add a new template into the template catalog or remove templates stored in the template catalog.

4.4.5 AxisBox

An AxisBox associates one attribute of the source data relation with the corresponding axis to arrange visualized record geometrically. Users can select one attribute of the source data relation by using a menu dialog. Then an AxisBox can normalize the value of selected attribute to arrange all visualized record in the visualization space. An AxisBox specify three attributes, `XCOORD`, `YCOORD`, and `ZCOORD`. These attributes are used for arranging visualized records in the visualization space.

4.4.6 ContainerBox

A ContainerBox evaluates input SQL statements and visualize retrieved records. A ContainerBox represents each record by applying a copy of a template box and arranges them in the visualization space. Therefore, A ContainerBoxes accepts a v-extended view that has the following four attributes at least, `TEMPLATENAME`, `XCOORD`, `YCOORD`, `ZCOORD`. When the input SQL statement is updated, a ContainerBox evaluates the input SQL and fetches retrieved record. Then a ContainerBox makes copies of template boxes according to values of the attribute `TEMPLATENAME` and substitutes values of other attributes for slot values of copied templates. Last a ContainerBox arranges copied template boxes geometrically according to values of three attributes, `XCOORD`, `YCOORD`, `ZCOORD`.

A ContainerBox has a visualization space for arranging visualized record. Usually a visualization space is limited in an enclosed area by the boundary of the ContainerBox. Furthermore a ContainerBox can extend its visualization space by lifting this limitation. In this case, A ContainerBox displays visualized records that are in the area as

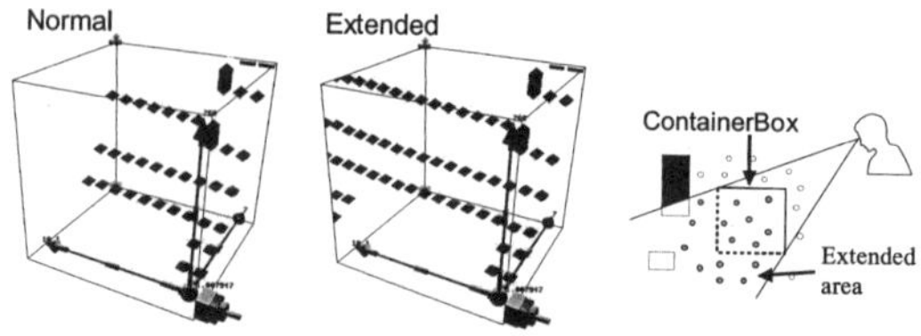

Figure 12: normal/extended visualization space

illustrated in Figure 12. By using this method for managing the visualization space, a ContainerBox can display more visualized record.

4.4.7 OverlayBox

An OverlayBox overlies one more visualization results. An OverlayBox allows users to visualize several visualization results in a single visualization space. In logically, this function is equivalent to the union operation on v-extended view. But our current implementation supports this function by evaluating input queries separately and visualizing each set of retrieved records in a single visualization space.

5 Visualization Examples

5.1 Basic example

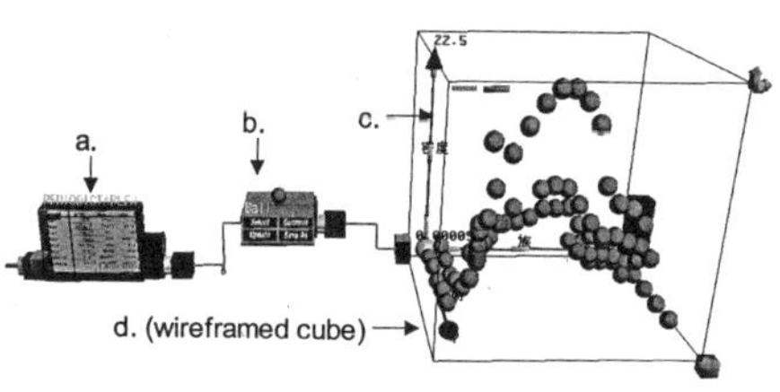

Figure 13: basic example

In this example the periodic table of the elements is visualized by our visualization system. The SQL statement is flowing from left to right. The TableBox specifies the relation `PERIODICTABLE` to visualize. The relation `PERIODICTABLE` consists of records corresponding to the elements. The TemplateManagerBox applies the template "Ball" for each record to visualize. Three AxisBoxes specify the coordinate system to arrange retrieved records geometrically. Three attributes, `E_GROUP`, `PERIOD`, and `DENSITY` are associated with three coordinate axes. Then the ContainerBox evaluates the input SQL statement and visualizes retrieved records. Users can select directly these visualized records by using a SelectBox. We give one example of this operation in the next subsection.

5.2 Overlay example

In this example two visualizations are generated. Each ContainerBox visualizes the relation `PERIODICTABLE` and arranges the elements using different coordinate systems.

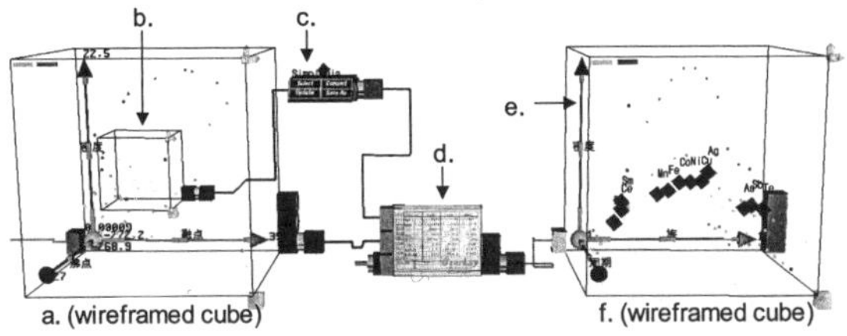

Figure 14: 'overlay' example

In this example all of the elements are visualized as colored dots. The SelectBox is dropped into the left ContainerBox to select visualized records it enclosed. The TemplateManagerBox apply the template "Simple Diamond" for each selected record, and the OverlayBox overlay the visualization of selected records and the visualization of all the elements. The right ContainerBox visualizes this overlaid result. Users can move the SelectBox dynamically, and the right ContainerBox updates its visualization immediately. Thus this coordination between these two visualizations is equivalent to a blushing-and-linkage coordination.

5.3 Nested visualization example

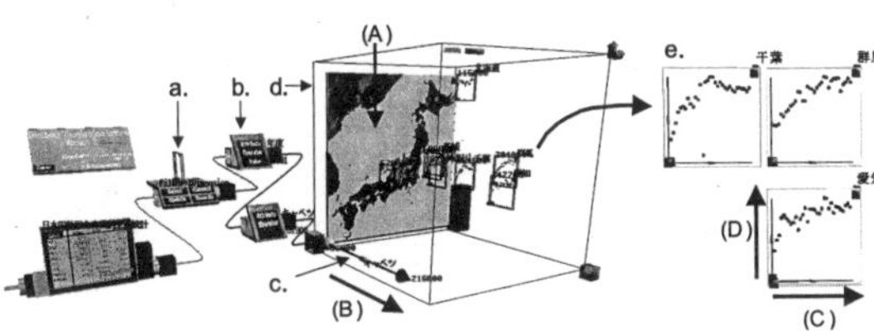

Figure 15: nested visualization example

This example is the visualization of the prefectural cabbage production in Japan. In this example a ContainerBox is used as a template to visualize each prefecture. Two small AxisBoxes are embedded in this template and this template is designed to visualize annual cabbage production changes of the corresponded prefecture. ContainerBoxes used as a template give users a nested visualization result. In this example the ContainerBox d (large wireframed cube) visualizes the cabbage production mounts of each prefecture in 1991. Moreover, each small ContainerBox e visualizes the annual cabbage production change of the corresponded prefecture.

6 Conclusion

In this paper we have proposed a new database visualization framework, and reported the visualization system based on this framework together with application examples. In our framework, visualization schemes are specified by database queries. In our visualization system, users can create these queries by interactively connecting operator boxes. In our visualization system, users can dynamically derive new visualizations from another and specify coordination among several visualizations. These features support users effectively to explore a large complex data set.

In our future work, we will extend our visualization framework to cope with a larger variety of visualization schemes and manipulations. For instance, aggregate functions have not been supported yet in our framework. Furthermore we will study the query evaluation optimization.

References

[1] Jock Mackinlay. Automating the Design of Graphical Presentations of Relational Information. em ACM Transactions on Graphics, 5(2), Apr, 1986.

[2] Stephen M. Casner. Task-analytic approach to the automated design of graphic presentations. em ACM Transactions on Graphics, 10(2), April 1991.

[3] Steven F. Roth, John Kolojejchick, Joe Mattis, Jade Goldstein. Interactive Graphic Design Using Automatic Presentation Knowledge. em Proc. ACM SIGCHI '94, April 1994.

[4] Alexander Aiken, Jolly Chen, Michael Stonebraker, and Allison Woodruff. Tioga-2: A Direct Manipulation Database Visualization Environment. em Proc. of the 12th International Conference on Data Engineering, February, 1996.

[5] Miron Livny, Raghu Ramakrishnan, Kevin Beyer, Guangshun Chen, Donko Donjerkovic, Shilpa Lawande, Jussi Myllymaki, and Kent Wenger. DEVise: Integrated Querying and Visual Exploration of Large Datasets. em Proceedings of ACM SIGMOD '97, May, 1997.

[6] Chris North, Ben Shneiderman. Snap-Together Visualization: A User Interface for Coordinating Visualizations via Relational Schemata. em Proc. ACM AVI 2000, May, 2000.

[7] Christopher Ahlberg, Erik Wistrand. IVEE: An information visualization & exploration environment. em Proc. IEEE Information Visualization '95, 1995.

[8] Y. Okada and Y. Tanaka. IntelligentBox:a constructive visual software development system for interactive 3D graphic applications. em Proc. of the Computer Animation 1995 Conference, 1995.

Information Modelling and Knowledge Bases XV
Y. Kiyoki et al. (Eds.)
IOS Press, 2004

Contextual Search in Large Collections of Information Resources

Mina AKAISHI*, Nicolas SPYRATOS** and Yuzuru TANAKA*

**Meme Media Laboratory, Graduate School of Engineering Hokkaido University, 060-8628 Sapporo, Japan*
***Laboratoire de Recherche en Informatique, Universite de Paris-Sud, LRI-Bat 490, 91405 Orsay Cedex, France*
E-mail: {mina |tanaka}@meme.hokudai.ac.jp, spyratos@lri.fr

Abstract. We propose a framework for searching large collections of information resources that we call *information bases*. Examples of such collections are large collections of files in a file system, or tables in a relational database, or objects and classes in object-oriented databases, or large collections of Web pages. The framework that we propose allows a user to define a sub-collection of resources of interest, to name these resources using familiar names (local to the sub-collection) and to refer to other sub-collections defined by the same user, or by a different user. We call such sub-collections user contexts, or simply *contexts*. The main goal of this paper is to provide a mechanism for context management in a web of inter-related contexts, i.e., a set of tools for creation or deletion of a context, insertion or deletion of objects in a context, search for objects of interest in a context, and traversal of contexts in search of a context of interest.

1. Introduction

The rapid proliferation of information sources in recent years, and the advent of the Internet have created a World Wide Web of interconnected resources. The Web represents today the largest collection of information resources that an individual has ever been able to access – and it is continuously growing at accelerating paces.

Several kinds of tools have been developed in recent years to help individual users to access Web resources. The so-called search engines are the most popular among these tools, as they allow users to access the Web resources they index using a very simple search mechanism, namely keywords or combinations of keywords.

There is however a price to pay by users for the simplicity of the search mechanism: the answers obtained from search engines usually contain large amounts of information that is not related to what the user had in mind. This problem comes from the fact that any given search engine indexes resources that cater to the interests of very large and highly heterogeneous populations of users.

So, on the one hand we have a large collection of information resources, that we shall call hereafter the *information base*, and on the other hand a very large and highly heterogeneous population of users. Clearly, what is needed here is a personalization mechanism that allows each user of an information base to define his (her) sub-collection of resources of interest. It is such a "customized" sub-collection that we call a user context, or simply *context.*

Intuitively, a context is a set of objects within which each object is associated with a set of names and a reference to some other context.

Perhaps the simplest example of context is the index, or directory, of a department store. In most department stores, this index is usually located on the ground floor, and looks like the table of Figure 1(a). It consists of a number of lines and each line contains one or more keywords, or descriptors, describing kinds of items plus a number indicating the floor on which such items can be found. For example, the first line contains the keywords "Perfumes" and "Cosmetics" plus the number 0 indicating that such items are found on the ground floor. Similarly, the sixth line indicates that furniture can be found on the fifth floor.

We can view the department store index as a context whose contents are triples of the form, < *line-number, descriptors, floor-number* >, as shown in Figure 1(b). Under this view, the line number in the triple is the object, the descriptors give the "semantics" of that object, and the floor number is the identifier of just another context – the floor context. Each floor context, in turn, is again a set of triples, where each triple consists of a floor sector number, a set of descriptors describing the items available in that floor sector and a sub-sector number - if the sector is divided into sub-sectors (or *Nil*, indicating that the floor sector is not divided into sub-sectors).

A customer entering the department store looks at (or "accesses") the index, and then examines one by one the triples of the index. Aided by the descriptors the customer selects a floor number, i.e., a new context. Once on the selected floor, the customer repeats the same steps but this time looking at the floor index to find the exact sector on the floor where the items of interest are located. Note however that the items themselves are *not* part of the sector context. In other words, the context mechanism just helps you find *where* the items of interest are.

It is important to note here that the notion of context is a "light-weight" abstraction mechanism that is different than the usual abstraction mechanisms used in modeling information systems (i.e., classification, attribution and inheritance). However, it can be used orthogonally together with those mechanisms.

There are only three types of entities in our context mechanism, namely object identifiers, context identifiers and descriptors; for simplicity, we shall call object identifiers simply *objects* and context identifiers simply *contexts*. We assume that the set of objects, the set of contexts and the set of descriptors are mutually disjoint sets. As a consequence, a context cannot belong to the contents of any context.

It is important to note that the context mechanism that we use is not concerned with the internal structure of the objects: they may be simple objects such as integers, characters, or strings, or they may be complex objects such as files, tables, classes, images, and so on; as long as they are identifiable, they can belong to the contents of a context. Actually, as we shall see, the information base itself is considered as a context.

It is also important to note that our context mechanism has a minimal interference with the normal operation of the information base: it can be implemented on top of the system managing the information base, at a minimal cost.

Perfumes, Cosmetics	ground floor
Women's Clothing	1st floor
Men's Clothing	2nd floor
Children's Clothing	3rd floor
Sports, Casual	4th floor
Furniture	5th floor
Restaurant	6th floor

(a) A department store index

< line# 1,	{ Perfumes, Cosmetics },	0 >
< line# 2,	{ Women's Clothing },	1 >
< line# 3,	{ Men's Clothing },	2 >
< line# 4,	{ Children's Clothing },	3 >
< line# 5,	{ Sports, Casual },	4 >
< line# 6,	{ Furniture },	5 >
< line# 7,	{ Restaurant },	6 >

(b) The index seen as a context

Fig. 1. An example of context

There are two main reasons for using a web of contexts on top of an existing information base:

(a) to allow users to define their own, personalized sub-collections, and to name objects using familiar names (local to the sub-collection);

(b) to speed-up searching for desired objects in the whole collection, by traversing appropriate contexts.

For example, if one sits at the University context, and wishes to access tourist information on Greece, the search will be much faster by traversing the National-Tourism-Organization context rather than the National-Education context (assuming the appropriate links exist).

Once again, we stress the fact that searching for desired objects is based on object names and object identifiers, i.e., without consideration of internal object structure: the internal structure can be described or "summarized" in the object name(s) which can be a piece of text, an image, a sound score, or even an "object viewer" – a concept to be explained later. Therefore, searching in a web of contexts is based on object names and object identifiers, and makes no use of the internal structure of objects. This is precisely the reason why, earlier on, we called our context mechanism a "light-weight" abstraction mechanism.

The main goal of this paper is to provide a mechanism for context management, in a web of inter-related contexts, i.e., a set of tools for creation or deletion of a context, insertion or deletion of objects in a context, search for objects of interest in a context, and traversal of contexts in search of a context of interest.

The remainder of this paper is organized as follows. In section 2 we define the notion of context that we use, as well as some auxiliary concepts. In section 3 we define the information base "directory" i.e., a system context that contains the information necessary for managing all user contexts and the basic operations of our context mechanism. In section 4 we describe the implementation of the proposed context mechanism based on the IntelligentBox system, a component-ware system developed at the Meme Media Laboratory. Finally, in section 5 we offer some concluding remarks.

2. Contexts

In this section, we present the notion of context that we use and the query language for context traversal. Our definitions are inspired from the notion of context presented in [1-4] with some extensions.

2.1 The notion of Context

A context consists of an identifier *c* plus a *content*. The content of *c* is a set of triples of the form, < *object-descriptors, object, object-references* >, where *object-descriptors* is a set of descriptions for the object and *object-references* is a set of contexts (eventually empty).

We note that, contrary to [1-4], we allow our contexts to have multiple references. As we shall see, this feature allows greater flexibility and provides for higher expressive power.
An object descriptor can be a piece of text, an image, a sound score, or even an "object viewer" – a concept to be explained later. As for the object references, they are contexts that contain information relevant to the object. It is important to note that descriptors and references are context dependent. An object can belong to different contexts and may have different names and/or different references in each context. This feature is useful when we want to view an object from different perspectives.

2.2 Accessing information through paths

Accessing information in a contextualized information base often involves navigating from one object to another by following references. From an object within a given context, we can reach any object that belongs to one of its references and, recursively, any object that lies on a path. Navigation is based on the notion of path. A path is a sequence of pairs of the form (c_i, t_i), i = 1, .., n, where

1/ c_i is a context and $t_i = <d_i, o_i, r_i>$ is a triple in the content of c_i, and

2/ c_{i+1} is in r_i, for i = 1, .., *n*-1.

We also define the concepts of descriptor path and object path as follows:

- a *descriptor path* is a dot-separated sequence of descriptors $d_1.....d_k$, where d_i is a descriptor in triple t_i, $i = 1,...k$.
- an *object path* is a dot-separated sequence of objects $o_1.....o_k$, where o_i is an object in triple t_i, $i = 1,...k$.

Paths form the basis for reaching objects in a context navigating through the references of objects.

2.3 Querying a Contextualized Information Base

The access to information is achieved using a path-language for context traversal. We introduce here two macro-operations that are inspired from [4] :

look-up(*c*, *d*) : this operation takes as input a context *c* and a descriptor *d* and returns the set of descriptor paths starting with a descriptor in the content of *c*, and ending with descriptor *d*.

cross-ref(*c*, *o*): this operation takes as input a context *c* and an object *o* and returns the set of all descriptor paths starting with a descriptor in the content of *c* and ending with one of the descriptors of *o*.

This is useful as we can find alternative representations of the same object in different contexts, as well as the descriptor paths to reach these representations.

3. Managing a Web of Contexts

We now turn to the question of how to manage a collection of contexts defined by users on top of a given information base. To this end, in this section, we describe a mechanism for creation or deletion of a context, insertion or deletion of objects in a context, search for objects of interest in a context, and traversal of contexts in search of a context of interest. Then, in the following section, we describe the implementation of our mechanism based on the IntelligentBox system [6].

The basic concept of our mechanism for context management is the information base *directory* i.e., a special context that contains the information necessary for managing all user-defined contexts. The idea behind the directory is to provide an entry point to the various contexts defined by the users. Therefore the directory acts as a registry where every newly defined context is registered (inserted) and from where every undesired context is un-registered (deleted). The directory can be referenced by any user-defined context in read-only mode, and supports the following operations:

(1) Context Creation

The creation of a new context is implemented by

asking for a new context, say c;

asking for a new object, say o;

adding to the contents of the directory a triple $< d, o, r >$, *with* $r = \{c\}$.

The object o acts as a surrogate for the context c (since its reference is c), we shall therefore refer to it as the *context surrogate*. The set d of descriptors contains user-defined descriptors of the object o - and therefore of the context c. We assume that d also contains a system-defined descriptor which is unique within the directory, we shall therefore refer to it as the *key* of o. Note that, according to the way contexts are created, for any two objects o, o' in the directory we have: $ref(o) \neq ref(o')$.
Access to a context is obtained only through the directory.

(2) Reference authorization

The first time that a context c wishes to refer to a new context c' an authorization is asked from the directory. The authorization is granted if c' is not deleted (see also the discussion below concerning the deletion of a context). One could of course use more sophisticated authorization mechanisms. However, this subject lies outside the scope of the present paper.

(3) The Information Base Context

We assume that the directory always contains a special object representing the *Information Base Context*, i.e., a context denoted by IBC and defined as follows :

$$contents(\text{IBC}) = \{ < \{\text{IB}\}, o, \varnothing > \mid o \text{ is an object in the information base}\}$$

In other words, the context IBC contains all the objects of the information base without any references to other contexts. Its presence serves to allow users that do not want to work with contexts to simply work with the information base (as usual).

(4) Context Deletion

The deletion of a context is implemented by simply putting to empty the reference of its surrogate in the directory. Since use of contexts as references is always done through the directory, a context deleted in this way will not be able to access.

The deletion of contexts poses the problem of "dangling references". Indeed, a problem arises when a context c' is referenced by some of the triples of a context c. This problem is dealt with by introducing a "shadow-context" to the directory, called the *usage context*. The usage context contains a triple of the form

< surrogate-key, surrogate-object, referenced-contexts >

for every surrogate object appearing in the directory. The third component of the above triple consists of all contexts referenced by the context whose surrogate object is the second component of the triple.

Whenever a context is deleted or the content of a context is updated the usage context is updated as well. Moreover, following any update of the usage context, a notification may have to be sent to contexts referencing deleted contexts (see the discussion below concerning context deletion).

(5) Insertion of a Triple in a Context

The insertion of a triple $< d, o, r >$ in a context c is implemented as follows:

if there is a triple $< d', o, r' >$ *in c*
then modify this triple as follows: $d' := d' \cup d$ *and* $r' := r' \cup r$
else add $< d, o, r >$ *to the contents of c*

We note that, in order to find contexts of interest to which one wants to refer (i.e., in order to find r' in the triple to be inserted) one has to always consult the directory. Indeed, at any moment, the directory contains all contexts that are currently present in the information base.

As we mentioned earlier, following an insertion, the usage context may have to be updated.

(6) Deletion of a Triple in a Context

The deletion of a triple from a context is performed by simply removing the triple from the contents and updating the usage contexts if necessary.

(7) Search for objects of interest in a context

The search for objects of interest in a context is done using object descriptors. The following operation is used:
search(*d*, *c*) : this operation takes as input a set *d* of descriptors and a context *c* and returns the set of all triples < *d'*, *o'*, *r'* > in c such that $d \cap d' \neq \emptyset$

(8) Traversal of contexts in search of a context of interest

Traversal of contexts is performed using the operations *look-up* and *cross-ref* seen earlier.

4. Implementation of Contexts in the IntelligentBox System

In this section we describe the implementation of the proposed context mechanism based on the IntelligentBox system, a component-ware system developed at the Meme Media Laboratory [5].

A web of contexts can be implemented in the form of what we call an *Information Access Space*. The basic components of such a space are what we call *media objects* that are software entities defined in the IntelligentBox system. We use two kinds of media objects, a *context space* and an *object space*, whose definitions will be given shortly. First we explain how contexts and their contents are mapped into context spaces and object spaces, respectively.

A context *c* is implemented as a context space, denoted *space(c)*, and each triple *t* in the contents of *c* is implemented as an object space, denoted *space(t, c)*. For each triple *t* in the contents of *c*, the object space *space*(*t*, *c*) is bound to the context space *space*(*c*). Roughly speaking, a context space consists of the object spaces into which its objects are mapped. Note however that an object space is bound to one and only one context space, thus if a triple *t* belongs to two different contexts, say *c* and *c'*, it will be mapped into two different object spaces, namely, *space*(*t*, *c*) and *space*(*t*, *c'*), respectively. The object space *space*(*t*, *c*) will be bound to the context space *space*(*c*), while the object space *space*(*t*, *c'*) will be bound to the context space *space*(*c'*).

In a context space, each object space of a triple models the descriptors and the references of the triple, and moreover it provides a *viewer* to the content of the object in that triple. As we shall see later, the viewer simply allows to inspect the content. We recall that the content of an object is *not* part of the context mechanism, i.e., the contents of objects are developed independently, and only their identifiers can appear in a context.

Given a collection of contexts, the set of context spaces into which the contexts are mapped is what we call the *Information Access Space* of that collection. In what follows, we describe the implementation of each of the basic components of an information access space, namely, a context space, an object space, an object descriptor, an object space reference and an object viewer.

(1) Information Access Module

Figure 2 shows the access mechanism to information bases from an IntelligentBox environment. We provide a database access interface and predefined template query as 3D components. A Query Definition Box receives some arguments as inputs, and then generates a query statement. A Database Proxy Box works as an interface between a database system and the IntelligentBox system. Through a Database Proxy Box, the

IntelligentBox system users can use a set of database functions in the form of boxes. A Data Manager Box reifies database records as Boxes. This box keeps an identification of the template Box(es) to materialize the database record. Arbitrary Boxes can be pre-registered in the Template Box Table that is a global variable in the IntelligentBox system. When the Data Manager Box receives the collection data, then the Data Manager Box makes copies of template Boxes that is pre-registered. Then each copy of the template Box is instantiated with the value of the corresponding element of the collection. The Data Set Manager Box distributes each element of the collection to each Box, which becomes an instantiation of the template model.

(2) Context Space

As we have seen, a context is a set of objects, in which each object is associated with a set of descriptors and a set of references. Similarly, a Context Space is a virtual space that includes a set of pointers to object spaces. A pointer to an object space is called an object space port (OSP) and a pointer to context space is called a context space port (CSP). The port is an entrance to access a target space.

Figure 3 shows the component structure corresponding to a context space. A CSP box holds the context-id *c* its slot #spaceID. An OSP Generator is constructed by the Information Access module. It receives the context-id *c* and reifies the object spaces that correspond to the contents of context *c*. A Query Definition Box generates a query to get contents of the context. Then a Database Proxy Box evaluates this query and sends the result to a Data Manager Box. A Data Manager Box reifies the result as a set of object spaces.

(3) Object Space

An object space is a 3D visualization of a triplet. Figure 4 shows the component structure corresponding to each object space. Each OSP of an OSP generator box is connected to a virtual 3D space, called an object space. In an object space, there are object descriptors, an object viewer and a set of references that correspond to the triplet data in the context. A reference is a set of pointers to context spaces, they are represented by CSPs.

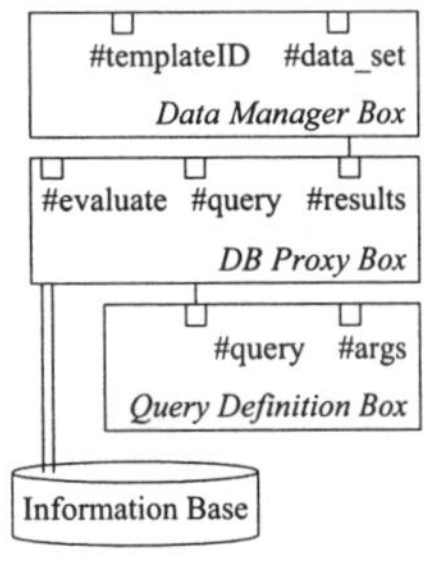

Fig. 2. An access mechanism to an information base from IntelligentBox.

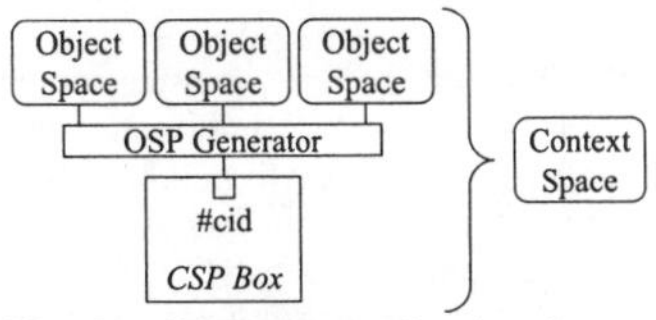

Fig. 3. A components structure of Context Space.

(4) Object Descriptor

An object descriptor can be a piece of text, an image, a music score and so on. Appropriate media object(s) are used as Object Descriptors. How to construct each object descriptor is up to the designer of an object descriptor. In Figure 5, an object-descriptor is text. We use a text Box to represent it.

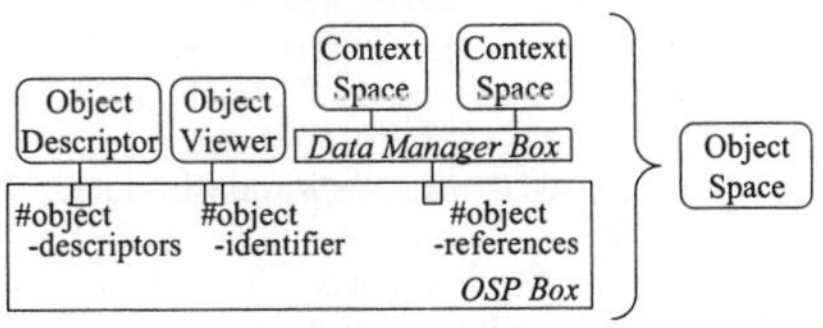

Fig. 4. A components structure of Object Space.

(5) Object Viewer

An object viewer is also an appropriate media object to represent an object. How to construct each object viewer is up to the designer of the object viewer. In Figure 5, an Image Viewer Box is used as an object viewer.

(6) Object Reference

An object reference is a set of context-ids. When a Data Manager Box receives a set of CIDs, it generates context spaces corresponding to the input data. In each context space, each OSP Generator automatically creates its own object spaces that are the contents of each context.

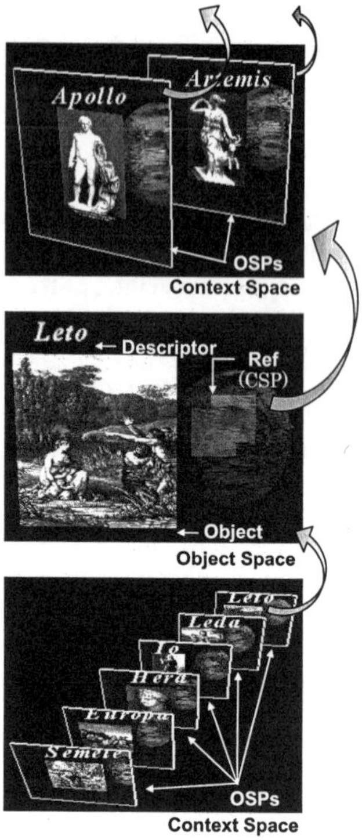

Fig. 5. An Exploration in a Context based Information Access Space

5. Concluding Remarks

We have proposed a framework for searching large collections of information resources based on context. This framework allows a user to define a sub-collection of resources of interest, to name these resources using familiar names (local to the sub-collection) and to refer to other sub-collections defined by the same user, or by a different user. The main goal of this paper is to provide a mechanism for context management in a web of inter-related contexts, i.e., a set of tools for creating or deleting a context, inserting or deleting the objects in a context, searching for objects of interest in a context, and traversal of contexts in search of a context of interest.

We have implemented these concepts in the form of what we call Information Access Space, based on the IntelligentBox System. As it stands now, our prototype allows for context traversal and querying of a collection of contexts. However, no update mechanism has been implemented so far.

Future work includes the implementation of update operations and the definition of a full fledged query language.

References

[1] M. Theodorakis and P. constantopoulos: Context-Based Naming in Information Bases, International Journal of Cooperative Information Systems, 6(3&4):269-292, 1997

[2] Teodorakis, M., Analyti, A., Constantopoulos, P., and Spyratos, N.: Context in Information Bases, Proc, of the 3rd Int. Conference on Cooperative Information Systems (coopIS '98), pp.260-270 (1998)

[3] M. Theodorakis, A. Analyti, P. Constantopoulos and N Spyratos: Querying Contextualized Information Bases, Proc. of the 24th Intern. Conference on Information and Communication Technologies and Programming, (ICT&P ' 99), 1999

[4] M. Theodorakis, A. Analyti, P. Constantopoulos and N. Spyratos: Contextualization as an Abstraction Mechanism for Conceptual Modeling, Proc. of the 18th Intern. Conference on Conceptual Modeling (ER '99), Paris, pp. 475-489, 1999

[5] Okada, Y. and Tanaka, Y.: IntelligentBox: A Constructive Visual Software Development System for Interactive 3D Graphic Applications, Proc. Of Computer Animation '95, pp.114-125 (1994)

[6] Itoh, M. and Tanaka, Y: WorldMirror and World Bottle: Components for Embedding Multiple Spaces in a 3D Virtual Environment, Journal of IPSJ, Vol. 42, No.10, pp.2403-2414 (2001)

[7] Ohigashi, M. and Tanaka, Y.: A Framework for the Virtual Reification of Database Records, IPSJ, Vol.42, No. SIG 1 (TOD8), pp80-91 (2001)

[8] M. Akaishi, H. YAMAMOTO, M. OHIGASHI, Y. TANAKA and N. Spyratos: 3D Visual Construction of a Context-based Information Access Space, the 12th European-Japanese Conf., pp.24-37. (2002)

Information Modelling and Knowledge Bases XV
Y. Kiyoki et al. (Eds.)
IOS Press, 2004

Finding Similar Stories by Using Sequences of Occurrence Vectors

Akira Ogiso* Akihiro Yamamoto†
Faculty of Technology and MemeMedia Laboratory
Hokkaido University
N 13 W 8, Sapporo 060-8628 JAPAN
Email : yamamoto@meme.hokudai.ac.jp

Abstract

The purpose of this research is to develop methods for managing text documents written in a natural language based on stories. Under defining a story as a sequence of events and every document is interpreted as a story, we try to find documents that are interpreted as a same story. In this paper we report some experimental results towards finding such documents, by abstracting every raw document with a sequence of occurrence vectors, which is a modification of well-known document vectors, by using some numerical function and Boolean function, and by using a refinement operator for generalization of documents.

1 Introduction

The purpose of this research is to develop a method for managing text documents written in a natural language based on stories. Stories have been used for transferring information for a long time. When we read books, magazines, or newspapers, or when we watch TV programs, we remember the contents as stories. Such experience in our everyday life suggests that stories might be used for managing information.

In order to achieve the purpose, we must define stories as an abstract data model. Our definition is that a *story* is a sequence of events, where an *event* is a minimum element that cannot be divided any more. We use these concepts as semantics of text documents. That is, a story is an interpretation of some text documents. This definition does not assume that every document telling a same story should be tell same events in a same order. For example, a sentence "He went to bed after he red a book" is equivalently represented as "He red a book before he went to bed." Under the definition, analysis of documents sentence by sentence would not be meaningful. In this paper, in order to find similarity of stories described to sentences, we propose a new method with which we compare two documents.

The first key idea for our method is that, instead of treating raw documents, we abstract them by translating every sentence into an *occurrence vector*, which is a modification of the document vector [1, 3]. An occurrence vector shows whether or not each keyword occurs in the original sentence. An abstracted document is a sequence of occurrence vectors, to which we could apply various methods based on mathematics. In fact we use the cosine function for defining similarity of two occurrence vectors.

The second idea is from the following consideration: Some two sequences from a same sentence in different order might be interpreted as a same story, but not all. For example, a text document would not keep its interpretation if we shuffled the sentences in it randomly. This means that some fragments of documents, which we will call a *window*, should represents an event, and that we must conjecture how long the windows when we look for documents of same stories. We determined it by experiments with documents of Japanese tales.

---

*At present, Mitsubishi Motors Corporation
†At present, Graduate School of Informatics, Kyoto University

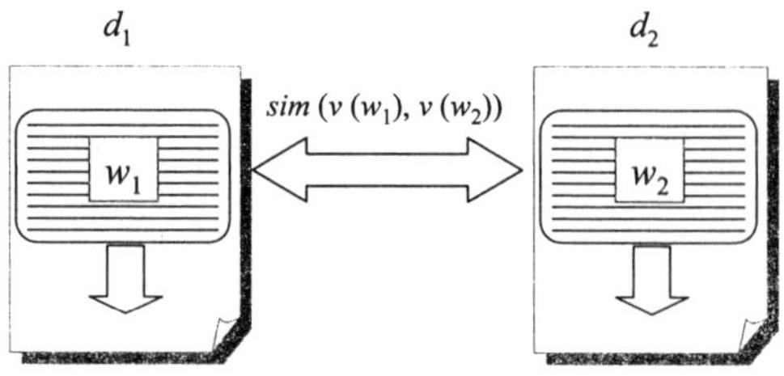

Figure 1: Finding similarity by sliding windows

2 Stories and Occurrence Vectors

Throughout this paper we treat the data type finite sequences. For a sequence σ, its i-th element is denoted by $\sigma(i)$ and its length is denoted by $\mathrm{len}(\sigma)$. For a natural number of n we define $n\sigma$ is a sequence of length $n \times \mathrm{len}(\sigma)$ such that $(n\sigma)(i) = \sigma([i/n] + 1)$.

A document d is a non-empty sequence of sentences, where a sentence is a minimum element which we never divide any more. The set of documents is denoted by $\mathcal{D}$. The concatenation of two documents or sentences is denoted by a dot $\cdot$. A *sub-document* of a document d is a subsequence of sentences in d. It is also called a *window* of d. We define the set of stories as a semantic domain for text documents. Let $\mathcal{E}$ be a set, each of which element is called an *event*. We define a *story* as a sequence of events. Two stories are same if they are same as sequences of events. The set of stories is denoted by $\mathcal{S}$. A *representation* r of stories is a one-to-one mapping from $\mathcal{S}$ to $\mathcal{D}$ satisfying that $r(s \cdot t) = r(s) \cdot r(t)$ for any two stories s and t. An *interpretation* of a subset $D' \subseteq \mathcal{D}$ is such a mapping i from D' to $\mathcal{S}$ that there is a representation r such that $r(i(d)) = d$ for every $d \in D'$.

An occurrence vector is defined as an abstraction of sentences. Let $\mathcal{K}$ be the set of key words and $\mathrm{B} = \{0, 1\}$. We assume that $\mathcal{K}$ is finite, with $\sharp(\mathcal{K}) = n$. Fix an enumeration $k_1, k_2, k_3, \ldots, k_n$ of the elements in $\mathcal{K}$. An occurrence vector $v(s)$ of a sentence s is an element $(b_1, b_2, \ldots, b_n)$ of $\mathbf{B}^n$ satisfying that $b_i = 1$ if the keyword k_i occurs in s and otherwise $b_i = 1$ for $i = 1, 2, \ldots, n$. For a window $w = s_1 s_2 \ldots s_m$, we define $v(w) = v(s_1)\, v(s_2)\, \ldots\, v(s_m)$ and call it the *occurrence sequence* of w. For vectors $\mathbf{u}$ and $\mathbf{v}$ in $\mathbf{B}^n$, we define $\mathbf{u} \cdot \mathbf{v} = (\mathbf{u}_1 \cdot \mathbf{v}_1, \ldots, \mathbf{u}_n \cdot \mathbf{v}_n)$ and $\mathbf{u} + \mathbf{v} = (\mathbf{u}_1 + \mathbf{v}_1, \ldots, \mathbf{u}_n + \mathbf{v}_n)$ where $\cdot$ and $+$ are Boolean multiplication and addition, respectively.

3 Finding Similarity of Stories

When two documents d_1 and d_2 are given, we detect similarity of the stories described with them in the following manner: At first we put a window w_i for each document d_i. Then, we compute the value $sim\big(v(w_1), v(w_2)\big)$, where sim is a function which defines similarity of two vectors. The pair of windows is slid from the heads of the each document to their ends with synchronization, as depicted in Fig. 1.

The length of the windows is determined by giving a the parameter $0 \le p \le 1$ so that the following holds for $i = 1, 2$:

$$\frac{\mathrm{len}(w_i)}{\mathrm{len}(d_i)} < p < \frac{\mathrm{len}(w_i) + 1}{\mathrm{len}(d_i)}.$$

The parameter p, called a *level* of abstraction, must help us to recognize similarity of the stories of the documents. In case that both of the windows w_1 and w_2 were too short, there would be almost no word which appears in common in them, and therefore the $sim\big(v(w_1), v(w_2)\big)$ would be very small even though the stories of the two documents were similar. On the contrary, in case that the windows were too long, words appearing in both of them would affect the similarity value, without depending on where they occurred in the documents. We determined the size by experiment as reported in the following section.

Now we formalize our method. Let a sequence of vectors δ_k^n such that $\mathrm{len}(\delta_k^n) = n$ and

$$\delta_k^n(i) = \begin{cases} (1, 1, \ldots, 1) & \text{if } 1 \le i \le k, \\ (0, 0, \ldots, 0) & \text{if } k + 1 \le i \le n. \end{cases}$$

(a) Two different documents for "Issun-boushi" (b) A document for "Issun-boushi" and shuffled

Figure 2: Results when $p = 0.7$

For any element of $\sigma \in (\mathbf{B}^n)^*$, we define

$$\sigma * \delta_k^{\mathrm{len}(\sigma)}(i) = \sum_{j=0}^{\mathrm{len}(\sigma)} \sigma(s+i) \cdot \delta_k^{\mathrm{len}(\sigma)}(i).$$

Below we write $\delta_k^{\mathrm{len}(\sigma)}(i)$ as $\delta_k(i)$. A *refinement relation* $\rightarrow_\delta$ is defined as a acyclic relation such that $\epsilon \rightarrow_\delta \sigma * \delta_n(0)$ and

$$\begin{aligned} & \sigma * \delta_{n-i}(0)\, \sigma * \delta_{n-i}(1) \ \dots\ \sigma * \delta_{n-i}(i) \\ \rightarrow_\delta\ & \sigma * \delta_{n-(i+1)}(0)\, \sigma * \delta_{n-(i+1)}(1) \ \dots\ \sigma * \delta_{n-(i+1)}(i+1) \end{aligned}$$

A *similarity* of two vectors in $\mathbf{B}^n$ is a reflexive and symmetric relation in $\mathbf{B}^n \times \mathbf{B}^n$. We extend the similarity to a relation between two occurrence vectors. Let σ and τ be $\in (\mathbf{B}^n)^*$. When we check the similarity of two documents using the refinement, we must firstly make their lengths equal. Secondly we must give a similarity of two vectors. Let σ and τ are two sequence. Then σ and τ are similar until level p w.r.t. $\rightarrow_\delta$ if there are natural umber I and series of refinements

$$\begin{aligned} & \epsilon \rightarrow_\delta \sigma_1 \rightarrow_\delta \dots \rightarrow_\delta \sigma_i \rightarrow_\delta \dots \rightarrow_\delta \mathrm{len}(\sigma)\sigma \\ & \epsilon \rightarrow_\delta \tau_1 \rightarrow_\delta \dots \rightarrow_\delta \tau_i \rightarrow_\delta \dots \rightarrow_\delta \mathrm{len}(\tau)\tau \end{aligned}$$

such that $I = [p \times \mathrm{len}(\sigma) \times \mathrm{len}(\tau)]$ and σ_i and that τ_i are similar for $i = 1, 2, \dots, I$, but not for $i = I+1, \dots, \mathrm{len}(\sigma)\mathrm{len}(\tau)$.

4 Experiments

In order to confirm that our method is consistent with our aim, we tried to find the level p to which two documents of a same story are similar. We used text documents written in Japanese for well-known tales: "Issun-boushi", "Cinderella", and "Momotaro". For each tale, we prepared several documents by different authors and publishers. As the similarity we used the *cosine* function

$$sim(\mathbf{v}, \mathbf{w}) = \frac{\mathbf{v} \cdot \mathbf{w}}{|\mathbf{v}| \times |\mathbf{w}|}.$$

of two vectors $\mathbf{v}$ and $\mathbf{w}$.

Because in Japanese no space is inserted between two words, we divide a document into words with a software tool named Chasen developed at Nara Institute of Science and Technology University (`http://chasen.aist-nara.ac.jp/`). More precisely speaking, Chasen extracts all morphemes, which is the minimum unit having meaning, and transforms each of the morphemes into its standard form. Since in its process Chasen infers the part of speech of each word, we use nouns, verbs, and adjectives as keywords, without using any stop-word-list.

The results are presented as graphs in Fig. 2, 3, and 4. In each graph in the figures, the x-axis is for the vectors in the sequence obtained by the refinement, and the y-axis is for the value of similarity.

The graph (a) in each figure is of the pair of different documents for "Issun-boushi". The graph (b) in Fig. 2 is of the pair of a document "Issun-boushi" for and the one obtained by shuffled the sentences of the first document. From the graphs in Fig. 2, we see that we cannot distinguish two documents for different stories in the case when $p = 0.7$. The graph (b) in Fig. 3 is of the pair of a document for "Issun-boushi" and one for "Momotaro". The graphs in Fig. 3 show that, if $p = 0.1$, we may not detect two different documents for one story. The graphs in Fig. 4 show that, if we choose a proper threshold for the similarity value, we can detect only the document which tell a same story.

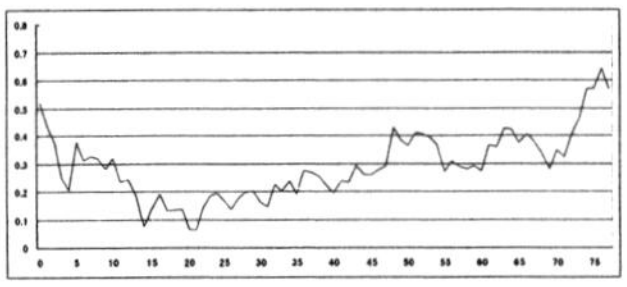

(a) Two different documents for "Issun-boushi"

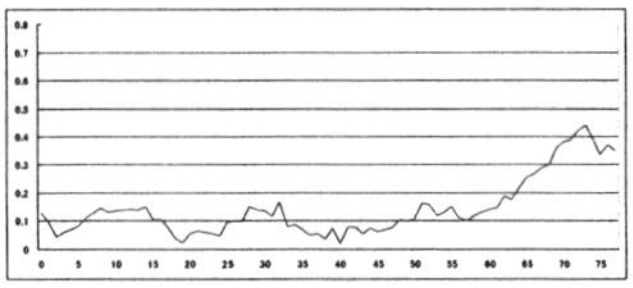

(b) Documents for "Issun-boushi" and "Momotaro"

Figure 3: Results when $p = 0.1$

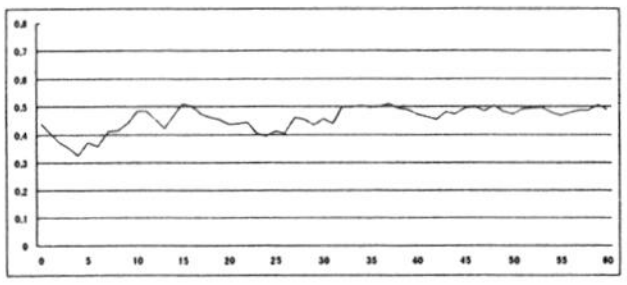

(a) Two different documents for "Issun-boushi"

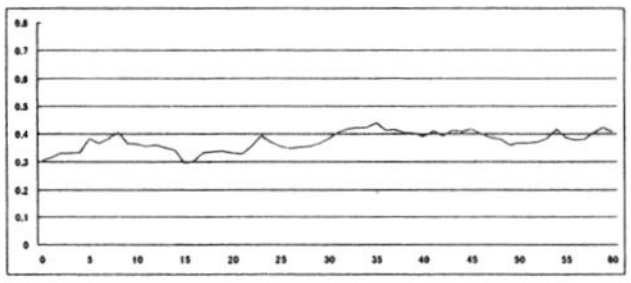

(b) A document for "Issun-boushi" and shuffled

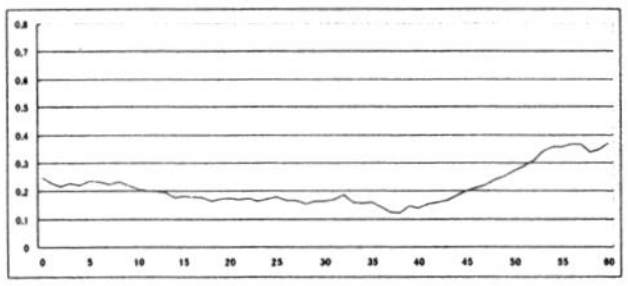

(c) Documents for "Issun-boushi" and "Momotaro"

Figure 4: Results when $p = 0.3$

5 Conclusion

In this paper we define fundamental concepts which are needed for managing text documents with stories. We also carried out experiments using text documents written in Japanese for well-known tales. We got such results as we had expected and conclude that our method is consistent to management of text documents with stories. Recently we improved our method by using document vectors based on the TF-IDF function [3], instead of using occurrences of words. Moreover, we have introduced generalization of words based on a thesaurus. The results from this improvement will be reported in near future.

References

[1] W. W. Cohen. Data Integration Using Similarity Joins and a Word Based Information Representation Language, *ACM Trans. on Inf. Sys.*, **18**(3):288–321, 2000.

[2] J. D. Ullman. *Principles of Dadabase and Knowledge-base Systems, Volume I, II*, Computer Science Press, 1988.

[3] G. Salton (ed.). Automatic Text Processing, Addison Wesley, 1989.

Information Modelling and Knowledge Bases XV
Y. Kiyoki et al. (Eds.)
IOS Press, 2004

Experiences in computer assisted XML-based modelling

Marko Niinimäki, Vesa Sivunen
Marko.Niinimaki@cern.ch, Vesa.Sivunen@cern.ch
Helsinki Institute of Physics at CERN, CH-1211 Geneva, Switzerland

Abstract.

Understanding the structure and functionality of the domain of interest and representing them in an intuitive, conceptual form is crucial in any effort to manage information about the domain. We adopt the view that documents contain information about the domain of application in a structural form. However, the structure in documents is often loose and modelling and management tools are seldom used in connection with document.

In an ideal situation, all the organization's documents are stored in an electronic form in the same database. In that case we say these documents form the organization's document database. Extensible Markup Language (XML) is now a widely accepted format for electronic documents. XML document type definitions are used to require a specific structure of documents. In our opinion, creating document type definitions corresponds to conceptual and logical database design in a database design process. We consider that this design can be supported with a suitable set of tools that help the designer concentrate on conceptual issues instead of implementation issues.

In this paper, we introduce a software called Meta Data Visualisation (MDV) that (i) assists the user with a graphical user interface in the creation of his specific document types, (ii) creates a database according to these document types, (iii) allows the user to browse the database, and (iv) uses native XML presentation of the data in order to allow queries or data to be exported to other XML based systems.

Our hypothesis is that using the methodology presented in this paper we gain XML databases that are useful and relevant, and with which MDV works as a user interface.

1 Introduction

The aims of this paper are (i) to study how XML can be used in the context of modelling and what were its benefits, and (ii) to outline an implementation of an XML-based modelling tool.

According to Reingruber and Gregory [19], a model in general is "a hypothetical or stylized representation"; it attempts to capture in meaningful form some larger, or in some cases smaller, object that exists or will exist. Modelling, naturally, is the process of forming these models. We call the object of modelling a domain of interest or, briefly, domain.

There are possibly dozens (if not hundreds) of different accounts of modelling in different domains – engineering, economics, medicine, and social sciences, to name just a few. In the scope of this paper we limit our interest to modelling in computer science and information studies, and in order to do so, we make some simplifying assumptions:

- Assumption 1: models and modelling are important tools for capturing information about the domain.
- Assumption 2: this information can be expressed in textual form, that we call documents.
- Assumption 3: the structure of the documents reflects the features of the domain.
- Assumption 4: these structured documents can be stored in a database and queries that take advantage of the structure of the documents can be supported by the database management system.

In computer science, modelling in the form of conceptual modelling, information modelling, database modelling, and data modelling has been applied at least in database design, artificial intelligence, and software design (see e.g. [11], [21], [12]). Despite the differences in terminology, it seems that most of the approaches emphasise the use of abstraction mechanisms to capture knowledge about the domain. Abstraction mechanisms allow us to state that there are objects, attributes of objects and different kinds of relations (of objects and attributes) in the domain of interest; briefly, they allow us to express the structure of the domain.

As Reingruber and Gregory [19] state, the model's representation relies on the adoption of a language. Using database terminology, a conceptual model is expressed by a conceptual schema using an appropriate language (see [20]). Semantic data models, like the Entity-Relationship model, and description logics (see [5], [2]) are among the best known languages created for the purposes of the representation of the model. Analysis of different languages from the point of view of their applications and expressive power, for instance, has been a source of many studies (see e.g. [16], [11], [3], [9]).

In order to eventually store and retrieve data, the conceptual schema will be translated into a logical database schema that can be implemented using a database management system (see [10]). The result of the implementation is a database that can be populated with actual data. In the context of this paper, and according to our assumptions, we consider the database to be a collection of structured documents.

Extensible Markup Language (XML) is a set of data representation conventions. A representation of something is called an XML document if the representation conforms with these conventions. These conventions do not state that a "real" document would always have an author or a title. In order to require such properties, we need to create a definition of our own, specific, type of a document. Naturally, this creation requires that we have knowledge about the domain of our documents and that we use this knowledge to impose a structure on our definition of such documents – for instance that each one of them has at least one author. Once we impose this requirement, the fact that each document has at least one author can be used in information retrieval, i.e. searching for documents based on the name(s) of the author(s).

The role of XML in this context can be summarised as follows:

- Constructing XML document types can be seen as modelling;
- It is possible to express abstraction mechanisms (stating that there are objects, attributes of objects and different kinds of relations) using XML;

- XML databases, their management software, and their query tools that take advantage of the structure of XML documents are readily available.

Meta Data Visualisation (MDV) software is a web application for managing XML-based data. The software supports both document type design and simple document management and query operations and contains its own database management system. Let us consider the database design process (as in [10]) to consist of requirements collection, conceptual database design, the choice of database management system software, logical database design, physical database design, and implementation. We can say that MDV supports all these steps in a trivial way, and additionally provides the user with a graphical user interface by which he can browse his data.

In order to illustrate the use of XML and MDV, we consider a domain of a wine farm. The user wants to model wines, their qualities and attributes, and their sales by bottles and barrels. The conceptual database design in this case equals to creating document types to correspond wine, wine bottle, barrel etc. This could be done by manually creating XML Document Type Definitions (DTDs), but most users would find it cumbersome. With MDV, the user creates these definitions interactively and then inserts his documents that are instances of these definitions.

Related work Several XML based web design frameworks like Expresso [15], Araneus [17] and WebML [4] (commercialized by WebRatio) are currently available. Many of them provide the user with sophisticated tools for web site building and work flow management. The scope of MDV is more limited but quite user friendly. The user of MDV does not need background knowledge about Entity-Relationship model or other modelling languages. Moreover, the user is provided with a simple, intuitive interface with categories (that contain documents) and methods for designing and creating documents.

Contents The rest of this paper is organized as follows. In Section 2 we define some terminology Section 3 presents how abstraction mechanisms can be expressed with XML and Section 4 describes by an example how to use MDV in modelling and XML based document management. Conclusions are presented in Section 5.

2 Terminology and conventions

XML (eXtensible Markup Language) is "the universal format for structured documents and data on the Web" [8]. As such, XML is a meta language – a language for describing other languages – which lets one design customised markup languages for different types of documents, using a declaration syntax defined in recommendation [6]. A particular XML language (like the one we use to describe documents in MDV) conforms to a grammar, that can be defined either using Document Type Definitions (DTDs) or XMLSchemas (see [8]).

According to the terminological conventions, an XML document consists of elements that are either entities or attributes (of entities). An XML processor (a computer program) can parse an XML document for as long as these conventions (and some further constraints) are not violated – even if there is no DTD for this document. The role of a DTD is to define valid element type names and attribute type names and in what order they must occur in the document. For further information about XML and examples of DTD's. see e.g. [13].

"XML document" in this paper is a technical term and refers to a well-formed string of characters by which elements (entities or attributes) are coded. Most documents that we encounter in real life are not XML documents; modelling is needed for representing in XML the information contained in real documents: we need to decide the format of XML in order to express the information in a meaningful form.

3 Representing documents using XML

It is our assumption that the structure of the documents reflects the features of the domain. In what follows, we shall study how to model documents and represent them in an XML format.

In electronic document management, we need to conceptualise the domain in order to find the relevant structures that the documents reflect. This kind of conceptualisation has been made in the field of Semantic Data Models (see e.g. [1], [14]). We adopt the following abstraction mechanisms since they appear frequently in documents and domains of documents (examples below)[1]:

- IS-A, i.e. the relation between a subtype and its supertype, like `WHITE WINE` IS-A `WINE`;
- Attribution, i.e. functional relations, like `WINE` having attributes of `country of origin` and `name`, at least;
- Association, i.e. named relations between objects of some types, like a relation of `precedes` between `BILL` and `REMINDER`;
- Aggregation, i.e. constructing something out of independent parts, like `BILL` would contain a `PERSON` as a recipient and payee;
- Grouping, i.e. creating finite sets of objects of a given type. For example a grouping of `BILLING ITEMS` is typical for bills.

Association can be seen as attribution, in a way that a `REMINDER` could have an an attribute `precedes`. Therefore, we omit association in further discussion.

Attribution can be represented trivially using XML attributes. However, since IS-A, aggregation, and grouping are basically relations, we adopt XLink, an XML language ([7]) to represent them.

4 Using MDV in designing and interacting with the database

Though the XML representation explained in Section 3 constitutes a solid XML foundation of representing documents, a set of these document type definitions probably means very little to a normal user. A user interface is needed for the user to add his own document types and relations in the database. Moreover, a user interface enables the user to enter, search, edit and delete actual documents, too.

The modelling features of MDV have been greatly influenced by Hull and King's accounts of Semantic Data Models ([1], [14]). The abstraction mechanisms that Hull and King discuss are those of IS-A, attribution, aggregation, and grouping, as explained in Section 3.

[1] In what follows, the names of types are written in uppercase and names of fields, attributes, and relations in lowercase.

As indicated by Hull and King in [14], attributes and aggregation can both be used in some situations.[2] This can confuse users, and therefore in MDV we impose a simplifying rule that seem to be quite intuitive to most users: an aggregate type is *just* an aggregate; it cannot have attribute fields.

In MDV, these abstraction methods are related to document types, that can be created or edited by the user. Document types may contain 0..n field types. In the simple case of Figure 1, a field is printable (string, enumeration, or picture). In this way, MDV implements simple attributes.

```
WINE                              Document id 5456
Grape: STRING                     Grape: Cabernet sauvignon
Name: STRING                      Name: Chateau Vieux Satigny
Country-of-origin: STRING         Country-of-origin: Switzerland
```

Figure 1: A simple document type and an example of its instance document.

Other abstraction methods are managed by MDV as follows:

- Functional relations: in MDV, fields that are not printable are called functional relations. In Figure 2, the user has created a type `WINE-BOTTLE`, that has a field `contains-wine`. `Contains-wine` can be filled with a document of type `WINE`. This is a method of implementing attributes whose values are non-printable.

```
WINE-BOTTLE                       Document id 5457
Contains-wine: WINE               Contains-wine: 5456
```

Figure 2: `WINE-BOTTLE` document type and an example of its instance document.

- IS-A: the administrator can derive a document type from an existing type. The new type will be a subtype of the existing one. In Figure 3, the user has derived `WHITE-WINE` from `WINE`.

```
WHITE-WINE                           Document id 5458
IS-A: WINE                           Grape: Sauvignon blanc
White-wine-quality: dry/medium/sweet. Name: Baccarat
Sparkling: yes/no.                   Country-of-origin: Switzerland
                                     White-wine-quality: dry
                                     Sparkling: yes
```

Figure 3: `WHITE-WINE` document type and an example of its instance document.

- Grouping: the administrator can create a grouping of an existing type. In Figure 4 a grouping `BOUGHT-WINE-BOTTLES` has been created.

- An aggregate (Cartesian product) is shown in Figure 5. As mentioned earlier, instead of aggregation (has-part in the figure), we could think of `WINE-BOUGHT-BY-BARREL` as a document type that has parts of type `WINE-BARREL` and `WINE`. We impose a limitation that an aggregate can only have has-part-fields. In this case, the functional relation (lower) implementation is better if we want to include the field `price` in the type.

[2] Hull and King discuss an example where the relationship of people and their businesses can be represented (i) by `PERSON's` attribute `works-for` whose values are `BUSINESSes` or (ii) by the aggregate `EMPLOYMENT` that has `person` and `business` as its parts.

```
BOUGHT-WINE-BOTTLES                    Document id 5459
GROUPING-OF: WINE-BOTTLE               GROUPING-OF values: 5456, 5457
```

Figure 4: BOUGHT-WINE document type and an example of its instance document.

```
WINE-BARREL                            Document id 5460
Made-of: STRING                        Made-of: Oak
Made-when: STRING                      Made-when: 1986
Size: STRING                           Size: 10 litres

WINE-BOUGHT-BY-BARREL                  Document id 5461
has-part-1: WINE-BARREL                has-part-1: 5460
has-part-2: WINE                       has-part-2: 5458

WINE-BOUGHT-BY-BARREL                  Document id 5461
Barrel: WINE-BARREL                    Barrel: 5460
Wine: WINE                             Wine: 5458
Price: STRING                          Price: 100 CHF
```

Figure 5: WINE-BARREL and two ways of implementing WINE-BOUGHT-BY-BARREL.

As an example, we demonstrate how to create the corresponding document types, relations and documents using MDV. The basic functionality of the software is explained in [18], so here we only provide a short summary of the main features.

Figures 6 and 7 illustrate how to create a new basic document type WINE. Figure 8 show how to add fields to it in order to achieve the type shown in Figure 1.

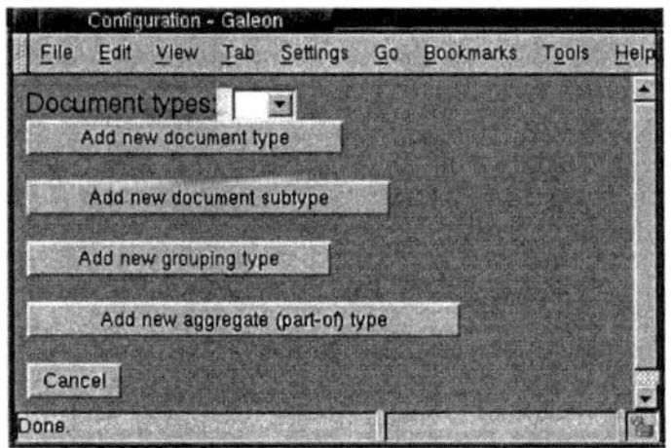

Figure 6: MDV document types configuration page.

Function relations with the interface: e.g. creation of type WINE-BOTTLE and a functional relation from it to WINE (WINE-BOTTLE contains WINE), as in Figure 2.

Subtypes, e.g. creating a new document type WHITE-WINE as a subtype of WINE, as in Figure 3.

Grouping: creating a grouping BOUGHT-WINE-BOTTLES, whose members are of type WINE-BOTTLE. The user creates a new grouping from the link "Add new grouping type" of the document type editor of Figure 6.

In an aggregation, only references to other (existing) document types are possible. The interface supports how to create a WINE-BOUGHT-BY-BARREL type that has wine-barrel (of type WINE-BARREL) and wine (of type WINE) as its parts. There, the user creates a field (part) wine in WINE-BOUGHT-BY-BARREL and states that only WINE documents can be this part.

There is naturally a user interface for creating and editing documents using MDV. As an example, let us assume the user creates a WINE document (corresponding to Figure 1), with the following values of fields: Grape Cabernet Sauvignon, Name Chateau X, Country-of-origin Switzerland.

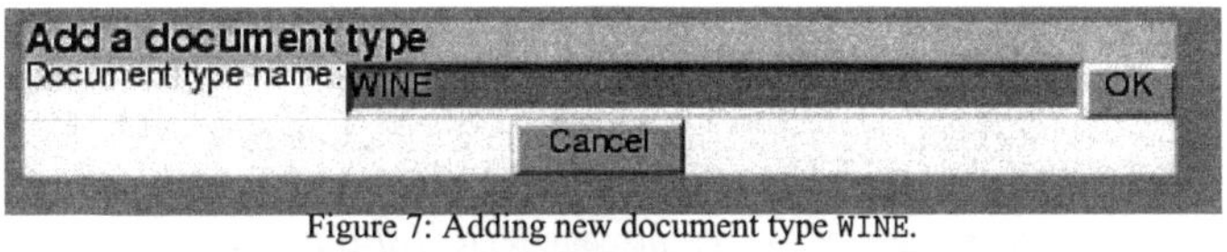

Figure 7: Adding new document type `WINE`.

Figure 8: Adding fields `Grape`, `Name` and `Country-of-origin` to `WINE`.

Our assumption 4 states that with structured documents, queries can take advantages of the structure. We have implemented a query interface, as follows:

- In Figure 8, the user stated that he wants to enable searching by `Country-of-origin` field;
- A new item, "Search by Country-of-origin" is now available in the user interface. The user types the name of the country of interest (e.g. Switzerland);
- A set of documents corresponding to the query is returned, in this case the document the user entered above.

5 Discussion and conclusions

Models and modelling are used in many areas to capture knowledge of the domain. There is a lack of suitable tools which can facilitate the modelling process. Our solution is the XML framework called Meta Data Visualisation. The MDV software assists user with a graphical user interface in the creation of the specific document types. The documents are stored into MDV's database. This database can be browsed and queried or data can be exported to other XML systems. We have demonstrated the functionality of MDV using a real life example that uses the abstraction methods (IS-A, attribution, aggregation, ..) in a natural manner.

A feature under development with MDV is a model browser that represents a graphical visualisation of the interconnections of document types. This will allow the users learn quickly about the information contained in the domain.

We believe that our methodology and the MDV software will help the modelling work and by using it one can create XML databases that are useful and relevant. MDV is open source software and it is downloadable at http://mdv.sourceforge.org.

References

[1] S. Abiteboul and R. Hull. IFO: A formal semantic database model. *ACM Transactions on Database Systems*, 12(4), 1987.

[2] A. Borgida. Description logics in data management. *IEEE transactions on knowledge and data engineering*, 7(1), 1995.

[3] D. Calvanese, M. Lenzerini, and D. Nardi. Description logics for conceptual data modeling. In J. Chomicki and G. Saake, editors, *Logics for Databases and Information Systems*. Kluwer Academic Publisher, 1998.

[4] S. Ceri, P. Fraternali, and A. Bongio. Web modeling language (webml): a modeling language for designing web sites. In *Proceedings of the Ninth International World Wide Web Conference, Amsterdam, May 15 - 19, 2000*.

[5] P. Chen. The entity-relationship model - towards a unified view of data. *ACM Transactions on Database Systems*, 1(1), 1976.

[6] The World Wide Web Consortium. Extensible markup language (xml) 1.0 (second edition), W3C recommendation 6 October. Available on: http://www.w3.org/TR/2000/REC-xml-20001006, 2000.

[7] The World Wide Web Consortium. Xml linking language (xlink) version 1.0. Available on: http://www.w3.org/TR/xlink/, 2001.

[8] The World Wide Web Consortium. Extensible markup language (xml). Available on: http://www.w3.org/XML/, 2002.

[9] F.M. Donini, M. Lenzerini, D. Nardi, and W. Nutt. The complexity of concept languages. *Information and Computation*, 134(1), 1997.

[10] R. Elmasri and S. Navathe. *Fundamentals of Database Systems*. Benjamin/Cummings, 2nd edition, 1994.

[11] G. Engels, M. Gogolla, U. Hohenstein, K. Hulsmann, P Lohr-Richter, G. Saake, and Ehrich H.-D. Conceptual modelling of database applications using an extended ER model. *Data and Knowledge Engineering*, 9(4), 1992.

[12] M. Fowler and K. Scott. *UML Distilled*. Addison-Wesley, 2nd edition, 2000.

[13] E.R. Harold and W. S. Means. *XML in a Nutshell*. O'Reilly, 2001.

[14] R. Hull and R. King. Semantic data modelling: Survey, applications and research issues. *ACM Computing Surveys*, 19(3), 1987.

[15] Jcorporate. Expresso framework. Available on: http://www.jcorporate.com, 2002.

[16] P. Lambrix. *Part-Whole Reasoning in Description Logics*. PhD thesis, Linköping Studies in Science and Technology No. 448, 1996.

[17] G. Mecca, P. Merialdo, and P. Atzeni. Araneus in the era of XML. *IEEE Data Engineering Bullettin, Special Issue on XML*, 1999.

[18] M. Niinimaki, M. Tuisku, and M. Heikkurinen. Patterns, XML and MDV platform, a case study. Technical report, Department of Computer and Information Sciences, University of Tampere, 2002.

[19] M. Reingruber and W.W. Gregory. *The Data Modeling Handbook, A Best-Practice Approach to Building Quality Data Models*. Wiley and Sons, 1994.

[20] Information processing systems Technical Committee ISO/TC 97. *Information processing systems – Concepts and Terminology for the Conceptual Schema and the Information Base*. ISO, TR 9007:1987 (E), 1987.

[21] H. P. Winston. Learning structural descriptions from examples. In H. P. Winston, editor, *Phychology of Computer Vision*. McGraw-Hill, 1975.

Information Modelling and Knowledge Bases XV
Y. Kiyoki et al. (Eds.)
IOS Press, 2004

Product Specifications Summarization and Product Ranking System using User's Requests

Kazutaka SHIMADA and Tsutomu ENDO

Department of Artificial Intelligence, Kyushu Institute of Technology,
Iizuka, Fukuoka 820-8502 Japan

Abstract. This paper proposes a method to integrate computer specifications retrieved from multiple Web sites, to extract characteristic-data of each computer based on integrated information, and to present products suitable for a user's request. The specifications written in HTML are converted into normal forms called table structure. The quantitative attributes such as speed, capacity and dimensions are extracted by comparing them with the mean or mode of all sample data, and the qualitative ones such as kind of processor and graphics chip are extracted using knowledge provided manually. The recommended products are dynamically determined from the extracted data by a user's request and relevance feedback. Moreover, a radar chart and Japanese sentences are generated from specifications. Experimental results show the effectiveness of our method.

1 Introduction

As the World Wide Web rapidly grows, a huge number of online documents are easily accessible on the Web. Finding information relevant to user needs has become increasingly important. One of the useful online documents is specifications for equipment about products such as personal computers and digital still cameras. In general, their specifications are presented in tabular form as shown in Fig. 1. Although they contain many kinds of data, it is not clear which ones are the characteristic-data among them. For example, consider users who want to buy a personal computer. They retrieve product information that includes specifications from Web sites of many computer makers. However, it is difficult for users except some experts to select a suitable computer for their own purpose from the several specifications. The reasons are as follows:

1. Each Web site provides its own product, and does not contain comparison with other maker's products.
2. Web pages of each site have various styles, and it is not easy to compare them with other maker's ones.
3. Extraction of characteristic-data and association of user's requests with specifications of each product require technical knowledge.

To satisfy a user's request, a Web-based system must integrate the information from the various sites into a single, coherent whole. Unfortunately, integrating information from diverse sources is very hard when information is presented in a simple structure[1].

The purpose of our study is to develop a multimedia summarization system. As the initial step, we focus on a table on the World Wide Web. We are developing a

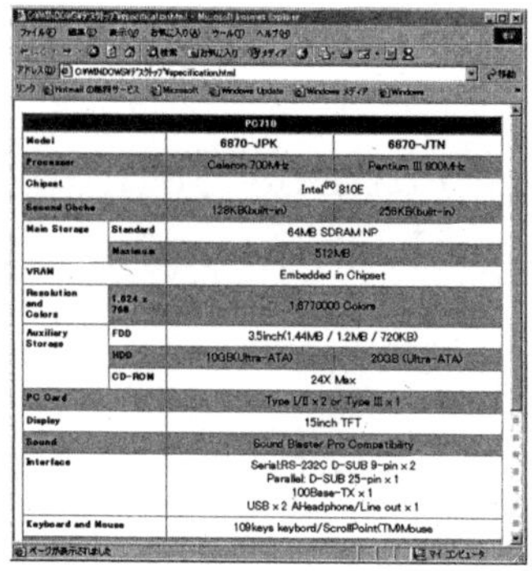

Figure 1: Specifications of products.

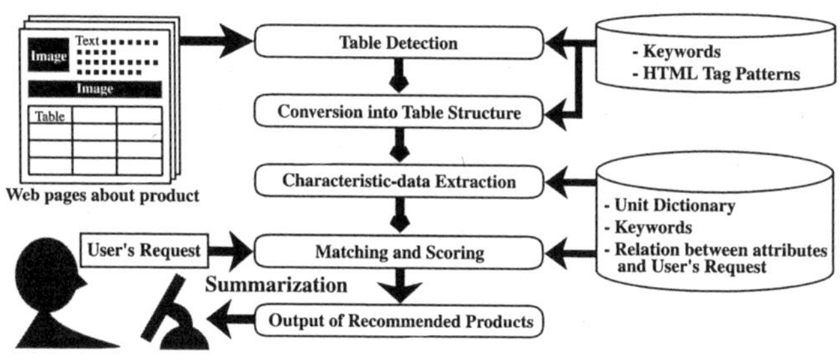

Figure 2: Outline of our system.

multi-specifications summarization system from multiple Web sites, focusing on personal computer products [2]. This paper proposes a method to integrate specifications presented in tabular form, to extract characteristic-data of each computer based on integrated information, and to present computers for a user's request. Figure 2 shows the process flow of our system. First, Web pages are retrieved from multiple sites by a file-downloading software. Product specifications are extracted from the Web pages. Then HTML-based specifications are converted into normal forms called table structure. These processes are available for other product specifications. Next, characteristic-data are extracted from the table structures. Finally, the recommended computers are dynamically determined by scoring these data according to a user's request and relevance feedback. Moreover, a radar chart and Japanese sentences are generated from specifications. We provide domain specific knowledge manually for the characteristic-data extraction and the sentence generation. The knowledge is the following: (1) Normal forms of attribute names, (2) Correspondence of an attribute with a unit, (3) The relevant technical terms such as "PCI" and "USB", (4) Kind of processor (e.g., Pentium III and Celeron), and (5) Relations between attributes and a user's request, (6) Frames for sentence generation.

2 Table Detection

Here we handle Web pages about computers as input. These pages are retrieved from multiple sites by a file-downloading software. The contents of the retrieved pages are not only tables but also text and images. The <Table> tag in an HTML document is not always a real table because it is often employed for a layout of the Web page. In order to extract the specifications from retrieved pages, we extract keywords and calculate their weights. We apply entropy to the weight. We divide documents $D = (d_1, ..., d_N)$ into D_{real} and D_{no}. D_{real} denotes the documents including specifications, and D_{no} denotes the documents not including specifications. The weight of $term_t$ is computed as:

$$ws_t = \frac{w_t^{D_{real}}}{w_t^{D_{no}}}$$

where

$$w_t^{D_{type}} = \log \sum_{k=1}^{M} tf(t,k) + \sum_{i=1}^{M} \frac{tf(t,i)}{\sum_{j=1}^{M} tf(t,j)} \log \frac{tf(t,i)}{\sum_{j=1}^{M} tf(t,j)}$$

$tf(t,i)$, $tf(t,j)$ and $tf(t,k)$ are the frequency of $term_t$ in $document_i$, $document_j$ and $document_k$ respectively. M is the number of documents in D_{real} or D_{no}.

First, our system extracts documents including specifications from downloaded Web pages. If $\sum_{t \in d_i} ws_t$ is more than or equal to a threshold, the system extracts the document. The threshold is $\frac{\sum ws_t}{2}$. Next, specifications are extracted from the document. The system computes $Score_j = \sum_{t \in table_j} ws_t \times num_j$ for $table_j$ in the document and extracts the $table_j$ maximizing $Score_j$. The num_j is the number of keywords in $table_j$. If $Score_j$ is more than or equal to a threshold, the system extracts the $table_j$ as specifications. The threshold is $\frac{\sum ws_t}{2} \times \frac{\#\ of\ keywords}{2}$. See [25] for the other methods and evaluation of table detection.

3 Table Structure Conversion

Specifications are expressed in the form of a two-dimensional table. Generally, the first column corresponds to the attribute of a PC. The rest of columns correspond to the data about each PC, and the cell in i-th row shows the value of the i-th attribute.

The serious problem in these tables is that the style of description in each cell is not standardized as follows: (1) the kind and name of attributes are not standardized, (2) some cell contains two or more values, (3) some attribute has subcategories (e.g., "Memory" in Fig. 3 (a)), and (4) two or more cells which contain the same value are unified (e.g., "256MB" in Fig. 3 (a)).

3.1 Definition of Table Structure

To solve above problems, we define a normal form called table structure. The table structure is a set of simple ternary lists:

(Nam Atr Val)

where Nam, Atr, and Val are a model name, an attribute name, and a value respectively. As regards most specifications of products, Nam is located at the top of ones and Atr is located at the left side of ones. Nam and Atr are often represented by a list form.

<table>
<tr><td colspan="2">Model Name</td><td>PC1</td><td>PC2</td></tr>
<tr><td colspan="2">CPU</td><td>400MHz</td><td>450MHz</td></tr>
<tr><td rowspan="3">Memory</td><td>Std</td><td>64MB</td><td>128MB</td></tr>
<tr><td>Max</td><td colspan="2">256MB</td></tr>
<tr><td>VRAM</td><td colspan="2">4MB</td></tr>
</table>

(a)

```
<table border="1">
   <tr>
       <td colspan="2"> Model Name</td>
       <td>PC1</td>
       <td>PC2</td>
   </tr>
   <tr>
       <td colspan="2">CPU</td>
       <td>400MHz</td>
       <td>450MHz</td>
   </tr>
   <tr>
       <td rowspan="3">Memory</td>
       <td>Std</td>
       <td>64MB</td>
       <td>128MB</td>
   </tr>
   <tr>
       <td>Max</td>
       <td colspan="2">256MB</td>
   </tr>
   <tr>
      <td>VRAM</td>
      <td colspan="2">4MB</td>
   </tr>
</table>
```

(b)

Figure 3: Specifications written in HTML.

Model Name		PC1	PC2
CPU		400MHz	450MHz
Memory	Std	64MB	128MB
Memory	Max	256MB	256MB
Memory	VRAM	4MB	4MB

Figure 4: Decomposed specifications.

3.2 Algorithm for Conversion

An algorithm to convert HTML-based specifications as shown in Fig. 3 (b) into table structures is as follows:

1. Decompose a unified cell by HTML tags, ROWSPAN and COLSPAN. Figure 4 shows an example of reformulated Fig. 3 (a).
2. Let c(i, j) denote a cell in the i-th row and j-th column. (Nam_k, Atr_k, Val_k) denotes the k-th list in table structures. Set $k = 1$. For each j ($1 < j$), do the following substeps:

   2.1 Set $\text{Nam}_k = \text{c}(1, j)$ (i.e., the model name of a PC is set to Nam).

   2.2 For each i ($1 < i$),

   (1) Set $\text{Atr}_k = \text{c}(i, 1)$ (i.e., the i-th attribute name is set to Atr).

   (2) Set $\text{Val}_k = \text{c}(i, j)$ (i.e., the value of the i-th attribute is set to Val).

   (3) Set $k = k + 1$.
3. For each list, do the following substeps using appropriate knowledge:

   3.1 Transform a word in a list into the normal form. We employ a manually constructed dictionary for the transformation. The number of keywords in

(PC1 CPU 400MHz)
(PC1 (Memory Std) 64MB)
(PC1 (Memory Max) 256MB)
(PC1 (Memory VRAM) 4MB)
(PC2 CPU 450MHz)
(PC2 (Memory Std) 128MB)
(PC2 (Memory Max) 256MB)
(PC2 (Memory VRAM) 4MB)

Figure 5: Table structures.

the dictionary is 50.
Ex. Monitor, Screen ⇒ Display

3.2 If the element Atr contains numerals with a unit such as "1024×768 dpi", transfer them to the element Val.
Ex. (PC1 (Resolution 1024×768dpi) ○) ⇒
(PC1 Resolution 1024×768dpi)

3.3 If the element Val contains two or more values, divide the list into several lists using symbols such as "/" and ",".
Ex. (PC1 Interface (USB×2, IEEE×1)) ⇒
(PC1 Interface USB×2)
(PC1 Interface IEEE×1)

3.4 If the element Val contains symbols with numerals and keywords such as "USB × 2", transform the Atr and the Val.
Ex. (PC1 Interface USB×2) ⇒
(PC1 (Interface USB) 2)

3.5 Parse the particular notations such as "[ ]" and "-" and rewrite them into normal forms.
Ex. (PC1 (Bays total [free]) 5[2]) ⇒
(PC1 (Bays total) 5)
(PC1 (Bays free) 2)

Figure 5 shows an example of table structure converted from HTML data (Fig. 3 (b)).

4 Characteristic-data Extraction & Summarization

Specifications contain many attributes and values about PCs. It is not, however, clear which ones are the characteristic-data. Our system extracts the attributes and values that characterize each PC. The attribute is classified into two categories: quantitative and qualitative. The typical example is listed in Table 1. Figure 6 shows a snapshot of our system. Our system has 3 features: (1) Scoring using 5 requests and attribute selection, (2) Score re-calculation using relevance feedback, and (3) Generation of a radar chart and Japanese sentences from specifications.

4.1 Characteristic-data Extraction using Quantitative Attributes

For quantitative attributes, the characteristic-data are extracted by comparing each value. The attributes that have the same value in all PCs are rejected. Table 2 shows

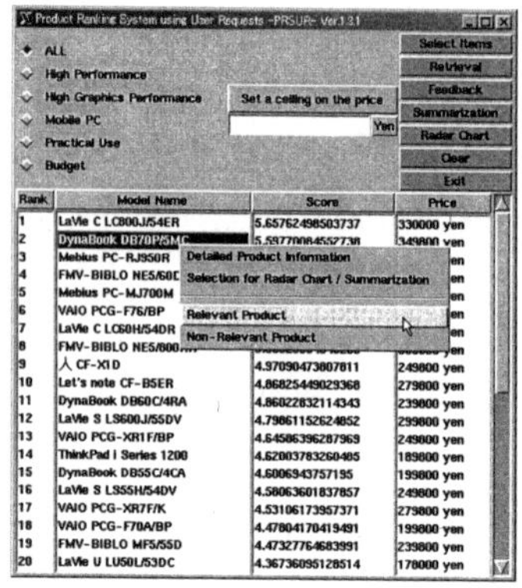

Figure 6: A prototype system.

Table 1: Classification of Attributes.

Quantitative	Qualitative
CPU Clock:MHz, GHz	CPU Processor
Memory: MB	Graphics
Display: inch	CD-R/RW
Weight: kg	DVD-ROM, DVD-RAM
Dimensions: mm, cm	Pre-installed-OS
...	...

the classification of unit for the comparison. There are two comparison processes: (1) extraction of attributes with the maximum or minimum value and (2) comparison with a standard value. The standard value is the mean or mode computed from sample data. Table 3 shows the classification of unit for computing the standard value. The following preprocessing is performed before computing the mean or mode:

- The unit of value is standardized: (mm ,cm), (MHz, GHz), and (KB, MB, GB).
- As for the data with the range, the maximum or minimum value is employed: (PC1 (Dimensions Height) 38-40mm) $\Rightarrow$ (PC1 (Dimensions Height) 38mm).

Each value obtains a score by comparing it with standard value. We define the scores: minimum, standard, and maximum points are 0, 5, and 10 points respectively. Our system calculates the value per 1 point from them. The calculation is exemplified in Fig. 7. Assume that "500MHz", "600MHz", and "1.1GHz" are the minimum, standard,

Table 2: The classification of units for comparison (in the case of Japanese specifications).

Maximum-Best	MHz, MB, GB, inch
Minimum-Best	W, yen, $, Kg
Dependent on an attribute	hours, mm

Table 3: The classification of units for standard value.

Mean	W, yen, $, mm, hours, Kg
Mode	MHz, KB, MB, GB, colors, inch

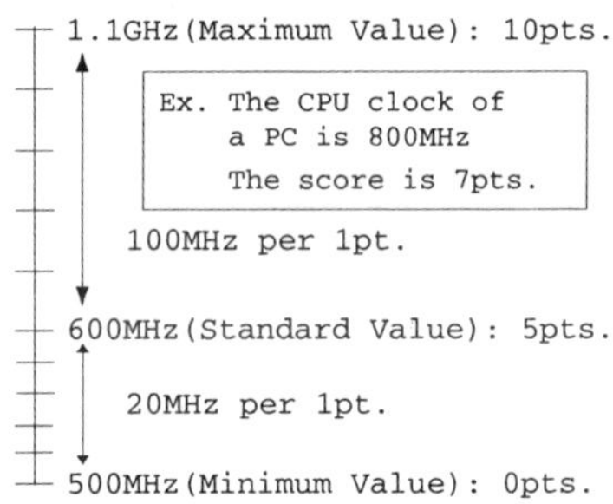

Figure 7: The calculation of the score.

and maximum value, which were calculated from all PCs, respectively. If the clock speed of a PC is "800MHz", the PC obtains 7 points.

Most data in specifications is a numerical value. By changing Table 2 and Table 3, our system can, in principle, extract the characteristic-data from the specifications of other products such as digital still cameras and cellular phones.

4.2 Characteristic-data Extraction using Qualitative Attributes

For qualitative attributes, we employ domain knowledge, which consists of keywords such as processor names, for the characteristic-data extraction. The number of keywords in domain knowledge is 23. The characteristic-data are extracted as follows:

1. Search a keyword from all table structures with qualitative attributes.
2. If the keyword exists in all products, it is not extracted as the characteristic-data.
3. If the keywords possess weight, score the weight to the PC with the keywords (e.g., Pentium4: 4, Pentium3: 3, and Celeron: 2).
4. Extract the data exceeding a threshold value as the characteristic-data.

4.3 Score Calculation by a User's Request

The characteristic-data extraction process is static. To find PCs that relate to a user's request, we define relationships between a user's request and attributes. Table 4 shows examples of the relationships. Our system can handle their 5 requests. Each attribute possesses weight. Moreover, a user can settle the weight of each attribute (from -1 to 4). Figure 8 shows the window for attribute selection. There are relationships between attributes. For example, "Weight" is related to "Dimensions" and "Battery Life". Their relationships are defined manually. Table 5 shows examples of the relationships between attributes. By clicking the "Related Items" button in Fig.8,

Table 4: The relationships between a user's request and attributes

Request	Attributes
High performance	CPU, Memory, Display, HDD, Interface
High graphics performance	Display, Graphics, CPU, Memory
Mobile PC	Battery life, Dimensions, Weight
Practical use	CPU, HDD, Price, Interface, Software
Budget PC	Price, Software, Memory, CPU

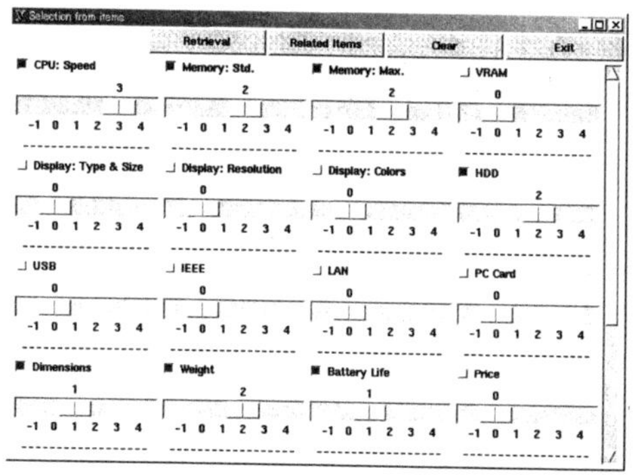

Figure 8: The window for attribute selection.

our system extends automatically the weights of the related attributes using the relationships, based on attributes selected by the user. The weight of a related attribute is calculated as follows:

$$uw(j) = \begin{cases} 0.5 & (uw(i) = 1) \\ -0.5 & (uw(i) = -1) \\ uw(i) - 1 & (\text{The others}) \end{cases}$$

where i and j are the attribute selected by a user and the related attribute respectively. $uw(j)$ is the weight of j by user's selections. Assuming that a user sets the weight of an attribute "Weight" to 2 and clicks the "Related Items" button, our system sets the ones of "Dimensions" and of "Battery Life" to 1.

The score calculation process is as follows:

1. Select the table structures with attributes relating to a user's request.
2. For each selected PC, compute

$$score(c, r) = \frac{\sum_{k=1}^{n}(w(a_k, r) + uw(a_k)) \times pt(a_k, c)}{\sum_{k=1}^{n} w(a_k, r)}$$

   where c, r and a_k are a PC, a user's request and an attribute respectively. $w(a_k, r)$ is the weight of a_k in the request. We define $w(a_k, r)$ manually. $pt(a_k, c)$ is the score calculated in Sect. 4.1 and 4.2.
3. Extract the PCs exceeding a threshold value.
4. Return them as the recommended computers in descending order for the score.

Table 5: Examples of the relationships between attributes

Attribute	Related attributes
CPU	Memory (Std. and Max.), HDD
Display	VRAM, Resolution, Colors
USB	IEEE, PC card
Weight	Dimensions, Battery life

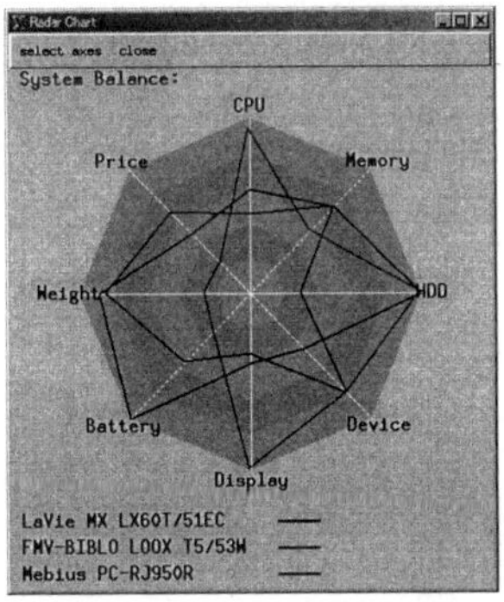

Figure 9: A radar chart.

4.4 Relevance Feedback

A single request is often insufficient because the weight is static. On the other hand, a user is often aware of the product which he/she needs by browsing the result of the search. Relevance feedback is an iterative process to improve the retrieval effectiveness [3]. Our system updates each weight during the relevance feedback. Assuming that a query consists of the weights of each attribute, the initial query is $\mathbf{Q}_0 = (w(a_1, r), ..., w(a_n, r))$. A new query $\mathbf{Q}_1$ is computed as:

$$\mathbf{Q}_1 = \mathbf{Q}_0 + \alpha \sum_{i=1}^{N^+} \mathbf{D}_i^+ - \beta \sum_{i=1}^{N^-} \mathbf{D}_i^-$$

where $\mathbf{D}^+$ and $\mathbf{D}^-$ are the vector for the relevant and non-relevant PC respectively. N^+ and N^- are the number of relevant and non-relevant PC chosen respectively. α and β tune the importance of relevant and non-relevant attributes respectively.

4.5 Generation of a radar chart and Japanese sentences from specifications

Our system can generate a radar chart and Japanese sentences from the characteristic-data of selected products by a user. The radar chart is generated by scores calculated in previous subsections. Figure 9 shows an example of a generated radar chart. "CPU", "Memory", "HDD", "Device", "Display", "Battery", "Weight" and "Price" are selected as default axes for the radar chart. A user can select each axis from attributes in specifications.

Table 6: Relationships between the topics and the attributes.

Topic	Attributes
Performance	CPU, Memory, Hard disk, etc.
Scalability	PCI, USB, PC card, etc.
Image processing	Graphics Chipset, Image processing soft, etc.
Display	Screen size, Resolution, VRAM, etc.
User-friendliness	Key size, Input device, etc.
Mobility	Weight, Dimensions, Battery life, etc.
Communication	Modem type, LAN, etc.
Sound	Speaker, Sound board, etc.
Soft	OS, Bundled software, etc.

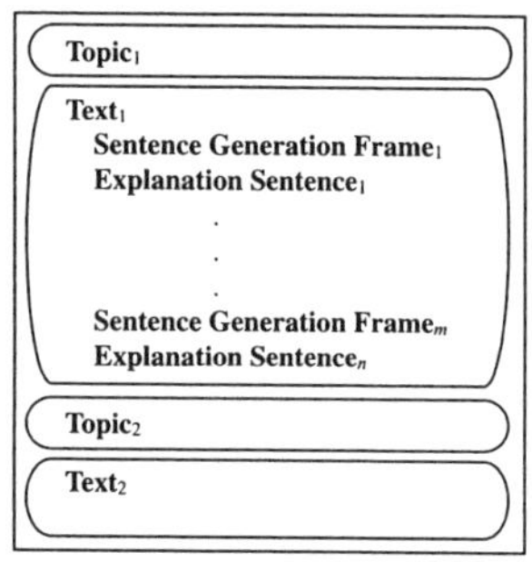

Figure 10: Document structure.

We define sentence generation frames (SG) and explanation sentences (ES) for sentence generation. Figure 10 shows document structure in our system. The number of topics is 9. Table 6 shows relationships between the topics and the attributes in specifications. Examples of SGs are as follows:

- Topic:
  [Topic] no {sugureta or yoi} [Nam]. (Japanese)
  [Nam] is excellent in [Topic]. (English)
- Text:
  [Nam] wa [Atr] ni [Val] wo {tousai or saiyou}. (Japanese)
  [Nam] is equipped with [Atr] of [Val]. (English)

[Topic], [Nam], [Atr], and [Val] are slots. Sentences are generated from SG of which the slots are filled with characteristic-data. The number of SGs is 27 frames. ESs are employed to generate additional information to supplement for the generated sentence by SGs. ESs possess the condition for generation, but do not possess any slots. An example of ESs is as follows:

- Condition: [Val] = "USB"
- ES: USB ha syuhenkiki wo tunagu interface desu. (Japanese)
  Universal Serial Bus, or USB, is an interface for connecting peripherals to your PC. (English)

The number of ESs is 35 sentences.

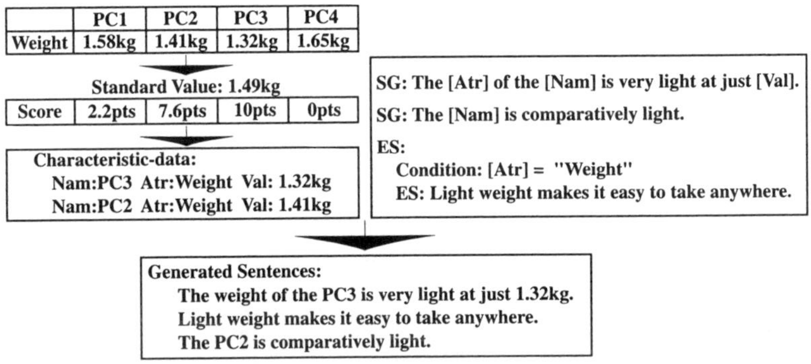

Figure 11: Sentence generation processing.

Our system re-calculates the scores of selected products by a user using the method described in subsection 4.1 and 4.2. [Nam] of SG for a topic is filled with the name of product of which the total of the characteristic-data of the attributes belonging to the topic is the maximum. If the score of characteristic-data is 5 or more, our system generates an additional sentence such as "[Nam] ha hikakuteki yoi ([Nam] is comparatively good)." Figure 11 shows an example of sentence generation processing.

5 Evaluation

In this section, we present experimental results to evaluate our system, and compare our approach with related work.

5.1 Table Detection and Conversion

To evaluate the table detection process, we used 200 documents from 5 Web sites. The number of documents including specifications was 100. The number of documents not including specifications was 100. We used 100 documents, which are 50 documents including specifications and 50 documents not including specifications, for weighting. We used recall and precision rates for the evaluation. The recall rate (R) and the precision rate (P) are computed as:

$$R = \frac{The\ Number\ of\ Documents\ Extracted\ Correctly}{Total\ Number\ of\ Correct\ Documents}$$

$$P = \frac{The\ Number\ of\ Documents\ Extracted\ Correctly}{Total\ Number\ of\ Extracted\ Documents}$$

The recall rate was 97% and the precision rate was 95%. We obtain the high recall rate and the high precision rate.

To evaluate the table conversion process, we used the 100 specifications including 247 products. The accuracy for the table conversion was 94%. The reason for the failure of the conversion is an error in HTML grammar: omission of </TD> tags or </TR> tags in a <TABLE> tag. If the HTML of specifications is described correctly, the accuracy for the table conversion rises to 100%.

		PC1	PC2	PC3
CPU		800MHz	700MHz	700MHz
Memory	Std.	64MB	64MB	64MB
	Max.	128MB	128MB	256MB
Hard Drive		15GB	15GB	10GB
Optical Device		external	external	internal
Display		11.3"TFT	12.1"TFT	10.4"TFT
VRAM		2.5MB	2MB	2MB
Resolution		1024×768pixels	800×600pixels	800×600pixels
PC card		TYPE II×1	TYPE II×1	TYPE II×1
Interface		USB×1, IrDA×1, LAN×1	USB×1, IrDA×1	USB×2
Key size		17mm	18mm	17mm
Battery Life	Std.	1.8hrs	2.5hrs	1.5hrs
	Max.	11hrs	5hrs	7hrs
Dimensions		270mm × 261mm × 29mm	270mm × 224mm × 33.7mm	257mm × 223mm × 29mm
Weight		1.6kg	1.98kg	1.5kg

Figure 12: Specifications in the experiment

5.2 *Characteristic-data Extraction*

We carried out the experiment of the characteristic-data extraction using the table structures converted from 66 specifications. Figure 12 shows an example, where each PC is the product of a different maker. The extracted values as the characteristic-data are shown in Table 7. In order to verify the accuracy for them, we compared them with a review in a magazine about PCs. The characteristics of the PCs in Fig. 12 are reviewed as follows:

PC1 Basic specs and a display are high performance. The user-friendliness and the mobility are comparatively good.

PC2 The user-friendliness.

PC3 The mobility and the scalability.

The clock speed of a processor and the capacity of a hard disk are the measures about basic specs. "Resolution" and the capacity of "VRAM" are the measures about performance of a display. Extracting the value of "Dimensions", "Weight" and "Battery Life" is appropriate because they are related to mobility. The maximum capacity of memory and expansion options such as "USB" are the measures about scalability. "Key size" is related to user-friendliness.

The number of characteristic-data extracted from 66 specifications is 365. Table 8 shows the correctness of the characteristic-data. Eval(1) in Table 8 denotes the number of characteristic-data, which we judged to be correct by the review. Eval(2) in Table 8 denotes the number of characteristic-data, which we could not judge to be correct or incorrect by the review (e.g., "IrDA" in Table 7). Although we could not judge the correctness of the characteristic-data in Eval(2) by the review, we considered that they were appropriate.

5.3 *User's Request and Relevance Feedback*

We evaluated a prototype system using a user's request and relevance feedback. We used 38 specifications about notebook PCs. Our system can handle 5 requests: (1) High Performance, (2) High Graphics Performance, (3) Mobile PC, (4) Practical Use, and (5)

Table 7: Extracted characteristic-data

PC Name	Attribute	Value
PC1	CPU	800MHz
	HDD	15GB
	Resolution	1024×768pixels
	VRAM	2.5MB
	Interface:IrDA	1
	Interface:LAN	1
	Dimensions	270mm × 215mm × 29mm
	Weight	1.6kg
	Battery Life Max.	11hrs
PC2	HDD	15GB
	Display	12.1"TFT
	Interface:IrDA	1
	Key size	18mm
	Battery Std.	2.5hrs
PC3	Memory Max.	256MB
	Optical Device	Internal
	Interface:USB	2
	Dimensions	257mm × 223mm × 29mm
	Weight	1.5kg

Table 8: Correctness of characteristic-data

	Correctness
Eval(1)	319/365
Eval(2)	46/365

Budget PC. We compared the result with recommended PCs in the magazine "Nikkei Best PC" [4]. Table 9 shows the ranking in the magazine of the product selected as the 1st by our system and the ranking in our system of the product selected as the 1st by the magazine. For the request (3) and (5), other results by our system also corresponded with the products ranked highly in the magazine. For the request (1) and (4), we obtained sufficient accuracy. Although some products ranked highly by our system did not correspond with the ones in the magazine for the request (2), two PCs recommended in the magazine were included in top five products of our result.

Next, we applied relevance feedback to the results. α and β for the relevance feedback were $\frac{1}{N^+}$ and $\frac{1}{N^-}$ respectively. The formula is well-known as Rocchio's formula [5]. Figure 13 shows an example of the recall-precision rate of the results using relevance feedback. In the case of Fig. 13, a user chose "Mobile PC" as a user's request first.

Table 9: The ranking in the magazine and our system.

Request	The ranking in the magazine	The ranking in our system
Request (1)	4th	3rd
Request (2)	8th	5th
Request (3)	1st	1st
Request (4)	4th	4th
Request (5)	1st	1st

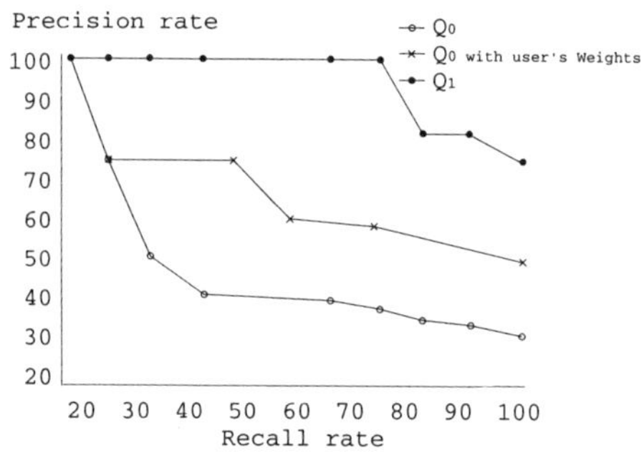

Figure 13: Recall-Precision rate.

Here, assume that the user attached importance to portability: the user put weight on the value of "Dimensions", "Weight" and so on rather than "CPU", "Memory" and so on. Next, the user judged the top 5 products based on the intention: relevant or non-relevant. The system re-calculated the score using $\mathbf{Q}_1$ obtained by user's feedback. "$\mathbf{Q}_0$ with user's weights" in Fig. 13 denotes the score calculated using attribute selection (Sect.4.3). The user set the weight of an attribute "Weight" to 3, and clicked the "Related Items" button. As a result, the recall-precision rate improved dramatically. The experimental results show the effectiveness of our system.

5.4 Generated sentences

We evaluated generated sentences with 8 graduate students. Figure 14 shows an example of the generated sentences. We employed 3 generated documents for the evaluation. The evaluation criteria of the generated sentences were as follows:

Eval(1) The grammatical accuracy.

Eval(2) The textual coherence.

Eval(3) The redundancy of expression.

Eval(4) The legibility.

8 graduate students classified the generated sentences into the following 5 categories:

Bad : 1pts.

Below average : 2pts.

Fair : 3pts.

Good : 4pts.

Excellent : 5pts.

Table 10 shows experimental results. Generated sentences were sufficient for summarization.

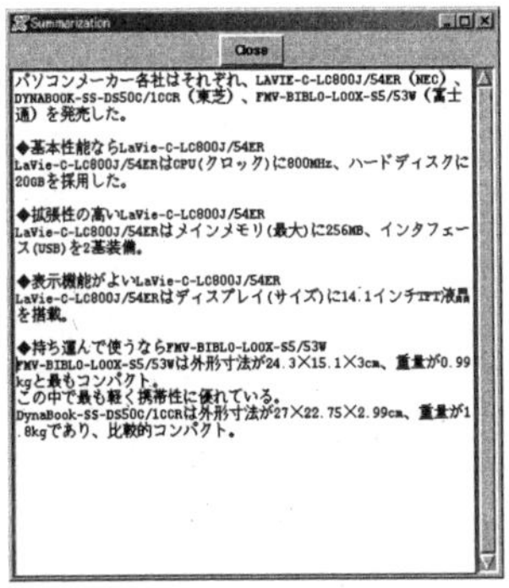

Figure 14: Generated sentences.

Table 10: Evaluation of generated sentences.

Eval(1)	Eval(2)	Eval(3)	Eval(4)
3.7	3.7	4.3	4.0

5.5 Related Work

Most of information extraction systems extract data from natural language text such as a newspaper article [6]-[10]. In their text-based systems, a large number of templates for pattern matching are necessary. One approach is to extract data from several articles [11]. The number of templates for the extraction system increases further. Moreover, newspaper articles lack information because they are a kind of summarized data. Therefore, specifications are among the best sources of data about products. As regards the need to change dictionaries in the extraction process, our system is easier than text-based systems because we employ units such as "MHz" and "GB" to extract characteristic-data from specifications.

On the other hand, there are several approaches to extract information using document structure such as itemization and tabular forms. Traditionally, they handle a document image [12] or plain text. Ng et al. have reported an approach that learns to recognize tables in free text [13]. Sato et al. have proposed a method for automatic generation of digests from the NetNews [14]. Kawai et al. have proposed a method for automatic extraction of relational information from itemized text [15]. However, they are different from table forms that we handle.

There are several approaches to deal with HTML-based documents. Although Chen et al. have reported a method for mining tables from HTML documents, their systems analyze only one table [16]. Hammer et al. have proposed a grammar-based tool for converting HTML pages into database objects [17]. They do not, however, deal adequately with the usage of structured data from tables. Therc is an approach to integrate several tables [18]. The purpose is to build ontologies from the World Wide Web via HTML tables. Our purpose is to extract the characteristic-data of each products by comparing several specifications with each other, and to present products suitable for a user's request.

As regards summarization, most of them deal with texts [19]. Our system summarizes tables into sentences. There are many report generation systems such as stock market summarization and textual weather forecasts from databases [20]. Our system performs not only text generation, but also radar chart generation and presentation of the product rankings.

There are many shopbots on the World Wide Web [21], [22]. Most of them compare only the prices of products with each other. Chai [23] and Budzikowska [24] have proposed a conversational dialog system for online shopping. Their system, however, compares products with same maker's ones. Our system can present the recommended products from several maker's specifications using a user's request and relevance feedback. The advantages of our system are as follows:

- A table-based information extraction system can be built with fewer patterns than a text-based system.
- It deals with specifications that contain many kinds of information about products.
- It can integrate several specifications retrieved from multiple sites by converting the HTML-based ones into normal forms called table structure.
- It can extract characteristic-data of each product, and find the products relevant to a user's request from multiple specifications.
- It can generate a radar chart and sentences as a summary from specifications.

6 Conclusions

In this paper, we have proposed a method of information extraction from specifications on the Web. Our system presents the recommended products using a user's request and relevance feedback. Moreover, a radar chart and Japanese sentences are generated from specifications. We obtained high recall and precision rates for the table detection process. The accuracy of the table conversion of HTML-based specifications into table structure was 94%. Most of the extracted characteristic-data were appropriate. We verified the effectiveness of our system. Our proposed system can be applied to specifications of other domain such as digital still cameras and cellular phones [26].

Some web sites and agents that compare some products already exist on the Web. However, most of them deal with only the prices of products. In comparison with traditional text-based information extraction systems, our system obtains much information because specifications contain more information than an article. Future work will include (1) construction of domain knowledge by machine learning, (2) information retrieval through man-machine dialogue, and (3) integration with other sources such as product images.

References

[1] W. Cohen, "The Whirl approach to information integration", IEEE Intelligent SYSTEMS, Vol.13, No.5, pp.20–24, 1998.

[2] A. Fukumoto, K. Shimada, and Tsutomu Endo, "Information extraction from specifications on the World Wide Web," Proceedings of PACLING 2001, pp.109–116, 2001.

[3] T. Tokunaga, "Information Retrieval and Natural Language Processing," Computation and Language Volume 5, University of Tokyo Press, 1999 (in Japanese).

[4] Nikkei Best PC, Nikkei Business Publications, Inc.

[5] J. J. Rocchio, "Relevance feedback in information retrieval", in The SMART Retrieval System: Experiments in Automatic Document Processing, Chapter 14, pp.313–323, Prentice-Hall, Inc., 1971.

[6] H. Matsuo and H. Kimoto, "A content extraction method from Japanese texts based on pattern matching using extraction patterns," Trans. IPSJ, Vol.36, No.8, pp.1838–1844, 1995 (in Japanese).

[7] F. Masui and J. Fukumoto, "Information extraction for listing of product information," Proceedings of Workshop Program The 4th Annual Meeting of The Association for Natural Language Processing, pp.56–63 (in Japanese).

[8] Y. Eriguchi and T. Kitani, "Information extraction from Japanese text using Tomita's generalized LR parse," Trans. IPSJ, Vol.38, No.1, pp.44–54, 1997 (in Japanese).

[9] S. Sekine, "Information extraction from text," IPSJ Magazine, Vo.40, No.4, 1999 (in Japanese).

[10] T. Wakao, "Information extraction from English text," Technical Report of IPSJ, NL114-12, pp.77–83, 1996 (in Japanese).

[11] J. Akamatsu, Y. Takao, H. Nagai, T. Nakamura, and H. Nomura, "Information extraction form newspaper articles of multiple products," Technical Report of IPSJ, NL140-9, pp.61–68, 2000 (in Japanese).

[12] J. Hu, R. Kashi, D. Lopresti, and G. Wilfong, "Medium-independent table detection," Proceedings of Document Recognition and Retrieval VII, pp.23–28, 2000.

[13] H.T. Ng, C.Y. Lim, and J.L.T. Koo, "Learning to recognize tables in free text," Proceedings of the 37th Annual Meeting of ACL, pp.443–450, 1999.

[14] M. Sato, S. Sato, and Y. Shinoda, "Automatic digesting of the NetNews," Trans. IPSJ, Vol.36, No.10, pp.2371–2379, 1995 (in Japanese).

[15] A. Kawai, T. Tsukamoto, K.Yamamoto, and T. Shiino, "Automatic extraction of relational information using document structure from itemization and tabular forms," IEICE Trans. Inf. & Syst., Vol.J81-DII, No.7, pp.1609–1620, 1998 (in Japanese).

[16] H.H. Chen, S.C. Tsai, J.H. Tsai, "Mining tables from large scale HTML texts," Proceedings of COLING2000, pp.166–172, 2000.

[17] J. Hammer, H. Garcia-Molina, J. Cho, R. Aranha, and A. Crespo, "Extracting semistructured information from the Web," Proceedings of the Workshop on Management of Semistructured Data, 1997.

[18] M. Yoshida, K. Torisawa, and J. Tsujii, "Extracting ontologies from World Wide Web via HTML tables," Proceedings of PACLING 2001, pp.332–341, 2001.

[19] M. Okumura and H. Nanba, "New topics on automated text summarization," Journal of Natural Language Processing, Vol.9, No.4, pp.97–116, 2002.

[20] R. I. Kittredge and A. Polguere, "The generation of reports from databases," In R. Dale, H. Moisl and H. Somers (eds.): A handbook of natural language processing, pp.261–304, 2000.

[21] D. Clark, "Shopbots become agents for business chance," IEEE Computer, Vol.33, No.2, 2000.

[22] R.B. Doorenbos, O. Etzioni, and D.S. Weld "A scalable comparison-shopping agent for the World Wide Web," Proceedings of the first International Conference on Autonomous Agents, 1997.

[23] J. Chai, V. Horvath, N. Kambhatla, N. Nicolov, and M. Budzikowska, "A conversational interface for online shopping," Proceedings of HLT2001, 2001.

[24] M. Budzikowska, J. Chai, S. Govindappa, V. Horvath, and N. Kambhatla, "Conversational sales assistant for online shopping," Proceedings of HLT2001, 2001.

[25] K. Shimada, K. Hayashi, and Tsutomu Endo, "Keywords and weighting for product specifications extraction," Proceedings of PACLING2003, 2003.

[26] K. Shimada, T. Ito, and T. Endo, "Characteristic-data extraction - Re-evaluation by the specifications of two products -," Technical Report of IEICE, TL2001-33, pp.27–34, 2001 (in Japanese).

[27] K. Shimada, T. Ito, T. Endo, "Classification of Images using Their Neighboring Sentences," Proceedings of PACLING, pp.250-256, 2001.9.

Author Index